W9-CUT-562

Instructor's Guide for

The Heath Anthology
of American Literature

Paul Lauter
Trinity College
General Editor

Juan Bruce-Novoa
University of California at Irvine

Jackson Bryer
University of Maryland

Elaine Hedges
Towson State University

Amy Ling
Georgetown University

Daniel Littlefield
University of Arkansas at Little Rock

Wendy Martin
The Claremont Graduate School

Charles Molesworth
Queens College, City University of New York

Carla Mulford
Pennsylvania State University

Raymund Paredes
University of California at Los Angeles

Hortense Spillers
Cornell University

Linda Wagner-Martin
University of North Carolina, Chapel Hill

Andrew Wiget
New Mexico State University

Richard Yarborough
University of California at Los Angeles

Instructor's Guide
for

The Heath Anthology of American Literature

Paul Lauter
General Editor

Edited by
Judith A. Stanford
Rivier College

D.C. Heath and Company
Lexington, Massachusetts Toronto

Part Openings:

page 1:   *An Indian Conjurer*, from a drawing by John White. North Wind
            Picture Archives.

page 61:   *Burning of the Stamp Act*, Library of Congress.

page 139:   *A View in the Rocky Mountains*, North Wind Picture Archives.

page 281:   Historical Picture Service, Chicago.

page 375:   Henry Dreyfuss Symbols Archive, Cooper-Hewitt Museum of
            Design, Smithsonian Institution, New York City.

page 539:   © Frank Siteman 1980, The Picture Cube.

Published simultaneously in Canada.

Printed in the United States of America.

International Standard Book Number: 0-669-12066-9

10 9 8 7 6 5 4 3 2 1

Contents

77 Emerging Voices of a National Literature: African, Native American, Spanish, Mexican

97 Enlightenment Voices, Revolutionary Visions

111 Patriot and Loyalist Songs and Ballads

114 The Federalist and Anti-Federalist Papers

117 United Voices, a National Literature

Early Nineteenth Century: 1800–1865   139

Late Nineteenth Century: 1865–1910   281

Contemporary Period: 1945 to the Present   541

623 Drama

633 Poetry

To the Instructor

*"Always a knit of identity, always distinction,
always a breed of life."*

Walt Whitman's words from "Song of Myself" apply to this instructor's guide as much as to *The Heath Anthology of American Literature*. Like the book, this guide represents the collaborative work of more than 200 American Literature specialists, each an expert on an individual author or period.

In addition to the headnotes in the text, which offer biographical details as well as interpretive discussions, contributing scholars have provided a wealth of material for this guide, drawing on their research and study as well as on their own classroom experiences.

This guide is arranged in the same order as the text, with each contributing editor providing information in the following categories:

Classroom Issues and Strategies

Major Themes, Historical Perspectives, and Personal Issues

Significant Form, Style, or Artistic Convention

Original Audience

Comparisons, Contrasts, Connections

Questions for Reading and Discussion/Approaches to Writing

Bibliography

In an attempt to preserve the diverse tone of this *Anthology*, I have changed very little of the original editors' submissions. Their widely varying approaches to each of the categories listed above suggests a broad range of teaching styles that provides you with options and possibilities we hope you will find useful.

Our thanks go to the contributing editors who "sponsored" many of the writers included in the *Anthology* and who have assisted in the preparation of this guide:

Elizabeth Ammons (Tufts University); William L. Andrews (University of Wisconsin—Madison); Francis R. Aparicio (University of Arizona); Elaine Sargent Apthorp (San Jose State University); Liahna Babener (Montana State University); Barbara Bardes (Loyola University of Chicago); Helen Barolini; Sam S. Baskett (Michigan State University);

Arethenia J. Bates-Millican (Southern University); Rosalie Murphy Baum (University of South Florida); Herman Beavers (University of Pennsylvania); Eileen T. Bender (Indiana University at Bloomington); Carol Marie Bensick (University of California at Riverside); David Bergman (Towson State University); Susan L. Blake (Lafayette College); Michael Boccia (New Hampshire College); Robert H. Brinkmeyer, Jr. (University of Mississippi); Carol A. Burns; John F. Callahan (Lewis and Clark College); James Campbell; Oscar Campomanes; Jean Ferguson Carr (University of Pittsburgh); Allan Chavkin (Southwest Texas State University); King Kok Cheung-Mare (University of Calfornia at Los Angeles); Beverly Lyon Clark (Wheaton College); C.B. Clark (California State University at Long Beach); Arthur B. Coffin (Montana State University); Constance Coiner (State University of New York at Binghamton); Martha E. Cook (Longwood College); Angelo Costanzo (Shippensburg University); Pattie Cowell (Colorado State University); John W. Crowley (Syracuse University); Martha Curry (Wayne State University); Walter C. Daniel (University of Missouri—Columbia); Cathy N. Davidson (Duke University); Jane Krause DeMouy; Dorothy L. Denniston (Brown University); Kathryn Zabelle Derounian (University of Arkansas at Little Rock); Margaret Dickie (University of Georgia); Raymond F. Dolle (Indiana State University); Sheila Hurst Donnelly (State University of New York at New Paltz); Carole Doreski (Emmanuel College); Sally Ann Drucker (North Carolina State University); Arlene A. Elder (University of Cincinnati); Everett Emerson (University of North Carolina at Chapel Hill); Bernard F. Engel (Michigan State University); Betsy Erikkila (University of Pennsylvania); Laraine Fergenson (Bronx Community College); Judith Fetterley (State University of New York at Albany); Lucy M. Freibert (University of Louisville); Susan Stanford Friedman (University of Wisconsin—Madison); Albert Furtwangler (Mount Allison University); Dianna Hume George (Pennsylvania State University at Erie-Behrend College); Leah Blatt Glasser (Mount Holyoke College); Wendell P. Glick (University of Minnesota); William Goldhurst (University of Florida); Rita K. Gollin (State University of New York at Geneseo); Suzanne Gossett (Loyola University of Chicago); Theordora R. Graham (Pennsylvania State University); Robert M. Greenberg (Temple University); Barry Gross (Michigan State University); James Guimond (Rider College); Minrose C. Gwin (Virginia Polytechnic Institute and State University); Alfred Habegger (University of Kansas); Joan F. Hallisey (Aquinas College); Jeffery A. Hammond (George Mason University); Earl N. Harbert (Northeastern University); Trudier Harris (University of North Carolina at Chapel Hill); Ellen Louise Hart (University of California at Santa Cruz); William L. Hedges (Goucher College); Joan D. Hedrick (Trinity

College); Allison Heisch (San Jose State University); Robert Hemenway (University of Oklahoma); Kristin Herzog; Donald R. Hettinga (Calvin College); Patricia Liggins Hill (University of San Francisco); Elvin Holt (Southwest Texas State University); Kenneth Alan Hovey (University of Texas at San Antonio); Gloria T. Hull (University of California at Santa Cruz); James M. Hutchisson (Washington and Jefferson College); Anne G. Jones (University of Florida); Joyce Ann Joyce (University of Nebraska); Nancy Carol Joyner (Western Carolina University); Rose Yalow Kamel (Philadelphia College of Pharmacy and Science); Carolyn L. Karcher (Temple University); Richard S. Kennedy (Temple University); Carol Farley Kessler (Pennsylvania State University); Elizabeth Keyser (Hollins College); Elaine Kim (University of California at Berkeley); Him Mark Lai; David M. Larson (Cleveland State University); Estella Lauter (University of Wisconsin—Milwaukee); Barry Leeds (Central Connecticut State University); James A. Levernier (University of Arkansas at Little Rock); Cliff Lewis (University of Lowell); Shirley Lim (Westchester Community College); Genny Lim; John W. Lowe (Louisiana State University); Juanita Luna-Lawhn (San Antonio College); Joseph Mancini, Jr. (George Washington University); Deborah E. McDowell (University of Virginia); Peggy McIntosh (Wellesley College); Nellie Y. McKay (University of Wisconsin—Madison); D.H. Melhem (The Union for Experimenting Colleges and Universities); Michael J. Mendelsohn (University of Tampa); Gabriel Miller (Rutgers University); Jeanne-Marie A. Miller (Howard University); Keith D. Miller (Arizona State University); James A. Miller (Trinity College); Joel Myerson (University of South Carolina); Charles H. Nichols (Brown University); Vera Norwood (University of New Mexico); Margaret Anne O'Connor (University of North Carolina at Chapel Hill); Genaro Padilla (University of California at Berkeley); Linda Pannill (Transylvania University); James W. Parins (University of Arkansas at Little Rock); Vivian M. Patraka (Bowling Green State University); John J. Patton (Atlantic Community College); James Robert Payne (New Mexico State University); Richard Pearce (Wheaton College); Michael W. Peplow (Lock Haven University); Ronald Primeau (Central Michigan University); Jennifer L. Randisi (California State University at San Bernadino); Geoffrey Rans (University of Western Ontario); John M. Reilly (State University of New York at Albany); Phillip M. Richards (Colgate University); Marilyn Richardson (Massachusetts Institute of Technology); Evelyn Hoard Roberts (St. Louis Community College at Meramec); James A. Robinson (University of Maryland); William H. Robinson (Brown University); Kenneth M. Roemer (University of Texas at Arlington); Judith A. Roman (Indiana University East); Nicholas D. Rombes, Jr. (Pensylvania State University);

Robert Rosen (William Paterson College); Deborah Rosenfelt (University of Maryland); Martin Roth (University of Minnesota); A. LaVonne Brown Rouff (University of Illinois at Chicago); Karen E. Rowe (University of California at Los Angeles); Doreen Alvarez Saar (Drexel University); Ramon Saldivar (University of Texas at Austin); George J. Searles (Mohawk Valley Community College); Cynthia Secor (HERS); David S. Shields (The Citadel); Thelma J. Shinn (Arizona State University); Frank Shuffleton (University of Rochester); Peggy Skaggs (Angelo State University); Catharine R. Stimpson (Rutgers University); Janis P. Stout (Texas A&M University); Claudia Tate (Howard University); John Edgar Tidwell (Miami University); Eleanor Q. Tignor (LaGuardia Community College); Jane Tompkins (Duke University); Steven C. Tracy (University of Cincinnati); Richard Tuerk (East Texas State University); Paula Uruburu (Hofstra University); Donald Vanouse (State University of New York at Oswego); Daniel Walden (Pennsylvania State University); Arthur E. Waterman (Georgia State University); Sybil Weir (San Jose State University); Judith Wellman (State University of New York at Oswego); James L. W. West, III (Pennsylvania State University); Thomas R. Whitaker (Yale University); Barbara A. White (University of New Hampshire); Marcellette G. Williams (Michigan State University); Norma Clark Wilson (University of South Dakota); James C. Wilson (University of Cincinnati); Kate Winter (State University of New York at Albany); Frederick Woodard (University of Iowa); Jean Fagan Yellin (Pace University); Amy Marie Yerkes (Pennsylvania State University); and Judy Yung.

Judith A. Stanford

Colonial Period

to 1700

The flyer

Native American Traditions

Contributing Editor: Andrew Wiget [p. 22]

Classroom Issues and Strategies

In the absence of real knowledge about other cultures or other periods in time, most students tend to project their own sense of appropriate behavior onto all other peoples and call it "universal human nature." The principal problem instructors face, not only with their students, but also with their own experience, is the recognition that people in other cultures understand the world and human behavior in significantly different ways. This difference means, in literary terms, that we may not be able to understand the motivation of characters or the significance of their actions without supplying a good deal of cultural information. To address this problem, instructors may choose to go over the notes, headnotes, and introductions supplied in the text as part of class discussion.

A second problem is that many students come to class with assumptions about how Native Americans lived, their historical relations with the United States, and their contemporary situation. Stereotypes include the notions that they were in perfect harmony with nature; that they were communalists and shared everything; that they did not believe in any form of individualism; and most frighteningly, that there are no more real Indians today. Concerning these stereotypes, I find it best to begin any discussion of Native American literature with an exploration of what students think they know about Native Americans, and I provide some basic background in terms of the population of the Native Americans as of the 1980 census, cultural information about modes of living and adaptation to particular environments, and historical information. I also make it a real point to emphasize that every society has evolved a useful and fitting adaptation to its environment. That adaptation we name *culture*. Culture is a system of beliefs and values by means of which a group of people structure their experience of the world. By working with this definition of culture, which is very close to the way current criticism understands the impact of ideology upon literature, we can begin to pluralize our notion of the world and understand that other peoples can organize their experiences in different ways.

3

A third problem arises because many forms of Native American literature employ different kinds of artistic devices that are unfamiliar or even antithetical to conventional Anglo-American notions of aesthetic response, such as acute brevity, much repetition, and cataloging. These devices often do not appeal to the contemporary reader. To address this problem, I illustrate how cultural conventions that students assume to be essential characteristics of literary experience have in fact changed over time. This is very easy to do. A classic example is to point out how conventional notions of what constitutes good poetry have changed significantly from the Renaissance through the early nineteenth century and up to the present day, noting that we recognize contemporary poetry as being marked by the absence of some features that used to be valued as significant in poetry.

I think the most important teaching strategy for Native American literature is to single out one text and embed it richly in its cultural and historical context. Work through a text with constant reference to the notes in the text. It is also very helpful to use films because they provide visual connections to the cultural environment. For instance, for the Zuni material I particularly recommend as good for a general Southwestern Native American world view, "Hopi: Songs of the Fourth World," a film by Pat Ferreiro.

In the Zuni story students are especially interested in images of transformation, and how the physical transformation of Zuni people resembles something like the scientific notion of evolution. In fact, this leads very productively to a discussion of symbols of transformation as models of evolution, and a discussion of physical evolution leads quickly to a discussion of social evolution. For instance, the antisocial and disorganized behavior of the Zuni people in the underworld is a behavioral reflection of a disorder that is also imaged in terms of their physical appearance. Thus, when their physical appearance is corrected, they have taken another step toward their social evolution as well. Students are also interested in monsters and what monsters might signify, and this leads to very fruitful discussions about psychology and imagination and the way in which monsters are composed of fragments of experience to symbolically represent forces that threaten one's sense of self or sense of order.

Major Themes, Historical Perspectives, and Personal Issues

Some very important themes evolve from this literature. Native American views of the world as represented in these mythologies contrast strongly with Euroamerican perspectives. Recognizing this is absolutely essential for later discussion of differences between Anglo Americans and Native Americans over questions of land, social organization, religion, and so on. In other words, if one can identify these fundamental differences through the literature very early on, then later it becomes easier to explain the differences in outlook between Native American peoples and Anglo-American peoples that often led to tragic consequences.

If culture is a system of beliefs and values by which people organize their experience of the world, then it follows that forms of expressive culture, like these myths, should embody the basic beliefs and values of the people who create them. These beliefs and values can be roughly organized into three areas: (1) beliefs about the nature of the physical world; (2) beliefs about social order and appropriate behavior; and (3) beliefs about human nature and the problem of good and evil.

The first three selections ("This Newly Created World," "Emergence Song," "Talk Concerning the First Beginning") all speak directly to the nature of the physical world. If we look closely at the Zuni story, "Talk Concerning the First Beginning," the story imagines the earth as hollow and the people coming out from deep within the womb of the earth. The earth is mother and feminine, and people are created not just of the stuff of the earth, but also from the earth. They are born into a particular place and into a particular environment. In the course of this long history, imagined as a search for the center (a point of balance and perfection), they undergo significant changes in their physical appearance, in their social behavior, in their social organization, and in their sense of themselves. By the time they have arrived at Zuni, which they call THE CENTER OF THE WORLD, they have become pretty much like their present selves. It is especially important to follow the notes with this selection and with the Navajo selection. Both of these stories talk about transformations in the physical world. The world is peopled by beings who are also persons like humans, all of the world is animated, and there are different nations of beings who can communicate with each other, who are intelligent and volitional creatures.

Both the Zuni story and the Iroquoian story also tell about how society should be organized, about the importance of kinship and families, about how society divides its many functions in order to provide for healing, for food, for decision making, and so on. The Iroquoian confederacy was a model of Federalism for the drafters of the Constitution, who were much impressed with the way the confederacy managed to preserve the autonomy of its individual member tribes while being able to manage effective concerted action, as the colonists—to their dismay—too often found out.

The last two stories about Raven are about a Trickster figure. Tricksters are the opposite of culture heros. Culture heros exist in mythology to dramatize prototypical events and behaviors; they show us how to do what is right and how we became the people we are. Tricksters, on the other hand, provide for disorder and change; they enable us to see the seamy underside of life and remind us that culture, finally, is artificial, that there is no reason why things must be the way they are, and so—if there is sufficient motivation—things change. Trickster provides for the possibility of change most often by showing us the danger of believing too sincerely that this arbitrary arrangement we call "culture" is the way things really are. When Raven cures the girl, for instance, he does so for the price of her sexual favors, and in so doing calls into question the not-always-warranted trust that people place in healing figures like doctors.

Significant Form, Style, or Artistic Conventions

Perhaps the most important thing that needs to be done is to challenge students' notions of myth. When students hear the word "myth," they succumb to the popular belief that mythology is necessarily something that is false. This is a good place to start a discussion about truth, inviting students to consider that there are other kinds of truth besides scientific truth (which is what gave a bad name to mythology in the first place). Consider this definition of myth: "The dramatic representation of culturally important truths in narrative form." Such a definition highlights the fact that myths represent or dramatize shared visions of the world for the people who hold them. Myths articulate the fundamental truths about the shape of the universe and the nature of humanity. It is also important to look at issues of form, such as repetition. Repetition strikes many students as boring. Repetition, however, is an aesthetic device. Repetition is used to create expectation. Consider the number three. Many aspects of our Euroamerican experience are organized in terms of three: how we start a race, "on your mark, get set, go"; three sizes—small, medium, and large; the colors of a traffic signal; and, of course, three little pigs. These are all commonplace examples, so commonplace, in fact, that initially most students don't think much of them. But there is no reason why we should begin things by counting to three. We could count to four or five or seven, as did the Zunis, the Chinooks, and the Hebrews, respectively. In other words, these repetitions have an aesthetic function: They create a sense of expectation and, when one arrives at the full number of repetitions, a sense of completeness, satisfaction, and fulfillment.

Original Audience

The question of audience is crucial for Native American literature, insofar as the original audience for the literature understands the world through its own experience much differently than most of our students do. As a result, it's important to reconstruct as much of that cultural and historical context for students as possible, especially when it has a direct bearing upon the literature. So, for instance, students need to know in discussing Zuni material that the Zunis and Hopis and Navajos are agricultural people and that corn and moccasins figure prominently as symbols of life. Rain and moisture and human beings are imagined in terms of corn, and life is understood as an organic process that resembles a plant growing from a seed in the ground, being raised up, harvested, and so forth. Historically it is important to realize, too, that visions of one's community and its history differ from culture to culture. So, for instance, the Hopi story of the Pueblo revolt imagines the revolt as a response to a life-threatening drought, which is caused by the suppression of the native religion by the Franciscan priest. This way of understanding history is very different from the way most of our students understand history today. Its very notion of cause and effect, involving as it does supernatural means, is much more closely related to a vision of history shared by Christian reconstructionists, seventeenth-century Puritans, and ancient Hebrews.

Comparisons, Contrasts, Connections

Various of these narratives lend themselves well to comparison with other texts, both Native American and non-Native American and Euroamerican. I always teach the Zuni creation story with readings from the Bible. Genesis 1–11 offers two versions of the creation of the world and a flood story, as well as opportunities to discuss social order in chapters 4, 5, and 10. Genesis 27, which relates the story of Jacob and Esau, provides a biblical Trickster figure in the person of Jacob. And finally the book of Judges, with its stories of Samson and Gideon, provides good examples of culture heros, as do other classics such as the *Aeneid*, the *Odyssey*, and the various national epics. These classical works are also good counterparts to the Navajo story of the Changing Woman's children, the hero twins, who are also on a quest to transform the world by ridding it of monsters, which, like Grendel or the Cyclops, are readily understood as projections of our fears and anxieties, as well as being interesting narrative agents. And the Iroquoian description of the confederacy is usefully compared with colonial political documents that envision various social orders, including the Declaration of Independence, the Constitution, and Federalist Papers.

Questions for Reading and Discussion/ Approaches to Writing

1. The number of works addressed in this section is so great and the material so varied that particular questions would not be useful. A good lead-in to all of these works, however, would focus on motivation of characters or significance of action. I would want students to identify some action in the narrative that puzzles them, and I would encourage them to try to explain the role of this action in the narrative and what might motivate it. They will not necessarily be successful at answering that question, but the activity of trying to answer will compel them to seek for meaning ultimately in some kind of cultural context. There is, in other words, a certain kind of appropriate aesthetic frustration here, which should not necessarily be discouraged, because it prepares the student to let go of the notion that human behavior is everywhere intelligible in universal terms.

2. I usually have students write comparative papers. I ask them to identify a theme—for example, man's relationship to animals, or attitudes towards death, or the role of women—and to write comparatively using Native American texts and a Euroamerican text that they find to be comparable.

Bibliography

Babcock-Abrahams, Barbara. " 'A Tolerated Margin of Mess': The Trickster and His Tales Reconsidered." *Journal of the Folklore Institute* 9 (1975): 147–86.

Fenton, William. "This Island, the World on Turtle's Back." *Journal of American Folklore* 75 (1962): 283–300.

Geertz, Clifford. "Religion as a Cultural System." In *The Interpretation of Cultures.* New York: Basic Books, 1973.

Radin, Paul. *The Trickster.* New York: Schocken, 1972.

Reichard, Gladys. "Literary Types and the Dissemination of Myths." *Journal of American Folklore* 34 (1914): 269–307.

Toelken, J. Barre. "The 'Pretty Language' of Yellowman: Genre, Mode and Texture in Navajo Coyote Narratives." *Genre* 2 (1969): 211–235.

Wheeler-Voegelin, Erminie, and R. W. Moore. "The Emergence Myth in Native America." *Indiana University Publications in Folklore* 9 (1957): 66–91.

Wiget, Andrew. "Oral Narrative." *Native American Literature*. Chapter One. Boston: Twayne, 1985.

The Literature of Discovery and Exploration

[p. 67]

Christopher Columbus (1451–1506)
The Virgin of Guadalupe
Alvar Nuñez Cabeza de Vaca (1490?–1556?)
A Gentleman of Elvas (fl. 1537–1557)
René Goulaine de Laudonnière (fl. 1562–1582)
Pedro Menéndez de Avilés (1519–1574)
Fray Marcos de Niza (1495?–1542?)
Pedro de Casteñeda (1510?–1570?)
Gaspar Pérez de Villagrá (1555–1620)
Samuel de Champlain (1570?–1635)

Contributing Editor: Juan Bruce-Novoa

Classroom Issues and Strategies

The primary problem that arises with teaching the Literature of Discovery and Exploration comes from students' lack of general historical knowledge of the period, compounded by the usual disinformation they learn in U.S. history as taught in this country. The other major problem is the question of whether or not these writings are, in fact, literature.

To address the first problem, I give the students a list of historical facts as they probably have learned them (i.e., dates of Jamestown, Plymouth, etc.), and we discuss this traditional way of teaching U.S. history. Then I give them a second list with the Spanish and French settlements included and discuss how this new context changes the way we conceive of U.S. history. Next I take time to explain the European backgrounds of the fifteenth and sixteenth centuries in which Spain, the first national state, was a dominant power and England a marginal and even second-rate power. Third, I emphasize the economic reality of colonization. Students must understand that none of the Europeans viewed the Native Americans as equals. The destruction of the Acoma people is just the start of a long U.S. tradition of subjugating conquered peoples and should not be read as a Spanish aberration. The Cabeza de Vaca experience is unique in that it prefigures not only captive literature but also migrant literature of the nineteenth and twentieth centuries: he and his comrades had to assimilate and acculturate to survive, working at whatever job they could get among a majority culture that did not necessarily need or want them around.

Students often ask why the Literature of Discovery and Exploration is important and how it relates to more conventional U.S. literature. You might suggest that they entertain a change in their traditional concept of the U.S. as an English-based country, considering the paradigm of a land that from the start was in contention by forces of several language groups and distinct origins. Students should be taught that this situation is still the same, in spite of the assumption that English won out. The forces present in this period are still contending for a place in U.S. territory.

Major Themes, Historical Perspectives, and Personal Issues

The headnotes specify two major themes: the newness of the experience and the need to relate it in European terms.

Another would be the strategies utilized to convince powerful readers of the benefits of the New World. These authors are constantly selling the unknown to potential investors and visitors. Here begins the tradition of hawking new property developments beyond the urban blight of the reader's familiar surroundings. Cabeza de Vaca introduces the familiar theme of wandering the back roads of the country—a sixteenth-century Kerouac. It is the theme of finding oneself through the difficult pilgrimage into the wilderness—a Carlos Castaneda *avant la lettre*.

Later, the encounters with the Native American population became more violent, introducing the theme of the subjugation of the native peoples, who would rather retain their own way of life. The arrogant assumption that one's own system is naturally superior to the native's way is again an indisputable characteristic of U.S. history.

Another theme is the sincerity of religious motivation, in spite of the contradicting evidence of economic ambitions. This conflict between the philanthropic ideals and the exploitative motivation still underlies U.S. foreign policy.

Significant Form, Style, or Artistic Conventions

First, the form of much of this material is the epistolary chronicle: a subjective report on the events without the limitations of supposedly objective historical science. It is a personal account like a memoir, but it is also a letter to a powerful reader, not the general public. It has no literary pretensions.

Second, the period is one of transition from the Middle Ages to the Renaissance, so there will be mixtures of characteristics from the two, the Medieval chronicle alongside the Renaissance epic of Villagrá.

Style is also hybrid. While most of these authors were educated well above the average commoner of the period, most of them were not trained in letters. Thus their writing is mostly unpretentious and direct. Again, Villagrá is an exception.

Most of these texts record personal experiences in the New World and thus have a ring of realism and direct contact with the earth and people. Purchas is an exception. His text is a typical propaganda piece by a distant observer, much more apt to rely on convincing metaphors than on the description of the real. In this he accurately reflects the British non-presence in this period, the desire to participate in what up to then had not been their project.

Original Audience

The audience then was specifically the powerful leaders. One can compare U.S. military reports on Vietnam or propaganda films on WWII like *Victory at Sea* to get a sense of nationalistic justification.

Now we must consider the audience to be those who should understand their past but have not had exposure to it. The material should be viewed as helping to retrain readers ignorant of their country's origins, and thus lacking in background to fully appreciate the ongoing evolution in the present.

Comparisons, Contrasts, Connections

There are plenty of writers in this section to compare and contrast. I would also recommend the contrast with Virginia and New England writers to get a sense of the newness encountered, the use of divine right to justify the project, and the determination to hold and civilize what is seen as wilderness.

Questions for Reading and Discussion/ Approaches to Writing

1. Ask students to review what they learned about this period in previous classes: who, what, where, when, why. Have them formulate a brief summary of the period according to this training. Have them compare it to the list of places and events you gave them at first and then to consider what the second list implies.
2. General assignments: Write about how this information changes their view of U.S. history. Write on the imagery used by the authors to characterize the New World.

Specific possibilities: On Cabeza de Vaca: Compare his experience with Robinson Crusoe's. On Villagrá: Compare his version with the Native American one in the anthology selections.

Bibliography

Frederick Turner, *Beyond Geography*.

Samuel Purchas (1577?–1626)

Contributing Editor: Kenneth Alan Hovey [p. 136]

Classroom Issues and Strategies

Students have difficulty with Purchas' witty and highly rhetorical style as well as trouble understanding the events surrounding the settlement of Virginia. Students need to understand the position of the Jamestown colony after the Indian massacre, and Purchas's message about the rights of the English and the benefits of settling also needs to be made clear.

Major Themes, Historical Perspectives, and Personal Issues

The major themes in Purchas's writing include the theology of colonialism in general, the importance of English nationalism, and mercantilism in competition with other countries and in the face of diminished resources at home. Another question that might be raised is how Purchas differs in his views, particularly of the Indians, from those who actually went to America. It is also worth pointing out that he was not a Puritan, but a strong member of the Church of England. Do his views, therefore, differ from the Puritans and are they like the Cavaliers' (Smith or Morton)?

Significant Form, Style, or Artistic Conventions

Much of the form in this piece is destroyed by the brevity of the selection and its choppiness, but some features should be pointed out. First, it is a promotional tract and therefore comparable to Smith's writings and various other early pieces and, second, it is a sermon of sorts, divided into points containing biblical references and repeated obeisances to the Christian God. Its style is clearly more ornate and rather scholastic compared to others.

Original Audience

One should note that Purchas is clearly in the employ of the colonial projectors. He is addressing prospective investors primarily, not the common man, and uses a superior tone to match their status, yet he is often deferential as well. A good job might have produced a better position for him in the Church of England.

Comparisons, Contrasts, Connections

Compare Purchas's work to Irving's explanation of the Spanish right to colonize the New World, found in Knickerbocker's *History of New York*. It satirizes the kind of self-serving rationalizing Purchas seems to epitomize from a modern point of view. Also, the connection to Smith is important since Purchas and the Captain worked together, and Purchas relied on and admired Smith.

Questions for Reading and Discussion/ Approaches to Writing

Students would find it helpful to outline the selections since they are fairly systematic, yet seem complicated. For a writing assignment, students could compare Purchas to the Smith selections or to Irving's piece, (from *History of New York*).

Bibliography

Material relating to the narrative portions of Purchas's volume are found in editions of Hakluyt's *Voyages*, of which Penguin has reprinted a useful selection.

The Literature of European Settlement

[p. 146]

John Smith (1580–1631)

Contributing Editor: Kenneth Alan Hovey [p. 149]

Classroom Issues and Strategies

The first problem that meets students in reading Smith is the extraordinary difference between the accounts he offers of his first appearance before Powhatan and the role of Powhatan's well-known daughter, Pocahontas. Not only do the differences call into question Smith's reliability but they reveal the way early "history" was commonly adapted to different audiences for different purposes. (See details below.)

Original Audience

Smith's first account (1608) may be the least exaggerated but was clearly written to highlight Indian grandeur and ignorance and to show how Smith took advantage of the latter for the benefit of Captain Newport, whose supporters Smith evidently hoped to please. In the account of 1624, written for a more general audience, Smith omits Newport from his account and adds piety, poetry, and Pocahontas to enhance the dramatic effect of the whole. In doing so, Smith transforms his own role from that of wily trader to pious hero of romance. The summary account of Pocahontas and himself written for Queen Anne shows Smith at his most ingratiating and courtly and Pocahontas at her noble and British best.

Comparisons, Contrasts, Connections

A practical side of Smith is seen in his expositions from *A Description of New England* and *Advertisements*. In the former, Smith as salesman offers important images of America as an Edenic land of plenty and its colonists as the true followers of Adam, Noah, and the Apostles. Such captivating images are frequently found in the Puritan and Cavalier literature of colonial America, but Smith casts his eye as well on the main chance, arguing that the colonies are simply a good investment, especially for industrious members of the middle class.

The idea of America as haven for the middle class, developed so fully a century later by Franklin, is restated from a different perspective in the *Advertisements*. There Smith bitterly attacks the overselling of America that has led to the false expectation of wealth gained without effort by absentee investors. Such expectations have led to the sending over of unfit colonists, the placing of unreasonable demands upon them by those in England, and the inevitable growth of mutual acrimony. Thus Smith, the man who would seem to be the very image of the American Cavalier, has come to favor the more independent and practical colonial practices of the Puritans of New England over the get-rich-quick schemes of his fellows in Virginia and their half-hearted backers in England. What the Puritans may lack in lineage, they more than make up for in industry and discretion. Smith, however, seems to stand alone in this, as in all his works, as the model of the well-born, discreet, and industrious man of "great spirit and small means" whom America really needs.

Edward Maria Wingfield (1560?–1613?)

Contributing Editor: Liahna Babener [p. 164]

Classroom Issues and Strategies

One problem is presented by the scarcity of historical information about Wingfield, and surprisingly, despite its centrality in the colonization of America, there is also very little particular data and few firsthand accounts of the Jamestown enterprise. Students have difficulty testing the assertions of Wingfield against the perceptions and recollections of other colonists, and difficulty sorting out the political, social, and personal ramifications of Wingfield's memoir. They may fail to appreciate the degree to which he views his experience from the frame of reference of a privileged Englishman who has inherited European attitudes toward the New World, the native peoples, government, and economic class.

A comparison with other eyewitness accounts (cf. John Smith, Frethorne letter in the anthology) helps clarify and balance Wingfield's point of view. Presentation of background on the settlement history of Jamestown is also useful, as is a review of the political, religious, and social issues that shaped colonization experiences in various regions of America, particularly New England, the Middle Colonies, and the South.

Students are most interested in the problems of maintaining discipline, managing provisions, and fostering cooperation. They like to explore the contrasts between settlements undergirded by strong religious ideology and those driven by economic ambitions (often reluctantly concluding that the former are more "successful" if also more regimented communities). Students also debate whether Wingfield is too timorous, whether he pads his case, and whether he manipulates their sympathies.

Major Themes, Historical Perspectives, and Personal Issues

1. The problem of leadership and political authority in early colonial government. Class, economic, and political conflicts among constituencies of colonists. The impact of these issues on evolution of colonial democracy. Relations between New World and mother country.

2. Wingfield's personal strengths and failings as a colonial administrator. The conflicts between the drive toward anarchy and the pressure for authoritarian government, where Wingfield is poised precariously between the two.
3. Conditions of life at Jamestown, including class stresses, daily life and its deprivations, illness and calamity, the absence of women, etc.
4. Can we begin to discern an image of America (as a culture in its own right, as distinct from its English occupants) in this document?
5. In what ways does the Jamestown experience as Wingfield tells it reflect the fact that it was an all-male society?

Significant Form, Style, or Artistic Conventions

We may view this document as a political treatise, apologia, manifesto, historical chronicle, and memoir. A consideration of the conventions of each genre and a comparison with other examples of each from the colonial period is illuminating. We may use it to discern the ethos of a male English gentleman, and explore the collision between his world view and the realities of life in Virginia under the devastating stresses of colonization.

Original Audience

Because the document is a self-defense, it is useful to determine whom Wingfield meant to address, and how his particular argument might appeal to his implicit audience. Would investors in the Virginia Company respond differently from fellow colonists? Would upper-class readers respond differently from the working class? Which groups might be alienated by his self-portrait and vision of leadership?

Comparisons, Contrasts, Connections

Compare express accounts of Jamestown settlement and issues of colonial governance by John Smith (*A True Relation of Occurrences and Accidents in Virginia*, 1608, and *General History of Va.*, 1624), George Percy (*A True Relation of . . . Moments Which Happened in Va.*, 1608), and Richard Frethorne ("Letters to His Parents"). Other documents that explore the pressures facing colonial executives and the crises of colonization and community include Bradford's *A Plymouth Plantation* and Morton's *The New English Canaan*. Especially suitable for its parallel case of deposed leadership and its differing vision of government is John Winthrop's "Speech to the General Court" included in his *Journal*. What differences between religiously and economically motivated settlements can be seen?

Questions for Reading and Discussion/ Approaches to Writing

1. (a) Discern the underlying world view of Wingfield, taking into account his background as an upper-middle-class male Englishman and perhaps a Catholic.
   (b) Identify his various strategies of self-justification. Are you sympathetic? Why or why not? Do you think his audience is won over? Explain.
   (c) Which issues seem more imperative: political struggles over power or economic struggles for provisions? What about military concerns about the colony's safety from Indians?
2. (a) Compare Wingfield's style of leadership to Bradford's, Morton's, Winthrop's, John Smith's.
   (b) Recreate a vivid picture of daily life at Jamestown.
   (c) How might the situation have been different if women had been present in the colony from the outset? If Wingfield had been an artisan or worker?
   (d) What were the particular obstacles to effective governance at Jamestown?

Bibliography

There is surprisingly little particularized history of Jamestown. I wanted to but couldn't find a recent social history of Virginia settlement. Wingfield appears as a footnote or brief entry in most textbooks or historical accounts of the Jamestown colony. In John C. Miller's chapter "The Founding of Virginia" in *This New Man, The American: The Beginnings of the American People* (1974) there is a substantive and articulate account of the colony's story. Richard Morton's treatment of the same material in the first two chapters of Vol. 1 of *Colonial Virginia* (1960) is also useful and very detailed, though, again, does not contain much express material on Wingfield. I had hoped to find a feminist reconsideration of the Jamestown experience to address the problems of a gender-imbalanced society, but found no sustained inquiry on that issue.

Richard Frethorne (fl. 1623)

Contributing Editor: Liahna Babener [p. 172]

Classroom Issues and Strategies

Virtually no historical data about Frethorne is available, so placing him in the context of the Jamestown colony is a bit difficult, since he settled near—rather than in—that assemblage.

In the absence of corroborating information, the writer's candor about his own experience is convincing. He used vivid details to describe his discontent, deprivation, and discomfort. The small specifics of daily life (quantities and kinds of food, items of clothing, catalogs of implements) and the data of survival and death (lists of deceased colonists, trade and barter statistics, numerical estimates of enemy Indians and their military strength, itemized accounts of provisions, and rations records) lend credibility to Frethorne's dilemma and enable students to empathize with his distress.

Students respond to reading Frethorne with questions like these:

What happened to Frethorne?

Did he remain in the New World, return home, or die?

Did he receive provisions from his parents?

Why is there no other historical record of his life or his fate?

Why was there so much rancor over provisions, and why couldn't the English authorities address the scarcity?

Major Themes, Historical Perspectives, and Personal Issues

I invite students to imaginatively recreate, through the detail in the text, the world Frethorne inhabited, gleaning his world view as a white, Christian, European (English), and presumably working-class man. What assumptions does he make about the mission of settlement, the character of the New World, the nature of the native peoples, the relationships between colonists? What does he expect in terms of comfort and satisfaction? What class attitudes does he reveal? Compare his implicit vision of the New World with the region he actually encounters. What religious, social, political, ethical beliefs does he bring to his account, and how do they shape his view of his experience? What can be inferred about the constraints upon indentured servants—and the lives they led—from Frethorne's record?

Significant Form, Style, or Artistic Conventions

1. Consider the "letter" as a literary genre, exploring issues of format, voice, reliability and self-consciousness of speaker, assumed audience, etc.
2. Discuss the letter as a social history document as well as a personal record and literary construct.
3. Discuss the strategies of persuasion and justification employed by the speaker. How does he win over his parents' support and pity through rhetorical tactics as well as emotional expression?
4. Consider the literary precedents and background of biblical allusion related to Frethorne's letter.

Comparisons, Contrasts, Connections

1. Use other letters and firsthand accounts from colonists in the New World: cf. letter from "Pond," a young Massachusetts settler, to his parents in Suffolk, England (repr. in Demos, John, ed., *Remarkable Providences, 1600–1760*. New York: George Braziller, 1972, p. 73).
2. Use Pond to compare New England and Jamestown experiences.
3. Use chronicles by Bradford, Smith, Wingfield—recording both personal and communal life in the colonies—to discover the diversity of such experiences, the impact of his background and ethos upon Frethorne's viewpoint in these letters. Use women's accounts to identify gender issues.
4. Use Calvinist pieces to set up relatively secular focus of Frethorne's chronicle.

Questions for Reading and Discussion/ Approaches to Writing

1. (a) Invite students to itemize the basic assumptions (world view components) that Frethorne brings to his experience—these then become the basis for class discussion (as we discern them from evidence in the document).
   (b) Ask students to try to determine what aspects of Frethorne's appeal have been calculated to move his parents to aid him. How does he use persuasive and manipulative techniques (or does he?) to affect them?

2. (a) Write out responses to (a) and (b) above.

   (b) Using other primary sources, imaginatively recreate the world of Jamestown by inventing your own letter or diary entry or newspaper story or other fabricated "document" that conveys a vivid sense of colonial life.

   (c) Write an imagined reply from Frethorne's parents.

Bibliography

There is no secondary source material on Richard Frethorne, so one must reconstruct his world to know him.

Edited anthologies of primary source documents (cf. Demos) that diversify the voices of recollection have been the most useful for doing so. Social histories of the colonial period and feminist reconstructions of the age and enterprise of settlement and of the authorial process have done the most to alert me to the matrix of issues one should explore when using a memoir or other personal document.

Thomas Morton (c. 1579–c. 1647)

Contributing Editor: Kenneth Alan Hovey [p. 176]

Original Audience

Most students have some knowledge of Puritans and their role in the settlement of New England, but very few are familiar with pioneering Cavaliers like Morton. His values, therefore, and their relation to the more familiar swashbuckling Cavaliers of Europe need to be carefully explained. According to his own self-description, Morton was the university educated son of a soldier, devoted to the British crown and old English ways, and a staunch supporter of the Church of England, its liturgy, and its holy days.

His portrait of the Indians is an attempt to show how, despite their uncivilized state, they share many values with the traditional Englishmen whom he takes to be his audience. The Indians' personal modesty, hospitality to strangers, respect for authority, and even religious views mirror those of England, and their contentment surpasses that of the English because of their greater closeness to nature. They are swashbucklers without the trappings of Europe, indulging in pleasures because they are natural and upholding authority because it allows indulgence. By contrast, the Pilgrims appear to be ill-educated rabble-rousers who despise all tradition and authority. Devoid even of common humanity, they serve their own self-glorifying appetites and deny the bounty that nature has left open to all.

Questions for Reading and Discussion/ Approaches to Writing

Morton is best read beside Bradford to bring out the full contrast between their views of Cavaliers, Indians, and Pilgrims. Morton also provides an interesting contrast in style to Bradford. Both works are highly rhetorical, but where Bradford uses his rhetoric to magnify God and humbly to minimize his poor persecuted people, Morton uses his to satirize those same people and to flaunt the superiority of his own wit and learning. All students should be able to pick out the clear cases of Morton's fictionalizing, especially in the account of Standish's response to Morton's escape, and some may see how he uses *Don Quixote* and medieval romance to shape his own mock-romance.

The contrast between Morton and Bradford can serve not only to establish the relative credibility of the two authors and the nature of their rhetoric, but to raise important moral questions about the whole colonial endeavor, especially with respect to the Indians. Were the Pilgrims, for instance, inhumane in denying the Indians firearms? Did Morton display true humanity in encouraging the Indians, male and female, to party with him and his men? To what extent could both groups be called hypocritical? Did British culture corrupt natural Indian ways or did Indian ways corrupt in different ways both the industrious Pilgrims and the pleasure-loving Cavaliers? Can the meeting of two such different cultures ever bring out the best in both, especially when each is itself divided into tribes or factions? Such questions rise naturally from much of colonial literature but perhaps most glaringly from Morton's work.

John Winthrop (1588–1649)

Contributing Editor: Nicholas D. Rombes, Jr. [p. 188]

Classroom Issues and Strategies

The sweeping nature of the journal encompasses social, political, economic, and "daily survival" issues. Thus, it might be wise to focus on an area, or areas, at least to begin with. When looking at cultural or historical implications, consult supplemental information. That is, although Winthrop's writings illuminate his biases and assumptions, they "shape" the history of the period as well as record it.

Students are generally shocked by the rigidity of Winthrop's view of the world. Their shock may be addressed by consulting outside sources (e.g., on the Hutchinson affair) and making them aware of Winthrop's assumptions concerning power, patriarchy, etc., as well as the position and voice of women in the Puritan community. However, it might be wise to note, as well, how our twentieth-century notions of what is fair and unfair can sometimes impose themselves upon the cultural environment Winthrop was operating within. Winthrop and the Puritans should be approached not only as philosophical political, and religious figures, but also as real people who struggled daily against nature, hunger, and disease.

Students are often curious about the distinctions between the Covenant of Works, the Covenant of Grace, and the Elect. Explore the notion of community and social structures and the role of the individual in these structures. Discuss Bible as typological model for Puritans, as well as Puritan conceptions of original depravity, limited atonement, grace, and predestination.

Major Themes, Historical Perspectives, and Personal Issues

Certainly, based on the selections in this anthology, it would be fruitful to focus on the Hutchinson controversy and its implications for the Puritan oligarchy. Examine the early Puritans' conception of liberty and its inextricable connections with their obligation to God. Likewise, the notion of a "city upon a hill" and the Puritans' link between America and the "new Israel" is important. Discuss as well the providential interpretation of events and the nature of hierarchy in the Puritan community.

Significant Form, Style, or Artistic Conventions

Winthrop had training as a lawyer; the style and form of *A Modell of Christian Charity* reflects this. Likewise, the entire self-reflexive nature of the Journal lends itself to examination: Who was Winthrop's audience? Where does the Journal belong in the convention of the personal narrative or spiritual autobiography? What was his purpose for writing?

Original Audience

Recent examinations of *A Modell of Christian Charity* suggest that the sermon was not only intended for those who would soon be settling in America, but also for those who were growing weary (and by implication becoming disruptive) during the long voyage aboard the *Arbella*. In what ways was Winthrop's audience (especially in the Journal) himself?

Comparisons, Contrasts, Connections

Perhaps compare Winthrop's sermons with those of Jonathan Edwards (who was writing a century later). Note how the style changed, as did the emphasis on religious experience (the experience becomes more sensory and less restrained). Compare Winthrop's vision of God's grace with Roger Williams's vision.

Questions for Reading and Discussion/ Approaches to Writing

1. (a) What motivated the Puritans to flee England?
   (b) Did the Puritans have a "blueprint" for organizing their new communities, or did the social structure evolve slowly?
   (c) From what type of social, cultural, religious, and economic background did Winthrop emerge?
2. (a) Examine Winthrop's 1645 speech in which he responds to charges that he exceeded his authority as governor. Is this speech a fruition (or expression) of the Puritan ambiguity between the value of religion and the value of individual liberty?
   (b) How did the Hutchinson controversy potentially threaten Puritan oligarchy?
   (c) Explore the "spiritual autobiography" and its characteristics. What philosophical purposes did it serve? What pragmatic purposes?
   (d) In *Modell*, have students trace image patterns Winthrop uses, i.e., allusions to Biblical passages, discursive form of sermon, etc.

Bibliography

Dunn, Richard S. "John Winthrop Writes his Journal." *William and Mary Quarterly* 41 (1984): 185–212.

Miller, Perry. *Errand into the Wilderness*. 1956. (Essays).

Morgan, Edmund S. "John Winthrop's 'Modell of Christian Charity' in a Wider Context." *The Huntington Library Quarterly* 50 (Winter 1987): 145–151.

Rutman, Darrett B. *Winthrop's Boston: A Portrait of a Puritan Town, 1630–1649*. Chapel Hill: University of North Carolina Press, 1965. (Look especially at Chapter I, "A City upon a Hill"; Chapter III, "The Emergence of Town Government"; and Chapter VI, "Diversity and Division.")

William Bradford (1590–1657)

Contributing Editor: Kenneth Alan Hovey [p. 210]

Significant Form, Style, or Artistic Conventions

The difficulty of teaching William Bradford rests in the fact that the group he headed, the Pilgrims, is familiar to most Americans in a highly popularized form. In elementary school, Americans learn that the Pilgrims were a virtuous people who, in the face of religious persecution in England, came to America, signed the democratic Mayflower Compact, landed at Plymouth, and after a hard year of hunting and farming, displayed their hospitality to the Indians and their thanks to God in a harvest feast of unrivaled home-cooking. Students coming to Bradford with this version in mind need to be shown that Bradford says almost nothing about a first thanksgiving, portrays the Pilgrims suffering and fasting more than feasting, is generally suspicious of the Indians, treats the Scrooby Church Covenant as far more important than the Mayflower Compact, and shows, unintentionally, how the strident religious position of his church naturally provoked the official persecution the Pilgrims received.

At a higher level, Americans generally learn that the Pilgrims were Puritans and that Puritans were rigid religious reactionaries who burned witches, opposed all pleasure, and condemned naysayers to the stocks in this life and hellfire in the next. Students on this level need to learn that in their day the Pilgrims (and Puritans generally) were religious progressives who rejected traditional religious holy days, ceremonies, and authorities; secularized marriage; multiplied rapidly; preferred beer to water; and adapted rapidly to changing times. Clearly the Puritans' devotion to the Bible, especially to the portrait of Israel in the Old Testament, resulted in their applying rigorous judgments to Indians, moral delinquents, and later, witches. But in his discussion of bestiality, Bradford shows a remarkable awareness of the dangers of such rigor and, in his portrayal of Morton, attacks what he considers the greater dangers of a laxity that exploited the Indians and the scapegraces it claimed to embrace and, further, that posed a threat to the whole colonial endeavor.

The most sophisticated students may have been taught a third view, that the Pilgrims were Calvinists and that Calvinists believed in double predestination, considered worldly prosperity as sign of predestined election, and therefore devoted themselves to the Protestant work ethic with a vengeance, rapidly becoming model capitalists. To such students, it is important to point out that the Pilgrim community was initially a communistic experiment in America. Bradford glorifies the Pilgrims in their impoverished unity in Holland and condemns them when their wealth divides them in America. Bradford undoubtedly emphasizes the this worldly providence of God, which upholds human effort, but contends that providence is displayed amid suffering and small means more than in success. Indeed, affliction is more often the sign of the saint in Bradford's view than prosperity. The Pilgrims are no more capitalists than they are hospitable, democratic pie-makers or pleasure-hating witch-burners.

Roger Williams (c. 1603–1683)

Contributing Editor: Raymond F. Dolle [p. 232]

Classroom Issues and Strategies

Williams was a controversialist who used his Cambridge training in medieval disputation to compose prolix, rhetorical, erudite arguments, supported with biblical and classical allusions and quotations. This style and complex syntax (often rambling, gnarled, and incomplete) is difficult for today's undergraduate to follow. The problem is often compounded by Williams's Puritan theology, formal subject matter, and didactic religious purpose. These may not immediately appeal to our students' tastes and interests. The problem is to make Williams comprehendible and relevant.

The selections in this anthology avoid much of Williams's most opaque prose, such as that in his most frequently anthologized tract, *The Bloody Tenent*. These selections exemplify the logic and structure of Williams's thoughts, and so allow us to appreciate the radical vision and hear the distinctive voice of America's most famous religious dissenter despite our problems with his language. Once students understand that Williams represents an early expression of the American ideals of religious toleration, equal rights, and individual freedom, they are usually willing to make the effort to read his writings.

Students admire Williams's rebellion against authority and his argument for individual liberty of conscience. Although they may not understand his religious beliefs, they respect his courage and determination to stand up for what he believed.

The satire of so-called "Christians" and "civilization" never fails to amuse students, many of whom see themselves as virtuous pagans. They should be encouraged to speculate on what Williams would think about modern America.

Parallels between the Indians' religious beliefs and Christian concepts often surprise students and stimulate discussion of the nature of religion.

Williams's apparent toleration of personal religious differences often confuses students because it seems to contradict his radical and extreme Puritanism. Students must be reminded that his acceptance into his colony of such sects as the Quakers does not mean he thought that their beliefs were acceptable. Rather, he believed that the free search for Truth and the liberty to argue one's beliefs would lead the elect to God.

Major Themes, Historical Perspectives, and Personal Issues

In order to understand the conflict between Williams and the Puritan leaders that led to his banishment, we need to understand the three extreme positions he expounded:

1. Civil magistrates should have no jurisdiction over religious matters, and Christian churches should be absolutely divorced from worldly concerns (i.e., separation of church and state)—a position destructive to the prevailing theocracy of Massachusetts Bay and Ply-

mouth. The elect had to be free to seek God as they believed right. His letter "To the Town of Providence" refutes the *reductio ad absurdum* charge that this position leads ultimately to political anarchy if individuals can claim liberty of conscience to refuse civil obedience.

2. The Puritans should all become Separatists because the Church of England was associated too closely with political authority—a position that jeopardized the charter and the relative freedom it granted.

3. The Massachusetts Bay Company charter should be invalidated since Christian kings have no right to dispose of Indian lands—a position again based on separation of spiritual and material prerogatives. Williams was a friend of the Narragansett Indians, a defender of their legal property rights, and an admirer of their natural virtue. He devoted much of his life to understanding their language and culture so that he could teach them about Christ. An "implicit dialogue" intended to bridge cultures for their mutual benefit, *A Key* exploits the paradoxical contrast between barbaric civility and English degeneracy. The savages had to be Christianized, but this colonizing process often had tragic effects. The importance of bringing knowledge of Christ to the Indians, despite this dilemma, created one of the central conflicts in Williams's life.

The banishment of Williams from the colony reflects basic conflicts and concerns in the patriarchal Puritan society of colonial New England. The community leaders felt an urgent need to maintain authority and orthodoxy in order to preserve the "city on a hill" they had founded. Any challenge to their authority undermined the Puritan mission and threatened the New Canaan they had built with such suffering. Of course, the zeal and pure devotion needed to continue the efforts of the founding fathers was too much to ask of most colonists, so their congregational social structure began to fracture almost before it was established. Not only did secular attractions, worldly concerns, and material opportunities distract immigrants, but also the strict requirements for church membership denied many full status in the community. Like Anne Hutchinson, Williams advocated attractive individualistic principles that threatened the prevailing system, and he was banished from Christ's kingdom in America in an attempt to hold the community of saints together.

Significant Form, Style, or Artistic Conventions

One of the most appealing rhetorical devices in these selections is Williams's use of analogy, metaphors, and emblems. The introduction to *A Key* (in fact, the title itself) invites attention to such figurative language, as in the proverb, "A little key may open a box, where lies a bunch of keys." The meaning and implications of such statements are fruitful points for class discussion. Other good examples are the ship metaphor in the letter to Providence and the emblematic poems at the end of the chapters in *A Key*.

Throughout *A Key*, especially in the General Observations, the satiric contrast between true natural virtue and false Christianity creates a tension that invigorates the text and makes it a unique example of the promotional tract tradition.

The catechism in the vocabulary lists is worth attention.

Original Audience

Although Williams usually wrote with particular readers in mind, his themes and subjects have universal relevance and can still reward readers today.

Williams tells us that he intended *A Key* "specially for my friends residing in those parts." In other words, he wants to instruct fellow missionaries and traders how to interact with his other friends, the Indians. He is determined to dispel the stereotypes and false conceptions of them as subhuman savages current in the early colonies. Images of the Indians in writings from Williams's contemporaries and earlier explorers should provide students with a clear sense of the audience, their assumptions, and their needs. Williams has much to say still about interracial understanding, respect, and harmony. Moreover, his observations are still keen insights into human nature.

The audience for the letter to Providence is again quite specific, with a particular misconception and need. Williams writes to settle a controversy over freedom of conscience and civil obedience. Again, this controversy is still alive, and we can consider Williams's statement in light of the writings on the subject by such men as Thoreau and Martin Luther King.

Comparisons, Contrasts, Connections

Williams's descriptions of the Indians can be compared to descriptions in many other texts, ranging from the orthodox Puritan attitudes toward the satanic savages, as in Mary Rowlandson's captivity narrative, to eighteenth- and nineteenth-century Romantic tributes to the Noble Savage.

Similarly, Williams is often seen as a forerunner of Jefferson and Jackson, but we must remember that he did not advocate liberty as an end in itself for political reasons, but rather as a means to seek God.

Questions for Reading and Discussion/ Approaches to Writing

1. (a) What can we infer about Williams's intentions from the fact that he chose to compose *A Key into the Language of America* as an "implicit dialogue" rather than as a dictionary?
   (b) Characterize the persona of the first-person narrator in *A Key*. What kind of person does Williams present himself as?
   (c) How is Williams's book like a key?
   (d) How do the various sections of each chapter in *A Key* relate to one another and to the whole work?
   (e) What lessons can a Christian learn from the Indians?
   (f) Why might Williams once have objected to Europe and the rest of the West being referred to as "Christendom"?
   (g) In what ways was a colony in the New World like a ship at sea?
   (h) What did Williams gain from his treaty with the Indians besides legal ownership of some land?

2. An anthology as innovative as the *Heath Anthology* calls for innovative pedagogy and assignments. Here are some alternatives to the traditional junior-level LITCRIT papers:
   (a) Personal Response Paper: Ask the students to compare one or more of Williams's observations to their own experiences and observations.
   (b) Creative Response Paper: Ask the students to write a letter back to Williams by a spokesman for the town of Providence refuting Williams's argument and defending the right to act as one believes one's religious beliefs demand.
   (c) Creative Research Paper: Assign supplemental readings from Winslow's biography of Williams (or other sources) related to his trial and banishment. Then ask the students to compose a transcript of the trial proceedings.

Bibliography

In addition to the books listed at the end of the headnote in the *Heath Anthology*, many useful articles on Williams are available. Here are some of the most recent:

Guggisberg, Hans R. "Religious Freedom and the History of the Christian World in Roger Williams' Thought." *Early American Literature* 12, no. 1 (Spring 1977): 36–48.

LaFantasie, Glenn W. "Roger Williams: The Inner and Outer Man." *Canadian Review of American Studies* 16 (1985): 375–94.

Peace, Nancy E. "Roger Williams—A Historiographical Essay." *Rhode Island History* 35 (1976): 103–13.

Teunissen, John J. and Evelyn J. Hinz. "Anti-Colonial Satire in Roger Williams' *A Key into the Language of America*." *Ariel: A Review of International English Literature* 7, no. 3 (1976): 5–26.

——. "Roger Williams, Thomas More, and the Narragansett Utopia." *Early American Literature* 11, no. 3 (Winter 1976–1977): 281–95.

Other sources published prior to 1974 can be located by using Wallace Coyle's *Roger Williams: A Reference Guide* (Boston: G. K. Hall, 1977).

Anne Bradstreet (c. 1612–1672)

Contributing Author: Pattie Cowell [p. 256]

Classroom Issues and Strategies

The main problem in teaching Bradstreet is the students' unfamiliarity with the Puritan context in which she wrote. Many students close off their reading of Bradstreet and other Puritan writers because they disapprove of what they know about Puritan theology. Offering brief background materials summarizing a few key elements of American Puritanism is helpful. In addition, consider beginning with and emphasizing the more personal—and accessible—poems. For example, students frequently pick up on the double message about the status of women poets in "The Prologue."

Major Themes, Historical Perspectives, and Personal Issues

Major themes include family, identity, spirituality, tension between faith and doubt, and history.

Other issues might be the status of poets, especially women poets, in seventeenth-century North America and literary ties across the Atlantic.

Significant Form, Style, or Artistic Conventions

1. Impact of Puritanism on Bradstreet's aesthetics.
2. British, French, and classical influences on Bradstreet's work.

Original Audience

Ask students to develop a description of Bradstreet's original readers through an exercise in historical imagination, in which they try to reconstruct the work's original context (demographics, geography, publishing circumstances, libraries or lack of libraries, means of communication, literacy, race and class and gender considerations, etc.). Next ask students to consider themselves as a contrasting audience through a discussion of how issues in Bradstreet's work relate or fail to relate to contemporary concerns.

Comparisons, Contrasts, Connections

Consider reading Bradstreet in comparison with either Edward Taylor's poems or with the work of contemporary British women writers, such as Katherine Philips.

Bibliography

Individual pieces in *Critical Essays on Anne Bradstreet*, ed. Pattie Cowell and Ann Stanford (Boston: G. K. Hall, 1983), especially:

Eberwein, Jane Donahue. " 'No Ret'ric We Expect': Argumentation in Bradstreet's 'The Prologue,' " pp. 218–225.

Richardson, Robert D., Jr., "The Puritan Poetry of Anne Bradstreet," pp. 101–115.

Stanford, Ann. "Anne Bradstreet: Dogmatist and Rebel," pp. 76–88.

White, Elizabeth Wade. "The Tenth Muse—A Tercentenary Appraisal of Ann Bradstreet," pp. 56–75.

Michael Wigglesworth (1631–1705)

Contributing Editor: Jeffrey A. Hammond [p. 282]

Classroom Issues and Strategies

Characterization provides a fruitful entry into Wigglesworth. Not surprisingly, student reactions to the figure of God in the poem usually initiate lively class discussion. But the character of God here is no more arbitrarily drawn than is the harsh Christ of *The Day of Doom*. Both figures function within the two poems as personifications of the legal side of the redemptive framework: the side corresponding to the Covenant of Works, original sin, and humanity's need for a Savior. Preaching manuals insisted that ministers were to stir up the fear of the Law by which hearers could find themselves convicted in sin. Puritans insisted that to the rude and headstrong, God would seem every bit as frightening as Wigglesworth portrays Him in the poem; readers terrified by Wigglesworth's depiction would thus feel their own need to repent. The stern God of "God's Controversy" would have pushed receptive readers toward the merciful God who existed *outside the poem*, and who still offered them a chance for salvation.

Major Themes, Historical Perspectives, and Personal Issues

The major themes for discussion would include: the Puritan sense of mission and special place in history; the genre of the jeremiad, in prose and in verse; and the relation of Wigglesworth's themes to the Restoration in England.

Among the personal issues to focus on would be: the Puritan urgency of conversion; psychological effects of the poetry; and the situational context of the verse: that it was often read aloud in families; that the form of the verse was designed to make it accessible, frightening.

Also noteworthy are Wigglesworth's use of poetry as a substitute for preaching and his attempt to reach the widest possible readership.

Significant Form, Style, or Artistic Conventions

Issues for discussion include:

1. Relation to *Bay Psalm Book* and ballad meter.
2. Closeness of biblical paraphrase—ask students to compare with Bible references and see how Wigglesworth adjusts his sources.
3. Relation to sermon form.
4. Relation to Old and New Testaments—balance of Law and Grace (i.e., theological underpinnings of the verse).

Original Audience

Audience is *very* important. Wigglesworth's verse was written to be *heard*, like a sermon. This poem, like his others, was written during a sense of decline in the Puritan mission for all "hearers," including children and illiterates. One key to teaching Wigglesworth, especially to undergraduates, is to approach his work as public and popular art, as opposed to the more private verse of Bradstreet and Taylor. Whereas they wrote to edify themselves or family members and friends, Wigglesworth aimed at a far broader readership. As a result, he was more obligated than they to teach basic principles of doctrine to uninitiated or unconcerned readers.

Comparisons, Contrasts, Connections

Contrast Wigglesworth's and Milton's meter/form and their portrayal of various figures. Contrast Bradstreet's and Taylor's private or familial approach with Wigglesworth's societal, communal, and historical focus.

Questions for Reading and Discussion/ Approaches to Writing

1. (a) Who was the poem written for?
   (b) How did it probably affect that audience?
   (c) What is the purpose of the poem? Does it succeed or fail?
2. What is the relation of the poem's structure to sermon form? Contrast "God's Controversy" with the more personal/private verse written by Puritans like Edward Taylor or Anne Bradstreet.

Bibliography

Crowder, Richard. "'The Day of Doom' as Chronomorph." *Journal of Popular Culture* 9 (1976): 948–59.

Hammond, Jeffrey A. " 'Ladders of Your Own': *The Day of Doom* and the Repudiation of 'Carnal Reason.'" *Early American Literature* 19 (1984): 42–67.

Minter, David. "The Puritan Jeremiad as a Literary Form." In *The American Puritan Imagination: Essays in Revaluation*, edited by Sacvan Bercovitch, 45–55. Cambridge University Press, 1974.

Pope, Alan H. "Petrus Ramus and Michael Wigglesworth: The Logic of Poetic Structure." In *Puritan Poets and Poetics: Seventeenth-Century American Poetic Theory and Practice*, edited by Peter White, 210–26. Penn State Press, 1985.

The Bay Psalm Book (1640)

The New-England Primer (1683?)

Contributing Editor: Jean Ferguson Carr [p. 295]

Classroom Issues and Strategies

Readers may assume that both of these texts are simply functional transmissions of doctrine and discipline, representing a narrow and dogmatic religious culture of merely antiquarian interest. The difficulty is to encourage readers to question their prejudgments both about Puritan culture and about religious/educational texts. Readers need to be taught how to read a text that has many parts, that is written not by a single author but by a group representing broader cultural interests and values. They need to see these texts as an emergent culture's effort to formulate values that can be taught and maintained.

For example, in reading the psalms, it is useful to compare the *Bay Psalm Book* version with those of the King James translation or others, noting the choices made and the interpretation those choices represent. Also, in reading the primer, consider what those lessons suggest about not only what the culture authorized teachers to enforce, but what the culture feared or had difficulty controlling.

Students are often unnerved by the old-style spelling, but with a little practice they can read the material smoothly. Once they are comfortable with these external issues, they are often surprised and impressed by the frankness with which such topics as death, sin, and governmental punishment are treated.

Major Themes, Historical Perspectives, and Personal Issues

The psalm book reflects a concern about making worship contemporary, particular to their time and place and special circumstances as pilgrims to a new land. The book's design and production stress the belief that faith must be attended to on a daily basis by each individual. The small books, written in English and in contemporary verse forms, could be carried into the home and the place of work, their lessons repeated to ward off the dangers and temptations of life in a "wilderness." The primer recognizes the difficulties of remaining faithful and obedient, and it values learning as a way to preserve from one generation to another "that part/which shall never decay," the cultural and religious values of the community which cannot be silenced by the state or death.

Significant Form, Style, or Artistic Conventions

John Cotton's preface is a fascinating document about translation, advocating use of the vernacular and defending "modern" poetry. The psalms are "contested" versions, retranslated to mark a cultural and religious difference from those versions widely used in Europe and England, as well as to distinguish the Massachusetts Bay Colony Puritans from the Plymouth Pilgrims, who used the Sternhold-Hopkins Psalter of 1562.

Original Audience

The psalm book, written and printed by the Puritans of Massachusetts Bay Colony in 1640, was designed to allow a whole congregation to sing psalms together in church and at home. Neither Cotton's essay nor the poems have been attended to by modern critics: The psalter has been generally treated as a simple "text" of antiquarian interest only. The primer was the chief educational text of the New England colonies for over a hundred years, from its first printing in 1683.

Comparisons, Contrasts, Connections

Melville's call for American readers to "boldly contemn all imitation, though it comes to us graceful and fragrant as the morning; and foster all originality, though, at first, it be crabbed and ugly as our own pine knots" ("Hawthorne and his Mosses," 1850) suggests how the psalms and Cotton's preface might usefully be reread. The *Bay Psalm Book* can be compared with the literary credos of Emerson and Whitman, which prefer originality over literary polish or imitative technical perfection. The primer could be used to frame discussions about attitudes toward learning and childhood, toward the propagation of cultural values through books. It serves as a useful anthology of cultural concerns to compare with such later textbooks as McGuffey's *Eclectic Readers* or Webster's *American Speller*.

Questions for Reading and Discussion/ Approaches to Writing

1. (a) Compare two versions of a psalm (perhaps King James, Isaac Watts, Bay Psalm, or a modern version). What do the changes suggest about what is valued by the translator? What do they suggest about how the translator understands the difficulties or possibilities of faith?

   (b) What does John Cotton's preface propose as the important considerations for poetry and religious song? What established values is he thus opposing?

   (c) What seem to be the daily conditions of life for the readers of the primer, as exemplified in the lessons' details? What did they have to fear or to overcome?

   (d) How does the primer envision the relationship of parent to child? Of state to citizen? Of God to person?

   (e) How do the lessons demark proper social relations? How do they suggest the community's ability to contain crime or misbehavior?

   (f) How does the primer propose to shape (control?) speech and writing?

2. (a) Compare the claims about poetry and national literature in Cotton's preface to one of the following texts: Emerson's "The Poet," Whitman's "Preface" to *Leaves of Grass*, Rebecca Harding Davis's *Life in the Iron Mills*, Melville's "Hawthorne and his Mosses."

   (b) Discuss how *The New-England Primer* represents both the importance and difficulty of learning cultural values and behavior.

(c) Compare *The New-England Primer* as a cultural artifact with a contemporary textbook for children. What seem to be the fears each text guards against? How does each text presuppose about childhood and children? How do they represent the relationship of school to children, of parents to children? What do they propose as the proper subjects for children?

Bibliography

Eames, W., ed. *The Bay Psalm Book* (Facsimile), 1903.

Ford, Paul, ed. *The New-England Primer* (Facsimile and introduction, pp. 1–53), New York: Teachers College Press, 1962.

Nietz, John. *Old Textbooks*. Pittsburgh: University of Pittsburgh Press, 1961.

Watters, David H. " 'I Spoke as a Child': Authority, Metaphor, and *The New England Primer*." *Early American Literature* 20, pp. 193–213.

Seventeenth-Century Wit

Nathaniel Ward (1578–1652)
Philip Pain (?–c. 1667)
John Fiske (1608–1677)
John Josselyn (c. 1610–post 1692)
John Saffin (1626–1710)
Roger Wolcott (1679–1767)

Contributing Editor: Kenneth Alan Hovey [p. 311]

Classroom Issues and Strategies

Students may find the language antique and thus difficult. The wit seems sometimes abstruse and sometimes silly while the ideas expressed can be conventional or fulsome.

Explain that the purpose of poetry in the seventeenth century was different than it is now (or since the Romantic Age). Poets were not trying to be original in idea or sincere in what they said, as today, but clever in expression, learned in word choice, and metrically perfect (whatever twists might have to be put in the syntax to accomplish this). Nathaniel Ward's poems, because they discuss poetry, would prepare students for the poetry of Pain and Fiske.

It would help students if you make a list of items presented in the headnote and have them define them and then find examples of these in the poems.

Major Themes, Historical Perspectives, and Personal Issues

The major theme is wit itself and how our "pious" forefathers used it to approach serious topics, especially death and God. The role of women figures prominently in the work of Nathaniel Ward and John Saffin. The theme of Nature is also important in the work of John Josselyn and Roger Walcott.

Significant Form, Style, or Artistic Conventions

Students should note the regular meter and rhyme and identify the different forms of wit, notably the conceit, the pun, the paradox, the anagram, the acrostic, and the emblems. Also prevalent are the high rhetorical expression of some poems (notably John Saffin's) and the low informal diction of others, (notably Nathaniel Ward's).

Original Audience

Allusions that are unfamiliar today were part of standard knowledge among literate seventeenth-century readers, especially allusions to the Bible and the Classics. Often, the Puritan faith was easily mixed with mythical terms derived from Rome and Greece. Late Renaissance writers, like their audience, accepted the joint authority of Revelation and Reason (embodied in antiquity) and naturally reconciled them, regarding ancient myth as entirely allegorical.

Comparisons, Contrasts, Connections

Aside from the other major American poets of the time (Bradstreet, Taylor and Willliams), these poets deserve comparison with their major influences, Donne, Jonson, and Herbert, all of whom reflect either metaphysical wit or neo-classical form. Other prose writers, like Purchas at one end and Mather at the other, reflect similarly witty and allusive styles in prose.

Questions for Reading and Discussion/ Approaches to Writing

You might make a list of the terms presented in the headnote and on the preceding pages and have the students define them (or give them definitions) and then have them find the defined features in the poems.

Simply "getting" the point is the trial for each student—and thus each student needs the help of the instructor. I doubt many students could write comfortably on poems so apparently arcane, though when understood, quite delightful.

Bibliography

A larger anthology of minor American seventeenth-century poetry would provide more examples of these forms and poets.

Mary Rowlandson (1636–1678)

Contributing Editor: Paula Uruburu [p. 317]

Classroom Issues and Strategies

One of the main problems in teaching Mary Rowlandson is getting the students to understand Rowlandson's covenant theology and how it affects her view of the Indians. Students find her constant quoting of the Bible tiresome and need to see that it is an integral part of her vision of the world. To address this difficulty, I explain the workings of Puritan covenant theology (the whole concept of the "errand into the wilderness") not only in Rowlandson's narrative, but also in Bradstreet's poetry and John Winthrop's *A Modell of Christian Charity*.

The narrative is best approached from several perspectives, including literary (what makes it a work of literature?); historical (where does fact mix with fiction?); and psychological (what factors may be affecting Rowlandson's interpretation of her experience?).

Students respond well to the personal diary-like quality of the narrative and the trials Rowlandson undergoes. Although most side with her, some also recognize the hardships the Indians have experienced at the hands of the colonists.

Major Themes, Historical Perspectives, and Personal Issues

It is important for the students to get the straight historical facts about King Phillip's War during which Rowlandson was taken captive. This allows them to see both sides of the issues that caused the "war" and to better understand the Indians' plight as well as Rowlandson's reaction to her eleven-week captivity.

Significant Form, Style, or Artistic Conventions

Discussion of the Indian captivity narrative as a genre is essential. Also, a background on Puritan sermons and their reliance upon the Word in the Bible is important since the movement/structure of the narrative juxtaposes real events with biblical comparisons or equivalents.

Original Audience

We discuss how the Puritans would have responded to the narrative and why Rowlandson wrote it. I ask students for their own reaction (with whom does their sympathy lie—the settlers or the Indians?). We then look at Benjamin Franklin's essay "Some Remarks Concerning the Savages of North America" for an ironic comparison/contrast and then discuss the changes in perception from his time until now.

Feminist perspective: In what ways does this narrative lend itself to a greater understanding of the woman's place in Puritan history? How does being a woman affect Rowlandson's point of view?

Comparisons, Contrasts, Connections

Using Bradstreet's poetry (especially "Some Verses Upon the Burning of our House") and Winthrop's sermon, give two different views of the details and effects of covenant theology on ordinary people's lives and how they were expected to respond to traumatic or trying events and circumstances.

Questions for Reading and Discussion/ Approaches to Writing

1. How does the *Narrative* demonstrate Puritan theology and thinking at work?
2. In what ways does Rowlandson use her experience to reaffirm Puritan beliefs? How does she view herself and her fellow Christians? How does she see the Indians? What do her dehumanizing descriptions of the Indians accomplish?
3. Are there any instances where she seems to waver in her faith?
4. Why does Rowlandson distrust the "praying Indians"?
5. How does she use the Bible and varied scriptural allusions in her analysis of her captivity and restoration?
6. Does her world view change at all during her eleven weeks of captivity? Why or why not?
7. How does the *Narrative* combine/demonstrate/refute what William Bradford in *Of Plymouth Plantation* and John Winthrop in *A Modell of Christian Charity* had to say about the Puritan's mission in the New World?

After addressing any number of the above questions, aimed at a basic analysis of the *Narrative,* an instructor can then continue with a discussion of the possible motives Rowlandson had for writing it. This aspect appeals to students who are most interested in trying to understand the human being behind the prose.

1. Compare and contrast the Indian captivity narrative with the slave narrative genre. What elements and conventions do they share? How do they differ?
2. Explain how Rowlandson's narrative reinforces her world view. Where (if at all) does her covenant theology fail her or seem insufficient to explain actions and events?

Bibliography

Primary Sources

Van Der Beets, Richard. *Held Captive By the Indians: Selected Narratives 1642–1836.* Knoxville: University of Tennessee Press, 1973.

Secondary Sources

Burke, Charles. *Puritans at Bay.* New York: Exposition Press, 1967.

Drimmer, Frederick, ed. *Captured By the Indians.* New York: Dover, 1961. A collection of fifteen firsthand accounts from 1750–1870.

Slotkin, Richard, and James Folsom. *So Dreadful a Judgment.* Connecticut: Wesleyan University Press, 1978. Puritan responses to King Phillip's War.

Edward Taylor (1642?–1729)

Contributing Editor: Karen E. Rowe [p. 342]

Classroom Issues and Strategies

Students may recoil from Taylor's overly didactic, seemingly aesthetically rough or unpolished poetry, in part because he seems too preoccupied with issues of sin and salvation, which they find alien. The fundamental need is to familiarize students with basic Puritan concepts, biblical sources and allusions, and the meditative tradition. This background allows students and teachers to move beyond the easy post-Romantic definition of the poetry as "lyric," which locks the class into a quick survey of only the occasional poems. Taylor may also seem both too easy ("doesn't he tell it all?") and too complicated, because of arcane word choices, the curious compounding of images, and the plethora of biblical images.

The organization of selections in the *Heath Anthology* permits one for the first time to trace Taylor's chronological development as a poet and also emphasizes a more personalized Taylor. By clustering the Meditations and engaging students in playing with the multiple meaning of curious words, the poetry comes alive as an intricate orchestration of recurrent themes and interconnected images. The point is to capture Taylor's imaginative flexibility as much as his tortured angst, while at the same time seeing it all as part of an overriding concern with personal preparation for heaven and with how Taylor as poet can best serve God—and in what language.

Students respond initially to the personal anguish and graphic degradations to which Taylor submits himself, yet they are also quick to recognize the pattern of self-abasement followed by Christ's intervention and re-elevation of humankind. Through class discussion, they revise their thinking about both the seeming lack of sophistication in Taylor's poetry and the dismissal of Puritan poets.

Major Themes, Historical Perspectives, and Personal Issues

Major, but different, themes and historical issues emerge from each selection. Metrical paraphrases of Psalms were acceptable "hymns" for Protestants, as reflected in the Massachusetts *Bay Psalm Book*, although Taylor models his poems on the earlier Sternhold-Hopkins Psalter. Important themes include Taylor's adoption of David as his model for the poet; the concept of poetry as an act/offering of ritual praise; distinctions between the godly (righteous) and ungodly; God's power as Creator and Lawgiver; the righteous man as the Lord's servant; Christ as a Rock and Redeemer; and God's voice as that which speaks truly, and which man's voice merely echoes. As Thomas Davis suggests, by "providing a means of fashioning his own experience in the framework of biblical and historical precedent, the paraphrases invited the poet to make poetry a central concern in his life," and with the emergence of an "authentic note of his own voice" point directly to the *Preparatory Meditations*.

Probably completed in 1680, *Gods Determinations* usefully introduces students to Taylor's major dilemmas as preacher and individual saint—how to ascertain *and* sustain the belief in one's place among God's Elect and what admissions standards to uphold for Church membership. In its historical context, *Gods Determinations* reflects Taylor's local need to found a frontier Church for the true Elect (1679). His battles were against both the wilderness and Indians without and Satan within. This mini-sequence from among the total thirty-five poems allows one to talk about the difficult progress from conversion to justification and sanctification in two ways. A narrative reading opens with the magnificent evocation of God's creation, then the "Souls Groan" for salvation and "Christs Reply" as a lover or mother to a lost child, followed by the ecstasy of accepted redemption set off against Satan's renewed attempts at casting doubt, and the final triumphant entry into "Church Fellowship rightly attended," whether on earth or in heaven. Hence, the poem becomes a narrative of a spiritual journey. Taylor's position is as narrator and as voice of the saint.

One can read the poems as a "debate," emphasizing various oppositions, between God and fallen man, the unworthy Elect soul and grace-giving Christ, the doubting soul and Satan the tempter, between Christ and Satan, hence between lowly earthly things and God's grandeur, being outside the covenant community of Elect saints and being within (the coach), between doubt and assurance, sin and salvation. The poems also anticipate later allegorical renderings of Christ's marital relationships with the Church and individual soul in terms of the Dove and the

Bride, set off against images of Satan as a mongrel cur and his deceptive seductions, hence a battle between loving faith/grace and distorting reason.

The Occasional Poems, which include eight numbered poems, were probably begun in the early 1680s, just as Taylor had completed *Gods Determinations* and was initiating the second version of the Psalm paraphrases and the early *Preparatory Meditations*. Because these poems are the most "lyrical," they are more accessible to modern students. But what motivates Taylor is a desire to meditate upon natural "occurants" in order to extract allegorical or spiritual meanings.

Taylor's fondness for extended metaphors is apparent in "Upon a Spider Catching a Fly" and his famous "Huswifery." The latter leads to discussion of Taylor's frequent use of spinning and weaving terms, frequently in relationship to poetic language or the need for the "Wedden garment" of righteousness that robes mankind for the Lord's Supper and union with Christ. "Upon Wedlock, & Death of Children" reveals Taylor at his most personal and usefully links with other poems from *Edward Taylor's Minor Poetry*, which traces his domestic relationship with Elizabeth Fitch from his courtship (1674) to her death (1689).

"A Valediction to all the World preparatory for Death" permits comparisons among different versions, showing Taylor's substantial revision of late poems even during a time of severe illness. Although only two of the total eight canticles are included in the *Heath Anthology*, they nevertheless display Taylor in the process of shedding worldliness, particularly all things that appeal to the senses and sensualities of the flesh. His "farewell" to the world, the flesh, and the devil is renunciatory and poignant, a meditation on "vanity of vanities, all is vanity" (Ecclesiastes 12:6–8) that evokes the very fondness for created nature that he appears to abjure.

"A Fig for thee Oh! Death" expresses Taylor's defiance of death, and it is a *memento mori* meditation that should be placed side by side with his later Canticles poems, in which he envisions the beauties of heaven. His anticipation of the final judgment and reunion of body and soul is a final affirmation of faith in the divine promise of eternal life.

As a complete sequence, the poems selected here trace Taylor's preoccupations over a lifetime:

- from the early focus on creation to the later renunciation of earthly vanities
- from his earliest attempt to map the soul's conflicts with Satan to his later celebration of Church fellowship, the Lord's Supper, and Christ as the divine host

- from his domestic espousal to his spiritual union with Christ as the eternal Bridgegroom
- from his questioning of poetic status to his desire to be another David or Solomon, singing hymns for all eternity
- from his entrance into the minister's life to his death—the end of a long preparation recorded in a virtual poetic autobiography

Significant Form, Style, or Artistic Conventions

Taylor's verse experiments range from the common meter of the Psalm paraphrases to the varied stanza and metrical forms in *Gods Determinations* and the Occasional Poems, and finally to the heroic couplets of "A Valediction to all the World preparatory for Death" and "A Fig for thee Oh! Death." Variety also appears in Taylor's choice of forms, including the Psalm paraphrases, a debate or narrative sequence of lyrics in *Gods Determinations*, elegies, love poems, a valediction and reflection on worldly vanities, and *memento mori*—all of which were commonplace among his English predecessors, such as John Donne, George Herbert, and Henry Vaughan. For a more in-depth study of form, students might be urged to read and compare Taylor's elegies on public figures with those on personal losses, such as "Upon Wedlock, & Death of Children" and "A Funerall Poem upon . . . Mrs. Elizabeth Taylor," all in *Edward Taylor's Minor Poetry*.

Taylor's form and style seem too predictable, because of the unchanging six-line, iambic pentameter, ababcc stanza of the Meditations. Discussion should relate his use of a disciplined, even caged and controlled, form to his concept of poetry as ritualistic praise, as a rational framework within which to explore (and contain) irrational impulses of the rebellious soul, as a stimulus to imaginative imagistic variations, and as a habitual exercise of spiritual preparation. These poems are meditative self-examinations, illustrating the Puritan requirement to prepare the heart and soul before entering the Church or partaking of (and administering) the Lord's Supper. They also mediate between Taylor's composition and delivery of his Sunday sermon.

Taylor's imagistic variations in *Preparatory Meditations* permits one to teach him in different combinations and ways. Structurally, the poems reflect differing manipulations of image patterns, such as the focus on a single metaphor (1.6, 2.24, 2.109); figural images and interpretations (2.1, 2.24, 2.26, 2.71, 2.50); allegorical panoramas of salvation history (2.50, 2.109); associational tumblings of images (1.20, 2.60B); magnifications and diminutions ("Prologue"); and allegorical love poems that anatomize the Bridegroom's and Spouse's beauties (2.115, 2.143).

Thematically, poems cluster around recurrent ideas, such as Christ's nature and life (1.20, 2.24, 2.43, 2.60B, 2.115); man's nature and estate (1.6, 2.1, 2.26, 2.50, 2.143); Old Testament types (persons, events, ceremonies) that foreshadow New Testament fulfillments in Christ (2.1, 2.24, 2.26, 2.50, 2.71); the Lord's Supper as sacramental feast (2.60B, 2.71, 2.109); the marriage of Christ to his Bride the Church and individual soul (2.115, 2.143); and the necessity of poetic praise ("Prologue," 2.43). As a study of Puritan preparation and aesthetics, the meditations also reveal the motivating cause in Taylor's need to celebrate the Lord's Supper with a cleansed soul, robed in the wedding garment of righteousness for the feast (2.26, 2.60B, 2.109, 2.143) and poetry's function as spiritual purging and preparation ("Prologue," 2.43).

Chronologically, the Meditations move from the first series' dichotomy between mankind (a "Crumb" yet "imprinted with the divine image") and the perfected, exalted Christ of the Ascension. In keeping with a reorientation in Taylor's preaching, the second series begins anew with the Old Testament typology (2.1, 2.24. 2.26, 2.50, 2.71). He then shifts to a Christological New Testament focus (2.43, 2.50) in poems corresponding to the *Christographia* sermons, then to Meditations on the Lord's Supper (2.60B, 2.71, 2.109), and finally the Canticles (2.115, 2.143), Taylor's most sensual love poems, which anticipate the heavenly union beyond death (as also in the "Valediction").

Finally, the poems can be organized to reflect the context and progress of mankind's existence, beginning with the magnificent creation in the "Preface" to *Gods Determinations* and the providential schema mapped out in Meditation 2.50, shifting to man's fallen nature (2.1, 2.26) yet divine aspiration (1.6), the necessity of Christ's intervention through the incarnation (2.24), shedding of blood (2.60B), and Ascension (1.20), and concluding with the anticipations of the espousal between Elect souls and Christ (2.115, 2.143), which the Lord's Supper commemorates and foreshadows (2.71, 2.109).

Original Audience

Taylor never published his poetry, although he carefully transcribed many poems in the manuscript "Poetical Works." A consideration of audience must therefore, take account of the fact that the elegies and perhaps *Gods Determinations* were written in a more public mode, but that the majority of his Occasional Poems, the *Preparatory Meditations* and the later "Valediction" and "A Fig for thee Oh! Death" are intensely personal, written it would seem for an audience of God or Christ alone, or as meditative self-examinations of Taylor's soul. As readers, we eavesdrop on Taylor, but we are not easily invited into the poems, except insofar as we identify with the Elect soul in its struggles or with Taylor as a representative pilgrim in his journey toward salvation.

Comparisons, Contrasts, Connections

Fruitful comparisons can be drawn both intratextually and extratextually. For the *Preparatory Meditations,* corresponding sermons are extant from *Upon the Types of the Old Testament* (Meditations 2.1, 2.24, 2.26, 2.71) and from the *Christographia* (Meditations 2.43, 2.50). Edward Taylor's *Treatise Concerning the Lord's Supper,* notably Sermon 4, yields excellent excerpts on the need to prepare for the Lord's Supper and the wearing of the "wedden garment" for the feast. Because Taylor habitually clusters poems on the same biblical text, providing students, for example, with all four Meditations (1.19–22) on Philippians 2:9, "God hath highly exalted him," contextualizes a reading of the selected Meditation 1.20. Similarly, a short typological series, such as 2.58–61, permits a study of Taylor's fascination with the Exodus of Israel from Egypt and with the various types that foreshadow man's spiritual journey to salvation under the New Testament, as well as a more specific contextualizing of Meditation 2.600 on the "Rock of Horeb." Meditation 2.109 is part of a series (2.102–111) on the Lord's Supper, and the Canticle series yields many examples of Taylor's interpretation of sensual imagery.

Comparisons with George Herbert's *The Temple* (Taylor owned it), particularly poems on the types, and with John Donne's sonnets on the Ascension, death, and Christ as Spouse, enable students to identify different poetic styles and place Taylor in a broader seventeenth-century meditative tradition.

One might also compare Anne Bradstreet's "The Prologue" and "Author to her Book" with Taylor's meditations on poetic craft in "Were but my Muse an Huswife Good," "Prologue" to the *Preparatory Meditations* and Meditation 2.43. Bradstreet's "Vanity of all Worldly Things" complements Taylor's "Valediction," and her poems "In Reference to Her Children 23 June, 1659" and "Before the Birth of One of her Children" work in tandem with Taylor's "Upon Wedlock, & Death of Children," as do Bradstreet's several elegies on various grandchildren ("In Memory of my Dear Grandchild Elizabeth Bradstreet" and "On my Dear Grandchild Simon Bradstreet"). Selections from the prose meditations of Bradstreet also provide an intriguing counterpoint to Taylor's poetic meditations.

Presentational and Strategic Approaches

It proves particularly helpful to provide students with background information about key Puritan concepts, some of which are detailed in the headnote for Edward Taylor's selections. Many of these should also be discussed in relationship to other Puritan texts. But one can also prepare handouts on areas such as the concept of typology by listing Taylor's sermons and poems on the types (see *Saint and Singer*); a diagram of Israel's tabernacle and temple, its furnishings, the role of the High Priest, and the significant ceremonies; excerpts from a good Bible dictionary on major biblical figures or events; or predistributed excerpts from key biblical passages related to a poem's imagery. Visual arts only approximate the verbal, but Vaughan's emblem of the stony heart from *Silex Scintillans* for "The Ebb & Flow" or a Renaissance painting of Christ's Ascension from Mediatation 1.20 instructively guide the textual analysis. A diagram labeling parts of the spinning wheel and spinning process illustrate Taylor's love of using weaving, looms, and webs as metaphors for poetry and the construction of the self in "Huswifery." Comparing metaphysical with typological conceits stimulates discussion about poetic technique (e.g., Meditation 2.24 on the Feast of Tabernacles). Finally, reading poems aloud in class captures the surprising personal voice and intensity of many poems.

Questions for Reading and Discussion/ Approaches to Writing

1. Specific questions can be generated easily for most poems, but it helps students (not only with Taylor but also with the study of other Puritan literature) to ask them to research key terms, using Donald Stanford's glossary, a well-annotated Bible with a concordance, such as the New Scofield Reference edition, Johnson's *The Poetical Works of Edward Taylor*, or the *Milton Encyclopedia*. Terms might include Elect/election, covenant, baptism, Lord's Supper, preparation, law, grace, typology, providential history, apostasy, marriage, the Dove, the Rock, first fruits, offerings/sacrifices, Adam and Eve, the Garden of Eden, the Fall, Passover, the Exodus, Christ's incarnation, the crucifixion and resurrection, and the Second Coming. One can assign students to look up the Bible verses mentioned in the footnotes or to read selections from Genesis, Exodus, Psalms, Canticles, the Gospel, Hebrews, and Revelation. Because of Taylor's playfulness with different meanings of a single image, students might be asked to look up in the *Oxford English Dictionary* the complete history of "fillet," "squitchen," "screw" and

"pins," "sally," "cocks," or "escutcheon" (one word each, perhaps). They might research the construction of the spinning wheel, thumbscrews and racks, tenon and mortise carpentry, the tabernacle and temple, and an alembic. Such preparation frequently alerts students to Taylor's multiple strands of imagery, his tricky, punning, even humorous use of language, and the variety of areas from which he draws images and metaphors (architecture, horticulture, heraldry, carpentry, clothing, bookbinding, warfare, alchemy, music, classical mythology, history, printing, domestic chores).

2. Obvious paper assignments involve interpretive readings of poems not otherwise studied in class. Advanced students can be encouraged to compare Genesis as the principal creation story with Taylor's rendering in Psalm 19, the "Preface" to *Gods Determinations*, Meditation 2.50, and his "Valediction to all the World preparatory for Death." Analysis of different strands of imagery that cut across several poems allows students to see Taylor's recurrent methods and themes, as in the water, blood, and wine associated with Christ and the Lord's Supper. Similar assignments might be made around the concept of the feast, marriage, the garden, reciprocal relationships (master and servant, tenant and landlord), or around broad areas of imagery, such as those from architecture (see "Preface" to *Gods Determinations* and Meditation 2.24).

Teaching Issues and Interpretation

Placing Taylor in the context of other Puritan literature becomes illuminating in two ways because it responds to the question of what is poetry supposed to be and do. First, Taylor's work shows how the Puritan emphasis on spiritual examination of the individual soul can take the form of meditative and autobiographical poetry. Poetry for Taylor is both an immediate preparation for his ministerial administering of the Lord's Supper *and* a lifelong preparation for eternal life. Students often stumble with Taylor's poetry because they do not understand how intensely Taylor renounces this world in favor of a spiritual life within and a heavenly life yet to come. But they can identify with the human psychology of doubt, fear, loss, and a need for some form of consoling grace, comfort, or higher being to give meaning to the innately corrupt heart.

Second, because Taylor is the most prolific poet of America's first two hundred years (the anomaly of a "poet in the wilderness"), his meditations open up the question of a supposed Puritan disdain for poetry. Taylor's own puzzling over the proper uses of poetic language appears in "Were but my Muse an Huswife Good," the "Prologue" to the

Preparatory Meditations, Meditation 2.43, and "Valediction to all the World." By setting Taylor in a seventeenth-century tradition of paraphrases of Psalms, Job, and Canticles and, thus, the sanctioned acceptance of Biblical poetry, and a respect for *Sola Scriptura* as the model of language to be imitated, students can begin to appreciate the roots of an American tradition of poetry. The association of Taylor with David and Solomon as biblical models of poets becomes a useful end point for discussion because it points to Taylor's hope for his role in heaven, validates poetry as a medium of spiritual expression acceptable to God, sets the standards for "a transcendent style," and defines poetry as a ritual (meditative) offering of praise and worship.

Bibliography

Selections from the *Preparatory Meditations* and *Gods Determinations* have been published by permission of Donald E. Stanford, ed. *The Poems of Edward Taylor* (New Haven: Yale Univ. Press, 1960) and the "Psalm Paraphrases," "Occasional Poems," "A Valediction . . .," and "A Fig for thee Oh! Death" by permission of Thomas M. and Virginia L. Davis, eds. *Edward Taylor's Minor Poetry* (Boston: Twayne, 1981).

Aside from sources already mentioned in the headnote's bibliography and the footnotes, the introductions to Taylor's published works by Donald Stanford, Norman Grabo, Thomas and Virginia Davis, and Charles Mignon always prove helpful. The most succinct biographical sketch is Donald Stanford's "Edward Taylor" in the *Dictionary of Literary Biography*. Key chapters on Taylor are found in Sacvan Bercovitch's *Typology and Early American Literature,* Albert Gelpi's *The Tenth Muse,* Barbara Lewalski's *Protestant Poetics and the Seventeenth-Century Religious Lyric,* Mason Lowance's *The Language of Canaan,* Earl Miner's *Literary Uses of Typology,* and Peter White's *Puritan Poets and Poetics.*

Samuel Sewall (1652–1730)

Contributing Editor: Carla Mulford [p. 385]

Classroom Issues and Strategies

Most students have trouble placing the reading of a diary within the context of traditional literary study. Students find Sewall's apparent preoccupation with merchant ships' arrivals, the costs of nutmeats and madeira, the problems of dress and so forth a little disarming, for they are used to finding meaning in texts according to standards (e.g., images, metaphors) artificially set up.

To address this issue, I stress two main points—one about aesthetics, the other about culture. Sewall's diary offers us a direct glimpse into the life of a private Puritan. Unlike the diaries of Winthrop, Edwards, Bradstreet, and other early writers, Sewall's diary was probably written for his eyes alone, not to be passed around among friends and family members. The diary offers us signs of real change, in both ideology and culture. Thus, the notations about practical affairs become signs of culture *and* signs of Sewall's life-preoccupations.

Fruitful discussion often arises when I ask students to compare Sewall's seeming preoccupation with material goods with their own preoccupation about name-brand clothes and cars and videotaped weddings. He works particularly well with a middle-class student body.

Major Themes, Historical Perspectives, and Personal Issues

I have successfully used the Sewell selections as a sign of a culture in transition, noting with students the seeming shift in Sewall's interests from spiritual to secular issues. (In a broader sense, from Christianity to capitalism, some students like to add.) I usually treat the fact that Sewall—very humanly—seems to have wanted to enter the church in order to get his first child baptized. I usually talk about the Salem witch trials and discuss Sewall's retraction of his behavior during the trials, along with his writing of the first Puritan anti-slaveholding tract, *The Selling of Joseph*.

And I usually conclude by talking about life for women—that Katherine Winthrop might seem silly (in her modish wish that Sewall wear a wig, for example) or, worse yet, covetous (in her wish that he hire horses and buy a coach for her) but that, given the system of coverture (under which men legally retained all that their wives nominally owned), Winthrop stood to lose a great deal if she married Samuel Sewall. As a widow, Katherine Winthrop was a fully empowered person. If she had married Sewall (note that she never *did* remarry), she would have lost all legal rights to property she had run *on her own*, and she would have had to move away from her family. Travel for women of Winthrop's social position was difficult. Women did not usually ride horses. A move of any distance from her daughter would have meant that Winthrop would need assistance in traveling to see her. Sewall seemed not to want to accommodate.

The poignancy of Sewall's last remark about her—that she would be a woman sorely missed in her community (this said when she was buried)—matches the poignancy of his having noted (when he parted from courting her for the last time) the dirty linen that she wore, linen that had once been noted as clean, if noted at all.

Significant Form, Style, or Artistic Conventions

Sewall's diary seems to have been private. Thus, we don't find the form of spiritual autobiography that we find in Winthrop's "Christian Experience" or in Edwards's diary of the early 1720s. Sewall's preoccupation with whether or not he is saved, in the early part of the selection, thus takes on a kind of urgency. He is not playing out a particular spiritual model (as in spiritual autobiography) but rather speaks from a particular need—to become himself a member of a church so that his daughter can receive baptism.

Comparisons, Contrasts, Connections

Contrast the diary with Winthrop's "Christian Experience" (as spiritual autobiography) and with Winthrop's journal. The first contrast will show the differences between public and private documentation of spiritual questioning; the second, the differences between public history and private meditation.

Contrast the diary with Taylor's *Preparatory Meditations*.

With regard to its more secular impulses, compare and contrast the diary with Sarah Kemble Knight's journal and with Franklin's autobiography.

Questions for Reading and Discussion/ Approaches to Writing

1. I usually ask students to note if they find any shift in Sewall's interests as evidenced in the *Diary*. They usually note the shift from sacred to secular interests. Sophisticated students note that Sewall has for the most part internalized the religious value system after which he strove so heartily early on, so that he is moved to act upon his dealings in the witch trials (and make the retraction) and his attitudes about slavery (and write the anti-slavery pamphlet, *The Selling of Joseph*), rather than simply to be obsessive about these issues privately.

2. Students usually enjoy writing about Sewall as a key sign of the cultural change taking place in America—from a spiritual commonwealth to a mercantile community.

Bibliography

Instructors ought to consult the complete *Diary of Samuel Sewall*, ed. M. Halsey Thomas. New York: 1973, 2 vols., in order to get the flavor of the original.

Cotton Mather (1663–1728)

Contributing Editor: Kenneth Alan Hovey [p. 399]

Major Themes, Historical Perspectives, and Personal Issues

The one work of Mather that immediately interests most students is his account of the famous Salem witchcraft trials. His opening explanation of why witchcraft arose among the Puritans deserves to be compared with Bradford's explanation of buggery among the Pilgrims. Both authors express the paradox that where God is most upheld so is the devil, yet Mather and Bradford are aware of the problems of such a paradox from a purely rational point of view. It is important to note how Mather carefully distances himself from the trials by various means, praising both opponents and supporters of the proceedings and arguing that the devil might have entangled events so that real witches would be confounded with the falsely accused and judgment rendered unsure. Except for the concluding note to the trial of Martha Carrier, Mather's reporting is quite dispassionate and allows students, therefore, to determine the truth for themselves. The *post hoc ergo propter hoc* arguments of the witnesses were not so easily dismissed by those who believed in an invisible world acting upon the visible, and the confessions of Carrier's children and avowed witches make it difficult to explain the phenomenon as the proverbial "witch hunt" of the self-serving opponents of the accused.

Comparisons, Contrasts, Connections

In the more important *Magnalia Christi Americana* Mather is, by contrast, far from dispassionate and unwilling to distance himself in any way. Students can easily pick out places where he editorializes personally. The most telling is at the end of his life of Eliot, when he essentially identifies himself with Eliot by linking him to his own grandfathers, Cotton and Mather. Such editorializing is what differentiates the *Magnalia* from its immediate predecessor *Of Plymouth Plantation*. The "General Introduction" corresponds closely in purpose to the opening of Bradford's work and the life of Eliot to Bradford's life of Brewster. But while Bradford humbly removes himself from his tale, speaking only infrequently and in the third person of himself, Mather constantly obtrudes his narrative "I" and his views on the reader. Such obtrusiveness makes sense if one realizes that Mather's real interest is not in conveying the facts of men's lives but in turning lives into instructive "examples," as the third paragraph of the introduction makes clear. On these examples, Mather hopes his readers will model themselves.

In Mather's portrait, Eliot is New England's exemplification of a host of Biblical models and the very personification of the word into which he anagrammatizes Eliot's name, "Toile." To foil this image of "indefatigable Eliot," Mather characterizes the Indians as the extreme opposite. The laziness of the Indians, especially the men, is depicted by Mather's close contemporary, William Byrd, as well. But where Byrd adds that he finds beauty in native women and truth in natural religion, Mather barely notices the women, despises all heathenism, and ridicules Indian language and practices.

Despite the heavy dose of instruction provided in the *Magnalia*, Mather refers to both it and the *Wonders of the Invisible World* as "Entertainments." Most of the entertainment value of these works is to be found in their style. Students might be urged to pick out passages from the *Magnalia* in which Mather's (and Eliot's) wit are most sparkling. Mather's most purely entertaining piece is the letter in which he tells how New England was "Entertained & overwhelmed with a *Snow*." This letter bears close comparison with Byrd's amusing letters, especially the one on breast enlargement. Byrd's letter is clearly a tall tale and Mather's avowedly a "Winter-tale," both written in remote America to delight a civilized British audience.

John Williams (1664–1729)

Contributing Editor: Rosalie Murphy Baum [p. 423]

Classroom Issues and Strategies

The popularity of the captivity narrative during the Puritan period is being repeated today among students who vicariously enjoy the narrators' experiences and realize the effect such narratives have had on popular frontier and Wild West adventure stories. To many students already familiar with Mary Rowlandson's 1682 *Narrative*, John Williams's 1707 narrative is especially welcome—not simply because it offers a male version of captivity, but also because it describes captivity both by the Indians (for eight weeks) and by the French (for two years). The primary difficulty students have in reading the narrative lies in their lack of knowledge of the French and Indian War and of the differences between Roman Catholicism and Puritanism.

Background information about the relationship between the French and English in North America can eliminate this difficulty and give students a more accurate idea of colonial history. To be stressed first is the fact that the hostilities between the French and the English in North America began as early as 1613 and that the period between 1613 and the Peace of Paris in 1763 was one in which some six extended conflicts, or "wars," resulted in captives, usually women and children, being taken from New England to Canada.

Students also need to be reminded of the theological and ritualistic differences that distinguished the Puritans from the Established Church of England. Roman Catholicism represented a structure and theology even more pernicious to Puritans that the structure and theology of the Church of England. In such a context, Williams's strong reaction to the Indians' taking him "to a popish country" (Québec) and to the efforts of the French Jesuits to convert him to Roman Catholicism becomes clear.

Major Themes, Historical Perspectives, and Personal Issues

The Redeemed Captive is, then, an excellent work to dramatize for students what the French and Indian Wars were about and to clarify the antagonism between Catholics and Puritans during this period. It is also a form of the jeremiad more readable and interesting to modern students than most of the Puritan sermons, histories, or personal narratives.

In addition, it illustrates "the significant mythic experience of the early white-Indian relationship" (Louise K. Barnett, *The Ignoble Savage*) and the "Puritan myth of 'America,' " "the first coherent myth-literature developed in America for American audiences" (Richard Slotkin, *Regeneration Through Violence*). Students can see in both Williams's and Rowlandson's narratives the way in which such accounts typically open with an Indian raid in which white settlers are brutally massacred and then proceed to describe the inhuman hardships Indians inflict upon their captives. The concept of the Indian is that of satanic beast. No attempt is made in these narratives to indicate that the Indian aggression is a part of the hostilities of decades and may have been provoked or equaled by white aggression. Little note is made of the decency or kindnesses of the Indians: such good fortune as the captive may experience is never attributed to the customs or virtue of the Indian but to God. Living conditions that are everyday parts of the Indian life or result from the normal state of travel at that time are regarded by captives as horrendous personal injuries being deliberately and cruelly inflicted upon them by the Indians. Clearly no cognizance is taken of the inherent difficulties that arise when two such disparate cultures come together under conditions of warfare.

Significant Form, Style, or Artistic Conventions

Of particular interest to many students will be the subject of the captivity narrative as a genre particularly American in its subject matter years before American writers—like Freneau, Bryant, Irving, Cooper, Hawthorne, and James—became concerned about the question of an inherently *American* literature. This genre was clearly, in its early stages, a religious statement, emphasizing redemptive suffering, with the captivity being either a test that God had set for his people or a punishment to guide them from their evil ways. Williams's narrative was such an excellent example of the type that Sunday School versions appeared as late as the 1830s and 1840s (e.g., Titus Strong's *The Deerfield Captive: an Indian Story, being a Narrative of Facts for the Instruction of the Young*).

Original Audience

Students should be reminded too, of course, that Williams is writing for a Puritan audience. Thus, for a people familiar with the jeremiad, he emphasizes God's wrath against his people for their shortcomings, but also rejoices in God's mercy and goodness toward his people. (See Sacvan Bercovitch, *The American Jeremiad*, for a study of the negative and positive sides of the jeremiad.) He assumes the satanic nature of the

Indians, particularly fearsome creatures by which God tests his people or punishes them. And he stresses the diabolical nature of the Jesuits, who, in their zeal to convert him to Roman Catholicism, make him attend a Latin Mass, urge him to pray to the Virgin Mary, and try to force him to kiss a crucifix.

Questions for Reading and Discussion/ Approaches to Writing

For their writing assignments, some students may wish to read other captivity narratives either to compare narratives of redemptive suffering or to trace the changes in the genre emerging during the propaganda and fictionalized thriller stages. Wilcomb E. Washburn's *Narratives of North American Indian Captivities* offers facsimile reprints of 311 such narratives dating from the late seventeenth century to the late nineteenth century.

But even without such additional reading, the possibilities for essays based upon Williams's narrative are considerable. Students may wish to discuss Williams's *The Redeemed Captive* as a jeremiad, comparing it to jeremiads they have read in other genres. They may wish to examine Williams's narrative techniques, especially with a view to the contribution the genre has made to the horror story or thriller. Students interested in women's studies or feminist criticism may wish to consider conceptual and stylistic differences between the narratives of Rowlandson and Williams. Students interested in Indian studies can compare attitudes toward the Indians in Williams and other authors studied (e.g., in Bradford, Roger Williams, Cotton Mather, Rowlandson, or, moving into a later period, Franklin, Freneau, Bryant, Cooper, Melville). Students familiar with Joseph Campbell's *The Hero With a Thousand Faces* can consider the archetypal nature of *The Redeemed Captive*, perhaps in the light of other works they have read.

Bibliography

Of particular value as background reading for teaching *The Redeemed Captive* is Wilcomb E. Washburn's "Introduction" to *Narratives of North American Indian Captivity: A Selective Bibliography* (1983), xi–lvv, and Edward W. Clark's "Introduction" to *The Redeemed Captive* by John Williams (1976), 1–25.

The Pueblo Indian Revolt and Spanish Reconquest, 1680–1692

Don Antonio de Otermín (fl. 1680)
Don Diego de Vargas (?–1704)

Contributing Editor: Juan Bruce-Novoa [p. 431]

Classroom Issues and Strategies

Students lack knowledge of the Spanish colonial system and its presence in New Mexico, but there is ample material in the popular lore to deal with this text. The revolt coincides with struggles with Native Americans on the East Coast and should be viewed as part of the general resistance effort by native peoples against European invasion. Furthermore, it should be placed in the context of ethnic aspirations to preserve group identity in the midst of a growing dominant culture.

Students respond to the question of Native American rights and the Spanish imposition of a foreign presence. They ask: What right did the Spanish have to be there if the Native Americans were there first? The logical conclusions are evident.

Major Themes, Historical Perspectives, and Personal Issues

The main historical theme is two-fold: on the one hand, the process of resistance by a conquered people to colonization by outsiders; on the other, the determination of great nations to hold their territory, even when the native inhabitants prefer independence.

Significant Form, Style, or Artistic Conventions

These are reports, not artistic creations. They continue the writing of conquest and discovery.

Original Audience

The audience was restricted to the powerful leaders. Modern readers now overhear private communications about events they can relate to only through the imagination.

Comparisons, Contrasts, Connections

One can compare the New England texts on Native American revolts. They share the sense of menace represented by the Native American, as well as the invaders' determination to retain the territory for God and country. One might also look at the letter of Cortes, focusing on the Aztec revolt that expelled the Spanish from Mexico City and the Spaniards' triumphant return.

Questions for Reading and Discussion/ Approaches to Writing

1. Ask the students to consider the question of Native American primacy in the Americas and the thorny dilemma of European presence. They should ponder the question of rights of possession to the land, keeping in mind the U.S. experience with the Native Americans everywhere in the country.
2. Have them write on what this event signifies in U.S. history. Does it shed any light on the basic character of U.S. existence?

Bibliography

There is very little on the specific subject. Read Frederick Turner's *Beyond Geography*.

Colonial Period

1700–1800

American Voices in a Changing World

Sarah Kemble Knight (1666–1727)

Contributing Editor: Kathryn Zabelle Derounian [p. 472]

Classroom Issues and Strategies

This journal is one of the most teachable colonial documents at the undergraduate level. While it is a close contemporary of such Puritan prose classics as Robert Calef's *More Wonders of the Invisible World* (1700), Cotton Mather's *Magnalia* (1701), and John Williams's *The Redeemed Captive* (1707), it differs from them in tone, content, and style. Students respond positively to Knight's humorous portrait of herself and her surroundings. Through this document—and others—a teacher can counterbalance the still all too common stereotype of Puritans as dour, somber, unsmiling, and morbidly pious.

Major Themes, Historical Perspectives, and Personal Issues

Themes

1. Position of women—especially women writers—in late seventeenth- and early eighteenth-century New England.

   In theory, Puritans used the typological significance of Eve's creation from Adam's rib as a way to stress women's dependence, domesticity, and intrinsic inferiority. Ninety-nine percent of women married at least once in Puritan New England, and a wife's major purpose was to serve God and her husband. Sermons, for example, frequently stressed the ideal woman's qualities of modesty, piety, humility, patience, charity, and so on. But in practice, of course, women were often far from ideal, and in a frontier society they sometimes had to take on men's work. Thus there is evidence that women became printers, stationers, writers, and innkeepers, for example—usually on the death of their father or husband. Sarah Kemble Knight is a case in point, and students might be asked to find textual evidence of Knight's business skills.

2. Views of the frontier/wilderness at this time.
3. Sociological issues like views of blacks, Indians, and other settlers in different colonies.

Personal Issues

Look carefully at the figure/character of the author/narrator.

Significant Form, Style, or Artistic Conventions

Discuss the genres of diary, journal and autobiography and also explain how this journal fits the fictional genre of the picaresque. Compare the popular, colloquial quality of this work with more academic works to understand what the ordinary Puritan citizen might think/read vs. what the well-educated, but few, members of the intelligentsia might think/read. Such a discussion inevitably involves other colonial works in these genres and helps students understand generic interrelationships. The diary (Sewall's is a prime example) focuses on externals; is unrevised, immediate, and fragmentary; may extend for many years; and usually has no audience in mind except the writer him- or herself. A journal, however (Knight's, for instance), focuses more on internal matters; may be slightly revised; may be written shortly after the fact; may extend over a shorter time period, sometimes to deal with a specific event like a courtship or a journey; should appear relatively coherent; and is probably written with a restricted audience in mind. The autobiography (and the sub-genre the spiritual autobiography) is often considered the most "literary" of the three related genres because it is more carefully structured and composed.

Original Audience

This work was not written with publication in mind, and indeed although written during 1704–1705 was not published until 1825. Like the work of other women writers and amateur authors, this might have been circulated among family and friends by the author, but it did not have a wider readership until it was actually published.

Comparisons, Contrasts, Connections

Compare with other women writers of the time: Anne Bradstreet and Mary Rowlandson, for example. Such comparisons do not reveal a direct influence or sense of tradition among women writers; rather, each person and her work must be considered separately. Contrast with journals of male contemporaries (other travel journals, for example).

Questions for Reading and Discussion

1. Look at Knight as heroine/protagonist of her story/journal.
2. Look carefully at how the wilderness is presented.
3. Look at exactly what she chooses to record in this journal.
4. Notice the lack of religious themes.

Bibliography

I attached a reading list to the headnote. Please see the suggested readings there.

William Byrd II (1674–1744)

Contributing Editor: Kenneth Alan Hovey [p. 491]

Major Themes, Historical Perspectives, and Personal Issues

William Byrd will come as a delightful surprise to students who come to colonial literature with an expectation of unrelieved Puritanism. As a Cavalier author, he picks up where Morton left off, only in Virginia one hundred years later. Much of his charm as a writer derives from the high polish he gives to even his most minor pieces, chiefly by the use of irony. This irony makes his writing constantly entertaining, but its real import is often elusive. Amid all the understatements and overstatements, the sarcasm and the wry humor, it is difficult to find a passage where Byrd does not have his tongue in his cheek or where he simply conveys his views in a straightforward manner.

In his letters he compares colonial America to early biblical times, both those of Eden before the fall and those of the promised land of Canaan under the patriarchs. The comparison is clearly overstated and leaves one doubting whether Byrd doesn't really prefer the fleshpots of Egypt and the fallen world of England. Furthermore, while America lacks the refined vices of England, its national blessings of ease and fertility lead to the crude sins of idleness and overindulgence, further encouraged by the importation of slaves and rum. Yet Byrd clearly glories in his own truly biblical mastership over bondmen and his moderate appreciation of alcohol, and he boasts of his own sexual potency under the guise of blaming American women for breeding like rabbits.

The entertainment provided by the contrasting highs and lows of the very personal *Secret History* is joined to a serious purpose in the contrasting panegyric and satire provided in the impersonal public *History of the Dividing Line*. But as in Byrd's letters, irony undermines virtually all moments of pure praise or blame. The New England Puritans are placed above the Virginians for their industry, but blamed for their fanatical religion. The North Carolinians are placed below the Virginians for their religious indifference and the idleness of their men, yet admired for their fertility and freedom. Indian males are lazier and female Indians dirtier than North Carolinians, but Indian natural religion is better than Carolinian indifference and Indian wives more innocent and faithful than white. Thus each group is ultimately viewed in a remarkably balanced though highly judgmental way, with neither civilized nor natural man monopolizing all good. Even nature itself, largely epitomized in both histories in the bear, is portrayed equivocally as the source of both good and evil to man, as reproduction and potential death. Byrd's confrontation with the bear, at least in his imagination, is the last of a whole series of events in both letters and histories in which British civilization is forced to confront American nature. By remaining at an always ironic critical distance, Byrd remarkably judges and accommodates both.

Jonathan Edwards (1703–1758)

Contributing Editor: Carol M. Bensick [p. 512]

Classroom Issues and Strategies

Problems that arise in teaching Jonathan Edwards include student prejudices, stereotypes, and preconceived notions of Puritans and preachers. Distorted images are often gathered from headnotes and selections in standard anthologies that tend to adopt an aridly "historical" approach and to reduce Edwards's text to his supposed "themes."

I've found it most effective to plunge students directly into the texts, deliberately avoiding any preliminary "informational" lecture on history and/or biography. It's almost impossible to argue them out of their fixed preconvictions; the only thing that really works is to show them, by immersing them from the start in the texts themselves. In class, I've found it works best to avoid lecturing and to start right in discussing passages. The most effective way I know of convincing students that a text is literary is by asking them to answer what they recognize as literary questions (e.g., about style, persona, imagery, tone, etc.).

Try asking students to read aloud; ask them to do line-by-line exercises in stylistic explication or to write "reader response" journals. Students deeply believe that Edwards is no fun—that he had no fun and he wants them to have no fun. You want to show (not tell) them that Edwards has *enormous* fun in the act of thinking and writing and that they can share it in the act of reading.

Major Themes, Historical Perspectives, and Personal Issues

My personal experience has been that my mention of historical or personal themes and issues tends to distract the students from the text itself; accordingly, I have become accustomed to stress passage explication and interpretation ("close reading") during class time. In exams and papers, I offer students opportunities to develop their own more general views of the author in contrast to others in the course. In general, however, I try to avoid offering interpretive grids for them to place over the texts and to discourage them from importing schemata from outside. I would rather leave them with a genuine personal sense of the author than a neat propositional summary of the content of his texts.

Significant Form, Style, or Artistic Conventions

Aspects to consider include: voice, tone, genre, implied audience, persona, public vs. private writing, and irony.

Original Audience

It's important to direct students' attention to signals within the texts indicating who the anticipated audience is. Particularly with the philosophical works, they need to be directed to notice that Edwards's audience, not just the local Northampton congregation as they tend to imagine, is the international world of letters and its posterity.

Comparisons, Contrasts, Connections

The old standard comparisons with Franklin, Mather, and to a lesser extent Woolman disserve Edwards. To help students *see* that Edwards is actually a cosmopolitan, not as they assume parochial, thinker, suggest comparisons with writers from other national traditions and from other time periods. Thus I might suggest students think about Edwards in comparison with Baudelaire, Oscar Wilde, or Sade. The old comparisons between Edwards and the writers of the so-called American Renaissance have been adequately shown by such recent critics as DeProspo to serve both parties badly (unless the comparatist is a visionary like Perry Miller).

Questions for Reading and Discussion/ Approaches to Writing

1. I'd be inclined to assign students a passage (or hand out a photocopy) without identifying Edwards as the author and ask them to freely speculate who the author (age, gender, profession, residence, etc.) might be.
2. The more specific a topic or assignment is to a specific text, the better I find it works. Each teacher must be the judge of what have emerged as the leading concerns in his or her own course in a particular term.

Bibliography

If a teacher is to induce direct, personal engagement with the author in his or her students, he or she must set the example; accordingly, the most important thing he or she can do by way of preparing is to read or reread the assigned texts afresh and not take refuge behind a predigested interpretation by an expert. Unless there is time to become a full-fledged specialist, a little reading will do more harm than good. The headnote has been designed to tell a nonspecialist all that should be necessary to present these texts in a nonspecializing course.

Elizabeth Ashbridge (1713–1755)

Contributing Editor: Liahna Babener [p. 579]

Classroom Issues and Strategies

Most students are unfamiliar with doctrinal differences between Anglican and Quaker faiths, upon which the *Account* hinges. They are uncomfortable with Quaker preaching practices and meetings, with their strongly religious orientation, and with their traditional notions of proper marital conventions. This discomfort sometimes alienates students or prevents them from empathizing with Ashbridge's dilemma. These anxieties, however, are almost always overcome by the power and poignancy of the text itself.

Providing background about religious and doctrinal tensions and gender patterns in colonial America is useful. Some emphasis on adopting a feminist critical strategy for reading is also helpful. Comparing other accounts of those who have been impelled by spiritual conviction to act against convention and law is illuminating. Reading some accounts of Christian dissenters and nonconformists helps. Also, a more precise look at Calvinist, Anglican, and perhaps Catholic documents of the period, drawn from the Great Awakening materials—set perhaps against deist and Enlightenment tracts with their secular emphasis—may be helpful.

Students enjoy discussing whether Ashbridge is heroic or perverse. They often identify with her independent spirit but lament her increasingly dour tone and her failed marriage. Some wonder whether she gave up too much for conscience's sake. Some students see the husband as abusive or imperious but cannot help but sympathize with his distress over losing a mirthful wife. Students also wonder if Quakers courted their social estrangement, contributing to their own victimization, and ask whether Quakers should be blamed or censured for their martyrdom.

Major Themes, Historical Perspectives, and Personal Issues

1. The expressly female dilemma of having to choose between conscience and husband, as well as the social stresses upon a woman who defies tradition and prescribed sex roles, threatening the stability of the patriarchal order.
2. The doctrinal and social conflicts between Anglicans and Quakers in early America; more broadly, the pressures from a predominantly Anglican, increasingly secularized culture to tame or compartmentalize religious fervor.
3. Making a living (as a woman) in colonial America.
4. Marriage, husbands' prerogatives, men's and women's ways of coping with marital estrangement.
5. Quaker doctrine, patterns of worship, and social customs.

Significant Form, Style, and Artistic Conventions

Study the document as an example of the genre of spiritual autobiography, of personal narrative, of female and feminist assertion (a kind of early "manifesto"), of social history, of eighteenth-century rationalism and at the same time revivalist ardor. Explore to what degree the document is confessional and to what degree it may be understood as contrivance or fiction. How is the author "inventing" herself as she writes? How does she turn her experience into a didactic instrument for the edification of her readers?

Original Audience

Social, historical, religious contexts are primary issues. The composition and publication history of the document—penned just before Ashbridge's death—is also interesting and illuminating. Consider the Great Awakening audience who may have read this account of religious conversion. Does the document create a sense of feminine solidarity? Are its intended readers primarily women?

Comparisons, Contrasts, Connections

Compare with other Great Awakening spiritual autobiographies, such as Jonathan Edwards's "Personal Narrative"; Puritan introspective literature; other chronicles of Quaker persecution in colonial America (Hawthorne's tale "The Gentle Boy" makes for instructive comparison); Franklin's more cunning and more secular *Autobiography*, an apt parallel. Many documents by eighteenth-century women (cf. the letters of Abigail Adams) make useful counterparts to consider women's roles and rights. Accounts of personal conversion experiences are also useful for comparison.

Questions for Reading and Discussion/ Approaches to Writing

1. (a) Characterize Ashbridge's spiritual struggle(s) and marital dilemma(s). Does she resolve the former at the expense of the latter?
   (b) In what ways do you empathize with Ashbridge in her conflict with her husband? With her husband? Why? How might you act differently from either or both of them in this situation?

(c) Does the community treat Ashbridge fairly following her conversion?

(d) What implicit moral and spiritual advice does the piece contain?

2. (a) Write a counterpart narrative (or defense) from the husband's point of view.

(b) Write an Anglican's critique of or comment upon Ashbridge's behavior.

(c) Invent an imaginative dialogue between Ashbridge and Jonathan Edwards (or any of the following) *in re* religious or gender issues: Anne Hutchinson, Anne Bradstreet, Samuel Sewall, Benjamin Franklin, etc.

Bibliography

Not much is to be found on Ashbridge. Best source available: "Elizabeth Ashbridge's *Account*" in Daniel B. Shea, Jr.'s, *Spiritual Autobiography in Early America* (Princeton: Princeton Univ. Press, 1968). A fairly thoroughgoing review of religious histories of America yields little or nothing on Ashbridge.

Feminist history and primary source collections on women's lives and firsthand documents are illuminating about gender roles in the period.

John Woolman (1720–1772)

Contributing Editor: James A. Levernier [p. 590]

Classroom Issues and Strategies

Students often have a difficult time reading eighteenth-century nonfiction prose. The issues it reveals seem dated and unexciting to them. A writer like Woolman comes across as a moral "antique" to students who would much prefer to skip over the entire period and move on to Melville, Hawthorne, and Poe in the next century.

I try to point out to students that Woolman is, in many ways, very contemporary. He almost single-handedly defied many of the conventional views of his day and was willing to stand up and take the heat for the things that he believed in. I also point out that the principles that Woolman uses to deal with the evils he perceives in society are by no means dated. Many of the issues he brings up still exist today but in different, more subtle, forms, and it is our responsibility to deal with those issues. Social injustices, bigotry, and poverty are, unfortunately, still very much with us today. Woolman offers us an example and guidance in such matters.

Students are often quite interested in Quakers and their culture. Most of them have heard something about Quakers, but they don't really understand them. They are usually quite moved by the conviction behind Woolman's writings and can identify with it. They want to know if he was typical of Quaker thinking and why they haven't been taught more about the effect of Quaker ideas on American culture.

Major Themes, Historical Perspectives, and Personal Issues

Woolman writes about many themes that should be emphasized:

1. Slavery as a historical issue.
2. Racism and prejudice as issues that are still very much alive today.
3. The responsibility of the individual for social injustices.
4. The need for conviction and passion in our moral and social lives.
5. The potential of any one person for bringing about true reform.

Significant Form, Style, or Artistic Conventions

In discussing Woolman, one needs to discuss the practice of keeping journals among Quakers and early Americans generally. Why did Quakers keep journals? Why did they publish them? An analysis of Woolman's simple and direct style is very useful to seeing the "art" in the *Journal,* since his style of writing very effectively underscores and enhances the power of his convictions. I also draw connections between journals written by Quakers and journals written by Puritans to the north. Quaker journals have an inner peace that Puritan journals often lack.

Original Audience

Woolman wrote the *Journal* and his *Plea for the Poor* for future generations. He certainly knew that the *Journal* at least would not be published in his lifetime. There is a rhetorical strategy behind the *Journal* that revisions within the work reveal. Clearly, Woolman wanted us to see the effects of the workings of the "Inner Light" in his own life so that we could perhaps begin to cultivate with equal effect the "Inner Light" he felt was within each of us. *Considerations* (I and II) were more immediate in their audience concerns; they are persuasive tracts, meant to bring about immediate action through a direct appeal to the consciences of those who read them.

Comparisons, Contrasts, Connections

Woolman can be tied to nineteenth-century American autobiographers, especially Henry David Thoreau and Henry Adams. The Quaker influence can also be connected to John Greenleaf Whittier, Emerson, and Whitman. The connections between the Quaker "Inner Light" and the type of transcendentalism expressed in Emerson's works, particularly in *Nature*, should be emphasized. Woolman also should be compared and contrasted to the journal writers and autobiographers of seventeenth- and eighteenth-century New England. John Winthrop, for instance, kept a journal for far different reasons and with far different results than did Woolman.

Questions for Reading and Discussion/
Approaches to Writing

1. (a) Would Woolman feel that his life and ministry made a difference to the world of today?
   (b) How would he feel about today's world? About social injustice in third world countries? About our response as individuals and as Americans to poverty and social injustice in other lands?
2. Comparison/Contrast papers are very useful ways to develop insights into Woolman. He can be compared, for example, to Bradford, to Emerson, to Adams, and to Whitman. Sometimes I ask students to envision three or more writers together in a room today discussing an issue. What would each writer say about the issue? Feminism, for example, or the atomic bomb. This device often helps students to enter the writer's world and better understand the imaginative process.

Poetry before the Revolution–English Forms in an American Idiom

[p. 611]

Ebenezer Cook (1667–1733)
Richard Lewis (1700?–1734)

Contributing Editor: Carla Mulford

Please consult the headnote in the text for complete information.

Poetry before the Revolution–A Collection of Poetry by Women

[p. 641]

Jane Colman Turell (1708–1735)
Bridget Richardson Fletcher (1726–1770)
Hannah Griffitts (1727–1817)
Mercy Otis Warren (1728–1814)
Lucy Terry (1730–1821)
Annis Boudinot Stockton (1736–1801)
Milcah Martha Moore (1740–1829)
Martha Brewster (1710–post 1759)
Ann Eliza Bleecker (1752–1783)
Anna Young Smith (1756–1780)
Sarah Wentworth Morton (1759–1846)
Poems Published Anonymously

Contributing Editor: Pattie Cowell

Classroom Issues and Strategies

The main problem with teaching poetry written by women prior to the Revolutionary War has been the absence of texts. The selection in the *Heath Anthology* remedies this difficulty. Students questions tend to center on cultural context rather than on literary appreciation, and this interest in the circumstances of these women's lives provides a useful entry to their works.

Major Themes, Historical Perspectives, and Personal Issues

These vary from poet to poet. Perhaps the emphasis should be on the diversity of their expression and form. But certainly themes of family, spirituality, politics, and identity recur.

Other issues: The status of women poets in colonial North America, cultural barriers to women writing, networking among women poets.

Significant Form, Style, or Artistic Conventions

Again, these vary from poet to poet. The emphasis should be on the diversity of their poetic forms. It is useful to point out that women wrote in every genre men used except the sermon.

Original Audience

First through an exercise in historical imagination, students should try to recreate the work's original context (demographics, geography, publishing industry circumstances, libraries or lack of libraries, means of communication, literacy, race and class and gender considerations, etc.). They should then profit from discussing issues in these poems that seem to speak to contemporary concerns.

Comparisons, Contrasts, Connections

Compare/contrast with contemporary male poets and contemporary female poets from England.

Bibliography

Cowell, Pattie. *Women Poets in Pre-Revolutionary America*. Troy, N.Y.: Whitston, 1981. Entries grouped by individual poets, so access to relevant material is relatively easy.

Individual entries in *American Writers Before 1800*, edited by James A. Lavernier and Douglas R. Wilmes. Westport, Conn.: Greenwood, 1983.

Watts, Emily Stipes. *The Poetry of American Women from 1632 to 1945*. Austin: University of Texas Press, 1977, 9–61.

Emerging Voices of a National Literature: African, Native American, Spanish, Mexican

[p. 678]

Jupiter Hammon (1711–1806?)

Contributing Editor: William H. Robinson [p. 679]

Classroom Issues and Strategies

Thanks to a history of racist American education, most modern students—black and white—are unwittingly almost completely unaware of, and often have difficulty believing in the documented reality of, early black American writers. Slave and free, literate and semi-literate, blacks in colonial times composed and even published verses and varieties of prose. Jupiter Hammond, in fact, published more than a half dozen verses and prose pieces (including one non-extant verse and one work twice reprinted).

Modern students and teachers (at all levels) ought to become aware of the fact that by exploiting the widest definition of "literature," black Americans have a literary tradition (dictated and black-written) that reaches back to 1645, but that only formally sanctioned, "acceptable" works reached print. It might be noted, for instance, that the title pages of most of Hammon's works include printed information showing that Hammon's verse and prose reached print only because of the "assistance" of (white) "friends."

One question often asked by students—a question that promotes lively discussion—is this: How could a slave, however literate, however indulged by his master, so publicly continue to urge fellow black slaves to comply so meekly with a slave system for some "pie-in-the-sky" notion of ultimate Christian acceptance?

Major Themes, Historical Perspectives, and Personal Issues

Because all of his writings are verse and prose expressions of Christian piety, it would seem clear that Hammon was an unordained minister of sorts, a man who enjoyed his prominence even though his persistently evangelizing piety met with black resistance. Students might explore the means by which Hammon tried to balance his personal exhortations for Christian docility against less pious black urgencies for secular and immediate freedom.

Significant Form, Style, or Artistic Conventions

Was Hammon's exclusive use of quatrains rhyming abab, with alternating lines of iambic tetrameters and iambic trimeters, deliberately so simplified to appeal more readily to a posited assumption of black people's short attention spans? Were his several references to his black reading and listening audiences as "children" unconscious or deliberate or derivative from the Christian imagery he found in the church hymnals from which he sang? Were his fatiguing uses of such quatrains and such imagery indicative of his own verse-making limitations?

Comparisons, Contrasts, Connections

To illustrate the range of displayed personality, poetic, and thematic differences among the earliest black American poets, the writings and what little is known of Hammon's life can be profitably compared and/or contrasted with the much more that is known of the life of Phillis Wheatley, Benjamin Banneker, John Marrant, Prince Hall, and even Lucy Terry, who composed a verse, "Bars Fight," in 1746.

Questions for Reading and Discussion/ Approaches to Writing

I have sometimes assigned a Hammon prose piece and asked my white students to react in a brief two- to three-page paper in two ways: as a free white contemporary of Hammon, and as a modern white American student. I have asked my black students to react as a black slave contemporary of Hammon, and as a modern black American student. I then have selected students to read and discuss their papers in class.

Bibliography

Brawley, Benjamin. *Early Negro Writers.* Chapel Hill: Univ. of North Carolina Press, 1935, 21–30.

Kaplan, Sidney. *The Black Presence in the Era of the American Revolution.* Washington, D.C.: Smithsonian, 1973, 171–78.

Ransom, Stanley. *America's First Negro Poet—Jupiter Hammon on Long Island.* Port Washington, N.Y.: Empire State Historical Publications Series No. 82, 1983, 12, 14–7.

Wegelin, Oscar. *Jupiter Hammon, American Negro Poet.* Miami, Fla.: Mnomosyne, 1969, *passim.*

Whitlow, Roger. *Black American Literature.* Chicago: Nelson Hall, 1973, 18–20, 24–5.

Prince Hall (1735?–1807)

Contributing Editor: William H. Robinson [p. 685]

Classroom Issues and Strategies

I have encountered no insurmountable problems in teaching Hall except to point out to students the differences (which may well have been "diplomatic") between Hall's almost illiterate manuscripts that were designed to be published and several of his other more acceptably normal manuscripts.

Although Hall wrote and published correspondence and wrote and co-signed almost a dozen petitions, I include him among examples of early American oratory.

Frequently asked student questions: In the two known Masonic "charges" that Hall published (1792 and 1797), where did he find the courage to be so outspoken? Could he find a presumably white Boston printer to publish the pieces?

Major Themes, Historical Perspectives, and Personal Issues

Hall was concerned with many aspects of racial uplift for black America and wrote about them all.

Significant Form, Style, or Artistic Conventions

As noted above, in class I note how Hall's nearly illiterate petitions, requiring an editor's "corrective" attention, may have been deliberately deferential. Hall was aware that not many white printers or publishers would readily publish manuscripts written by obviously literate blacks.

Original Audience

I point out the real differences in tone and general deference between Hall's petitions designed for white Boston legislators and other prominent whites, and the tone and racial outspokenness in his "charges," formal annual addresses to his fellow black Masons.

Comparisons, Contrasts, Connections

Although no black writer contemporary with Hall was so widely concerned with racial uplift, his work might be compared with Phillis Wheatley's letters, which are also concerned with black uplift and even "proper" Bostonian antislavery protest.

Questions for Reading and Discussion/ Approaches to Writing

I have asked students to compare the differences in tone and understanding of biblical injunctions between Jupiter Hammon and Prince Hall.

Bibliography

Crawford, Charles. *Prince Hall and His Followers*. New York: The Crisis, 1914, 33.

Kaplan, Sidney. *The Black Presence in the Era of the American Revolution*. Washington, D.C.: Smithsonian, 1973, 181–92.

Walker, Joseph. *Black Squares and Compass*. Richmond, Va.: Macon, 1979, *passim*.

Gustavus Vassa (Olaudah Equiano) (1745–1797)

Contributing Editor: Angelo Costanzo [p. 694]

Classroom Issues and Strategies

Students have no prior knowledge of Equiano's life and work. To them, he is a strange African whose eighteenth-century writing style seems oddly fanciful at times. To address this knowledge gap, I give background information on the history and sociology of the eighteenth-century slave trade, placing in this context Equiano's life story—his kidnapping, Middle Passage journey, slavery in the Western world, education, religion, and seafaring adventures. I also describe his abolitionist efforts in Great Britain, and I say something about his use of neoclassical prose in the autobiography.

I use Equiano as an introduction to American slave narrative literature and demonstrate the important influence of autobiographical form and style on the whole range of African-American literature up to the present day, including its impact on such writers as Richard Wright, Ralph Ellison, Alice Walker, and Toni Morrison.

Students are particularly interested in the way the whites conducted the slave trade in Africa by using the Africans themselves to kidnap their enemies and sell them into slavery. Equiano was sold this way. Also their interest is aroused by Equiano's fascinating descriptions of Africa as a self-sufficient culture and society before the incursions of the whites. Students are moved by the graphic scenes of slavery, the Middle Passage experience described by Equiano, and his persistent desire for freedom. Most of all, they enjoy reading the first-person account of a well-educated and resourceful slave whose life story is filled with remarkable adventures and great achievements.

Major Themes, Historical Perspectives, and Personal Issues

The students need to know about the slave trade and the condition of slavery on the Caribbean islands. As for the literary aspect of Equiano's work, the students should be instructed about the genre of spiritual autobiography, its structure, methods, and styles. In particular, information should be given on how spiritual autobiography was used in the formation of the new genre of slave narrative literature, mainly the three-part structure of slavery, escape, and freedom that corresponds to the spiritual autobiography's three parts that describe the life of sin, conversion, and spiritual rebirth.

Equiano's great autobiography illustrates influences from several popular schools of personal writing current in the eighteenth-century Western world. Among these are the spiritual autobiographical writings of St. Augustine and John Bunyan, the descriptive travel literary works of Daniel Defoe and Jonathan Swift, and the secular stories that display a hardworking youth's rise from rags-to-riches in the commercial world. The latter pattern can be seen quite well in Benjamin Franklin's *Autobiography*, a work that shares some interesting parallels with Equiano's narrative. Equiano, like Franklin, is an enterprising young man rising up in life and playing numerous roles that help to develop his character in a free world of possibility. Both Equiano and Franklin use self-ironic humor to depict their adventures, and frequently they see themselves acting the role of the picaro figure—a stratagem used many times for survival purposes.

Another eighteenth-century mode of writing observed in Equiano's work is the primitivistic style that is related to the noble savage ideal. Equiano was aware of this type of writing, especially in the books on Africa by Anthony Benezet, the Quaker antislavery writer; when Equiano recalled his early days in Africa, he relied heavily on his reading in the primitivistic literature. However, Equiano's autobiography is remarkable in the account he gives of his African days because his re-creation is a mix of primitivistic idealism and realistic detail, in which he never expresses shame or inferiority regarding his African heritage. Africa is an edenic place whose inhabitants follow their own cultural traditions, religious practices, and pastoral pursuits. But although Africa is a happy childhood land for Equiano, he is not blind to the evil events that lately have befallen his people.

The Europeans have entered to plunder, enslave, and introduce the despicable inventions of modern technological warfare. Equiano himself is a victim of that situation when he is kidnapped and sold into slavery. His early experiences in the American colonies are recreated with a sense of awe and wonder as the young picaro slave observes the Western world's marvels. He is saved from a life of plantation slavery, but his seafaring service gives him the opportunity to witness firsthand the brutal practices of slavery in several areas of the world. Equiano's life story is a journey of education in which he goes from innocence in edenic Africa to the cruel experience of slavery in the West.

Significant Form, Style, or Artistic Conventions

I always discuss Equiano's work in conjunction with the whole genre of spiritual autobiography. I show how Equiano adapted the autobiographical form to the new slave narrative. I also explain the primitivistic elements in his work and say something about the eighteenth-century neoclassical style of writing.

In accordance with the pattern of spiritual autobiography, Equiano's narrative follows the three-part structure of spiritual and physical enslavement, conversion and escape from slavery, and subsequent rebirth in a life of spiritual and physical freedom. Not until he gains his physical liberty is Equiano able to build his character along personal, religious, and humanitarian lines of development. This is the reason he places his manumission paper in the center of his narrative and records his jubilation on attaining his freedom. From that point on in the autobiography, Equiano uses a confident, exuberant, and crusading tone and style as he relates his immersion in the honorable aspects of Western society while he denounces the West's inhumane practices of slavery.

Original Audience

I emphasize the fact that Equiano's reading audience was mostly composed of American and European abolitionists. His immediate purpose was to influence the British political leaders who were debating the slave trade issue in Parliament in the late 1750s. However, Equiano's work was read and discussed by numerous religious and humanitarian readers on both sides of the Atlantic. His work went through nineteen editions and was translated into several languages. It appeared in print well into the middle of the nineteenth century, and its influence on the whole range of slave narrative literature was strong.

Comparisons, Contrasts, Connections

The best comparison is with Frederick Douglass's *Narrative* (1845), which follows the three-part pattern of spiritual and slave autobiographical work. Douglass's work depicts the same search for identity involving the attainment of manhood, education, especially the ability to read, and the securing of physical and spiritual liberations.

Questions for Reading and Discussion/ Approaches to Writing

1. Questions may deal with definitions of primitivism, form of autobiography (spiritual and secular), history of slave trade and slavery, and eighteenth-century writing styles.

2. (a) Describe the primitivistic elements in Equiano's description of his stay in Tinmah.

   (b) What kind of picture does Equiano paint of his African slave experiences as opposed to his later encounters with slavery in the Western world?

   (c) What signs of European influence does Equiano observe during his slave journey to the coast?

   (d) Discuss the reversal situation of the cannibalistic theme demostrated by Equiano's initial meeting with the white slave traders on the African coast.

   (e) What are some of the white world's magical arts Equiano observes with a sense of awe and wonder?

   (f) Equiano's account of the talking book is a commonly described experience in early slave works. What significant traits of the young enslaved person does the story reveal?

Bibliography

Andrews, William L. *To Tell a Free Story: The First Century of Afro-American Autobiography, 1760–1865.* Urbana: University of Illinois Press, 1986. (See especially Chapter 2.)

Costanzo, Angelo. *Surprising Narrative: Olaudah Equiano and the Beginnings of Black Autobiography.* Westport, Conn.: Greenwood Press, 1987. (See especially Chapter 4.)

Davis, Charles T., and Henry Louis Gates Jr., eds. *The Slave's Narrative.* New York: Oxford University Press, 1985. (See Paul Edwards' essay, "Three West African Writers of the 1780's.")

Much of my research and writing has centered on Equiano. As a result, a great deal of the information required for an understanding and appreciation of Olaudah Equiano's great work can be found in my book.

Phillis Wheatley (1753–1784)

Contributing Editor: William H. Robinson [p. 712]

Classroom Issues and Strategies

One of the difficulties in teaching Wheatley comes in trying to illustrate that she certainly was much more racially aware, and antislavery, in her letters (which were intended to be private) than in her more widely known verses (written for a general white public).

I show how, in spite of her fame and the special indulgence of the Wheatley family who owned her, Phillis was necessarily aware of her blackness; for example, in racially segregated church pews, in the widespread menial work (street sweeping and the like) that blacks were forced to do, and in the general lack of educational facilities for Boston blacks.

Students (and even scholars) are sometimes wary of the authenticity of Phillis's poetic abilities and, accordingly, ask germane questions. Such students and scholars are disabused of their doubts when confronted with copies of extant manuscripts of verses and letters written when Phillis was known to have not been in the company of whites.

Major Themes, Historical Perspectives, and Personal Issues

It is important to note that Phillis was very much aware of herself as a *rara avis*, who worked hard to show that, given the training and opportunity, blacks could write verse as well as any comparably educated and advantaged Bostonian.

Significant Form, Style, or Artistic Conventions

Familiar with rhetorical devices of classical prosody (especially as practiced by English masters, Pope, Milton, etc.), Phillis preferred a predominant usage of the Neoclassical couplet, which, on occasion, constrained her seemingly natural tendencies towards Romanticism.

Original Audience

Most of her verse was written for prominent white figures of her day—e.g., General Washington, several prominent Boston divines—but in several of her elegies and her "Nature pieces" she wrote some lines that have continuing value to audiences of today. Her work was published largely at the behest of the whites for whom she wrote.

Comparisons, Contrasts, Connections

No other colonial black versifier wrote with Phillis's obviously superior sophistication, and comparison of her work with that of black contemporaries is usually done at the expense of the other writers.

Questions for Reading and Discussion/ Approaches to Writing

I have asked students to examine Phillis's verse and letters for instances of her acquired Boston gentility and of her racial awareness and of herself as "the Colonial Boston poet laureate."

Bibliography

Mason, Julian. *Poems of Phillis Wheatley, Revised and Enlarged.* Chapel Hill: Univ. of North Carolina, 1989, 1–39.

Robinson, William H. *Critical Essays on Phillis Wheatley.* Boston: G. K. Hall, 1982, *passim.*

——. *Phillis Wheatley and Her Writings.* New York and London: Garland, 1984, 3–69, 87–126.

Samson Occom (Mohegan) (1723–1792)

Contributing Editor: A. LaVonne Brown Ruoff [p. 728]

Classroom Issues and Strategies

Students lack knowledge of tribal history, of the religious background of the period, and of the execution sermon as a genre. Providing information on these topics is essential. A discussion topic that captures students' interest is why execution sermons were so popular.

Major Themes, Historical Perspectives, and Personal Issues

1. Identify the Mohegans as a tribe and give some sense of their background. A member of the Algonkian language family, the Mohegans originally were the northernmost branch of the Pequots, the fiercest of the New England tribes. During the 1637 war with the English, the Pequots were massacred near what is now Stonington, Connecticut. Led by their chief Uncas, the Mohegans, who sided with the English in the war, joined in the massacre. After the war, they remained at peace with the English but resumed hostilities with their old enemies, the Narragansetts. For a brief period, the Mohegans, then numbering 2,000, greatly expanded their territory. However, this had shrunk drastically by the end of the seventeenth century. English settlers, who regarded the nomadic Mohegans as idle thieves, issued orders to remove them from the towns. Uncas and his sons further decreased Mohegan territory by making large land transfers to the whites. By the end of the century, the Mohegans were no longer independent. The first successful attempt to gather them into Indian villages was made in 1717. Eight years later, the Mohegans numbered only 351 and were split into two opposing camps, located one-half mile apart on the west side of the Mohegan river between New London and Norwich, Connecticut.
2. Popularity of the execution sermon in the period. (See below.)
3. Structure and general content of execution sermons. All this is included in the text headnote and in the following section.

Significant Form, Style, or Artistic Conventions

Occom's sermon is a typical example of the popular genre of the execution sermon. The first publication in New England to combine the offender's "True Confession" with the "Dying Warning" was Increase Mather's *The Wicked mans Portion* [sic] (1675). His *A Sermon Occasioned by the Execution of a Man found Guilty of Murder* [sic] (1686) expanded the literary form by including the murderer's complete confession as allegedly taken down in shorthand. The 1687 second edition added a discourse between the prisoner and minister, designed to introduce realism. Lawrence Towner argues that the genre demonstrated that New Englanders committed crimes and were led to contrition. Because the listeners to the sermons and readers of the "True Confessions" and "Dying Warnings" were at worst minor sinners, it was necessary to trace the criminal's career back to its origins and to generalize about the nature of crime. As criminals increasingly became outsiders (blacks, Indians, Irishmen, or foreign pirates), the tone of the True Confessions and Dying Warnings changed from moral suasion to titillation. So popular became the genre that in 1773, the year after the publication of Occom's sermon, eleven separate publications dealing with the condemned prisoner Levi Ames were printed. Wayne C. Minnick suggests that the authors of execution sermons ranked among the "best educated, most influential men of their society" (78).

Original Audience

It is important to get students to understand the religious milieu of the period, which responded to execution sermons as a form of spiritual confession. This can be compared with the confessions of the contemporary born-again fundamentalists. The sermon was sometimes delivered in church on the Sunday or Thursday before the execution, but most frequently just before the time appointed for the hanging. Audiences numbered between 550 and 850.

Comparisons, Contrasts, Connections

Increase and Cotton Mather and Jonathan Edwards—the structure and general themes of their execution and other sermons—can be compared. These preachers emphasized dramatic conversion, which Edwards described as a three-stage process: (1) Fear, anxiety, and distress at one's sinfulness; (2) absolute dependence on the "sovereign mercy of God in Jesus Christ"; and (3) relief from distress under conviction of sin and joy at being accepted by God (Goen 14). This process, reflected in Occom's sermon, became the norm in the Great Awakening and in subsequent revivalism. Evangelists also used emotional extravagance in their sermons.

Questions for Reading and Discussion/ Approaches to Writing

1. Call attention to the structure and the concept of redemption through confession of sin.
2. I don't assign a paper on this work. If I did, it would be in terms of asking students to write about the extent to which Occom follows the standard structure and basic content for such sermons (see text headnote).

Bibliography

Conkey, Laura E., Ethel Bolissevain, and Ives Goddard. "Indians of Southern New England and Long Island: Late Period." In *The Northeast*, edited by Bruce G. Trigger, 177–89. *Handbook of North American Indians*, vol. 15. Washington, D. C.: Smithsonian, 1978. Valuable introduction to these tribes.

Goen, C. C. *Revivalism and Separatism in New England, 1740–1800. Strict Congregationalists and Separate Baptists in the Great Awakening.* New Haven: Yale Univ. Press, 1962.

Heimert, Alan. *Religion and the American Mind: From the Great Awakening to the Revolution.* Cambridge: Harvard Univ. Press, 1966.

Jennings, Francis. *The Invasion of America; Indians, Colonialism, and the Cant of Conquest.* New York: Norton, 1976. Standard work on the subject, with lengthy bibliography.

Minnick, Wayne C. "The New England Execution Sermon, 1639–1800." *Speech Monographs* 35 (1968): 77–89.

Salwen, Bert. "Indians of Southern New England and Long Island: Early Period." In *The Northeast*, edited by Bruce G. Trigger, 160–76. *Handbook of North American Indians*, vol. 15. Washington, D. C.: Smithsonian, 1978. Informative introduction to these tribes.

Sturtevant, William C., ed. *Handbook of North American Indians*, vol. 15. Washington, D. C.: Smithsonian, 1978.

The Northeast, edited by Bruce G. Trigger. vol. 15. *Handbook of North American Indians*, edited by William C. Sturtevant. Washington, D. C.: Smithsonian, 1978. The articles on the execution sermon by Minnick and Towner are especially good.

Towner, Lawrence L. "True Confessions and Dying Warnings in Colonial New England." In *Sibley's Heir. A Volume in Memory of Clifford Kenyon Shipton*, 523–39. Boston: Colonial Soc. of Massachusetts and Univ. Press of Virginia, 1982.

Washburn, Wilcomb E. "Seventeenth-Century Indian Wars." In *The Northeast*, edited by Bruce G. Trigger, 89–100. Good overview of these wars.

Hendrick Aupaumut (Mahican) (?–1830)

Contributing Editor: Daniel F. Littlefield, Jr. [p. 751]

Classroom Issues and Strategies

Some students may be concerned about the deviations from "standards" in matters of syntax and grammar, so you might ask them to examine these deviations in such writers as Madam Knight. Have them consider the Southwestern humorists of the nineteenth century, for example, as models of the ways writers play on the deviations for literary effect. Suggest to students that Aupaumut's style may be seen as an example of "authentic" English dialect of an American Indian. Have them compare the Fus Fixico letter by Alexander Posey in the 1865–WWI section for a literary use of an Indian's English dialect.

Students are amazed at how little the questions of race/political power, race/social bias, and race/fear have changed in two hundred years. And expect to hear this question: "Could Indians actually write back then?"

Major Themes, Historical Perspectives, and Personal Issues

1. Indian identity, racial self-consciousness. (Aupaumut is painfully aware that he is an Indian writing about Indians. He is also aware of his odd position in defending the U.S. when the Indians have ample reason to doubt it. Note the *I–they* posture he takes.)
2. Ethnic identity in the emerging new nation.
3. Indian-white relations, colonial period to period of Indian removal.

Significant Form, Style, or Artistic Conventions

Have the students investigate the narrative's structure.

Original Audience

An Indian, having visited tribes in the old Northwest, is making recommendations concerning the posture the U.S. should take toward those tribes. His report indicates that he advised the tribes how they should act. Also, the piece is a defense of himself against accusations that he betrayed his trust. While his audience was mainly public policy makers, the piece speaks with pointed relevance today about the American Indians' (reasonable) distrust of federal policy makers. (Some things have not changed in the past two hundred years.)

Comparisons, Contrasts, Connections

The "assimilated" Indian, since the "Praying Indians" of the Puritan period, has been in an anomalous position. Aupaumut is caught between the expectations of two societies. Compare this position with that of Copway, Apes, and Boudinot. For relevant texts related to the Indians' distrust of the Europeans, see relevant sections of Smith, Bradford (more relevant to Aupaumut), Franklin, the Pueblo Revolt texts, and Delgado.

Fray Carlos José Delgado (1677–post 1750)

Contributing Editor: Carla Mulford [p. 756]

Classroom Issues and Strategies

The text seems like a report, with little literary value. Students will also tend to read it according to the stereotype of the cruel Spaniard exploiting the Native Americans.

Teachers must emphasize that this type of document was common in early stages of development everywhere during the colonization and settlement phases of U.S. history. The letter demonstrates that Spanish settlements shared a paradigmatic experience with those of other national groups. However, it should be made clear that the point here is not the image of the abusive Spaniard, but the vigorous defense of the native population by a Spaniard. This could be compared to Roger Williams' texts on Native Americans, stressing that the debate over the treatment of the original inhabitants was encoded as a theme in American writing by all the colonizing groups. It can also be shown that this text prefigures contemporary themes: the defense of third world peoples by U.S. religious groups against their exploitation and abuse by the U.S. government and its mercenaries, i.e., in Salvador and Nicaragua; it can even be seen as an allegorical prefiguration of the current defense of the environment against polluting exploiters.

Significant Form, Style, or Artistic Conventions

Delgados' language is very accessible. Problems may arise from a mis-understanding of his religious and political position within the colonial system. Missionaries were often at odds with the political leaders because the former were charged with the defense of the converted peo-ples. Also, the converts were assigned to the mission as workers within an economic unit that supposedly functioned in a cooperative manner and was supposed to teach the members to integrate themselves into the larger economic system as equals. The civil officials, however, wanted to exploit that labor at less than market value, and to do so they had to cir-cumvent the protective organization of the mission. The only voice of opposition came from the missionaries, who had recourse to a separate line of communications to centralized powers. They functioned some-what like the investigative press of our time. It is important, then to emphasize to students that they must see beyond the content to the ques-tion of genre: denunciatory reporting, a prefiguration of investigative and documentary journalism. Writing was operating in a checks-and-balances system, attempting to protect the civil rights of an oppressed class. This type of exposé would become more popular in nineteenth- and twentieth-century fiction.

Francisco Palou (1723–1789)

Contributing Editor: Juan Bruce-Novoa [p. 762]

Classroom Issues and Strategies

Students think that the text is an anachronism, coming late in history. While the East Coast is in the midst of its independence struggle, Serra and Palou are still founding missions. Students have been taught to think of Spain as finished internationally after the Great Armada.

One must explain that the eighteenth century was one of expan-sion and renewed vitality for Spain. Its missionaries and soldiers were moving on all fronts, founding new cities in Texas and northern New Mexico, moving into the Mississippi and Ohio valleys, solidifying their position in the Caribbean basin, and spreading north along the Pacific Coast to counter the southern movement of the Russians from Alaska. Missionaries were the Spanish equivalent of frontiersmen, but they prove how much better organized the Spanish expansion system was. Also, students should be told that the treaty between France and England in 1763 acknowledged Spain's traditional claim to the Mississippi Valley, which was disputed by the French.

Students often question the purpose of the missionary project. It has become fashionable to denounce Serra as an exploiter of Native Americans, so instructors may find it necessary to prepare a defense. More useful, however, is to turn the discussion toward a consideration of how models are always ideologically based and serve the purpose of social indoctrination.

Major Themes, Historical Perspectives, and Personal Issues

Consider the following: the theme of personal sacrifice and determination in the face of great odds; the theme of the traditional moving of borders farther into the territory of the non-Christian that comes from Spain's reconquest of their own territory from the Moors (700–1492).

There is also the literary motif of creating models of culture behavior in texts that will be used to teach the young.

Significant Form, Style, or Artistic Conventions

The form is biography. Students should consider the task of depicting the life of another, the choices made to emphasize certain traits, the strategies used to convince the reader of the author's objectivity and reliability.

There is also the similarity to the writing on the lives of the saints. Students might consider which virtues are held up for imitation in different settings and times.

Original Audience

Readers then were much closer to the ideals, probably coming from the novices of religious orders. They were much more willing to believe in the values reflected in the life of Serra. Now there is little sense of divine mission in life nor of the virtue of extreme sacrifice for the common good. Students must be urged to comprehend the energy of societies in expansion.

Comparisons, Contrasts, Connections

Compare this to Cotton Mather, as the headnote mentions. Both writers attempt to create models for new generations who have forgotten their founding fathers. One could also pick a favorite section from John F. Kennedy's portraits of courage to compare with Serra.

Questions for Reading and Discussion/ Approaches to Writing

Pose the question of role models in society in different periods. Ask students to consider where the models come from and what purpose they fulfill. How do they differ then and now?

Two Mexican-American Oral Tales: "The Llorona, Malinche, and Unfaithful Maria" and "The Devil Woman"

Contributing Editor: Andrew Wiget [p. 771]

Classroom Issues and Strategies

Students may be caught up in the tension between that which is apparently historical and that which is fantastic in legend. There is a tendency to read this story as possibly biographical, and that need not be discouraged. A consultation with the secondary sources, especially Kirtley, will indicate the potential for exploring historical references in this legend. One the other had, students may rush very quickly to try to generalize, in a Jungian sense, about universal symbols representing different dimensions of human nature. A third tendency would be to read this as kind of a gothic horror story. In other words, the fundamental problem with this story is genre, and how genre conventions shape the reading experience.

I mention, for those who are interested in exploring the historical basis of the story, some other references pointed out in Kirtley, and also the frequent newspaper accounts of incidents of family violence in which parents have been responsible for murdering children and children murdering parents. Such discussion helps root the legend in real experience. On the other hand, the story is not limited to being a biography and, in fact, is found almost everywhere Mexican-Americans have settled in sizable numbers. The real issue is why people should want to bring such a horrific story with them. What function does it serve?

Students respond well to being asked to share current popular legends. Most, for instance, have heard of the lovers parked in a desolate area who hear a radio bulletin describing the escape of a murderer who has a hook instead of a hand. You might consult any of Jan Brunvand's popular books, such as *The Vanishing Hitchhiker*, *The Choking Doberman*, and *The Mexican Pet*, all of which contain good discussions of very popular contemporary urban legends.

Major Themes, Historical Perspectives, and Personal Issues

The major theme in this story is the role of women, and how women imagine their value and their identity. Clearly the role of women in this tradition is intimately tied to marriage and the legitimacy of offspring. These topics are much debated today, and yet their value is evident in this story, where transgressing those values leads to catastrophic consequences. Moreover, those values are really social values and not only involve a woman's sense of her own identity, but a woman's sense of a man's identity, and a man's part in creating a woman's identity. In other words men, as much as women, are implicated in the horror of this story.

Finally, this story is about social status, since in most cases one version of this story (that represented by the text of "The Llorona, Malinche, and Unfaithful Maria") has to do with class differences between an aristocratic man and a lower-class woman. In colonial Hispanic society, aristocratic men frequently kept lower-class mistresses, fathered children by them, and reserved them as a second "family," though they would marry an aristocratic woman in order to have a legitimate family. This was a well-known custom, tacitly approved of by both men and women in the aristocracy. This story speaks directly to the abuse of persons through this class-structured system.

Significant Form, Style, or Artistic Conventions

The primary questions for this story have to do with genre of legend, and with the relationship between oral folklore and the written literature of the elite. The response to the issue of genre has already been discussed. The second issue, however, is equally interesting. If written literature is produced by and for the elite class, who are literate, then the aristocratic man in this story represents precisely the kind of person who would participate in that literate culture. This story, on the other hand, is the product of an oral culture and represents its commentary on the behavior and values of that literate, aristocratic class. In other words, the tension between classes is reflected in the choice of genre (legend or fiction) and in the mode of transmission (oral or literate). The legendary is precisely that category that is not yet fiction, that is rooted in the historical but exaggerated. Fiction, however, begs the question of facility entirely, and so suggests the entire reality is imagined. Clearly the choice of genre reflects the interests of the oral versus the literate classes in maintaining this particular tradition.

Original Audience

A good exercise to demonstrate to students that a story is not limited to a specific time and place but can be adapted to other settings is to ask them to write a version of the story set in modern times. What kinds of changes would they make in the story? What elements would they retain?

Comparisons, Contrasts, Connections

This story can be usefully compared to those ethnic literary traditions that depend upon legendary material as subtext, as well as to Anglo-American writers such as Hawthorne and Irving who use legendary material in their short fiction. In each case, it's very useful to ask how legends serve to create an imaginative response to historical and social realities.

Questions for Reading and Discussion/ Approaches to Writing

1. What would drive this woman to kill her children? What do these stories suggest about the relationship between men and women? About class? About the role of marriage and children in creating women's identities?
2. Students might compare this legend to the urban legends mentioned above.

Bibliography

Barakat, R. A. "Aztec Motifs in 'La Llorona.' " *Southern Folklore Quarterly* 39 (1965): 288–96.

Kirtley, Bacil. "La Llorona and Related Themes." *Western Folklore* 19 (1960): 155–68.

Perez, Soledad. "Mexican Folklore from Austin, Texas." In *The Healer of Los Olmos and Other Mexican Lore*, edited by Wilson H. Hudson. Texas Folklore Society Publications, 24 (1951): 71–76.

Enlightenment Voices, Revolutionary Visions

Benjamin Franklin (1706–1790)

Contributing Editor: David M. Larson [p. 776]

Classroom Issues and Strategies

The primary problem involved in teaching Benjamin Franklin in an American literature course is persuading students to view Franklin as a writer. The myths surrounding Franklin and the fact that he writes in genres many students view as informational rather than literary hinder students in viewing his work as literature. In addition, many students have problems because they lack the historical knowledge to deal effectively with occasional writing such as Franklin's.

For providing historical knowledge it is necessary that students learn some basic history to provide context for Franklin's works. In order to persuade students to treat Franklin as a writer, it is useful to apply the techniques of literary analysis (particularly persona and irony).

Students usually respond to and are rather disturbed by the protean quality of Franklin's personality and the variety of his achievement. They want the "real" Franklin to stand up and make himself known, and they want to know how he accomplished so much.

Major Themes, Historical Perspectives, and Personal Issues

Franklin's contribution to the creation of an American national identity is perhaps the most important theme that needs to be emphasized. In connection with this, the students can discuss his role in the shift in the American consciousness from an otherworldly to a this-worldly viewpoint. Franklin's abandonment of Puritanism in favor of the enlightenment's rationalism reflects a central shift in American society in the eighteenth century. In addition, his works reflect the growing awareness of America as a country with values and interests distinct from those of England—a movement that, of course, finds its climax in the Revolution. Franklin's participation in the growing confidence of the eighteenth century that humanity could, through personal effort and social reform, analyze and deal with social problems reveals the optimism and self-confidence of his age, as do his scientific achievements. His belief that theory should be tested primarily by experience not logic also reflects his age's belief that reason should be tested pragmatically. Perhaps most important, in the *Autobiography* Franklin creates not only the classic story of the self-made man but also attempts to recreate himself and his career as the archetypal American success story. Since such varied writers as Herman Melville (*Israel Potter*, "Bartleby, the Scrivener," and *Benito Cereno*), Mark Twain, Thoreau (the "Economy" chapter of *Walden*), William Dean Howells (*The Rise of Silas Lapham*), and F. Scott Fitzgerald (*The Great Gatsby*) respond to the myth Franklin creates, the *Autobiography* can be used as a basis for examining the question of what it means to be an American and what the dominant American values are.

Significant Form, Style, or Artistic Conventions

Franklin must be viewed as essentially an eighteenth-century writer. The eighteenth century's didacticism, its refusal to limit literature to *belles lettres*, its ideal of the *philosophe* or universal genius, and its emphasis on the rhetoric of persuasion all need emphasis. In this connection, students need to become familiar with the use of personae in eighteenth-century writing, with both straightforward and satiric means of rhetorical persuasion, and with the ideal of the middle style in English prose. In addition, students studying Franklin need to become familiar with the conventions of political and other persuasive writing, with those of scientific writing, with those of the letter, and, especially, with the conventions of satire and autobiography in the period. Since for most students the eighteenth century is foreign territory and since the study of eighteenth-century writers has especially been neglected in American literature, students need to learn the ways in which the ideals and practice of literature in Franklin's age differ from the romantic and post-romantic works with which most of them are more familiar.

Original Audience

Since almost all of Franklin's writing is occasional, prompted by a specific situation and written for a particular audience, a consideration of situation and audience is crucial for understanding his work. Each of the satires, for example, is designed for a particular audience and situation. Also, *Poor Richard's Almanac* can be best appreciated when it is viewed as a popular publication for a group of nonliterary farmers and mechanics. In contrast, Franklin's French *bagatelles* are written for a very sophisticated audience who would savor their complex persona and ambiguously ironic tone. The *Autobiography* is designed not merely for Franklin's contemporaries but for posterity as well. Consequently, one of the most interesting features of the study of Franklin as a writer is an examination of the ways in which he adapts his style, tone, organization, and personae to a variety of audiences and situations.

Comparisons, Contrasts, Connections

Franklin can usefully be compared to a host of different writers. The traditional comparison between Franklin and his Puritan predecessors remains useful. For example, while Puritan spiritual autobiographies emphasize their authors' dependence upon God for grace and salvation and their inability to achieve virtue without grace, Franklin's *Autobiography* focuses on his own efforts to learn what is virtuous in this world and to put his discoveries to use in his life. Franklin retains the Puritan concern for self-improvement but removes its otherworldly orientation. Similarly, Cotton Mather's and Franklin's views of the importance of benevolence can usefully be compared and contrasted. And Edwards's thought, with its attempt to understand this world in the light of Puritan assumptions about God and his divine scheme for humanity, can be contrasted with Franklin's, which focuses on this world, largely ignores the next, and sees morality and experience as more important than faith.

Franklin's works also need to be compared to those of the great eighteenth-century English prose writers. In his preference for reasonableness, common sense, and experience over emotion or speculation, Franklin shows his indebtedness to the English writers of the early eighteenth century and to the new scientific spirit promoted by the Royal Society. Franklin's style owes much to the example of Defoe and Addison and Steele; his satiric practice—especially his mastery of the creation of diverse personae and, at times, his use of irony—reflects his familiarity with Swift's satire, even though Franklin's effects are very different.

And Franklin's ideas, persuasive methods, assumptions, and empirical bent can usefully be compared to and contrasted with those of his great British contemporary and pamphlet opponent, Samuel Johnson.

Also, Franklin's achievements in such diverse fields as science, literature, politics, and diplomacy can be compared to the achievements of the eighteenth-century philosophers, such as Voltaire, Rousseau, and Diderot, with whom he was classed in his own age.

Finally, it is useful to compare Franklin's stylistic and persuasive methods and his intellectual assumptions with those of his younger contemporary, Thomas Jefferson.

Questions for Reading and Discussion/ Approaches to Writing

1. The study questions that are useful before students read Franklin depend entirely on the works that they have read previously. Since students in a historical survey of American literature usually approach Franklin after reading heavily in Puritan literature, it is useful to ask questions that force students to confront the similarities and the differences between Franklin and his Puritan predecessors.

2. With Franklin, paper topics can be historical (focusing on Franklin's contribution to any number of events or ideas), comparative (comparing Franklin's works to those of American, British, or European writers), cultural (focusing on Franklin's pertinence to American culture at any stage past the eighteenth century), or narrowly literary (focusing on any number of facets of Franklin's artistry as a writer). The success of a topic depends largely on the extent to which it ties in with the approach taken by the teacher during the course.

Bibliography

The end of the headnote contains books useful for any study of Franklin. In addition there are a few articles on Franklin as a writer that might be especially profitable for teachers to examine. I would suggest:

Larson, David M. "Benevolent Persuasion: The Art of Benjamin Franklin's Philanthropic Papers." *The Pennsylvania Magazine of History and Biography* 110 (April 1986): 195–217.

Lemay, J. A. Leo. "Franklin and the Autobiography: An Essay on Recent Scholarship." *Eighteenth-Century Studies* 1 (December 1963): 258–75.

———. "Benjamin Franklin." In *Major Writers of Early American Literature*, edited by Everett Emerson. Madison, Wis.: University of Wisconsin Press, 1972.

Levin, David. "The Autobiography of Benjamin Franklin: The Puritan Experimenter in Life and Art." *Yale Review* 53 (December 1963): 258–75.

Lynen, John F. "Benjamin Franklin and the Choice of a Single Point of View." In *The American Puritan Imagination: Essays in Revaluation*, edited by Sacvan Bercovitch, 173–95. London, Cambridge Univ. Press: 1974.

Sayre, Robert F. *The Examined Self: Benjamin Franklin, Henry Adams, Henry James*. Princeton: Princeton Univ. Press, 1964. (The chapter on Franklin is quite good.)

Spiller, Robert E. "Franklin on the Art of Being Human." *Proceedings of the American Philosophical Society* 100 (August 1956): 304–15.

John Leacock (1729–1802)

Contributing Editor: Carla Mulford [p. 882]

Major Themes, Historical Perspectives, and Personal Issues

Although the writings of John Leacock seem to have been as popular as those of, say, Francis Hopkinson, and although parts of Leacock's biblical parodic satire *The First Book of the American Chronicles of the Times* were as widely reprinted in newspapers as the Federalist Papers, they have largely been lost to American literary historians. Their loss from American literary history probably results from the efforts of nineteenth-century historians to find continuity in the very discontinuous early American culture. If the founding American ideology was taken by our nineteenth-century historians (like the New Englander Moses Coit Tyler) to be a distinctively Puritan ideology, then those historians sought to create an American past—amid the instability of late nineteenth-century American society—that was coherent and continuously Puritan. Indeed, except for the writings of Benjamin Franklin (which found their own odd historical-interpretive path), the writings from the Middle Atlantic States and especially Philadelphia—that is, the largest trade and industrial area for the fifty mid-century years of the eighteenth century—along with writings from the South were for the most part noticed for their "quaintness" only, if noticed at all.

Other reasons, too, might be adduced for the loss to American literary history of the genre—anthologized here for the first time—of biblical parodic satire, despite its popularity in the colonies. Its loss probably results in large measure from the parodic form itself, which brought a possibility for double-voicing that could direct satire not only at England but *at other colonies.* Nineteenth-century literary historians tended not to discuss the inter-colonial contention rife during the federal period, and they tended to blur the problems texts like Leacock's satire—and even the Federalist Papers—addressed.

Perhaps, too, readers in the past felt uncomfortable with biblical imitation that was not fully and clearly reverential toward the Bible. In addition, the fact that *The First Book of the American Chronicles of the Times* imitated (or parodied) the Bible could have caused dislike among "romantic" readers, who argued that parody was the enemy of inspirational, original (romantic) creations. Its parodic form and its political intent no doubt contributed to the neglect in the American literary past of the *American Chronicles*, one of the most humorous pieces of early American literature.

The selections here from Leacock's biblical parodic satire and from his play allude to the Puritan self-justification in terms of a necessary indigenous right to have riches and freedom, a right provided both by God (given as a New Canaan) and by the Indians (given as a representative, native republicanism). Precisely because of the form of the text as biblical parodic satire, *The First Book of the American Chronicles of the Times* at once celebrates and calls into question the Puritan sense of a hegemonic destiny. This is not to say that the satire is anti-American. The satire is clearly anti-British in support of the American cause of freedom. But the satire questions, as well, the American attitude about military glory, which seems (within the context of this complicated satire) not far different from British (and especially Puritan, as represented by Oliver Cromwell) military vainglory.

Leacock's writings reproduced here would fit well in a syllabus that calls for students to read and discuss writings and issues of Native Americans, Puritans, and/or Philadelphians and to treat questions of genre in early American literature.

Bibliography

For further discussion of John Leacock and his writings, see under "John Leacock" in *Dictionary of Literary Biography: Volume 31, American Colonial Writers,* 1735-1781, edited by Emory Elliott (Detroit: Gale, for Bruccoli-Clark, 1984) and in *Philadelphia: Three Centuries of American Art* (Philadelphia: Philadelphia Museum of Art, 1976).

Dallett, Francis James, Jr. "John Leacock and *The Fall of British Tyranny*." *Pennsylvania Magazine of History and Biography* 78 (1954): 456–75.

Mulford, Carla. *John Leacock's The First Book of the American Chronicles of the Times, 1774–1775*. Newark: Univ. of Delaware Press, 1987.

Mulford [Micklus]. "John Leacock's *A New Song, On the Repeal of the Stamp Act*." *Early American Literature* 15 (1980): 188–93. *The Fall of British Tyranny* in *Trumpets Sounding: Propaganda Plays of the American Revolution*, edited by Norman O. Philbrick. New York: Benjamin Blom, 1976.

J. Hector St. John de Crèvecoeur (1735–1813)

Contributing Editor: Doreen Alvarez Saar [p. 890]

Classroom Issues and Strategies

Letters is a very accessible text; the greatest difficulty in teaching it is establishing the cultural context—the political rhetoric of the Revolution—which makes structural sense of the whole.

Generally, students read the text as the simple story of a farmer and as "truth" rather than as fiction. The teaching challenge is to get students to see how political ideas structure the text. One way into the text is to have the students read letter II and count the references, both direct and indirect, to the way society should be organized. In the opening section of the letter, James compares his situation to the state of other farmers in other nations. Later in letter II, note how the supposedly neutral descriptions of animals are used to talk about the conduct of humans in society.

Students are generally intrigued by the idea that members of the colonies were actually against the Revolution.

Major Themes, Historical Perspectives, and Personal Issues

In the course of *Letters*, through the character of James, Crèvecoeur describes for his reader how social principles laid out by the new American society operate in the life of an individual American. There are many interesting themes that can be pointed out in the text: the nature of the American character—the work ethic, the responsibility of the individual, anti-intellectualism; the farmer as a prototype of the American character; the treatment of slaves; the view of new immigrants and their ethnicity; literary resonances such as the escape from civilization in letter XII and stereotypical American characters. One theme that is frequently overlooked is James's desire not to participate in the Revolution. Students believe that all colonists accepted the righteousness of the Revolutionary cause. A discussion of James's feelings helps students recognize the constancy of division in society and is useful for later discussions of the social and literary reactions to the Civil War and the Vietnam War.

Significant Form, Style, or Artistic Conventions

Eighteenth-century Americans did not share our modern idea that politics and art must be kept separate. Thus some forms of eighteenth-century writing do not conform to common notions about genres and form. For an interesting discussion of the social form of the American novel, see Jane Tompkin's discussion of Charles Brockden Brown's novels in *Sensational Designs*. Further, the form of *Letters* is related to other less common genres like the philosophical travel book, which was often epistolary in form (Montesquieu's *Persian Letters* is a good example).

Original Audience

When students read *Letters*, they find its substance very familiar because much of this material has become part of the mythology of America. Students need to be reminded that *Letters* was one of the first works describing the character of the average American. Also, its American readers were a society of colonials who had just overturned centuries of tradition and were attempting to define themselves as something new, in order to distinguish themselves from those who were exactly like them but born under monarchical governments in Europe. European readers were trying to make sense of this "new man."

Comparisons, Contrasts, Connections

Letters is a good literary expression of the political principles in the Declaration of Independence and Paine's *Common Sense*. It is very useful to read *Letters* in tandem with Book II of Timothy Dwight's *Greenfield Hill*, which is another imaginative creation of the "ideal" average American.

Bibliography

For a quick introduction to the political rhetoric of the period, instructors might read:

pp. 82–86 in *A Cultural History of the American Revolution* by Kenneth Silverman (excerpted in *Early American Literature*, edited by Michael Gilmore).

Chapters 1 and 2 of Gordon S. Wood's *The Creation of the American Republic*.

Doreen Alvarez Saar's "Crèvecoeur's 'Thoughts on Slavery': Letters from an American Farmer and the Rhetoric of Whig Thought" in *Early American Literature* (Fall 1987), 192–203.

John Adams (1735–1826)
Abigail Adams (1744–1818)

Contributing Editor: Albert Furtwangler [p. 925]

Classroom Issues and Strategies

Part of the difficulty in teaching John Adams is that he is one of the so-called Founding Fathers—one of the great, revered, mythical figures who wore ruffles and powdered wigs and foresaw the destiny of America. Part of the delight in reading the Adamses is that they restore such statuesque personages to human life.

Major Themes, Historical Perspectives, and Personal Issues

Adams' correspondence is as a lively memoir of the founding father that reveals a realistic view of his political contemporaries. The perspective on how women fit into society (whether they should vote, etc.) at that time is discussed in John Adams' correspondence with Abigail Adams.

Original Audience

Much of Adams' writing takes its force from being directed to the mind of a strong antagonist or a well-educated contemporary. Adams loves to flourish an allusion or refine the nuances of an idea that he and his reader already know in detail.

The original audience for Adams' letters was each other; a grand-son, Charles Francis Adams, published Abigail Adams' letters in several collections, beginning in 1840.

Comparisons, Contrasts, Connections

These selections make a lively contrast to the impersonal rationality of the Federalist essays or the Declaration of Independence. Or they can be used to reinforce and highlight the sparkling self-awareness of Ben-jamin Franklin or the political fun of John Trumball's poetry. And of course, the selections about women in public life anticipate a large litera-ture about the full dimensions of American freedom.

Bibliography

A student who would go further with the Adamses is confronted by a daunting row of books. John Adams wrote thousands of pages of legal and controversial prose that now require expert annotation. Fortu-nately, many of his papers have been recently edited with insight and imagination. The nineteenth-century edition of his *Works*, 10 vols. (Boston, 1850–56) was prepared with skill and tact by his grandson, Charles Francis Adams; this same editor directed attention to Abigail Adams by publishing her letters in several collections, beginning in 1840. *The Adams Papers* is an ongoing project of the Massachusetts His-torical Society, recipient of the Adams Family Trust by deed of gift from the Adams family in 1956. A microfilm edition of the family papers, 1639–1889, was issued in the late 1950s and can be found in major research libraries. Since the 1960s these papers have been expertly edited and issued by Harvard University Press. *The Diary and Autobiogra-phy of John Adams*, 4 vols., appeared in 1961. The volumes of *Adams Family Correspondence* began in 1963. Other series include *Papers of John Adams* and *Legal Papers of John Adams*. These books may intimidate a novice, but there is an engaging, illustrated selection that provides a rapid overview of Adams' career, tones, moods, and perceptions: John Adams: *A Biography in His Own Words*, ed. James Bishop Peabody (New York: Newsweek Books, 1973).

Several special collections bring out Adams' play of mind. The most famous is *The Adams-Jefferson Letters*, ed. Lester J. Cappon, 2 vols. (Chapel Hill: University of North Carolina Press, 1959)—which also con-tains some strong exchanges between Abigail and Jefferson. A shorter selection appeared as *Adams and Jefferson: "Posterity Must Judge,"* ed.

Adrienne Koch (Chicago: Rand McNally, 1963). There are revealing and often angry remarks about Adams' greatest contemporaries in *The Spur of Fame: Dialogues of John Adams and Benjamin Rush*, 1805–1813, ed. John A. Schutz and Douglass Adair (San Marino, Calif.: The Huntington Library, 1966). Adams also pitted himself against many European political thinkers by marking up the margins of their books. These annotations have been ingeniously turned into dialogues in Zoltan Haraszti, *John Adams and the Prophets of Progress* (Cambridge, Mass.: Harvard Univ. Press, 1952). Adams debated a trenchant loyalist in a series of newspaper essays, which has been summarized and discussed in Albert Furtwangler, *American Silhouettes* (New Haven: Yale Univ. Press, 1987), Ch. 3; this book also treats the abiding strains between Jefferson and Adams in Chapter 6.

The most recent full biographies are listed below. Mention should also be made of Peter Shaw, *The Character of John Adams* (Chapel Hill: Univ. of North Carolina Press, 1976) and of Bernard Bailyn, "Butterfield's Adams: Notes for a Sketch," *William and Mary Quarterly*, 3rd ser., 19 (1962), 238–56. The latter, a review essay on the *Diary and Autobiography* volumes, analyzes the young John Adams and Abigail Smith and the strength that was forged between them.

Primary Works

Diary and Autobiography of John Adams, ed. L. H. Butterfield, 4 vols., 1961; Adams Family Correspondence, 1963; *The Book of Abigail and John: Selected Letters of the Adams Family 1762–1784*, ed. L. H. Butterfield, Marc Friedlaender and Mary-Jo Kline, 1975; *The Adams-Jefferson Letters*, ed. Lester J. Cappon, 2 vols., 1959.

Secondary Works

Page Smith, *John Adams*, 1962; Charles W. Akers, *Abigail Adams: An American Woman*, 1980.

Thomas Paine (1737–1809)

Contributing Editor: Martin Roth [p. 936]

Major Themes, Historical Perspectives, and Personal Issues

From the perspective of contemporary feminism, Paine displays a mixture of insight and blindness. In his "Occasional Letter to the Female Sex," he is sensitive to the oppression of women. In fact, he acknowledges it to be universal, and he links it somehow with their being adored by men—as if the adoration were the other side of their oppression. On the other hand, he seems to believe that women can properly be identified with their beauty—"when they are not beloved they are nothing"—and motherhood (their only "call" on men). And the tag from Otway suggests that men and women are totally opposite species, contrasting as brutes and angels.

Nature and Reason are not abstract principles for Paine. They are not categories through which it is useful to think about things, but dynamic principles that Paine almost literally sees at work in the world. Reason in *Common Sense* is masculine, a most concrete actor pleading with us to separate from England or forbidding us to have faith in our enemies. Nature is feminine; "she" weeps, and she is unforgiving as part of her deepest nature. Should these agencies be regarded as philosophical principles? As deities? Are they coherent characters? Can they be identified by collecting all their behaviors and their metaphoric qualifications?

How do we think about Paine as an author, a writing "I"? One of his works is presented as having been written by an embodied principle of "common sense," and another piece, *The Age of Reason,* a work on the general truth of religion, opens in an extremely private, confessional mode. But he writes in this way to prove that he could have no private motives for misleading others. What kind of stakes are being waged by writing a work on religious truth just before you die? Is there any distinction for Paine between the private and the public I, the private and the public life? Notice how many statements fold back upon the self: "it is necessary to the happiness of man that he be mentally faithful to himself" and "my own mind is my own church."

Paine evokes the splendor of the visible world to close a unit opened by the notion of a privileged book, a "revealed" book, a bible. How are the book and the world opposed to each other? One of these ways is as writing and speech; although, actually, the world transcends the distinction between writing and speech: it "speaketh a universal language" which "every man can read." Could Paine's distrust and rejection of the Bible be applied to those other "revealed" and "privileged" pieces of writing, literary "masterpieces"? Much of Paine can be read as an attack on the book, a motif that connects him with Mark Twain at the end of the next century.

In *The Rights of Man*, Paine assumes that the right to engage in revolution is inalienable. How does he understand this? Can time and complexity alter this characteristic of the nature of things? What is a government for Paine? The metaphors that he uses should again remind us of Twain, images of stealth and deceit, images of theatricality used for purposes of fraud.

Family is crucial here too as Paine examines the absurdity of hereditary aristocracy. In this as in almost everything he does, the later writer that Paine most evokes is Mark Twain, here the Mark Twain of *A Connecticut Yankee* and *The American Claimant*. Among the resemblances to Twain that should not be overlooked is a vein of extremely cunning black humor in much of *The Age of Reason*.

Thomas Jefferson (1743–1826)

Contributing Editor: Frank Shuffleton [p. 957]

Classroom Issues and Strategies

Jefferson does not write in traditionally conceived literary genres, i.e., fiction, poetry, etc., but his best writing is in the form of public addresses, letters, and a political and scientific account of his home state. One must persuade students to see the cultural significance of these forms and then lead them to see the artful construction of image and idea to move readers. In other words, move them past the initial resistance, often expressed as "This isn't literature," to the recognition that the texts work (perform) as literature.

Students are particularly interested in discussing the notion of equality, and most people in general want to talk about Sally Hemings. The contradiction between Jefferson's egalitarianism and his racism (real or apparent) also provokes discussion.

Major Themes, Historical Perspectives, and Personal Issues

For Jefferson, the values of political and moral equality, the scientific interest in variety and complexity in nature and culture, and a kind of skepticism, a doubt that absolute truth can be unequivocally attained in any generation, put him in the line of Emerson and William James. At the same time, the fact that he seems to represent the voiceless and the marginal as a political leader even while his own interests and social position put him among the white male elite of his time points to certain tensions in his positions, of which he was not himself always aware.

Significant Form, Style, or Artistic Conventions

Jefferson published only one full-length book, his *Notes on the State of Virginia*, but the Declaration of Independence and his letters are also significant literary achievements. The Declaration matters because of its significance for our national culture, the letters because of their frequent power to express Jefferson's public ideals and commitments, the importance of the many ideas and issues that fall under his consideration, and the clarity of his consideration. We should remember that Jefferson's sense of the historical moment conditioned practically everything he wrote.

Original Audience

The distinction between private audience, as for personal letters, and public audience, as for the Declaration, is interesting to pursue because Jefferson blurred them in interesting ways. Some of his letters were published, usually against his will but not without his recognition that personal letters could always become public, and yet he was somewhat reluctant to publish *Notes on the State of Virginia*.

Comparisons, Contrasts, Connections

Comparisons are effective; for example, the Declaration to Puritan sermons, *Notes on the State of Virginia* to Crèvecoeur's *Letters* or to Bartram's *Travels*. It is also helpful to get students to think about the importance of history and politics as central matrices for eighteenth-century thought, the move toward science and natural history as the nineteenth century approached, and the different ways we in the late twentieth century have for ordering our knowledge of the world.

The Declaration is a kind of jeremiad in Sacvan Bercovitch's sense of the term, which involves an ironically affirmative catalog of catastrophes, an admission of sins to cast them out. *Notes*, Crèvecoeur, and Bartram can be seen as different ways of defining the American landscape, the place of America.

Bibliography

Useful essays on a variety of topics appear in *Thomas Jefferson: A Reference Biography*, ed. Merrill D. Peterson (New York: Scribner's, 1986). See also its bibliographical essay.

Cunningham, Noble E, Jr. *In Pursuit of Reason: The Life of Thomas Jefferson*. Baton Rouge: LSU Press, 1987. A convenient one-volume biography.

Lehmann, Karl. *Thomas Jefferson, American Humanist*. New York: Macmillan, 1947. Discusses Jefferson's ideas in terms of his grounding in the classics.

Miller, John C. *The Wolf By the Ears: Thomas Jefferson and Slavery*. New York: Free Press, 1977. A thorough and balanced view of Jefferson's changing views on race and slavery.

Peterson, Merrill. *Thomas Jefferson: A Reference Biography*. New York: Scribner's, 1986. Contains authoritative essays on Jefferson's interests and the issues in which he found himself involved. Has a useful bibliographical essay.

Patriot and Loyalist Songs and Ballads

Contributing Editor: Rosalie Murphy Baum [p. 994]

Classroom Issues and Strategies

Most students enjoy Patriot songs and ballads but approach Loyalist works with shyness and curiosity. Their studies in elementary, middle, and high school have led them to think of the Revolutionary War as a completely justified and glorious chapter in American history; they tend not to be aware of the Loyalist (Tory) view of the conflict. At the same time, however, their consciousness of recent American history and international events (e.g., the Vietnam War, the Iran-Iraqi conflict, the Israeli-Palestinian struggles) have made them increasingly aware of the complexity of historical events and of the need to understand both sides of issues. The fact that the songs and ballads reflect and articulate two conflicting *American* views about a momentous period can be of great interest to students once they overcome their qualms about literature that questions or criticizes national decisions and actions.

Major Themes, Historical Perspectives, and Personal Issues

Reading the Patriot and Loyalist songs and ballads provides a glimpse of the popular sentiments being expressed in newspapers, periodicals, ballad-sheets, and broadsides during the Revolutionary period. The selections in the text represent various forms: the song and the ballad, the selection addressed to the public at large and the selection addressed to the child, the work expressing the Patriot or Loyalist position and the work commemorating the life of a particular hero. The usual themes of the Patriot and the Loyalist writers are summarized in the introduction to the selections.

A good glossary of literary terms can offer students information about the usual form and conventions of the song and ballad. Students should anticipate uneven work in popular songs and ballads, written in haste and for immediate practical purposes. At the same time, however, they may wish to examine what in these works accounted for their great popularity during the period and their survival through the years. Of particular interest might be an imaginative reconstruction of the response of both Patriot and Loyalist to either a Patriot or a Loyalist song.

Probably the most important facts students need to consider before reading Patriot and Loyalist songs and ballads are: (a) at the time of the Revolutionary War, the Loyalists were Americans just as much as were the Patriots (Rebels or Whigs); (b) the Loyalist group included some of the leading figures in the country at the time (e.g., Chief Justice William Allen, Rev. Mather Byles, Samuel Curwen, Joseph Galloway, Governor Thomas Hutchinson, Rev. Jonathan Odell, Chief Justice Peter Oliver, Rev. Samuel Seabury, Attorney General Jonathan Sewall), figures whom students tend not to recognize because of the usual emphasis in the classroom upon only Patriot figures; (c) whatever knowledge the students have of Loyalists probably comes from the remarks and writings of Patriots and thus is heavily slanted. The classroom emphasis on Patriot leaders and Patriot arguments, of course, distorts the political complexion of the time and does not help the student to appreciate the complex issues and emotional turmoil of a period in which it is believed that about one-third of the people were Patriots, one-third Loyalists, and one-third neutrals, with Loyalists being especially strong in Delaware, Maryland, New Jersey, New York, and Pennsylvania.

Comparisons, Contrasts, Connections

The sentiments of these works, both Patriot and Loyalist, can be compared very successfully with the ideas expressed by prose writers like John Adams, Benjamin Franklin, Thomas Jefferson, and Thomas Paine, Patriots who are frequently anthologized. Students, however, may also be interested in reading a few of the Loyalist prose writers, such as Rev. Samuel Seabury ("A View of the Controversy Between Great Britain and Her Colonies") and Joseph Galloway ("Plan of a Proposed Union Between Great Britain and the Colonies" or "A Candid Examination of the Mutual Claims of Great Britain and the Colonies"). Students interested in popular culture may wish to pursue the difficult question of what characteristics distinguish popular literature, like these songs and ballads, from serious literature, like the poems of William Cullen Bryant, Walt Whitman, or Emily Dickinson. There could be considerable controversy about where the poetry of Philip Freneau should fit in such a comparison.

Approaches to Writing

Some students may simply wish to report on additional Patriot and Loyalist songs and ballads and can consult Frank Moor's *Songs and Ballads of the American Revolution* (1855, 1964) for the most complete collection. Other students may wish to consider the degree to which the Revolutionary War was very much a civil war. They might compare such a struggle to the conflict between the disparate cultures of the whites and Indians reflected in Puritan literature, or draw parallels between the civil conflict in America and similar hostilities in countries throughout the world today.

Bibliography

Two kinds of information can be particularly useful for students or instructors in studying the Patriot and Loyalist songs and ballads. The introductions to *Prose and Poetry of the Revolution* (1925, 1969), edited by Frederick C. Prescott and John H. Nelson, and to *The World Turned*

Upside Down (1975), edited by James H. Pickering, give excellent, brief overviews of the period and of the literature.

William H. Nelson's *The American Tory* (1961) offers an excellent discussion of Loyalist views.

Wallace Brown's *The King's Friends* (1965) attempts to identify who the Loyalists were and to determine their motives for remaining loyal to the king.

The Federalist and Anti-Federalist Papers

Contributing Editor: Donald R. Hettinga [p. 1007]

Classroom Issues and Strategies

A significant problem in teaching these essays is getting students to see the intensity of the debate; too often it is hidden from them by what they consider archaic and wooden prose.

While there doesn't seem to be a magic formula that can make eighteenth-century prose come alive for twentieth-century students, there are a couple of strategies that may help: (1) Hand out point-counterpoint editorials from a current newspaper (*USA Today* frequently has brief ones) to make the analogy between the constitutional debate and our contemporary situation. (2) Ask two students who are fairly good orators to face off in front of the class, one reading the first three or four paragraphs from Hamilton's #6 and the other reading the first three or four paragraphs from the essay of the "Centinel." (3) To get at the issue of persona, ask students to describe and to compare the persons that they imagine as they read Papers #6 and #10. Since both are writing about similar issues under the same pseudonym, the differences should become readily apparent.

Once students are introduced to the historical background of the time, they are very interested in noting the flux the country was in. Some may also be intrigued by the conflict between states' rights and federal rights, particularly in education and religion.

A good issue for discussion is one that underlies all these essays—the nature of humanity: Are people naturally good? Are they essentially self-interested? Should leaders try to influence citizens to cooperate?

Major Themes, Historical Perspectives, and Personal Issues

These two Federalist Papers tell us quite a bit about the Federalist writers. As the papers demonstrate their belief in the power of written texts to serve as unifying instruments, they also reveal the following attitudes or ideas of their authors:

1. Their assumption that history provides usable lessons.
2. Their assumption of a historically literate audience.
3. Their particular admiration for classical precedents.
4. Their assumption that people are not naturally good.
5. Their fear of abuses of power.
6. Their sense of the uniqueness of the American situation.
7. Their fear of factions.
8. Their great respect for the Baron de Montesquieu's *The Spirit of the Laws*.

While some of these same assumptions and fears are present in "Centinel's" essay, some uniquely Anti-Federalist positions are also evident:

1. The fear of aristocracy.
2. A belief in the militia and the fear of a standing army.
3. The fear of a conspiracy.

Significant Form, Style, or Artistic Conventions

Students need to see these essays as pieces serially written for newspaper publication and only later anthologized in book form. If they can recognize this, then perhaps they can begin to see the urgency in the rhetoric of these writers. Teachers can help here by directing students to particularly arch or passionate passages in the essays and discussing the fear or cultural tension that the writer is attempting to cover with that rhetorical strategy.

Original Audience

One effective strategy is to compare the references and allusions of a contemporary political speech with the classical allusions that pepper these essays. What this reveals is that current politicians assume audiences with much briefer cultural memories.

Another interesting strategy is to ask students to come up with pseudonyms that current political writers might use if writing anonymously were as popular today as it was in the eighteenth century. It's worth noting, of course, that one reason writers of the early republic wrote anonymously is that ideas were, in that period, more important than personality. Questioning the reason for the shift in our current culture may prompt a stimulating discussion.

Comparisons Contrasts, Connections

Alexis de Tocqueville makes numerous telling observations about the political behavior of citizens in a democracy, and a teacher might want to pick a favorite passage for comparison. However, chapters three and four of volume two of *Democracy in America* may serve well to raise another perspective on the issue of the effect of centralized power.

To see an American complaining about the loss of individual rights in a democracy, see James Fenimore Cooper's *The American Democrat* (1838).

Questions for Reading and Discussion/ Approaches to Writing

1. Since *faction* is not a current political term, ask students to list various political or special-interest groups and to think of these when Hamilton or Madison refers to political factions.

   Another useful strategy is to ask students to list public figures who have fallen from power because of sexual indiscretions, vanity, or any of the other faults that Hamilton points to in Paper #6. Substituting Gary Hart for Pericles or Jimmy Swaggart for Cardinal Wolsey may help the text come alive for them.
2. Have students write a letter to the local newspaper arguing for or against another constitutional convention or for or against abolishment of one of the rights in the Bill of Rights.

Bibliography

Ferguson, Robert A. " 'We Hold These Truths': Strategies of Control in the Literature of the Founders." *Reconstructing American Literary History*, edited by Sacvan Bercovitch. Harvard English Studies 13: 1–28. Cambridge: Harvard Univ. Press 1986.

Lerner, Ralph. "The Constitution of the Thinking Revolutionary." In *Beyond Confederation: Origins of the Constitution and American National Identity* edited by Richard Beeman, Stephen Botein and Edward C. Carter II, 38–68. Chapel Hill: Univ. of North Carolina Press, 1987.

Storing, Herbert J. *What the Anti-Federalists Were For: The Political Thought of the Opponents of the Constitution.* Edited by Murray Dry. Chicago: Univ. of Chicago Press, 1981. Note in particular Chapter 1, "Introduction," 3–6; Chapter 5, "The Federalist Reply," 38–47.

Wood, Gordon S. *The Creation of the American Republic, 1776–1787.* Chapel Hill: Univ. of North Carolina Press, 1969.

United Voices, a National Literature

[p. 1022]

Judith Sargent Murray (1751–1820)

Contributing Editor: Amy M. Yerkes [p. 1024]

Classroom Issues and Strategies

The primary problem I have encountered in researching Judith Sargent Murray is that her writings are for the most part unavailable, except on microfilm. Thus students would not have quick access to much of her work. Another problem would be the diversity and incongruous nature of her work: she dealt with so many issues and worked in all genres.

Finally, there is an apparent contradiction between Murray's Federalist agenda and her platform for feminist reform. She maintains that society must be based on a strict adherence to order—political, social, family, and personal order—while promoting a change of women's place within that order. This hierarchical Federalist platform is also in conflict with Murray's Universalist religious beliefs, which argue for each individual's ability to establish a direct link with God.

The writings of Judith Sargent Murray can best be made accessible to students if the presentation is tightly organized around the social, political, and literary issues they address.

Major Themes, Historical Perspectives, and Personal Issues

Murray was interested primarily in literary nationalism—especially with reference to drama—Federalism, Universalism, the education and equality of women. These are the themes that should be emphasized in a presentation of Murray's works. Murray drew from the philosophies of Locke and Rousseau, respectively, in her development of the *Gleaner* persona and her ideas on education; a basic understanding of these philosophies would be helpful to students.

Significant Form, Style, or Artistic Conventions

Murray's most successful literary work is her *Gleaner* essay series; while the topics of the essays are progressive, the form is rather conventional, following such famous prototypes as the essays of Addison and Steele. The development of Murray's persona of Mr. Vigillius, however, is extremely interesting; his interaction with the audience, his reporting style, and his personality allow for interesting discussion.

Her poems, plays, and novel again follow rather conventional forms based on British prototypes. Murray was primarily interested in developing a new content for her work rather than establishing new literary forms.

Original Audience

Since much of Murray's work was originally printed in journals, any consideration of audience should address the readers of these periodicals and the serial nature of the presentation. Furthermore, she was appealing to a very diverse audience: readers who would adhere to her conservative Federalist agenda as well as those liberals who were interested in women's issues. Her ability to embrace such diversity in subject and audience is an important point of emphasis.

Comparisons, Contrasts, Connections

Murray's writings beg comparison with her better-known contemporaries, and it is astonishing to realize that she preceded many of these contemporaries in addressing certain issues. For example, her essay *On the Equality of the Sexes* offers an argument very similar to that found in Mary Wollstonecraft's *A Vindication of the Rights of Woman*. Fruitful comparisons can be made between *The Story of Margaretta* and contemporary sentimental novels such as Hannah Webster Foster's *The Coquette* and Susanna Rowson's *Charlotte Temple*. Murray's two plays exhibit an interest in rendering the American experience—an interest shared by contemporary playwright Royall Tyler.

Questions for Reading and Discussion/ Approaches to Writing

1. Of particular interest in her essays on the equality and education of women are the strategies she adopts to prove this equality. Students might be asked to analyze these strategies and to determine why she adopted them.

   Secondly, since the concept of order is all-pervasive, students might be asked to consider what link exists between the insistence on social and personal order and the demand for a more equal education and status for women.

2. Students could explore Murray's guidelines for developing and promoting American literature (in this case drama) by focusing on the prologues and epilogues she wrote for well-known American plays.

   A more complete understanding of Murray's agenda for the education of women can be achieved by revealing how she adheres to and where she departs from Rousseau's theories on education.

   The questions mentioned in the above section also serve as writing assignments and paper topics.

Bibliography

There is relatively little secondary work on Judith Sargent Murray. The only biography is entitled *Constantia: A Study of the Life and Works of Judith Sargent Murray, 1751–1820*, by Vena Bernadatte Field (Orono, Me.: University Press, 1931).

A brief but helpful critical evaluation of Murray's work is by Bruce Granger in *American Essay Serials from Franklin to Irving*, Chapter VIII (Knoxville: University of Tennessee Press, 1978).

There are helpful, although brief, references to Murray in *Liberty's Daughters: The Revolutionary Experience of American Women 1750–1800* (Mary Beth Norton, 1980), and *Revolution and the Word: The Rise of the Novel in America* (Cathy Davidson, 1986).

Finally, Pattie Cowell offers an insightful overview of Murray's poems in *Women Poets in Revolutionary America 1650–1775* (1981).

Philip Freneau (1752–1832)

Contributing Editor: David S. Shields [p. 1042]

Classroom Issues and Strategies

Some of Philip Freneau's poems require an explanation of the changing political context of the 1770s through 1790s so that their arguments may be understood. Freneau's religious poetry, with its striking absence of scriptural allusion and Christian doctrine, may prove rather alien to students of traditional Christian background.

Discriminations between the beliefs of Patriots and Loyalists, Whigs and Tories, must be supplied for the poems of the 1770s. Discussion of the split of the American revolutionaries into Federalist and Jeffersonian factions during the 1790s is also helpful. "To Sir Toby" is an excellent poem with which to examine the legal justifications of slavery employed during the late 1700s.

I find that the early American political cartoons provide a useful way of introducing students to the context of Freneau's politics. (Michel Wynn Jones' *The Cartoon History of the American Revolution* is a good source.) Sometimes I get a reproduction of one of the newspapers in which a Freneau poem first appeared to show how closely his world-view was tied to the journalism of the era.

Major Themes, Historical Perspectives, and Personal Issues

Freneau was a radical advocate of political democracy. As the chief literary spokesman for the Jeffersonian program, he is an original expositer of certain powerful American political myths: of universal liberty, of the reasonability of the common man, of the superior morality of the life of the farmer to that of the commercial enterpriser. These myths still inform political discourse.

As a nature poet, Freneau presents little difficulty to the student, for his arguments are simple and his language straightforward.

"The House of Night" sometimes risks being reduced to a grade B horror movie rather than an exercise in the sublime.

Significant Form, Style, or Artistic Conventions

Freneau cultivated a variety of styles, most of which were suited to the newspaper readership of common Americans he envisioned as his audience. As a political poet, he employed the usual neoclassical devices of parody, burlesque, and mock confession in his satires; in his political admonitions he practiced "Whig sentimentalism" in his antislavery verse and the "progress piece" in his historical ruminations. In general Freneau was an eighteenth-century neoclassicist in his political verse. His nature studies and theological speculations, however, looked forward to romanticism, particularly in its representation of a natural world suffused with divine vitality.

Original Audience

Revolutionary and post-revolutionary Americans were immersed in political rhetoric. The common reader knew a surprising amount of political theory. An interesting exercise is to isolate the imagery in the poems connected with various political systems—monarchy, aristocracy, republicanism, democracy—and construct the mental picture that Freneau projected for his readers.

Comparisons, Contrasts, Connections

Freneau's nature poems work well with those of William Cullen Bryant. The closest analogue to his political poetry is found in Francis Hopkinson (not frequently anthologized) and Joel Barlow.

Questions for Reading and Discussion/ Approaches to Writing

1. I do not usually guide a student's reading of the text with questions. I do, however, usually suggest that a student pay particular attention to the adjectives Freneau employs.
2. I will take a poem from a Federalist Connecticut wit (Richard Alsop, Timothy Dwight, or Lemuel Hopkins) and ask the students to contrast the ideals of government, citizenship, and policy found in it with those expressed in a political poem by Freneau.

Joel Barlow (1754–1812)

Contributing Editor: Carla Mulford [p. 1071]

Major Themes, Historical Perspectives, and Personal Issues

The writings of Joel Barlow were early anthologized among those of his Connecticut contemporaries of 1785-87, when Barlow and David Humphreys, John Trumbull, Timothy Dwight, and a few others engaged in collaborative writing projects and called themselves the Connecticut or Hartford wits. In the first half of the twentieth century, scholars tended to follow the lead of nineteenth-century literary historians and continued to rank Barlow among his conservative contemporaries. Leon Howard's groundbreaking *The Connecticut Wits* (1943) confirmed Barlow's association with this group, and Howard's influence has continued within the scholarly community. Cecelia Tichi's more timely *New World, New Earth: Environmental Reform in American Literature from the Puritans through Whitman* (1979) continues the Howard interpretation, but clearly within a different context. The interpretation is promulgated in literary and biographical handbooks: the recent commentator cited in the headnote to the Barlow readings, for instance, is Jeffrey Walker, in the Barlow entry in *American Writers Before 1800*, eds. James A. Levemier and Douglas R. Wilmes. As a corrective to these assessments of Barlow, scholars should consult the work, cited below, of Arner, Lemay, Mulford, and Richardson.

Original Audience

Central to the reinterpretation of Barlow's writings is an understanding of the audience to which Barlow was addressing his writings. Barlow seems to have believed, in his early years, that patrons of the arts could be found in America. As a poet seeking patrons in the eastern portion of the new nation—from New Hampshire to Georgia—Barlow would predictably have bespoken the traditional Christian assumptions about God, home, and country to be his readers' beliefs. But given his own reading of Henry Home, of Lord Kames, of dissenting minister Dr. Richard Price, and of historian William Robertson, Barlow most likely personally espoused a conception of the progress of morals not necessarily Judeo-Christian in orientation—despite his Revolutionary War chaplaincy. His potentially deistic interests, in fact, seem to have entered even the rather conservative (in terms of religion) poem, *The Vision of Columbus* (see the

Christensen citation below). Given the context of Barlow's writing during his earliest years, then, there seems little reason to continue the assumption that he necessarily held the beliefs he propagandized. His interests and his readings continued, through his life, to be philosophical, republican, scientific, and propagandist.

Bibliography

The standard biography of Barlow remains the critical biography by James Woodress, *A Yankee's Odyssey: The Life of Joel Barlow* (Philadelphia: Lippincott, 1958).

The standard critical references have been those by Howard and Tichi.

For a reassessment of Barlow's work, see:

Arner, Robert. "The Smooth and Emblematic Song: Joel Barlow's *The Hasty Pudding*." *Early American Literature*, 7 (1972): 76–91.

Lemay, J. A. Leo. "The Contexts and Themes of 'The Hasty Pudding.' " *Early American Literature* 17 (1982): 3–23.

Mulford, Carla. "Radicalism in Joel Barlow's *The Conspiracy of Kings* (1792). In *Deism, Masonry, and the Enlightenment: Essays Honoring Alfred Owen Aldridge*. Newark: Univ. of Delaware Press, 1987, 137–57.

Richardson, Robert O. "The Enlightenment View of Myth and Joel Barlow's Vision of Columbus." *Early American Literature* 13 (1978): 34–44.

See also Merton A. Christensen, "Deism in Joel Barlow's Early Work: Heterodox Passages in *The Vision of Columbus*," American Literature 27 (1956): 509–29.

Royall Tyler (1757-1826)

Contributing Editor: Carla Mulford [p. 1089]

Classroom Issues and Strategies

Students have trouble reading dramatic works, whether they are written by Shakespeare or O'Neill. But they especially have trouble with Tyler's "The Contrast," which they think wooden, stilted, and clumsy. They sometimes even take the central character—and the hero—as a stiff Steve Martin-like buffoon. There's much to do here.

I spend half a class talking about the values of the culture in which this play was produced and saw overnight success. I tell them especially about the belief, held by the elite culture, that morality could be reified, that is, could find actual material manifestation in language and action. This conception that high culture, if demonstrated fully and well, would produce in the masses a liking for high culture and a desire to emulate high culture fascinates them because it seems to them unbelievably naive. Then I have pointed out to them that this attitude seems to have dominated the Reagan White House. They don't always agree—and we use the play as a kind of test case.

Major Themes, Historical Perspectives, and Personal Issues

Tyler picked up on the key high culture themes—frugality, industry, sobriety—spoken most fully by Crèvecoeur and Franklin but by other writers of the revolutionary era as well. These themes are in the play, and the students can readily identify them in the contrasts Tyler sets up for dramatic effect. Students also find the discussions about dress and behavior very intriguing, and they sometimes like to discuss the culture's attitudes about "manly" behavior.

For students who like to do biographical reading, the fact that Tyler was himself involved in quelling the Shays's disturbance has proved interesting. For those who prefer source study, it's useful to note Tyler's reliance upon Sheridan's *School for Scandal*.

Significant Form, Style, or Artistic Conventions

As its title suggests, contrast is the defining principle behind the play. The central contrast is one between Europeanized foppishness, a result of luxury, and American forthrightness, a result of sobriety and industry, "manly" virtues. Manly and Maria, the two characters who wed at the end of the play, represent the new American virtues, while Dimple, Charlotte, and Laetitia represent the degrading decadence of European values.

Students like to note the other contrasts within the play, from discussions about hooped dresses to types of reading material to behavior of servants. Jonathan is considered the "type" of primitive American goodness, an unknowing bumpkin who has lived outside citified life.

Comparisons, Contrasts, Connections

For similar themes, see Crèvecoeur and Franklin.

For similar themes and generic contrasts, see Hannah Webster Foster and Susanna Rowson. The women characters here are particularly useful matter for class discussion.

Questions for Reading and Discussion/ Approaches to Writing

1. Given the Puritans' proscription of dramatic presentation, what might have been the cultural changes that allowed finally for the flourishing of drama in America?
2. Students who like biographical inquiry might find it useful to pursue the Shays's Rebellion issue.

   Students who enjoy source study like to write on the comparisons and contrasts between Richard Brinsley Sheridan's *School for Scandal* and Tyler's play. Interesting analyses of the contrasts in the play have arisen from their papers.

   Some students may want to consider the extent to which the prologue and epilogue reflect the play's content. In this vein, see Judith Sargent Murray's writing on the play in the anthology entry for Murray.

Bibliography

For biographical matters, see:

Tanselle, G. Thomas. *Royall Tyler*. Cambridge, Mass.: Harvard Univ. Press, 1967.

For matters of interpretation, see three excellent articles:

Pressman, Richard S. "Class Positioning and Shays's Rebellion: Resolving Contradictions in *The Contrast*." *Early American Literature* 21 (1986): 87–102.

Siebert, Donald T. "Royall Tyler's 'Bold Example': *The Contrast* and the English Comedy of Manners." *Early American Literature* 13 (1980): 3–11.

Stein, Roger B. "Royall Tyler and the Question of Our Speech." *New England Quarterly* 38 (1965): 454–74.

Hannah Webster Foster (1758–1840)

Contributing Editor: Lucy M. Freibert [p. 1131]

Classroom Issues and Strategies

Teaching Hannah Foster's *The Coquette* poses four problems: (1) the lack of name recognition of both author and work, (2) the questioning of quality, as the work has previously been excluded from the canon, (3) twentieth-century prejudice against didacticism associated with the "sentimental" tradition to which the seduction novel belongs, and (4) the effort required on the student's part to extract the plot from the epistolary structure.

Strategies for dealing with these problems include the following: (1) The lack of recognition may be explained by pointing out that in the latter part of the nineteenth century, publishers, influenced by academics and critics, discontinued the publication of works by women, who had been extremely popular in the earlier part of the century. (2) The high quality of *The Coquette* stems from the careful use of voice to create distinctive characters and from the depth of social analysis of sex roles, customs, manners, and conventions underlying the content of the letters. (3) Foster eliminated didacticism and sharpened her work through astute handling of characterization and voice. Eliza, assertive, speaks with unique rhythm, tone, vocabulary, and intensity. Her voice, echoing Mrs. Richman's, bespeaks the security that Eliza desires, could she have it on her own terms. (4) Small group discussions enable students to clarify questions about the plot structure.

The issue students bring up most frequently is the dependence of men in these novels on the money they would acquire by marriage to women of means. The question asked by both male and female students is Why didn't Sanford expect to have a regular job? A question frequently asked by young men is Why didn't Eliza want to marry? Young women want to know Why didn't Eliza get herself a job? These questions are asked by people from middle- and lower-middle-class families. Students in other economic circumstances might have very different queries.

Major Themes, Historical Perspectives, and Personal Issues

Teaching Hannah Foster's *The Coquette* (1797) within the context of the National Period offers students opportunities to acquire historical, cultural, and literary insights. As Walter P. Wenska, Jr., points out in *"The Coquette* and the American Dream of Freedom" (*Early American Literature* 12, no. 3 [Winter 1977–78]: 243–55), *The Coquette* raises "the question of freedom, its meaning and its limits, in a new land newly dedicated to births of new freedoms," a theme treated subsequently by many American writers. Wenska sees Eliza Wharton as a rebel who seeks a freedom not typically allotted to her sex, and he shows how she consistently rejects the advice of friends who encourage her to settle into the "modest freedom" of marriage.

Like Wenska, Cathy N. Davidson in "Revolution and the Word: *The Rise of the Novel in America"* (New York: Oxford University Press, 1986) recognizes *The Coquette* as much more than "simply an allegory of seduction." Davidson reads it as "less a story of the wages of sin than a study of the wages of marriage" and as "a dialogical discourse in which the reader was also invited to participate if only vicariously." Davidson's analysis of *The Coquette* is indispensable reading for anyone who would teach the novel seriously. Two other works that offer valuable historical and cultural insights are Mary Beth Norton's *Liberty's Daughters: The Revolutionary Experience of American Women, 1750–1800* (Boston: Little, Brown, 1980) and Linda K. Kerber's *Women of the Republic: Intellect and Ideology in Revolutionary America* (Chapel Hill: University of North Carolina Press, 1980).

Significant Form, Style, or Artistic Conventions

The American novel had its origin in the seduction novel appropriated from the British sentimental tradition of Samuel Richardson and his followers. To make the sensational story of the "ruin" of an innocent girl palatable to readers steeped in Puritan thought, early novelists emphasized the factual and educative nature of their works. Alexander Cowie in *The Rise of the American Novel* (1948) says that didacticism was, in fact, a *"sine qua non* of the early novel."

Although the novel as genre had come into its own by the time Foster wrote *The Coquette*, authors continued to claim basis in fact in order to justify the publication of risqué materials. The Preceptress in Foster's *The Boarding School* explains the prevailing objections: " 'Novels, are the favorite and the most dangerous kind of reading, now adopted by the generality of young ladies. . . . Their romantic pictures of love, beauty, and magnificence, fill the imagination with ideas which lead to impure desires, a vanity of exterior charms, and a fondness for show and dissipation, by no means consistent with that simplicity, modesty, and chastity, which should be the constant inmates of the female breast. . . .' "

While voicing opposition to the novel in general, Foster and other novelists characterized the reading of their own works, which were "founded on fact," as warnings, to keep young women from peril. As Lucy Sumner's last letter in *The Coquette* (LXIII) states: "From the melancholy story of Eliza Wharton, let the American fair learn to reject with disdain every insinuation derogatory to their true dignity and honor." In *The Boarding School*, a former student justifies reading Samuel Richardson's novels by claiming "so multifarious are his excellencies, that his faults appear but specks, which serve as foils to display his beauties to better advantage."

Original Audience

A very effective way of handling student inquiries as to who read *The Coquette* is to read to the class a passage from Elias Nason's biography of Susanna Rowson. Writing in 1870, Nason describes the readership of Rowson's best-selling novel, *Charlotte Temple*, with which *The Coquette* competed during the National Period, as follows:

"It has stolen its way alike into the study of the divine and into the workshop of the mechanic, into the parlor of the accomplished lady and the bed-chamber of her waiting maid, into the log-hut on the extreme border of modern civilization and into the forecastle of the whale ship on the lonely ocean. It has been read by the grey bearded professor after his "divine Plato"; by the beardless clerk after balancing his accounts at night, by the traveler waiting for the next conveyance at the village inn; by the school girl stealthfully in her seat at school."

Insofar as this description applies to *Charlotte Temple*, it likely applies to *The Coquette*.

It is much too early to say whether current interest in novels like *The Coquette* will be lasting or whether the novelty of discovering these earlier writers will wear off. It is exciting to the current generation of students that these books are now available. How they will react when they become teachers is pure speculation.

Comparisons, Contrasts, Connections

Novels that invite comparison and contrast with *The Coquette* are William Hill Brown's *The Power of Sympathy* (1789) and Susanna Rowson's *Charlotte Temple* (1794), with which it competed for favor through the early decades of the nineteenth century. Frank L. Mott discusses the popularity of these novels in *Golden Multitudes: The Story of Best Sellers in the United States* (New York: Macmillan, 1947).

All three works treat the seduction theme and claim to be based on fact. The British title of *Charlotte Temple* was *Charlotte, A Tale of Truth* (1791); the seduction possibly involved Colonel John Montrésor, a cousin of the author (Richard D. Birdsall, "Susanna Haswell Rowson," *Notable American Women* 3 [Cambridge: Harvard University Press, 1971]). *The Power of Sympathy* drew on the seduction of Frances Theodora Apthorp by her sister's husband, Perez Morton (William S. Kable, "Editor's Introduction," *The Power of Sympathy* [Columbus: Ohio State University Press, 1969]); and *The Coquette*, on the seduction of Elizabeth Whitman of Hartford, Connecticut, by a person of disputed identity (Aaron Burr and Pierrepont Edwards, son of Jonathan Edwards, being among the "accused"). Extensive, yet inconclusive, discussion of the Elizabeth Whitman story appears in Jane E. Locke's "Historical Preface" to the 1855 edition of *The Coquette* (Boston: William P. Fetridge and Company, 1855), Caroline Dall's *The Romance of the Association: or, One Last Glimpse of Charlotte Temple and Eliza Wharton* (Cambridge: Press of John Wilson and Son, 1875), and Charles Knowles Bolton's *The Elizabeth Whitman Mystery* (Peabody, Mass.: Peabody Historical Society, 1912).

Significant differences separate *The Coquette* from *The Power of Sympathy* and *Charlotte Temple*. Characters in *Charlotte Temple* follow relatively stock patterns. Only the villainous Madmoiselle La Rue and Belcour display individuality. Charlotte, generally passive, succumbs easily to La Rue's temptations and threats, Montraville's persuasion, and Belcour's deceit. The characters in Brown's novel have interesting potential. Harriot, for example, displays strong powers of observation, and Ophelia speaks forcefully. But they employ the same voice as Rowson's narrator—the voice and style of the sentimental novel.

Questions for Reading and Discussion/ Approaches to Writing

1. Students should be asked to consult the *Oxford English Dictionary* for the meanings of *coquette* and *rake*, paying special attention to the changes in meaning through time. They might also be asked to investigate the concept of *dowry*, noting what brought about the end of the practice of providing a dowry. Ask them to find out whether the epistolary form is used in novels today.

2. Paper topics may include the following:
   argumentative—Eliza Wharton and Peter Sanford are/are not equally responsible for Eliza's death, or Eliza Wharton's fall was entirely her own fault.

analytic—a character study of Eliza Wharton using her letters alone, or a character study using only the letters of others.

research paper—compare *The Coquette* to a British epistolary seduction novel, focusing particularly on social issues.

research paper (nonliterary)—a study of property rights of men and women in eighteenth-century America.

Bibliography

Helpful sources have been provided above. Both students and teachers might find quick access to the beginnings of the American novel in the introduction, didactic, melodrama, and satire/humor sections of *Hidden Hands: An Anthology of American Women Writers, 1790-1870*, edited by Lucy M. Freibert and Barbara A. White (New Brunswick, N.J.: Rutgers University Press, 1985).

Susanna Haswell Rowson (1762–1824)

Contributing Editor: Laraine Fergenson [p. 1153]

Classroom Issues and Strategies

Some students may be put off by Rowson's moralizing, which is rather heavy at times. Another problem might be the author's eighteenth-century language and style of writing. Where extreme difficulty is likely to occur (such as in the use of "eagerly" for "anxiously"), a note is provided in the text, but some students may find old-fashioned and excessively quaint such lines as "I am snatched by a miracle from destruction!" or "It is not too late to recede from the brink of a precipice, from which I can only behold the dark abyss of ruin, shame, and remorse!"

The best way to deal with both problems mentioned above is by an examination of the audience Rowson intended to reach and her purposes in writing. As she saw it, she was arming young women for existence in a perilous world inhabited by seducers and false friends. This world that Rowson depicted was dominated by a rigid moral code (to which Rowson apparently subscribed, although she knew that violations of it were dealt with very harshly). Keeping in mind this audience, described explicitly in the author's preface as the "young and thoughtless of the fair sex," the modern reader can understand both Rowson's emphasis and her language.

Students are interested in Rowson's notion of sisterhood. Although in other writings, she warns unmarried girls about associating with women of damaged reputations, lest their own suffer, in *Charlotte Temple*, she clearly approves of Mrs. Beauchamp's befriending Charlotte. Perhaps it is significant that Mrs. Beauchamp is a safely married woman, but she is obviously a foil to La Rue, who, established as Mrs. Crayton, shows detestable hypocrisy in shunning Charlotte as a fallen woman. Rowson's idea that women should take care of each other and not join in heaping insults upon a betrayed sister is similar to ideas in the writings, in the next generation, of Margaret Fuller, who in 1845 published *Woman in the Nineteenth-Century*, our first feminist book.

Major Themes, Historical Perspectives, and Personal Issues

1. The need for Rowson: Redressing the balance.

   Ellen B. Brandt's "Introduction" to *Susanna Haswell Rowson: America's First Best-Selling Novelist* (Chicago: Seabra Press, 1975) makes the following statement:

   "Whether we consider her historical importance as an influential and well-loved editor, educator, and public figure; her literary importance as America's first best-selling novelist and, probably, our first genuine 'lady-of-letters'; or her cultural importance as a commentator on the lives and customs of American women of her era; we must come to the conclusion that Susanna Haswell Rowson was one of the most interesting, dynamic and productive personalities of the early national period. Yet, for reasons still not clearly defined, she has all but disappeared from course curricula, literary studies, and bibliographies of this period, a "forgotten" woman in the archives of our cultural history." (vii)

   This statement, all too true, is a good place to begin a discussion of Rowson.

2. Historical background.

   In the preface to her useful work on Rowson, Patricia Parker states:

   "Rowson lived during a crucial period of our nation's history, as it turned from provincial colony to preindustrial nation. She herself strongly identified with the political objectives of the new republic and came to consider herself American despite her British birth, as she lived most of her life in this country.

   "Her writings reflect an increasing concern with freedom and democratic principles, both politically and sexually. To study her song lyrics and theatrical compositions during the 1790s is to understand the popular taste of the American public who were trying to decide how to live with their newly acquired independence."

Some of Rowson's song lyrics have been excerpted in the sources mentioned above, and an interesting discussion might come from reading them in class. Also, her role in the early American theatre and her association with Thomas Wignell could be discussed.

The importance of the American Revolution should also be noted. It affected Rowson personally, and she was one of the first writers to use the Revolutionary War as the background for her novels. Montraville and Belcour are both British soldiers being sent to America to fight against the rebels. Charlotte, wondering about La Rue's desertion of Belcour, reflects that she thought only true love had made her follow the man to the "seat of war." Montraville, seducing Charlotte, says: "I thought that you would for my sake have braved the dangers of the ocean, that you would, by your affection and smiles, have softened the hardships of war. . . ."

Significant Form, Style, or Artistic Conventions

Plot, Characterization, and Structure of Charlotte Temple

An instructor presenting selections of *Charlotte Temple* would do well to read the entire novel in order to appreciate its structure and the sophistication of its characterization. By explaining the motivations of the characters at length, Rowson makes their actions believable and, in doing so, invalidates the charge that she was a writer of melodrama. Her portrayal of Charlotte is masterful. The girl's naive and ingenuous character is rendered convincingly. Rowson details the progress of her seduction with sympathy and keen psychological insights into the workings of her mind.

Rowson devotes considerable time in this short novel to describing Charlotte's parents, and with good effect. Lucy Eldridge Temple and her father had been driven to a debtor's prison by the machinations of an unscrupulous man who had designs on Lucy. Her refusal, under intense pressure, to submit to the kind of arrangement Charlotte has with Montraville brings disaster to the household, but the Eldridges and Temple never doubt that she has done the right thing. It is thus doubly poignant that Lucy's daughter Charlotte should yield as she does. It is ironic and also perfectly understandable that a couple so idealistic, so perfectly loving, and so trusting could produce a child as dangerously naive as their Charlotte.

Montraville too is well-drawn. Although he plays an evil role in the story, he, like Clyde Griffiths in *An American Tragedy*, is no villain. Attracted to Charlotte and unable to resist seducing her, though he knows that her lack of fortune will make marriage inexpedient, he abandons her because he believes his deceitful friend (who has placed Charlotte in a compromising position in order to alienate her from Montraville) and because he cannot resist the charms of Julia Franklin, his new love. Although Montraville brings great evil upon Charlotte, he, like her, is not so much evil as weak, and he suffers intense pangs of conscience—and eventually an early death—for what he has done. By making Montraville a sympathetic human being instead of a stock-figure of evil, Rowson lends plausibility to her story, and she accomplishes her goal, which is to show that yes, such things can really happen—even to the most well-meaning people.

Original Audience

Consider the idea, mentioned in the headnote, that the subtitle, *A Tale of Truth*, may have been intended to present the work to Americans with a Puritan heritage as somewhat more worthwhile than just a novel.

The most striking point to make about the audience of this book is that it was quite clearly intended to be female. Thus this book is by a woman and for women.

Not only was this true in colonial times, but throughout the nineteenth century and into the early twentieth, the book's readership was largely female. As discussed in the headnote, it was described disparagingly as appealing to an audience of "housemaids and shopgirls." In her Preface to *Susanna Rowson* [Boston: Twayne, 1986], Patricia Parker attributes this phrase to Carl Van Doren's *American Novel*. A lively classroom discussion might center on the reasons for the book's appeal to such an audience—assuming the accuracy of Van Doren's observation, which might also be subject to discussion. Instructors might raise the issue of the vulnerability of women of lower socio-economic status and hence their identification with Charlotte.

Comparisons, Contrasts, Connections

Rowson has sometimes been compared to Samuel Richardson, the eighteenth-century English author of *Pamela* and *Clarissa*. Richardson is known for the epistolary form, and in *Charlotte* letters (often ones that do not get delivered) play an important role. But even more striking is the emphasis on seduction in both Richardson and Rowson. Ellen Brandt writes of the "Clarissa theme" as follows: "The loss of female virginity without the sanction of marriage must lead rapidly and inexorably to the death of the transgressor-victim" (p. 26).

It is also instructive to compare *Charlotte Temple* to *An American Tragedy* by Theodore Dreiser. The plots have many similarities: In both a self-indulgent young man of little personal wealth, but wealthy connections, seduces a poor girl and then falls in love with another woman, who offers not only superior attractiveness, but money as well. In both, the young man, seeing the first girl as an obstacle to his material and romantic happiness with the second, regrets his rashness in seducing the first, who is pregnant and dependent on him. In both novels the seduced women die. Although Montraville does not plot to kill his mistress, as Clyde plans to and in effect does kill Roberta, Charlotte dies through his neglect.

This eighteenth-century American author saw and depicted a very bad world indeed—for women. But—and this point must be emphasized—her solution to the evil was not to change that world, but to help develop in women the strength, wisdom, and common sense they would need to deal with it as it was. Where Dreiser saw Roberta and Clyde as victims of social and economic inequality, Rowson saw Charlotte and Montraville as victims of individual failings—treachery, weakness, and sinful folly. Whereas Dreiser's novel is a sweeping indictment of the class system in supposedly egalitarian America, Rowson's *Charlotte Temple* is an indictment of personal evil and weakness.

Questions for Reading and Discussion/ Approaches to Writing

1. It might be helpful to consider the historical period in which the novel is set. Students might also want to look up more information on Rowson than is provided in the brief headnote, because her life was truly fascinating.

2. One topic on which students might write is the critical evaluation of the novel. Since this question is still open, students will find much room for originality.

   Another interesting assignment is to write a comparison/contrast essay on *Charlotte Temple* and *An American Tragedy*. (This assignment would be for students who have read the whole of both novels; thus it might be suitable as a term paper assignment or a special individual project.)

   Students in a class stressing the creation of literature might be assigned to write a moralistic story of their own, trying to focus on a specific purpose and audience as Rowson does.

Bibliography

The preface to Patricia Parker's *Susanna Rowson* (Boston: Twayne, 1986), mentioned above and in the headnote, is very helpful.

Robert Vail's study, "Susanna Haswell Rowson, the Author of *Charlotte Temple*: A Bibliographical Study," also mentioned in the headnote, provides much useful information.

The chapter on Rowson in Constance Rourke's *The Roots of American Culture* (New York: Harcourt, Brace & Co., 1942) is an interesting presentation of Rowson as a feminist.

Charles Brockden Brown (1771–1810)

Contributing Editor: Carla Mulford [p. 1163]

Classroom Issues and Strategies

Undergraduates find Brown peculiar when compared to other writers of the era, and they tend to say, "He reminds me of Poe," without realizing that Poe wrote a generation after C. B. Brown. They are unused to first-person narratives of Brown's order if they have been in a chronologically arranged survey course. They have been used to first-person narratives that explore particular models of behavior, like the spiritual autobiography. Brown, writing in the absence of particular religious ideologies or political agendas, puzzles them. Some students like him immensely; others find him obtuse and irrational.

I play upon students' surprise at Brown's narrative, and I stress that *if* Brown's narratives seem irrational, then perhaps that was part of Brown's point, that life itself is unpredictable according to rational plans. I show them that at the time when most writers were attempting to find ways to model the federalist political agenda, Brown was questioning the assumptions of the model—that life could be organized like a coherent machine and that people could be taught "moral" behavior. If students can't quite see it this way, then I talk with them about various means by which authors more familiar to them (Poe, Conrad, Hawthorne) have represented the unconscious and seemingly irrational behavior.

Major Themes, Historical Perspectives, and Personal Issues

If students want to explore Brown's life, they find ample interesting material in his letters about authorship. Most biographies on Brown—there are a few readily available—quote from letters.

Significant Form, Style, or Artistic Conventions

Two key issues are raised by Brown's writing:

Brown's first-person narratives differ from those most students will be accustomed to from earlier writers. Brown's narrators, like Althorpe, the narrator of this story, are often unreliable. Students are intrigued by the exploration of psychology that Brown offers them. (They have been trained to think such complexity available only in twentieth-century authors, or in Poe.)

Second, because of the first-person narrative form, the intense psychological issues Brown renders often take on a motif of "the double." In this narrative, young Althorpe, the narrator, has his double in both the unnamed man to whom Constantia Davis is engaged and in the anticipated intruder, Nick Handyside. This is a minor sample of Brown's often-central motif of the double. (See *Wieland, Edgar Huntly*.)

Comparisons, Contrasts, Connections

We talk about the federalist audience that would have liked Foster and Rowson, in order to put Brown's work in a relief of "conscious" narrative. This enables students to see just how extraordinary Brown's narrative attempts were.

We then, later on (in covering Poe and Hawthorne), discuss the extent to which later authors used some of Brown's interests and techniques. Hawthorne considered Brown one of the best American writers, and he regretted Brown's inability to find an appreciative audience.

Many students then like to make comparisons between Brown and recent authors.

Questions for Reading and Discussion/ Approaches to Writing

Students have written fruitful papers on doubles in Brown; Brown's implied attack against the "rational" federalist agenda of his day; Brown's relationship to Poe and Hawthorne.

Bibliography

There are many, many studies on Brown. Recent articles have played upon the issues of family and disintegration. Teachers should pursue those articles that might interest them, after reading discussions of books and articles in the entries (well-indexed) in each annual volume of *American Literary Scholarship*.

*Early
Nineteenth
Century*

1800–1865

Myths, Tales, and Legends

[p. 1214]

Jane Johnston Schoolcraft (Ojibwe) (1800–1841)

Contributing Editor: James W. Parins [p. 1216]

Classroom Issues and Strategies

Establishing a framework for discussion is the primary difficulty with teaching Schoolcraft. The instructor needs to address the prehistoric nature of the original oral tales and aspects of the oral tradition itself, and, in addition, explain how the tales were enhanced stylistically and rhetorically once they were written down. The dual audiences (of the original tales and the written versions) need to be addressed as well.

As a helpful teaching strategy, draw parallels with other oral tales, for example, Njal's *Saga, Beowulf,* and the *Iliad.* All these existed first in the oral tradition and were later written down. All included super- or preternatural elements.

Students usually have questions on the differences in social values in the American Indian and "mainstream" cultures.

Major Themes, Historical Perspectives, and Personal Issues

Themes should be approached in the same ways that the teacher approaches other works. Of particular importance are creation myths or stories that explain how things came to be.

Significant Form, Style, or Artistic Conventions

Students can compare the author with others writing in the "standard" style of the time, Hawthorne and Irving, for example.

Original Audience

Teachers need to address the preliterate society for which the tales were originally composed as well as the non-Indian audience Schoolcraft was writing for. Points to be made include the following: The style was embellished for the non-Indian audience; students should be directed to find examples. Schoolcraft's Romantic style differs from some other narratives, including slave narratives.

Comparisons, Contrasts, Connections

Oral texts from other traditions can be compared and contrasted. Cusick's work is especially helpful for comparison within the American Indian context.

David Cusick (Tuscarora) (?–1840)

Contributing Editor: James W. Parins [p. 1225]

Classroom Issues and Strategies

Establishing a framework for discussion is essential. The teacher needs to address the prehistoric nature of the original oral tales and aspects of the oral tradition itself. In addition, it is helpful to explain how the tales were enhanced stylistically and rhetorically once they were written down. The dual audiences (of the original tales and the written version) need to be addressed as well.

Note, also, that Cusick's language is at times difficult for modern readers to understand. This difficulty may be addressed by stressing careful reading and drawing parallels with other oral texts.

Students usually have questions on the differences in social values in the American Indian and "mainstream" cultures.

Major Themes, Historical Perspectives, and Personal Issues

Themes should be approached in the same way that the teacher approaches other works. Of particular importance are creation myths or stories that explain how things came to be.

Significant Form, Style, or Artistic Conventions

Questions might include investigation of style and vagueness in the plot-line. Students also might be asked to account for the language difficulties encountered in the work.

Original Audience

Teachers need to address the preliterate society for which the tales were originally composed as well as the non-Indian audience Cusick was writing for. In addition, Cusick had an Indian audience in mind, since one of his purposes was to make sure the tales were preserved.

Comparisons, Contrasts, Connections

Oral texts from other traditions can be compared and contrasted. Schoolcraft's work is especially helpful for comparison within the American Indian context.

Tales from the Hispanic Southwest

Contributing Editor: Genaro M. Padilla [p. 1228]

Classroom Issues and Strategies

Students may need to be reminded that these tales are usually performed orally. So, instructors should help students recreate the oral tradition out of which they emerge. I often read these tales aloud and try to actually reconstruct the performative features of the tale.

Major Themes, Historical Perspectives, and Personal Issues

See headnote.

Significant Form, Style, or Artistic Conventions

Again, the cultural value attached to oral tradition and collective audience should be borne in mind.

Original Audience

The best/ideal audience is youngsters who are still shaping their social and ethical beliefs.

Comparisons, Contrasts, Connections

Other folk tale types should be useful, especially those sustained by other immigrant groups—Italians, Greeks, etc.

Questions for Reading and Discussion/ Approaches to Writing

1. (a) What are our common ideas about death? Why do we avoid discussing death?
   (b) How do stories entertain us into ethical behavior?
2. (a) Students might compare these tales with others they have heard or read.
   (b) They might consider the "usefulness" of the moral tales in a largely secular world.

Washington Irving (1783–1859)

Contributing Editor: William Hedges [p. 1238]

Classroom Issues and Strategies

Students generally know the two short stories ("Rip" and "Sleepy Hollow"). With the selections from *History*, it is wise to avoid tipping off students in advance to Irving's attitude toward the treatment of Native Americans by European-Americans; see if they can penetrate through the technically sophisticated irony to Irving's scathing condemnation; some may be tempted to read the passage as approving the harsh treatment. (Note that, strictly speaking, the passage is concerned with Latin America, not America as a whole. But students can be asked whether it has relevance to North American policies relating to Indians.)

Emphasize Irving's humor before getting too serious. Give students a chance to talk about what they find entertaining in the selections and why. Also, try comparing responses of male and female students to "Rip Van Winkle." How sympathetic are each to Rip? Look at the story as the first in a long line of texts by male American writers in which a male protagonist forsakes civilized community life for the wilderness (or the sea) on a quest of sorts and perhaps joins forces with a male companion(s). Consider the psychological or cultural significance of such narratives, as well as the role of and attitude toward women they portray.

Major Themes, Historical Perspectives, and Personal Issues

History: racism, its guises and rationalizations; what it means to be truly civilized—or savage.

"Rip Van Winkle": loss (and discovery?) of identity; a challenge to American values, the work ethic. Does Rip himself represent anything positive? George III vs. George Washington (is the story anti-republican?); is the story sexist?

"Sleepy Hollow": artificiality vs. naturalness; Puritan-Yankee intellectual pretentiousness, hypocrisy, greed, and commercialism as threats to an American dream of rural abundance and simple contentedness; the uses of imagination.

Significant Form, Style, or Artistic Conventions

With the *History* selection, questions of burlesque irony, the reliability of the narrator: Is Irving's persona, the peculiar Diedrich Knickerbocker, a party to the irony? Is he being deliberately ironic himself (saying just the opposite of what he believes about treatment of Native Americans), or does he seem duped by the defenses of brutal mistreatment that he offers? Does it matter which? Could it be either one—or both? Is the reader being played with?

The two stories were written ten years after the *Knickerbocker History*. *The Sketch Book*, from which the two stories come, is generally taken to be the beginning of Irving's transformation into a romantic writer of sorts. What romantic elements can be seen in "Rip" and "Sleepy Hollow"?

These two stories are also, arguably, the beginning of a new genre, the short story. If so, what makes these narratives short stories as opposed to earlier kinds of tales?

Original Audience

Relate Irving's commercial success beginning with *The Sketch Book* to the burgeoning of American popular culture in the early nineteenth century. Discuss *The Sketch Book* as context of "Rip" and "Sleepy Hollow" and the huge vogue for "sketch" books, literary annuals, and gift books that follows.

Comparisons, Contrasts, Connections

Compare the selection from *History* with Franklin's Swiftian satires, "The Sale of the Hessians," "An Edict by the King of Prussia"—or Swift's "A Modest Proposal" itself.

Compare and contrast the rural felicity of the inhabitants of Sleepy Hollow with Crèvecoeur's idealization of American rural life in the *American Farmer* or Jefferson's famous agrarian pronouncements in query XIX of *Notes on Virginia*.

What distinguishes Irving as a short story writer from Hawthorne or Poe?

Questions for Reading and Discussion/ Approaches to Writing

1. The humor of the *Knickerbocker History*—have students read sections of it.
2. Political satire and opinion in the *History*—consider specifically the anti-Jeffersonianism of the section on Governor Kieft. Prepare a personal interpretation of one of the two stories.
3. Papers on varying or contrasting approaches to "Rip" or "Sleepy Hollow," consulting some of the interpretations listed in the bibliography. Discuss the humor in either story.

Bibliography

Fetterly, Judith. Ch. on "Rip Van Winkle" in *The Resisting Reader* (1978). A feminist interpretation.

Hedges, William L. Article on the *History* in Stanley Brodwin, ed., *The Old and New World Romanticism of Washington Irving* (1986). *Knickerbocker*'s politics and Irving's disorienting humor.

Hoffman, Daniel. Ch. on "Sleepy Hollow" in *Form and Fable In American Fiction* (1961). Folkloristic interpretation, Native American humor.

Martin, Terence. "Rip, Ichabod, and the American Imagination." *American Literature* 31 (1959): 137–49.

Ringe, Donald A. "New York and New England: Irving's Criticism of American Society." *American Literature* 21 (1967): 455–67. Irving's pro-Dutch, anti-Yankee posture.

Roth, Martin. Chs. on *Knickerbocker* and on the two stories, in *Comedy in America: The Lost World of Washington Irving*. Very original criticism, mythic and cultural.

Seelye, John. "Root and Branch: Washington Irving and American Humor." In *Nineteenth-Century Fiction* 38 (1984): 415–25. Very solid, well-balanced approach.

Young, Philip. "Fallen from Time: The Mythic Rip Van Winkle." *Kenyon Review* 22 (1960): 547–73. Jungian, the motif of the long sleep in world literature.

Zlogar, Richard J. "Accessories that Covertly Explain: Irving's Use of Dutch Genre Painting in 'Rip Van Winkle,'" *American Literature* 54 (1982): 44–62. Argues story is critical of Rip.

James Fenimore Cooper (1789–1851)

Contributing Editor: Geoffrey Rans [p. 1280]

Classroom Issues and Strategies

Students initially find Cooper verbose, long-winded, and his characters repetitious. I have found it better not to insist on Cooper's formal powers at the outset, nor even on his obvious importance as an innovator and initiator in American fiction. Rather, it is effective to invite the students to discuss the substantive issues that arise in a reading of Cooper. Their importance and typicality in the American literary experience remain alive to students in various historical transformations, and Cooper presents them in unresolved and problematic formations.

While the passages selected in the *Heath Anthology* raise obvious and important issues—of empire, of political theory, of nature versus civilization, law, conservation, religion, race, family, American history—one Leather-Stocking novel should be studied in its entirety. Depending on where the instructor places most emphasis, *The Pioneers, The Last of the*

Mohicans, and *The Deerslayer* are the most accessible. In any case, any study of even the selected passages requires some "story-telling" by the instructor.

The discussion of *The Pioneers* or other novels can become, as well, a discussion of the competing claims on the student's attention to form and content: whether form is always possible or desirable; whether the unresolved issues in history are in any sense "resolved" in works of art; how the desire for narrative or didactic closure competes with the recognition of an incomplete and problematic history and political theory. Approach questions of empire, race, progress, civilization, family, law, and power, and lead back from them to the literary issues.

Major Themes, Historical Perspectives, and Personal Issues

1. Historical myth and ideology. How do they differ? How do they interact?
2. Nature/civilization
3. Law
4. Power and property
5. The land
6. Violence
7. Race
8. Gender and family
9. Cooper's contradictory impulses: see Parrington (10)
10. Hope/disappointment

Significant Form, Style, or Artistic Conventions

1. Didacticism, resolved and unresolved
2. Romance—the Scott tradition: see Orlans (10)
3. Myth
4. Romanticism
5. Conventions of description and dialogue, epic and romantic
6. Epic
7. For advanced students: the question of the order of composition, and the literary effect on the reader of anachronism

Original Audience

I stress how the issues that were urgent to Cooper and his readers (they are evident in the novels, but see also Parrington) are alive today. Some attention should be given to the demand for a national literature, and the expectations of the American Romance (see Orlans).

Indispensable reading for this period is Nina Baym's *Novelists, Readers and Reviewers* (Ithaca: Cornell Univ. Press, 1984).

Comparisons, Contrasts, Connections

Here are some pursuable issues:

1. Crèvecoeur: slavery, Indians, the agrarian ideology and its betrayal.
2. Relate to other writings on the encounter of white and red—see Smith, Winthrop, Williams, Crèvecoeur, Franklin, Jefferson.
3. Stowe—on race, slavery, Christianity and its betrayal, didacticism—Twain, Frederic Douglass.
4. The nonfiction writers of the Revolution and the New Republic: Jefferson, the Federalists.
5. Faulkner: race, history. Carolyn Porter's chapters on Faulkner (see 10) might seem relevant to Cooper to some instructors.
6. Catherine Sedgewick's *Hope Leslie*. Seek and you shall find.

Questions for Reading and Discussion/ Approaches to Writing

1. Before starting Cooper, an assembly of the issues raised in the course about form, the canon, and the literature of Colonial, Revolutionary and New Republican times should be given by the instructor.
2. I have found the following areas particularly fruitful for student essays on Cooper:
   (a) Confusion, contradiction, and resolution
   (b) Myth versus reality
   (c) Race
   (d) Law and justice
   (e) Power in all its forms: class, race, military, political, and property

Bibliography

The chapters on Cooper in the following books (subtitles omitted):

Bewley, Marius. *The Eccentric Design*. New York: Columbia Univ. Press, 1961.

Fisher, Philip. *Hard Facts*. New York: Oxford Univ. Press, 1985.

Marx, Leo. *The Machine in the Garden*. New York: Oxford Univ. Press, 1964.

Orlans, G. Harrison. "The Romance Ferment after *Waverly*." *American Literature* 3 (1932): 408–31.

Parrington, Vernon L. *Main Currents in American Thought*. Vol. 2. New York: Harcourt Brace, 1927.

Porter, Carolyn. *Seeing and Being*. Middletown: Wesleyan Univ. Press, 1981. The chapters on Faulkner.

Rans, Geoffrey. "Inaudible Man: The Indian in the Theory and Practice of White Fiction." CRAS VII (1977): 104–15.

Smith, Henry Nash. *Virgin Land*. New York: Vintage, 1950.

Tompkins, Jane. "Indians: Textualism, Morality, and the Problem of History." CI, 13 (1986): 101–19.

———. *Sensational Designs*. New York: Oxford Univ. Press, 1985.

Catharine Maria Sedgwick (1789–1867)

Contributing Editors: Barbara A. Bardes and Suzanne Gossett [p. 1308]

Classroom Issues and Strategies

There may be some difficulty in helping students compare early nineteenth-century attitudes toward Indians, who are here referred to as savages, to Sedgwick's treatment of Native Americans, which is so different from that of her contemporaries. Students need to understand Sedgwick's complex attitude toward the early Puritan colonies, combining patriotism and objections to Puritan oppressiveness. It is also important to note the place of women in the early American republic, as important teachers of the political culture yet subordinate within the home.

Emphasize that Sedgwick occupied an unusual position as an important woman writer with sympathy for those without power in the society. Present some biographical and historical background, first on Sedgwick and then on Puritans. Be sure students know the legend of Pocahontas.

Major Themes, Historical Perspectives, and Personal Issues

1. Sedgwick's picture of solidarity between women (Hope and Magawisca).
2. Sedgwick's sympathy for the Indians who are being destroyed by the English settlers. The sympathy is evident because the Indian massacre repeats an English one and is also shown in the discussion of the marriage of Faith Leslie to an Indian.
3. The political significance of Hope and Magawisca's defiance of the Puritan magistrates: the way in which both Indians and women are excluded from the political system. The emphasis throughout on the political and personal need for liberty and independence. Contrast Magawisca's defiance of the English with the historical Pocahontas's marriage to an Englishman.
4. The place of the family in the political order and the place of women within the family. The family is seen as the primary unit in politics and each family is represented by its male adult members. Wives and children's interests are represented by the men and they have no public voice in political decisions.

Significant Form, Style, or Artistic Conventions

Sedgwick is important for her participation in the creation of a national literature. Both the extensive descriptions of nature and the topics are specifically American. Formally this novel shows development from those of earlier women, e.g., Susanna Rowson.

Original Audience

The blend of historical fact and adventure made *Hope Leslie* acceptable reading for young women. The novel was very popular.

Comparisons, Contrasts, Connections

The novel should be compared with *The Last of the Mohicans*, published one year earlier. Sedgwick refers to Cooper's novel in the text. But she countenances marriage between an Indian and a white woman, and she shows sympathy for the motives of the Indian attack on the white settlers. In addition, she puts women at the center of her novel, rather than on the margins, and does not make them merely the means of alliance between men.

Questions for Reading and Discussion/ Approaches to Writing

1. (a) Compare the discussion of the Indian massacre in Hope Leslie with the massacre in *The Last of the Mohicans*.
   (b) Consider how Sedgwick equates her two heroines, Magawisca and Hope Leslie.
   (c) What is the basis for Magawisca's refusal of Puritan authority? Is it defensible?

2. (a) Consider the political implications of the parallel judgment scenes in *Hope Leslie*, when Everell is "tried" by the Indians and Magawisca is tried by the Puritans.
   (b) Compare Cooper's and Sedgwick's attitudes towards relations between the Indians and the white settlers.
   (c) Consider Sedgwick's female characters in this novel: In what ways do they fit the stereotype of the early nineteenth century and in what ways do they express Sedgwick's own vision of women in the republic?

Edgar Allan Poe (1809–1849)

Contributing Editor: William Goldhurst [p. 1322]

Classroom Issues and Strategies

Students confuse Poe's narrator with the author, so that in stories involving drug addiction and murders, students often say "Poe this" and "Poe that" when they mean the narrator of the tale. Poe's reputation for alcohol abuse, drug abuse, poverty, and bizarre personal habits—all exaggerated—often comes up in classroom discussion and should be relegated to the irrelevant. Students ask: "Was he an alcoholic?" "Was he a drug addict?" "Was he insane?" I quickly try to divert attention from such gossip to the themes of Jacksonian America, asking them to ponder the nature and value of Poe's vision.

I have a slide lecture, largely biographical, which always is well received. Lacking such materials, I would recommend a line-by-line reading of the major poems, with explanations as you go along. Particularly "The Raven" and "Ulalume" are understandable by this method. I would also prepare students for effects late in "Ligeia," then have them read aloud the last few pages of this tale. I always prepare the class for the Poe segment with a quick review of President Andrew Jackson's policies and what is meant by "Jacksonian Democracy." I believe this to be essential for a study of Poe.

Major Themes, Historical Perspectives, and Personal Issues

Stress Poe's affinities with mainstream America. He was culturally informed, rather than isolated, reclusive, and warped. I have spent years studying his ties to Jacksonian popular culture. It is unrealistic to ask all teachers to be informed to this extent; but the point should be made, and repeatedly.

Significant Form, Style, or Artistic Conventions

Poe's fictional architecture is unparalleled. Stories such as "The Purloined Letter" and "Ligeia" have definite form and symmetry. On another level, while most critics align Poe with the Gothic tradition, I emphasize his links with the sentimental writers of his time and earlier.

The "cycle" form practiced by many painters of his time is reflected in poems such as "The Raven."

Original Audience

It is important to establish the fact that death literature was common in Poe's day, owing to the high mortality rate among the young and middle-class citizens. In some ways Poe participated in the "consolation" movement of this time, by which he attempted to comfort the bereaved.

Comparisons, Contrasts, Connections

Poe compares with James Fenimore Cooper, Washington Irving, Charles Brockden Brown, Wm. Gilmore Simms, Donald G. Mitchell—in fact, he relates in revealing ways to most of his contemporaries.

Questions for Reading and Discussion/ Approaches to Writing

1. I always ask students to express their concept of Poe the man and Poe the author before we begin our studies. Later, I hope they have changed their image from the stereotype to something closer to reality. I also ask the students to mention more recent figures who compare to Poe. If they say Stephen King, I argue the point. I try to introduce them to Rod Serling and Alfred Hitchcock.
2. Explain the steps involved in the "Initiation Ritual," and then ask the students to trace the initiation pattern in Poe stories. It works out very well for all concerned.

Bibliography

I would definitely recommend notes in an annotated Poe edition, such as Harvard's *Works* by Poe, edited by T. O. Mabbott, or the *Short Fiction* edited by the Levines. This legwork is an absolute minimum requirement for teaching Poe.

I would add two articles that answer a lot of questions:

Sands, Kathleen. "The Mythic Initiation of Arthur Gordon Pym." *Poe Studies* 7:1 (June 1974).

Whipple, William. "Poe's Political Satire." *Texas U. Studies in English* 35 (1956).

For advanced courses I would recommend my own "Self Reflective Fiction by Poe: Three Tales," *Modern Language Studies* XVI: 3 (Summer 1986).

Humor of the Old Southwest

Davy Crockett (1786–1836)
Mike Fink (1770?–1823?)
Augustus Baldwin Longstreet (1790–1870)
George Washington Harris (1814–1869)

Contributing Editor: Anne G. Jones [p. 1427]

Classroom Issues and Strategies

The most crucial problem is getting them read at all. These writers are typically included in anthologies but excluded in syllabi—*vide* the syllabi in *Reconstructing American Literature*. Secondly, the dialect and spelling are forbidding. And finally, this work comes with its set of literary critical stereotypes: it has been a favorite of many of the more conservative literary historians, who tend to see it mainly as grist for Twain and Faulkner mills. Finding new ways to think about the material could be a problem.

Thinking about these writings in the light of gender, race, and class makes them accessible and interesting to students. Indeed, the selections have been chosen with gender issues especially in mind. Having students prepare to read them aloud as a performance should help make the dialect more accessible. And suggesting innovative pairings—with Marietta Holley, with rap lyrics, with "Legend of Sleepy Hollow," for example—should enliven the reading further.

Major Themes, Historical Perspectives, and Personal Issues

The construction of gender on the frontier seems a major project of this writing. The texts can be analyzed closely to see how they construct both manhood and womanhood, and how those constructions differ from mainstream American engendering of the period. The strong and sexual woman in particular appears anomalous; these texts both present and demonstrate some ambivalence about such figures. Class issues are crucial too, particularly in the relation between the voices in the texts: the controlling, omniscient, standard English voice and the disruptive, "carnival" voice in the "Dedicatory" set up the most familiar opposition, one that takes various forms in the selections.

Significant Form, Style, or Artistic Conventions

Much of this material is transcribed from or inspired by anonymous oral sources. And if students have performed selections, the question of the relation between oral and written texts can be foregrounded. The use of language in these selections is a second major stylistic concern; the vigor and power of this writing is attractive, and invites students to look closely at specific linguistic strategies—metaphors and similes, concrete vs. abstract diction, etc. And the stories by Harris and Longstreet offer two ways of rendering plot, the one loose and almost episodic, and the other tightly controlled.

Original Audience

The audience for this work most likely consisted of educated white men, "gentlemen of some means with a leisurely interest in masculine pursuits," as Cohen and Dillingham put it. They were likely, too, to be Southerners and proslavery Whigs. The audience's relation to the texts, then, was at least a step removed from the primary characters; these tales and stories seem to enable identification with the "masculinity" of the Crocketts and Finks and even Suts, and at the same time allow an "educated distance" from that identification. What happens now, when the audience has vastly changed? How many different ways can these texts be read? How does audience determine a text's meaning?

Comparisons, Contrasts, Connections

Washington Irving ("Legend" inspired much Southwest humor); Hannah Foster and Susanna Rowson (see Cohen and Dillingham: gender issues); Harriet Jacobs and Frederick Douglass (struggle with voices); Marietta Holley (women's vs. men's humor); Mark Twain and William Faulkner (do they revise the tradition? how? what do they retain?).

Questions for Reading and Discussion/ Approaches to Writing

1. (a) Do the women in these selections surprise you? Think about how and why. To what uses is this "strong woman" put in the selections? What do you think has happened to this figure of woman? Does she survive anywhere in our literature?
   (b) What can you say about the structure of each selection?
   (c) How many voices can you hear in these selections?

(d)   What type of manhood is constructed in these pieces? How does "The Death of Mike Fink" fit in?

(e)   What does Sut want from the quilting party? Why does he do what he does?

2. (a)   Consider "Mrs. Yardley's Quilting Party" in the light of Elaine Hedges's book on quilting, *Hearts and Hands*.

(b)   Consider some implications of the various types of narration.

(c)   How do language and subject converge in the "Dedicatory" and another text of your choice?

(d)   How is the "strong woman" used in these selections?

Bibliography

Cohen, Hennig, and William B. Dillingham, eds. *Humor of the Old Southwest*. Athens: Univ. of Georgia Press, 1975, xiii–xxviii. The introduction is useful for information, but also as a representative of a particular critical position on the material. The remarks on gender are particularly provocative.

Curry, Jane. "The Ring-Tailed Roarers Rarely Sang Soprano." *Frontiers* II: 3 (Fall 1977): 129–40.

Explorations of an "American" Self

[p. 1450]

George Copway (Kah-ge-ga-gah-bowh) (Ojibwe) (1818–1869)

Contributing Editor: A. LaVonne Brown Ruoff [p. 1451]

Major Themes, Historical Perspectives, and Personal Issues

The Ojibwe, also known as the Ojibwa and Chippewa (particularly in the United States), are numerically the largest tribe in the United States and Canada. A member of the Algonkian language family, they are spread out around the western Northern Great Lakes region, extending from the northern shore of Lake Huron as far west as Montana, southward well into Wisconsin and Minnesota, and northward to Lake Manitoba. In early historic times, the Ojibwe lived in numerous, widely scattered, small, autonomous bands.

Families hunted individually during the winter but gathered together as groups during the summer. Thus, the term "tribe" is appropriate in terms of a common language and culture but not in terms of an overall political authority. In the seventeenth century, they were mainly located in present-day Ontario. Their hereditary enemies were the Hurons and Iroquois on the east and the Fox and Sioux on the west.

Bibliography

Densmore, Frances. *Chippewa Customs*. *Bulletin of the Bureau of American Ethnology*, No. 86. Washington, D. C., 1929. Minneapolis: Ross and Haines, 1976. Essential work.

Landes, Ruth. *Ojibway Religion and the Midewiwin*. Madison: Univ. of Wis. Press, 1968. Basic work on the subject.

The Northeast. Ed. Bruce G. Trigger. Vol. 15. *Handbook of North American Indians*. Ed. William C. Sturtevant. Washington, D. C.: Smithsonian, 1978.

Robers, E.S. "Southwestern Chippewa." In *The Northeast*, edited by Bruce G. Trigger, 760–71.

Ritzenthaler, Robert E. "Southeastern Ojibwa." In *The Northeast*, edited by Bruce G. Trigger, 743–59.

Tanner, Helen Hornbeck. *The Ojibwas: A Critical Bibliography*. Bloomington: Indiana Univ. Press, 1976.

Vizenor, Gerald (Ojibwe). *The People Named the Chippewa. Narrative Histories*. Minneapolis: Univ. of Minn. Press, 1984.

Warren, William Whipple (Ojibwe). *History of the Ojibways, Based on Traditions and Oral Statements*. Collections of the Minnesota Historical Soc., 5 (1885). Rpt. Intro. by W. Roger Buffalohead. Minneapolis: Ross and Haines, 1957; Minneapolis: Minnesota Hist. Soc., 1984.

Ralph Waldo Emerson (1803–1882)

Contributing Editor: Jean Ferguson Carr [p. 1467]

Classroom Issues and Strategies

Students reading Emerson for the first time are often uncomfortable with reading extended pieces of prose; their sense of how to handle such length and complexity leads them to try to summarize or extract "Emerson's philosophy" or "message." The unfamiliarity of Emerson's many references (to other writers, to topical events, to scientific discoveries, to religions and practices of many cultures) and the difficulty of the vocabulary and sentence structure are also daunting. It is difficult for students to enter into the controversies Emerson provokes because they have been encouraged to see him as the "first American writer" and have little knowledge about the English and continental traditions he both evokes and revises.

It seems very important to address Emerson not as the proponent of a unified philosophy or movement (e.g., Transcendentalism or Romanticism), concerned with his audience and his peers, but as an American scholar/poet/seer. This might lead to, for example, focusing on what specific definitions or categories Emerson faces (categories such as what is "literary" and what is "poetic," what authorizes a scholar as "learned"). And it leads to paying attention to how Emerson characterizes his audience or reading public, how he addresses their difficulties and expectations, and how he represents his "times." Working from Emerson's journals can be extremely useful in this context; students can see a writer proposing and reflecting and revising his own articulations. Emerson's vocabulary and references can be investigated not simply as a given style, but as material being tested, often being critiqued as it is being used. His method of writing can be investigated as a self-reflective experimentation, in which Emerson proposes situations or claims, explores their implications, and often returns to restate or resituate the issue.

It can be particularly useful to have students read some of Emerson's college journals, which show his uncertainty about how to become an "American scholar" or "poet." The journals, like "The American Scholar," show Emerson teaching himself how to read differently from the ways advocated by past cultures and educational institutions. They show him sorting through the conflicting array of resources and texts available to a young man in his circumstances and times.

Students can also situate Emerson in a range of cultural relationships by using Kenneth W. Cameron's fascinating source books that reprint contemporary materials, such as *Emerson Among His Contemporaries* (Hartford, Conn.: Transcendental Books, 1967), or *Ralph Waldo Emerson's Reading* (Hartford, Conn.: Transcendental Books, 1962), or *Emerson the Essayist* (Raleigh, N.C.: Thistle Press, 1945).

Major Themes, Historical Perspectives, and Personal Issues

Emerson's concern with proposing the active power of language—both spoken and written—in constructing an emergent culture that will be different from the cultures of Europe is a central interest. His attention to what it means to make something "new," and his concern about the influence of the past, of books and monuments, mark him as an important figure in the production of a "national" literature. Emerson's investigation of reading as creative action, his efforts to examine the authority and effects of religious and educational institutions, help frame discussions about literature and education for subsequent generations. As a member of the Boston cultural and religious elite of the early nineteenth century, Emerson reflects both the immersion in and allegiance to English culture and the struggles of that American generation to become something more than a patronized younger cousin. Emerson's tumultuous personal life—his resignation from the ministry, the deaths of his young wife, son, and brothers, his own ill health—tested his persistence and seemingly unflappable energy and make his advocacy of "practical power" not an abstract or distanced issue.

Significant Form, Style, or Artistic Conventions

Emerson challenges and investigates formal traditions of philosophic and religious writing, insisting on the interpenetration of the ideal and the real, of the spiritual and material. His speculations about self-reliance move between cultural critique and personal experience, as he uses his own life as a "book" in which to test his assumptions and proposals. The essays often propose countercultural positions, some of which are spoken by imaginary bards or oracles, delivered in the form of fables or extended metaphors. Emerson's essays enact the dramatic exchanges in which arguments suggest the authority and limitations of what is spoken in the world as "a notion," as what "practical men" hold, or as what a "bard" might suggest. Emerson's journals show him rethinking the uses of a commonplace book, examining his own past thoughts and reactions as "evidence" of cultural changes and problems. Emerson argues for a "new" mode of poetry, one that emulates the "awful thunder" of the ancient bards rather than the measured lines of cultured verse.

Original Audience

Many of Emerson's essays were initially delivered as lectures, both in Boston and on his lecture tours around the country. His book *Nature*, the volumes of *Essays*, and his poems were reprinted both in Boston and in England. Several of his essays ("Love," "Friendship," "Illusions") were bound in attractive small editions and marketed as "gift books." His poems and excerpts from his essays were often reprinted in literary collections and school anthologies of the nineteenth century. Emerson represents the audiences for his work in challenging ways, often imagining them as sleeping or resistant, as needing to be awakened and encouraged. He discusses their preoccupation with business and labor, with practical politics and economy; their grief over the death of a child. He uses local and natural images familiar to the New Englanders at the same time he introduces his American audiences to names and references from a wide intellectual range (from Persian poets to sixth-century Welsh bards to Arabic medical texts to contemporary engineering reports). He has been a figure of considerable importance in modern American literary criticism and rhetoric (his discussions about language and speech, in particular), in American philosophy (influencing William James, Dewey, and more recently William Gass), and in discussions about education and literacy.

Comparisons, Contrasts, Connections

Emerson has been particularly significant as a "founding father," a literary figure that younger writers both emulated and had to challenge, that American critics and readers have used to mark the formation of a national literature. He is usually aligned with the group of writers living in or near Concord, Massachusetts, and with the Boston educational and literary elite (for example, Bronson Alcott, Nathaniel Hawthorne, Margaret Fuller, Henry David Thoreau). He also is usefully connected with English writers such as Carlyle, Wordsworth, and Arnold. Whitman proclaimed a link with Emerson (and capitalized on Emerson's letter greeting *Leaves of Grass*); Melville proclaimed an opposition to Emerson (and represented him in his satire *The Confidence-Man*). It is useful to consider Emerson's effect on younger writers and to consider how he is used (e.g., by such writers as T. S. Eliot) to represent the authority of the literary establishment and the values of the "past."

The following women writers make intriguing comments about Emerson in their efforts to establish their own positions: Elizabeth Stuart Phelps, Louisa May Alcott, Rebecca Harding Davis, Lucy Larcom (also the delightful mention of reading Emerson in Kate Chopin's *The Awakening*). Many writers "quote" Emersonian positions or claims, both to suggest an alliance and to test Emerson's authority (see, for example, Douglass's concern about "self-reliance" in his *Narrative*, Hawthorne's portrait of the young reformer Holgrave in *The House of Seven Gables* or of the reformers in *The Blithedale Romance*, Davis's challenging portrait of the artist in "Life in the Iron Mills").

Questions for Reading and Discussion/ Approaches to Writing

1. (a) How does Emerson characterize his age? How does he characterize its relation to the past?

    (b) What does Emerson see as the realm or purpose of art? What notions of art or poetry is he critiquing?

    (c) How does Emerson represent himself as a reader? What does he claim as the values and risks of reading? What does he propose as a useful way of reading?

2. (a) Emerson's writings are full of bold claims, of passages that read like self-confident epigrams ("Life only avails, not the having lived"; "Power ceases in the instant of repose"; "What I must do is all that concerns me, not what the people think"; "Travelling is a fool's paradise"). Yet such claims are not as self-evident asthey may appear when lifted out of context as quotations. Often they are asserted to be challenged, or tested, or opposed. Often they propose a position that Emerson struggled hard to maintain in his own practice, about which he had considerable doubts or resistance. Select one such claim and discuss what work Emerson had to do to examine its implications and complexities.

    (b) Emerson's essays are deliberately provocative—they push, urge, outrage, or jolt readers to react. What kinds of critiques of his age is Emerson attempting? And how? And with what sense of his audiences' resistance? How do these function as self-critiques as well?

(c) Test one of Emerson's problematic questions or assertions against the particular practice of Emerson, or of another writer (e.g., Whitman, Hawthorne in *The Blithedale Romance*, Rebecca Harding Davis, Frederick Douglass). Examine how the issue or claim gets questioned or challenged, how it holds up under the pressure of experience. (Some examples of passages to consider: "The world of any moment is the merest appearance"; "The poet turns the world to glass, and shows us all things in their right series and procession"; "Every mind is a new classification.")

Bibliography

Buell, Lawrence. "Ralph Waldo Emerson." In *The American Renaissance in New England*, edited by Joel Myerson, vol. 1 of *Dictionary of Literary Biography*, 48–60. Detroit: Gale Research Co., 1978.

Levin, David, ed. *Emerson: Prophecy, Metamorphosis, and Influence*. Papers of the English Institute. New York: Columbia Univ. Press, 1975.

Matthiessen, F. O. *American Renaissance: Art and Expression in the Age of Emerson and Whitman*. New York: Oxford Univ. Press, 1941.

Myerson, Joel, ed. *Emerson Centenary Essays*. Carbondale, Ill.: Southern Illinois Univ. Press, 1982.

Packer, Barbara. "Uriel's Cloud: Emerson's Rhetoric." In *Emerson's Fall*, 1–21. New York: Continuum Press, 1982.

Porte, Joel, ed. *Emerson: Prospect and Retrospect*. Cambridge, Mass.: Harvard Univ. Press, 1982.

Sealts, Merton M., Jr., and Alfred R. Ferguson, eds. *Emerson's "Nature"—Origin, Growth, Meaning*, 2nd ed. Carbondale, Ill.: Southern Illinois Univ. Press, 1979.

Yoder, Ralph A. "Toward the 'Titmouse Dimension': The Development of Emerson's Poetic Style." *PMLA* 87 (March 1972): 255–70.

Sarah Margaret Fuller (1810–1850)

Contributing Editor: Joel Myerson [p. 1580]

Classroom Issues and Strategies

Students have problems with Fuller's organization of her material and with nineteenth-century prose style in general. The best exercise I have found is for them to rewrite Fuller's work in their own words. My most successful exercises involve rewriting parts of *Woman in the Nineteenth Century*. Students are amazed at the roles given to women in the nineteenth century and wonder how these women endured what was expected of them.

I ask students to reorganize the argument of Fuller's work as they think best makes its points. This process forces them to grapple with her ideas as they attempt to recast them.

Major Themes, Historical Perspectives, and Personal Issues

Transcendentalism, women's rights, critical theory, gender roles, profession of authorship, all are important themes in Fuller's writing.

Significant Form, Style, or Artistic Conventions

I deal exclusively with Fuller's ideas, not her form or style.

Original Audience

I give a background lecture on the legal and social history of women during the period so students can see what existing institutions and laws Fuller was arguing against.

Comparisons, Contrasts, Connections

Woman in the Nineteenth Century: Emerson's "Self-Reliance" and Thoreau's *Walden* for the emphasis on individual thought in the face of a society that demands conformity; L. M. Child's novels for depictions of gender roles. *Summer on the Lakes*: Emerson's "The American Scholar" for a discussion of literary and cultural nationalism.

Questions for Reading and Discussion/ Approaches to Writing

The topics I've received the best responses to are:

1. Compare "Self-Reliance" or *Walden* to *Woman in the Nineteenth Century* as regards the responsibilities of the individual within a conformist society.
2. Discuss whether Zenobia in Hawthorne's *The Blithedale Romance* is a portrayal of Fuller, as some critics suggest.
3. Compare or contrast Fuller's ideas on critical theory to Poe's.
4. Compare Fuller's solution to the assignment of gender roles to Kate Chopin's in *The Awakening* or Theodore Dreiser's in *Sister Carrie*.

Bibliography

Read Robert N. Hudpseth's chapter on Fuller in *The Transcendentalists: A Review of Research and Criticism*, ed. Joel Myerson (NY: MLA, 1984) and see Myerson's bibliographies of writings by and about Fuller; also read in Hudspeth's ongoing edition of Fuller's letters.

Frederick Douglass (1818–1895)

Contributing Editor: James A. Miller [p. 1637]

Classroom Issues and Strategies

Readers tend to read Douglass's *Narrative* sympathetically but casually. Although they readily grasp Douglass's critiques of slavery in broad and general terms, they tend to be less attentive to *how* the narrative is structured, to Douglass's choices of language and incident, and to the ideological/aesthetic underpinnings of these choices.

I find it useful to locate Douglass historically within the context of his relationship to the Garrisonian wing of the abolitionist movement. This requires students to pay more attention to the prefatory material by Wendell Phillips and William Lloyd Garrison than they normally do. I also try to focus their attention on the rhetoric and narrative point of view that Douglass establishes in the first chapter of his *Narrative*.

Questions students often ask include:

How does Frederick Douglass escape?
How does he learn to write so well?
Is Douglass "typical" or "exceptional"?
Why does Anna Murray appear so suddenly at the end of the narrative?
Where is she earlier?
What happens to Douglass after the narrative ends?

Major Themes, Historical Perspectives, and Personal Issues

Paying careful attention to the unfolding of Douglass's consciousness within the context of slavery draws attention to the intersection of personal and historical issues in the *Narrative*. The movement from slavery to "freedom" is obviously important, as is the particular means by which Douglass achieves his freedom—the role literacy plays in his struggle.

Significant Form, Style, or Artistic Conventions

Douglass's command of the formal principles of oratory and rhetoric should certainly be emphasized, as well as his use of the conventions of both sentimental literature and the rhetoric and symbolism of evangelical Christianity. In short, it is important to note how Douglass appropriated the dominant literary styles of the mid-nineteenth-century American life to articulate his claims on behalf of African-American humanity.

Original Audience

Through a careful examination of Douglass's rhetorical appeals, we try to imagine and re-create Douglass's mid-nineteenth-century audience. We try to contrast that audience to the various audiences, black and white, that constitute the reading public in the late twentieth century.

Comparisons, Contrasts, Connections

Linda Brent, *Incidents in the Life of A Slave Girl*—for a contrasting view of slavery through a woman's eyes and experiences. Thoreau's *Walden*—for a view from one of Douglass's contemporaries. The *Autobiography* of Benjamin Franklin—for another prototype of American autobiography.

Questions for Reading and Discussion/ Approaches to Writing

1. What is the function of the prefatory material? Why does Douglass add an appendix?
2. What is the relationship of literacy to Douglass's quest for freedom? Of violence?
3. What idea of God animates Douglass?
4. How does Douglass attempt to engage the sympathies of his audience?

Bibliography

Gates, Henry Louis, Jr. "Binary Opposition in Chapter One of *Narrative of the Life of Frederick Douglass, An American Slave, Written by Himself.*" In *Afro-American Literature: the Reconstruction of Instruction*, edited by Robert B. Stepto and Dexter Fisher. New York: Modern Language Association, 1978.

Gibson, Donald B. "Reconciling Public and Private in Frederick Douglass' *Narrative.*" *American Literature* 57 (Dec. 1985): 549–69.

Kibbey, Ann. "Language in Slavery: Frederick Douglass' *Narrative.*" *Prospects: An Annual of American Cultural Studies* 8 (1985): 163–82.

O'Meally, Robert G. "Text Was Meant To Be Preached." In *Afro-American Literature: the Reconstruction of Instruction*, edited by Robert B. Stepto and Dexter Fisher. New York: Modern Language Association, 1978.

Sekora, John. "Comprehending Slavery: Language and Personal History in Douglass' Narrative of 1845." *College Language Association Journal* 29 (1985): 157–70.

Stepto, Robert B. "Narration, Authentication and Authorial Control in Frederick Douglass' *Narrative* of 1845." In *Afro-American Literature: the Reconstruction of Instruction*, edited by Robert B. Stepto and Dexter Fisher. New York: Modern Language Association, 1978.

Stone, Albert C. "Identity and Art in Frederick Douglass' Narrative." *College Language Association Journal* 17 (1973): 192–213.

Sundquist, Eric J. "Slavery, Revolution and the American Renaissance." In *The American Renaissance Reconsidered*, edited by W. B. Michaels and Donald E. Pease. Baltimore: Johns Hopkins University, 1985.

Harriet Ann Jacobs (1813–1897)

Contributing Editor: Jean Fagan Yellin [p. 1723]

Classroom Issues and Strategies

Primary problems that arise in teaching Jacobs include:

1. The question of authorship: Could a woman who had been held in slavery have written such a literary book?
2. The question of her expressions of conflict about her sexual experiences.
3. The question of veracity: How could she have stayed hidden all those years?

To address these questions, point to Jacobs's life: She learned to read at six years. She spent her seven years in hiding sewing and reading (doubtless reading the Bible, but also reading some newspapers, according to her account). And in 1849, at Rochester, she spent ten months working in the Anti-Slavery Reading Room, reading her way through the abolitionists' library.

Discuss sexual roles assigned white women and black women in nineteenth-century America: free white women were told that they must adhere to the "cult of domesticity" and were rewarded for piety, purity, domesticity, and obedience. Black slave women were (like male slaves) denied literacy and the possibility of reading the Bible; as Jacobs points out, in North Carolina after the Nat Turner rebellion, slaves were forbidden to meet together in their own churches. Their only chance at "piety" was to attend the church of their masters. They were denied "purity"—if by "purity" is meant sex only within marriage—because they were denied legal marriage. The "Notes" to the standard edition of *Incidents* read: "The entire system worked against the protection of slave women from sexual assault and violence, as Jacobs asserts. The rape of a slave was not a crime but a trespass upon her master's property" (fn 2, p. 265). Denied marriage to a man who might own a home and denied the right to hold property and own her own home, the female slave was, of course, denied "domesticity." Her "obedience," however, was insisted upon: not obedience to her father, husband, or brother, but obedience to her owner. Slave women were excluded from patriarchal definitions of true womanhood; the white patriarchy instead formally defined them as producers and as reproducers of a new generation of slaves, and, informally, as sexual objects. Jacobs is writing her narrative within a society that insists that white women conform to one set of sexual practices and that black women conform to a completely contradictory set. Her awareness of this contradiction enables her to present a powerful critique; but it does not exclude her from being sensitive to a sexual ideology that condemns her.

Discuss also the history of Anne Frank—and of others who hid for long periods to avoid persecution (e.g., men "dodging" the draft during World War II and the Vietnam War, etc.).

Major Themes, Historical Perspectives, and Personal Issues

Themes: The struggle for freedom; the centrality of the family and the attempt to achieve security for the family; the individual and communal efforts to achieve these goals; the relationships among women (among generations of black women; between black slave women and slaveholding white women, between black slave women and nonslaveholding white women); the problem of white racism; the problem of the institution of chattel slavery; the issue of woman's appropriate response to chattel slavery and to tyranny: Should she passively accept victimization? Should she fight against it? How should she struggle—within the "domestic sphere" (where the patriarchy assigned women) or within both the domestic and the "public sphere" (which the patriarchy assigned to men)? How can a woman tell her story if she is not a "heroine" who has lived a "blameless" life? How can a woman create her own identity? What about the limits of literary genre? What about the limits imposed on women's discussion of their sexual experiences?

Historical Issues: The institution of chattel slavery; patriarchal control of free women in the antebellum period; the struggle against slavery (white abolitionists, black and white abolitionists, within the free black community, within the slave community); the historic struggle against white racism (in the antebellum North); the historic effort of the antislavery feminists, among the Garrisonian abolitionists, who attempted to enter the public sphere and to debate issues of racism and slavery (women like Sarah and Angelina Grimké, like Amy Post, who suggested to Jacobs that she write her life story, and like Lydia Maria Child, who edited it); the Nat Turner revolt; the 1850 Fugitive Slave Law; the publication of *Uncle Tom's Cabin*; the firing on Fort Sumter.

Personal Issues: The narrator constructs a self who narrates the book. This narrator expresses conflict over some of her history, especially her sexual history (see above). She is rejected by her grandmother, then later accepted (but perhaps not fully); near the end of her book, she wins her daughter's full acceptance. All of this speaks to the importance of intergenerational connections among the women in this book. Near the conclusion, the narrator expresses her deep distress at having her freedom bought by her employer, a woman who is her friend: she feels that she has been robbed of her "victory," that in being purchased she has violated the purity of her freedom struggle. Writing the book, she gains that victory by asserting control over her own life.

Significant Form, Style, or Artistic Conventions

Incidents appears to be influenced by (1) the novel of seduction and (2) the slave narrative. It presents a powerful, original mix of the conventions of both of these genres. What is new here is that—in contrast to the seduction novel—the female protagonist asserts her responsibility for her sexual behavior, instead of presenting herself as a powerless victim. This is a new kind of "fallen woman." In contrast to the type of the slave narrative, *Incidents* presents not a single male figure struggling for his freedom against an entire repressive society, but a female figure struggling for freedom for her children and herself with the aid of her family and much of a black community united in opposition to the white slavocracy. Even from within that slavocracy, some women assert their sisterhood to help. The language in *Incidents* suggests both the seduction novel and the slave narrative. The passages concerning Brent's sexual history are written in elevated language and are full of evasions and silences; the passages concerning her struggle for freedom are written in simpler English and are direct and to the point—or hortatory, in the style of Garrisonian abolitionism.

Original Audience

I have touched on this above, in discussing history. Jacobs's Linda Brent writes that she is trying to move the women of the North to act against slavery: these, I take it, were free white women who were not (yet) committed to abolitionism and who were not (yet) engaged in debate in the "public sphere." In class, we talk about the ways in which Jacobs's Linda Brent addresses her audience in Chapter 10, and the ways in which, as a writer reflecting on her long-ago girlhood, she makes mature judgments about her life.

Comparisons, Contrasts, Connections

Incidents can fruitfully be compared/contrasted with the classic male slave narrative, Frederick Douglass's 1845 *Narrative*. It can also be read in connection with *Uncle Tom's Cabin*, *The Scarlet Letter*, and with "women's" fiction, much of which ostensibly centers on a woman's sexual choices and possibilities, and on women's intergenerational relationships.

Questions for Reading and Discussion/ Approaches to Writing

Study questions: Find a troubling passage. What is troubling? Why? What does this suggest? Why do you think that *Incidents* was believed the production of a white woman, not of a former slave? Why do you think that *Incidents* was thought to be a novel, not an autobiography?

Bibliography

I think that the letters appended to the Harvard University Press edition, and that the Introduction to that edition, should prove useful. In addition, the secondary works cited in the text headnote should prove of interest and of help.

Issues and Visions in Pre-Civil War America—Indian Voices

[p. 1752]

William Apes (Pequot) (1798–?)

Contributing Editor: A. LaVonne Brown Ruoff [p. 1753]

Classroom Issues and Strategies

The instructor should address attitudes toward the Indians and explain problems faced by Indians in the early nineteenth century. Consider presenting historical material on what had happened to East Coast Indians. The Pequot history (Apes's tribe) is briefly outlined in the section of the headnote on teaching strategy.

Students often ask why Indians turned to Christianity and used it as an appeal to their white audiences.

Major Themes, Historical Perspectives, and Personal Issues

1. Indian–white relations—especially the impact of the Indian Removal Bill.
2. Emphasis among American Indian authors and slave narrators on achieving equality through Christianity.

Significant Form, Style, or Artistic Conventions

1. Use of persuasive, oratorical style and appeal to emotions of audience.
2. Use of series of rhetorical questions to audience about what Indians have suffered.
3. Use of biblical quotations to support position.

Original Audience

1. Religious orientation of audience, which would have expected appeals to Biblical authority.
2. Prejudice toward Indians of early-nineteenth-century audiences.

Comparisons, Contrasts, Connections

Compare with speeches by Indians, Copway's autobiography—sections on worth of Indian and picture of Indian family life, which buttress Apes's arguments for treating Indians as human beings.

Compare with slave narratives, which also argue for essential humanity of people of all races.

Questions for Reading and Discussion/ Approaches to Writing

1. (a) Relationship between publication of this document and debate over passage of Indian Removal Bill. Also relationship to miscegenation bill in Massachusetts passed around this time.
2. (a) Compare/contrast the oratorical styles used by Apes and Douglass.
   (b) Compare and contrast the oratorical style used by Apes and the American Indian orators such as Logan and Seattle.

(c) Discuss Apes's and the slave narrators' criticisms of the treatment of Indians and slaves by white Christians.

(d) Discuss the influence of Christianity and its concept of the essential equality of all men under God as expressed by Apes and Copway and by slave narrators such as Douglass.

Bibliography

Listed in headnotes. Best general article on Apes is Kim McQuaid's. Mine deals with Apes's autobiography. On the context, the articles in *The Northeast* are excellent.

Elias Boudinot (Cherokee) (c. 1802–1839)

Contributing Editor: James W. Parins [p. 1760]

Classroom Issues and Strategies

The need to establish a historical context is one big difficulty. Boudinot seeks to and succeeds in breaking the stereotype of the Indian established by Irving's "Traits of Indian Character" and other writing that established the Indian as uneducated and shiftless.

Two major issues that interest students are cultural discontinuity and the position of minorities in American culture.

Major Themes, Historical Perspectives, and Personal Issues

Major themes include the perceptions of minorities by the dominant society, the role of the government in protecting the minorities against the majority, and the social responsibilities of the majority toward minorities.

Significant Form, Style, or Artistic Conventions

In many ways, Boudinot is using "standard" methods of persuasive discourse in use at the time. Students should examine his oratorical and rhetorical devices including diction and structure.

Original Audience

It is important to stress that Boudinot was trying to persuade his white audience to take a particular course of action.

Comparisons, Contrasts, Connections

Boudinot was writing in the oratorical mode used by mainstream writers at the time. Compare with works by Emerson, Frederick Douglass, and Chief Seattle.

Questions for Reading and Discussion/ Approaches to Writing

Students should explore the historical situation in which the address was written, should do comparative studies, and should examine rhetorical and oratorical devices.

Bibliography

See any history of the Cherokees.

Chief Seattle (Suquamish) (1786–1866)

[p. 1769]

Please consult the headnote in the text for complete information.

John Rollin Ridge (Cherokee) (1827–1867)

Contributing Editor: James W. Parins [p. 1772]

Classroom Issues and Strategies

The question of assimilation of a minority figure into white society should be raised. The historical context needs to be firmly established and the implication of assimilation should be addressed, especially as it relates to the loss of culture. The introduction should be consulted carefully as it will help in this regard.

Major Themes, Historical Perspectives, and Personal Issues

The major themes include Ridge's views on progress and how it comes about, the tensions between the dominant society and minorities, and the Romantic aspects of his poetry.

Significant Form, Style, or Artistic Conventions

In his poetry, Ridge follows many of the Romantic conventions common in American and British literature of the period. His prose reflects a vigorous editorial style that spilled over from his journalism into his other prose literary efforts.

Original Audience

Ridge was writing for a white, educated audience. His work is relevant now in terms of the majority-minority relations and is valuable in a historical context.

Comparisons, Contrasts, Connections

Any of the contemporary poets can be fruitfully compared. Contemporary prose writers include Mark Twain, Joaquin Miller, and Bret Hart.

Questions for Reading and Discussion/ Approaches to Writing

Topics include the Romantic elements in his work, the idea of progress in nineteenth-century society, and his attitudes toward the American Indians. The latter subject is interesting because of Ridge's ambiguity toward this topic.

Bibliography

No shorter comprehensive studies exist. Refer to the introduction, as it was written with this in mind.

Issues and Visions in Pre-Civil War America—The Literature of Abolition

David Walker (1785–1830)

Contributing Editor: Paul Lauter [p. 1781]

Classroom Issues and Strategies

The first problem with teaching this author is the militance of Walker's *Appeal.* Some students (especially whites) are troubled by the vehemence with which he attacks whites. *They*, after all, don't defend slavery, so why should *all* whites be condemned? Some (especially students of color) prefer not to get into open discussion where their sympathies with Walker's views will necessarily emerge. Some also don't like his criticism of his fellow blacks.

A second problem is the rhetoric of the *Appeal*. It uses techniques drawn from sermons (note especially the biblical references) and from the political platforms of the day. Most students are unfamiliar with religious or political rhetoric of our time, much less that of 150 years ago.

One way of beginning to address these problems is to ask students whether they think Georgia officials were "correct" in putting a price on Walker's head and in trying to get his *Appeal* banned from the mails. This can be put in the form of "trying" the text, with arguments for prosecution and defense, etc. Is Walker guilty of sedition, of trying to foment insurrection?

Another approach can be to use a more recent expression of black militance, e.g., Stokely Carmichael on black power: "When you talk of black power, you talk of building a movement that will smash everything Western civilization has created." How do students feel about that? Would Walker approve? Sometimes an effective way to begin class discussion is by reading aloud brief *anonymous* student responses.

Major Themes, Historical Perspectives, and Personal Issues

It's critical for students to understand the difference between "colonization" schemes for ending slavery (which would gradually send blacks back to Africa) and Walker's commitment to immediate and unconditional emancipation.

If they have read earlier (eighteenth-century) expressions of black protest (e.g., Prince Hall, Gustavas Vassa), it's important and useful to see how Walker departs from these in tone, as well as in audience and purpose.

Ultimately, the question is what does Walker want to happen? Blacks to unite, to kill or be killed, if it comes to that?

Significant Form, Style, or Artistic Conventions

To some extent the rhetorical questions, the multiple exclamation points, the quoting of biblical passages, the heated terminology are features of the period. It can be useful to ask students to rewrite a paragraph using the comparable rhetorical devices of our day. Or, vice versa, to use Walker's style to deal with a current political issue like the level of unemployment and homelessness among blacks.

Original Audience

This is a central issue: The *Appeal* is clearly directed to black people, Walker's "brethren." But since most black slaves were not literate, doesn't that blunt the impact? Or were there ways around that problem?

Why isn't Walker writing to whites, since they seem to have a monopoly of power? Or is he, really? Does he seem to be speaking to two differing audiences, even while seeming to address one?

Comparisons, Contrasts, Connections

The Walker text is placed with a number of others concerned with the issue of slavery in order to facilitate such comparisons. While some share the religious rhetoric (e.g., Grimké), others the disdain of colonization (e.g., Garrison), others the appeal to black pride (e.g., Garnet), others the valorization of a black revolutionary (e.g., Higginson), all differently compose such elements. What links (values, style) and separates them?

Questions for Reading and Discussion/ Approaches to Writing

1. How does Walker's outlook on slavery (on whites, on blacks) differ from X (X being any one of a number of previous writers— Franklin, Jefferson, Vassa, Wheatley)?
   Why would the government of Georgia put a price on Walker's head?
2. I like the idea of asking students to try adapting Walker's style (and that of other writers in this section) to contemporary events. It helps get them "inside" the rhetoric.

Bibliography

There are not many sources to consult; the best of these are already cited in the primary and secondary bibliographies in the text.

William Lloyd Garrison (1805–1879)

Contributing Editor: Paul Lauter [p. 1792]

Classroom Issues and Strategies

Students often don't see why Garrison seemed so outrageous to his contemporaries. Of course slavery was wrong; of course it had to be abolished. There seems to be a contradiction between the intensity of his rhetoric and the self-evident rightness (to us) of his views.

He may also strike them as obnoxious—self-righteous, self-important, arrogant. That's a useful reaction, when one gets it. Even more than Thoreau, who students "know" is important, Garrison may be seen (and be presented in history texts) as a fringy radical. He tends to focus questions of effectiveness, or historical significance, and of "radicalism" generally.

It can be useful to ask whether Garrison is an "extremist" and, if so, whether that's good or bad. (Some may recollect Barry Goldwater on the subject of "extremism.") Garrison was committed to nonviolence; but wasn't his rhetoric extremely violent? Are his principles contradicted by his prose?

Particularly effective presentational strategies include asking these questions:

Would you like to work with/for Garrison? Explain your reasons.
What would Garrison write about X (an event expressing prejudice/discrimination on campus or in the community)?

Students often ask these questions:

Why was Garrison important? *Was* he important?
Why was he involved in so many reforms?
Didn't his many commitments dilute his impact?
Wasn't he just a nay-sayer, opposed to everything conventional?

Major Themes, Historical Perspectives, and Personal Issues

Students are not generally familiar with the difference between colonization as an approach to ending slavery and Garrison's doctrine of immediate and unconditional emancipation.

They are even less familiar with the implications of evangelical Christianity, as interpreted by people like Garrison. They have seldom been exposed to concepts like "perfectionism," "nonresistance," "millennialism." The period introduction sketches such issues.

It can be important to link Garrison's commitment to abolitionism with his strong commitments to women's rights, temperance, pacifism. If students can begin to see how these were connected for Garrison and others, they will have a significant hold on antebellum evangelical thinking.

The issue raised by Tolstoi (see headnote) is also significant: What human interactions are, or are not, coercive? How is political activity, like voting, coercive? What alternatives are there?

Significant Form, Style, or Artistic Conventions

Students can find it interesting to analyze a typical passage of Garrisonian rhetoric—e.g., "I am aware, that many object to the severity of my language. . . . Tell a man whose house is on fire, to give a moderate alarm. . . ." One finds in that paragraph the whole range of his rhetorical techniques.

How does he compare with an Old Testament prophet like Jeremiah?

Original Audience

Since the work included in the text is the lead editorial for the *Liberator*, the question of audience (or audiences) is crucial. In the passage noted above, Garrison is arguing *against* a set of unstated positions—those who claim to be "moderates," the apathetic. Indeed, throughout the editorial, he addresses a whole range of people, most of whom—when one looks closely—he assumes disagree with him. In a way, the editorial can be used to construct the variety of opposed viewpoints, and if students can do that, they may also be able to discuss why Garrison takes his opponents on in just the ways he does.

Comparisons, Contrasts, Connections

The Garrison text is placed with a number of others concerned with the issue of slavery in order to facilitate such comparisons. While some share the passionate rhetoric (e.g., Walker), others the disdain of colonization, others the sense of commitment and the view that people can achieve change (e.g., Grimké), all differently compose such elements. What links (values, style) and separates them?

He is particularly interesting in comparison with Grimké and Thoreau on the issue of civil disobedience, which doesn't come to the surface in this editorial, but is implicit in it. In particular, Garrison does focus on the idea that "What I have to do is to see, at any rate, that I do not lend myself to the wrong which I condemn" (to quote Thoreau). His emphasis on satisfying his own conscience is important, but is that a sufficient criterion for action? Is this editorial what Thoreau means by "clogging with your whole weight"?

Questions for Reading and Discussion/ Approaches to Writing

1. (a) What is Garrison arguing against?
   (b) How has he changed is own position regarding the abolition of slavery?
   (c) Is it sufficient to "satisfy" one's own conscience? What does that mean?
2. (a) One can easily find quotations suggesting that Garrison was an ineffective windbag. How do students respond to such accusations?

(b)   Do you think his approach would be effective today regarding racism in American society?

(c)   Are Garrison's objectives and his style at war with one another?

Bibliography

Tolstoi's comments on Garrison (see headnote) illustrate his influence on the nineteenth century—and also underline the issue of coercion and rationality.

Lydia Maria Child (1802–1880)

Contributing Editor: Jean Fagan Yellin [p. 1795]

Classroom Issues and Strategies

To some, Child's writings appear all too commonplace, not radically different from writings that twentieth-century readers associate with ladylike nineteenth-century writers. Yet Child is radical, although it is sometimes difficult for today's students to understand this. They often ask about her relationship to the feminist movement.

She wrote about the most controversial issues of her time, and she published her writings in the public sphere—in the political arena which, in her generation, was restricted to men. Today's readers need to read Child carefully to think about what she is saying, not merely to be lulled by how she is saying it. Then they need to think about the tensions between her conventional forms and her highly unconventional content.

Focus on problematic passages. What do you do with the first sentence of her Preface to the *Appeal?* It reads like the beginning of a novel—as a private, emotional appeal to readers, not as an appeal to their intellects and not a public political appeal. Yet it is public and it is political. How does Child's narrator present herself? How does she define her audience? What are the consequences of all of this?

Major Themes, Historical Perspectives, and Personal Issues

Major themes: Chattel slavery and white racism; women's rights; life in the cities; problems of class in America; social change and "Progress."

Historical and personal issues: Garrisonian abolitionism; the movement for women's rights; the development of the Transcendental critique of American society; women's role in American journalism; the discovery of urban poverty in America; the invention of the Tragic Mulatto in American fiction.

Significant Form, Style, or Artistic Conventions

Child characteristically uses an unexceptional style and appears to be writing from a posture relegated to women novelists and to common-sense male news analysts. But she is saying things that are quite different from other writers of fiction *in re*: attitudes about race and gender, just as she is saying things that are quite different from other journalists *in re*: attitudes about class and race and slavery and women's rights. Look at her language and her syntax. Then try to locate the places in her text where she does not say the expected, but instead says the unexpected.

Original Audience

With Child, this seems easy because—as her style suggests—she appears to be appealing to the common man and the common woman; she is not writing for a "special" audience of "advanced thinkers."

Comparisons, Contrasts, Connections

Perhaps it would be interesting to contrast Child's newspaper rhetoric with that of Garrison—or even to contrast her *Appeal* with Angelina Grimké's *Appeal* and with Sarah Grimké's *Letters* in terms of language and syntax and logic—and of course audience. Like Jacobs and the Grimkés, Child is an American woman who condemns chattel slavery and white racism and attempts to assert women's rights. In what ways does she approach these issues differently from Jacobs and the Grimkés? And it would be interesting to read Child in relation to Emerson and Thoreau, who were developing critiques of American capitalist culture as Child was doing.

Questions for Reading and Discussion/ Approaches to Writing

I try to stress the exceptional: Why was Child's membership in the Boston Atheneum revoked when she published the *Appeal*? What is so terribly outrageous about the book? Why might she have omitted Letter 33 from the edition of *Letters*? How could this letter have affected the sale of the book? It is hard, today, to see Child as a threat. Why did she appear a threat in her own time? Why doesn't she appear a threat today?

John Greenleaf Whittier (1807-1892)

Contributing Editor: Elaine Sargent Apthorp [p. 1813]

Classroom Issues and Strategies

Students may be put off by various features of the poetry, such as: the regularity of meter (which can impress the twentieth-century ear as tedious—generally we don't "hear" ballads well anymore unless they are set to music); conventional phrasing and alliteration; place-names in "Massachusetts to Virginia"; effect of stereotyping from a clumsy effort to render black dialect in "At Port Royal."

I think we can take clues from such responses and turn the questions around, asking why, in what context, and for what audience such poetry would be successful. Consider reasons why one might want to give his verses such regular meter, such round and musically comfortable phrasing; consider the message of the verses, the political protest the poet is making—and the mass action he is trying to stimulate through his poetry. This could lead to a discussion of topical poetry, the poetry of political agitation/protest, as a genre—and of Whittier's work as a contribution to that tradition.

Some activities that can bring this home to the students include (1) having students commit a few stanzas to memory and give a dramatic recitation of them to the class (when one has fallen out of one's chair shouting defiantly, "No fetters on the Bay State! No slave upon our land!" one knows in one's own body why declamatory poetry is composed as it is), and (2) comparing samples of topical poetry and song by other authors (e.g., poetry of the Harlem Renaissance; the evolutions of "John Brown's Body," "The Battle Hymn of the Republic," and "Solidarity Forever"; union ballads ["The Internationale"] and protest songs of the Great Depression [Woody Guthrie's "Deportees," for example], and contemporary popular songs of protest, like "Man in the Mirror," "The Way It Is," etc.).

One can use the same general strategy in discussing other thorny elements in the students' experience of the poetry, i.e., asking why a person working from Whittier's assumptions and toward his objectives would choose to compose as he did. What might the effect of all those place-names be on an audience of folk who came from all of those places? How do we respond to a song that mentions our home town? Which praises it for producing us? Which associates us, as representative of our town, with other towns and their worthy representatives? Assuming that the poet did not mean to convey disrespect to the speakers of the dialect he sought to represent in "At Port Royal," we could ask why he would try to represent the dialect of the enslaved. (Even without recourse to evidence of Whittier's views on Afro-Americans, this is easy enough to demonstrate: summon up some Lawrence Dunbar or Robert Burns or Mark Twain and consider briefly the difficulties writers face in trying to represent on paper the elements of speech that are uniquely oral—inflexion, accent, etc.)

When you talk in class about these poems as instruments in abolition agitation, students may want to know how blacks responded to Whittier's poetry; whether Whittier read aloud to audiences; whether readers commited the poetry to memory and passed it on to others (including nonliterate others) by recitiation.

Major Themes, Historical Perspectives, and Personal Issues

Naturally one would have to speak about the abolition movement, as these poems were written to express and to further that cause.

Specific to understanding Whittier as abolitionist, it would be good to point out that the first abolition society was founded by Quakers (a few words about John Woolman and about the Quaker beliefs that led so many of them to labor against slavery—inward light, reverence for all souls, etc.)

Specific to understanding some of the appeals Whittier makes in "Massachusetts to Virginia," one should remind the student of the Revolutionary and democratic heritage of Massachusetts—the state's role in the Revolutionary War, its founding by religious dissenters, its tradition of the town meeting, and so forth.

Significant Form, Style, or Artistic Conventions

Aside from the issue of topical poetry, it would be appropriate to talk a little bit about the "fireside poetry" that was popular throughout the century in the United States—the characteristics of poetry of sentiment, the kind of audience to which it appealed, and the expectations of that audience. In a way this was the most democratic poetry the nation has produced, in that it was both effectively popular and written expressly to appeal to and communicate with a wide audience. To speak of it as popular rather than elite culture might be useful if one is scrupulous to define these as terms indicating the work's objectives and function rather than its aesthetic "quality" or absolute "value." The artists worked from different assumptions about the function of poetry than those that informed the Modernist and post-Modern poets of the twentieth century. The audience for poetry in America was as literate as primary education in "blab" schools and drilling in recitation from McGuffey's readers could make it. Good poetry was something you could memorize and recite for pleasure when the book was not in hand, and it was something that stimulated your emotions in the act of reading/reciting, recalling to a harried and overworked people the things they did not see much in their day's labor and the values and feelings an increasingly commercial and competitive society obscured.

Original Audience

It would also be useful to point out that the audience Whittier sought to cultivate were Northern whites who had no firsthand experience of conditions in slave states, whose attitude toward blacks was typically shaped more by what they had been told than by personal encounters with black Americans, free or slave. To get such an audience to commit itself to agitation on behalf of American blacks—when that entailed conflict with Southern whites, and might imperil free white labor in the North (if masses of freed blacks migrated to Northern cities to compete for wage-labor)—was a task and a half. He would have to draw his audience to this banner by identifying his cause with that audience's deepest beliefs and values (such as their Christian faith, their concern for their families and for the sanctity of the family bond, their democratic principles and reverence for the rights of man, their Revolutionary heritage, etc.).

Comparisons, Contrasts, Connections

These poems work well in tandem with other topical/protest poetry and song and/or with another abolition piece. One could compare the effects of Whittier's poetry with the effects of a speech or essay by Frederick Douglass, Wendell Phillips, Henry Highland Garnet, Theodore Weld, the Grimké sisters, Garrison, etc.

Questions for Reading and Discussion/ Approaches to Writing

1. I would alert the class in advance to the function these poems were designed to fulfill, i.e., to stir listeners and readers to outrage on behalf of slaves and to action defying slaveholding states. How do you get an audience to care for people not related to them, outwardly "like" them (skin color, dialect, experiences, etc.), or as a source of profit by association or alliance? Can you ask strangers to risk life, prosperity, and the cooperation of other powerful Americans whose products they depend upon, to liberate what Southerners defined as property—perhaps violating the Constitution in doing so.

   It might be fruitful to ask that they compare Whittier's topical/protest poetry to the work of a poet like Dickinson—asking that they bracket for the moment questions of which they prefer to read and why, in order to focus instead on the different relationship established between poet and audience. How does Dickinson seem to perceive her calling/duty as a poet? How does Whittier perceive his calling/duty as a poet? To what extent does Dickinson challenge/disrupt the expectations and the shared assumptions of her culture? For what purpose? Toward what effect? Does Whittier engage in this or not? Why (given his objectives)?

2. This is a very challenging assignment, but it really stimulates an appreciation of Whittier's achievement and is a hands-on introduction to topical poetry—to the effort to employ the aesthetic as a tool for persuasion and political action.

   Have students compose a short poem designed (1) to awaken audience to concern for an issue or for the plight of a neglected, abused, disenfranchised, or otherwise suffering group, and (2) to stimulate assent in the broadest possible audience—agitating as many as possible while offending as few as possible. Then have the students report on the experience: What problems did they have in composing? How did they opt to solve those problems? Why did they choose the approach and the language they chose? Compare their solutions to Whittier's. At stake would be the quality of the students analyses of their own creative processes, not so much the instructor's or class's opinion of the poem's effectiveness (though such reader response might form part of the "material" the students would consider as they analyzed and evaluated the task of composing this kind of poetry).

Bibliography

Instructors in search of materials on the poet may start with Karl Keller's bibliographical essay on Whittier studies in *Fifteen American Authors Before 1900* (Robert Rees, editor, Madison: Univ. of Wisconsin Press, 1984) which can direct instructors to studies that explore a variety of questions about the poet's life and work.

Two studies I have found useful for their emphasis on Whittier as abolitionist poet/political activist are: (1) Albert Mordell's *Quaker Militant, John Greenleaf Whittier* (Boston: Houghton Mifflin, 1933) and (2) Edward Charles Wagenknecht's *John Greenleaf Whittier: A Portrait in Paradox* (New York: Oxford Univ. Press, 1967). In Wagenknecht I would refer the reader to the chapters "A Side to Face the World With" and "Power and Love."

John Pickard's introduction to Whittier, *John Greenleaf Whittier: An introduction and interpretation* (New York: Barnes and Noble, 1961) provides a good tight chapter on Whittier's abolition activities (ch. 3).

Angelina Grimké Weld (1805–1879)

Sarah Moore Grimké (1792–1873)

Contributing Editor: Jean Fagan Yellin [p. 1825]

Classroom Issues and Strategies

Angelina Grimké's *Appeal to the Christian Women of the South* is filled with Biblical quotations and allusions; it is written as an evangelical appeal, as the appeal of a Christian woman to other Christian women to act to end chattel slavery. Not only is the language that of evangelical abolitionism, but the logic is as tightly constructed as a Christian sermon. In short, it is difficult to read. In like manner, the language in Sarah M. Grimké's *Letter on the Equality* is Latinate, stiff, and formal. Her language, too, makes slow going for the relatively inexperienced reader.

Try teaching Angelina Grimké's *Appeal to the Christian Women of the South* as a religious argument. The informing notion here is that slavery is sin, and that immediate abolition of slavery means immediate abolition of sin, perhaps immediate salvation. Grimké's tactic is to legitimize—using Biblical references—the unprecedented involvement of American women in the public controversy over chattel slavery. She is arguing that slavery is sin and must be ended immediately; and she is arguing that women not only can end it, but that they are duty-bound as Christians to do so.

Read Angelina Grimké's *Letters to Catharine Beecher* as a completely different version of the same argument. Where *Appeal* was couched in religious rhetoric and theological argument, *Letters* is written from a political perspective; it is useful to compare/contrast these, to see where/how Grimké is moving intellectually and formally.

Consider the following approach with Sarah Grimké's *Letters on the Equality of the Sexes and the Condition of Women, Addressed to Mary S. Parker, President of the Boston Female Anti-Slavery Society*: Help students discover that the title suggests the letter's three parts: (1) concerning the equality of the sexes, which, Grimké argues, was created by God; (2) concerning the condition of woman, which, she argues, is oppressive and which was imposed not by God but by man; (3) concerning the way to rectify the current sinful situation: by women uniting, organizing, and acting, as in the Boston FASS under the leadership of Parker. The title spells out the argument of the *Letters*; it is basically theological.

Major Themes, Historical Perspectives, and Personal Issues

In a letter she had impulsively written to the abolitionist William Lloyd Garrison, Angelina Grimké had aligned herself with the abolitionists. Garrison published the letter without her consent, and she was condemned by her meeting (she had become a Quaker [Orthodox]) and even by her sister, her main emotional support. She stuck by her guns. However, although she refused to recant, she was for a time unable to decide what action she should next take. Writing the *Appeal to the Christian Women of the South* was the first public abolitionist document that Angelina Grimké wrote *as* a public document, to be printed with her name on it. Here she commits herself, as a Southern woman of the slaveholding class, to abolitionism—and to an investigation of women's activism in the antislavery cause.

A. E. Grimké wrote the *Letters to Catharine Beecher* for the weekly press during the summer of 1837, while she was traveling and lecturing as an "agent" of the American Anti-Slavery Society. She wrote them in response to an attack on her lecturing that Catharine Beecher had published as *An Essay on Slavery and Abolitionism, with Reference to the Duty of American Females, Addressed to A. E. Grimké*. Beecher, a leading educator, developed the notion of the moral superiority of females and, asserting the importance of the home, argued that women should oppose slavery within the domestic circle but should not enter the public political sphere—as Angelina Grimké was doing. In her *Letters*, Angelina Grimké responds to Beecher's attack. The *Letters* should also be read in relation to the abolitionists' petitions—to local, state and national legislative bodies—to end slavery and to outlaw various racist practices. These petitions were circulated by men and, as Grimké urges here, by women as well. Historians have traced the later petition campaigns of the feminists to these antislavery petition campaigns.

In *Letters*, Sarah Grimké raises a number of feminist issues—the value of housework, wage differentials between men and women, women's education, fashion, the demand that women be allowed to preach (she was bitter that she had not been permitted to do so), etc. And she discusses the special oppression of black women and of women held in slavery.

Significant Form, Style, or Artistic Conventions

Angelina Grimké's *Letters* should be read and contrasted with Grimké's *Appeal*.

Sarah Grimké's *Letters* should be read and contrasted with Margaret Fuller, then with Stanton, et al. This is a beginning. American feminist discourse emerges from this root.

Original Audience

Angelina Grimké's *Appeal*: Audience is stated as the Christian women of the South; by this Grimké means the free white women—many of them slaveholders, as she herself had been—who profess Christianity. It is worthwhile examining the ways in which she defines these women, and exploring the similarities and differences between her approach to them and the patriarchal definition of true womanhood being generally endorsed at the time. The patriarchy was projecting "true womanhood" as piety, purity, domesticity and obedience. Angelina Grimké urges her readers to break the law if the law is immoral—to be obedient not to fathers, husbands, and human laws, but to a Higher Law that condemns slavery. And she urges them to act not only within the "domestic sphere" allocated to women, but also within the "public sphere" that was exclusively male territory.

Angelina Grimké's *Letters*: Written directly to Catharine Beecher, these were published weekly in the abolitionist press, then compiled into a pamphlet that became an abolitionist staple.

Sarah Grimké's *Letters on the Equality*: Like Angelina's *Letters to Catharine Beecher*, these were published in the weekly press, then collected and published as a pamphlet.

Comparisons, Contrasts, Connections

As suggested above, Angelina Grimké's *Appeal* and her *Letters to Catharine Beecher* present an interesting comparison. Both might be read in light of *Uncle Tom's Cabin*.

Compare Angelina Grimké's *Appeal* with Lydia Maria Child's *Appeal in Favor of that Class of Americans Called Africans* and with later feminist writings and appeals.

re: Sarah Grimké's *Letters*: See suggestion above.

Questions for Reading and Discussion/ Approaches to Writing

Direct students' attention to the epigraph to Angelina Grimké's *Appeal*. Why Queen Esther?

Bibliography

See the primary and secondary works listed in headnote.

Henry Highland Garnet (1815–1882)

Contributing Editor: Allison Heisch [p. 1838]

Classroom Issues and Strategies

Ideas that seem radical in one era often become common sense in another and thus may appear obvious to the point of being uninteresting. Furthermore, out of its historical context, Garnet's "Address to the Slaves of the United States" may be hard for students to distinguish from other, more moderate abolitionist appeals.

Garnet's diction is primarily that of a highly literate nineteenth-century black man who has had a white education in theology. Students will understand what he's saying, but unless they can *hear* his voice they'll have trouble feeling what he means.

To teach Garnet effectively, his work should be presented in the context of wider (and, of course, two-sided) debate on abolition. Second, it's important to pay attention to the form of this address and to its actual audience: Garnet is speaking before the National Negro Convention (1843). Is he speaking to that audience or is he trying to communicate with American slaves? The former, obviously. Ideally, some of this should be read aloud.

Despite his radicalism, Garnet fits comfortably into a tradition of "learned" nineteenth-century religious/political orators. As such, Garnet is a fine representative of the abolitionists who made the argument against slavery in part by demonstrating their intellectual equality with whites. But there is another strain of American abolitionists—perhaps best represented by Sojourner Truth—who made the same argument on personal and emotional grounds, and whose appeal belongs to another great American tradition, one that is in some sense almost anti-intellectual in its emphasis on the value of common sense and folk wisdom. Particularly since those two traditions are alive and well in contemporary America, it is useful to place them side by side.

Major Themes, Historical Perspectives, and Personal Issues

It may be useful to point out that Garnet's appeal failed (by a single vote) to be adopted by the Convention. Why might this have happened? Garnet's speech is steeped in Christianity, but he seems to advocate violence in the name of Christianity. When is the use of force legitimate? Useful? How is his position different from those taken by contemporaries such as Frederick Douglass? Garnet's audience is implicitly exclusively male; how can one be so opposed to slavery and yet so unconcerned about women's rights?

Significant Form, Style, or Artistic Conventions

Although this speech was eventually printed (1865), it was obviously written for oral delivery. Nevertheless, Garnet's pretext is that he is writing a letter; could his pretended audience of slaves have actually received such a letter? Certainly not. What is the rhetorical purpose of pretending to address one audience while actually addressing another? Could Garnet's "Address" be regarded as a sermon? If so, can a sermon also be a call to arms? It is useful to approach the "Address" as a piece of argumentation, to see how Garnet makes his case, and to show how it builds itself through repetition (e.g., the repeated address to "Brethren") and through the chronological deployment of names of famous men and famous deeds to his conclusion, which is a call for armed resistance.

Original Audience

The simplest way to evoke a discussion of audience is to ask a set of fairly obvious questions: What is the stated audience? What is the "real" audience? How large an audience would that have been in the 1840s?

Comparisons, Contrasts, Connections

First, and most obvious, Garnet can be contrasted with Martin Luther King to discuss theories of resistance and passive resistance. (Consider especially the "Letter from Birmingham Jail" with its "real" and "implied" audiences.) It is also useful to have students read the "Address" against Lincoln's Gettysburg Address or the Second Inaugural (to compare form and content). Garnet may be read against David Walker (to show similarities and differences, the evolution of the radical position) and against Frederick Douglass (to discuss styles of persuasion).

Questions for Reading and Discussion/ Approaches to Writing

Questions *before* reading: Who or what is Garnet's real audience? Why does he pretend to be writing a letter?

Bibliography

Bremer, William. "Henry Highland Garnet." In *Blacks in White America Before 1865*, edited by Robert Haynes. New York, 1972.

Quarles, Benjamin. *Black Abolitionists*. New York: 1969.

Schor, Joel. *Henry Highland Garnet*. Westport, Conn.: Greenwood, 1977.

Wendell Phillips (1811–1884)

Contributing Editor: Allison Heisch [p. 1847]

Classroom Issues and Strategies

Students tend not to know enough history (or, for that matter, geography) to understand the setting for *Toussaint L'Ouverture*. In addition, Phillip's view of race and racial difference will strike some students as condescending: he sets out to "prove" that Toussaint is "okay" and seems to imply that his sterling example proves that some blacks are "okay" too. This is not the sort of argumentation that we like nowadays, for we've understood this as tokenism.

A quick history/geography lesson here (including Napolean and the French Revolution) is in order. Also, review the attitudes toward race generally taken in this period. I've given background reading in Stephen J. Gould's *The Mismeasure of Man* as a way of grounding that discussion. It is equally useful to pair Phillips with a figure such as Louis Agassiz to show what style of thought the "scientific" view of race could produce. Yet, students can and do understand that styles of argument get dated very readily, and this can be demonstrated for them with various NAACP sorts of examples.

Students often ask, "Is this a true story?" (Answer: Sort of.)

Major Themes, Historical Perspectives, and Personal Issues

Phillips's emphasis on the dignity of the individual. The idea of the hero (and the rather self-conscious way he develops it—e.g., in his emphasis on Toussaint's "pure blood," and his deliberate contrast of Toussaint with Napolean). It's useful to show Toussaint as Phillips's version of "the noble savage" (an eighteenth-century British idea still current in nineteenth-century America).

Significant Form, Style, or Artistic Conventions

This piece needs to be placed in the broader context of circuit-speaking and in the specific context of abolitionist public speaking. It should also be located in the debate over slavery.

Original Audience

Phillips's assumptions about his audience are very clear: There is little doubt that he addresses an audience of white folks with the plain intent of persuading them to adopt his position, or at least to give it a fair hearing. Students may very well say that Phillips *has* no contemporary audience, and that is probably true. It's useful, however, to point out that long after Phillips's death black students memorized this piece and recited it on occasions such as school graduations. Thus, while the people who first heard this piece were certainly very much like Phillips, his second (and more enduring) audience was an audience of black people— largely students—who probably knew and cared nothing about Phillips, but embraced Toussaint L'Ouverture as their hero. That phenomenon—the half-life of polemic—is very interesting.

Comparisons, Contrasts, Connections

It is useful (and easy) to present Phillips with other white abolitionists (such as Garrison and Thoreau) or to read Phillips against black orators (F. Douglass, H. H. Garnet, David Walker). Another tack is to put him in a wider spectrum of white antislavery writing: Read him with John Greenleaf Whittier or even Harriet Beecher Stowe. One approach to take is to compare his oratorical style with that of Garnet or Douglass. Another is to show the breadth of antislavery writing, particularly with reference to the particular genres involved. If the students don't notice this, it's important to point out that this is an antislavery piece by implication: Phillips does not address the subject directly.

Questions for Reading and Discussion/
Approaches to Writing

1. I like to have students identify the intended audience for me: How do they know to whom Phillips is speaking?
2. From Phillips's vantage, what are the traits of this ideal black hero? (Part of the point here is to get them to understand Phillips's emphasis on Toussaint's appreciation for white people and to see what kinds of fears he implicitly addresses.)
3. In what ways is this effective (or ineffective) as a piece of argumentation?
4. Is this piece propaganda? And, if so, what *is* propaganda? What are the differences (in terms of content and specifics) between Phillips's argument and one that might be made in a contemporary civil rights speech?

5. A good topic for getting at the heart of the matter (a very good paper topic) is a comparison of Toussaint L'Ouverture and Uncle Tom.

Bibliography

Bartlett, Irving. *Wendell Phillips, Brahmin Radical.* Boston: Greenwood, 1973.

Bode, Carl. *The American Lyceum: Town Meetings of the Mind.* New York: S. Illinois Univ. Press, 1968.

Komgold, Ralph. *Two Friends of Man: The Story of William Lloyd Garrison and Wendell Phillips and their Relationship with Abraham Lincoln.* Boston, 1950.

Stewart, James Brewer. *Wendell Phillips, Liberty's Hero.* Baton Rouge and London: Louisianna State Univ. Press, 1986.

Thomas Wentworth Higginson (1823–1911)

Contributing Editor: Paul Lauter [p. 1858]

Classroom Issues and Strategies

It's almost impossible for students to connect the apostle of Nat Turner with the "mentor" of Emily Dickinson; a Christian minister, a colonel of a black Civil War regiment; an active feminist; an important nineteenth-century editor. All these roles were filled by T. W. Higginson, yet only the first two aspects are represented by the texts. So the real issue is whether or not he is significant. And if he is, why?

If students know Higginson at all, they will probably know him as the man who, in putting Dickinson poems into print, disgracefully smoothed them out, changing her words, her punctuation, even her meanings. Why read such a fellow? Why in the world did Dickinson write to him?

At the same time, he doesn't smooth out Nat Turner. Yet, like any historical writer, he "constructs" Nat Turner in a particular way. The nature of that "construction" is not easy to define.

Sometimes it's useful to begin from an example of what Higginson (and Todd) did to a Dickinson poem. Their choices say something about Dickinson, about nineteenth-century sensibilities, and—with Higginson's and Dickinson's letters—about their unique relationship. The revised

Dickinson also raises the question of why one might want to include Higginson in this anthology.

At one point in the 1960s, students had heard about William Styron's "Confessions" of Nat Turner. It may still be useful to bring up some of the summary accounts in magazines like *Newsweek* of Styron's version and the controversy that surrounded it. Higginson's picture is, of course, quite different, yet both can be understood, among other ways, as serving certain historical needs in their audience.

Major Themes, Historical Perspectives, and Personal Issues

Is there any unity at all to Higginson's life as minister, military man, activist, writer, editor, mentor? More than most, Higginson's extraordinarily varied career expresses a nineteenth-century commitment by a well-to-do white man to racial, gender, and class equality—in politics, in social relations, and in culture. His sensitivity—and his limitations—say a great deal about the power as well as the constraints upon that kind of progressive politics, and about the forms of culture it inspired. To see why Dickinson sought him out and yet would not be limited by him reveals a great deal about the cultural revolution her writing represents, as well as about the strengths of what Higginson can be taken to illustrate.

The essay on Nat Turner also is very useful in relation to the other abolitionist writers, especially Walker and Garrison. Though Nat Turner's rebellion came after Walker's *Appeal* and the beginning of *The Liberator*, there are ways in which it was taken, literally and symbolically (as Higginson implies), as an outgrowth of such writings.

Significant Form, Style, or Artistic Conventions

Higginson commands a fine and varied prose style, and it can be very rewarding for students to examine certain of his paragraphs—like the initial one on the files of the Richmond newspaper, the early one on the participants in the rebellion, the one on the lives of slaves not being "individualized," and the final one of the essay.

Original Audience

The essay and the letter can be usefully compared on this ground. They are not very distant in time, yet quite distinctly conceived because of audience.

The essay was written before the Civil War began, yet was published only after. What does that say about the limits of "acceptable" discourse? What does the essay imply about the readership of the *Atlantic*, where it was published?

Comparisons, Contrasts, Connections

Higginson's construction of Nat Turner can usefully be compared with Phillips's portrait of Toussaint, with Frederick Douglass's self-portrait (as well as with his picture of Madison Washington), and with the black characters of Melville's "Benito Cereno." All these texts involve the issue of the "heroic slave"—what constitutes "heroism" in a slave. Underlying that is the issue of what constitutes "humanity," since for many Americans, black people were not fully human.

Questions for Reading and Discussion/ Approaches to Writing

How does Higginson account for Nat Turner's motivations, actions?

Why did the essay on Nat Turner remain unpublished until after the Civil War began?

Why, given Higginson's letter about Emily Dickinson and her letters to him, did she wish to write to him?

What does Higginson's relationship to Dickinson (and the way he helped publish her poems) tell you about the kind of culture he represents?

What are the predominant features in Higginson's portrait of Nat Turner? What are the alternative views of Nat Turner between which he is choosing? Is Higginson's Nat Turner a hero or a terrorist?

Bibliography

Henry Irving Tragle's *The Southampton Slave Revolt of 1831* and Herbert Aptheker's *Nat Turner's Slave Rebellion* contain useful brief materials on Nat Turner, including the text of his "confessions," as compiled by Thomas Gray. The view of Nat Turner in that and other texts usefully contrasts with Higginson's.

If one is interested in the problem of how writers construct historical accounts (an issue quite relevant to Melville's "Benito Cereno," for example), such materials provide a useful case in point.

Mary Boykin Chesnut (1823–1886)

Contributing Editor: Minrose C. Gwin [p. 1873]

Classroom Issues and Strategies

It is important to consider Mary Chesnut and her work in context. Chesnut is well known for her criticism of slavery and patriarchy. Yet she is also very much a member of the wealthy planter class in her views on race. In addition, this is a massive work—close to 900 pages. It is, therefore, difficult to find "representative" sections that capture the breadth and sweep of the work as a whole.

In teaching Chesnut consider these strategies:

1. Provide historical context with attention to the intersections of race, class, and gender in Southern culture. Consider especially the position of white women in a patriarchal slave society. Students also need to understand the rise and fall of the Confederacy.
2. Require students to read and report on diverse sections of the work.

Students often ask questions related to Chesnut's "feminism" and her attitude toward race. For example, why does she blame black women for being sexual victims of white men? How implicated is she in the patriarchal order?

Major Themes, Historical Perspectives, and Personal Issues

1. This is an important *social* history of the Civil War era in the South.
2. At the same time, it is interesting both as a woman's autobiography—a *personal* history of struggle and hardship—and as a remarkable story of the trauma experienced by both white and black women in the Civil War South.

Significant Form, Style, or Artistic Conventions

This autobiography is a combination of a journal written on the spot and reminiscences of the Civil War period. (See *The Private Mary Chesnut* for the former.) There is, therefore, a fascinating *combination* of the personal and the public in Woodward's edition.

Original Audience

Hundreds of war reminiscences were published in the forty to fifty years after the Civil War. Poorly edited versions, both called *A Diary from Dixie*, were published in 1905 and 1949. Installments of the first edition were published in *The Saturday Evening Post*. Readers then were more interested in the actual events of the war years so vividly portrayed by Chestnut.

Comparisons, Contrasts, Connections

I would suggest a contrast/comparison to a black woman's slave narrative, perhaps Harriet Ann Jacobs's (pseud. Linda Brent) *Incidents in the Life of a Slave Girl*, which also decries white men's sexual misuse of female slaves—from the point of view of the victim. (Also see *Uncle Tom's Cabin* for similar themes.)

Questions for Reading and Discussion/
Approaches to Writing

1. (a) Describe how Chesnut created this massive volume.
   (b) Describe the life of an upper-class white woman in the Old South.
   (c) Describe the editorial history of this volume.
2. (a) Compare to slave narrative, abolitionist or pro-slavery fiction, realistic or plantation fiction, or modern woman's autobiography.
   (b) Discuss Chesnut's relationships and attitudes toward: black women, her own husband and father-in-law, female friends (e.g., Varina Davis), or her own slaves.
   (c) Describe how fictional techniques bring life to the diary format.

Bibliography

Gwin, Minrose. *Black and White Women of the Old South: The Peculiar Sisterhood in American Literature.* Univ. of Tennessee Press, 1985. Chapter 2.

Jones, Anne Goodwyn. "Southern Literary Women, and Chronicles of Southern Life." In *Sex, Race, and the Role of Women in the South*, edited by Joanne V. Hawks and Sheila L. Skemp. Univ. Press of Mississippi, 1983.

Woodward, C. Vann. *Mary Chesnut's Civil War*. Yale Univ. Press, 1981.
Introduction.

——, and Elisabeth Muhlenfeld. *The Private Mary Chesnut*. Oxford Univ.
Press, 1985. Introduction.

Abraham Lincoln (1809–1865)

Contributing Editor: Elaine Sargent Apthorp [p. 1882]

Classroom Issues and Strategies

The big difficulty with Lincoln is that his words are so familiar to students, who have received those words, or the echo of them, by a hundred indirect sources, and who sometimes conflate the Gettysburg Address with the Pledge of Allegiance—and not by accident. (Similarly, the man himself has been rendered unreal by his status as a culture hero and icon; part of the reconstruction process entails restoring personhood to this historical figure—reconstructing his statesmanship and character by describing the context in which he grew and worked, the forces he had to contend with as a politician and as President, etc.) Another problem is how to make the words live in their original context—so that by stripping them temporarily of their canonization in the store of U.S. holy scriptures, we can see why they were so appropriated—what it was about these words that moved Americans in the aftermath of the war. And what about Lincoln's construction of these statements has made them so emblematic of culture ideals we still cherish (however vague their application).

To give the meanings back to the words, we need to (1) restore vividly the historical context in which these speeches were composed and to which they were addressed and (2) read slowly and explicate together as we go. What precedents and values is he calling to his listeners' minds? What does he ask them to focus on? What doesn't he choose to talk about, refer to, or insinuate?

Major Themes, Historical Perspectives, and Personal Issues

I've tried to canvass these in the headnote. It's important that the students know, for example, that the battle of Gettysburg was in many respects the turning point in the Civil War. It was the farthest advance the Confederate forces were to make. In addition, it was the bloodiest and most costly battle (in sheer number of lives lost on both sides) in what was a devastatingly bloody war (over 600,000 battle casualties over four years, with another million and more dead from disease via infected wounds, malnutrition, inadequate medical attention).

Students should know something of how Lincoln was perceived in the North and South during his presidency, the polarized forces with which he had to contend even among the nonseceding members of the Union, his concern for maintaining the loyalty of slaveholding border states and holding out hope for reunion with the Confederate states, in tension with the pressure he felt from the radical Republicans who urged the emancipation of slaves by executive proclamation, and so forth. This kind of information helps us to interpret both of the Lincoln documents in our selection.

Significant Form, Style, or Artistic Conventions

Again, see headnote on style—Biblical allusions and cadence, lawyer's cutting and distinguishing, simplified syntax and diction. In a discussion of oratory as it was practiced in this period, point out ways in which Lincoln participated in and departed from the practice of oratory that was considered eloquent in that day (e.g., Edward Everett who preceded Lincoln on the podium at Gettysburg).

Original Audience

1. The audience could tolerate, and indeed expected, long, florid, syntactically complex speeches. They were, at the same time, both more literate and more aural than we are (we're more visual, attending to images rather than words or sounds).
2. The audience were Christians. War had bitterly divided North from South; politicians debated while many people experienced death at Rebel or Yankee hands. Lincoln had to consider how to appease the vindictive rage/triumph/urge-to-plunder of the conquering Union supporters while establishing foundation for political and economic reconstruction and rebuilding. He had to rally maximum support (reminding North and South of their common faith; characterizing the war as a war for the Union's democratic survival, not as a war to free slaves or alter the economic order of society—use Union and Constitution; obscure State's Rights).

3. Consider our own time, and our longing for the rock of humane statesmanship that Lincoln has represented in the popular mind. Consider the motives behind his canonization after assassination, when he had been so unpopular while alive in office. Consider the uses Lincoln's been put to, by politicians, etc. Consider the evolutions in public perception of Nixon, Kennedy, etc.

Comparisons, Contrasts, Connections

1. A bit of Everett's speech at Gettysburg for comparison with Lincoln's little Gettysburg Address.
2. Samples of Biblical prose for comparison with Lincoln's.
3. Elements of debates with Stephen Douglass in 1858, again for comparison.
4. Dr. Martin Luther King's "Letter from Birmingham Jail," "I Have a Dream," etc., to discover the uses of Lincoln for other politically active people/groups.

Bibliography

Studies on Lincoln's life and career exist in flourishing and staggering abundance, and most of them examine the language of his speeches and other public and private documents to help develop their interpretations of Lincoln's character, attitudes, and policies as they evolved.

Steven B. Oates's *With Malice Toward None* offers what is finally a sympathetic and admiring account of Lincoln, but it is tempered and qualified by a scrupulous confrontation with inconvenient evidence and careful consideration of the poles of controversy in Lincoln studies between which he means to place his own interpretation.

There are also a number of essays that explore Lincoln's writings as works of literature, which trace one or more of the several strands of law, rural imagery, backwoods humor, Shakespeare, and the Bible, which inform Lincoln's rhetoric. Entire books have been devoted to establishing the historical contexts in which Lincoln developed the Gettysburg Address or the Emancipation Proclamation, but for the instructor on the go nothing beats Jacques Barzun's *Lincoln the Literary Genius* (Evanston, Illinois: Evanston Publishing Co., 1960). It's short but covers much ground and offers perceptive close analysis of Lincoln's rhetorical techniques and style—both identifying these elements and suggesting their effects and implications.

One more recent study that employs analysis of Lincoln's speeches is Charles B. Strozier's psychoanalytic study of Lincoln, *Lincoln's Quest for Union: Public and Private Meanings* (Urbana and Chicago: Univ. of Illinois

Press, 1987; Basic Books 1982), chapters 6–9 but especially chapter 7, "The Domestication of Political Rhetoric."

Issues and Visions in Pre-Civil War America—Women's Voices

[p. 1886]

Sarah M. Grimké (1792–1873)

See material under "Angelina Grimké Weld" and "Sarah Moore Grimké" earlier in this guide.

Elizabeth Cady Stanton (1815–1902)

Contributing Editor: Judith Wellman [p. 1893]

Classroom Issues and Strategies

There are no major problems with the selection from Stanton's autobiography, which reads well, in a fresh, personal, and modern style. Students do, however, benefit from some introduction to the Seneca Falls Declaration of Sentiments.

I usually ask students to analyze the Declaration of Sentiments in two ways:

1. How it is like/unlike the Declaration of Independence? It is almost identical to the Declaration of Independence in the preamble, except for the assertion that "all men and women are created equal." It is also divided into three main parts, as is the Declaration of Independence. Instead of grievances against King George, however, the Declaration of Sentiments lists grievances of women against the patriarchal establishment. Supposedly, the women tried to use the same number of items in 1848 as the Second Continental Congress incorporated in 1776, but the 1848 document actually contains one or two fewer.

2. How many grievances of 1848 are still issues for feminists today? Asking students to list them or to compare them with the issues raised at the 1977 Houston convention, ending International Women's Year, works well.

Professors might ask students to imagine they were present at the Seneca Falls convention. Would they have signed this document? Why or why not?

Students might also imagine they were Elizabeth Cady Stanton in 1848. What was her state of mind? Does this document reflect her personal life or only her political ideals?

Ask students (individually or in groups) to select the one or two grievances from 1848 that they would consider important issues today and to defend their choices in writing or in class discussion. Or ask them to choose one or two contemporary issues that did not appear in the Declaration of Sentiments and to consider why they are important today but were not stated publically then.

Students are often amazed that women were citizens without citizenship rights. They are also amazed at how many issues from 1848 are still unresolved. They have no trouble agreeing that "all men and women are created equal" but they do not always agree on what that means.

They ask about how well this Declaration was received (widely reported, mixed reception), and they are curious about the relationship between Elizabeth and Henry (difficult even for scholars to figure out).

Major Themes, Historical Perspectives, and Personal Issues

1. What was the political and legal position of women in the early Republic? Were women, for example, citizens? What did citizenship mean for women?
2. What alternative vision did the women and men who signed the Seneca Falls Declaration of Sentiments propose for women?
3. To what extent did the Declaration of Sentiments reflect issues in Stanton's personal life, as well as in her political ideals?

Significant Form, Style, or Artistic Conventions

Contrast between the Declaration of Sentiments, with its attempt to reflect revolutionary writing and therefore revolutionary, egalitarian ideals, and Stanton's own account of her life, designed to emphasize her own experiences, which results in a more direct and personal style.

Original Audience

Professors might emphasize the universal character of the Declaration of Sentiments. It was not designed to appeal to some Americans only but to all Americans.

Comparisons, Contrasts, Connections

Comparisons with the Declaration of Independence and with the report from the Houston convention are both useful.

Questions for Reading and Discussion/ Approaches to Writing

1. Professors might ask students to imagine they were present at the Seneca Falls convention. Would they have signed this document? Why or why not?

   Students might also imagine they were Elizabeth Cady Stanton in 1848. What was her state of mind? Does this document reflect her personal life or only her political ideals?

2. Ask students (individually or in groups) to select the one or two grievances from 1848 that they would consider important issues today and to defend their choices in writing or in class discussion. Or ask them to choose one or two contemporary issues that did not appear in the Declaration of Sentiments and to consider why they are important today but were not stated publicly then.

   Ask students to respond to the question, What does "all men and women are created equal" really mean? Think about equality of condition, equality of rights, equality of opportunity.

Bibliography

Flexner, Eleanor. *Century of Struggle*. Rev. ed. Cambridge, Mass.: Harvard Univ. Press, 1979. Chapter 5.

Griffith, Elisabeth. *In Her Own Right: The Life of Elizabeth Cady Stanton*. New York: Oxford Univ. Press, 1984. Chapter 4.

Melder, Keith. *Beginnings of Sisterhood: The American Women's Rights Movement, 1800-1850.* New York: Schocken Books, 1977. Chapters 8 and 10.

Stanton, E. C. "Address Delivered at Seneca Falls," July 19, 1848. In *Elizabeth Cady Stanton, Susan B. Anthony: Correspondence, Writings, Speeches* edited by Ellen Carol DuBois, 27–35. New York: Schocken, 1981.

Fanny Fern (Sara Willis Parton) (1811–1872)

Contributing Editor: Barbara A. White [p. 1899]

Classroom Issues and Strategies

When not influenced to think otherwise, students tend to respond very positively to Fern's writing. They may have difficulty relating her work to their other readings; often students are familiar only with the white male American literary tradition, which they have been taught is "the" tradition.

If alternative works, critical of the white male tradition, have been read earlier in the course, Fern can easily be fit in. Otherwise, it is necessary to explain the existence and nature of a countertradition.

I have found Fern most accessible to students when presented as primarily a humorist and satirist, rather than a "sentimentalist," and a journalist rather than a novelist. However, I try to avoid setting her up as an exception, as Nathaniel Hawthorne did, a writer "better" than the typical "scribbling woman." Ann Douglas Wood sets Fern apart for her refusal to disguise her literary ambition and conform to prevailing rationales for women writing, and Joyce W. Warren tries to rescue her from classification as a sentimentalist instead of a satirist; Warren includes no "sentimental" pieces in her selection from Fern's work. One might argue, however, that Fern should be recognized as the author of "A Thanksgiving Story" as well as "Critics," and that while she was more outspoken than most of her sister authors, she also resembles them in many ways.

Major Themes, Historical Perspectives, and Personal Issues

The rights of women and the problems and status of female authors are obvious Fern themes. I believe it is also important to emphasize Fern's treatment of class, since she is unusual for her time in portraying domestic servants and factory workers as well as middle-class women.

Students have been responsive to approaching Fern through the issue of names and their symbolism. When I was in graduate school studying nineteenth-century American literature, female writers other than Emily Dickinson were mentioned only to be ridiculed as having three names. To use more than two names, like Harriet Beecher Stowe, or two initials, like E. D. E. N. Southworth, was to be *ipso facto* a poor writer, and it was just as bad to adopt an alliterative pseudonym like Grace Greenwood or Millie Mayfield. I don't recall the professors ever referring to Grata Payson Sara Willis Eldredge Farrington Parton, "Fanny Fern."

The "Grata Payson" was supplied by the writer's father, who named her after the mother of a minister he admired; the rest of the family objected to "Grata," and in the first of a series of symbolic name changes, she became "Sara," discarding the influence of the father and his orthodox religion. Later in life Fern explained her pen name as inspired by happy childhood memories of her mother picking sweet fern leaves. In a further repudiation of patriarchal tradition Fern, although she is often referred to in literary histories as Sara Parton, did not use that name; she preferred her pseudonym, extending it to her personal life and becoming "Fanny" even to family and friends.

Ann Douglas Wood (see headnote) views the *nom de plume* "Fanny Fern" as an emblem of Fern's "artistic schizophrenia." She points out that "Fern" is a woodsy, flowery name typical of "sentimental" writers, while "Fanny" suggests the rebel (Fern, who was given the nickname "Sal Volatile" at the Beecher school, once remarked, "I never saw a 'Fanny' yet that wasn't as mischievous as Satan"). Wood, noting the two different types of sketches Fern wrote, concludes that she possessed "two selves, two voices, one strident and aggressive, the other conventional and sentimental." Mary Kelley in *Private Woman, Public State* (Oxford, 1984) also stresses Fern's "dual identity" in arguing the thesis that female authors of the nineteenth century experienced a split between their private selves and public identities. (Teachers who plan to assign *Ruth Hall* should also see Linda Huf's comments on this issue in her chapter on the novel in *A Portrait of the Artist as a Young Woman* [Ungar, 1983].

Although the "split personality" approach interests students and helps illuminate the cultural coritext in which women wrote, it can be overdone. Early in her career Fern was obviously searching for a voice, trying out the more conventional approach in pieces like "Thanksgiving Story" and expressing herself more daringly in "Soliloquy of a Housemaid." But it could be argued that once she established herself, she successfully united the Fanny and the Fern in her writing—and in her life shed the identity given her by men and became the person she herself created. In any case, it is typical of Fern, who possessed the unusual ability to mock herself, to create a final irony by making fun of her pen name. She advised budding authors in search of a pseudonym to "bear in mind that nothing goes down, now-a-days, but *alliteration*. For instance, Delia Daisy, Fanny Foxglove, Harriet Honeysuckle, Lily Laburnum. . . ."

Significant Form, Style, or Artistic Conventions

Fern's writing is especially useful for getting students to think about style and tone, and the discussion can be related both to the split personality issue raised above and the question of literary worth. Although some students have considered Fern's style human and spontaneous, probably accounting in large measure for her popularity, others have criticized it as too loud ("noisy," "braying"). They tend to view the italics, capital letters, and exclamation points with suspicion ("unprofessional," "feminine," "schoolgirl"). One student claimed that a writer who employs expressions like "Heigho!" and "H-u-m-p-h!" cannot be "taken seriously." He could not explain why, any more than most students (or critics) have been able to explain successfully what "sentimental" means and why it's bad to be so.

Original Audience

The question of literary value can easily be related to that of audience. Fern's "A Thanksgiving Story" lends itself to discussion of these issues. The question of whether "A Thanksgiving Story" is "worse" than the other selections by Fern and how so, can be used to provoke discussion of the standards by which literature is judged (and who does the judging) and of the differences between nineteenth- and twentieth-century readers.

Comparisons, Contrasts, Connections

Fern's work can easily be compared and contrasted with that of just about any woman of her time. She can also be paired with male writers, such as Walt Whitman (*Fern Leaves* and *Leaves of Grass*) and Ik Marvel (Donald Grant Mitchell), the essayist, who gained fame at about the same time as Fern. Or she can be treated along with other nineteenth-century humorists.

If Fern's relationship with Walt Whitman is to be emphasized, see J. F. McDermott, "Whitman and the Partons" (*American Literature* 29 [Nov. 1957] 316–19) and William White, "Fanny Fern to Walt Whitman: An Unpublished Letter" (*American Book Collector* 11 [May 1961] 8–9). In "Fern Leaves and Leaves of Grass" (*New York Times Book Review*, April 22, 1945) it is suggested that Whitman imitated *Fern Leaves* in choosing both his title and his binding, particularly the floral designs on the cover. Fern's review of *Leaves of Grass* is reprinted in Warren, pp. 274–77.

Questions for Reading and Discussion/ Approaches to Writing

1. I prefer to have students read her without any initial intervention.
2. For the intrepid—have students try to imitate Fern's style. This demonstrates that it's not "natural," i.e., easy, but you may not be forgiven for this assignment. It is also illuminating to compare the original version of "Soliloquy of a Housemaid" (in Warren) and the collected version in this anthology—so that students can see how Fern revised her seemingly slapdash work.

Sojourner Truth (c. 1797–1883)

Contributing Editor: Allison Heisch [p. 1908]

Classroom Issues and Strategies

One reason why Sojourner Truth has not appeared in conventional American literature anthologies until now is that the texts are stenographic transcriptions of spontaneous speeches. Thus, even the orthography is "made-up." Students may tend to dismiss this as nonliterature. Also, the interior structure of the speeches does not follow expected expository modes (i.e., there's no "beginning," "middle," and "end"), so they are vulnerable to rigidly "logical" analysis.

Sojourner Truth offers a wonderful opportunity to raise large questions: What is literature? And what is American literature? Are speeches literature? Is it literature if you don't write it down yourself? What is the purpose of literature? It is useful to set these speeches for the students in the context of antislavery meetings, to describe where and how they were held, and also who participated. Students may have difficulty with these texts; old-fashioned close reading in class will help.

I like to talk about "unpopular ideas": Sojourner Truth has several of these! It is also useful to place her in the tradition of oral literature.

Responses to Truth vary widely, depending on the class. Some students may make the argument that she is hostile to men. Generally discussion goes in the direction of contemporary issues involving women.

Major Themes, Historical Perspectives, and Personal Issues

Why did racial equality take precedence over equality of the sexes? How can we explain the conflict between racial and gender equality? What is the difference between Sojourner Truth's argument and the contemporary argument for "comparable worth"?

Significant Form, Style, or Artistic Conventions

Ordinarily, we are able to separate a writer from her work. In this case, we have not only oral presentation, but also a style of presentation in which the speaker presents herself as the major character in the work. In some sense, therefore, she is the subject of her work. To what literary and quasi-literary categories could you assign these speeches (fiction, autobiography, prophesy)? How do they "violate" traditional genre boundaries? Where does oratory end and drama begin? These speeches provide a splendid opportunity to demonstrate to what extent our literary categories are a construct, one that not only defines and makes rules, but one that also excludes.

Original Audience

Because Sojourner Truth's speeches were transcribed and preserved by her admirers, it is by no means clear how her original audiences really responded. We have the laudatory side only. Just the same, it is apparent that to many of her contemporary listeners, she was a figure of mythic proportion. To get at the issue of audience, it's useful, first, to have the students identify the issues of continuing importance that she raises. Second, it is helpful to show them a contemporary parallel (such as Barbara Jordan's "We the People" speech) as a means of generating discussion.

Comparisons, Contrasts, Connections

Frederick Douglass ("What to the Slave Is the Fourth of July?") and Henry Highland Garnet ("An Address to the Slaves of the United States") show the tendency of abolitionist literature to regard slavery as a phenomenon affecting black men and, coincidentally, to consider the abuse of black women largely as an affront to their husbands and fathers. Compare Frances Ellen Watkins Harper (almost anything) to demonstrate the common view that women could exercise power through their men and that the needs of the race were best served by guaranteeing black men their rights.

Questions for Reading and Discussion/
Approaches to Writing

1. What issues does Sojourner Truth raise that you consider to be of contemporary importance?
2. Compare the positions on civil rights taken by Frederick Douglass and Sojourner Truth.

Bibliography

Lerner, Gerda. "While the water is stirring I will step into the pool." *Black Women in White America: A Documentary History*. New York: 1973.

Stanton, Elizabeth Cady, et al. "Sojourner Truth." *History of Woman's Suffrage*, 3 vols., 1881-1886. New York: 1970.

Frances Ellen Watkins Harper (1825–1911)

Contributing Editor: Elizabeth Ammons [p. 1915]

Classroom Issues and Strategies

Two primary problems in teaching Harper are: (1) the high-culture aesthetic in which students have been trained makes it hard for them to appreciate Harper and find ways to talk about her; (2) most students' ignorance of nineteenth-century Afro-American history deprives them of a strong and meaningful historical context in which to locate Harper's work.

To address the first problem, I ask students to think about the questions and methods of analysis that they are accustomed to bring to the study of literature in the classroom. What do we look for in "good" literature? Their answers are many but usually involve the following: It should be "interesting" and deal with "important" ideas, themes, topics. It should be intellectually challenging. The style should be sophisticated—by which they mean economical, restrained, and learned without being pretentious. It should need analysis—i.e., have many hidden points and many "levels" of meaning that readers (students) do not see until they get to class. Then we talk about these criteria: "Interesting" and "important" by whose standards? Theirs? *All* of theirs? Whose, then? *Why* is intellectually hard literature judged better than "easy" literature? Why is lean, restrained, educated style "better" than fullsome, emotional, colloquial, or vernacular style (except for keeping professors employed)?

The point here is to talk about the aesthetic students have been taught in school to value and to ask these questions: Where does it comes from? Whose interests does it serve (in terms of class, race, ethnic group, and gender—both now and in the past)? What values does it reflect, morally and spiritually (intellect is superior to feelings, transmitting tradition is a primary goal of high-culture literature, etc.)? Thinking about our own aesthetic assumptions and expectations in these ways proves a good way of getting us to see that what we probably accept unquestioningly as "good art" (whether we "like" such art or not) is just one definition of "good art." We can now ask: What aesthetic is Harper writing out of? Is hers the aesthetic we have just described, and is she simply not very good at it, or—at best—only half-way good at it? Or is she speaking and writing out of a different aesthetic—perhaps a mix of what we are familiar with plus other things that many or all of us are not familiar with?

To address the second problem, the historical ignorance that can hamper students' understanding of Harper, one useful strategy is to assign a few short reports for students to present in class. The topics will depend on what selections by Harper one is teaching, and what resources are available, but might include such things as racist stereotypes of black people in newspaper cartoons in the nineteenth century; women's resources against wife-abuse in the nineteenth century; the formation of the WCTU (Women's Christian Temperance Union); the division between white feminists and black people created by the fight for the Fifteenth Amendment; the founding of the National Association of Colored Women. Such reports can give a sense of the intense climate of controversy out of which Harper wrote and can involve the students in the process of creating historical context for Harper. Also, having students prepare these reports in pairs or small groups is a good way of spreading the work around, counteracting problems of nervousness about making presentations, and having them work corporately rather than individually—which is particularly appropriate for Harper.

Harper, like many other nineteenth-century writers, wrote to be heard, not just read. Therefore, a good strategy is to have students prepare some of her work outside of class to deliver in class.

Major Themes, Historical Perspectives, and Personal Issues

Two major themes I emphasize in Harper are, first, her commitment not to individual psychology, ethics, development, and fulfillment but to the *group*. Harper, like Emerson, is ever the teacher and preacher, but the philosophy that she comes out of and lives is not, like his, individualistic—not focused on the self or Self. It is group-centered. I think that this is one of the most important points to make about Harper. Therefore I ask my students to think about this question: Is the classic dominant-culture American schoolroom theme of the Individual vs. Society relevant to Harper? If so, where and how? If not (and often it is not), what question(s) about America does Harper place at the center? If we use her, a black woman, as "the American"—that is, if we follow her lead and place her at the center rather than at the margin—what does "America" mean? What dominant theme(s) define Harper's America?

Second, I emphasize that Harper is a political writer and a propagandist. Art and politics are not alienated for her but inseparably dependent: art is not above politics; it is the tool of politics. I ask the class to think about our customary high-culture disdain for art in the "service" of politics, our disdain for art as propaganda. Why do we have that disdain? What art is not political?

Significant Form, Style, or Artistic Conventions

Often Harper writes and speaks in popular forms. I ask the class to identify the forms and think about how they work. The sermon, the political stump-speech, melodrama, the ballad, African-American story-telling, and vernacular verse are among the forms Harper draws on. How do these forms work? What devices do they rely on (e.g., accessibility rather than abstruseness; repetition of the familiar; audience response/recall/participation; deliberate emotion-stirring, etc.)? We talk about the appropriateness of these characteristics of form, style, and artistry to Harper's mission of reaching and affecting large numbers of people, including people not often written for or about with respect by white writers.

Original Audience

The question of Harper's current audience inevitably comes up in the discussion of aesthetics. Because we have been taught not to value the kind of literature she created or to know much about or take seriously the issues she addressed (group justice as opposed to individual development; wife abuse and alcoholism in the nineteenth century; voter fraud and corruption; lynching; divisions between black feminists and white feminists; employment barriers to middle-class blacks in the nineteenth century; black women as the definers of women's issues), most of us have not been exposed to Frances Ellen Harper. Clearly this will continue to change as the authority for identifying what is good, valuable, and important expands to include people traditionally excluded from the profession of professor (women, people of color). Or will it? I ask how many students in the class plan to be teachers and scholars?

In her own time Harper was very popular and widely acclaimed, especially among black people. She was the best-known black poet between Phillis Wheatley and Paul Laurence Dunbar. "The Two Offers" is probably the first short story published in the U.S. by any black author. For many years *Iola Leroy* was considered the first novel written by a black American woman. Harper's public speaking was uniformly praised as brilliant. In light of the gap between Harper's reputation in her own day and the widespread ignorance about her today, audience as a social contruct—as something that doesn't just "happen" but is contracted by identifiable social forces (economics; the composition of the teaching profession in terms of race, gender, and class)—and the issue of why we teach the authors we teach are central to discussion of Harper.

Comparisons, Contrasts, Connections

Many other writers compare well with Harper, but especially other black women writers in the anthology: Harriet Jacobs, Sojourner Truth, Alice Dunbar-Nelson, and Pauline Hopkins. Comparing these writers can give a glimpse of the range of black women writers' work to the nineteenth century, which was broad. It is very important to teach more than one or two black women writers before 1900 and to make comparisons. Otherwise there is a tendency to generalize one author's work and point of view into "the black woman's" perspective, of which there was not one but were many. That point—the existence of great difference and variety as well as common ground—should be stressed.

Questions for Reading and Discussion/ Approaches to Writing

1. Preparing an oral delivery, as suggested above, is an excellent way to get "inside" a work. Also a good exercise is to ask the class to choose one piece and extrapolate from it the aesthetic principles governing it. Before class they should try to arrive at a statement of what a particular poem or speech or piece of fiction does—the effect it is designed to have on the reader/listener—and how it accomplishes that end. Then have them form small groups and work together to make up and write down "A Brief Writer's Guide for Young Writers by Frances Ellen Watkins Harper" to discuss in class.

2. A good assignment for Harper is to ask students to think about her as a Black Woman Writer. What did each of these three terms mean to her? How do the three terms clash? How do they cooperate?

Issues and Visions in Pre-Civil War America—Voices from the Southwest

[p. 1944]

As indicated in the introductory essay to this section, one of the dominant literary forms practiced by Mexican Americans in the nineteenth century was the personal narrative. The nineteenth century was a time of great change for Mexican Americans. During just the first fifty years, Mexican Americans from Texas to California witnessed the transfer of their lands, their citizenship, and, to some extent, their destinies from Spanish to Mexican to American hands. In this period of inexorable, sometimes wrenching and perplexing transition, a good number of Mexican-Americans—hardly any with established literary ambitions— determined to set down their versions of political and historical events, to commit to posterity some record of their embattled culture, and, certainly not least, to fix their places of prominence among their people. Among the most important of these chroniclers were Juan Seguin (1806- 1890) of Texas and Mariano Vallejo (1808-1890) of California.

(Contributed by Raymund A. Paredes)

Juan Nepomuceno Seguin (1806–1890)

Contributing Editor: Genaro Padilla [p. 1944]

Major Themes, Historical Perspectives, and Personal Issues

Student should have some background information on American settlement in Texas in the early 1830s and events leading up to the battle of the Alamo (1836) as well as the gradual increase of tension leading to U. S.–Mexican War in Texas.

Seguin was born in San Antonio into a prominent Texas Mexican (*tejano*) family which had close ties with Stephen F. Austin, the leader of the first American settlers in Texas. Seguin rose to power rapidly in San Antonio, being elected *alcalde* at age eighteen. When events in Texas veered toward revolution in 1835, he sided with the Anglo separatists and organized a company of *tejano* volunteers.

The section of Seguin's *Personal Memoirs* printed here reveals an aspect of the Texas War for Independence little known among American readers: the invaluable participation of *tejanos* alongside the more celebrated figures of Sam Houston, Jim Bowie, and Davy Crockett. Like their American brothers-in-arms, the *tejanos* despised "the tyrannical government of Santa Anna" and yearned for representative and responsive government. In a clear and unadorned style, Seguin recounts the "efficiency and gallantry" of his *tejano* troops as they rode from San Antonio to San Jacinto.

After performing heroically at San Jacinto, the battle that assured Texas independence, Seguin returned to San Antonio to resume his political career. An ardent supporter of the Republic of Texas, he served in its Senate from 1838 to 1840, at which time he was elected mayor of San Antonio. He was the last Mexican American to occupy that office until the 1980s.

Seguin's tenure as mayor was disastrous, largely because the growing Anglo population, with its intense and long-standing resentment of Mexicans, would not trust nor defer to a *tejano*. By 1842, the *tejanos* of San Antonio were moving away in the face of continuous intimidation and violence from Anglos. After a series of death threats, Seguin relocated his family in Mexico, the country against which he had taken up arms only six years before.

In Mexico, Seguin was coerced into military service and found himself in combat against American troops in the Mexican War of 1846-48. After the war, Seguin returned to Texas, by now homesick and thoroughly disillusioned. He lived there quietly until 1867 when, for reasons not altogether clear, he crossed the Rio Grande one last time, remaining in Mexico until his death.

(Biography and historical information contributed by Raymund Paredes.)

Bibliography

See material on Mariano Guadalupe Vallejo, immediately following.

Mariano Guadalupe Vallejo (1808–1890)

Contributing Editor: Genaro Padilla [p. 1952]

Classroom Issues and Strategies

Students' lack of historical knowledge about the United States Mexican War (1846–1848), especially events in California can, be a problem. Some historical background needs to be given; Vallejo should be read as a colonized subject. His historical personal narrative gives the Mexican version of events.

Students often wonder why Vallejo seems politically contradictory. They ask whether he wrote other material and are curious about his social position.

Major Themes, Historical Perspectives, and Personal Issues

Vallejo's sense of betrayal comprises an important and intriguing theme. From the selection one can surmise that he actually favored American annexation of California, but was summarily imprisoned by a group of Americans he refers to as "thieves."

Like Seguin, Mariano Vallejo was born into a prominent family, in his case in Monterey, California. Vallejo early decided to pursue a career in both politics and the military and by age twenty-one had been elected to the territorial legislature and had distinguished himself in various campaigns against the Indians. Again like Seguin, Vallejo supported the American presence in his region, hoping that the *yanquis* would bring both prosperity and stability. Accordingly, Vallejo became one of the most prominent *California* supporters of the American annexation of California.

The movement toward American control of California accelerated with the Bear Flag Revolt of 1846. Vallejo was inexplicably taken prisoner by the troops of John C. Fremont and held for two months, an experience that should have raised doubt in Vallejo's mind about his pro-American sympathies. But Vallejo persisted in his allegiance and eventually served in the state's first senate. In the early 1850s he filed for validation of his Mexican land-grants, only to lose much of his property in a ruling by the United States Supreme Court. By the 1860s his fortune and influence had declined considerably, and a wiser Vallejo sat down to compose a "true history" of his territory, free of myths and lies. After a series of mishaps and distractions, he completed his five-volume chronicle and donated it to H. H. Bancroft, the celebrated California historian. Vallejo lived quietly thereafter, tending to the 280 acres of land he had left of his once-vast empire. Like Seguin, he looked back on his support of American expansion with great bitterness.

In "Six Dollars an Ounce," Vallejo writes of an economic revolution that changed California as decisively as San Jacinto changed the course of Texas history. He recounts how the Gold Rush of 1849 threw California into a frenzy. Previously reasonable men gave up respectable trades and careers to pursue the yellow metal. As Vallejo tells it, the Gold Rush unleashed the meanest of human qualities—distrust, avarice, and violence among them—and accelerated the destruction of traditional *California* culture. In the Americanization of California, Vallejo notes that he witnessed change but not progress.

(Biographical and historical information contributed by Raymund Paredes.)

Significant Form, Style, or Artistic Conventions

The Vallejo selection should be thought of as autobiographical historiography.

Original Audience

It was written as a revisionist version of historical events that Vallejo wished Americans would hear.

Comparisons, Contrasts, Connections

Comparison might be made with native American orations on tribal displacement, uncertainty, subjugation.

Questions for Reading and Discussion/
Approaches to Writing

1. What is the standard version of the Bear Flag Revolt in California in 1846?
2. How does the Vallejo version humanize the Mexican populace?

Bibliography

Padilla, Genaro M. "The Recovery of Chicano Nineteenth-Century Autobiography." *American Quarterly* 40, no. 3 (Sept. 1981).

Pitt, Leonard. *The Decline of the Californios.* Los Angeles: University of California, 1969. A good background history of events during the period.

Issues and Visions in Pre-Civil War America—A Concord Individualist

[p. 1964]

Henry David Thoreau (1817–1862)

Contributing Editor: Wendell P. Glick [p. 1964]

Classroom Issues and Strategies

Students of the '80s are less sympathetic toward Thoreau's nonconformist moral, social, and political ideas than they were in the '60s. As social scientists and educators have pointed out, students are more materialistic, more inclined to major in business fields than in the arts and humanities. The instructor, therefore, has the burden of inducing students to see Thoreau as a serious, thoughtful human being addressing universal problems rather than as a maladjusted iconoclast.

Thoreau speaks cogently to a multitude of present-day problems. For example, the instructor can cite a plethora of contemporary examples of Thoreau's dictum that "the ways by which you may get money almost without exception lead downward." Current scandals in military procurement, venality in ex-White House officials, corruption in insider trading, are but a few. And, of course, Thoreau's perceptions of the ecological linkage of all life and the danger to human kind of destroying the earth's environment have proved prophetic and sound. To students who resent Thoreau's anti-religious bent, it can be pointed out that many of his ideas are Christian.

Thoreau's political theory, that the individual conscience takes precedence over the law and the Constitution, invariably elicits controversy. I have found historical references and textual comparisons to the political theory of John Winthrop, Jefferson, and John Stuart Mill to be illuminating. The relation of individual rights to state authority is a critical and continual issue in democratic societies.

Students' questions frequently center around Thoreau's perceived idiosyncrasies—his bachelorhood, for example: "Of course he could be free to live his own life without restriction. He had no wife, no children, no dependents, no social responsibilities, paid no income taxes, etc."

Thoreau's response might be: "Of course this is true. But my point is that many restraints upon our freedoms are self-imposed; all of us can be more free to do what we desire than we realize."

Major Themes, Historical Perspectives, and Personal Issues

Thoreau's debt to English Romanticism and to Emersonian Transcendentalism are important as historical contexts. Thoreau's championing of human rights, his opposition to black slavery, his insistence upon the moral responsibility of the writer to use language to tell the truth, and (to repeat) his belief in the interrelationship of all life forms are all major themes. As a person, he resolutely refused to defer to public opinion when his principles were at stake.

Significant Form, Style, or Artistic Conventions

Thoreau's angle of vision is patently that of the American Romantic deeply influenced by the insights of Kant and Coleridge and Carlyle. But Thoreau's style differs markedly from that of Emerson, whose natural expression is through abstraction. Thoreau presents experience through concrete images; he "thinks in images," as Francis Matthiessen once observed, and employs many of the resources of poetry to give strength and compressed energy to his prose. Widely read himself, he is very allusive, particularly to classical literature, and is one of America's most inveterate punsters.

Original Audience

Students majoring in the life sciences will find Thoreau's studies of flora and fauna of interest. Students concerned with such problems as pollution of the environment will naturally respond to him. Students of philosophy will relate him to Kant, and should be counseled to read the writings of Cavell, the Harvard philosopher, on Thoreau. Students of economics will recognize that Thoreau was remarkably knowledgeable as to the economic theories of his time.

Since Thoreau's reputation did not build appreciably until 75 or so years after his death, it is clear that few of his contemporaries understood how far in advance of his age his ideas were.

Comparisons, Contrasts, Connections

Walden is *sui generis* though there are contemporary writers, e.g., Wendell Berry and E. B. White who have clearly been influenced by this book in both style and thought. N. C. Wyeth, the American painter, confessed to being "an enthusiastic student of Thoreau." Of major twentieth-century writers, Robert Frost has probably been most indebted to Thoreau. Martin Luther King's philosophy of passive resistance to the state is clearly borrowed from Thoreau's "Resistance to Civil Government." Some Thoreau scholars have discerned Thoreau's influence in Yeats, Tolstoy, and Gandhi.

Questions for Reading and Discussion/ Approaches to Writing

1. Teaching methodologies will vary, of course, with instructors. Rather than prescribing in advance what I feel students should look for in a writer as subtle as Thoreau, I prefer to let them in their first reading discover what they can on their own, particularly if they are English majors experienced in reading literature. With introductory students, I sometimes lift seminal sentences from the texts ahead of time and ask them to decide from contexts what the sentences mean. For example, what is the meaning of "Our sills are rotten" or " Time is but the stream I go a-fishing in"?

2. Writing assignments will vary depending on the literary maturity and sophistication of the students. In general, however, I have found most successful assignments calling attention to the remarkable contemporaneity of Thoreau's ideas—on morality, values, the environment, industrialization, political theory. Assignments in genre are less successful because Thoreau's works do not fit neatly into any genre; and assignments in Thoreau's aesthetics are taxing for most undergraduates and often dampen student interest.

The Flowering of Narrative

[p. 2063]

Nathaniel Hawthorne (1804–1864)

Contributing Editor: Rita K. Gollin [p. 2065]

Classroom Issues and Strategies

Some students find Hawthorne too gloomy, dense, and complex. Few understand Puritan attitudes concerning self, sin, etc., as they evolved into Emersonian antithetical attitudes.

To address these issues, try approaching Hawthorne as a riddler and wry joker. Introduce recurrent patterns and devices (character, theme, image, etc.). Lay out the basic facts and show how they contrast both within and among his works.

Try tracing the following:

Strategies of irony and self-deprecation, concern with vocation, and problems of strategies for financial support (from earliest letters onward)

Psychological conventions (based on Scottish school of philosophy, incorporating earlier literary conventions and self-observation)

Interrelationships of notebook entries and subsequent fiction

Family experiences (intimacy, deprivation) in his life and in his fiction

Students respond well to Hawthorne's self-mockery and forms of ironic self-presentation (in letters and prefaces as well as through narrators' and authorial voices). They are also interested in these themes in Hawthorne's life and works: relation of men to women; adults to children; authority figures to marginal individuals. Devices such as alternative possibilities; use of subconscious (dreams, reveries); and the relationship of fact/fantasy, past/present, clear statement/suggestion provide lively discussion topics.

Major Themes, Historical Perspectives, and Personal Issues

Themes: Individual vs. society, self-fulfillment vs. accommodation or frustration, guilt vs. innocence, hypocrisy vs. integrity, love vs. hate, exploitation vs. hurting, fate vs. free will.

Historical Issues: Puritan and Whig ideas of self and history and those prevalent in Hawthorne's day. Mid-nineteenth-century marketplace values; Jacksonian democracy.

Personal Issues: His Puritan heritage and Manning family mercantile values; fatherless boy, unassertive mother, and idolizing sisters; Salem past, present; Bowdoin College; political oppression; being published.

Significant Form, Style, or Artistic Conventions

1. Sketch vs. short story—audience expectations, narrative
2. Romance vs. novel
3. Imagery: Cluster and patterns (dark vs. light, natural vs. unnatural, positive vs. negative)
4. Characters: Recurrent "types" and their interrelationship; authorial intrusion or objective display
5. Psychology vs. probing (dreams, reveries, author's comments)
6. Particular narrative antecedents: Biblical parable, Spenserian romance, allegory (Dante, Bunyan, etc.), Gothic horror tale, sentimental tale, fairy tale, etc.
7. Reworking of notebook into fiction and earlier and later fictional forms

Original Audience

"Then"

1. For the tales and sketches: nature of publishers vs. audience for gift books and periodicals, reasons for and consequences of anonymous publication; reviews; contexts (what *else* was in the same gift book and periodical as a Hawthorne tale); probable date of particular periodical or gift book; price and payment and circulation, illustration, correspondence about work with editor or friends; use of historic materials as "revision," use of domestic details and sentimental approach, roles of women, inclusion of children, involvement of reader by narrator.

2. For the collections: Hawthorne's reasons for selection and sequence, choice of publisher, reviews and advertisements.
3. For the novels: Hawthorne's aims as expressed in letters and journals and prefaces and through narrator; marketing, sales, and reviews; two-volume vs. three-volume format and size of issue in U.S. and England.

"Now"

Changing audience expectation vs. genre, canon, national identity, gender of author.

Comparisons, Contrasts, Connections

Irving—Use of American past including folktales, popular myth, specific settings

Poe—Use of Gothic settings, themes, characters

Melville—Profound examination of human mind, dark truths

James—Sensitive hero/narrator, psychological scrutiny

Conrad—Journeys to heart of darkness, parallel of outer and inner experience

Jewett—Minute attention to nature of world and unheroic characters

Welty—Comic irony, ambivalence, anti-authoritarianism

Flannery O'Connor, Updike, Borges—Queries concerning mystifying complexities of human behavior, dark comedy

Questions for Reading and Discussion/ Approaches to Writing

1. (a) Traditions of the self inherited by or contemporary with Hawthorne, e.g., Puritan, Romantic (Wordsworthian, Emersonian, etc.)
   (b) Attitude toward art in general and fiction in particular in nineteenth-century America (including definitions: picturesque, sublime, gothic, etc.)
2. (a) Comparison of first and last "views" of a particular character.
   (b) Ambivalent treatment of: women, writers, artists.
   (c) Tracing a recurrent image or symbol or theme or myth (e.g., fortunate fall).

(d) Asking whether there is an identifiable hero or victim. Asking about various authorial stand-ins.

(e) Asking about how readers are specifically addressed and the reasons.

Bibliography

I would give names of critics rather than particular articles.

Instructors may want to leaf through books by these authors, using indexes for information on texts they are teaching:

Nina Baym
Michael Colacurcio
Richard Biodherd
Hyatt Wayonner
Richard Harden Fogle
Roy Harvey Male
Rita Gollin

Caroline Kirkland (1801–1864)

Contributing Editor: Judith Fetterley [p. 2286]

Classroom Issues and Strategies

Most of the students I have taught love Caroline Kirkland. They find her eminently contemporary. Her prose style is accessible, she is funny, and she deals with a subject familiar to nearly all Americans—the frontier. Some students are put off by her middle-class bias and perspective; they find her attitudes toward the locals patronizing and they object to the fact that (unlike Jewett) Kirkland provides very little space for the stories of any of these people as told by themselves.

Kirkland's letters sound like they were written yesterday to the student reading the letter. One obvious way of breaking open the text and inviting discussion is to ask students to pick one of her "natives" and have them write what they imagine that person would say about their new neighbor, Caroline Kirkland, if they wrote a letter to one of their friends who has moved farther west.

Students often wonder why they have never heard of Kirkland before. They want to know what else she wrote. They wonder why she is so concerned with issue of manners and ask what happened when she published her book.

Major Themes, Historical Perspectives, and Personal Issues

Kirkland is accessible in part because she is writing about a subject that has been made central to the study of American culture—the frontier, the movement west of white settlers. Kirkland is important because she is dealing with this phenomenon from the point of view of the woman who was required, often not of her own will, to follow the man to his new home. She writes specifically of the cost to women of the male model of "upward mobility"—the pattern of constantly moving on under the guise of improving one's position. This theory of "improvement" of course takes no account of the woman's position, which is usually worsened as a result. Thus the most important feature of Kirkland for the survey course is the fact that she inserts the woman's perspective into this male cultural pattern. Kirkland's work thus provides the context for discussing the commitment of the mid-century women writers to values of home, domesticity, etc.

Kirkland is equally important as an example of a relatively early American woman writer who successfully established a voice. The instructor should be familiar with Kirkland's essay "Literary Women," collected in *A Book for the Home Circle* (1853), and included in the forthcoming volume of Kirkland's work from the Rutgers Press American Women Writers series. Kirkland was well aware of the prejudices against women writers and of the strictures governing what they were and were not supposed to write. Her decision to lace her text with literary references may in part have stemmed from her desire to define herself clearly as a literary woman and to defy the strictures and the stereotypes. In a context where there was so much harassment of women writers, her voice is remarkably clear and confident. She writes with a sense of authority and conviction that is not modulated through any other agency. She writes because she likes to write, not because she is trying to save the world or support her children. She is a rare example of an early American woman writer who wrote carefully and published only what she felt was well written.

Significant Form, Style, or Artistic Conventions

First, Kirkland defines herself as a realist. Since American literary history has been based, until very recently, on a study of the works of male

American writers, the governing generalization insists that realism in American literature is a post-Civil War phenomenon. However, American women writers were experimenting with realism in the decades before the Civil War and Caroline Kirkland was among the first, the most explicit, and the most articulate. Clearly defining herself against the romantic views of the West provided by contemporary male writers, Kirkland claims to write the truth about Michigan, which means that she intends to include the difficulties that face women who try to put together three meals a day in the wilderness, the state of the Michigan roads with their enormous pot holes, and the general slovenliness of the "natives." So certainly any discussion of Kirkland needs to address her conception of realism and the general contours of American literary history that emerge from including women writers in the map of the territory.

Second, Kirkland identifies herself as participating in a tradition set by women writers. She ends her preface to *A New Home* with a reference to "Miss Mitford's charming sketches of village life" and with a "humble curtsey." It is important to explore the degree to which Kirkland establishes throughout her text her connection to a tradition of women writers presenting a woman's point of view. As is clear from the preface, Kirkland embraces an iconography that clearly identifies her as a woman writer (men don't curtsey) and she wishes to remind her readers that they are reading a work written by a woman. In the process of so doing, she is also attempting to explore the nature of a woman's aesthetics. Implicitly, and on occasion explicitly, she is asking, what kind of book does a woman write, given the nature of woman's experience and perspective?

One can also raise here the question of genre—to what extent is Kirkland's voice, her authority, tied to her use of a relatively unconvention-ridden genre, namely the letter home? Is she freed to do her best because she is not trying to be a great writer but is trying only to write interesting letters to the folks back home? Students might be encouraged to look into the use of the letter as a form for published writing by both men and women in the nineteenth century.

Original Audience

As I have said earlier, Kirkland is useful for raising the larger question of the relation of the nineteenth-century American women writers to their audience. Nineteenth-century white middle-class American male writers had problems establishing an audience, a sense of who they were writing to. A new view could and should question these assumptions. Hawthorne's preface to *The Scarlet Letter*, the chapter on the Customs

House, can serve perhaps as a paradigm for the male situation. Here Hawthorne reveals his fear that he is speaking to no one except himself. Kirkland, on the other hand, has a very clear sense of the "you" at the other end of her letter. One can certainly raise with students the question as to why it is that Kirkland might have such a clear sense of audience. To what degree does it have to do with the world she describes women as inhabiting—a world in which loved ones are left behind, a world in which the letter (and think of the implications of this fact—here we look forward to *The Color Purple*) was left in the hands of women, a world in which there was a clear sense of community and of someone who would want to know what was happening to their daughters who had gone west?

It seems fairly obvious that Kirkland assumed her readers would be of the same social class as herself. Whether or not she assumed her readers would be primarily women is a more complex question. My own sense of Kirkland leads me to believe that she assumed a readership made up of men as well as women, that she was not of that group of women writers who were writing essentially to women even though they knew and hoped that men might read their books and thus overhear their conversation. But I also think Kirkland took her women readers seriously and wrote at least in part to educate them.

Comparisons, Contrasts, Connections

I have already suggested many points of comparison. I will just reiterate them here. Kirkland can be compared with many male writers in terms of her presentation of the frontier and the experience of westward and "upward" mobility. She can also be compared with many male writers in terms of her attitudes toward and handling of the issue of class. A writer like Hawthorne is so completely class bound that class is never even an issue in his work. In many of the classes I have taught on Kirkland, I have been able to use students' anger at Kirkland's classism to raise the issue of class prejudice in writers like Hawthorne. Many students have come to realize that writers like Hawthorne protect themselves, albeit unconsciously, against charges of classism by simply never raising class as an issue. Kirkland is at least aware that American society is profoundly affected by the issue of class. Kirkland can also be compared to male writers in terms of the question of audience, as discussed above.

Kirkland can be fruitfully compared with other nineteenth-century American women writers in terms of the issue of voice. Students can compare the authority with which Kirkland speaks to the less secure voice of certain other women writers. She can also be compared with other women writers in terms of her commitment to realism and in terms of her commitment to presenting the woman's story.

Bibliography

I refer the instructor to the discussion of Kirkland in Annette Kolodny's *The Land Before Her* and in my own *Provisions*.

There is also a Twayne series book on Kirkland that is useful for an overview but does not provide much in the way of criticism and would not be of much use in the classroom.

The Rutgers Press American Women Writers series has a volume of Kirkland under contract and the introduction to that volume should be very useful.

Harriet Beecher Stowe (1811–1896)

Contributing Editor: Jane Tompkins [p. 2307]

Classroom Issues and Strategies

The primary problems you are likely to encounter in teaching Stowe are (1) the assumption that she is not a first-rate author because she has only recently been recognized and has traditionally been classed as a "sentimental" author, whose works are of historical interest only; (2) by current standards, Stowe's portrayal of black people in *Uncle Tom's Cabin* is racist; and (3) a lack of understanding of the cultural context within which Stowe was working.

In dealing with the first problem, you need to discuss the way masterpieces have been selected and evaluated. Talk about the socio-economic and gender categories that most literary critics, professors, and publishers have belonged to in this country until recently, explaining how class and gender bias have led to the selection of works by white male authors.

The second problem calls for an explanation of cultural assumptions about race, which would emphasize the way—historically— scientific beliefs about race have changed in this country between the seventeenth century and our day. For her time, Stowe was fairly enlightened, although her writing perpetuates stereotypes that have since been completely discredited.

The third problem requires that the instructor fill the class in on the main tenets of evangelical Protestantism and the cult of domesticity, which were central to Stowe's outlook on life and to her work. Beliefs about the purpose of human life (salvation), the true nature of reality (i.e., that it is spiritual), the true nature of power (that it ultimately resides in Christian love), and in the power of sanctity, prayer, good deeds, and Christian nurture would be crucial here.

One useful device is to have different groups of students (three or four in each group) read some of the classic works of American criticism—e.g. F. O. Matthiessen, Richard Chase, R. W. B. Lewis, D. H. Lawrence—and then report to the class why the assumptions that underlie these works made it impossible for their authors to include Stowe or other women authors in their considerations. The purpose is to demonstrate how critical bias determines from the start what work will be thought important and valuable and which will be completely ignored or set at a discount. (The groups meet with me to plan their presentation to the class beforehand. Usually I encourage them to use an imaginative format—e.g., talk show, debate, allegoried dramatization.)

Students love to talk about Augustine St. Clair and to speculate whether Uncle Tom or George Harris is the real hero of *Uncle Tom's Cabin*.

Major Themes, Historical Perspectives, and Personal Issues

Two of the historical issues that are important have already been referred to: evangelical Christianity, and the cult of domesticity. To this should be added the abolitionist crusade in the 1850s, the furor over the passage of the Fugitive Slave Law, and the change in the temper of the country after the Civil War—a turn from moral to social reform, and from romanticism to realism in literature—which accounts for the change in the temper and tone of Stowe's writing in this period.

Significant Form, Style, or Artistic Conventions

The Biblical overtones of much of Stowe's prose, the emotionalism of her rhetoric, her addresses to the reader, and the highly oratorical nature of her prose need to be discussed in relation to the predominance of sermons and religious writing in the 1850s and of the view of language which held that words should appeal to the feelings and make ideas accessible to as wide a range of people as possible. In other words, the ideology of Stowe's style is evangelical and democratic, rather than elitist, aestheticizing, aiming for clarity and form over formal innovation.

It should be stressed that Stowe was a brilliant writer of dialogue, one of the masters of American realism before realism became the dominant literary mode; she also had a powerful grasp of literary character. (It is no accident that three of the characters in *Uncle Tom's Cabin* have become bywords in American culture—little Eva, Uncle Tom, and Simon Legree). Stowe also exploited the philosophical possibilities of the novel as a genre, discussing, and dramatizing in fictional form complex theological, moral, and political issues of her day.

Original Audience

The astounding popularity of Stowe's first novel is worth noting—she was probably the best-known American of her time throughout the world. *Uncle Tom's Cabin* appealed to people regardless of social class, although it was unpopular in the South, after its initial reception there (which was favorable in some quarters) and was met with only a qualified enthusiasm by black readers in the North. Changes in beliefs about race, gender, religion, and literary value have made *Uncle Tom's Cabin* somewhat less universally appealing today, though it still retains its power to move readers in a way that very few works of the period do.

Comparisons, Contrasts, Connections

Stowe can be usefully compared to Emerson, whose vision of ideal existence, as put forward in essays like "Self-Reliance" and "The American Scholar" is sharply at odds with hers. Emerson's emphasis on individual integrity and self-cultivation, envisioning a time when "man will deal with man as sovereign state" contrasts with Stowe's ideal of a community of co-workers, bound together by Christian love, mutual sympathy, and a common purpose (for instance, the Quaker kitchen scene in *Uncle Tom's Cabin,* and the circle of women around Miss Prissy in *The Minister's Wooing*).

Hawthorne is another author whom it is interesting to compare with Stowe: His view of slavery was diametrically opposed to Stowe's—he condoned it—and his approach to writing, as well as to life in general, is skeptical where hers is believing; self-doubting where hers is self-trusting; detached and withdrawn where hers is active and participatory.

Questions for Reading and Discussion/ Approaches to Writing

1. Discussion questions should depend on the interest of the instructor.
2. Papers comparing Stowe to other authors, on Stowe's literary development, on her use of local color realism; interpretations of individual scenes or chapters from *Uncle Tom's Cabin*; the function of idealism as an ideal in Stowe's work.

Herman Melville (1819–1891)

Contributing Editor: Carolyn L. Karcher [p. 2400]

Classroom Issues and Strategies

The primary problems I have encountered in teaching Melville are the difficulty of the language and the complexity of the narrative point of view. This is particularly true of "Benito Cereno," but *Billy Budd* and "The Paradise of Bachelors and the Tartarus of Maids" also present problems for students unaccustomed to allusive and circuitous language and a complex narrative stance. Students usually find "Bartleby" and "The Encantadas" much more accessible.

Each of the Melville selections demands a somewhat different strategy. What works best for me is to group the stories with texts developing similar themes, instead of teaching all the Melville selections as a unit. For example, I use a unit on the Transcendentalists (Emerson, Thoreau, and Margaret Fuller) to introduce such themes as individualism vs. social responsibility (Emerson); alienation and the critique of industrial capitalism (Thoreau's *Walden*); the critique of patriarchy and of marriage as an institution, the parallels between the oppression of women and the enslavement of blacks, and the deconstruction of "true womanhood" and "woman's sphere" as ideological concepts (Fuller's "The Great Lawsuit"). Following this unit, I group "Bartleby," "The Paradise of Bachelors and the Tartarus of Maids" and the Hunilla sketch in "The Encantadas" with Rebecca Harding Davis's "Life in the Iron-Mills," Elizabeth Drew Stoddard's "Lemorne versus Huell," and analogous texts the *Heath Anthology* will make available.

I generally try not to overwhelm students with long analyses of style and point of view, but some brief treatment of these matters is indispensable, especially in the case of "Benito Cereno." I often begin by reading key passages aloud to the students and having them analyze the tone of Melville's rhetoric. When they actually hear the tone, they can usually pick up the undercurrent of satire in "The Paradise of Bachelors," the smug insensitivity of Bartleby's employer, and the sense that both Delano and the reader are being subtly mocked.

The question of tone leads easily into the issues of narrative point of view and audience. It is, of course, essential for students to realize that Bartleby's story is narrated by his boss and that "Benito Cereno," though in the third person, is narrated primarily from Delano's point of view, except for the Deposition, which represents Benito Cereno's point of view. After establishing these facts, I ask the students to consider why Melville did not choose instead to narrate his stories from the viewpoints of Bartleby, Babo, and the factory operatives in "Tartarus of Maids."

It is extremely effective to emphasize the continuing applicability of Melville's insights to our own times. Some of the issues his fiction raises are more relevant than ever. Many students (and their parents) work at jobs as meaningless and dead-end as Bartleby's and identify strongly with him. One student described the law copyists as "living xerox machines." Of course, the disparities between rich and poor are even more glaring now than at the time Melville wrote "The Paradise of Bachelors and the Tartarus of Maids" and the phenomenon called the "feminization of poverty" adds another relevant twist to those disparities. In the '60s "Benito Cereno" evoked Malcolm X and the Black Panthers. Today it evokes the struggle in South Africa. *Billy Budd* has perhaps never been more relevant than during the Reagan era, with its wholesale glorification of militarism and its rollback of democratic rights in the name of national security.

The most persistent questions my students raise are why Melville chose to address issues of such vital importance through literary strategies so oblique and circuitous, and whether these strategies were at all effective in subverting his readers' ideological assumption, let alone transforming their political consciousness.

Major Themes, Historical Perspectives, and Personal Issues

A major source of Melville's continuing power is the prescient insight he displays into the central problems of our culture: alienation; violence against women and the repression of the "feminine in man" that usually accompanies it; the widening gap between a decadent ruling class and the workers it immiserates; racism and an ever-more-brutal assault against the world's peoples of color; an unbridled militarism that threatens our very existence while demanding that we resign our civil liberties and human rights in the name of national security. Thus the most effective way of teaching Melville is to encourage students to draw contemporary lessons from the historical predicaments he dramatizes so compellingly.

Each story, of course, centers around a different theme. In teaching "Bartleby" and "The Paradise of Bachelors and the Tartarus of Maids," I emphasize Melville's critique of capitalism and the alienation it produces. "The Communist Manifesto" and Marx's essays "Estranged Labor," "The Meaning of Human Requirements," and "The Power of Money in Bourgeois Society," from *The Economic and Philosophic Manuscripts of 1844* are extraordinarily relevant to these two stories and illuminate them in startling ways. However, I find it preferable to let Marx indirectly inform the approach one takes to the stories, rather than to get sidetracked into a discussion of Marx. A secondary theme in "Bartleby" is the Christian ethic of Matthew 25, which Melville counterpoises against the capitalist ethic of Wall Street (see Bibliography for useful articles on this subject).

"The Paradise of Bachelors and the Tartarus of Maids" naturally invites a feminist as well as a Marxist approach. Margaret Fuller's "The Great Lawsuit" provides a ready-made framework for a feminist analysis of that story. The Hunilla sketch in "The Encantadas" likewise shows that Melville's sympathy of women as victims of patriarchy extended to classes of women invisible to most of his peers, and here, too, Fuller is very relevant. Though "Benito Cereno" and *Billy Budd* do not focus on women, a feminist approach can enrich the students' understanding of key episodes and subthemes.

In "Benito Cereno," for example, Delano's racist stereotypes not only prevent him from recognizing that slave revolt has occurred on board the *San Dominick*, but distort his perception of the African women's role in that revolt. Just as Babo protects his fellow rebels from discovery by catering to Delano's stereotypes about blacks as faithful slaves, so the African woman Delano ogles does so by catering to his stereotypes about African women as sexual objects and primitive children of nature. By reading between the lines of the Deposition from a feminist perspective, we see that the African women have probably been sexually victimized by both their master and Don Benito and that they have played an active role in the revolt. Melville's references to the "inflaming" songs and dances they sing while their men are fighting indicate his probable familiarity with such sources as Equiano's narrative, which speaks of African women's participation in warfare.

Similarly in *Billy Budd*, Melville connects his critique of militarism and the dehumanization it generates with a critique of Western culture's polarization of masculine and feminine. The feminine imagery Melville uses to describe Billy suggests that he represents what Vere later calls the "feminine in man," instructing his drumhead court that "she must be ruled out" of their deliberations. It also suggests that one of the roots of Claggart's and Vere's homosexual attraction to Billy is his embodiment of the "feminine in man" that they have repressed in themselves and must continue to repress by killing Billy. Here again, Margaret Fuller's analysis of the ways in which patriarchy victimizes men as well as women is relevant.

"Benito Cereno" obviously needs above all to be set in the contexts of the antebellum slavery controversy and of the prior historical events to which the story refers (summarized in the footnotes): the Spanish Inquisition; the introduction of African slavery into the Americas under Charles V; the African slave trade and its relationship to the activities of sixteenth- and seventeenth-century English buccaneers; the Santo Domingo slave uprising of 1797–1804; the slave revolt on board the Spanish ship *Tryal* that the real Captain Delano had helped suppress; and the uncannily similar slave revolt that occurred on board the Spanish slave-trading schooner *Amistad* in 1839 (for useful articles on these aspects of the story, see the Bibliography below). As mentioned under history above, the easiest means of teaching "Benito Cereno" in historical context is to assign it in conjunction with such texts as Olaudah Equiano's, Frederick Douglass's, and Harriet Beecher Stowe's *Uncle Tom's Cabin*, and other selections the present anthology makes available.

Billy Budd reverberates with implications for the nuclear age and its strategy of Mutually Assured Destruction (MAD). Teachers should not be afraid to exploit the story's contemporary relevance, but they should also set the story in its twin historical contexts—1797, the date of the action, and 1886–1891, the period of composition. See H. Bruce Franklin's "From Empire to Empire," cited below, for an invaluable discussion of these historical contexts.

I have tried to provide biographical facts germane to the stories in the introduction and notes. Teachers might point out, however, that "Bartleby" draws on Melville's experiences of working as a clerk for a brief period and also reflects attitudes he must have associated with his brother Allan, a lawyer; that Elizabeth Shaw Melville's debilitating pregnancies, as well as an actual visit to a paper mill, helped generate the feminist insights Melville displays in "The Paradise of Bachelors and the Tartarus of Maids"; that Judge Lemuel Shaw's conservative views on slavery and controversial role as the first northern judge to send a fugitive slave back to his master may explain the circuitous form Melville adopts in "Benito Cereno"; and that the suicide of Melville's son Malcolm in 1867 may have some bearing on *Billy Budd*.

Significant Form, Style, or Artistic Conventions

The traditional grouping of Melville with Hawthorne and Poe obscures not only the social vision, but the concept of art differentiating Melville from such canonical figures. Unlike them, Melville persistently rejects "the symmetry of form attainable in pure fiction," holding instead to the principle that "Truth uncompromisingly told will always have its ragged edges." Teachers should point out the way in which Melville deliberately subverts formalist conventions in "Benito Cereno" and *Billy Budd*, by appending the Deposition and the three chapters of sequel that force readers to determine the truth for themselves. It might also be useful to point out that the concept of art Melville articulates at the end of *Billy Budd* directly opposes Vere's doctrine of "measured forms" (see Edgar A. Dryden, cited below). By contextualizing Melville with writers like Olaudah Equiano, Frederick Douglass, Lydia Maria Child, Margaret Fuller, Rebecca Harding Davis, Harriet Beecher Stowe, and Elizabeth Stuart Phelps, among others, teachers might suggest comparisons between their aesthetic of "Art for Truth's Sake" (as Phelps called it) and Melville's concept of literature as "the great Art of Telling the Truth" (delineated in his review "Hawthorne and His Mosses"). Although Melville's short fiction is much less accessible and more oblique than the protest writings of these other authors, it is important to remember that four out of his first five books were autobiographical accounts of his life as a sailor—a genre not very different from the slave narrative. All five are filled with explicit and passionate social protest, culminating in *White-Jacket's* powerful appeal for the abolition of flogging in the navy, another parallel with the slave narrative.

Stylistically, I like to emphasize Melville's use of irony and grim humor. If one adopts Babo's point of view in reading "Benito Cereno," one is struck again and again by the humor of the story. The shaving scene is one of the best examples, and I like to go over it at length, beginning with the way in which Babo responds to Don Benito's slip of the tongue about Cape Horn by suggesting that Don Benito and Delano continue the conversation while he shaves his master.

"Bartleby," too, presents many examples of Melville's incisive irony and grim humor. See, for instance, the scene in which Bartleby announces that he will "do no more writing" and asks the narrator, "Do you not see the reason for yourself?"—to which the narrator, who does not see, responds by postulating that Bartleby's vision has become "temporarily impaired."

Original Audience

I generally let the subject of audience come up spontaneously, which it nearly always does. The students often infer—correctly—that Melville was writing for an audience linked by sympathies of class and race to the lawyer in "Bartleby," the bachelors in "Paradise," and Captain Delano in "Benito Cereno." I then talk a little about Melville's social milieu and the readership of *Harper's* and *Putnam's*. (The latter was moderately antislavery, and distinctly more progressive than *Harper's*, which Lydia Maria Child characterized as proslavery; nevertheless, its readers shared the attitudes Delano exemplifies.)

The question of audience is related to the literary strategy Melville adopted. In discussing Melville's rhetoric and the discomfort it provokes in a reader who has an obscure sense of being made fun of, we speculate about whether Melville hoped to jolt readers into thinking about the implications of their attitudes.

Comparison, Contrasts, Connections

See suggestions above under "Classroom Issues and Strategies." I also suggest grouping "Benito Cereno" with Equiano's, Douglass's, and Jacobs's narratives, Stowe's *Uncle Tom's Cabin*, and antislavery writings by Lydia Maria Child and others.

Bartleby has often been seen by critics as a Thoreau-like figure in his passive resistance, but Thoreau's perspective on industrialization, capitalism, and alienation actually contrasts with Melville's, which is closer to Marx's.

Davis's story makes an ideal pairing with "Paradise and Tartarus." Her narrator, like Melville's, is an outsider complicit by her class position in the oppression of the workers with whom she sympathizes, but also sharing some aspects of their oppression. Davis, like Melville, projects herself into workers of the opposite sex. And issues of class and gender intersect in both "Life in the Iron-Mills" and "The Paradise of Bachelors and the Tartarus of Maids."

The reasons for grouping "Benito Cereno" with other works about slavery are obvious, but teachers can help students make specific connections between the slaves on board the *San Dominick* and Douglass's battle with Covey, between the African women among them and Equiano's reminiscences of women's participation in battle, between the *San Dominick's* "true character" as a slave ship and Equiano's description of the slave ship that transported him across the Atlantic, between Melville's use of the Deposition (and of the three appended chapters in

Billy Budd) and Child's use of newspaper accounts at the end of "Slavery's Pleasant Homes."

At the same time, one can contrast Melville's rhetorical strategy with the more direct strategy of appeal for the reader's sympathy than other antislavery writers adopt. One can further contrast the male and female writer's perspectives on slavery. For Melville and Douglass, the slave's attempt to reclaim his "manhood" by fighting back and risking his life for freedom is central, while the female slave's attempt to defend her children and to resist the violation of her humanity through rape is peripheral. For Stowe and Jacobs the reverse is true; Child balances the two perspectives in "Slavery's Pleasant Homes."

Billy Budd invites comparison with Thoreau's essay on civil disobedience, which casts an ironic light on the arguments Vere uses to have Billy sentenced to hanging. If teachers decide to group *Billy Budd* with the writings on slavery, rather than with those on industrialism and the oppression of women, they can underscore the parallels Melville suggests between the condition of sailors and that of slaves (a theme he develops at great length in *White-Jacket*). The Black Handsome Sailor who appears in the opening pages of *Billy Budd* and incarnates the ideal of the Handsome Sailor more perfectly than Billy also provides a strong, positive counter-image of blacks, offsetting the seemingly negative stereotypes presented in "Benito Cereno." Formally as well, the two stories have much in common and invite comparison with "Slavery's Pleasant Homes."

Questions for Reading and Discussion/
Approaches to Writing

I do not like to use study questions because I find them too directive. I prefer to train students to become attentive readers through more indirect strategies. My principal strategy (borrowed from H. Bruce Franklin) is to give students a quiz requiring them to analyze several key passages in the text, prior to class discussion. (The lawyer's description of the place he assigns Bartleby in his office would be a good choice. So would the passage about the "odd instance" Delano observes of "the African love of bright colors and fine shows.")

I can, however, supply some questions I regularly ask in the course of class discussion.

Questions for class discussion of "Bartleby":

1. What does the subtitle of "Bartleby" suggest? What is the significance of Wall Street and the walls in the story?

2. What is the significance of the information that the narrator provides about himself and his employees at the beginning of the story? How does it prepare us to understand Bartleby and the narrator's attitude toward him?

3. Why does Melville tell the story from the point of view of the employer rather than of the office staff or of Bartleby himself? What effect does this narrative strategy have on the reader?

4. How reliable is the narrator? Are there any indications that he might be obtuse or unreliable? Give examples.

5. What incident unleashes Bartleby's passive resistance? What escalates it at each point?

6. What assumptions govern the question that the narrator asks Bartleby: "What earthly right have you to stay here? Do you pay any rent? Do you pay my taxes? Or is this property yours?"

7. What ethic does Melville implicitly oppose to the ethic of Wall Street? (This question leads into a discussion of the New Testament echoes running through the story.)

8. Why does the narrator conclude that Bartleby "was the victim of innate and incurable disorder"? How does it affect our responses to the story if we accept this conclusion?

9. What is the significance of the postscript the narrator appends to the story? What psychological (or ideological) purpose does it serve for the narrator? What symbolic purpose does it serve for Melville?

10. How much has the encounter with Bartleby changed the narrator by the end of the story? Is the narrator "saved"?

Questions for class discussion of "Paradise and Tartarus":

1. What contrast does the opening of "Paradise" draw between the Bachelors' haven and the outside world? How does Melville develop the implications of the opening passage in the rest of the sketch?

2. How might the fate of the medieval Knights Templars be relevant to the nineteenth-century Templars?

3. Read out loud the paragraphs about the survival of Templars in modern London and ask: What effect does this imagery have? What attitude does it create toward the Templars?

4. Read out loud the description of the Templars' banquet and ask: What is the significance of this imagery? What associations does it suggest to you? (The teacher might amplify the discussion by pointing out the parody of Plato's *Symposium* suggested by dubbing the field-marshall/waiter "Socrates.") What bearing does this description have on the second sketch of the pair?

5. What role does the narrator play in each of the two sketches? How would we situate him vis-à-vis the bachelors of the first sketch and the factory owner and workers of the second sketch?

6. What business takes the narrator to the paper mill? What might his "seedsman's business" symbolize?

7. Why does Melville link these two sketches as a pair? What devices does he use to cement the links? What connections does he invite readers to make between the bachelors and the maids, between Temple Bar and the New England paper factory? How is the contrast between the bachelor of the first sketch and maids of the second sketch continued within the second sketch?

8. Read out loud the passage describing the landscape of Devil's Dungeon and ask what its imagery suggests.

9. What is the significance of the imagery Melville uses to describe the factory? (Read aloud passages drawing the students' attention to the girls' dehumanization and the machine's preemption of their reproductive functions.)

10. What is Melville critiquing in this pair of sketches? Why does he link the economic to the sexual, production to reproduction?

11. Depending on the order in which assignments are made, teachers can also ask questions about:

　　—the continuities linking "Bartleby" with "Paradise and Tartarus"

　　—the similarities and differences between Melville's and Rebecca Harding Davis's critiques of industrial capitalism

　　—the extent to which Melville shares the concerns Margaret Fuller articulates in "The Great Lawsuit."

Questions for class discussion of "Benito Cereno":

1. Through whose eyes do we view the events in the story? Where in the text does Melville shift into Delano's point of view? Whose point of view does the Deposition represent? (N.B. I have found again and again that students confuse third-person narrative with omniscient point of view and a character's subjective point of view with first-person narrative. Unless instructors take special care, students will end up referring to Delano as the narrator in their papers and exams.)

2. Why doesn't Melville choose to write the story from Babo's point of view? What might his purpose be in confining us to Delano's and later Benito Cereno's point of view? What limitations does this narrative strategy impose on us as readers?

3. How reliable are Delano's perceptions of reality? What tendencies in particular make him an unreliable interpreter of the behavior he

sees manifested on board the *San Dominick*? (Draw the students' attention to the racial assumptions embedded in his perceptions of the oakum-pickers and hatchet-polishers; in his endorsement of the "contrast in dress, denoting their relative positions," that distinguishes Don Benito from Babo; in his ogling of a naked African woman and his failure to realize the terrible irony of the possibility that she might be one of "the very women Mungo Park saw in Africa, and gave such a noble account of'; in his belief that the blacks are "too stupid" to be staging a masquerade and that no white would be "so far a renegade as to apostatize from his very species almost, by leaguing in against it with negroes"; in his ludicrous misinterpretation of Babo's intent in using the flag of Spain as a bib. Obviously there will not be time to discuss all these passages, but one or two should be singled out for discussion.)

4. The best example of how Delano's racism keeps him from recognizing that the blacks have staged a revolt is the episode in which he sees Babo use the flag of Spain as a bib for Don Benito, but misinterprets it as an "odd instance of the African love of bright colors and fine shows." How does that episode originate? (Draw the students' attention to Don Benito's slip of the tongue and Babo's quick invention of the shave as a ruse to prevent further inopportune slips. Use an analysis of the episode to show how brilliantly Babo manipulates Delano's prejudices.)

5. What attitude toward slavery does Delano exhibit? How does his attitude differ from Benito Cereno's? (Point out passages showing Delano's envy of Don Benito, even as he feels the Yankee's superiority to the decadent slaveholding aristocrat; most crucial is Delano's insistence on pursuing and capturing the *San Dominick* with its cargo of slaves "worth more than a thousand doubloons.")

6. Most of the confusion in interpreting "Benito Cereno" arises from the latter part of the story. It is easy to see that Delano's view of blacks as stupid is wrong, but does Melville present Benito Cereno's view of blacks as a corrective to stereotype, or merely as another stereotype? Does the Deposition represent the "truth"?

7. How does the language of the Deposition differ from the language Melville uses elsewhere in the text? What makes us take it for the "truth"?

8. What is Benito Cereno's interpretation of events, as opposed to Delano's initial interpretation? How does he explain the slaves' revolt?

9. Does the Deposition indirectly provide any alternative explanations of why the blacks may have revolted? What does it tell us about the blacks' actual aims? How do they try to achieve those aims? (If necessary, point out the hints that the slave women have been sexually abused by Aranda and Cereno; also consider the conversation between Cereno and Babo during the revolt, when Babo asks Cereno to transport the blacks back to Senegal and promises that they will abide by the rationing of water and food necessary to effect such a long voyage.)

10. Does Melville provide any clues to an interpretation of the story that transcends the racist stereotypes of Delano and Cereno? (Point out the allusions to the ancient African civilizations of Egypt and Nubia; the allusion to Ezekiel's Valley of Dry Bones; the symbolism of the San Dominick's "shield-like stem-piece" and the way in which the identities of the masked figures get reversed at the end of the story.)

11. What is the narrative point of view of the few pages following the Deposition? How do you interpret the dialogue between the two captains? Does it indicate that either Delano or Cereno has undergone any change in consciousness or achieved a new understanding of slavery as a result of his ordeal?

12. What seems to be the message of the scene with which the story ends? What do you think Melville was trying to convey through the story? How does the story continue to be relevant or prophetic?

Questions for class discussion of Billy Budd:

1. Why does Melville begin the story with a description of the Handsome Sailor? What does this figure seem to represent? What is the significance of the fact that the first example Melville cites of the Handsome Sailor is "a native African of the unadulterate blood of Ham"? What characteristics does Billy share with the Black Handsome Sailor? What is the purpose of the analogies Melville suggests between the "barbarians" of pre-Christian Europe, Africa, and the South Seas? In what respects does Billy fail to conform fully to the Handsome Sailor archetype?

2. What are the historical contexts of the story? What is the purpose of the historical background Melville supplies on the Nore and Spithead mutinies? (Note that the story takes place only a few years after the American War of Independence against Britain and that it begins with an impressment, recalling the frequent impressment of American sailors by the British—one of the grievances that led to the War of 1812. See H. Bruce Franklin's

"From Empire to Empire" for a full discussion of the story's historical contexts.)

3. What is the significance of Billy's being impressed from the *Rights-of-Man* to the *Bellipotent*?

4. What relationship does Melville set up between Billy, Claggart, and Vere? What qualities does each represent? Why are Claggart and Vere attracted to Billy? In what ways is he a threat to them?

5. How do you interpret Melville's definition of "Natural Depravity"? To whom does it most obviously apply in the story? To whom else might it also apply? (A number of critics have pointed out the applicability of the passage to Vere as well as Claggart.)

6. How does the tragedy occur? How might it have been avoided?

7. How does Melville invite the reader to judge Vere's behavior and decision to hang Billy? What passages, dialogues, and scenes must we take into account?

8. What tactics and arguments does Vere use to sway his officers? What are the political consequences (in real life as well as in the story) of accepting Vere's arguments? Do you see any contradictions in Vere's arguments, or do you find them rational and persuasive? Is Melville's description of "Natural Depravity" at all relevant to an evaluation of Vere's conduct at the trial ("Toward the accomplishment of an aim which in wantonness of atrocity would seem to partake of the insane, he will direct a cool judgment sagacious and sound")?

9. How do you interpret the many Biblical allusions in the story? In what ways do they redefine or amplify the meaning of the story? What relationship(s) do you see between the religious and political interpretations the story invites? How does Melville characterize the role of the chaplain?

10. After the hanging, Vere forestalls possible disturbances by ordering the drums to muster the men to quarters earlier than usual. He then justifies his action by explaining how he views art and the purpose it serves: "With mankind forms, measured forms, are everything; and that is the import couched in the story of Orpheus spellbinding the wild denizens of the wood." Does Melville endorse this concept of art in *Billy Budd*? How does the form of the story jibe (or conflict) with Vere's ideal of "measured forms"? How does the glorification of the Handsome Sailor, and the imagery used to describe him, jibe (or conflict) with Vere's view of "the wild denizens of the wood"?

11. What is the effect of the three sequels Melville appends to the story? What further light do they shed on Vere and on the political interests governing his decision? To whom does the story give the last word?

12. Depending on the order of assignments, teachers can invite students to draw connections between:

—the status of slaves, sailors, and factory workers

—the legal arguments Vere uses in his role as prosecuting attorney at Billy's trial, and the portrayal of lawyers and the law in "Bartleby" and "Paradise and Tartarus"

—Thoreau's essay on civil disobedience and Vere's defense of martial law and the Articles of War

—Vere's insistence that "the heart, sometimes the feminine in man, be ruled out" and Fuller's critique of the rigid sexual stereotypes that patriarchal ideology imposes on men and women.

Since I group readings together, I also try to formulate paper topics that involve comparisons and contrasts of several readings. Most of the following topics are thematic. Instructors who would prefer formalist topics that focus exclusively on Melville's stories might adapt some from the questions for class discussion listed above.

In their fiction, Stoddard, Davis, and Melville dramatize problems of nineteenth-century American life that Emerson, Thoreau, and Fuller comment on philosophically. Show the relationship between the ideas of any of these thinkers and a story by Stoddard, Davis, or Melville. Examples:

1. Use Thoreau's discussion of alienation in *Walden* as a framework for analyzing "Bartleby." In the process, compare and contrast the two authors' political perspectives.

2. Compare and contrast Thoreau's, Melville's, and/or Davis's critiques of industrialism and capitalism in *Walden*, "The Paradise of Bachelors and the Tartarus of Maids," and "Life in the Iron-Mills."

3. Apply Fuller's analysis of women's oppression to Stoddard's "Lemorne versus Huell," Melville's "The Paradise of Bachelors and the Tartarus of Maids," and/or Davis's "Life in the Iron-Mills."

4. Apply Fuller's critique of middle-class concepts of "true womanhood" to the women portrayed in Davis's "Life in the Iron-Mills" and Melville's "The Encantadas" and "The Paradise of Bachelors and the Tartarus of Maids." ("Benito Cereno" can also be included if it has already been assigned.)

5. Use Thoreau's essay on civil disobedience as a framework for analyzing *Billy Budd* and the issues it raises.

Choose some aspect of slavery explored in the assigned readings, and compare and contrast the perspectives these various works provide on it.

1. The issue of slave resistance and rebellion (can include violent and nonviolent, individual and collective resistance).
2. The issue of Higher Law vs. the law of the land.
3. The contrast between the masters' and the slaves' viewpoints and values (e.g., Douglass and Jacobs and their fellow slaves vs. their masters; Uncle Tom, Chloe, Cassy, etc., vs. the Shelbys, St. Clares, and Legree; Babo vs. Cereno and Delano).
4. Religion and slavery, or religion and militarism (can include the indictment of the church's hypocrisy, the use of the Bible to support or condemn slavery, the theme of apocalyptic judgment, the use of typology and religious rhetoric and symbolism).
5. Comparative analysis of the rhetorical techniques, purposes, and intended audiences of three writers among those assigned, or of the metaphors each writer uses to describe slavery and structure his/her narrative.
6. The use of irony in the antislavery argument (can analyze the different types of irony found in slave songs, Douglass's and Jacobs's narratives, Child's antislavery writings, *Uncle Tom's Cabin*, and "Benito Cereno").
7. The image of Africa and the portrayal of the slave trade in Equiano's narrative and "Benito Cereno."
8. Double meanings and the theme of appearance vs. reality in any of the assigned readings.
9. The theme "Slavery proved as injurious to her as it did to me" (a quotation from Douglass's *Narrative* as applied to the individuals who people the assigned works, or to the North and the South, blacks and whites, oppressed and oppressing classes, the American nation in general).
10. The picture of slave life and the slave community that emerges from any three of the assigned works (preferably three representing different racial, regional, or gender perspectives).
11. The theme "Slavery is terrible for men, but it is far more terrible for women," as dramatized in several of the assigned readings.

Bibliography

Ideally, acquaintance with *Typee*, *Redburn*, and *White-Jacket* would be extremely helpful for teaching the stories in the anthology from the perspective suggested here. The introduction and notes to the selections quote liberally from these three works, however, and several of the critics cited below summarize their bearing on *Billy Budd*.

For a broader intellectual context, teachers who have time to read "The Communist Manifesto" and perhaps Marx's essays "Estranged Labor," "The Meaning of Human Requirements," and "The Power of Money in Bourgeois Society," from *The Economic and Philosophic Manuscripts of 1844* will find them extremely relevant to both "The Paradise of Bachelors and the Tartarus of Maids" and "Bartleby." In particular, Marx discusses workers' reduction to commodities, and their enslavement to machines, and their resulting alienation.

For a complete bibliography, covering all of Melville's short fiction except *Billy Budd* and including overviews of the stories' reception, see Lea Bertani Vozar Newman's *A Reader's Guide to the Short Stories of Herman Melville* (Boston: Hall, 1986). Forthcoming will also be the second volume of Brian Higgins's *Herman Melville: An Annotated Bibliography* (Boston: Hall), covering all Melville criticism published since 1930. For an excellent reconstruction of the stories' chronology, circumstances of composition and publication, and contemporary reception, see Merton M. Sealts's Historical Note in the Northwestern-Newberry edition of *The Piazza Tales and Other Prose Pieces, 1839–1860* (Evanston and Chicago: 1987, 457–533). The volume also reprints the chapter of Delano's *Narrative* that Melville used as a source.

For a biographical study that situates Melville and his family in the context of contemporary politics, see Michael Paul Rogin, *Subversive Genealogy: The Politics and Art of Herman Melville* (New York: Knopf, 1983), especially Chapters 6 and 9.

For challenges to the stereotype of Melville as a writer indifferent or hostile to women, see Kristin Herzog's chapter on Melville in *Women, Ethics, and Exotics: Images of Power in Mid-Nineteenth-Century American Fiction* (Knoxville: Univ. of Tennessee Press, 1983), as well as the essays in the February 1986 issue of *Melville Society Extracts*.

Listed below are the critical studies I have found most useful for illuminating the Melville selections in this anthology, and for developing approaches toward teaching them.

For books containing relevant discussions of more than one story, see Rogin, cited above; Marvin Fisher, *Going Under: Melville's Short Fiction and the American 1850s* (Baton Rouge: Louisiana State Univ. Press, 1977), especially the chapters on "Bartleby" and "The Paradise of Bachelors and the Tartarus of Maids"; and H. Bruce Franklin's chapter on Melville in *The Victim as Criminal and Artist: Literature from the American Prison* (New York: Oxford Univ. Press, 1978), as well as his earlier sections on "Bartleby" and "Benito Cereno" in *The Wake of the Gods: Melville's Mythology* (Stanford: Stanford Univ. Press, 1963) (although dated, the discussion of "Benito Cereno" contains pertinent information on Charles V and slavery in the Americas); Joyce Sparer Adler, *War in Melville's Imagination* (New York: New York Univ. Press, 1981), especially the chapter on *Billy Budd* and Robert K. Martin, *Hero, Captain, and Stranger: Male Friendship, Social Critique, and Literary Form in the Sea Novels of Herman Melville* (Chapel Hill: Univ. of North Carolina Press, 1986), especially the chapter on *Billy Budd* and pp. 105–106 on "The Paradise of Bachelors."

On "Bartleby," in addition to the books cited above see Stephen Zelnick, "Melville's Bartleby, The Scrivener: A Study in History, Ideology, and Literature," *Marxist Perspectives* 2 (Winter 1979/80): 74–92; and Donald M. Fiene, "Bartleby the Christ," in Raymona E. Hull, ed., *Studies in the Minor and Later Works of Melville* (Hartford: Transcendental Books, 1970): 18–23.

On the Hunilla sketch, see Robert Sattelmeyer and James Barbour, "The Sources and Genesis of Melville's 'Norfolk Isle and the Chola Widow,'" *American Literature* 50 (November 1978): 398–417.

On "The Paradise of Bachelors and the Tartarus of Maids," in addition to the books cited above see Beryl Rowland, "Melville's Bachelors and Maids: Interpretation Through Symbol and Metaphor," *American Literature* 41 (November 1969): 389–405.

Two books situate Melville in the slavery controversy: Carolyn L. Karcher, *Shadow over the Promised Land: Slavery, Race, and Violence in Melville's America* (Louisiana State Univ. Press, 1980), especially Chapters 1 and 5; and Rogin, *Subversive Genealogy* cited above. See also Eric J. Sundquist's superbly researched article, "*Benito Cereno* and New World Slavery," in Sacvan Bercovitch, ed., *Reconstructing American Literary History* (Cambridge, Mass.: Harvard Univ. Press, 1986): 93–122. On the relevance of the Spanish Inquisition to *Benito Cereno*, see John Bernstein, "'Benito Cereno' and the Spanish Inquisition," *Nineteenth-Century Fiction* 16 (March 1962): 345–50. Sidney Kaplan discusses the *Amistad* case in "Herman Melville and the American National Sin: The Meaning of 'Benito Cereno,'" *Journal of Negro History*, 42 (January 1957): 11–37, but interprets the story as an endorsement, rather than a critique, of racism. For Black perspectives on the story's dramatization of slavery and racism, see Charles E. Nolim, *Melville's "Benito Cereno": A Study in Meaning of Name Symbolism* (New York: New Voices, 1974); and Joshua Leslie and Sterling Stuckey, "The Death of Benito Cereno: A Reading of Herman Melville on Slavery," *Journal of Negro History*, 67 (December 1982): 287–301. The latter argues convincingly that Melville shows an understanding of African culture based on reading Mungo Park.

Study of *Billy Budd* should begin with the indispensable notes provided by Harrison Hayford and Merton M. Sealts in their 1962 edition

(Univ. of Chicago Press). Besides pointing out innumerable parallels between *Billy Budd* and Melville's other works, of which *White-Jacket* and *Israel Potter* are the most relevant, Hayford and Sealts sum up previous criticism. Among recent critics, Milton R. Stern formulates the most persuasive version of the pro-Vere interpretation in his 1975 Bobbs-Merrill edition of the story. Offering the strongest rebuttals and the most satisfying readings of the story are Adler (cited above) and H. Bruce Franklin, "From Empire to Empire: *Billy Budd, Sailor,*" in A. Robert Lee, ed., *Herman Melville: Reassessments* (London: Vision, 1984). Containing pertinent historical information, despite a strained thesis, is Stanton Gamer, "Fraud and Fact in Herman Melville's *Billy Budd*" *San Jose Studies* 4 (May 1978): 82–105. Edgar A. Dryden, *Melville's Thematics of Form: The Great Art of Telling the Truth* (Baltimore: Johns Hopkins Univ. Press, 1968) 209–16, analyzes the way in which the form of *Billy Budd* subverts Vere's doctrine of "measured form."

William Wells Brown (1815–1884)

Contributing Editor: Arlene Elder [p. 2584]

Classroom Issues and Strategies

A major problem will be the students' unfamilarity with the details of slavery, especially, in this case, with slave auctions and the existence of very fair-skinned slaves. They will also be puzzled by the stilted descriptions of the protagonists and will need to be provided with some background on the formulas for depicting heroes and heroines, as well as villains, in the popular fiction of Brown's day.

It would be extremely useful to recount briefly Brown's own history and to emphasize that he was self-taught after his escape from slavery and, therefore, influenced strongly both by his reading and by the popular ideas current during his time, for instance, common concepts of male and female beauty. Reading the class a short historical description of a slave auction and some commentary about the sale of persons of mixed blood, since even one drop of Negro blood marked one legally as black, hence enslaved, would also provide a context for the chapters from *Clotelle*.

One might provoke a lively discussion by quoting some of the negative comments on writers like Brown present in "The myth of a 'negro literature' " by LeRoi Jones (Amiri Baraka) in *Home Social Essays* (New

York: William Morrow, 1966) or Addison Gayle, Jr.'s, designation of Brown as "the conscious or unconscious propagator of assimilationism" (*The Way of the New World, The Black Novel in America*, New York: Anchor, 1976, p. 11). Any denigration of functional or committed art by critics with New Critical persuasions would also serve this purpose.

Students are interested in the verification of the sale of "white" slaves: the historical basis for Clotelle as the alleged daughter of Thomas Jefferson; questions of nineteenth-century popular characterization as a source for Brown's handling of his protagonists; the whole genre of the slave narrative; and theoretical issues such as art vs. propaganda.

Major Themes, Historical Perspectives, and Personal Issues

1. Brown's own personal experience as an aide to a slave trader.
2. The sexual exploitation of both female slaves and white wives by slave owners.
3. The historical role of Christianity as both an advocate of slavery and, for the slaves, a source of escapism from their situation.
4. The presence of rebellious slaves who refused to accept their dehumanization.

Significant Form, Style, or Artistic Conventions

One needs to place *Clotelle* within the dual contexts of the black literary traditions of slave narrative and folk orature and the mainstream genre of popular nineteenth-century drama and fiction. This dual influence accounts for what appears to be the incongruous description of Jerome, for instance, who could be seen, in his manly rebellion against an unfair beating as a fictional Frederick Douglass but also is described in a totally unrealistic way both to appeal to racist standards of beauty and to correspond to images of heroes in popular white novels.

Original Audience

Of equal influence on Brown's composition of *Clotelle* are his two very different audiences, the white middle class and the black "talented-tenth," with very different, sometimes conflicting, expectations, histories, aesthetics, education, and incomes, to whom Brown and other nineteenth-century black novelists had to appeal. Interestingly, there is still no homogeneous audience for black writing, *Clotelle* included, because American society is still not equal. Therefore, it should not surprise an instructor if the selections arouse extremely different responses from various class members.

Comparisons, Contrasts, Connections

Brown's intertwined aesthetic and political complexities are echoed not only in the writing by other nineteenth-century African-American novelists but also in the work of all ethnic American writers, especially those of the present day, for whom issues of constituency and audience are extremely complicated. It is for this reason that *Clotelle* is extremely useful to demonstrate not only common subjects and themes with the slave narratives but, as interesting, the influence of society upon artistic choices and the paradoxical position of the ethnic artist vis-à-vis African- and Euro-American literary heritages and his or her mixed constituency.

Questions for Reading and Discussion/ Approaches to Writing

1. Chapter II:
    (a) How is the idea as well as the historical reality of slaves being treated as dehumanized property expressed in Brown's language and imagery?
    (b) How does the auction process reveal the complete dichotomy between the interests of the slaves and those of their traders and owners?
    (c) What is the intended effect of Brown's description of Isabella on the auction block?
    (d) Why does Brown link the image of the auction block with that of the church spires in this chapter?
2. Chapter X:
    (a) What is the symbolic/thematic effect of Brown's description of Isabella's garden?
    (b) What does this chapter reveal about the sexual exploitation of both female slaves and the wives of the white masters? What contradiction does it suggest about the possibly comforting concept of a "good master"?
    (c) Have we been given enough information to explain Linwood's behavior? How do we account for Isabella's continued kindness toward him?
3. Chapter XI:
    (a) Why doesn't Linwood accept Isabella's offer to release him from his promise to her?

    (b) Do you think a nineteenth-century reader might react differently from a modem one to the unbelievability of Linwood's mutterings in his sleep? If so, why?

    (c) What is the function of religion for Isabella?

4. Chapter XVIII:

    (a) How do you explain Brown's incongruous physical description of Jerome?

    (b) Who are George Combe and Fowler, and why are they alluded to here?

    (c) What do the allusions to certain well-known lovers reveal about Brown's reading?

5.

    (a) Comparison with details of slave life, especially female concubinage found in Harriet A. Jacobs, *Life of a Slave Girl, Written by Herself* (Cambridge, Mass.: Harvard Univ. Press, 1987).

    (b) Discussion of Isabella and Clotelle as representatives of the popular "tragic octoroon" stereotype.

    (c) Comparison of *Clotelle* with another nineteenth-century African-American novel about a female slave and her liberation, Frances E. W. Harper's *Iola Leroy* (Philadelphia, 1892).

    (d) Discussion of Jerome as a "counterstereotype" intended to refute negative popular images of blacks. A look at Frederick Douglass's *Narrative of the Life of Frederick Douglass* (Boston, 1845) as well as Thomas Dixon, Jr.'s, *The Clansman* (1902) would provide polar contexts for this subject.

Bibliography

Dearborn, Mary. *Pochahantas' Daughters, Gender and Ethnicity in American Culture.*

Gates, Henry Louis, Jr. *"Race," Writing and Difference.*

Kinney, James. *Amalgamation: Race, Sex, and Rhetoric in the Nineteenth-Century American Novel.*

Takaki, Ronald T. *Violence in the Black Imagination.* (Especially Part III on Brown and *Clotelle*).

Alice Cary (1820–1871)

Contributing Editor: Judith Fetterley [p. 2596]

Classroom Issues and Strategies

Students are turned off by what they perceive as her didacticism, the morals attached to the ends of the stories. They also have trouble with what they perceive as her Christian dogma or perspective. And occasionally they perceive her stories as sentimental.

These problems are endemic to the reading of texts by nineteenth-century American women writers. They are useful and interesting problems to encounter in the classroom because they raise quite clearly the issue of aesthetic value and how the context for determining what is good art changes over time. The instructor needs to be aware of how contemporary critics have addressed this issue. The single best book for the teacher to have and use is Jane Tompkins's *Sensational Designs*. The instructor might wish to assign the last chapter of this book, "But Is It Any Good?" to the class, since this chapter raises directly the questions most of them have about nineteenth-century women's texts.

Compared to other nineteenth-century American women writers, Cary is minimally didactic, Christian, or "sentimental." So, in teaching her, my approach consists of comparing her work with that of writers who are much more didactic, Christian, and "sentimental" and asking how it is that she avoids these patterns. What fictional techniques has she developed to tell the story she has to tell without in fact resorting to didacticism, etc.? This usually leads into a discussion of the form of the short fictional piece, and more specifically into a discussion of regionalism. (See the forthcoming *Norton Anthology of American Women Regional Writers*, edited by Fetterley and Pryse.)

Students respond to the issue of storytelling—how women tell stories and the relation between their telling of stories and their context of domestic work. They are also interested in the issue of landscape—how Cary manages to create a mood through her description of the landscape and how she manages to convey the open-ended nature of her stories. Their lack of plot in the conventional sense is worthy of discussion as is the fact that Cary tells stories about women's lives and experience from the point of view of a female narrator.

Major Themes, Historical Perspectives, and Personal Issues

It is important to emphasize that Cary was essentially a self-made writer. She had little formal education, little support from family or extended personal context; yet she made herself into a poet whose name was known throughout the country. Her decision to move to New York in 1850 represented an extraordinary act of self-assertion for a woman at the time. She determined that she needed to get out of the "provinces" in order to have the literary career she wished and she did it. She set up a household in New York that included two of her sisters and she supported this household by her own work. She is an example of the way in which nineteenth-century American women writers were able to set up supportive networks that were based on connections with other women. She is an example of a nineteenth-century American woman writer who was genuinely financially independent of men. She ran her house, earned the money for it, and handled her money herself.

In terms of literary themes, it is important to emphasize the fact that Cary began to write seriously about her Ohio neighborhood after she left it for New York. She saw herself as trying to present a realistic picture of this neighborhood and to create a place in literature for the region, but she was able to do this only after she had left it for New York.

Significant Form, Style, or Artistic Conventions

It is important to point out that Cary thought of herself primarily as a poet. Her reputation during her lifetime and thereafter was based on her poetry. The conventions that governed poetry by women in the nineteenth century by and large produced a body of poetry that is not of interest to the late twentieth-century reader. The novel was also a highly determined form. Women were expected to write certain kinds of novels, to produce "women's fiction" with the appropriately feminine perspective and set of values. The short fictional sketch, however, was a relatively undetermined territory. It was not taken as seriously as were the novel and poetry and no theory existed as to what kind of fictional sketch a woman should or should not write in order to demonstrate that she was in fact a woman. As a result, in writing her clovernook sketches Cary was on her own, so to speak. She was able to write organically, to let the shape of the fiction emerge from the nature of the story she wished to tell. As a result, her short fiction holds interest for the contemporary reader; it seems fresh, new, not written to fulfill convention or previously determined script, but deriving from some deep personal place that produces a uniquely marked and signed prose. Thus any discussion of Alice Cary needs to address the role that the form of the fictional sketch plays in creating fiction that interests us. In other words, the issue of form is central to the discussion of Alice Cary. Specific features of this form include: the freedom this form gives to focus on character and setting as opposed to plot; the lack of closure in many of Cary's sketches; the intermingling of realism and surrealism. For a fuller discussion of these and other issues relative to the form of the sketch in relation to Alice Cary, I refer the instructor to my "Introduction" to the Rutgers Press edition of the short fiction of Alice Cary, *Clovernook Sketches and Other Stories*.

It is also important to discuss the issue of realism in relation to Cary. Since American literary history, until very recently, has been based on a study of male writers, the predominant view is that realism began in America after the Civil War. However, women writers were experimenting with realism in the decades before the Civil War. Cary's "Preface" to the first volume of Clovernook sketches, published in 1852, lays out her theory of realism and the instructor should be familiar with it. She sees herself as participating in the effort to write about American subjects and she sees herself as doing something "new" in choosing to write about these subjects as "they really are." In making this choice she is in effect following the lead of writers like Caroline Kirkland and participating in the development of realism as a mode suited to the needs and interests of women writers in the nineteenth century. Alice Cary thus provides the instructor with the opportunity to at once raise the issue of the bias in literary history and the issue of the development of realism as an American mode.

Original Audience

As I have indicated above, Cary's primary audience during her lifetime was for her poetry. Her short fiction was not a big popular success and was not reprinted. But the nineteenth century, as I said before, did not take the genre of short fiction as seriously as it did that of poetry and the novel. So in a way this does not tell us much about how well her short fiction was received by her readers. Her short fiction, much of which was initially published in periodicals, may well have been as popular as that of any other contemporary writer, male or female. The point is that the genre itself was not as popular. Interestingly enough, however, Cary's greatest critical successes came from her short fiction. Once again, though, this may simply indicate that the genre itself was not taken very seriously.

Comparisons, Contrasts, Connections

Cary can be fruitfully compared with a number of different writers in a number of different contexts. She can be compared with writers like Poe and Hawthorne in her use of fiction as dream work and projection. She creates the same kind of uncanny, eerie, dreamlike atmosphere that they do. She can also be compared with them in terms of her use of the first-person narrator and the complexities of that narrator's relation to the story she tells and the characters she creates. She can also be compared with them in terms of her use of setting.

She can be compared with nineteenth-century women writers like Caroline Kirkland for her use of realism and for her commitment to telling the woman's side of the story. She can also be compared with other nineteenth-century women writers for her ability to avoid some of their didacticism, Christian moralizing, and "sentimentality."

She can be most interestingly compared to Emily Dickinson in her ability to place herself and her imagination at the center of her work. Very few nineteenth-century American women writers were able to overcome the dicta that required of women self-effacement in literature as in life. Dickinson overcame it by virtue of not publishing. Cary overcame it through her use of the nonconventional form of short fiction. Her work is remarkable for the sustained development of first-person narration. Her collections of Clovernook sketches are as much about the narrator as they are about anything else. She creates a remarkable I/eye for her work.

Bibliography

I refer the instructor to the discussion of Alice Cary in *Provisions* and to the "Introduction" to the Rutgers Press volume of Cary's short fiction, *Clovernook Sketches and Other Stories*. Also to Kolodny, *The Land Before Her*.

Elizabeth Stoddard (1823–1902)

Contributing Editor: Sybil Weir [p. 2614]

Classroom Issues and Strategies

Stoddard's cryptic narrative style and the limitation of the point of view to the female narrator may make it difficult for students to follow the plot sequence. Also, students unfamiliar with the conventions of senti-mental fiction may miss much of Stoddard's satire.

With Stoddard, I may begin discussion by asking a student to review the plot. Before students read the story, I lecture on the senti-mental conventions in fiction, emphasizing the use of a courtship plot structure, and that the fiction often endorses a self-sacrificial heroine. Stoddard, in contrast, begins with a marriage and satirizes the heroine's penchant for self-abnegation.

Major Themes, Historical Perspectives, and Personal Issues

I would link historical and personal issues by raising questions about nineteenth-century assumptions about woman's place, woman's sphere, and woman's nature; Stoddard questions, for example, her culture's assumption that female self-sacrifice is a virtue. By beginning with a seemingly unhappy marriage, Stoddard calls into question sentimental fiction's assumption that women will be happiest when married.

The ending raises several problems: Does it implicitly condone the violence with which the story begins? Does the ending validate patriar-chal values by confirming the wisdom of the male doctor and validating the institution of marriage? Is it a "cop-out"?

Significant Form, Style, or Artistic Conventions

The primary questions have to do with Stoddard's use of the literary tra-ditions of her day, the traditions of sentimental fiction, gothic romance, and regional prose. In addition to her departure from the standard courtship plot, Stoddard satirizes other conventional elements as in her satirical presentation of the narrator's diary and in her mocking depic-tion of Mrs. Bowman's religious character. She draws upon the tradition of regional realism to sketch Marlow, the Massachusetts seacoast village, modeled after her hometown of Mattapoisett. For her characterization of Gerard, she draws upon the gothic tradition, in particular the Byronic heroes found in the Brontës, whom Stoddard greatly admired.

I would also emphasize Stoddard's importance "as an experimenter in narrative method. She anticipates modern fiction in using a severely limited mode with minimal narrative clues" (Buell and Zagarell, "Biographical and Critical Introduction," p. xxiii).

Original Audience

"The Prescription" was first published in *Harper's New Monthly Magazine*, suggesting that Stoddard's fiction was considered to appeal to a middle-class, educated audience. In fact, neither Stoddard's short fiction nor her novels were ever popular or recognized beyond a small circle of intellectuals and writers. Presumably, the audience of her own day was put off both by her elliptical style and by her satirical questioning of their favorite assumptions about female virtue, self-abnegation, and religious piety.

Comparisons, Contrasts, Connections

I would compare Stoddard's fiction with Stowe's and Alcott's: for example, in what ways does Stoddard's characterization depart from Stowe's emphasis on religious piety or Alcott's affirmation of domestic feminism? How, and to what extent, do all three writers emphasize the self-reliance of their heroines?   Other appropriate comparisons and contrasts, depending on what the students have read, have to do with point of view (what is the effect of the first-person narration) and with the use of local color.

An illuminating comparison with a later writer measures the limitations of Stoddard's feminism: Gilman's "The Yellow Wall-Paper" also features a doctor's prescription for an unhappy marriage but Gilman undercuts the prescription, which embodies patriarchal values, whereas Stoddard seemingly affirms the effectiveness of the prescription and therefore the desirability of the patriarchal institution of marriage.

Questions for Reading and Discussion/ Approaches to Writing

1. What is the effect of the first-person narration?
2. In what ways does the narrator change during the course of the story?
3. What do you make of the ending? Does it weaken the story? Does it implicitly affirm male violence?

Harriet E. Wilson (c. 1808–1870)

Contributing Editor: Marilyn Richardson [p. 2628]

Classroom Issues and Strategies

Students usually have little sense of the historical period. Some discussion of the reality of free blacks, both in the North and in the South, is useful, along with some background on the abolitionist movement and its literature.

Major Themes, Historical Perspectives, and Personal Issues

While antislavery writers agreed about the urgent need to abolish slavery, there was considerable difference of opinion on the role emancipated blacks might be expected/allowed to play in American society. This book points the finger at the so-called liberal North where, even during the height of the abolitionist period, profound issues of caste and class, as well as overt racism, prefigure struggles to come during Reconstruction and up to the present day.

To date, there is only one edition of *Our Nig* readily available. Gates, as editor, has provided an extensive discussion of these issues in his introductory essay.

Bibliography

Andrews, *Sisters of the Spirit*, Richardson, *Maria W. Stewart*, Harper, *Iola Leroy*, Jacobs, *Incidents in the Life of a Slave Girl*, all give excellent insight into black women's nineteenth-century experience, North and South. Three excellent anthologies, Lerner, *Black Women in White America*, Loewenbert and Bogin, *Black Women in 19th Century American Life*, and Sterling, *We Are Your Sisters*, all provide background information that could be useful with this text.

The Emergence of American Poetic Voices

[p. 2638]

Native American Oral Poetry

Contributing Editor: Andrew O. Wiget [p. 2641]

Classroom Issues and Strategies

The Inuit and Aztec poetry requires the introduction of cultural background in order to understand some of its themes and imagery, but it is much more accessible than "Sayatasha's Night Chant." The Inuit and Aztec poetry, because it is expressive of individual emotional states, is much closer to the Western lyric poetry tradition, and therefore more readily apprehended by students than the long Zuni chant. "Sayatasha's Night Chant," on the other hand, is difficult for students for a number of reasons, which if properly addressed, make it a rich aesthetic experience.

First of all, it is absolutely essential to consciously and deliberately refer students to the notes, which supply important contextual information that is culture-specific and necessary for understanding the poems. This is less urgent in the more accessible poetry of the Aztecs and the Inuit, but it is demanded by texts such as "Sayatasha's Night Chant." Second, in the case of "Sayatasha's Night Chant," which I think will pose the most problems for students, one can enrich the cultural context of the poem by teaching it in conjunction with the Zuni "Talk Concerning The First Beginning." This origin story establishes some of the fundamental symbols that are expressive of the Zuni world view and some of the fundamental themes, so that if the students read "Sayatasha's Night Chant" following upon the emergence story, they can carry forward some of the cultural information acquired from reading the origin story to support their reading of "Sayatasha's Night Chant."

In discussing the Eskimo poetry, begin by inviting students to consider the physical environment in which the Inuit peoples live and the need for powerful social bonds in face of the overwhelming power and intimidating scale of the natural world of the arctic. By the same token, begin the discussion of Aztec poetry with a presentation of the scale and scope of the Aztec military, political, economic, and social achievement. In both cases the poetry then stands against this powerful cultural contextualization and effectively discloses its key themes sometimes by contrast to one's expectations (as in the case of Inuit poetry).

Students are very responsive to the Aztec and Inuit poetry. Its thematic concerns and its formal structure very much resemble their own prior experiences with Western poetic forms and themes. Consequently it's easy to stimulate discussion about attitudes toward death as in Aztec poetry, or feelings of alienation and man's place in the physical universe that occur in Inuit poetry. "Sayatasha's Night Chant" will be difficult, as students really do need to be walked through the poem. On the other hand, when such a reading is accomplished, students begin to ask all sorts of questions about how ritual functions in a society, including their own, and they begin to make connections between symbols of life and fertility that they find in Zuni poems and symbols of life and fertility that abound in the cultural lexicon of their own experience. Moreover, they readily confess that they understand the value of ritual, and the role of language in relationship to ritual, in ways that they had not before, when ritual in their minds was identified almost exclusively with the notion of routine. And they see real differences between Native American and Euroamerican views of nature.

Major Themes, Historical Perspectives, and Personal Issues

The Inuit and Aztec poetry is relatively accessible to students, who recognize in it some fundamental human emotions that have literary expression in Euroamerican traditions as well. The Inuit poetry is remarkable for its juxtaposition of human beings against the natural world. Nature is viewed as an enormous arena that dwarfs Man, who is continually struggling to secure his existence. Much of the Inuit view of nature corresponds rather well to the notions of the Romantic sublime. This is a nature that the Inuit face with a combination of awe, terror, and humility, as reflected in the Copper Eskimo "Song" and Uvavnuk's "Moved." On the other hand, the "Improvised Greeting" suggests that in the presence of such an overwhelming nature, which isolated people, the experience of social contact was a cause for tremendous joy. And yet as the "Widow's Song" suggests, alienation from one's community left one isolated and trapped in one's self. (Inuit poetry can be very reflective.) Orpingalik's song speaks to a loss of competence and power in one's old age that undermines one's sense of accomplishment and identity. A good poem to read to workaholics, whose identity rests in their work!

Aztecs understood the act of creating poetry as a way of achieving immortality. Because they experienced life as passing away, they looked to create an ideal world through the images articulated in their poetry. In this they felt they were imitating their principal deity, Omeoteotl, the creator of the universe. This being achieved immortality through creativity, and the Aztec poets sought to do the same.

Significant Form, Style, or Artistic Conventions

Students need some initial help in understanding images like flowers in Aztec poetry. They might also need assistance in seeing some of the potent juxtapositions that occur in the Inuit poetry. For example, the despairing woman in the "Widow's Song" who holds an amulet (a token of religious faith) in her hands while she stares angrily at the Northern Lights, which taunt her with their beauty and promise.

In the case of "Sayatasha's Night Chant" there is much ritual language and students need help in working through the characters and in understanding the ritual actions that are a key to the poem. The notes should be helpful in this regard, especially notes one, three, and eight. Ritual poetry is very formulaic and repetitive. Students are frequently frustrated by repetition and aggravated by the apparent lack of spontaneity and the stiltedness of the language. It is useful to point out to students that in serious religious settings spontaneity is not valued, not only at Zuni but in ritual contexts throughout the world, including the Euroamerican cultures.

It's also good to develop with them some understandings of the importance of key symbols like water and corn as symbols for life. Water, especially, is something that they ought to be able to relate to.

Original Audience

I make it a point to try to reconstruct the cultural context of the poem's origin in order to recover for the students the aesthetic force that these poems must have had for their original hearers. I remind them of the terrible and frightening confrontation that man has with the physical environment in the arctic and how people cling to each other under such circumstances. Understanding the relationship between the physical and the social worlds in Inuit life, I think, is a necessary precondition for understanding the poetry.

Comparisons, Contrasts, Connections

The Aztec and Inuit poetry compare well in theme and form to British and American Romantic lyric poetry. Certainly the Aztec poetry compares well with Western poetry in the elegaic tradition. The Inuit and Aztec poems also offer opportunities for comparing and contrasting the role of poetry as a vehicle for self-expression and for the creation of individual identity, another important romantic theme. Certainly one can contrast "Sayatasha's Night Chant," in which the individual identity of the speaker of the poem is totally submerged in his ritual role or persona, with the "I" of the Inuit and Aztec poetry that reflects the personal identity of the poet/subject.

Questions for Reading and Discussion/ Approaches to Writing

1. I would draw students' attention in the Eskimo poetry to the place of man in the physical universe and the relationship of the individual to society, and in the Aztec poetry, to the images of flowers and to the function of poetry. In "Sayatasha's Night Chant" I would focus on important images such as cornmeal and invite them to make connections between symbols that they discover in "Sayatasha's Night Chant" and their antecedents in the Zuni origin myth, "Talk Concerning the First Beginning."
2. Aside from obvious thematic papers, focused around topics such as nature, death, ritual, and so on, I would invite them to write on broader topics such as the role of poetry in these societies and to compare how poetry functions in these societies with the ways in which poetry has functioned in the Western tradition.

Bibliography

Bunzel, Ruth. "Zuni Ritual Poetry." *47th Annual Report of the Bureau of American Ethnology* (1930):611–835.

Geertz, Clifford. "Religion as a Cultural System." In *The Interpretation of Cultures*. New York: Basic Books, 1973.

Leon-Portilla, Miguel. *Pre-Columbian Literatures of Mexico*. Norman: Univ. of Oklahoma Press, 1969.

Lowenstein, Tom, trans. "Introduction," *Eskimo Poems From Canada And Greenland*. Pittsburgh: University of Pittsburgh Press, 1973.

Wiget, Andrew. "Aztec Lyrics: Poetry in a World of Continually Perishing Flowers." *Latin American Indian Literatures*, 4 (1980): 1–1 1.

——. "Oratory and Oral Poetry." In *Native American Literature*. Boston: Twayne, 1985.

——. "Sayatasha's Night Chant: A Literary Textual Analysis of a Zuni Ritual Poem," *American Indian Culture and Research Journal* 4 (1989): 99–140.

Songs and Ballads

Contributing Editor: Paul Lauter [p. 2671]

Classroom Issues and Strategies

Students immediately ask, "Is it literature?" The songs raise all of the issues about "popular culture," including their "quality" as literary texts, their changeableness from version to version, their audience, their relationship to music. Can they be, should they be, studied in a literature classroom rather than in a music classroom?

It is useful to play versions of the songs and ballads—especially the spirituals. Surprisingly few students have ever actually heard such a song, and they often find them powerful. But this can be overdone—after all, the musical vocabulary is, on the whole, even more remote from student culture than are the texts. A less inhibited or more skilled instructor may wish to involve students in the singing; indeed, some may be able to lead a class, and that experience can pay off significantly when one gets to the question of audience.

It can be important to confront directly the question of what constitutes the domain of "literature." Who decides what is included there? And on what basis? If these texts are, as some are, extraordinarily simple, does that remove them from what we think of as significant literature? Are questions of audience and function involved? What are—and have been—the functions of such songs? Who sings them, and when, and why? Are these significant literary questions?

Another issue best confronted directly is the question of the mutability of such songs. Is it a good thing or a bad thing that people change them?

Major Themes, Historical Perspectives, and Personal Issues

Obviously, the spirituals draw deeply on the Bible, especially the Old Testament. Many are built on a fundamental analogy between black slaves and the Hebrews. They can also be read ethnographically, for they express a good deal about the character and functions of religion and other forms of culture in the slave period.

Both the songs of black and white communities interestingly focus on everyday experiences of work, courting, religion (as well as on eschatological visions).

Significant Form, Style, or Artistic Conventions

The headnote points to a number of formal features, like refrains and repetitions, qualities of language, characteristic patterns of imagery, the ways in which songs are taken up, reframed, renewed. It can be useful to discuss how these songs are similar to and different from more "formal" poetry and also from one another.

Original Audience

The most interesting issue may be how, in the origins of such songs, the distinction between creator/singer and audience did not, on the whole, exist. The end of the Introduction to the period considers that issue. Raising this problem allows a class to explore the difference between culture as a commodity produced by persons other than oneself, and culture as an integral part of human life, serving a variety of functions, including discharging grief, inspiring hope, and offering opportunities, in the *singing*, for physical and psychological expression. The song, Bernice Reagon has pointed out, is only the vehicle or perhaps excuse for the singing.

Comparisons, Contrasts, Connections

This unit is designed to allow, indeed, encourage, comparisons between varieties of poetic texts from very different cultures.

Questions for Reading and Discussion/ Approaches to Writing

1. (a) How are these songs similar to/different from more formal kinds of poetry?

   (b) What patterns of imagery, features of language, do you notice?

   (c) What are the structural features common to some or all of these songs?

2. (a) Make up an additional verse to . . . . (Useful since it helps students see the formal features of a text, and also to overcome their wariness of "poetry.")

   (b) Should such songs (or other forms of popular culture) be taught in literature courses?

Bibliography

The first chapter of Lawrence Levine's *Black Culture and Black Consciousness* offers important insights about the functions and structure of spirituals.

William Cullen Bryant (1794–1878)

Contributing Editor: Allison Heisch [p. 2692]

Classroom Issues and Strategies

Most of the Bryant selections in the anthology are ruminative poems about the nature of life and the nature of nature. Some students really like this sort of thing, but substantial numbers are allergic to it.

The most effective strategy I have found is to provide visual backup in the form of a Hudson River School slide show. A fancy version would parallel English Romantic poets (esp. Gray, Cowper, and Wordsworth) and painters (e.g., Constable and Turner).

Bryant is a fine example of a writer who was not only popular but famous in his day. He can be used to open a discussion of the social and historical implications of such popularity (why it comes and why it goes), the essentially political character of anthologies (yes, even this one), and the idea of "fame" in connection with contemporary poets and poetry.

For students (and they are many) who do not naturally respond to Bryant, the questions generally run to "Why are we reading this?" Or, more decorously, "Why was he so popular?" Yet, they do respond to him as an example of how the American high culture invented itself. In an altogether different vein, the personal philosophy expressed in "Thanatopsis" has some enduring appeal.

Major Themes, Historical Perspectives, and Personal Issues

Bryant is very useful as a means of demonstrating the imitative mode through which New Englanders of an intellectual bent sought to establish an acceptable American literary voice. This is easily demonstrated by pairing his poems with comparable English productions. He can also be linked to the Transcendentalists—though with great caution, since much more is going on.

Significant Form, Style, or Artistic Conventions

Again, he should be shown in connection with his English models. It's useful to point out the self-conscious regularity of these poems both in connection with their particularly derivative subject matter and in contrast with the form and subjects of those contemporary poems and songs (well represented in this anthology) that were not informed by the dominant English literary culture

Original Audience

I have usually talked about Bryant's audience in connection with the expansion of publishing in nineteenth-century America—especially magazines and newspapers. Ordinarily, students have no idea what a nineteenth-century newspaper would have looked like or contained. They never expect them to contain poetry. To demonstrate the probably contemporary audience, I have found it useful to collect and read commercially-produced greeting cards.

Comparisons, Contrasts, Connections

Freneau's "The House of Night" may be read with "Thanatopsis" to demonstrate both the imitation of dominant English poetic forms and transatlantic lag-time in creating them for American audiences. Obviously, Bryant may be read with Emerson and Thoreau as a pre- or proto-Transcendentalist. It is interesting to contrast Bryant's earnest view of nature with Emily Dickinson's ironic one. Bryant's poem on Abraham Lincoln against Whitman's ("When Lilacs Last . . . Bloom'd") makes a memorable contrast between Anglophile American poetry and poetry with a genuine American accent.

Questions for Reading and Discussion/ Approaches to Writing

1. (a) Based upon what you can glean from these poems, what sort of religious and philosophical outlook does this writer have?
   (b) Compare the view of nature in poems such as "To a Water-fowl" and "The Yellow Violet" with that in "The Prairie."
2. Bryant's "Thanatopsis" is often read as a proto-Transcendentalist poem; yet it was discovered and rushed to publication by Bryant's father, who by all accounts was a Calvinist. Some options:
   (a) Provide a Calvinist "reading" of "Thanatopsis."
   (b) Locate, compare, and explain potentially "Transcendental" and "Calvinist" elements in the poem.
   (c) Argue that it's one or the other (very artificial, but effective).

Bibliography

Brown, Charles H. *William Cullen Bryant*. Scribner, 1971.

Henry Wadsworth Longfellow (1807–1882)

Contributing Editor: Allison Heisch [p. 2702]

Classroom Issues and Strategies

If students have encountered Longfellow before taking a college course, the poems they know are not in this anthology: *Evangeline, The Song of Hiawatha, The Courtship of Miles Standish*. The Longfellow of this anthology is our late twentieth-century "revisionist" Longfellow, and except in poems such as "A Psalm of Life," he is almost unrecognizable as a writer who might have written those famous poems. If students have not actually read Longfellow, but merely heard of him (the typical case), they want to know why he's so famous.

Longfellow *is* accessible, and the fact is that in almost any class there will be students who adore "A Psalm of Life" and students who cannot stand it. Such a division, of course, presents the teacher with an ideal point of departure.

Although Longfellow is now very unfashionable, he is nevertheless an excellent vehicle for teaching about poetry either to the unlimited or the turned-off. Oddly enough, students in general respond to the story of his life almost more readily than to his poetry. That, therefore, is a good place to begin. They often ask about his fame. Some respond very positively to his sentimentalism, which can be tricky.

Major Themes, Historical Perspectives, and Personal Issues

Longfellow's themes in the poems in this collection are nearly indistinguishable from those of his contemporaries in England. It's useful to show him, therefore, as an example of the branch of American literature that created itself in admiring imitation of English literature. He is also that rare thing, a genuine celebrity of a poet, whose fame has not subsided and whose stature has shrunk accordingly. Many of the poems we now admire most are from his later years, and conform better to modern taste than the poems for which he was famous in his lifetime. Thus, he can be used as a good example of the ways in which changing literary tastes alter literary reputations.

Significant Form, Style, or Artistic Conventions

Longfellow's poems are not only accessible in their meaning, but they are also highly regular in their form. It is very simple to teach metrics with Longfellow because he provides easy and memorable examples of so many metrical schemes. These can be presented in connection with Longfellow's personal history, for he is of course an academic poet, and as such a poet writing often self-consciously from a learned perspective. Thus, nothing with him seems wholly spontaneous or accidental.

Original Audience

Two points are easy and convenient where audience is concerned: First, the fact that Longfellow was in his time as popular as a rock singer might be in ours. Second, the fact that while he was writing for an audience descended from transplanted Englishmen, he was nevertheless trying to create for them an American poetry crafted from "native" materials, thereby making chauvinist myth. Admittedly, it's hard to get to that point from the selections in the present anthology, but since "The Jewish Cemetery at Newport" was originally part of *The Courtship of Miles Standish*, a way *can* be found.

Comparisons, Contrasts, Connections

There are many directions to travel here: First, locate Longfellow in New England with Emerson and the Transcendentalists; second, locate him as a (necessary?) predecessor to Whitman, and then compare their views of America; third, set his view of life and nature against that of native poets.

Questions for Reading and Discussion/ Approaches to Writing

1. (a)   To whom is he writing? What is his message?
   (b)   Translate "A Psalm of Life" *literally* and say whether you agree or disagree.
   (c)   What are Longfellow's favorite words?
2. How has Longfellow changed or maintained his essential view of life between "A Psalm of Life" and "Aftermath"?

Bibliography

Because his poetry is more impressive taken together than individually analyzed, Longfellow has commanded whole books more often than single articles.

Wagenknecht, Edward. *Henry Wadsworth Longfellow*. New York: Ungar, 1986.

Walt Whitman (1819–1892)

Contributing Editor: Betsy Eikkila [p. 2709]

Classroom Issues and Strategies

I use the 1855 versions of "Song of Myself" and "The Sleepers" because I think these poems represent Whitman at his unrevised best. I begin with a biographical introduction, stressing Whitman's active engagement as radical democrat and party journalist in the major political conflicts of pre-Civil War America. The inscription poem "One's-Self I Sing" and his vision of the poet balanced between pride and sympathy in the 1855 Preface serve as a good introduction to "Song of Myself." I usually begin by asking the students to talk about Whitman's free verse technique. What ordering devices does he use in the opening lines to achieve his poetic design: these include repetition, biblical parallelism, rhythmic recurrence, assonance, and consonance.

Section 15 is a good illustration of the ways Whitman's catalog technique serves as a democratizing device, inscribing the pattern of many and one. By basing his verse in the single, end-stopped line at the same time that he fuses this line—through various linking devices—with the larger structure of the whole, Whitman weaves an overall pattern of unity in diversity. This pattern of many and one—the *e pluribus unum* that was the revolutionary seal of the American republic—is the overarching figure of *Leaves of Grass*.

I present "Song of Myself" as a drama of democratic identity in which the poet seeks to balance and reconcile major conflicts in the body politic of America: the conflict between "separate person" and "en masse," individualism and equality, liberty and union, the South and the North, the farm and the city, labor and capital, black and white, female and male, religion and science. One can discuss any of the individual sections of the poem in relation to this conflict. Moments of particular conflict and crisis occur in sections 28 and 38. I ask the students to discuss the specific nature of the crisis in each of these sections. Both involve a loss of balance.

In section 28, the protatonist loses bodily balance as he is swept away by an erotic, masturbatory urge. Ask the students to think about why a masturbation fantasy occurs in a poem about democracy. Ask them to think about why the masturbatory fit is represented in the language of political insurrection? These questions lead to interesting observations about the relation between political power and power over the body. Masturbation is, in effect, the political ground on which Whitman tests the theory of democracy. Within the democratic economy of his poem, the turbulence of the body, like the turbulence of the masses, is part of a natural regenerative order.

If section 28 involves a loss of bodily balance, section 38 involves a loss of self in empathetic identification with others. In discussing the crisis in section 38, ask the students what Whitman means by the lines: "I find myself on the verge of a usual mistake"? This will usually lead back to the end of section 3, where the poet begins identifying with scenes of suffering, carnage, and death. Some of these scenes are linked with the nation's history: the hounded slave, the Texas war, the American Revolution. The poet appears to be on the verge of losing faith in the divine potency of the individual and the regenerative pattern of the whole. He resolves the crisis by remembering the divinity of Christ as a living power existing within rather than outside of every individual.

The resolution of this crisis leads to the emergence of the divinely empowered poet who presides over the final passages of the poem, declaring his ultimate faith in the "form, union, plan" of the universe. Here you might want to discuss the relation between this poetic affirmation of democratic faith and union and the fact of an American Union that was in the throes of dissolution.

Since Whitman's poetic development corresponds with stages in his own and the nation's history, a chronological presentation works well in the classroom. After discussing "Song of Myself," you might want to discuss other 1855 poems such as "The Sleepers" and "There Was a Child Went Forth." "The Sleepers," which was toned down in later versions, represents in both its form and its content the half-formed, erotically charged, and anxiety ridden fantasies of the dream state. The poem anticipates Freud's "unconscious" and the literary experiments of the surrealists. But the poem is revolutionary not only in its psychosexual dimension. The poet also descends into a kind of political unconscious of the nation, dredging up images of regeneration through violence associated with Washington and the battle for American independence, the slave as black Lucifer, and the Indian squaw.

If you have time to do later work by Whitman, the 1860 poems might be grouped together since they correspond with a period of both personal and national crisis. This crisis is most effectively represented in "As I Ebb'd with the Ocean of Life"; within the context of *Leaves of Grass*, "Out of the Cradle Endlessly Rocking" appears to respond to this crisis. Ask the students to comment on the differences between the "amative" poems of *Children of Adam* and the "adhesive" poems of *Calamus*. This will lead to a discussion of Whitman's sexual politics.

Women students have particularly strong and mixed reactions to "A Woman Waits for Me": they are attracted by Whitman's celebration of an erotically charged female body, yet are repelled by the fact that she seems rhetorically prone. The students will usually note that Whitman's poems to men seem more immediate and personal than the poems of *Children of Adam*. "In Paths Untrodden" reflects Whitman's split at this time between the public culture of democracy and his desire to tell secrets, to "come out" poetically by naming his hitherto unspeakable passion for men. You might want to remind the students that the term "homosexual" did not yet exist, and thus Whitman was breaking the path toward a language of male love. His invention is particularly evident in "When I Heard at the Close of the Day," where the power and tenderness of his feelings for his lover are linked with the rhythms of a

completely natural order. The "confessional" note in the poems anticipates the later work of Allen Ginsberg, Robert Lowell, and Sylvia Plath.
Ask the students to reflect on why it was the poems of *Children of Adam*
and not *Calamus* that most shocked the literary establishment. It was
really not until Allen Ginsberg wrote his comic tribute to Whitman, "In a
Supermarket in California," that Whitman, the homosexual poet, came
fully out of the closet—at least in America.

I usually begin discussion of the war poems by asking how the
experience of fratricidal war might affect Whitman as the poet of
national union. This will lead to reflections on the tragedy of the Civil
War. The poems of *Drum-Taps*—which proceed from militant exulta-
tion, to the actual experience of war, to demobilization and
reconciliation—might be read as an attempt to place the butchery of the
war within a poetic and ultimately regenerative design. Ask the students
to compare Whitman's war poems with his earlier poems. They are at
once more formally controlled and more realistic—stylistic changes that
are linked with the war context. "A March in the Ranks Hard-Prest, and
the Road Unknown" and "The Artilleryman's Vision" are proto-modern
poems in which the individual appears as an actor in a drama of history
he no longer understands nor controls. Whitman's ambivalence about
black emancipation is evident in "Ethiopia Saluting the Colors." "Vigil
Strange I Kept on the Field One Night" and "As I Lay with My Head in
Your Lap Camerado" are particularly effective in suggesting the ways
the wartime context of male bonding and comradeship gave Whitman a
legitimate language and social frame within which to express his love for
men.

In discussing Whitman's famous elegy on the death of President
Lincoln, it is interesting to begin by asking what remains unsaid in the
poem. For one thing, Lincoln is never named as the subject within the
context of the poem; his death becomes representative of all the war
dead. By placing Lincoln's death within a timeless regenerative order of
nature, Whitman's "Lilacs" also "covers over" the fact of Lincoln's unnatural and violent assassination. Although the vision of battle in section
15 is often passed over in critical considerations of the poem, this bloody
sight of "battle-corpses" and the "debris" of war is, I believe, the
unspeakable honor and real subject of the poem.

Democratic Vistas (1871) might be read either as an introduction to
or a conclusion to the study of Whitman. In the essay, he struggles with
the central tensions and paradoxes of American, New-World experience.
These conflicts intensify and are more urgently addressed in the post-
Civil War period as the unleashed force of market capitalism and the
dynamic of modem civilization appear to spin out of control. "Who bri-
dles Leviathan?" Whitman asks in *Democratic Vistas*. It is a fitting ques-

tion with which to conclude the study of Whitman and to begin the study of the modern world.

Emily Dickinson (1830–1886)

Contributing Editors: Peggy McIntosh and Ellen Louise Hart [p. 2838]

Classroom Issues and Strategies

Students may have problems with the appearance of the poems—with the fact that they are without titles; that they are often short and compact, compressed; that the dash is so often used in the place of traditional punctuation. Some students will be put off by the grammatical elisions and ellipses, and some by the fact that the poems often do not quickly display a central, controlling metaphor or an easily identifiable narrative theme. Students who are already intimidated by poetry may find the poems difficult and unyielding. Some, however, may find Dickinson's brevity and conciseness startling and enjoyable. Those who have false notions that everything in poetry means or symbolizes something else, and that the reader must crack the code and come up with a "solution" to each poem's meaning, will be frustrated by Dickinson or will read the poems with atrocious insensitivity. Dickinson's work requires intense concentration, imagination, and unusually high tolerance for ambiguity.

One final problem lies with the biography and concerns students' tendency to dismiss Dickinson as an "old maid" or as a woman who "missed out on life" by not marrying. One student asked, "Why didn't she just move to Boston and get a job?" Students want to know about Dickinson's life and loves, her personal relationships with both men and women; they are curious about why she chose not to publish; they are interested in her religious/spiritual life, her faith, and her belief in immortality. They want to know what the dilemmas of her life were, as they manifested themselves in her writing: What her psychic states were, what tormented her, what she mourned, what drove her close to madness, why she was fascinated with death and dying. Addressing these questions allows the opportunity to discuss the oversimplifying and stereotyping that results from ignorance of social history as well as insistence on heterosexism.

Students should be prepared for the poems by being encouraged to speculate. An instructor can invite students to explore each poem as an experiment, and to ease into the poetry, understanding that Dickinson was a poet who truly "questioned authority" and whose work defies authoritative readings. All of her difficulties as listed above can be seen as connected with her radically original imagination.

Students can be directed toward approaching these poems with "lexicon" in hand, as Dickinson wrote them. Here is the perfect opportunity for an exercise with the OED. Students can be asked to make a list as they read of words that begin to seem to them particularly Dickinsonian, "Circumference," for example. They can also list characteristic phrases or images. The selection of poems can be parceled out in certain groupings in which linked images, emotions, or descriptions of natural phenomena are easily recognizable.

Students can be assigned to write journals in which they record their first impressions and discoveries, as well as later commentary on poems and further stages of interpretation. Asking people to read poems out loud will help them to learn to hear the poet's voice and to tune their ears to her rhymes, rhythms, and syntax. Above all, the instructor should not pretend assurance about Dickinson's meanings and intentions.

It works well to have students make a selection of poems on a theme or image cluster, and then work in groups with the selected poems, afterwards presenting their readings. Such group work can create flexibility while giving students confidence in their own perceptions.

Another presentation that is very useful is the kind of demonstration Susan Howe gives and which some other teachers now use. Make a copy of a Thomas Johnson version of a poem and then make a typed transcription of the same poem using Franklin's *Manuscript Books*. This can lead to interesting discussions of editing questions involved with Dickinson: how to represent the line breaks and the punctuation; how to render these unpublished poems in print.

Major Themes, Historical Perspectives, and Personal Issues

Students need to know something about Dickinson's life, her schooling, religious upbringing and subsequent rebellion, her family members, and the close friends who became the audience for her poems. (Much of this is outlined in the headnote.) They will be helped by having some historical sense of women and men in nineteenth-century New England. They need information on women's habits of reading and writing, on friendships among women, religious revivalism, and life in a small college town like Amherst. Awareness of class, class-consciousness, and social customs for families like the Dickinsons and their circle of friends will help prevent questions like the one cited above on why Dickinson didn't just move and "go for it" in a city. Students should be discouraged from discussing the poems as "feminine" or as demonstrating "the woman's point of view."

A discussion of homophobia is necessary. Here the headnote should be helpful. The love poems are not exclusively heterosexual. Students should be encouraged to examine the erotics of this poetry without being limited to conventional notions of gender. Dickinson uses a variety of voices in these poems, writing as a child (often a boy), a wife-to-be, a woman rejected, and as a voice of authority which we often associate with maleness. These voices or roles or "poses," as they are sometimes called, need to be identified and examined. Here are the multiplicities of self. Do we need to reconcile these voices? What happens when we don't? Students may reflect on or write about multiplicities of experience, perspective, and voice in themselves.

Significant Form, Style, or Artistic Conventions

Information should be provided about other American and British writers publishing at this time, those whom Dickinson read, those especially popular at the time but not as well known, as well as those still recognized: Emerson, Longfellow, Stowe, Helen Hunt Jackson, Elizabeth Barrett Browning, George Eliot, Dickens.

Dickinson's poetry is very dissimilar to poetry being published at the same time. Attention needs to be drawn to this fact and to the originality, the intentional and consistent innovativeness, of her style. Questions of style can also lead to observations concerning the thin line between poetry and prose in Dickinson's letters.

Students need to know about the publishing and editing history of the poems, to understand how Dickinson worked—collecting poems into packets, identifying words for revision, sending poems to various recipients, and apparently avoiding publication during her lifetime. There is also the question of the editing: What did a given poem look like when early editors published it, and when Thomas Johnson published the same poem in the variorum edition? (Students should be made familiar with Thomas Johnson's variorum as well as Ralph Franklin's *Manuscript Books of Emily Dickinson*.) What did the variorum edition of the poems bring to Dickinson scholarship? What was available before? What has F. W. Franklin's publication of the manuscript books meant? And what about Susan Howe's argument that Dickinson's original line breaks must be honored? Some students may wish to take up the question of how to represent in type Dickinson's marks of punctuation.

Original Audience

Students should look at Franklin (or photocopies of pages from Franklin) to see how the "packets" or "fascicles" looked. Reading poems sent in letters or with letters is a way of considering audiences, both Dickinson's immediate audience and her writing for posterity. The variorum edition identifies poems sent in letters; the three volumes of *Letters* list many enclosed poems.

Comparisons, Contrasts, Connections

Dickinson can be read with her contemporaries, the American and British writers of her time. She may also be read in the context of twentieth-century New England writers, Robert Frost and Robert Lowell, for example, or with current New England women writers, May Sarton and Maxine Kumin, for example. A regional sense is a strong thread in Dickinson's writing. She may be read in the context of experiments in modernism, in relation to e. e. cummings, for example. Dickinson also fits within a continuum of American women poets from Anne Bradstreet and Phillis Wheatley through Amy Lowell, Gertrude Stein, Edna St. Vincent Millay, H. D., Marianne Moore, Sylvia Plath, Anne Sexton, Adrienne Rich, Audre Lorde, and Judy Grahn. (This, of course, is only one selection, which represents many of the best-known American writers. There are other such lists.)

Questions for Reading and Discussion/ Approaches to Writing

Cumbersome term papers "arguing" a single thesis on Dickinson are usually quite out of tune with her own multifaceted sensibility and intelligence. Reading a poem as a statement of a creed, i.e., as a "proof" that Dickinson believed this or that, is usually fatal to common sense. We suggest that the following 15 writing assignments on Dickinson will suit a variety of students with a variety of learning styles.

1. All her life, Emily Dickinson seems to have felt she was encumbered by structures that did not fit her, whether structures of religion, belief, value, language, thought, manners, or institutions. If you share her feeling, give some examples of her sense of the problem and then some examples of your own sense of it, in your life.

2. 1862, a year in which Dickinson wrote more than 300 poems, seems to have been a year of great emotional intensity for her. Drawing on poems from 1862 given in this anthology, trace some recurrent themes or designs in the poems of that year.

3. Kathleen Raine has written: "For the poet when he begins to write there is no poem, in the sense of a construction of words; and the concentration of the mind is upon something else, that precedes words, and by which the words, as they are written, must constantly be checked and rectified."

   If this quotation rings true for you, choose one or more poems and discuss the "something else" and the process by which Dickinson apparently revised toward it, using Johnson's three-volume edition, which shows all known revisions.

4. You are Emily Dickinson. An acquaintance who does not know you very well has just suggested that the time you spend alone must feel somewhat empty. Write a fragment of a letter or a poem in which you respond as you think she might.

5. Many of Dickinson's poems are not so much about ideas or themes, as about the process of seeing or coming to see, or guess, or know. Trace the *elements of process* in one or more poems; then imitate the sense of process in a passage of poetry or prose of your own.

6. What do you appreciate about Emily Dickinson, and what do you think she hoped readers would appreciate about her?

7. Read Jay Leyda's collection of documents about Emily Dickinson's year of college in *The Years and Hours of Emily Dickinson*, and read Dickinson's letters from her year away. Compare your own college experience with hers. Considering both the pressures on you and the pleasures you experience, how do you differ from or resemble her?

8. Dickinson's poems have both authority and obliqueness, as suggested in her line "Tell all the Truth but tell it slant." Discuss examples of Dickinson's techniques of slantwise style and some of their effects on you as reader.

9. Reading Dickinson is a personal matter, and readers' perceptions of her change continually. On each of three different days, begin an essay entitled "On Reading Emily Dickinson." Do not work for consistency, but rather for a fresh account of your perception on each day.

10. For many English and American poets, moments of "seeing" accurately have often been moments of affirmation. For Dickinson, they were often moments of pain. Discuss any aspects of the poems on pain that interest you, shedding light, if possible, on her words "A nearness to Tremendousness/An Agony Procures. . . ."

11. Richard Wilbur wrote:

"At some point Emily Dickinson sent her whole Calvinist vocabulary into exile, telling it not to come back until it would subserve her own sense of things. . . . Of course, that is not a true story, but it is a way of saying what I find most remarkable in Emily Dickinson. She inherited a great and overbearing vocabulary which, had she used it submissively, would have forced her to express an established theology and psychology. But she would not let that vocabulary write her poems for her."

Analyze some of the religious poems which seem to you unorthodox or surprising, and then write a short piece of your own, in poetry or prose, in which you use the vocabulary of a religious tradition in an unusual way that "subserves your own sense of things."

12. Write four alternative first paragraphs to a paper entitled "Emily Dickinson."

13. Imagine a conversation between Emily Dickinson and any one of the other women writers read for this course. What might they have to talk about? Add a third woman (perhaps yourself) to the conversation if you like. Draw on all the sources of evidence that you have.

14. Dickinson used traditional hymn meter, but her poems are not like traditional hymns. Choose the words to any hymn you know, and rewrite them until they sound as much like Dickinson as possible. You may virtually have to abandon the original hymn.

15. Emily Dickinson's first editors thought they were doing her a favor by changing certain words, repunctuating her poetry, and standardizing the line breaks. Using the three-volume Johnson edition and the Franklin manuscript books, judge for yourself, in the case of two or three poems in which changes were made.

Bibliography

See the bibliography in the headnote to the anthology selection. Also:

Howe, Susan. "Women and Their Effect in the Distance." In *Ironwood* 28, "Dickinson/Spicer: A Special Issue." Vol. 4, no. 2 (Fall 1986): 58–91.

Leyda, Jay. *The Years and Hours of Emily Dickinson.* 2 vols. New Haven: Yale Univ. Press, 1960.

McNeil, Helen. *Emily Dickinson*. New York: Virago/Pantheon Pioneers, 1986. This is a short, readable critical biography of Dickinson that is informed by the theories of feminism as well as deconstruction. This text talks of Dickinson in current critical language. As a biography, it is more convenient for the teacher with little time than sifting through Sewall's book. McNeil uses Sewall's research for the text, so it is very helpful. We recommend a run through the entire text of 181 pages; in a pinch the introduction and the first two chapters, "Dickinson and Knowledge" and "Dickinson and Difference" provide a starting place.

Miller, Christanne. *Emily Dickinson: A Poet's Grammar*. Cambridge: Harvard Univ. Press, 1987. Chapter 2: "A Grammar."

Morris, Adalaide. " 'The Love of Thee—a Prism Be': Men and Women in the Love Poetry of Emily Dickinson." In *Feminist Critics Read Emily Dickinson*, edited by Suzanne Juhasz. Indiana Univ. Press, 1983.

Rich, Adrienne. "Vesuvius at Home: The Power of Emily Dickinson." In *On Lies, Secrets, and Silence: Selected Prose 1966–1978*. New York: Norton, 1979.

Wilbur, Richard. "Sumptuous Destitution." In *Emily Dickinson, a Collection of Critical Essays*. Englewood Cliffs, N.J.: Prentice Hall, 1963.

Late
Nineteenth
Century

1865–1910

The Development of Women's Narratives

[p. 34]

Julia A. J. Foote (1823–1900)

Contributing Editor: William L. Andrews *[p. 35]*

Classroom Issues and Strategies

One of the primary problems in teaching Julia Foote is her intensely religious view of life as contrasted to the secularism of today's students. Students often wonder whether she was self-deceived in thinking herself authorized by the Holy Spirit to assert her will over those of the general mass of people in her church. It is important, therefore, to emphasize the relationship of Foote's religious world-view to her feminism. She supports her feminism by citing biblical precedent.

Major Themes, Historical Perspectives, and Personal Issues

Major themes include Foote's search for her authentic self, the black woman's search for power and voice in male-dominated religious institutions.

Significant Form, Style, or Artistic Conventions

How does Foote turn a straightforward narrative of her life into an argument for Christianity, feminism, and holiness?

Original Audience

I stress to the students that Foote is addressing someone in particular—ask them how they can identify who this is?

Comparisons, Contrasts, Connections

Interesting comparisons can be made with slave narrators like Frederick Douglass, since Foote and Douglass are both concerned with affirming their sense of a spirit within that owes its allegiance only to transcendent ideals.

Bibliography

Andrews, William L. ed. *Sisters of the Spirit: Three Black Women's Autobiographies of the Nineteenth Century.* Bloomington: Indiana Univ. Press, 1986. Discusses and annotates Foote's entire autobiography.

Rebecca Harding Davis (1831–1910)

Contributing Editor: Judith Roman [p. 41]

Classroom Issues and Strategies

Problems in teaching Davis include: dialect, allusions, confusing dialogue, hard-to-identify speakers, vague frame story, religious solution, and the juxtaposition of sentimental language with religiosity and realism. To address these problems consider the following:

1. Explain the dialect (see the footnotes).
2. Try to ignore the allusions; most are not important to the heart of meaning.
3. The names of characters, their jobs, the speakers, and their roles need to be clarified.

   Kirby, son of Kirby the mill owner—He is aware of the problems of the workers but sees them as insoluble; he takes the attitude of Pontius Pilate.

   Dr. May, a town physician—He is idealistic, sympathetic to the workers, but naive about reality and thus unintentionally cruel to Hugh.

   "Captain"—The reporter for the city paper.

   Mitchell, Kirby's intellectual brother-in-law, visitor to the South—He is cold, cynically socialistic.

4. Discuss frame story. Careful readers will find inconsistencies in the frame narratives that explain the narrator's perspective. Early in the story, the narrator "happens" to be in the house, apparently a visitor, but at the end of the story, the house and statue of the korl woman seem to belong to her. The story of the Wolfe family is said to be set thirty years in the past, so how did the narrator come to know it in such intimate detail? One of my students suggested that the narrator may be Janey, who has somehow risen above her environment and become a writer, a solution that is provocative but unsubstantiated by the text.

5. Show how Davis is ambiguous about religious solution. She espouses it, but her realistic picture of the problem is so vivid that it seems impossible to the reader that just Quaker kindness will solve the problems.

6. The swing between romanticism and realism is at the heart of this author.

Some students find this work depressing, but some like it. They can be asked to compare the situation of the poor today, especially the homeless and uneducated and today's immigrants, the Hispanics and other recent immigrant groups. Students can also be interested in a discussion of religion's role in comforting and/or silencing the poor.

Major Themes, Historical Perspectives, and Personal Issues

"Life in the Iron-Mills" is an accessible text that poses no major problems for students. It can be assigned and discussed in a single class meeting. Many students reject the "naturalistic" view inherent in the story that the characters could do little to help themselves. Contemporary students, educated to believe in the Alger myth, are eager to protest that Hugh could have lifted himself out of his poverty or moved to the city to become an artist.

Perhaps a greater problem may be students' unwillingness to see the feminist subtext of the story discovered by Tillie Olsen. The story deals quite openly with the life of an iron-worker; how, then, do we find in it the story of a thwarted "spinster" fiction writer? To make this reading credible, students will need to know something of Davis's life story (see headnote); the position of unmarried women in society (their dependence on their families, the lack of socially acceptable ways for a woman to earn a living, and the impossibility of living alone); and the incredible isolation of writers who lived anywhere in America outside of Boston and perhaps New York at this period. In the context of a traditional American literature survey, Davis's frustration could be related to that of writers like Cooper and Irving and the sense of the U.S. as an artistic wilderness that prevailed early in the century.

Significant Form, Style, or Artistic Conventions

As far as style, many would have found the work oppressively realistic and unpleasant. The Hawthornes used words like "gloomy" and even "mouldy" to describe Davis's writing.

Original Audience

The work was written for an upper-middle-class and upper-class audience, the readers of the *Atlantic* who were the elite of the country at the time. Many had familiarity with languages and the literary allusions in the work as well as intimate knowledge of the New Testament. Most were "liberal" Christians and although some were social reformers, virtually all believed the individual Christian had a responsibility to people like Hugh and Deb. The audience was highly receptive to Davis's message.

The difference in the audience now is that college students come from a broader spectrum of society. This has two effects: first, some of them may have worked in factories or come from blue-collar families and have experience closer to that of Hugh and Deb; second, the language of the text is apt to be more difficult for them. The excess of punctuation is an impediment. The sentimental exclamations probably differ little from some kinds of contemporary popular literature that students may have encountered.

Comparisons, Contrasts, Connections

Davis can be compared to:

1. Hawthorne, who had an influence on Davis, especially *House of the Seven Gables*; American Romantic literature
2. Dickens—sentimental realism
3. Popular literature of today
4. Novels of social criticism, such as *Uncle Tom's Cabin*; even later muckraking novels, such as *The Jungle*

Questions for Reading and Discussion/ Approaches to Writing

1. What is the purpose of the rhetorical questions posed by the author/narrator at various points in the story? Do they refer simply to the prospect of salvation for a man convicted of stealing, or do they imply the naturalistic view that Hugh's theft is excused by his unfortunate environment and heredity? Some students may recognize what is probably religious rhetoric in the questions: perhaps the teacher can simply encourage students to seek additional possibilities.

2. They could write a paper discussing the story as a transitional work between Romanticism and realism, using traits outlined in Richard Chase's *American Novel and Its Tradition*.

Bibliography

Tillie Olsen's essay in the Feminist Press edition is probably the most accessible place to go for additional information. It is highly personal but helpful.

Louisa May Alcott (1832–1888)

Contributing Editor: Elizabeth Keyser [p. 68]

Classroom Issues and Strategies

"Actress," the third chapter of Louisa May Alcott's novel *Work*, provides an ideal introduction to the author, for throughout her career Alcott was concerned with women's action—both on and off stage. Some of her heroines, like Jean Muir of *Behind a Mask* and Christie Devon of this selection, are professional actresses; more often her heroines, like those of Jane Austen, Charlotte Brontë, and Edith Wharton, appear in amateur theatricals or tableaux vivants. Even when off stage, most of her heroines strike poses and assume disguises, play roles and contrive scenes. On stage, ironically, they frequently express the inadmissible; off stage, the constrained and artificial nature of many women's lives.

Major Themes, Historical Perspectives, and Personal Issues

In "Actress" we find that the professional actress acquires a measure of power and independence but that the theater in many ways mirrors larger society. The chapter opens with Christie "resolving not to be a slave to anybody." And by becoming "Queen of the Amazons" she seems to have escaped that subservient condition. Further, in becoming an actress, Christie continues to declare her independence to Uncle Enos. At the thought of his disapproval "a delicious sense of freedom pervaded her soul, and the old defiant spirit seemed to rise up within her." Yet to obtain her role, Christie must first subject herself to dehumanizing scrutiny. In fact, her manager's examination reminds us of the slave market scenes in *Uncle Tom's Cabin*. And her Amazon troupe is described as "a most forlorn band of warriors . . . afraid to speak, lest they should infringe some rule." Far from being true Amazons, capable of terrorizing their male enemies, the show girls cower in terror of male authority. Christie recovers some of her enthusiasm on opening night, but the narrator tells us that her warlike trappings are "poor counterfeit." Even the "grand tableau," in which the martial queen stands triumphantly over the princess she has rescued, seems not so much a reversal of as a variation on the familiar male script.

Significant Form, Style, or Artistic Conventions

While a number of critics have recognized the importance of the drama in Alcott's life and art, not all of them view her use of it as consistently subversive. As early as 1943 Madeleine Stern, in "Louisa Alcott, Trouper," provided an account of Alcott's youthful dramatic activities and perceived that both her sensation and her autobiographical fiction was indebted to them. Since then Sharon O'Brien and Karen Halttunen (among others) have discussed Alcott's adolescent melodramas: O'Brien sees them foreshadowing Alcott's inability to reconcile "the energetic, assertive self represented by her tomboy period with an adult female identity"(365); Halttunen views them as subverting her father's use of allegorical drama "to control every aspect of self-expression" (237–238).

Comparisons, Contrasts, Connections

Alcott's use of theatricals can be fruitfully compared to that of Jane Austin in *Mansfield Park*, Charlotte Brontë in *Jane Eyre* and *Villette*, and Edith Wharton in *House of Mirth*. Interesting comparisons might also be drawn between Christie's experience as a professional actress and that of Dreiser's Carrie.

Questions for Reading and Discussion/ Approaches to Writing

Students should debate whether Christie's retirement from the stage reflects Alcott's conservatism, her view that public exposure hardens and coarsens women, that acting—and perhaps public action—are incompatible with womanliness. More likely, however, Alcott is pointing out the pitfalls of any highly competitive endeavor, especially in fields still dominated by men. Even today women enter these fields, as Christie did, in a spirit of defiance only to find themselves conforming to and having their talents co-opted by the very establishment they had hoped to challenge.

Bibliography

Alcott, Louisa May. *Work: A Story of Experience*. Introduction by Sarah Elbert. New York: Schocken, 1977.

Auerbach, Nina. "Afterword." *Little Women*. New York: Bantam, 1983.

Elbert, Sarah. *A Hunger for Home: Louisa May Alcott and Little Women*. Philadelphia: Temple Univ. Press, 1984.

Fetterley, Judith. "Impersonating 'Little Women': The Radicalism of Alcott's *Behind a Mask*." *Women's Studies* 10 (1983): 1–4.

Halttunen, Karen. "The Domestic Drama of Louisa May Alcott." *Feminist Studies* 10 (1984): 232–54.

Keyser, Elizabeth. "Alcott's Portraits of the Artist as Little Woman." *International Journal of Women's Studies* 5 (1982): 445–49.

———. "Domesticity versus Identity: A Review of Alcott Research." *Children's Literature in Education* 16 (1985): 165–75.

———. "Women and Girls in Jo's Boys." *International Journal of Women's Studies* 6 (1983): 457–71.

Langland, Elizabeth. "Female Stories of Experience: Alcott's *Little Women* in Light of *Work*." In *The Voyage In: Fiction of Female Development*, edited by Elizabeth Abel, Marianne Hirsch, and Elizabeth Langland, 112–27. Hanover, N.H.: Univ. Press of New England, 1983.

O'Brien, Sharon. "Tomboyism and Adolescent Conflict: Three Nineteenth-Century Case Studies." In *Women's Being, Women's Place: Female Identity and Vocation in American History*, 351–72. Boston: G. K. Hall, 1979.

Stern, Madeleine B. "Louisa Alcott, Trouper: Experiences in Theatricals, 1848-1880." *New England Quarterly* 16 (1943): 175–97.

Harriet Prescott Spofford (1835–1921)

Contributing Editor: Thelma J. Shinn [p. 81]

Classroom Issues and Strategies

Students often lack appreciation for "domestic imagery"—symbols and images drawn from female experience but used to represent universal values. In addition, they also are often inadequately aware of the transitional elements from romance to realism evident in the writings of Spofford and her contemporaries.

To address these issues, show contemporary appreciation of Spofford in better known authors (such as Dickinson and Whittier). Help students discern the *patterns* of imagery so that they do not dismiss individual images as "popular" or "sentimental." Point out the metaphorical implications of the setting which, while realistic (with its historical roots in Spofford's family), is also part of the romantic tradition.

Major Themes, Historical Perspectives, and Personal Issues

Major themes include:
> The Female Artist
> Humanity as Animal vs. Spirit
> Music/Art as Communication
> Romance vs. Realism (particularly in defining naturalism)
> The Forest in American Literature
> Importance of Popular Culture (well-known songs)
> Preservation of Family History (true incident)

By basing "Circumstance" on an incident in the life of her maternal great-grandmother, Spofford shifts time and place to enter Hawthorne's "neutral territory, . . . where the Actual and the Imaginary may meet." While Hawthorne turns back two centuries to the suggestion of a historical event in *The Scarlet Letter*, however, Spofford chooses a closer time and a specific personal/historical moment. In doing so, she reflects the female consciousness that personal events—events recorded orally and handed down from mother to daughter—define human history perhaps more accurately than official records. In these records she finds a circumstance that can embody female and human experience in finite and infinite terms.

Although *circumstances* refers to essential and environmental conditions in which we find ourselves, the singular form specifically refers, according to *Webster's New Collegiate Dictionary*, to "a piece of evidence that indicates the probability or improbability of an event." While the existence of God cannot be proved, Spofford can present a "circumstance" that indicates for her its probability. And so she has in this story. The religious theme is all the more powerful because it is couched in the "Actual" and discovered by a woman not given to the "Imaginary." Spofford reveals Hawthorne's "neutral territory" to be the world in which we live, and it is her journey through this world that the narrator must find evidence of the omnipresence of God.

Significant Form, Style, or Artistic Conventions

Spofford anticipates the styles and themes of the realists, even of the naturalists who will surround her later writing career. Already in this 1860 story, her narrator must abandon her romantic notions of nature ("If all the silent powers of the forest did not conspire to help her!") and face that "the dark, hollow night rose indifferently over her." At the same time, she has recognized the naturalistic corollary to nature's indifference in humanity's animal antecedents. Impending death by a "living lump of appetites" forces her to acknowledge the self-loathing as the beast "known by the strength of our lower natures let loose." The primitive cannibalism of humanity seems to be reflected in her fear of becoming a part of the beast again: "the base, cursed thing howls with us forever through the forest." Such pessimistic reflections indeed bring misery, as they will to later writers. "The Open Boat" finds Stephen Crane's correspondent (also reflecting a true incident in Crane's own life) similarly trapped in nature and discovering its indifference to him.

Original Audience

Consider the following:

1. The time period during which the story was written and the New England setting.

2. The fact that the story was first published in a periodical.
3. The Puritan background of Spofford's contemporary audience.
4. The familiarity of the audience with the popular music mentioned.

Comparisons, Contrasts, Connections

Useful comparisons may be made with the following works:

> Emily Dickinson, "Twas like a maelstrom . . ."
> Nathaniel Hawthorne, "Young Goodman Brown"
> Stephen Crane, "The Open Boat"
> Henry James, "The Beast in the Jungle"

Questions for Reading and Discussion/ Approaches to Writing

1. What songs do *you* know that she might be singing in each category? Where did you learn these songs? From whom?
2. (a) Find parallels in your experience to the story, its themes its particulars (consider sharing family stories).
   (b) Examine the roots of a genre (oral roots of fiction, for instance)
   (c) Interpret one art through another (art and music here)
   (d) Also try traditional thematic and stylistic approaches and comparisons to other stories.

Bibliography

Fetterley, Judith. *Provisions*. Bloomington: Indiana Univ. Press, 1985.

Halbeisen, Elizabeth K. *Harriet Prescott Spofford: A Romantic Survival*. Philadelphia: University of Pennsylvania Press, 1935.

Elizabeth Stuart Phelps (1844–1911)

Contributing Editor: Carol Farley Kessler [p. 92]

Classroom Issues and Strategies

For many students the nineteenth-century style with its many allusions and complicated syntax presents a problem. It may be difficult for a few of the male students to enter the viewpoint of the heroine, but many students—especially women—find this a profoundly rewarding novel to read.

To address these issues, first I acknowledge to a class that Phelps's style sometimes causes a problem. I explain that she was an anxious person, that in *Avis* she was tackling taboo subjects—such as the view that marriage is not good for women, and that women are as creative as men. I ask students to note other taboo viewpoints that arise. Then I ask them to consider how they write when they are afraid of how people may react to their ideas. Phelps's writing is sometimes precious, over-written—the tactic of a worried person. I also point out that sometimes contorted language occurs with personally difficult or socially controversial subjects; students need to consider the possible emotional significance of the text for its author. The problems of style can inform us.

Women respond strongly, positively to this realistic novel depicting women's three-role status (mother-wife-person), which they recognize as unresolved in the 1990s as in the 1870s. Men may be less aware of the potential for overwork entailed in this three-role status; however, some will be sons of single or divorced mothers, hence more aware of the dilemma of women's unpaid, often invisible labor. They, rather than the instructor, may be guided to provide explanations to less-aware men. Also women (and some men) need the conscious support of an instructor to feel safe enough to respond with emotional honesty to male (and some female) classmates who don't understand the issues Phelps tackles.

Perry Miller Adato's thirty-minute film on "Mary Cassatt" (1844-1926), a Philadelphia artist who worked in Paris, provides an overview of the status of the nineteenth-century creative woman.

Erica Jong's essay, "The Artist as Housewife: The Housewife as Artist," in *Ms.* (October 1972), reprinted in *The First Ms. Reader* (New York: Warner, 1973, pp. 111–22), demonstrates surprisingly little contrast between 1877 and 1972.

The marriage/career conflict engages students' attention, as does the general contemporary relevance of the concerns of Phelps's novel. They wonder, especially the women, why these problems continue to exist. They wonder how to solve them. They take the issues addressed by the novel very personally.

Major Themes, Historical Perspectives, and Personal Issues

An overview of these matters is Kessler's Introduction to *The Story of Avis* (New Brunswick, N. J.: Rutgers, 1986, pp. xiii-xxvi, plus notes).

Themes include role conflict and overload for women, conditions needed for creativity, the reality of unhappy marriages for women, freedom with singleness and constraint with marriage, possibilities emerging from atypical choices.

Historical issues: The novel attacks the socialization of women to be "true women" (Phelps's essay, in the Rutgers reprint of *Avis*, elucidates the role construct of true womanhood—to be compassionate, cheerful, submissive, selfless); it espouses women's movement beliefs in women's right to meaningful work and emotional support.

Personal issues: Avis seems to be an ideal composite of Phelps, her mother, and female relatives (see "A Literary Legacy" in *Frontiers* 5 [Fall 1980] 28–33). The longest publication gap in Phelps's career occurs between *The Silent Partner*, 1871, and *The Story of Avis*, 1877: consider Tillie Olson's view that "censorship silences" (see her *Silences* [New York: Delta, 1979], p. 9). In a 1903 letter to Harriet Prescott Spofford, Phelps wrote, "The married are hampered in what they can say. I remember that when I wrote *Avis* I said 'were I married, I could not write this book' " (*Avis*, Introduction, p. xxxi).

Significant Form, Style, or Artistic Conventions

Form/Convention: A feminized version of the Grail legend, hence a romantic quest, though this is not particularly evident in the two excerpted chapters; Bildungsroman/Künstlerroman—the growth and development of the protagonist/artist; American literary realism, contemporaneous with Henry James and William Dean Howells; also New England regionalism.

Style: Emotionally loaded, highly allusive and imagistic; "avis" = Latin for bird: the caged bird, according to Ellen Moers in *Literary Women*, 1976, pp. 245–51, is characteristic of women's writing; ironic social commentary; occasional Christian sentiment.

Aesthetics: Art for truth's sake—"art implies truthful and conscientious study of life as it is," notes Phelps in her autobiography (*Chapters from a Life*, 1896, p. 261); "life *is* moral responsibility," essential to beauty, she believes; didactic function of literature. She assumed the seriousness of her mission as author.

Original Audience

One reviewer found the book unacceptable, especially for young female readers; on the other hand, feminist Lucy Stone was sure it was destined for "a permanent place in English literature." Currently its return to availability was noted favorably (*Legacy* 2 [Spring 1985]: 18). Student reports on standard reference articles—AWW, 1982; DAB, 1936; NAW, 1971—provide a challenge as each presents a very different viewpoint on Phelps, a combination of differing audience and historical period.

Comparisons, Contrasts, Connections

Henry James's early Künstlerroman, *Roderick Hudson*, 1875, in which the artist is overcome by a disappointment in love and commits suicide; Louisa May Alcott, "Diana & Persis" (written in 1879; in *Alternative Alcott*, 1988, edited by Elaine Showalter), in which two friends discover that maybe marriage and art can mix; Kate Chopin, *The Awakening*, 1899, in which a woman resists an eventless life and strikes for independence; Willa Cather, *The Song of the Lark*, 1915, a novel depicting the origins and development of artistic genius. Avis has a stronger character than James's Roderick Hudson, but has less optimism than Alcott's Persis, less impatience and rebelliousness than Chopin's Edna Pontellier, less firm commitment to her art than Cather's Thea Kronborg.

Questions for Reading and Discussion/
Approaches to Writing

1. (a) Discuss the conflict between caring and creativity that Avis experiences. How does Phelps plot this?
   (b) Delineate how marriage figures in the plot pattern of entrapment and escape.
   (c) What ideas about relationships between women and men presented in the novel are still historically unrealized?
   (d) At the end of the novel, Phelps argues that making A Woman will take three generations. How, in the chapters read, does she provide support for this hypothesis?

2. (a) Keep a reading journal of responses to the daily assignments, with notations of specific (i.e., page, paragraph, word) support for generalization noted.
   (b) In-class paragraphs written during the first fifteen minutes providing detailed support for an opinion about the novel, on topics assigned for later class discussion.
   (c) Individual reports relating supplementary articles or other literary selections to the *Avis* chapters.

Bibliography

Legacy: A Journal of Nineteenth-Century American Women Writers provides critical articles about authors of Phelps's era.

Recent reprints of Phelps's best novels—*The Story of Avis*, *The Silent Partner* (about a mill town social worker), *Doctor Zay* (about a homeopathic physician)—contain useful introductions or afterwords.

In addition, *Woman in Sexist Society* (ed. Vivian Gornick and Barbara K. Moran, NAL, 1972) contains three relevant articles: Jessie Bernard, "The Paradox of the Happy Marriage," 145–62; Linda Nochlin, "Why Are There No Great Women Artists?" 480–510; and Margaret Adams, "The Compassion Trap," 555–75.

Sarah Orne Jewett (1849–1909)

Contributing Editor: Elizabeth Ammons [p. 110]

Classroom Issues and Strategies

I've encountered some problems teaching Jewett's *Country of the Pointed Firs* because at first it seems dull to students, but they love "A White Heron" (hereafter WH) and I'm confident that they will also respond enthusiastically to "The Foreigner" (hereafter F), though I have not taught it. (There is, by the way, a film of WH that many people find excellent.)

Students often don't like the ending of WH (the author's intrusion) and are baffled by it; they wonder about Sylvia's mother—what's Jewett saying about her?—and about why the girl's grandmother sides with the man. Also they wonder why the bird is male.

Major Themes, Historical Perspectives, and Personal Issues

Both of these stories are characteristic of Jewett not only in focusing on women but also in focusing on women-centered or women-dominated space, geographic and psychic. The existence and meaning of such space is probably the most basic theme in Jewett.

Female-defined space is celebrated in F, which shows the boundaries of such space transcending the physical world and also national and ethnic barriers. The bonds between women find expression in and are grounded in the acts of mutual nurture, healing, story telling, shelter, feeding, touching, and transmission of wisdom denigrated in the dominant culture as witchcraft. Female-defined reality is threatened but then reaffirmed, at least for the present, in WH, in which the intrusion of a man from the city into the grandmother/cow/girl-controlled rural space upsets the daily harmony, and potentially the life-balance itself, of nature.

Historically these stories explore the strength and depth of female bonding at a time when same-sex relationships between women in Western culture were being redefined by sexologists such as Freud and Havelock Ellis as pathological, deviant. Jewett recognizes in WH the threat posed to same-sex female bonding by the allure of heterosexuality in the person of the hunter, who is sexy and deals in violence and death: if Sylvia falls for him, she will be participating, symbolically, in her own death (the killing and stuffing of the heron). In F, written later, Jewett sets against a stormy background a story affirming women's love, despite divisions of region, nationality, and culture.

Sororal, filial, maternal, erotic: bonds between women in Jewett's work no doubt reflect her own feelings and those of women close to her. While she numbered men among her friends and associates, her closest, most intimate friends were women. Debate about whether to call Jewett a lesbian writer exists because the term was not one Jewett would have used; our highly sexualized twentieth-century view of same-sex romantic and erotic attachment may very well not be a historically accurate way to describe Jewett's world, fictive or biographical. So labels need to be carefully thought about. Whatever terminology is used, though, the central, deep, recurrent theme in Jewett's work is love between women.

Significant Form, Style, or Artistic Conventions

F uses many features of the traditional Western ghost story to tell a love story. The storm, the cat, the ghost—the tale is deliberately encoded with ghost-story trappings, yet is in the end not scary but healing. The story is formally interesting to think about therefore as a transformation of something Poe or Hawthorne might do into a narrative that instead of scaring or depressing, succors. A kind of serious fierce maternalization of masculine form? Certainly WH plays with masculine form, reproducing in its structure the build to a high climax (literally the tippy-top of a tree) that both traditional, white, Western dramatic structure (exposition/conflict/complication/climax/resolution) and, it can be argued, male-dominated heterosexual relations inscribe. Then at the end of WH Jewett disrupts and undoes this tight, linear pattern with a flossy, chatty final paragraph so exaggeratedly "feminine" in character as to call attention to itself. One question often asked by students is: Why does the narrative voice switch like this in the end? One answer is that, just as Sylvia's decision thwarts the hunter, the narrative switch at the end deliberately deconstructs the traditional inherited masculine narrative pattern of climax-oriented fiction grounded in aggression and conflict that has preceded.

Original Audience

Jewett was widely read and admired in the late nineteenth century, but until recently she has been dismissed in the academy as minor, regional, slight. Her recent revival reflects in large part the increasing numbers and strength of women in the profession of professor and scholar. Not of interest (threatening?) to a predominantly white, male, heterosexual group of critics and scholars, Jewett is now finding an increasingly large audience as women gain power within the system of higher education. That is, Jewett is the beneficiary of a new group of people being able to define what is "interesting" and "important." Thus Jewett, when we ponder the question of audience, vividly raises highly political issues: who defines what is "good" and worth studying? How do the politics of gender and sexual orientation shape the politics of the classroom, without their ever even being acknowledged? What writers and kinds of writers are currently being excluded or denigrated because of the composition of the profession of professor?

Comparisons, Contrasts, Connections

Jewett is often compared quite productively with Mary Wilkins Freeman, a fellow New England writer. Jewett admired Harriet Beecher Stowe's New England writing and therefore is fruitfully thought of in conjunction with Stowe. Willa Cather was encouraged by Jewett to write full time and, particularly on the topic of women's relationships with each other, Cather's work is very interesting to compare and contrast with Jewett's. As a regionalist—a writer engaged in trying to capture in detail and with great accuracy and sensitivity life as it was experienced in a particular region, rather than attempting to fill in a huge and more diffuse canvas, Jewett compares illuminatingly with other regionalists, especially across regions: Kate Chopin and Alice Dunbar-Nelson focusing on New Orleans, Hamlin Garland picturing the northern Midwest, Abraham Cahan on the Lower East Side in New York.

Questions for Reading and Discussion/ Approaches to Writing

1. F: Who is the Foreigner? Is this story racist?
   WH: Who/what does the heron symbolize? Why is the cow in the story? Why does it matter that Sylvia is nine years old?
2. These two stories together and individually lend themselves well to traditional kinds of textual analysis of symbols, imagery, characterization, authorial point of view, and so forth: for example, animal imagery and symbolism in either or both; nature as a character in either or both; comparing the portraits of old women in the two stories.

Bibliography

Two sources for essays are:
Critical Essays on Sarah Orne Jewett (Boston: G. K. Hall, 1984) and *The Colby Library Quarterly: Special Issue on Jewett* (March 1986). WH and F are discussed from various points of view in a number of excellent essays in these two volumes.

Mary E. Wilkins Freeman (1852–1930)

Contributing Editor: Leah Blatt Glasser [p. 135]

Classroom Issues and Strategies

A problem that can arise when teaching Mary Wilkins Freeman is the tendency among students to oversimplify, to bring to her work a set of one-dimensional feminist formulas into which any of her heroines can be reduced and misunderstood. Often students will miss her capacity for paradox and the complexity of her work. They will either ignore her most interesting contradictions or they will become angry at the way in which her heroines fail to satisfy easy models of feminist behavior.

The best strategy is to provide a full context for Freeman's work in terms of both her life and period and to select particularly paradoxical passages for class discussion. It is especially enlightening to discuss the endings of her stories, which often disappoint students or trouble them. Have students consider possible revisions of these endings and then discuss why Freeman might have chosen to conclude as she did.

Students may wish to consider the title of "The Revolt of 'Mother' " and its implications. What is the nature of Sarah's "revolt"? Why does Freeman put "mother" in quotation marks? Students may be interested to know that Freeman's father, Warren Wilkins, gave up his plan of building the house Eleanor, Freeman's mother, had hoped for. Instead, the family moved in 1877 into the home in which Eleanor was to serve as hired housekeeper. Freeman's mother was thus "deprived of the very things which made a woman proud, her own kitchen, furniture, family china; and she had lost the one place in which it was acceptable for her to be powerful: her home" (Clark 177).

Another interesting comment is this one, made by Freeman in the *Saturday Evening Post*, published December 8, 1917 (long after the publication of the story). Freeman disparages her story for its lack of realism:

In the first place all fiction ought to be true and "The Revolt of 'Mother' " is not true . . . . There never was in New England a woman like Mother. If there had been she certainly would have lacked the nerve. She would also have lacked the imagination. New England women of that period coincided with their husbands in thinking that the sources of wealth should be better housed than the consumers.

"A Church Mouse" provides a good example of Freeman's duality. Ask students to study the tone and quality of Hetty's early expressions of determination with her final plea to the community. Focus also on passages that depict the role of work in Hetty's life. The sunflower quilt, for example, plays an important part in the story as it serves the function of both dividing Hetty from the other churchgoers and celebrating her capacity as an artist. Hetty's battle to establish her right to live alone and to do the work she loves may be compared with aspects of Freeman's life.

As the story progresses, students may notice that the action moves from an individual plea to a collective demand. Moreover, Freeman achieves what Hetty does; she rebels, but she does so safely and she is heard—her story is published in *Harper's Bazaar*, a woman's magazine that would reach a similar audience composed largely of women. As indicated above, Hetty's position in the church behind the sunflower quilt she has made in church suggests a context for Freeman's feelings about the role of work in her life.

Freeman wrote "Old Woman Magoun" during her unhappy marriage to Dr. Charles Freeman. It is one of the few short stories written during this period in which she managed to maintain her mastery. It is interesting to consider Freeman's experience of marriage in relation to the fears she invests in Old Woman Magoun of losing the young Lily to men like Nelson Barry and Jim Willis. In a letter to a newly-married friend, Harriet Randolph Hyatt Mayor, she had written, "I shall find the old you. It will never be lost. I know how you fell . . . I am to be married myself before long . . . . If *you* don't see the old *me*, I shall run *until I find her*" (Kendrick 205). Unfortunately, Freeman was forced to part with the "old me" until her husband's alcoholism and abusive behavior finally ended in his being committed to the New Jersey State Hospital and her separation from him.

Students may wish to consider the nature of Old Woman Magoun's extreme actions. A close study of the scene in which she allows Lily to eat the poisoned berries will yield a lively discussion. Reward for being recognized as a writer caused Freeman to say "I felt my wings spring from my shoulders, capable of flight." In this scene, she has Old Woman Magoun give wings, in a sense, to her grandchild for a flight that will not bring her "home" as Mary Wilkins Freeman's "wings" did.

Major Themes, Historical Perspectives, and Personal Issues

The major themes of Freeman's work illuminate aspects of her life. Mary Wilkins Freeman's words to describe the feeling of receiving her first acceptance and check for a short story provide an interesting context: "I felt my wings spring from my shoulders, capable of flight, and I flew home" (*New York Times*, April 1926). Her statement characterizes the dilemma this remarkable turn-of-the-century New England writer faced, the paradox that she expressed in almost all of her work. Feeling "capable of flight" because of the power of her capacity as a writer, Freeman nevertheless could only fly "home." Most striking in her life and work is the haunting echo of two inner voices: a voice that cries out for rebellious flight, another voice that clings to the safety of home. The heroines of Freeman's short stories, even as they rebel, struggle with this conflict. Students may compare the heroines of "A Church Mouse," "The Revolt of 'Mother,' "and "Old Woman Magoun," listening for the ways in which Freeman invests the women with power and yet simultaneously limits their power, bringing their rebellious "flights" to what Freeman considered "home"—the realities of nineteenth-century New England.

It is important to explore her depiction of relationships between women, her focus on the role of work in women's lives, the way in which she explores the psychology of rebellion as characters rebel, submit, or face the consequences of their rebellion. Of particular interest in offering a biographical context is the intensity of Freeman's relationship with

Mary Wales, with whom she lived for twenty-five years. Her stories reflect a great understanding of female friendships.

Significant Form, Style, or Artistic Conventions

Freeman has often been categorized as a local colorist, a New England writer of the post-Civil War period whose primary talent lay in depicting the peculiarities of her region. This has tended to minimize her work. Certainly she does offer a vivid sense of life in New England. Most significant, however, is the way in which she moves beyond region to offer a focus on the psychology of women's conflicts at the turn of the century. Her use of dialect may be compared with Twain's as she manages to bring us the voices she knew with fine precision.

Original Audience

This is an interesting question. Freeman published in magazines for young women (*Harper's* primarily) and her audience consisted largely of women readers. She was influenced at times by her editors' demands for "gentility" in accordance with their sense of the codes of female behavior at the turn of the century. Consequently Freeman's endings often couch rebellious content in acceptable, domestic scenes of female submission. The shift in Hetty's behavior in "Church Mouse" is interesting in this context as is the reunion of Sarah and her husband in "Revolt of 'Mother.'

Comparisons, Contrasts, Connections

It is fruitful to compare Freeman with male peers such as Twain, James, and Howells. Her capacity for psychological portrait compares well with Henry James and many of her heroines may be compared with the heroines in James's short fiction. She did participate in a project with James, a collaborative novel, entitled *The Whole Family: A Novel by Twelve Authors* (Harper & Brothers, 1908). Her chapter in this novel should be compared with the chapter by James, particularly on the themes of rebellion and repression. Both writers held a fascination with patterns of repression and rebellion, although Freeman's focus was almost entirely upon women in this light. Twain's use of dialogue may also be explored in relation to Freeman's. Finally, she should be compared with other American women writers at the turn of the century (particularly Sarah Orne Jewett, Edith Wharton, Willa Cather).

Questions for Reading and Discussion/
Approaches to Writing

1. (a) Study the role of work in each story in relation to the development of Freeman's heroines.

   (b) Analyze the conclusions of "A Church Mouse" and "The Revolt of 'Mother.'" What seems paradoxical or unexpected? How do these conclusions relate to earlier stages of revolt in each story?

   (c) Note the image of wings in "Old Woman Magoun" and consider possible contests. What does the final scene suggest?

   (d) Note references to madness in each story. What might Freeman be suggesting in each case?

2. Students enjoy focusing on the development of Freeman's heroines, their contradictions and strengths. Consider a paper on the attitudes toward women the story suggests and its influence on the heroine's actions. Ask students to study a particular scene or set of images (Sarah Penn's work in her house: "She was an artist"; Hetty's quilt in "Church Mouse." Does Freeman's work suggest anything about her sense of the artist?) Study the death scene in "Old Woman Magoun." What do you make of the language of the old woman as she eases the child into death?

Bibliography

A useful and brief discussion of Freeman's life and work can be found in *Legacy: A Journal of Nineteenth Century American Women Writers* Volume 4, Spring 1987 ("Profile: Mary E. Wilkins Freeman" by Leah B. Glasser).

Useful biographical material can also be gleaned from *The Infant Sphinx: Collected Letters of Mary E. Wilkins Freeman* intelligently edited and introduced by Brent L. Kendrick. Her letters, though cautious and unrevealing on the surface, hint at the intensity of her relationship with her childhood friend Mary Wales. Freeman lived with Wales for over twenty years and it is likely that much of her focus on friendships between women was drawn from this relationship. The difficulties of her marriage are also apparent in many of her letters written during that trying period of her life. The numerous letters she wrote to her editors reveal Freeman's seriousness about her career.

The two existing biographies on Freeman are useful, although somewhat outdated: Foster's *Mary E. Wilkins Freeman* and Westbrook's *Mary Wilkins Freeman*.

Interpretive studies of her work can be found in Clark's Afterword to *The Revolt of Mother and Other Stories*, Marjorie Pryse's Introduction and Afterword to *Selected Stories of Mary E. Wilkins Freeman,* and Leah Glasser's essays "Discovering Mary E. Wilkins Freeman" in *Between Women* and "The Stranger in the Mirror" in *The Massachusetts Review* (Summer 1984).

For a good sampling of Freeman's short stories through the successive phases of her career, see *Selected Stories of Mary E. Wilkins Freeman* (New York: Norton, 1983).

Freeman's novels are not as strong as her short stories; the novel most representative of her talent is *Pembroke* (1894).

The Shoulders of Atlas (1908), *Madelon* (1896), and *By the Light of the Soul* are fascinating examples of Freeman's duality as protagonists are continuously caught between rebellion and submission.

Students may find it interesting to compare the chapters written by Mary Wilkins Freeman and Henry James, her contemporary, in the collaborative novel entitled *The Whole Family: A Novel by Twelve Authors* (New York: Harper & Brothers, 1908).

Pauline Elizabeth Hopkins (1859–1930)

Contributing Editor: Jane Campbell [p. 172]

Classroom Issues and Strategies

Problems include the students':

1. Unfamiliarity with racial issues, both today and at the turn of the century.
2. Alienation from diction and style of the day.
3. Unfamiliarity with the novel *Contending Forces,* leading to difficulties understanding and interpreting the excerpts.

The following strategies are helpful:

1. Introduce Hopkins by putting her into context, fleshing out the headnote to explore some historical, social, and racial particulars during the two periods she fictionalizes in CF.
2. Briefly describe romance conventions, eliciting comparisons with the contemporary popular romance. Emphasize Hopkins's stylistic similarities to other writers of her day.
3. Review novel and plot, as described in the headnote.
4. Make Hopkins accessible by exploring the contemporary nature of several issues she explores, e.g., rape, color prejudice, racism.

I strongly recommend peer interaction in teaching Hopkins. Students might work in small groups or in pairs to raise questions about barriers to their enjoyment of the excerpts from CF. I suspect male students, by and large, will need coaxing to identify with the excerpts. Such problems as students raise may then be tackled by the class as a whole.

I would use journal writing, as well, giving students an opportunity to consider how CF does or does not seem relevant to our times or to their personal lives. Journals can also lead to fruitful comparisons with other works read so far in the course.

White students generally seem shocked by historical particulars and contemporary examples of racism, Klan activities, discrimination, and rape, but they also express gratitude about learning of these issues. Students of color, while painfully cognizant of such issues, may be open to sharing their awareness that these issues are pertinent today. The more sophisticated and bold nonwhite students may be willing to cite specific examples.

When I explore Hopkins from the perspectives offered here, I find the students raise very few questions that I am called upon to answer. That is, once these bases have been covered in writing and discussion, students seem to feel all their questions have been answered, either during discussion with me or with their peers.

Major Themes, Historical Perspectives, and Personal Issues

I would emphasize mob rule and lynching, the convergence of racism and sexism, interracial blood lines, voting disenfranchisement, job discrimination against blacks, and color prejudice. The instructor should also stress Hopkins's emphasis on feminist issues such as rape, female bonding and empowerment, and women's collective political action.

Significant Form, Style, or Artistic Conventions

It is essential that students grasp the obstacles facing an Afro-American woman of Hopkins's day. Her ability to transcend cultural, racial, and sexist barriers in order to write fiction is extraordinary. I would also make sure that students understand that Hopkins is one of a handful of black women writers who managed to surmount these obstacles.

Fitting Hopkins into the nascent tradition of African-American writers would involve discussion of cultural/literary conventions of the time, e.g., the tragic mulatto, educated diction.

I would also detail the primary conventions of women's romance:

1. Entertaining, fast-paced narrative
2. Beautiful, extraordinarily talented, strong heroine who overcomes numerous obstacles and serves as a model for her audience
3. Emphasis on pleasures of homemaking, love, and motherhood—usually derided as "the cult of domesticity" by male critics
4. Villains seeking to compromise heroine's virtue
5. Marriage as joyous conclusion to narrative

Hopkins, like her female contemporaries, chose the romance as an appropriate vehicle for appealing to a wide audience.

Original Audience

I seek to elicit theories (from students who read "romance novels" today) about the appeal of such books. Why do they read them? What elements are satisfying about such books? Eventually, it becomes evident that writers such as Hopkins could profitably mine this genre, interweaving politics and entertainment, thus raising the consciousness of a large audience.

Comparisons, Contrasts, Connections

If any students have read contemporary black novels, such as Alice Walker's *The Color Purple* or Maya Angelou's *I Know Why the Caged Bird Sings*, they will discover parallels, specifically rape and abuse of black women. Romances such as *Charlotte Temple* and *Uncle Tom's Cabin* or others included in *Reconstructing American Literature* might link Hopkins with white authors concerned with similar issues and using the same literary mode to present them.

Questions for Reading and Discussion/ Approaches to Writing

1. Explore how "Ma Smith's Lodging-House—Concluded" delineates educated from uneducated characters. Why do you suppose such distinctions were important to Hopkins?

   What did you learn from "The Sewing Circle" about African-Americans during Hopkins's day? Do these selections seem "dated" in any ways? Explain.

   Could a novel similar to *Contending Forces* be written today? Explore what differences you might expect.

What differences and similarities can you find between *Contending Forces* and *Work X* (X being anything the student might be familiar with)?

Might there be other African-American writers of Hopkins's time whose work has been lost, writers we have not yet rediscovered? Why might their works have been lost?

How do you account for the resurgence of interest in early Afro-American women writers?

2. Writing assignments are variations on study and journal questions offered above.

Quite honestly, I am opposed to assigning paper topics. I feel strongly that part of the writing process involves the writer generating her/his own topic.

Bibliography

See the headnote. Each of the sources listed under Secondary Works is either an article or a chapter or an introduction. Campbell, Tate, and Washington are the most recent and perhaps current. The introductions to the Schomburg editions of Hopkins are excellent, as well.

Regional Voices, National Voices

[p. 192]

African-American Folktales

Contributing Editor: Susan L. Blake [p. 194]

Classroom Issues and Strategies

Students with little grasp of racial oppression may have difficulty seeing the metaphorical qualities of African-American folktales. To address these issues, the class should discuss the historical contexts of the tales, not only in slavery, but also black experience at the times of the tales' collection.

Major Themes, Historical Perspectives, and Personal Issues

The main theme is the tales' commentary on oppression.

Significant Form, Style, or Artistic Conventions

1. The characterization of the trickster-hero (or anti-hero) and the relationship between antagonists.
2. The relationship between historical experience and folk fiction. Compare, for example, the told-for-true tale "Malitis" with other food-stealing stories. How does the retort function in these stories?
3. The variation in style among the tales. What evidence do we find of individual storytellers' concerns and vision? Of collectors' intrusion?

Original Audience

More obviously than written texts, folktales represent interaction between storyteller and audience. Discuss how the race, class, and historical experience of various audiences—the storyteller's neighbors, the folktale collector, the students in the class—may affect the telling and hearing of the tale.

Comparisons, Contrasts, Connections

Folktales are ideal texts for comparative study because they are based on common motifs and varied according to group experience as well as individual talent. The notes in Dorson's *American Negro Folktales* provide extensive references to European, African, and African-American variants of these tales. Comparisons might also be drawn with folktales the students know, contemporary African-American humor, and the fiction of such writers as Langston Hughes, whose Simple stories update the "John and Old Marster" tales, and Toni Morrison, whose *Song of Solomon* is based on the tale of the flying Africans.

Questions for Reading and Discussion/ Approaches to Writing

Try to translate a tale into realistic terms. How does the tale interpret social relationships? How does consideration of the tale's social basis affect your enjoyment of it?.

Samuel Langhorne Clemens (Mark Twain) (1835–1910)

Contributing Editor: Everett Emerson [p. 214]

Classroom Issues and Strategies

I find no problems teaching Twain. He is much loved and admired. The question might be asked, "Why is it that Mark Twain's writings and personality are so appealing?" I share my affection for the author with my students. I note that Mark Twain's readers enjoy *Huckleberry Finn* more if they know some Shakespeare and something about the French Revolution. Both of these loomed large in the author's consciousness when he wrote his masterpiece.

Mark Twain began his career as a humorist. In both *Huckleberry Finn* and all of his other better pieces, an important aspect of his work is the speaker's presentation of himself. What connection does this interest in the speaker or teller have to Mark Twain's humor?

Students are interested but edgy when I raise the question of the word "nigger" in the book. They ought to know that the term was used not long ago by many blacks as well as unsympathetic whites. But the appearance of the word in the book, despite the historical accuracy of the use of the term, needs careful consideration.

Major Themes, Historical Perspectives, and Personal Issues

I think it important to see how the shorter works by Mark Twain in the anthology shed light on *Huckleberry Finn*. I also suggest that the book (*Huckleberry Finn*) be read as the education of a racist, and that the limits of the education that Huck receives be recognized. Huck loses *some* of his prejudiced attitudes toward one particular black. Huck is free and easy with Jim because he regards Jim as his inferior. He records no regret when it appears that Jim has perished in the riverboat accident.

Significant Form, Style, or Artistic Conventions

Mark Twain was always attempting to escape from the established standard of literary propriety, as the Notice posted at the beginning of *Huckleberry Finn* shows. Why was he attempting to escape? Was he successful?

Original Audience

I remind my students that though the setting is the antebellum South, the book was written after Emancipation; it ought to be recognized that the book is not so much an antislavery novel as is *Uncle Tom's Cabin*. But the mind-set that put property values ahead of human values made slavery possible and did not disappear after the Civil War.

Comparisons, Contrasts, Connections

I invite comparison with John Milton and James Joyce. I invite a consideration of Mark Twain's availability to readers. I suggest that one might ask if this availability has any unfortunate consequences.

Questions for Reading and Discussion/ Approaches to Writing

1. What is the role of Tom Sawyer in Huckleberry Finn? If you have read *The Adventures of Tom Sawyer*, what is the difference between Tom in the earlier book and in *Huckleberry Finn*?
2. What aspects of *Huckleberry Finn* are as vital today as they were one hundred years ago? What in the book helps you understand an earlier era in American history, different from our own?

Bibliography

Robinson, Forrest G. *In Bad Faith: The Dynamics of Deception in Mark Twain's America*. 1986, 1–2, 111–22.

George Washington Cable (1844–1925)

Contributing Editor: James Robert Payne [p. 431]

Classroom Issues and Strategies

Students need to have some knowledge of southern American history as distinct from the historical emphasis on the Northeast that generally prevails in American history and literature courses. They should have a sense of the historical pluralism of southern American society, understanding that it includes American Indians, blacks, Hispanic Americans, exploited poor whites, as well as the conservative white elite, which tends to be the object of most attention. Cable's perception of multicultural southern America is central to his fiction.

Students need to be reminded that not all southerners supported slavery before the Civil War nor did all support segregation after the Civil War. For example, George Washington Cable, a middle-class white native of Louisiana, actively supported civil rights through his writings and through ordinary political work.

To break up tendencies to stereotype the South, students may be reminded that many southern cities voted against secession from the Union before the Civil War, and the voting was by white males only. Cable's fiction is expressive of pluralism in southern life and values.

Students are interested in the character of Charlie and his discourse. They wonder to what extent his speech in the story can be taken ironically. More generally, interest is expressed in the situation and status of Indians at the time and place of the story. Students also express interest in the moral issues of the story: they ask to what extent would Colonel De Charleu cheat "Injin Charlie" and does Colonel De Charleu learn better at the end?

Major Themes, Historical Perspectives, and Personal Issues

1. A central theme of Cable's fiction is the impact of the complex history of the American South on modern southern life. In his sense of the profound influence of history on the present, Cable anticipates the later master southern fictionist, William Faulkner.

2. An issue that might be regarded as more personal concerns Cable's relation to New Orleans Creoles (in New Orleans, people of French or Spanish ancestry who preserved elements of their European culture). Creoles felt that their fellow New Orleanian betrayed them by what they saw as Cable's excessively biting satire and critique of the Creole community in his fiction.

Significant Form, Style, or Artistic Conventions

Cable needs to be taught as a southern American realist author (at least insofar as his early, most vital fiction is concerned) who combines tendencies of critical realism (in his critique of southern social injustice and hypocrisy) and local color realism (in his evocation of old New Orleans and plantation Louisiana in all their exoticism).

Yet unlike the work of his fellow realists of the North, such as William Dean Howells and Henry James, Cable's greatest works, *Old Creole Days*, *The Grandissimes*, and *Madame Delphine*, are historical "period" fictions.

Original Audience

In Cable's day, many southerners objected to what they saw as Cable's unjust and disloyal criticism of southern social injustice. More specifically, Cable's New Orleans Creole readers expressed offense at what they regarded as Cable's excessively harsh satire (amounting to caricature, as they saw it) on the Creole community. Cable found his readership by publishing his fiction in *Scribner's Monthly*. It was a readership much like that of his fellow authors William Dean Howells and Henry James, essentially middle class, "genteel," and mostly outside the South. Cable's audience today admires his work as giving the best depiction of old New Orleans and of Louisiana as well.

Comparisons, Contrasts, Connections

1. *Mark Twain*—The greatest of all southern writers of Cable's day, Mark Twain, is comparable to Cable in certain important ways. Both were essentially liberal southerners whose writings effectively criticized problems in southern life. Both Mark Twain and Cable also convey their love and understanding of their region through their endeavors to convey its varied dialects, complex social relationships, and dramatic history.

2. *Kate Chopin*—Cable shares with his fellow Louisiana writer Kate Chopin a strong interest in the Louisiana French-American community and the tensions between the French and Anglo communities, as well as a concern for the situation of women in the South of their day.

Questions for Reading and Discussion/
Approaches to Writing

1. (a) Consider and contrast values dramatized in the portrayal of "Injin Charlie" in relation to the portrayal of Colonel De Charleu.

   (b) Consider how the critical realist Cable undercuts romantic myths of the "noble aristocracy" of the "Old South."

2. (a) In an essay, discuss the significance of Cable's method of representing American language in relation to his themes. Hint: Remember that American language does not always mean English. Consider his representation of communication in French and, depending on which of Cable's works are being studied, other languages.

(b) Consider residual romantic tendencies in the fiction of the southern realist George Washington Cable.

(c) In an essay, discuss and demonstrate—with specific references to passages of Cable's fiction—how Cable undercuts ethnic stereotyping in his work.

Bibliography

Butcher, Philip. *George W. Cable.* New York: Twayne, 1962. Short, highly readable, solid book-length study of Cable and his work.

Clark, William Bedford. "Cable and the Theme of Miscegenation in *Old Creole Days* and *The Grandissimes.*" *Mississippi Quarterly* 30 (Fall 1977): 597–609.

Eaton, Richard Bozman. "George W. Cable and the Historical Romance." *Southern Literary Journal* 8 (Fall 1975): 84–94.

Fulweiler, Howard W. "Of Time and the River: 'Ancestral Nonsense' vs. Inherited Guilt in Cable's 'Belles Demoiselles Plantation.' " *Mid-continent American Studies Journal* 7 (Fall 1966): 53–9.

Hubbell, Jay B. *The South In American Literature: 1607–1900.* Durham, N.C.: Duke Univ. Press, 1954. Section on Cable.

Petry, Alice Hall. *A Genius in His Way: The Art of Cable's Old Creole Days.* Rutherford, N.J.: Fairleigh Dickinson Univ. Press, 1988. Short, readable, stimulating new study of Cable's best short fiction.

———. "Universal and Particular: The Local-Color Phenomenon Reconsidered." *American Literary Realism: 1970–1910* 12 (Spring 1979): 111–26.

Pugh, Griffith T. "George Washington Cable." *Mississippi Quarterly* 20 (Spring 1967): 69–76.

Turner, Arlin, ed. *Critical Essays on George W. Cable.* Boston: G. K. Hall, 1980.

———. *George W. Cable: A Biography.* Baton Rouge: Louisiana State Univ. Press, 1966. The best single source on Cable by far.

Charles Waddell Chesnutt (1858–1932)

Contributing Editor: William L. Andrews [p. 445]

Classroom Issues and Strategies

Classroom issues include: How critical or satirical of blacks is Chesnutt in his portrayal of them? Does he treat them with sympathy, even when they behave foolishly? Is Chesnutt's satire biting and distant or self-involving and tolerant?

There's rarely one source of authority in a Chesnutt story. Different points of view compete for authority. Get the students to identify the different points of view and play them against each other.

Stress that Chesnutt's conjure stories were written in such a way as not to identify their author as an African-American. How effective is Chesnutt in this effort?

Students want to know what Chesnutt's social purposes were in writing his conjure stories. How could stories about slavery have any bearing on the situation of blacks and on race relations at the turn of the century—when Chesnutt wrote—and today?

Major Themes, Historical Perspectives, and Personal Issues

Major themes include: Chesnutt's attitude toward the Old South; the myth of the plantation and the happy darkey, the mixed-blood (monster or natural and even an evolutionary improvement); miscegenation as a natural process, not something to be shocked by.

Significant Form, Style, or Artistic Conventions

Chesnutt wrote during the era of literary realism. What is his relationship to realism, its standards, its themes, its ideas about appropriateness of subject matter and tone?

Original Audience

I stress that Chesnutt wrote for genteel magazine readers much less critical and aware of their racism than we. How does he both appeal to and gently undermine that audience's assumptions?

Comparisons, Contrasts, Connections

Chesnutt wrote to counter the stories of Thomas Nelson Page and Joel Chandler Harris. Chesnutt might also be compared to Dunbar and Douglass as depicters of blacks on the plantation before the Civil War.

Bibliography

Read the chapter on the dialect fiction in William L. Andrews, *The Literary Career of Charles W. Chesnutt* (Baton Rouge: LSU Press, 1980).

Paul Laurence Dunbar (1872–1906)

Contributing Editors: Elaine Hedges and Richard Yarborough [p. 473]

Classroom Issues and Strategies

In many ways Paul Laurence Dunbar can be viewed as the end of one tradition in African-American literature and the beginning of another. Wishing to be a "professional" writer, Dunbar opted for "mainstream" publishing with little or no apparent regard for the compromises that could result. As a partial result of his choice, he erroneously became known to later generations as a "dialect" poet who had willingly used negative stereotypes of his own people in order to satisfy a white reading public. In fact, there are those who now maintain Dunbar's work is devoid of substance. While it may seem that he sacrificed posterity's opinion of him, during his lifetime he was considered to be the symbol of African-American authorship and a "spokesman for his race."

Little known are the many essays Dunbar wrote dealing with American race relations and other contemporary issues that appeared between 1897 and 1905, during the height of his popularity. It is perhaps no wonder that shortly after his death and extending up to the 1940s, his name was often associated with institutions in the African-American community. Practically gone now are the various Paul Laurence Dunbar Literary Societies that flourished throughout the country, but the housing projects and the schools bearing his name still exist in many cities. Who, then, is this man who evokes such negative reactions among modern critics but whose name is known to the literary and non-literary through the various Dunbar High Schools from coast to coast?

Scholars are still undecided upon the actual effect of William Dean Howells's well-meaning support. Clearly, the critic made much of Dunbar as a "full blooded Negro" and of the dialect poems, which Dunbar compared to the work of Robert Burns. The fact that many of his poems were not authentic black dialect at all but were rather Dunbar's attempt to render the Hoosier dialect of James Whitcomb Riley, one of his literary idols, escaped Howells and later critics who praised the poet's use of dialect. Almost universally overlooked were his poems in standard English, which are now too often dismissed as imitative or lacking "racial fire."

Significant Form, Style, or Artistic Conventions

Since much has been made of Dunbar's use of plantation tradition, it must be remembered that his actual knowledge of slavery was limited to the tales that he heard from his parents. Born and reared in a post-Civil War period in the North, Dunbar knew little of southern life. Furthermore, it must be remembered that despite the mystique that has developed about late-nineteenth-century American literature, Paul Laurence Dunbar wrote at a time when American poetry was in a state of transition. Popular poetry was cast in a romantic mold, and the best of it was extremely didactic. Even for those who believed—as did Dunbar— that poetry represented "the highest calling," contemporary models were scarce. Although Emily Dickinson had died in 1886, her work was virtually unknown until the 1930s. Emerson had died in 1882 and Whitman in 1892. William Stanley Braithwaite's determination to give respectability to American poetry through his anthologies and Harriet Monroe's attempt to put poetry in the mainstream of world literature were yet to come.

Original Audience

During Dunbar's productive period, fiction was still being controlled by those magazine editors who were convinced that stories of the antebellum South were the best portraits of a vanquished region. Joel Chandler Harris and other such southern writers had popularized the plantation tradition within the local color movement. Whatever else it was, this post-Civil War literary regionalism was a form of nationalism. There appeared to be the tacit belief that through sectional awareness would come a sense of unity. The basic premise seemed to suggest that to know a locale was to understand it. However, as much as local color was actually presented during the latter part of the nineteenth century, the literary tradition was one that emphasized a sentimental approach to life, one characterized—more or less—by external pleasantries. Seldom were the popular writers concerned with the impact of region upon character. At the same time, there was not a great deal of interest in a realistic portrayal of African-American life. And for a writer—such as Dunbar, who wanted to ride the crest of fashionable literary traditions— using that which was in demand was another way of insuring sales. Consequently, as he looked at the slave mother, the faithful slave, or the comic antics that took place in the quarters, he did so with a detachment that some recent critics find objectionable and others find intolerable. Yet as a northerner, he did not readily identify with southern blacks and saw no reason why he should have shied away from using them in his fiction and poetry.

Comparisons, Contrasts, Connections

All things considered, Dunbar's great sense of optimism can be understood. While British romantic poets were his major models, he grew up in an America that considered such poets as Henry Wadsworth Longfellow and James Whitcomb Riley as "true" poets, that looked upon such sentimental works as Eugene Field's "Little Boy Blue" and Will Carleton's "Over the Hills to the Poorhouse" as the epitome of poetic genius. This was not a day that found Emerson's verse and poetic theory or Walt Whitman's poetic innovations to be representative. While there was a long African-American poetic tradition, few knew of it. Consequently, within the parameters of what was known and what was popular in his own day, Paul Laurence Dunbar created.

Questions for Reading and Discussion/ Approaches to Writing

For "Mr. Cornelius Johnson, Office-Seeker":

1. What did the Reconstruction Amendments to the U.S. Constitution (1865–1870) accomplish? What did they fail to do?
2. In what way does the story of Cornelius Johnson transcend its time and place? On the basis of your response, does this story meet the test of "universality" often used to define "a classic"?
3. Given the method of character presentation, do you—as the reader—sympathize with Cornelius Johnson? Do you find any weaknesses in him that might tend to explain his predicament?

For Dunbar's poetry:

1. By "scanning" Dunbar's poetry, does a reader learn anything about Dunbar's poetic technique?

2. Identify examples of racial stereotypes in "When Malindy Sings," "An Ante-Bellum Sermon," and "We Wear the Mask." Try to remove yourself as much as possible from the emotional, the sentimental, and the intensely subjective, then examine your beliefs by discussing the following question: In your opinion do racial stereotypes serve any purpose?

3. From your knowledge of Frederick Douglass, does Dunbar's poem entitled "Frederick Douglass" transmit important information about the nineteenth-century leader?

Alexander Lawrence Posey (Creek) (1873–1908)

Contributing Editor: Daniel F. Littlefield, Jr. [p. 489]

Classroom Issues and Strategies

Students should have no problems with the lyrics but may have difficulties with the dialect in the Hotgun poem and the Fus Fixico letter.

Present these matters in the same way one would present them in relation to other dialect writers of the period: e.g., Clemens, Cable, Chesnutt, Dunbar, Chopin. Present the lyrics as one would the lesser lyrics of a Bryant or a Longfellow, for instance.

Students are interested in the question of Indian-U.S. relations, not only in Posey's time but before and after. They are also curious about the "Americanization" of Indians like Posey (e.g., his romantic lyrics, his classical education, etc.). This issue leads untimately to questions of assimilation and cultural discontinuity.

Major Themes, Historical Perspectives, and Personal Issues

1. Passing of the Indian (that foolish concept of the "vanishing American"). The interesting point is that Posey, and many other Indian writers, bought the idea to some extent.

2. Romanticizing the "great" man, whether he is Sequoyah or Crazy Snake or Yadeka Harjo. (Why would an Indian choose these as great men?)

3. The Noble Savage (Crazy Snake *is* one in the poem).

4. Indian humor—most students are surprised to find that Indians have any.

Significant Form, Style, or Artistic Conventions

Discuss with the students the same questions that apply to any lyrical poetry, to any dialect poetry, and to any dialect prose, especially the professional dialect humorists, the "Phunny Phellows" of the late nineteenth century. Posey's dialect fits squarely into the local color movement. If we can have Harte in the West, Cable and Chopin in Louisiana, Garland in the Midwest, why not Posey in the Indian Territory?

Original Audience

Posey published most of his poems in Indian Territory newspapers and magazines. He wrote for a Western audience. Posey, like many Indians at the turn of the century, witnessed a great attrition in Indian culture as the U.S. pushed a policy of assimilation. He attempted to document the passing of Indian folk heroes, great and small. Recent American Indian writing deals in large measure with attempts at rediscovering what has been lost. Writers like Posey anticipate the themes of many contemporary American Indian or Chinese or Japanese or Chicano writers.

Bibliography

The most complete treatment of Posey's life today is the highly romanticized "Memoir" by William E. Connelley in Minnie Posey, ed., *The Poems of Alexander Lawrence Posey* (Topeka: Crane, 1910). All other studies derive from this.

John Milton Oskison (Cherokee) (1874–1947)

Contributing Editor: Daniel F. Littlefield, Jr. [p. 497]

Classroom Issues and Strategies

Students are interested in the insistence that Indians conform to the expectations of Anglo-dominated society vs. the social exclusion of blacks of the same period.

Major Themes, Historical Perspectives, and Personal Issues

1. Imposition of one's ideology upon another
2. Cultural roots of personal world views
3. Racial-cultural biases, stereotyping

Significant Form, Style, or Artistic Conventions

The story should be dealt with in the context of the short story form. It relates to the local color writing of the late nineteenth and early twentieth century.

Original Audience

The piece was written for a popular audience during a period when federal policy aimed to move the Indian into mainstream American society, to eliminate cultural differences, to make the Indian, as it were, a red white person. In retrospect, present-day readers see the failure of such policies. But on another level, the story has something to say to the reader who is concerned about the imposition of one's ideology upon the unwilling, whether that ideology is religious, social, or political.

Comparisons, Contrasts, Connections

In its harsh tone and didacticism, the story can be compared well with some of Chesnutt's or those of other black writers of the period.

Alice Dunbar-Nelson (1875–1935)

Contributing Editor: Gloria T. Hull [p. 504]

Classroom Issues and Strategies

The state of African-American literature when these two stories were published (1899–1900) was the transition period between post-slavery Reconstruction and the flowering of black literature in the nineteen-teens (1915 ff into the Harlem Renaissance)—before Booker T. Washington's *Up From Slavery* (1901) and W. E. B. Du Bois's *The Souls of Black Folk* (1903) had articulated the terms of a racial debate that highlighted the difference between old and new ways of conceptualizing and pre-senting (politically and artistically) black American culture. There was continuing richness in folk literature, but it still did not represent an extensive scribal tradition. Two black men-of-letters had achieved national recognition—Paul Laurence Dunbar for his dialect poetry (which, despite its original genius, still used familiar minstrel and planta-tion motifs) and Charles Chesnutt, author of *The Conjure Woman* and *The Wife of His Youth* (1899), stories that featured a tale-telling trickster fig-ure and the "color line," respectively. Clearly, Dunbar-Nelson is helping to define a nascent modern tradition, and doing so in ways that avoided limitations and stereotypes but also skirted race.

One must remember, too, the context of nineteenth-century pop-ular fiction with its penchant for narrative modes and devices we now eschew—romance, melodrama, moralizing, etc. Of particular relevance is the flourishing of the local color tradition, in which women writers excelled. The South and Louisiana had its representatives, and Dunbar-Nelson wrote and was read in the light of George Washington Cable and Kate Chopin. In an early letter to her, Paul Laurence Dunbar said:

> Your determination to contest Cable for his laurels is a com-mendable one. Why shouldn't you tell those pretty Creole stories as well as he? You have the force, the fire and the artistic touch that is so delicate and yet so strong.
>
> Do you know that New Orleans—in fact all of Louisiana—seems to me to be a kind of romance land . . . . No wonder you have Grace King and Geo. W. Cable, no wonder you will have Alice R.[uth] M.[oore] [Dunbar-Nelson's maiden name]

Major Themes, Historical Perspectives, and Personal Issues

Race and racism within the U.S. is a contextual given. One of the spe-cific results/manifestations that is relevant is *intra*-racial color prejudice, especially the prejudice against darker-skinned black people and the hierarchy of color. These contexts relate to Auguste in "Pearl." So does the phenomenon of "passing" (usually economically motivated). Dunbar-Nelson herself casually passed on occasion—to see a theatrical performance, to have a swim at a bathing spa, to travel comfortably.

Auguste does so in a much more serious and sustained way for, in the eyes of the Irish politicians, his free black grandfather makes him just as much a "nigger" as Frank and the others.

The ambiguous racial status of the Louisiana Creoles is an even further refinement on the race/racism theme. Their admixture of

French-Spanish-Indian-black-white blood, their often free status, their closed/district society/culture, etc., set them apart. Readers did not (do not?) tend to see these Creole characters as black/African-Americans, but as some kind of non-white exotics.

Significant Form, Style, or Artistic Conventions

Race and the African-American writer. There has always been feeling and discussion on the black writer's proper role/stance with regard to her/his racial roots and the use of this material. This has been complicated by the pseudo-argument of whether one wants to be a "black writer" or a "writer" (recall the shibboleth of being "universal").

Original Audience

Answering questions like this was also affected by questions of audience and readership, since the authors had to write for predominantly white or mixed audiences. Furthermore, whites controlled the mass markets. Black newspapers and journals furnished independent outlets, but these were comparatively few and small. Clearly, Dunbar-Nelson was writing for a larger, mostly white readership. She had also learned from experience that this audience did not accept controversial treatments of blacks or black-white relations.

Comparisons, Contrasts, Connections

Dunbar-Nelson has usually been taught—if at all—as a very minor female poet of the Harlem Renaissance, partly because of that period's notoriety and also because only a few of her poems have been available. Literary historians knew/know of her "Creole stories," but they have not been easy to access. It radically alters our view of her to see that poetry was the least significant genre for her and short fiction the most important. After *Violets* and *St. Rocque*, she wrote two other collections that were never published (though a few individual stories were): *Women and Men*, more nature and original Creole and non-Creole materials, and *The Annals of 'Steenth Street*, tales of Irish tenement youth set in New York City. She also wrote various other types of stories until she died.

Bibliography

Possible further reading: Two other Dunbar-Nelson stories: "The Goodness of St. Rocque," which typifies, perhaps, her mode in these works, and "The Stones of the Village," an even more overt and tragic handling of race, passing, and the black Creole; plus "Brass Ankles Speaks," an autobiographical essay about growing up in New Orleans as a "light nigger," which Dunbar-Nelson wrote pseudonymously toward the end of her life.

Secondary criticism: The biographical-literary chapter devoted to Dunbar-Nelson in Gloria T. Hull, *Color, Sex, and Poetry: Three Women Writers of the Harlem Renaissance* (Bloomington: Indiana Univ. Press, 1987), and the Introduction to *The Works of Alice Dunbar-Nelson*.

William Dean Howells (1837–1920)

Contributing Editor: John W. Crowley [p. 510]

Classroom Issues and Strategies

Students are usually unfamiliar with Howells and his central position in nineteenth-century American literature. If they have heard of him at all, they are likely to have picked up the (still) prevailing stereotype: that Howells was a genteel prude whose realism could not possibly be of any interest to contemporary readers. Another problem is that students are not often sensitive to quiet irony in what they read; they are not prepared to hear the subtle nuances in Howell's narrative voice—or to read between the lines in his treatment of sexuality, which he handled with Victorian decorum but did *not* avoid as a subject.

It is useful to tell students about the history of Howell's literary reputation: his contemporary fame, his fall from grace during the 1920s, his currently anomalous position in the canon. Students are usually pleasantly surprised by Howells, in part because his prose is not "difficult" (like James's) and because they find more complexity than they had expected. It is best to start, perhaps, with the "Editor's Easy Chair" selection, which introduces students to his characteristic tone and prepares them to recognize his use of the dramatic method in the fiction: the apparent (but only apparent) narrative detachment, the embodiment of themes in the characters' dialogue and interactions.

I have sometimes introduced Howells by reading from the famous account of the Whittier Birthday Dinner in 1877, as reported in *My Mark Twain*. The narrative is very engaging and amusing; it catches students' attention. It is also revealing of Howell's "inbetweenness" in the literary culture of his time and of the collision of East and West, decorum and humor. Howells often seems remote from the world of current students.

They may wish to know why they are reading him at all—a question that can usher in a discussion of canon formation.

Major Themes, Historical Perspectives, and Personal Issues

The personal theme I would emphasize—because it is not well recognized—is Howells's neuroticism: his history of psychological perturbation and its bearing on his sensitivity to undercurrents of motive in his characters. I would also stress his role as the "Dean" of American letters as indicative of the changing means of literary production in the late nineteenth century. It is also important that Howells's career spanned virtually the entirety of American literature up to his time: from the romantics to the forerunners of modernism.

Significant Form, Style, or Artistic Conventions

Obviously, the key issue for Howells is literary realism: what it means, how it came to develop in America. Since realism has become something of a whipping boy for poststructuralist theory, it makes sense to use Howells to examine the enabling ideological assumptions of realism. There is in Howells, however, especially in his later work, a strong debt to Hawthorne and the American romance. This side of his work is not well known.

Original Audience

Howells was acutely aware of the female dominance of the audience for fiction in the period. He clearly imagined that he was writing for women primarily and believed further that he had a moral responsibility not to offend the sensibilities of young women readers. Insofar as the current audience for literature has been "masculinized" by modernism, Howells's work may sound out of key in the same way that much women's fiction from the period does. In this sense, Howells is best understood as a "woman's" writer.

Comparisons, Contrasts, Connections

Howells makes a nice contrast to almost any American fiction writer of the period because his work assimilated so many of its literary discourses. One conventional way of placing Howells is to put him between James and Twain, his closest literary friends—or to compare him to the generation of his literary sons (Crane, Dreiser, Norris, etc.). A fresher approach would be to pair him with women writers, many of whom he helped to establish. In this regard, "Editha" is a useful text.

Questions for Reading and Discussion/ Approaches to Writing

Although the general approach to teaching literature—and my own approach—seems to have become broader and more theoretical, I still find that students do not know how to read closely enough; they don't understand basic literary codes. With realism, it is especially important to stress the role of reader inference, and I tend to assign topics that focus closely on workably small bits of text.

Bibliography

For a general orientation to recent Howells criticism, I know nothing better than my own omnibus surveys, published as "Howells in the Seventies" and "Howells in the Eighties" in *ESQ:A Journal of the American Renaissance* (1979, 1986-87). See also the recent Howells issue of *American Literary Realism* (1988), which contains several articles and a bibliography keyed to individual Howells texts.

The standard biographies are still Edwin H. Cady, *The Road to Realism/The Realist at War*, and Kenneth S. Lynn, *William Dean Howells*.

Henry James (1843–1916)

Contributing Editor: Alfred Habegger [p. 548]

Classroom Issues and Strategies

In "Beast" James's late style will be a problem. In "Daisy Miller" students may well miss the important social nuances of the language used by the characters and the narrator. Most of us take for granted certain usages—"ever so many," "it seems as if," "I guess," "quaint"—that are indications of the Millers' lack of cultivation. Also, there are some genteelisms in their speech—Mrs. Miller's "the principal ones." Then there's the narrator's somewhat inflated diction—"imbibed," "much disposed towards."

Distribute ahead of time a short list of usages, divided according to categories, and ask the students to add some usages from their own reading of "Daisy Miller."

Another problem that should be mentioned is point of view. Tell the students ahead of time that both "Daisy" and "Beast" use the same technical device of restricting the reader's perspective to what one character sees and knows. Ask them to decide what character this is. Give examples, find exceptions where the narrator speaks out.

"Daisy Miller": Some students inevitably despise Daisy for her occasional social crudity and inexperience. A good tactic to deal with this attitude is to emphasize such matters right at the start, trusting to other students to feel that they must speak up and defend Daisy's naturalness and boldness. I also recommend getting the obvious fact that the Millers represent vulgar new money out in the open from the start; otherwise, some rather slow reader will triumphantly announce this fact later on in order to simplify the heroine's character.

Students will appreciate some facts about Rome. The story takes place before the floor of the Colosseum was excavated and before the cause of malaria was discovered. The 1883 Baedeker guide reminded tourists of the traditional danger of malaria: "In summer when the fever-laden *aria cattive* [bad air] prevails, all the inhabitants who can afford it make a point of leaving the city." Some students will have no experience of Giovanelli's type—the public dandy and lounger.

Students consistently enjoy analyzing and judging (with great ferocity) the various characters. I am often surprised at the harsh judgments passed on Daisy's flirtatiousness and game playing.

"Beast": Few students respond well to "Beast," partly because of the aridity of the lives portrayed. The students may want to know why the story is so long, why it delays the revelation of Marcher's emptiness.

Major Themes, Historical Perspectives, and Personal Issues

In "Beast" I like to stress Marcher's eerie hollowness, the fact that he isn't quite alive and doesn't know it (until the end). In "Daisy Miller" students will probably need a detailed explanation of the Colosseum scene, where Winterbourne finally makes up his mind about Daisy, not only deciding that she isn't respectable but showing her by his behavior that he scorns her as beyond the pale. He learns the truth about her (and his own feelings for her) too late, of course—just like Marcher.

Significant Form, Style, or Artistic Conventions

"Daisy Miller" may be presented as a classic instance of nineteenth-century realism in presenting "a study" of a modern character-type. Simultaneously, since the story follows Winterbourne's point of view, James's subject becomes a double one and also concerns the male character's process of vision and understanding. In this sense, the story is about Winterbourne's "studying."

In "Beast" the emphasis on the man's process of vision becomes even more salient. The lack of objective detail points to modernism.

Original Audience

For "Beast" students need to be told that the two characters are late nineteenth-century or early twentieth-century English, and that Weatherend is an upper-class country house frequented by weekend guests.

In "Daisy Miller" students will need help in grasping the leisure-class European social code: the importance of restraint, public decorum, the drawing of lines. When Daisy looks at Winterbourne and boasts of having had "a great deal of gentleman's society," she doesn't know (though Winterbourne and James do) that she is coming on precisely as a courtesan would.

Comparisons, Contrasts, Connections

Many valuable comparisons can be drawn between "Daisy Miller" and "The Beast in the Jungle." Both stories tell of an aborted romance in which the man distances himself emotionally until it is too late. This fundamental similarity can help bring out the real differences between the works, especially the fact that "Daisy Miller" supplies a good deal of pictorial background and social realism, while "Beast" focuses far more intensively on Marcher's state of mind and perceptions. "Beast" may also profitably be compared with Eliot's "Prufrock."

Questions for Reading and Discussion/ Approaches to Writing

1. Ask students to pay attention to those situations in "Daisy Miller" where one character tries to gauge or classify another. They may notice that Winterbourne's social judgment is much shakier than at first appears. Not only does he misread Daisy (in the Colosseum) but he is wrong in pronouncing Giovanelli "not a gentleman." Giovanelli turns out to be a respectable lawyer.

2. I like to ask students to compare and contrast the scene in the Colosseum where Winterbourne decides Daisy is a reprobate and laughs in her face to the scene in *Huckleberry Finn* where Huck decides to go to hell out of friendship with Jim. One character gives way to a rigid social exclusion, the other defies it.

Bibliography

The preface that James wrote for "Daisy Miller" in the New York edition is illuminating but must be used with care. The preface was written about thirty years after the story, and James's attitudes had changed somewhat. Now he was much more uneasy about the vulgarity of speech and manners of American women, and he decided he had been too easy on the Daisy Miller type. Hence he labeled this story "pure poetry"—a way of calling it romance rather than realism.

Two helpful and somewhat contrasting studies: Wayne Booth's discussion of "Daisy Miller" in *The Rhetoric of Fiction* and Louise K. Barnett, "Jamesian Feminism: Women in 'Daisy Miller,' " *Studies in Short Fiction* 16, no. 4 (Fall 1979): 281–87.

It's difficult to know whether Daisy Miller is a historically accurate type. Respectable single women did not apparently go out alone in the evening in New York of the 1870s, but they did not require a duenna when accompanied by a man.

Kate Chopin (1851–1904)

Contributing Editor: Peggy Skaggs [p. 626]

Classroom Issues and Strategies

Chopin's irony is too subtle for some students, who may see her female characters as cold, unloving, unfeeling women. They have difficulty understanding that the protagonists in, say, "A Respectable Woman" and "The Story of an Hour" really do love their husbands, although in the one case the wife seems sure to commit adultery and in the other the wife exults in her freedom when she believes that her husband has died in an accident. The same students almost surely will judge Calixta (but probably not Alcée) in "The Storm" very harshly. Students almost always respond to Chopin's treatment of the relationship between men and women. Often the male students dislike such characters as Mrs.

Mallard and Mrs. Baroda intensely. Often, also, they judge the mother in "A Pair of Silk Stockings" to be uncaring about her children and frivolous in spending her little windfall. In other words, students today still hold many of the notions about women that inspired Chopin's best irony and satire.

Class discussions usually help a great deal to clear up such misunderstandings. These discussions are based on a very close reading of the text, calling attention to the myriad small clues Chopin always provided but readers do not always observe. "The Storm," being a sequel to "At the Cadian Ball," becomes much clearer in characterization and theme when students understand the groundwork that was laid in the earlier work. Indeed, without such explanation, "The Storm" hardly makes sense to many students.

Since Chopin wrote everything she produced during the last decade of the nineteenth century but was too advanced in her thinking to be accepted until the last quarter of the twentieth century, she offers a fine vehicle for exploring the intellectual and aesthetic tides of American thinking and American literature. In important ways, she summarizes the nineteenth century with her fine mixture of romanticism, realism, and naturalism. But in other ways, she predicts the latter part of the twentieth century with her feminism and existentialism. I like to close one century and begin the next with her works.

Major Themes, Historical Perspectives, and Personal Issues

Chopin's feminism certainly is a major theme, but an instructor must be careful not to overstate it. Chopin seems to have believed that men and women alike have great difficulty reconciling their need to live as discrete individuals with their need to live in close relationship with a mate; these conflicting needs lie at the center of her work.

Significant Form, Style, or Artistic Conventions

Since Chopin's works contain clear elements of romanticism, transcendentalism, realism, naturalism, existentialism, and feminism, her stories can help students understand these literary modes and the directions in which American literature has developed during the last century and a half. Chopin's style offers opportunities to point out the virtues of conciseness; strong, clear imagery; symbolism; understatement; humor; and irony.

Original Audience

I discuss the intellectual background against which Chopin was writing in the 1890s. I share with the students some of the vitriolic reviews received by *The Awakening* in 1899. I trace the history of Chopin's literary reputation from the time the critics buried her in 1899 until a Norwegian resurrected her work in 1969.

Comparisons, Contrasts, Connections

Chopin admired Maupassant's stories enormously, and she translated a number of them into English. Many writers have noted his strong influence, especially apparent in the sharp, ironic conclusions Chopin favored in many stories ("The Story of an Hour" and "Désirée's Baby," for example). The influence of Hawthorne, Whitman, and Henry James has been noted by various critics, also.

Questions for Reading and Discussion/ Approaches to Writing

1. I try to get students to look for irony, simply because so many of them are prone to miss it in Chopin's work.
2. Writing a character study of Mrs. Mallard in "The Story of an Hour" sometimes helps a student to accept that she can be both grief stricken and relieved that her husband is dead.

   A similar assignment focused on the protagonist in "A Respectable Woman" occasionally forces a student to admit that Mrs. Baroda tries valiantly to resist her temptation.

   If the class has read Whitman, I often have them write an essay about how the two authors use lilacs as a symbol or how they both emphasize the importance of both body and spirit.

Bibliography

Particularly useful is the new book *Approaches to Teaching Chopin's "The Awakening,"* edited by Bernard Koloski (New York: MLA, 1988). The backgrounds, biographical information, discussion of critical studies, bibliography, and aids to teaching all contain information useful for teaching Chopin's short stories as well as the novel.

Mary E. Papke's chapter, "Chopin's Stories of Awakening," discusses "The Story of an Hour" and "A Pair of Silk Stockings."

In *Kate Chopin* (Boston: Twayne Publishers, 1985), I discuss each of the stories in this anthology as well as everything else Chopin wrote.

Ambrose Bierce (1842–1914)

Contributing Editor: Cathy N. Davidson [p. 652]

Classroom Issues and Strategies

Two primary problems present themselves. First the details are grotesque. The procession of bloody, dying men and the macabre humor of the small child mounting one as he would a pony (or his father's slaves "playing horsey") often disturbs students very much. This, of course, is exactly Bierce's intention. Second, the ending seems like a gratuitous trick. Is is necessary that the child be deaf and dumb? Realistically, this is necessary since the child does not hear the great battle—we are told so explicitly. But it's also important symbolically: the temptation to war is so great in male culture that even this small child learns it, even though there is so much he does not understand.

To address these issues, first I read some conventional war accounts and war stories—or even the lyrics to war songs. I then read aloud the most grotesque parts of Bierce. I next ask my students which is, in its consequence, the more violent. We then discuss protest literature and Bierce's disgust that several prominent generals of the Civil War were rewriting the incomparably brutal history of that war. Second, we go through the story isolating how the child learns, what he knows and doesn't. The picture book lesson at the beginning makes the point that a child is already learning values at the earliest age, prelinguistically. These are *powerful* messages, calls to violence.

Try reading some definitions from the *Devil's Dictionary*. "*War*, n. A by-product of the arts of peace. War loves to come like a thief in the night; professions of eternal amity provide the night." "*Peace*, n. In international affairs, a period of cheating between two periods of fighting."

I usually give a full biographical lecture on Bierce because he was such a character and such a successful muckraker. Students are always fascinated by his disappearance—no skeleton was ever found. (Several expeditions were mounted and, since he was over 6' tall and had a full head of pure white hair, the rumors of his every move were rampant: but there has never been confirmation of his death.) Brigid Brophy insists he did not die but merely came back again when the world was more ready for his wild, stylistic experiments. According to Brophy, he now writes under the nom de plume of "Jorge Luis Borges." (Actually, since Borges died recently, I suppose that must mean Bierce finally did, too.)

Major Themes, Historical Perspectives, and Personal Issues

War, the tendency toward violence, the idea that we fear what we do not know but perhaps should most fear what we know (i.e., ourselves, our fellow humans, those people we love who nonetheless perpetuate the values of violence). The child sees nothing wrong with war until it literally comes home—the burned house, the dead and probably raped body of the mother. Note, too, the rampant animal imagery throughout the story. Early critics called it an "allegory" and it is.

Significant Form, Style, or Artistic Conventions

Unlike most so-called naturalists, Bierce blamed humans, not Fate, for determining the course of human existence. However, he was a naturalist in his use of macabre and even lurid details that force the reader to see the full implications of war. Stylistically, he brilliantly mimics the actions of the boy (as well as his perceptions, devoid of sound and often sense, since, as a small child, he lacks the experience to know what is harmful, what not: bears are cute in the picture books, so is war) and of the dying soldiers. The famous passage of the ground in motion and the creek relies on repetition to heighten the sense of relentless violence. Allegory is another important genre to discuss and elucidate here.

Original Audience

I always discuss the memoirs of the Civil War veterans as well as the beginning of America's full-fledged attempt at imperialism in Latin America, the Spanish-American War. Bierce, in his other capacity as a journalist, vociferously denounced the war that William Randolph Hearst bragged he started (saying people buy newspapers during wars). Bierce was fired from that job but went on to other newspapers where he was equally adamant in his opposition to the war. He died (or rather disappeared) sometime in 1914, over 70 years old, when he went to Mexico to see Pancho Villa first-hand. Carlos Fuentes' *The Old Gringo* is a retelling of Bierce's journey into Mexico where peasants still insist Bierce wanders the Sierra Madres.

Comparisons, Contrasts, Connections

Stephen Crane learned his craft from Bierce. Hemingway later borrowed some of his techniques. Bierce is highly regarded by postmodernists such as Fuentes as well as Jorge Luis Borges and Julio Cortazar.

He is said to be similar to Guy de Maupassant or O. Henry. But while both of those authors use trick endings, most of Bierce's "tricks" have some larger metaphysical purpose.

Questions for Reading and Discussion/ Approaches to Writing

1. I let students be surprised by the ending and horrified by the language. I try not to give anything away before they get to the story.
2. I've sometimes had them do historical research on the Spanish-American War.

Bibliography

I have a long section on "Chickamauga" in my *Experimental Fictions of Ambrose Bierce*.

Hamlin Garland (1860–1940)

Contributing Editor: James Robert Payne [p. 658]

Classroom Issues and Strategies

Discussion and explanation of Garland's populist values and political activities definitely enhances an appreciation of his fiction, as does some consideration, however brief, of his interest in Henry George's economic theories. Relate the populist movement of late nineteenth-century America to present-day grievances and problems of American farmers. More generally, compare social and political tensions between southern, midwestern, and western American regions on one hand, and the northeastern region on the other in Garland's day and today.

Garland's profound empathy for the life situation of the rural and small-town midwestern farm woman requires discussion and may be productively studied in relation to Garland's biography. If feasible (depending on student interest), compare Garland's "single-tax" notions (derived from Henry George, 1839-97) with present-day tax reform schemes. What would be the social impact of such schemes, then and now?

Students express interest in Garland's representation of the impact on rural society of national economic policies and laws. They are also interested in comparing the role of women in rural America as given in Garland's writings with what they perceive as the role of women in rural areas today. Students will also compare the impact of land speculators and monopoly industries on society today with the impact of such forces as represented in Garland's writings.

Major Themes, Historical Perspectives, and Personal Issues

1. Central to much of Garland's best fiction and autobiography is an attempt to contrast actual conditions of American farm families with nineteenth-century (and earlier) idealizations of farm life.
2. As we see in his story "Up the Coulé" and elsewhere, Garland was very interested in the drama inherent in relations between farm families and their urbanized children.
3. Garland's theme of white America's injustice to Indians, apparent in his novel *The Captain of the Gray-Horse Troop* and his collection the *Book of the American Indian*, is very important though neglected in teaching and writing about Garland.

Significant Form, Style, or Artistic Conventions

1. If the instructor is interested in such conventions as "realism" and "naturalism," Garland may be taught as a transitional figure between the relatively genteel realism of William Dean Howells and the harsher naturalism we associate with Stephen Crane (as in *Maggie*, 1893) and Theodore Dreiser (as in *Sister Carrie*, 1900).
2. Consider represented speech in Garland's fiction, including suggestions of German language, as we see in "Up the Coulé," as indicative of Garland's efforts toward realism.

Original Audience

Although Garland's early fiction, such as that collected in *Main-Travelled Roads* (which includes "Up the Coulé"), shocked many with its frank portrayal of the harshness of actual farm life, as Garland perceived that life, by the end of his career, particularly through such works as *A Son of the Middle Border*, Garland was a recognized, even beloved, chronicler of the opening up and settlement of the American Midwest and West. In Garland's day, many rural midwesterners read *A Son of the Middle Border* as their region's analogue to Benjamin Franklin's *Autobiography*. Readers today value Garland's work as giving a most authentic dramatization of post-Civil War midwestern rural life.

Comparisons, Contrasts, Connections

Emile Zola (1840–1902)—French naturalist author who endeavored to convey an accurate picture of the poor and marginalized of France in his day. Compare and contrast with Garland's drama of the harsh life on nineteenth-century American farms.

Willa Cather (1873–1947)—Compare Cather's presentation of rural midwestern life to Garland's. Is the picture that Cather gives us more balanced, varied, and perhaps more positive than Garland's generally bleak views?

John Steinbeck (1902–1947)—With particular reference to Steinbeck's *The Grapes of Wrath* (1939), compare unrest of farmers in 1930s (Steinbeck) to that in the late nineteenth century (Garland).

Questions for Reading and Discussion/ Approaches to Writing

1. Items that follow refer specifically to Garland's story "Up the Coulé":
   (a) As you read, recall a time when you returned to your parental home after a considerable period of absence during which you achieved, perhaps, a new sophistication. Compare your experience, feelings, and family tension to family tensions and feelings represented in "Up the Coulé."
   (b) Compare Garland's portrayal of farm life to your experience of farm life.
2. Discuss Garland's fiction against the background of the populist movement of late-nineteenth-century America.
   (a) Research Garland's autobiographies, especially *A Son of the Middle Border* and *A Daughter of the Middle Border* and trace autobiographical tendencies in Garland's fiction.
   (b) Research Henry George's "single-tax" theories (see George's *Progress and Poverty*, 1879) and compare George's ideas and themes with ideas implicit in Garland's *Main-Travelled Roads* series.
   (c) Compare and contrast themes and values of Garland's *A Son of the Middle Border* to Franklin's *Autobiography*.

Bibliography

Ahnebrink, Lars. *The Beginnings of Naturalism in American Fiction.* Cambridge, Mass.: Harvard Univ. Press, 1950, 63–89. European influences on Garland.

Bledsoe, Thomas. Introduction. In *Main-Travelled Roads.* New York: Rinehart, 1954.

Folsom, James K. *The American Western Novel.* New Haven, Conn.: College and Univ. Press, 1966, 149–55, 180–84. On Garland's writings about Indians.

Gish, Robert. *Hamlin Garland: The Far West.* Boise State Univ. Western Writers Series, No. 24. Boise, Idaho: Boise State Univ., 1976.

McCullough, Joseph B. *Hamlin Garland.* Boston: Twayne, 1978. Short, readable, solid introductory book.

Pizer, Donald. "Hamlin Garland's *A Son of the Middle Border:* Autobiography as Art." In *Essays in American and English Literature Presented to B. R. McElderry, Jr.,* edited by Max L. Schultz, 76–107. Athens: Ohio Univ. Press, 1967.

———. *Hamlin Garland's Early Work and Career.* Berkeley: Univ. of California Press, 1960. Best treatment of Garland's most vital years as fictionist.

———. "Herbert Spencer and the Genesis of Hamlin Garland's Critical System." *Tulane Studies in English* 7 (1957): 153–68.

Taylor, Walter F. *The Economic Novel in America.* Chapel Hill: Univ. of N. C. Press, 1942, 148–83. On Garland's social and economic views.

Walcutt, Charles C. *American Literary Naturalism, A Divided Stream.* Minneapolis: Univ. of Minn. Press, 1956, 53–63.

Stephen Crane (1871–1900)

Contributing Editor: Donald Vanouse [p. 689]

Classroom Issues and Strategies

Stephen Crane's works present sudden shifts in tone and point of view, and frequently the works end without establishing either certainty about characters or resolution of thematic issues. Crane's imagery is vivid, but the works seldom provide final interpretations (e.g., the empty bucket in "A Mystery of Heroism"). These qualities contribute to Crane's multi-layered irony.

The instructor should attempt to shift the focus from *resolving* issues of plot or character (e.g., "Is Collins a hero?") to showing the students that Crane seems to encourage the reader to *enrich* and *re-evaluate* ideas about patterns of action and thought. Crane asks questions rather than providing answers.

Consider using the poems to introduce some of his major themes. Crane seems to have valued them quite highly as expressions of his sense of the world. In like manner, the pace and drama of "A Mystery of Heroism" and "The Bride Comes to Yellow Sky" make them easier as doorways to Crane than the more stately and ambitious reflectiveness of "The Open Boat."

Like other scholars, students in class often are concerned with Crane's attitude toward God. It is useful—if complex—to invite them to look at "God Lay Dead in Heaven," "A Man Said to the Universe," "Do Not Weep, Maiden, For War Is Kind," "Chant You Loud of Punishments," and "When a People Reach the Top of a Hill." These poems, along with the "prayer" in "The Open Boat" indicate the *variety* of religious experience in Crane.

Major Themes, Historical Perspectives, and Personal Issues

Crane writes about extreme experiences that are confronted by ordinary people. His characters are not larger-than-life, but they touch the mysterious edges of their capacities for perception, action, and understanding.

In his themes and styles, Crane is an avant-garde writer.

Significant Form, Style, or Artistic Conventions

Crane's works reflect many of the major artistic concerns at the end of the nineteenth century, especially naturalism, impressionism, and symbolism.

His works insist that we live in a universe of vast and indifferent natural forces, not in a world of divine providence or a certain moral order. "A Man Said to the Universe" is useful in identifying this aspect of Crane. But Crane's vivid and explosive prose styles distinguish his works from those by many other writers who are labeled naturalists.

Many readers (including Hamlin Garland and Joseph Conrad, who were personal friends of Crane) have used the term impressionist to describe Crane's vivid renderings of moments of visual beauty and uncertainty. Even Crane's "discontinuous" rendering of action has been identified as impressionist.

In "The Open Boat," Crane has been seen as a symbolist. Perhaps it is most appropriate to see the story as a skeptical balancing of concern with vast archetypes with an equal concern with psychology of perception: personal and cultural symbol grids.

Original Audience

Crane had a popular audience as well as a cultivated, literary audience during his lifetime.

Crane was a "star" journalist, and he published many of his best fictional works in the popular press. Nonetheless his comment that a newspaper is a "collection of half-injustices" indicates his skepticism about that medium of communication.

Comparisons, Contrasts, Connections

Crane's relationship to naturalism links him to such writers as Frank Norris, Theodore Dreiser, and John Dos Passos.

Crane's brief free-verse poems invite comparison with those of Emily Dickinson (Howells read them to him), and with a number of twentieth-century poets, particularly those influenced by imagism (Carl Sandburg, Amy Lowell, Pound, Williams, for example). In brevity and in the authors' desire to escape conventional poetic rhetoric, these poems are comparable to Crane's. There are, of course, some vast differences in subject.

Questions for Reading and Discussion/ Approaches to Writing

1. Why does Crane use the term "Mystery" in the title of his war story? What is the mystery? Or do you find more than one?
2. In "The Bride" Crane seems interested in the role of women. Does the story show a shift of power from male violence?
3. In "The Open Boat," Crane seems very interested in what the correspondent learns. What does he learn about nature? Or about seeing nature? Or his relationship to other human beings?

4. How useful is "A Man Said to the Universe" in understanding the correspondent's experience?
5. "There Was a Man with a Tongue of Wood" and "Chant You Loud of Punishments" are poems about poetry. What do these poems say about Crane's ambition or purpose as a poet?

Crane's vivid prose makes him particularly valuable in developing student skills in discussing literary style.

Also, his spare and startling structures (especially "endings") provide useful occasions for assignments on literary structure.

Crane's relationship to naturalism provokes questions about individual freedom and responsibility.

Bibliography

Ralph Ellison's essay in *Shadow and Act* (1964) (first published as the Introduction to *The Red Badge of Courage and Four Great Stories by Stephen Crane*, New York: Dell, 1960) brings fresh insight to the issue of Crane's value to American culture.

Jack London (1876–1916)

Contributing Editor: Joan D. Hedrick [p. 725]

Classroom Issues and Strategies

In young readers, London sometimes inspires an uncritical identification. His heroes and his ideologies are bigger than life; he himself often has no proper distance from them. On the other hand, more sophisticated readers sometimes are impatient with London's romanticism and overstatement.

Careful analysis of the strengths of London's art—his selection of detail, his vivid descriptions, his mythic plots—is effective in restoring the balance of both the undercritical and the overcritical reader. Because London led a colorful life and drew heavily on his experiences in his writing, biographical approaches are effective.

Individualism is a volatile and heady topic in America, and in naturalistic stories of rebirth the heroes sometimes rise to megalomaniacal proportions. "To Build a Fire" is remarkable in that London uses this stark focus on the individual to suggest the limits of individualism. "The man" has no class or social ties—not even a name. That his only companion is a creature of another species, a dog who is his "toil-slave," hints at the reality of unbreachable class differences that contribute to the man's isolation and ultimate death. Written after London's "long sickness," a period of profound disillusionment in which London questioned whether his admission to the literary establishment had been worth the price, "To Build a Fire" contrasts man's hubris with his frailty and finitude.

Students respond to London's two-fisted approach to life and want to know details of his life. This can be an opportunity to explore the contradictions that a writer from the working class experiences as he modulates his tone, language, and experience to appeal to a middle-class literary audience.

Major Themes, Historical Perspectives, and Personal Issues

The major themes I emphasize are social mobility and the American dream in a period of severe economic depression and centralization. As America became an urban, industrial nation, the farming population was replaced by a burgeoning middle class that earned its living in more sedentary ways. A nostalgia for the primitive and primordial fueled a literary marketplace that obliged with stories of prehistoric man and tales of the exotic outdoors. The Alaskan Gold Rush, from which "To Build a Fire" takes its setting, is itself an illustration of the dislocations of the 1890s. The Panic of 1893 initiated a deep depression that left those disappointed in the American Dream ready at the hint of gold to believe in it again.

Significant Form, Style, or Artistic Conventions

Naturalism is the literary movement that provides the best context for "To Build a Fire." Naturalism has been understood as a dialectic between free will and determinism (Charles Child Walcutt, *American Literary Naturalism, A Divided Stream* [Minneapolis: Univ. of Minnesota Press, 1956]), but it is probably most intelligible through social history. The appeal of naturalistic tales is often escape. The urban problems of unemployment, labor wars, and poverty are left behind for a spare scenario in which an individual can be tested. A stock naturalistic device involves taking an "overcivilized" man from the upper classes into a primitive environment where he must live by muscle and wit. Frank Norris uses this device in *Moran of the Lady Letty*, as does London in *The Sea-Wolf*. *The Call of the Wild* also fits this pattern, although here the hero is a dog. Buck, a dog of northern ancestry who has been raised in Southern California, is kidnapped and taken to Alaska where he must adapt to snow and the rule of the club.

In another common naturalistic pattern, the hero who stays in the city either becomes an ineffectual dandy or degenerates into a lower-class brute. Frank Norris's *Vandover and the Brute*, set in San Francisco, traces the downward arc of Vandover's career from a Harvard education through the urban horrors of drink, dissipation, and aimless drifting to his ultimate reward: he literally becomes a primitive brute when he falls victim to lycanthropy and finds himself barking like a wolf. London treats these materials more realistically, yet employs the same pattern whereby the city is associated with degeneration and the open country with rebirth. Both *Burning Daylight* and *The Valley of the Moon* contrast the vitality of the heroes in the country to the dissipation and bad luck they encounter in the city.

Original Audience

In discussing London's working-class origins, I encourage students to consider the ways in which he had to transform and compromise his material in order to appeal to a middle-class literary establishment. For the middle class, Alaska represented an adventure, a lark; for the working class, it recapitulated the struggle to survive that was a daily part of their urban lives. Thus it provided what Earle Labor has called a "symbolic wilderness" in which to enact different class agendas.

Comparisons, Contrasts, Connections

"To Build a Fire" is related to such naturalistic tales as Stephen Crane's "The Open Boat," and is part of the ethos of the strenuous life that rose out of the decadence of the 1890s. Such stories of escape from civilization have obvious links to the "classic" male initiation stories, or what Nina Baym has called "melodramas of beset manhood," from Cooper's *Deerslayer* to Twain's *Adventures of Huckleberry Finn* to Hemingway's stories of *Men Without Women*. Women are often associated with the evils of civilization—although the opposite side of the stereotype are the sentimental stories London wrote in which females redeem the heroes through a cloying domesticity (*White Fang*, *Burning Daylight*, and *The Sea-Wolf*). For their treatment of naturalistic themes, comparisons between London and Norris are helpful in delineating the preoccupations of the writers of the 1890s.

Questions for Reading and Discussion/ Approaches to Writing

When I teach London's *Martin Eden,* I ask students to compare his story of a self-made man to that of either Theodore Dreiser's *Sister Carrie* or Maimie Pinzer's *The Maimie Papers* and analyze the difference that gender makes in the story of success.

Bibliography

The best work on London's Alaskan stories is in James McClintock's *White Logic: Jack London's Short Stories* (Grand Rapids, Michigan: Wolf House Books, 1975).

For a biographical context for London's writing, see Joan Hedrick, *Solitary Comrade: Jack London and His Work* (Chapel Hill: Univ. of N. C. Press, 1982), Chapters 1–2, pp. 3–47.

Issues and Visions in Post-Civil War America

[p. 738]

Standing Bear (Ponca) (1829–1908)

Contributing Editor: Daniel F. Littlefield, Jr. [p. 739]

Classroom Issues and Strategies

It is difficult to provide a historical framework for Standing Bear, though this can be overcome by acquainting students with the modes, conventions, and protocol of Indian oratory, getting them to understand the word as a spoken record of a nonliterate culture. It might be useful to place the dispossession of the Poncas of lands that were traditionally theirs alongside the economic aspirations of immigrants to America and the excesses of the Gilded Age as evidenced in the literature.

Major Themes, Historical Perspectives, and Personal Issues

Three major themes are: an understanding of those who were victimized by national goals of Manifest Destiny; the rights of those outside constitutional protection; and the dehumanization of people in the march of nineteenth-century progress.

Significant Form, Style, or Artistic Convention

Introduce the modes, conventions, and protocol of Indian oratory.

Comparisons, Contrasts, Connections

Concerning the theme of destruction of Indian cultures in the late nineteenth century, Indian writers like Eastman, Zitkala-Sa, and Oskison offer useful points of comarison. The position of the Indians as non-white peoples in America might be usefully compared and contrasted to the position of other such groups, like the African Americans.

Bibliography

See primary and secondary works listed with the text headnote.

Ghost Dance Songs

[p. 742]

Please refer to the headnote in the text for complete information.

Charles Alexander Eastman (Sioux) (1858–1939)

Contributing Editor: Daniel F. Littlefield, Jr. [p. 745]

Classroom Issues and Strategies

Students need to know what the Ghost Dance movement was, its importance to the Indians, and reasons why U.S. officials viewed it as something that had to be suppressed. They also are curious about the status of an assimilated Indian like Eastman. Supply background on these issues. It is also helpful to deal with Eastman's work in the same manner as you would an autobiographical narrative written by any other author of the same period.

Major Themes, Historical Perspectives, and Personal Issues

Discuss cultural ignorance, social discontinuity, national goals vs. cultural integrity, cultural assimilation, the narrator as an "in-between" person.

Significant Form, Style, or Artistic Convention

Attention can be focused profitably on the form of the autobiographical narrative, touching on such matters as narrative control, style, self-revelation, etc.

Comparisons, Contrasts, Connections

Compare the autobiographical works of other Indians, such as Zitkala-Sa, John Joseph Mathews, and Thomas Whitecloud, as well as any other autobiographical works, especially by writers who belong to other racial or cultural minorities.

Bibliography

The list of primary and secondary works in the headnote is comprehensive.

Marietta Holley (pseud. "Josiah Allen's Wife") (1836–1926)

Contributing Editor: Kate H. Winter [p. 754]

Classroom Issues and Strategies

The regional dialect and peculiar orthography in Holley's work may initially prove difficult for students. It is helpful to read the early part of the chapter aloud so student readers can catch the rhythm of the language and see the humor in the odd spellings. Equally helpful is Jane Curry's recorded rendering of Samantha's voice in the tape cassette that accompanies *Samantha Rastles the Woman Question.*

Have students list the unfamiliar language usages and colloquialisms they encounter in their college community. Discuss what is amusing and/or revealing about these, what values are implicit in their use, and their use as a means of establishing community. Students often want to know whether Holley's audience found it difficult to read dialect and whether they took pleasure in it.

Ask students to examine the Declaration of Independence before reading the Holley selection. A journal or freewriting assignment could follow in which students respond to what they understand to be the values implicit in that document. Or you might ask students to rewrite the Declaration of Independence in their vernacular.

Students often have difficulty understanding how women might feel religiously disenfranchised, so we do some quick exercises demonstrating the power of exclusion—for example, not allowing anyone with blue eyes to speak in class for a set period. In addition we discuss briefly the patriarchal structure of Christian religious practice and its impact.

Major Themes, Historical Perspectives, and Personal Issues

Much of the book is taken up with Samantha's descriptions of how the local church women are refurbishing and maintaining the church counterpointed with her disagreements over Josiah's wrong-headed interpretations of Scripture. Samantha uses feminist arguments to explain away or circumvent the difficulties in Biblical texts that excluded women: there may have been an error in translation; or the context within which the Scriptures were written rendered the literal meaning irrelevant to modern times; or the writer (St. Paul, for example) was just one man giving his personal opinion. The chapter included here extends the disagreement to interpreting the Declaration of Independence, thereby linking religious with legislative hypocrisy.

The language issues inherent in this text also provide an excellent opportunity to have students look at sexism in language, the significance of dialect (which students are apt to be familiar with from their own usages), and the standardization of English. Most classes can address questions about the ability of language to exclude or include privileged groups.

Through Samantha, Holley tackled the prevailing ideas of what gifts, responsibilities, and rights "Nater" and law had given women and men.

Significant Form, Style, or Artistic Conventions

In addition to showing the faults in the logic of the brethren, Holley was attempting to reproduce phonetically the patois of upstate New Yorkers. Holley captures the style and character of much upstate New York fiction as does Philander Deming, whose Adirondack stories are gems of local color writing, and Irving Bacheller, whose novels of New York's North Country preserve an era and place long since lost.

Holley's audience often thought her spellings were the result of her being an uneducated country woman; only more sophisticated readers recognized that she, like Twain, adopted a persona for the distance it provided between audience and writer and the comic effect of the naive commentator.

As the headnote indicates, Holley's work blends several American literary traditions including the verbal play of the male literary comedians. She also turned humorist Ann Stephens's vernacular humor and Frances Witcher's humorous modes to her own ends. Her style includes the elements of anticlimax, misquoted Scripture, decorative spelling, puns, malapropisms, comic similes, mixed metaphors, extravagant images, language reversals, and proverbs and maxims. She handles these techniques with the same flair and assurance that the male writers who dominated the tradition did. Furthermore, there is the comic irony of her saying one thing, doing another, and having Josiah deny the reality or validity of both. While the literary and social value of the satiric humor of the male writers in the tradition has rarely been debated, Holley's place in the canon of American humor—because of her subject matter—has been small and narrow.

Original Audience

In addition to the work described above, I sketch for students the political background. In 1888, the National Methodist Conference (the "Brethren" of the title) had refused to seat four duly elected women delegates. Holley's response to the outrage was this book, which is dedicated to "All women, who work trying to bring into dark lives the brightness and hope of a better country." The author's intimate friend within the church hierarchy, Bishop John Newman, and his wife, provided her with most of the background material and arguments that informed the debates. At the back of the first edition, the publishers append six of the speeches delivered in deliberation at the conference. Students may wish to contrast the rhetoric in them with Samantha's.

Comparisons, Contrasts, Connections

Two other texts included in this collection make useful corollary reading for this chapter. In Mary Wilkins Freeman's "A Church Mouse," we see the local colorist's use of dialect and dialogue that also marks Holley's work and a similar struggle between patriarchal habit and the newly feminized Christianity of the late nineteenth century. The conflict that Freeman depicts is underlaid by the bedrock of prejudice that Josiah represents in Holley's work. Students may want to consider what assumptions about gender differences form the basis for Josiah's and the townspeople's arguments. Holley's fiction is particularly subversive because of Samantha's willingness to work at the role of country wife while she chips away at the granite convictions about male superiority that her husband Josiah clings to. A look into Charlotte Perkins Gilman's *Herland*, especially chapter 10 on religion, also provides parallel material for discussion.

Questions for Reading and Discussion/ Approaches to Writing

I attempt to give writing tasks that invite the students to connect their own experience with what is in the text so that they begin to "own" the ideas and feelings. For example: have students write imitations of a short piece—even a paragraph—to approximate stylistic features; have them rewrite a piece in their own words to help them see the importance of the language community in shaping a text; ask them to transform a text by rewriting it in another genre—perhaps a news story, poem, dialogue, letter, etc. With any of these methods, the students get a glimpse of the decisions informing the author's choice of language and genre and contribute to their understanding of the creative process in a cultural context.

Charlotte Perkins Gilman (1860–1935)

Contributing Editor: Elaine Hedges [p. 760]

Classroom Issues and Strategies

Usually students respond well to "The Yellow Wall-Paper" and don't have serious difficulty with it. Background information on medical treatment of women in the nineteenth century—especially Dr. S. Weir Mitchell's "rest cure"—is useful (mentioned in the headnote). Naive students sometimes wonder why the woman can't just leave; they need to understand the situation of married women in the nineteenth century.

Since the chapter from *Herland* is an excerpt from a utopian novel, some discussion of the tradition and nature of utopias, what their purposes are, is useful. Alert students to the fact that utopias discuss ideas, often at the expense of narrative action. Gilman's emphasis on motherhood might strike some students as excessive or old-fashioned, and many will have trouble accepting her ideas about sex. The issue of motherhood, like many others Gilman raises in the chapter, can all be discussed in relation to contemporary realities. (One can point out that we live in a society that officially venerates motherhood but in actuality offers few social services for mothers.) Regarding Gilman's ideas on sex, one can ask students to consider the extent to which it is a physiological necessity or a learned behavior.

Major Themes, Historical Perspectives, and Personal Issues

Consider "The Yellow Wall-Paper" as a critique of male power, of marriage, and of medical treatment of women. Students can be asked how relevant these critiques are today, whether similar situations still exist.

Regarding the theme of madness, can madness be liberating? Compare Emily Dickinson's poem, "Much madness is divinest sense."

The themes or issues in the chapter from *Herland* are the heart of the matter, and the excerpt can elicit good discussion of them, since they are all still relevent. The chapter asks us to question or examine our received opinions about marriage, wifehood, the home, love, sex (and the relation of sex to love), motherhood, friendship, and what it means to be "feminine." Students can be asked whether Gilman's observations still have validity. They can be asked before reading the chapter to write a definition or a paragraph describing their understanding of one or more of the topics, then compare with what Gilman says.

Significant Form, Style, or Artistic Conventions

In "The Yellow Wall-Paper" less sophisticated students have a tendency to identify the narrator with Gilman (especially since the story is based on an episode in her life). Discussion of the literary convention of first-person point of view and of differences between an author and her persona is useful.

Students will want to deal with the symbolism in the story, especially the symbolism of the wallpaper, and also of the room to which the narrator is confined. They usually enjoy this.

With the chapter from *Herland*, conventions of utopian fiction, the use of role reversal throughout the chapter, and the use of satire and irony are primary stylistic and conventional concerns.

Original Audience

I discuss Gilman's difficulty in getting "The Yellow Wall-Paper" published, and ask students to consider why it might have disturbed her contemporaries. (It was rejected by one editor on the grounds that it would make readers too miserable.) Why has it also been read as a gothic thriller rather than a story about the sexual politics of marriage?

I discuss the rediscovery of the story and reasons for its current popularity: why do they think it has become a "classic" for feminist (and other) readers? Is it easier today to accept Gilman's analysis of male power?

Contemporary critics have noted that Gilman wrote *Herland* during World War I, a time when women, especially feminists like Gilman, seeing the old order breaking up, might have had hopes of a new order in which women would enjoy greater equality. Current revival of interest in the work is due to our interest once again in challenging traditional sex roles.

Comparisons, Contrasts, Connections

In the same section of the anthology, other entries dealing with marriage and with male-female power relations include: Elizabeth Stuart Phelps's, some of Chopin's stories, Freeman's (where the women try to resist more). "The Yellow Wall-Paper" could also be compared/ contrasted to the comic treatment of husband-wife relations and male assertions of power in the Marietta Holley selection. And I've already mentioned Dickinson. One could also compare and contrast Gilman's use of gothic elements with Poe's.

Marriage and motherhood are treated in selections by Phelps, Chopin, Freeman, Holley. Many of these discuss the actualities, as opposed to Gilman's focus on the ideals in *Herland*.

Questions for Reading and Discussion/ Approaches to Writing

One could ask students whether men today want to marry women as independent as those in Herland? Do today's men find such women sexually attractive?

Bibliography

My afterword to the Feminist Press edition of "The Yellow Wall-Paper" is the most succinct analysis of it, with a biography of Gilman. Also: "Introduction," Ann J. Lane, ed., *Herland* (N.Y.: Pantheon, 1979)

W. E. B. Du Bois (1865–1963)

Contributing Editor: Frederick Woodard [p. 782]

Questions for Reading and Discussion/ Approaches to Writing

"The Song of the Smoke" is a poem of celebration of blackness. It was written during a period of great social and political weakness of black people. List the attributes of blackness celebrated in the poem and suggest how each attribute contributes to a positive image. Consider why Du Bois may have felt it necessary to write of blackness in such exalted terms.

Ask students to characterize the effect of verbal repetition, rhythm, and variation of line length in the poem. How do these characteristics relate to the central metaphor, "smoke"?

"The Damnation of Women" is an expression of Du Bois's concern for the right of women to choose for themselves the life worth living. What is the basis for this belief? How does this belief relate to feminism? What role, in Du Bois's estimation, does economics play in the subordination of women? What specific details indicate Du Bois's appreciation for independent thinking and action in women.

Select an edition of the volume *The Souls of Black Folk* and peruse the beginning of each chapter. Find lines of poetry and a musical score. Consider the possible significance of these two art forms to the major theme of the book. Note that "Of the Sorrow Songs" contains comments on the music and names the songs.

The "veil" is one of Du Bois's most famous symbols. Consider possible meanings for it in "Of Our Spiritual Strivings." In regard to possible meanings for the "veil," what may be at the beginning of the essay, particularly his boast of living "above the veil"?

Relate the section in "Of Our Spiritual Strivings" out of which the famous Du Bois passage on twoness comes (beginning with "After the Egyptian and the Indian, the Greek and Roman" and ending with, "Shout, O Children!/Shout, you're free!/For God has bought your liberty!") to a reading of "The Unhappy Consciousness," a chapter in Hegel's *Phenomenology of Mind*. Then develop a list of supporting evidence to justify the probable influences of the Hegelian argument on Du Bois's thinking in his essay. Additional reading in Hans-Georg Gadamer, *Hegel's Dialectic: Five Hermeneutical Studies*, translated by P. Christopher Smith (New Haven: Yale Univ. Press, 1976) should provide excellent analysis of Hegel's ideas and method. See particularly Chapters 2 and 3.

Note throughout the essays collected here that Du Bois uses the terms Negro, black, and African-American almost interchangeably. On closer examination you may discern a specific context that differentiates the usage of each term. Develop a rationale for usage of each term in a specific context.

"Of the Sorrow Songs" is considered one of Du Bois's most enduring statements on African-American folk art. Using the content of the essay, trace the evolution of the African song to a unique American folk expression.

Corridos

Contributing Editor: Raymund Paredes [p. 798]

Classroom Issues and Strategies

Major problems anticipated are the following: students' lack of familiarity with Chicano culture generally; lack of familiarity with musical forms, especially Mexican; and lack of familiarity with teaching music—in this case, ballads—as literature.

Probably the most useful piece of advice is to regard the lyrics of the ballads as narrative poems that treat some aspect of Mexican-American (or Chicano) history; e.g., cattle drives, political injustice, racial hostility. *Corridos* represent the collective wisdom and perspective of Mexican Americans; they occupy a place in Chicano culture somewhat analogous to the place of blues in African-American experience. It's worthwhile to do a bit of reading in Mexican-American history for context: start with Americo Paredes's *With His Pistol in His Hand*. It is most useful to listen to *corridos*, to engage them as musical performances. *Corridos* are available in most record libraries.

Major Themes, Historical Perspectives, and Personal Issues

In this group of *corridos*, it's important to note that American cowboy culture derives largely from Mexican culture: the *corrido* "Kiansis I" lauds the superiority of Mexican cowboys over their Anglo counterparts. The point is that Mexican Americans have resented the appropriation of their culture without due recognition. "Gregorio Cortez" and "Jacinto Treviño" are epic ballads that deal with Mexican/Mexican-American responses to "American" injustice and bigotry.

Significantly, the ballads make no distinction between a Mexican citizen and resident like Treviño and a resident of the United States like Cortez. Both are "Mexicanos" who fight for their community's rights and dignity. "El Contrabando de El Paso" relates the experiences of a young Mexicano who is enticed into smuggling and then betrayed by his "friends." The ballad poignantly relates the fears of the Mexican immigrant in a strange land.

Significant Form, Style, or Artistic Convention

The *corrido* has certain standardized qualities of form and meter but these are not easily discernible in English translation. In Spanish, *corridos* normally appear in four-line stanzas with an abcd rhyming pattern and a *one*-two-three strumming pattern. *Corridos* often end with a *despedida*, an explicit farewell that marks the end of the song.

Original Audience

Corridos are songs of the people, usually composed anonymously and typically focused on a significant personal or cultural event. *Corridos* have achieved widespread popularity through both oral and mechanical (phonograph records, radio, etc.) transmission. *Corridos* are well known in virtually all Chicano and Mexican communities.

Comparisons, Contrasts, Connections

The *corrido* tradition, in terms of form and function, may be compared with the blues. Both are tremedously important expressive forms in their respective cultures, representing certain values, attitudes, and historical perspectives. It is, of course, critical to understand the primacy of oral expressive forms in cultures traditionally denied the tool of literacy.

Questions for Reading and Discussion/ Approaches to Writing

Students should be familiarized with the historical literary importance of musical forms, beginning, perhaps, with the transformation of Greek folk songs into Homeric epics. The ballad tradition in England, Scotland, and other European locations might also be considered as providing a historical context. Students might be asked to write on any of these background issues.

Writing assignments explicitly on *corridos* might include a broader study of the genre. There are extensive collections of *corridos* in Spanish. Students might be asked to write about *corridos* from a particular period, a particular locale (e.g., Texas), or about a particular subject (such as Mexican immigration to the United States).

Bibliography

The most useful general reference for *corridos* in the United States is Americo Paredes's *With His Pistol in His Hand*; also helpful are "Songs of Mexican Migration" in J. Frank Dobie's *Puro Mexicano* and Merle Simmons's *The Mexican Corrido*.

Upton Sinclair (1878–1968)

Contributing Editor: James C. Wilson [p. 813]

Classroom Issues and Strategies

The most difficult problem in teaching *The Jungle* is how to approach a text in which literary qualities are subordinated to political purpose. *The Jungle* does not lend itself to the kinds of literary discussions that most of us are accustomed to. Its literary shortcomings are obvious.

One way to begin discussing *The Jungle* would be to approach it as a political novel. Work with your students to define the genre of the political novel. Compare *The Jungle* to other political novels the students might have read. Discuss the criteria by which we evaluate—or should evaluate—a political novel. Should our criteria include social and/or political considerations? (It might be useful here to draw a parallel between a political novel and a postmodern novel, for example, in which ideas overshadow the other ingredients of the fiction.)

Students generally respond to Sinclair's portrait of the unsanitary conditions in the meat-packing industry. They tend to be interested in the history of *The Jungle*—how it was written, the federal legislation that was passed because of the public reaction to it, etc.

Major Themes, Historical Perspectives, and Personal Issues

Any discussion of *The Jungle* should mention the unsanitary conditions in the Chicago meat-packing industry at the turn of the century and the federal legislation that Congress passed as a result of the national furor that Sinclair's muckraking novel created. However, it is equally important to emphasize that *The Jungle* was—and is—primarily an indictment of wage slavery. Sinclair's purpose in writing the novel was to document the inhumane treatment of working men and women in industrial capitalism and to argue that socialism provided the only solution to the problem.

Significant Form, Style, or Artistic Conventions

Questions of style and form often seem irrelevant to *The Jungle*. However, it is possible to discuss the primitive, at times brutal, prose of the novel as an appropriate vehicle to convey the quality of human life that Sinclair found in the stockyards of Chicago: working men and women reduced to the level of the dumb beasts they were butchering on the killing fields.

Comparisons, Contrasts, Connections

The Jungle should be considered in the context of three separate but related literary movements in America. First, the novel comes out of the muckraking era. The Muckrakers—so named by Theodore Roosevelt because they, like the Man with the Muckrake in *Pilgrim's Progress*, looked down at the filth and ignored the celestial crown—exposed and attempted to correct graft and corruption in both government and business. The most famous of the Muckrakers, in addition to Sinclair, were Lincoln Steffens and Ida Tarbell, whose major works, *The Shame of the Cities* and *History of the Standard Oil Company* respectively, appeared in 1901.

The Jungle also has its roots in American naturalism, with its first twenty-one chapters conforming, in both form and content, to the typical naturalistic novel of that period. For example, both style and psychological complexity are subordinated to the necessary machinations of the plot—the inevitable movement toward chaos and disintegration. Jurgis and his family, like the heroines of Stephen Crane's *Maggie*, Frank Norris's *McTeague*, and Theodore Dreiser's *Sister Carrie* are victims of hereditary, environmental, social, and economic forces beyond their control—forces that shape their lives in an impersonal, mechanistic way.

Of course, what distinguishes *The Jungle* from these other examples of American naturalism is the turn toward socialism in the last four chapters, which allows Sinclair to end his novel on an optimistic note. The fact that Sinclair was a socialist, and that he used his writing as a vehicle to express his socialism, identifies him with the group of radical writers and artists that was centered in Greenwich Village (where the radical socialist magazine *The Masses* was published) and that included Floyd Dell, Randolph Bourne, Lincoln Steffens, Max Eastman, and John Reed. Sinclair, like these other socialist writers of the Progressive Era, understood that journalism and fiction could be used as political tools. Sinclair's critique of American capitalism has much in common with his fellow socialists in the pre-World War I period.

Questions for Reading and Discussion/ Approaches to Writing

1. (a) Discuss *The Jungle* as an indictment of wage slavery and compare it to other works of literature that attack antebellum slavery (e.g., Harriet Beecher Stowe's *Uncle Tom's Cabin*).

   (b) Discuss Sinclair's portrait of industrial capitalism in *The Jungle*. Look at the connection between the meat-packing industry and the other institutions represented in the novel. Look at the function of money and the false sense of security it promises. Look at Jurgis's response to hardship: "I will work harder."

   (c) Discuss Sinclair's portrait of European immigrants in *The Jungle*. Discuss his portrait of the American city at the beginning of the twentieth century and compare it to other treatments of the American city in similar novels.

2. (a) Examine one or more of the major works of other American writers referred to as Muckrakers (especially Lincoln Steffens's *The Shame of the Cities* and Ida Tarbell's *History of the Standard Oil Company*). Compare these works to *The Jungle*. What common values and assumptions do all of these works share?

   (b) Explore Sinclair's connection with the radical writers who wrote for *The Masses* (1911–1917). Read Sinclair's novel *King Coal* (1917) and compare its treatment of the Colorado mine wars of 1913–14 with Max Eastman's in "Class War in Colorado" (*The Masses*, June 1914) and John Reed's treatment of the famous Patterson, New Jersey, textile strike in "War in Patterson" (*The Masses*, June 1913).

   (c) Examine Sinclair's theory of literature in *Mammonart* (1925) and an early essay entitled "Our Bourgeoisie Literature—The Reason and the Remedy," published in the October 8, 1904, issue of *Collier's*.

Bibliography

Especially helpful are the chapters on *The Jungle* in the following critical biographies of Sinclair:

Bloodworth, William A., Jr. *Upton Sinclair*. Boston: Twayne, 1971.

Harris, Leon. *Upton Sinclair: American Rebel*. New York: Thomas Y. Crowell, 1975.

Also, Harvey Swandos's article, "The World of Upton Sinclair" (*Atlantic Monthly*, Dec. 1961, pp. 96–102), contains an important discussion of *The Jungle* as an historical document.

Henry Adams (1838–1918)

Contributing Editor: Earl N. Harbert [p. 828]

Classroom Issues and Strategies

Explain Henry Adams's point of view as an outsider even when he writes about his own life. Note also his allusive, old-fashioned prose style, which is so different from that of (for example) Hemingway. Discuss Adams's lack of dependence on the economic rewards that his writings might bring, and his unusual authorial attitudes. Also important is an extended exploration of the meaning and usefulness of his key symbols.

In teaching Henry Adams, especially the entries included in the *Heath Anthology*, I have enjoyed the largest success when I emphasized the following five themes:

1. Although born into a tradition of elite political, social, and intellectual leadership, Henry Adams yet remained essentially an observer rather than a participant in the robust American life of the 1860–1912 period. Writing in all literary forms, his point of view is that of an outsider—even when he tells about his own life (as the third-person narration in the *Education* demonstrates).

2. A writer by choice, tradition, and careful training, Adams's economic independence allowed him always to do the work of his choice; namely, to pursue a broadly cultural and historical study of the past and present (represented in the selections from *Chartres* and the *Education*).

3. As a pioneer in intellectual history, as well as an interested student of science, Henry Adams sought to measure the European twelfth century against the American late nineteenth and early twentieth century. His method concentrated on the vital principles that characterized both eras. Thus, the medieval virgin (religion) appears first in *Chartres* and later is compared and contrasted with the modern dynamo (the force of electric power), when the conjunction becomes explicit in Chapter 25 of the *Education*. The same symbolic progression Adams uses to suggest the path of his personal intellectual voyage to increased understanding.

4. Adams's poem defines this intellectual journey in a more personal and perhaps a more compelling form. In particular, it reveals the deference (or even skepticism) that prevents the author from accepting simplistic judgments on history, religion, and other topics that he discusses.

5. As Adams shows in the letter to James, at its best, the thought and writing of Henry Adams resists what he finds to be the narrow parochialism of American experience. Building on this belief, Adams attempts to move his readers toward some larger understanding—even at some artistic cost in didacticism and possible misinterpretation.

As a practical minimum preparation for any instructor, and as the next step for any interested student, I recommend a careful reading of the entire *The Education of Henry Adams*, edited by Ernest Samuels.

Major Themes, Historical Perspectives, and Personal Issues

1. Henry Adams's life of privilege, born into a family that had achieved three generations of elite political and intellectual leadership.

2. Henry Adams's displacement from that role in the U.S. from 1860 to 1918.

3. Henry Adams's life-long concern with finding in history (human experience) some key to understanding and useful application.

4. Henry Adams's reclusive, "anti-confessional" pose as author (vs. moderns).

Significant Form, Style, or Artistic Conventions

Consider the definitions of autobiography and biography as matters of traditional literary form, modified in Henry Adams's work.

Original Audience

I raise the question of the audience for the private printings of both works, to make the contrasting attitudes of Henry Adams more comprehensible. Thus, reading becomes relative to audience.

Comparisons, Contrasts, Connections

It is fruitful to compare Adams's work to Rousseau's, *Confessions*, Gosse's, *Father and Son*, and St. Augustine's, *Confessions*.

Bibliography

Samuels, Ernest, ed. *Major Writers of America (II) The Education of Henry Adams.* Introduction.

New Explorations of an "American" Self

Booker Taliaferro Washington (1856–1915)

Contributing Editor: William L. Andrews [p. 851]

Classroom Issues and Strategies

Students typically ask questions like these: Why was Washington such an accommodationist? Why did he seem so ready to accept the values of the dominant culture and political system? Why was he always so restrained and unwilling to say anything to upset the white supremacy status quo? I point out Washington's training at Hampton Institute, where he learned very early what white people wanted and how little could be accomplished without pleasing them. Also note that Washington is trying to build a source of black power in the South and cannot do so unless he makes his work seem apolitical (when it isn't).

Consider also these questions: What is the best way for a minority group to advance their own cause when faced with either outright hostility or fear and mistrust? Is Washington's tactic the most effective? What are its costs and advantages?

Major Themes, Historical Perspectives, and Personal Issues

What is Washington's relationship to Douglass, the leader whose mantle he adopted? What kind of realism is Washington advocating and how does it accord with literary realism? How does Washington fit into the tradition of the Franklinesque self-made man?

Significant Form, Style, or Artistic Conventions

What sort of slave narrative is Washington writing, in contrast to Douglass's? Compare the first two chapters of both men's autobiographies to see where they resemble each other and differ. Generally Washington poses as a man of facts, not feelings, but does he sometimes betray strong feelings?

Original Audience

Stress the willingness of turn-of-the-century readers to believe a black man who is full of optimism about progress. How might such a message be received today—with how much suspicion?

Comparisons, Contrasts, Connections

Compare to Douglass and Chesnutt, especially in their depiction of slavery. Why would Washington play down the horrors of slavery?

Bibliography

I recommend the chapter entitled "Lost in a Cause" in Robert Stepto's *From Behind the Veil* (Urbana: Illinois Univ. Press, 1979).

Abraham Cahan (1860–1951)

Contributing Editor: Daniel Walden [p. 877]

Classroom Issues and Strategies

Students need to understand the following: (1) the Eastern European Jewish culture out of which Cahan came; (2) New York City as a fast-changing urban and technologized environment in the late nineteenth and early twentieth century; and (3) the nature of ethnicity in the context of the forces of Americanization.

To address these topics, I require I. Howe and E. Greenberg, Introduction to *Treasury of Yiddish Stories* (for the European culture), and Moses Rischin, *The Promised City: New York's Jews 1880–1920*, for the culture of New York City. For an introduction to Cahan as a realist, see Jules Chametzky, *From the Ghetto*.

I also use the following films:

1. *The Inheritance* (a documentary made by Amalgamated, 1964).
2. *The Distorted Image* (a set of slides on stereotyping by B'nai Brith, Anti-Defamation League).
3. *The Chosen* (film of Chaim Potok's novel).
4. *Hester Street* (film of Cahan's novel)
5. *The Pawnbroker* (film of Wallant's novel)

Students tend to identify with Cahan's attempts to find himself, a newcomer, a Jewish immigrant, in urban New York. They are surprised that this man, as an editor and novelist, was such a big influence in the 1900–1940 era. They tend to ask about the Eastern European culture, what New York was *really* like in the 1910s, 1920s, and why and how people struggled for identity in the face of overt oppression, poverty, and discrimination.

Major Themes, Historical Perspectives, and Personal Issues

Help students understand the parallel themes of ethnicity/identity and assimilation/Americanization. In *Yekl*, Cahan begins to address these themes; in *The Rise of David Levinsky* (1917) he was able to develop character and relationships in the context of the turn-of-the-century culture.

Significant Form, Style, or Artistic Conventions

Cahan was a realist who had mastered English. His style bore the impress of his Russian literary and cultural background, as well as having come out of an Eastern European Jewish culture.

Original Audience

It is necessary to prepare a word-list or glossary of those few Yiddish words that are used. A contemporary American audience has to learn to tune in the late nineteenth- and early twentieth-century Russian and Jewish cultures from which Cahan came.

Comparisons, Contrasts, Connections

The classic Russian authors, like Tolstoi, Dostoyevsky, and Turgenev, should be mentioned and briefly explained. W. D. Howells and his circle were also an influence on Cahan. Lastly, Yiddish authors like Mendele and Sholom Aleichem should be referred to. All were influences on Cahan, who absorbed their work even as he reflected the culture of New York City in the 1890–1913 era.

Questions for Reading and Discussion/ Approaches to Writing

1. (a) Explain the religio-cultural ethos of nineteenth century Eastern European Jewry.
   (b) What was the literary culture of nineteenth century Russia?
2. Abraham Cahan: Russian Jewish Realist.
   Abraham Cahan: Yiddishist, Reformer, Novelist.
   Abraham Cahan: Editor and Mediating Influence.
   Abraham Cahan: American Democratic Pragmatic Socialist

Bibliography

To understand the Eastern European Jewish background, I recommend the Introduction to I. Howe and E. Greenberg, *Treasury of Yiddish Stories*.

For the culture of the Lower East Side, New York, I suggest Moses Rischin, *The Promised City: New York's Jews 1880–1914*.

For an introduction to Cahan as a realist, see Jules Chamatzky, *From the Ghetto*.

Edith Maud Eaton (Sui Sin Far) (1865–1914)

Contributing Editor: Amy Ling [p. 884]

Major Themes, Historical Perspectives, and Personal Issues

If students are to appreciate the work of Edith Eaton fully, they must be given its historical and social context, namely the reception of Chinese by dominant Americans before and during her period. Students should know that though the Chinese were never enslaved in this country, as were Africans, they were brought here in large numbers as indentured laborers, coolies, whose status was not much better than that of slaves. In fact, Chinese were not permitted free immigration and naturalized citizenship until 1943, long after African-Americans and American Indians were recognized as American citizens. Initially attracted to California by the discovery of gold in the mid-nineteenth century, by the 1860s thousands of Chinese laborers were enticed here to construct the mountainous western section of the transcontinental railroad. Almost from the beginning, prejudice against them was strong. They were regarded as an alien race with peculiar customs and habits that made them unassimilable in a nation that wanted to remain white; and their hard-working, frugal ways, their willingness to work for lower wages than whites, rendered them an economic threat and thus targets of racial violence.

Into this environment, Edith Eaton came as a small child from England, living first in Hudson City, New York, and later settling in Montreal. Though her writing career began on the Montreal newspaper, *The Star*, she was to make her mark in the United States (she lived most of her adult life in Boston, Seattle, and San Francisco), writing articles and short stories using the Chinese pseudonym Sui Sin Far.

Edith Eaton's autobiographical essay and her stories, of which "In the Land of the Free" is an example, show what it was to be a Chinese woman in the white man's world. Though Eaton herself was only one-half Chinese (and one-half English), she was devoted to her mother and to the cause of counteracting the hatred and prejudice against her mother's people so pervasive during her own formative years. She took the Chinese name of a flower popular among the Chinese (Sui Sin Far means narcissus) and courageously asserted her Chinese heritage, even though this background was not evident on her face.

In "Leaves" she describes through personal anecdotes, chronologically arranged, her growing awareness of her own ethnic identity, her sensitivity to the curiosity and hostility of others, the difficulty of the Eurasian's position, and the development of her racial pride. The other theme apparent in "Leaves," and in many of her short stories, is Eaton's defense of the independent woman. The biographical fact that Eaton herself never married and the intimate details of this woman's journal entries would indicate that she is telling her own story, but she refrained from identifying herself out of a delicate sense of modesty.

"In the Land of the Free" is typical of Edith Eaton's short fiction. Her themes are of utmost importance: exposure of racial insensitivity, the human costs of bureaucratic and discriminatory laws, the humanity of the Chinese. The creation of rounded characters is a secondary concern. Lae Choo is little more than maternity personified, maternity victimized by racial prejudice. But the very portrayal of a Chinese woman in the maternal role—loving, anxious, frantic, self-sacrificing—was itself a novelty and a contribution, for the popular conception of the Chinese woman, whose numbers were few in nineteenth-century America, was that of a sing-song girl, prostitute, or inmate of an opium den. In Lae Choo, Eaton gives the reading public a naive, trusting woman whose entire life is devoted to the small child that the law of "this land of the free" manages to keep away from her for nearly one year. By the end of the story, the irony of the title becomes forcefully apparent.

Edith Eaton hoped to effect a change by means of her pen, to be the pioneer in bridging the Occident and the Orient, but the last article she published, less than a year before her death on April 7, 1914, was still a plea for the acceptance of working-class Chinese in America. She asserts that many former laundrymen become college graduates and influential people, that half the Chinese children in the Sunday School class she visited in San Francisco wore American clothes, while in eastern public schools, all the children wore American clothes. The pathetically shallow arguments she makes reflect not her thinking but that of the opposition. At the time of her death, the newspapers were full of stories about keeping Asian children out of public schools in reaction to the murder of a white woman by her Chinese "houseboy," and the Chinese Exclusion Act had been extended indefinitely.

Bibliography

Anonymous. *Marion, the Story of an Artist's Model. By Herself and the Author of Me.* New York: Watt, 1916. Biography of Sara Eaton Rosse by Winnifred Eaton. Includes anecdotes of the Eaton family life with Edith referred to as Ada.

Anonymous. *Me, a Book of Remembrance.* New York: Century, 1915. Winnifred Eaton's autobiography.

Sui Sin Far. (Pseud. of Edith Maud Eaton.) "Leaves from the Mental Portfolio of an Eurasian." *Independent* 66 (January 21, 1909): 125–32.

——. *Mrs. Spring Fragrance.* Chicago: A. C. McClurg, 1912.

Watanna, Onoto. (Pseud. of Winnifred Eaton.) *A Japanese Nightingale.* New York: Harper, 1901.

Mary Austin (1868–1934)

Contributing Editor: Vera Norwood [p. 901]

Classroom Issues and Strategies

Students have difficulty responding to Austin's strident individualism and her vacillation between ardent feminist and male-identified writer. The best approach is to provide contextual background that reveals that Austin was not alone in her struggles to write from both inside and outside her culture.

Once we have addressed some of the difficulties of voice in this autobiography, I have the best luck with teaching what I think Austin as a writer was best at evoking. Her strength was in describing and evaluating the interior domestic spaces of her house and the natural and built environments of the Midwest and Far West, thus raising questions about the sort of material world women valued and created. Teaching sections of the autobiography in conjunction with *The Land of Little Rain* and *Lost Borders* encourages literature students to think about various ways in which women have created appropriate spaces and changed the places they settled, both indoors as craftswomen and outdoors as gardeners and preservationists.

The main question Austin's autobiography engenders is how accurate a reflection she provides of late-nineteenth-century women's lives. Not that this is an issue with the particular selection made for the anthology, but Austin's depiction of the American Indian and Hispanic populations of the Southwest raises more questions and issues than the gender-related material. Teachers who branch out into other of her regional works will need to be prepared for these questions.

Major Themes, Historical Perspectives, and Personal Issues

Austin was a Progressive Era writer, deeply involved in supporting regional diversity, multicultural perspectives, and environmental preservation. Students understand her authorial voice better when they know something about her work in these areas. Austin belonged to a generation of creative women struggling to shift from nineteenth-century lives as private, housebound, husband-and-father dominated people, to twentieth-century roles as modern, independent individuals influencing social and political trends. Students should also know something of her private circumstances: the long separation and eventual divorce from her husband, the birth of a retarded daughter, the necessity that she write a great deal to earn her living—each played a part in the sometimes contradictory voice appearing in her work.

Significant Form, Style, or Artistic Conventions

Obviously, some familiarity with autobiographical conventions is useful. Gender is an important variable when reading any autobiography. We discuss male and female voices, stressing that women began to write after men had established the basic form and so their works often combined male traditions with female experimentation. In Austin's case, the experiment is in her use of different voices for the visionary, individualistic persona and for the traditional, good daughter.

Original Audience

Austin's audience in her time was more male than currently. Her reputation as a political activist and writer was with regionalists and environmentalists, among whom the leading lights were men. In many ways, her autobiography was written with an eye to setting herself off from the "ordinary" woman of her generation, of claiming a specialness that would put her in the male leagues while also encouraging other women to break free from gender-role proscriptions. In the process of this somewhat divisive attempt, however, she created a persona with a strong feminist character. In our time, it is that visionary woman who speaks to a much larger audience of women readers. For this audience Austin is less interesting for what she did in the public sphere of environmentalist politics than for her scathing critique, and frustrated rejection, of the nineteenth-century gender role model offered her by her mother.

Comparisons, Contrasts, Connections

I teach Austin with Sarah Orne Jewett and Charlotte Perkins Gilman. All three worked in approximately the same time period and struggled with the same gender-role restrictions. Jewett and Gilman are particularly useful in tempering some of the negative reactions students have to Austin's voice. Also useful are Benjamin Franklin's and Frederick Douglass's autobiographies. Teaching these with Austin provides students with a better understanding of the genre in which Austin worked.

Questions for Reading and Discussion/ Approaches to Writing

1. The main introduction I make to any autobiography is to suggest that students think about what sort of people have written their life story. Generally, such authors are engaged in an act of self-creation, which assumes that there is something unique to their life. I ask students to look at strategies the author uses to present herself as, in some way, remarkable. With autobiographies by women this becomes a particularly useful question to begin the study of how gender comes into play in issues of genre.

2. Selecting comparative/contrastive passages from the writers mentioned above and having students look for similarities/differences has been successful. With Austin, Jewett's story "The White Heron" provides a good starting point for looking at landscape values as they are impacted by gender. Also, "The Basket Maker" chapter in *The Land of Little Rain* offers an opportunity for students to analyze how material from the autobiography matches Austin's more "fictional" work. This is a good exercise for demonstrating how much Austin created her autobiographical persona out of her earlier writing.

Bibliography

Really the best additional reading a teacher could seek is more Austin. Mary Austin was a prolific, wide-ranging writer and one should be aware of the work on which her reputation is based. I would advise reading some of the stories in *Lost Borders* and a few chapters of *Land of Little Rain* as the best preparation for teaching Austin.

Gertrude Bonnin (Zitkala-Sa) (Sioux) (1876–1938)

Contributing Editor: Kristin Herzog [p.910]

Classroom Issues and Strategies

Without a knowledge of Zitkala-Sa's life and the near impossibility for an American Indian woman of her time to publish independently, students will wonder where these stories fit in. It is important to point out the extreme difficulties of a writer trying to preserve a tribal heritage and yet to communicate to a white audience.

Besides dealing with matters of biography, history, and style, I think approaching these early American Indian authors from the religious perspective (Native American spirituality versus enforced assimilation to Christian beliefs) is effective in helping students to sense the very basic dilemma of a writer, a problem of cultural and spiritual identity that goes deeper than mere issues of civil rights, important as they are.

Students easily identify with the aspect of social criticism or rebellion, but may not find the style particularly attractive because they do not know the historical and biographical background and the tastes of the literary market at this time.

Major Themes, Historical Perspectives, and Personal Issues

Zitkala-Sa is a transitional writer whose life and work are expressing deep conflicts between tradition and assimilation, literature and politics, Native American religion and Christianity. If we focus on the tension between her artistic and her political commitments, she can be seen in the middle between Susette LaFlesche, whose fiction was almost submerged by her political speaking and writing, and Leslie Marmon Silko, who is able to create a blend of traditional and modern fiction that organically incorporates a political stance.

Nor by far are all of her political activities reflected in her writings, but in her editorials for the *American Indian Magazine*, for example, she discussed controversial issues like the enfranchisement of American Indians, Indian contributions to military service during World War I, corruption in the Bureau of Indian Affairs, and allotment of tribal lands. The selections reprinted here from *American Indian Stories* are neither essays of cultural criticism nor strictly autobiographical accounts. They are an attempt at turning personal experience as well as social criticism into creative "stories."

One aspect of Zitkala-Sa's imbalanced, but path-breaking, attempt to merge cultural criticism and ascetic form is her struggle with religion. In Parts IV and V of "School Days," she vividly describes the little girl's nightmares of the palefaces' devil and the bitterness she felt when a schoolmate died with an open Bible on her bed, listening to the "superstitious ideas" of the paleface woman taking care of her. While Charles Eastman in *Indian Boyhood* (published in 1902, two years after "School Days") uses the word "superstition" for some of his Sioux traditions, Zitkala-Sa turns the matter around: Christianity to her is superstitious.

Similarly, "Why I Am a Pagan" is an unusual statement in her time. Its sentimentality and self-consciously "poetic" language can partly be ascribed to the popular journal style of the time. There is daring in her point of view. Interestingly, she does not satirize a white preacher, but one of her own kin whom she sees as tragically duped by the Christian "superstition." Even though we learn from other sources that she and her husband denounced the Peyote religion and therefore to some extent hampered the fight for American Indian freedom of religion, the fact remains that she asserted the dignity of Indian religion and put her finger on two blindspots of Christianity that are being overcome only in our time: the disregard for nature and the disrespect for other cultures. What Christian theology is learning today from ecology and anthropology as well as from some of its own forgotten roots, Native American writers learned from their ancient tribal traditions.

Significant Form, Style, or Artistic Conventions

The selections from "The School Days of an Indian Girl" expose the blatant injustice of stripping a child of language, culture, religion, and familiar surroundings. At the same time they express the irony that the maltreated student is extremely unhappy upon returning home and finally feels the urge to return to the place of her earlier sufferings. While the style is sometimes stilted or sentimental, it is at other times direct and powerful, as, for example, in the passage on the hair cutting. In learning about American Indian customs and beliefs ("short hair was worn by mourners, and shingled hair by cowards"), we are made to experience the trauma of the child. In hearing the mother's desperate cry for help from the spirits of her departed warrior brothers, we can sense the tragic family divisions caused by forced assimilation.

Comparisons, Contrasts, Connections

The many years of literary silence in Zitkala-Sa's life seem to indicate a serious break between artistic endeavors on the one hand and relentless activism on behalf of American Indian health, education, legal representation, and voting rights on the other. However, in her few creative works she actually anticipated the concerns of contemporary writers. In blending autobiography with creative narrative, elements of tribal traditions, and social criticism, she helped to pave the way for those recent writers who have focused more clearly and more comprehensively on their own traditions.

Questions for Reading and Discussion/ Approaches to Writing

1. (a) What is your knowledge of American life around 1900 in terms of what you have "absorbed" in a lifetime? In terms of consulting recent scholarly works?

    (b) What do you suppose were the difficulties of a Native American woman writer in writing for a white audience around 1900?

2. (a) How are literary art and protest merged in Zitkala-Sa's work?

    (b) How did Zitkala-Sa pave the way for contemporary American Indian writers like Leslie Marmon Silko or Paula Gunn Allen (in case contemporary American Indian women authors have been read in the class)?

Bibliography

Allen, Paula Gunn. *The Sacred Hoop: Recovering the Feminine in American Indian Traditions* (Boston: Beacon, 1986), 82.

Dockstader, Frederick J. *Great North American Indians: Profiles in Life and Leadership*. New York: Van Nostrand, 1977, 40f.

Eastman, Charles A. *Indian Boyhood*. New York: McClure, Phillips & Co., 1902, 172, 177. Christianity and superstitions. See also Hertzberg, *The Search for an American Indian Identity*, especially 256ff. and 262.

Fisher, Alice Poindexter. "The Transformation of Tradition: A Study of Zitkala-Sa and Mourning Dove, Two Transitional Writers." Ph.D. Diss., City Univ. of New York, 1979, 36. On the quality of the passage on hair cutting.

Fisher, Dexter. "Zitkala-Sa: The Evolution of a Writer." *American Indian Quarterly* 5 (August 1979): 229–38.

Hertzberg, Hazel W. *The Search for an American Indian Identity: Modern Pan-Indian Movements.* Syracuse: Syracuse Univ. Press, 1971 Describes her political activities.

Littlefield, Daniel F., Jr., and James W. Parins. *A Biobibliography of Native American Writers, 1772–1924.* Metuchen, N.J.: Scarecrow Press, 1981, 17f. For a list of writings by Zitkala-Sa. See also the Supplement to this volume, 1985, 16.

Olsen, Tillie. *Silences.* New York: Delta/Seymour Lawrence, 1978. Helpful in explaining to students the many reasons for a break in creativity, especially as it pertains to women and members of minorities.

Schöler, Bo. Introduction to *Coyote Was Here*, p. 10.

Stout, Mary. "Zitkala-Sa: The Literature of Politics." In *Coyote Was Here: Essays on Contemporary Native American Literary and Political Mobilization,* edited by Bo Schöler, 74. Aarhus, Denmark: Dept. of English, Univ. of Aarhus, 1984.

Young, Mary E. "Bonnin, Gertrude Simmons." *Notable American Women, 1607–1950: A Biographical Dictionary,* Vol. I.

Mary Antin (1881–1949)

Contributing Editor: Richard Tuerk [p. 923]

Classroom Issues and Strategies

One primary problem involves students' unfamiliarity with the time period treated in *The Promised Land,* especially with aspects of the Great Migration and of immigrant settlement in America in the late nineteenth and early twentieth centuries. Especially important is conveying to them the kinds of conditions the newly arrived immigrant encountered in large eastern cities. Students are also unfamiliar with the kinds of conditions the immigrants lived in in the Old World.

I use slides made from photographs by people like Jacob Riis to try to give the students a feeling for life in the immigrant quarters. I also use books containing photographs by people like Roman Vishniak to give them a feeling for Old World Orthodox Jewish life. Frankly, I find that photographs have a stronger impact on my students than simple descriptions and statistics do.

Most of the questions I hear from students concern life in the Old World; however, most material treating Old World life has been omitted from the anthology. Other questions involve the urban environment of the newly arrived immigrant. Strangely enough, few of my students question Antin's idea that total assimilation is desirable.

Major Themes, Historical Perspectives, and Personal Issues

Antin's emphasis on Americanization and total assimilation deserves careful scrutiny. I try to discuss the values of an ethic of assimilation as well as the problems it presents. I usually contrast Antin with at least one author—usually Ludwig Lewisohn, although Leslie Marmon Silko would do as well—who questions the ethic of assimilation. Particularly apt books for contrast are Lewisohn's *Up Stream* and Silko's *Ceremony*. I also discuss the related theme of initiation in Antin's book.

The work may be treated in terms of its sociological content, that is, in terms of what it reveals about the expectations and possibilities of an immigrant girl in America around the turn of the century. It also may be treated in terms of the role of the public schools in helping (perhaps forcing) the immigrant to come to terms with American culture and society. However, the work may also be treated as a piece of literature.

Significant Form, Style, or Artistic Conventions

As I see it, *The Promised Land* is basically a tale of initiation, even of rebirth. Antin's being reborn as an American provides her with her principal form in terms of her contrasting Old World and New (the anthology does not contain material dealing directly with her Old World life) and in terms of her growth in the New World. The book is, among other things, a study in radical discontinuity in terms of the relations of Antin's Old World life to her New World life and of continuous growth in terms of her New World life.

Original Audience

Antin says that she is writing for all Americans, and her statement seems correct. I mention the tremendous popularity of her work and its use, either in whole or in part, in classrooms in public schools throughout America. Chapters from it became parts of textbooks used from coast to coast.

Comparisons, Contrasts, Connections

Other works of initiation are especially useful for comparison, especially those dealing with initiation into American society. Ethnic tales of initiation make instructive objects of comparison, works like Leslie Marmon Silko's *Ceremony*, Ludwig Lewisohn's *Up Stream*, O. E. Rolvaag's *Giants in the Earth*, and Richard Wright's *Black Boy*.

Even more helpful, however, is comparing Antin's book with Mark Twain's *Adventures of Huckleberry Finn*. These works are in many ways very similar yet at the same time radically different, especially in terms of their evaluations of American society. Whereas Antin desires assimilation above all, Huck learns to loathe the idea of being assimilated into American society.

Questions for Reading and Discussion/ Approaches to Writing

1. In what ways is Antin's experience in the New World unique? In what ways is it typical?

   In what ways is she unique? In what ways is she typical? As you read the selection, it might help to bear in mind that she insists that she is representative of all young immigrants.

   What is her attitude toward public schools?

   How realistic is her evaluation of America?

2. Compare Antin's attitude toward public schools with your own attitude; what incidents in her life and in yours are responsible for the similarities and differences in those attitudes? Trace the steps by which Antin shows herself becoming Americanized.

Bibliography

"Assimilation in Jewish-American Autobiography: Mary Antin and Ludwig Lewisohn." *A/B: Auto/Biography Studies* 3.2 (Summer 1987): 26–33.

Guttman, Allan. *The Jewish Writer in America: Assimilation and the Crisis of Identity*. New York: Oxford Univ. Press, 1971. Sec. 2, ch. 3. "The Rise of a Lucky Few: Mary Antin and Abraham Cahan."

Liptzin, Sol. *The Jew in American Literature*. New York: Bloch, 1966. Ch. 8. "The Promised Land."

Rubin, Steven J. "Style and Meaning in Mary Antin's *The Promised Land*: A Reevaluation." *Studies in American Jewish Literature* 5 (1986): 35–43.

Tuerk, Richard. "The Youngest of America's Children in Mary Antin's *The Promised Land*." *Studies in American Jewish Literature* 5 (1986): 29–34.

Modern Period

1910–1945

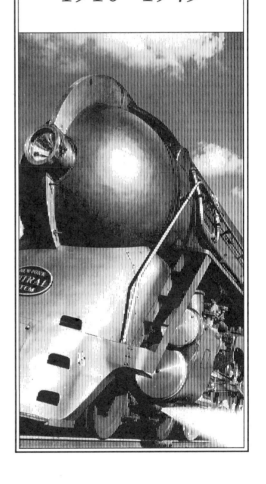

Toward Modernism

[p. 961]

Edwin Arlington Robinson (1869–1935)

Contributing Editor: Nancy Carol Joyner *[p. 962]*

Classroom Issues and Strategies

There are few problems in teaching Robinson other than the general problem of teaching any poetry. His lack of flamboyance (or, more positively put, his subtlety) might be a problem for some. Robert Stevick has said that "Robinson's poetry deserves the attention it does not contrive to attract" (Barnard, *Centenary Essays*, 66).

To introduce Robinson's subtlety, read the poems out loud and more than once. Robinson once told a reader who confessed to being confused about his poetry that he should read the poems one word at a time. Robinson was very sensitive to the sound of words and complained of not liking his name because it sounded like a tin can being kicked down the stairs. He also said that poetry must be music. This musical quality is best perceived by reading his poetry aloud.

Major Themes, Historical Perspectives, and Personal Issues

Robinson is a "people poet," writing almost exclusively about individuals or individual relationships rather than on more common themes of the nineteenth century. He exhibits a curious mixture of irony and compassion toward his subjects—most of whom are failures—that allows him to be called a romantic existentialist. He is a true precursor to the modernist movement in poetry, publishing his first volume in 1896, a decade notable from the point of view of poetry in America only because of one other publication, the first, posthumous, volume of poems by Emily Dickinson. As the introduction emphasizes, many of Robinson's poems are more autobiographical than their seeming objectivity indicates immediately.

Significant Form, Style, or Artistic Conventions

Although Robinson's subject matter and philosophical stance differ markedly from that of his predecessors', his form is unremittingly traditional. He considered movies, prohibition, and free verse "a triumvirate from hell," and said that if free verse were as easy to write as it was difficult to read, he was not surprised there was so much of it. In his early work Robinson experimented with difficult French forms, like the villanelle and rondeau, but his longer work is written almost exclusively in blank verse. Robinson is one of America's greatest practitioners of the sonnet and the dramatic monologue.

Original Audience

Literate adults, then and now.

Comparisons, Contrasts, Connections

Critics have pointed out that Robinson is a descendant of Anne Bradstreet, and in their deceptively plain style and solitary careers they make an interesting comparison. Sometimes Robinson and Masters have been confused, with people mistakenly assuming that Masters had an influence on Robinson, when the reverse must be true.

The most obvious and fruitful writer for comparison/contrast is Robert Frost, only five years younger than Robinson but nearly twenty years behind him in publication. They share a New England background, contemporaneity, and allegiance to formal writing, but they were decidedly different in life-style, in personality, and finally in their poetry, with Robinson's being the more honest. (Biographers of both poets report that Frost was extremely jealous of Robinson but the reverse was not true.)

"Aunt Imogen" and "A Servant to Servants" or "Home Burial" make an interesting comparison in the two men's presentation of women protagonists. A friend gets students in her class to examine the metrical pattern of "Leonora" by asking them to name the tune most appropriate for it, which is "The Battle Hymn of the Republic."

Questions for Reading and Discussion/ Approaches to Writing

1. Comparison of Frost's and Robinson's presentation of women
2. Robinson on marriage
3. Biographical connections in some poems
4. Imagery in "Eros Turannos" and "Leonora"
5. Robinson's successful failures

Bibliography

Coxe, Louise O. *Edwin Arlington Robinson: The Life of Poetry.* New York: Pegasus, 1969.

Joyner, Nancy Carol. "Edwin Arlington Robinson." *Dictionary of Literary Biography*, Vol. 54, 366–88.

Squires, Radcliffe. "Tilbury Town Today." In *Edwin Arlington Robinson: Centenary Essays*, edited by Ellsworth Barnard, 175–84. Athens: Univ. of Ga. Press, 1969.

Ellen Glasgow (1873–1945)

Contributing Editor: Linda Pannill [p. 972]

Classroom Issues and Strategies

Glasgow fails to make the New Woman convincing. The philosopher Judith Campbell takes her iconoclastic new book from a muff and presents it ("my little gift") to the lover for whom she is willing to sacrifice a career. She does not perceive his jealousy of her own job offer. In dialogue she repeats his words back to him. That Judith Campbell seems more like a southern belle than a philosopher speaks to the power over heroine and perhaps author of an old-fashioned ideal of womanhood and to the difficulty for writers of Glasgow's generation who are working to create new characters and plots.

When teaching Glasgow's work, symbolism is a good place to start. Estbridge's idealism and his ruthlessness are seen in fire images: the portrait of Savonarola over a fireplace, the "flame" of love, "burned his boats," burning his papers, the reference to the Grand Inquisitor. Other symbols include Judith's veils, the storm, Estbridge's name (East?

China?), the Christmas setting (connected with his feeling "born anew" and her initials), the doctor's garden. Judith is compared to a cypress, presumably like the one that did not survive. The remaining tree is a tough ailanthus, common though originally from China. Estbridge feels Judith is the "temptation" to disobey society's rules, but after all he will stay in his fallen garden with his sick wife. (That the younger colleague is named Adamson reinforces the Edenic motif, a favorite of the author's.)

The burden on a woman of trying to live up to a man's ideal, a theme throughout Glasgow's work, is interesting to the students. Yet they find Glasgow herself old-fashioned in her preoccupation with romantic love and with the goodness and beauty of her heroines. Along with the dire plots and the reappearances of weak male characters this calls for an explanation that students will seek first in the author's life. They should be encouraged to look beyond.

Major Themes, Historical Perspectives, and Personal Issues

Because of wide reading on the subject, Glasgow considered herself something of a philosopher. Like Judith Campbell, she wrote, and like her she had an affair in New York with a married man, by some accounts also a doctor. In *The Woman Within* the author depicts a conflict in her own life between woman and artist roles, love and ambition. Neither choice seems right.

Significant Form, Style, or Artistic Conventions

Irony underlines John Estbridge's self-centeredness and Judith Campbell's self-sacrifice, traits Glasgow thought typical of men and women. Judith gives up an appointment at Hartwell College, previously her heart's desire, to run off with Estbridge. He misses the appointment with Judith to accept a faculty appointment. His is the "Professional Instinct," hers the "instinct to yield." A too-obvious irony is the timing of the traffic accident that gives Estbridge the opportunity to betray Judith (or the author the opportunity to rescue her).

Original Audience

Both Raper (in *The Sunken Garden*) and Godbold point to a letter from Pearce Baily, prominent New York neurologist, advising Glasgow on the story. "The Professional Instinct" deals, of course, with a doctor who has helped a writer in her work. Ellen Glasgow decided not to publish the short story and seems not to have finished revising.

Comparisons, Contrasts, Connections

Mary Hunter Austin and Willa Cather, like Glasgow, were long considered regional writers, though not all their work is set in the desert Southwest or Nebraska, as not all Glasgow's is set in Virginia. Recent feminist scholarship emphasizes these authors' concern with sex roles and their problematic self-concepts as women writers.

Questions for Reading and Discussion/ Approaches to Writing

1. (a) Explain the allusion to Savonarola.
   (b) Why is the point of view effective?
   (c) Consider Tilly Estbridge and Judith Campbell as foil characters.
   (d) What seems to be the target of Glasgow's satire?
   (e) To what extent is the reader prepared for the ending?
   (f) To what extent is Glasgow the literary realist she considers herself?
2. (a) Why might Glasgow have chosen not to publish the story?
   (b) To what extent are both Judith Campbell and John Estbridge autobiographical characters?
   (c) Ellen Glasgow considered herself a feminist. How is the feminism of her period (not our own) reflected in the story?
   (d) In Glasgow's version of society, what kinds of power, if any, do women have?
   (e) How might the influence of Darwinism and Social Darwinism be seen in Glasgow's depiction of the relationship between the sexes?

Bibliography

Glasgow, Ellen. *The Woman Within*. New York: Harcourt, Brace, 1954. Chapters 1, 8–9.

Wagner, Linda. *Ellen Glasgow: Beyond Convention*. Austin: Univ. of Texas Press, 1982. Chapter 1.

Edith Wharton (1862–1937)

Contributing Editor: Elizabeth Ammons [p. 985]

Classroom Issues and Strategies

In my experience, students divide sharply on Wharton. Some love her work, responding particularly to the elegance and precision of her prose and the sharpness of her wit; others don't like her at all, finding it hard to "get into" her fiction because she seems so cold, the prose seems so detailed and self-conscious, and the subject matter is so elite.

Mainly I try to get the two groups talking/arguing with each other. The result usually is that each can appreciate the point of view of the other, and we can start there: with a view of Wharton in which she is both marvelously accomplished as a stylist within a particular aesthetic and—in some ways on the very same grounds—limited as a writer by class and temperament.

One issue students are very interested in is sexuality in Wharton's fiction, ranging from what birth control was available at the time and in the class she wrote about to what her own attitudes toward sex were. Another question is: Why care about all these rich privileged people in Wharton's fiction? Who cares? (One response I give to this is that the top of the pyramid gives a very good sense of what the whole culture aspires to since those are the people that everyone envies and wishes to be—or is supposed to envy and wish to be. Wharton's fictive world tells us a lot about how the whole culture works and what it values and is supposed to value.) Finally a question that often gets asked is "What other works by Wharton would you recommend reading?" A good sign.

Major Themes, Historical Perspectives, and Personal Issues

Major themes in Wharton's work include the effects of class on both behavior and consciousness (divorce, for example, often horrifies the established upper class as much for its offense against taste as for its violation of moral standards); the American belief in progress as actual and good (many "advances" Wharton welcomed; others she was contemptuous of); the contrast between European and American customs, morality, and sensibility; the confinement of marriage, especially for women; women's desire for and right to freedom in general, and particularly sexual and economic freedom, and the reality that, usually, desire and right are thwarted; the preference of powerful, white, usually upper-class men for childish dependent women; the complexity and pain of relationships between women within patriarchal culture, including (and especially) rivalry and animosity among women.

Historically, Wharton was both the product and the beneficiary of a highly developed, even if recent, high-culture tradition of brilliant, educated women able to write and publish fiction for a living. Before Wharton, in France and England George Sand, Madame de Staël, Jane Austen, George Eliot, Mrs. Gaskell, and the Brontës had used fiction to examine many of the issues that engaged Wharton: marriage, the restraints of class, the repression of "respectable" women's sexual desire, the structure of patriarchal power, and the desire of middle-class white women for respectable, paid work. In the United States, in addition to popular women novelists in the nineteenth century, artistically ambitious women writers such as Elizabeth Stuart Phelps and Sarah Orne Jewett preceded Wharton. Contemporary with Wharton was a whole group of accomplished women fiction writers—Chopin, Austin, Hopkins, Glasgow, Cather, Stein. The point is that Wharton's work, historically, is rooted not only in the tradition of social and psychological realism commonly associated with Howells and James (writers she admired), but also in the realism and social criticism of women writers publishing before and contemporary with her who were concerned with many of the same issues that engaged Wharton, particularly issues centered on women's experiences and problems.

Personally, Wharton treated many of the issues of her own life in her fiction: her estrangement from and anger at her mother; her frustration with the limitations placed on women, and especially women of the upper class; her miserable marriage and the stigma against divorce, again particularly in her class but also generally; her fear of the ways in which cautiousness and selfishness can corrupt one's soul; her knowledge that female sexuality, despite society's repression of it, was a potent source of creativity.

Significant Form, Style, or Artistic Conventions

"The Valley of Childish Things" is a parable, but the other selections here are classic conventional modern short stories in terms of form and effect. Wharton can be used to show perfect mastery of conventional form. Her taut, elegant prose and expert command of dramatic structure beautifully manipulate the conventional Western short story pattern of exposition/conflict/complication/climax/resolution. Typically the climax appears almost at the very end of a Wharton story, creating a very long, strong build-up of anticipation and then a swift, deft finish.

You can practically teach the standard modern Western short story—at its best—from a Wharton story.

Original Audience

Wharton was a best-selling author at the turn of the century and into the 1920s; she was also highly acclaimed by critics. After the 1920s she was taught less and less in schools and universities until before and following World War II she was virtually untaught. She was viewed as a disciple of Henry James and he, but not she, was taught. In the late 1960s and then on through the 1980s Wharton has steadily and dramatically regained both an academic audience and a general readership, clearly as a result of the most recent wave in the women's movement. In other words, her work attracts attention now for the very reasons it was generally dismissed in the middle of the twentieth century: its focus on women and women's experiences and its emphasis on social context, customs, pressures, and manners as human variables rooted in time, class, gender, nationality, and culture.

Comparisons, Contrasts, Connections

Useful contrasts could include authors such as Harriet Beecher Stowe or Frances Ellen Watkins Harper, who wrote fiction for explicit and avowedly political ends; Mark Twain, who was interested in communicating an almost felt sense of a very different America, the rural Midwest and the white South; Upton Sinclair (whose politics Wharton did not like but whose right to say what he wanted she vigorously defended), who identified with the working class and the poor and wrote muckrakers; or Jack London, who celebrated much of the same white masculine power-ethic that Wharton disliked. Another good contrast is Henry James; though often cited as Wharton's mentor (he was one), James is also quite different from Wharton: he is much wordier, more intrusive and self-indulgent authorially, and inclined to Victorian notions of self-sacrifice and self-immolation.

Questions for Reading and Discussion/ Approaches to Writing

1. When I use study questions for Wharton, I use standards closely keyed to the piece at hand: e.g., for "Roman Fever": Where does the hatred between the two women come from? What is its source? What is the source of the source? For "The Other Two" I might

ask: Where do Wharton's sympathies lie in this story? On what do you base your opinion?

2. In addition to standard analytical/critical papers that ask students to work out an interpretative position by arguing closely from the text (which works very well for Wharton), I have found that Wharton is a good author to use for creative-writing paper assignments, which I do in "straight" English courses on the theory that one excellent way of getting inside poetry or fiction is to try to create some yourself, even if you're not very good at it. For Wharton I might ask students to reread "The Valley of Childish Things" and then write their own gender parable for the late twentieth century of about the same length and structural strategy. For "Roman Fever" I might ask them to write a short story about the two middle-aged women from Barbara's point of view. I spin off Wharton either formally or specifically in subject matter; also I give a rather directed assignment, since one of my goals is to get students to think more about a particular piece by Wharton, how it works or what it says. I have learned that if the creative assignment is too loose, it can let them wander so far from the Wharton text that they discover no more about it than they knew before writing.

Bibliography

Relatively little Wharton criticism focuses on the short stories, so often it is necessary to adapt general criticism on her. Two of the most provocative books are: Elizabeth Ammons, *Edith Wharton's Argument with America* (1980), and Cynthia Griffin Woolf, *A Feast of Words: The Triumph of Edith Wharton* (1977).

Good articles can be found in Harold Bloom, ed., *Edith Wharton* (1986) and a forthcoming volume, *Critical Essays on Edith Wharton*, to be published by G. K. Hall.

Edgar Lee Masters (1869–1950)

Contributing Editor: Ronald Primeau [p. 1033]

Classroom Issues and Strategies

Some students expect—even demand—that poetry be very "difficult" to be deemed worthwhile. When Masters is relatively simple in form and message, that throws them. To address this issue, talk about popular arts, the oral tradition, the enormous popularity of *Spoon River*, and the fact that all poetry need not be academic.

Masters provides a good chance to talk with students about what they think poetry is or ought to be and how the literary establishment can or cannot control popular opinion. Use some multimedia presentations, reading out loud. Bring in some actors from university theater.

Students are interested in events from the poet's life and factors that led him to write this kind of poetry. They wonder how any book of poems could have been *that* popular. No TV back then, they suspect.

Major Themes, Historical Perspectives, and Personal Issues

Consider what it means to live in small-town America, how it is attractive to try to sum up a lifetime on a gravestone, the importance of peer pressure and what others think. Think about Masters's life as a lawyer and how that affected his poetry.

Significant Form, Style, or Artistic Conventions

It is important to discuss basic elements of form and meter in order to see how Masters alluded to, and modified, existing conventions. It is crucial to see that he was outside developing critical norms and how that has clearly limited his inclusion in the critical canons.

Original Audience

Spoon River reached a mass audience when it was written and still sells better than most poetry. Today, however, the audience is largely academic and concerns are more in the direction of scholarship and how to teach the works rather than popularity and whether they speak to an age. Discuss with students questions of popular taste and the split between mass art and high art.

Comparisons, Contrasts, Connections

Compare with Thornton Wilder's *Our Town*. Perhaps even show a video if there's time. There are recordings of *Spoon River*—and a musical. Read Masters alongside Whitman. Talk about how he hid copies of Shelly and Goethe behind law books when people thought he was supposed to be working.

Questions for Reading and Discussion/ Approaches to Writing

1. (a) Who are these speakers?
   (b) To whom are they speaking?
   (c) What is our role as readers?
   (d) What have you underlined or written in the margin and why?
   (e) Which of these characters would you like to know better and why? What was Spoon River like as a place?

2. (a) Discuss the conflicts between standards for "high" art and "mass" art. Who sets criteria and how?
   (b) Compose your own gravestone biography and message to the world—à la *Spoon River*.
   (c) Write a portrait of your home town—à la *Spoon River*.

Bibliography

Flanagan, John T. *The Spoon River Poet and His Critics*. Metuchen, N.J.: Scarecrow, 1974. A very useful reference guide.

Primeau, Ronald. *Beyond Spoon River: The Legacy of Edgar Lee Masters*. Austin: Univ. of Texas, 1981. Reevaluates Master's place in the American tradition; see Chapters 1–2 for useful background on Masters.

Willa Cather (1873–1947)

Contributing Editor: Margaret Anne O'Connor [p. 1039]

Classroom Issues and Strategies

It's hard to do justice to a novelist by looking at a single short story, but "Old Mrs. Harris" promises to be a better representative story to introduce Cather and her major concerns as a writer than any story previously anthologized. More than any other, "Old Mrs. Harris" treats the midwestern locale of her best known Nebraska novels. It is also extremely autobiographical, an emphasis that offers an instructor the advantage of introducing the life history of this important novelist as more than mere background information.

The headnote to this Cather story stresses biographical information which should prompt questions that will stimulate classroom discussion. Philip Gerber's bare-bones chronology in his Twayne volume on Cather is an accurate outline and an excellent choice for a chronology to supply to students. Sharon O'Brien's more detailed and topic-oriented chronology (in her edition of five of Cather's book-length prose publications for the Library of America in 1986, pp. 1296–1318) would be an excellent biographical summary for instructors to have at their disposal.

Since this story is about a family and one important plot element features a young girl's impatient hunger to go to college, instructors have a natural way to involve student readers in the story through questioning students' own reasons for being in college, the depth of their own commitment to knowledge compared to that of the young woman, and a then/now discussion of options open to young women.

Cather is often considered a regional writer, but one who wrote knowledgeably of many regions in her best known works—Nebraska, New Mexico, Canada, and even Virginia in her last novel. This story presents an excellent opportunity to discuss class members' perceptions of midwesterners vs. southerners, the class structure of small town America in the 1890s, the religious, class, gender, age, and ethnic differences that all come into play in the story. Discussing any of these questions would enhance students' awareness of the complexity that underlies the calm prose style of this story.

Major Themes, Historical Perspectives, and Personal Issues

Published as a story in *Ladies' Home Journal* in the fall of 1932, the original title of "Old Mrs. Harris" was "Three Women." The story could be said to concern the life of WOMAN and the options she has, the ages of a woman as represented by "old Mrs. Harris" and the two generations that follow her, as well as the temper of the time and place—Skyline, Colorado, in the early 1890s—in relation to the generations of women described there.

Significant Form, Style, or Artistic Conventions

Point of view is very important in the story; there is no single first-person narrator or Jamesian "central consciousness" directing the story. Instead a third-person omniscient narrator goes into the minds of key figures in the narrative to present their reactions. Students often agree with contemporary reviewers of the story that the last two paragraphs are a great departure from the established technique of the rest of the story—very "old-fashioned" and intrusive. What is the effect of this "shift"? Compare it to the ending of Sarah Orne Jewett's "The White Heron." What does each author hope to achieve in their closing commentary?

Original Audience

The themes of this story are timeless. Still, it is set in the past and said much about the need for forbearance to Depression-era readers who were its first audience. One excellent point for discussion might be just how much Americans of the 1990s value the patience that Mrs. Harris and Mandy exhibit in the story. In the story, patience is more often seen in the older characters, and the impatience of youth is specifically lamented in the last paragraph.

Comparisons, Contrasts, Connections

Compare Cather to Sarah Orne Jewett. Cather knew Jewett and admired her work. She even wrote an appreciative preface to a two-volume edition of Jewett's stories in 1925. An expanded version of the preface appears in the essay "Miss Jewett" in *Not Under Forty* (1936), an essay that makes it clear that Cather saw herself as aspiring to achieve many of the strengths as a writer that she found in Jewett's work.

Questions for Reading and Discussion/ Approaches to Writing

1. (a) In your reading of the story, who is the most important character? In your reading, who is the most reliable narrator? Who is the "hero"? Who is the most sympathetically presented character?

   (b) Cather used "Three Women" as the title of this story when she published it in a magazine, but "Old Mrs. Harris" when it appeared in a collection. What is the difference in emphasis? Which title do you prefer and why?

   (c) Describe the Templeton marriage. Whose fault is it that this family's life is less than perfect? Does the story attempt to place blame on husband or wife?

   (d) How does this story treat the issue of "motherhood"?

   (e) How is the southern background of the Templeton family important to the story?

    (f)   Discuss the economic and social structure of Skyline, Colorado. Who's on top? On the bottom? Why? Who is inside the structure and who is outside? Where do the Templetons fit? The Rosens?

2. One writing assignment I would suggest is in the form of a reading "quiz." Before discussing the work in class on the day it is the assigned reading, ask students to write a one-sentence summary of the story. Ask everyone to exchange papers and have students read aloud sentences that described a different central issue than the one each of them selected as at the heart of the story. These responses should lead easily into the study questions given above.

Bibliography

For the most part, the recent biographies by O'Brien and Woodress and book-length critical studies such as those by David Stouck and Susan Rosowski present the most sensitive readings of Cather's life and work.

One particularly fine "older" source is *Willa Cather: A Pictorial Memoir* (Lincoln: Univ. of Nebraska Press, 1974), with photographs by Lucia Wood and text by Bernice Slote. It's an excellent brief introduction to the world of Willa Cather.

Marilyn Arnold has an extremely useful discussion of "Old Mrs. Harris" in *Willa Cather's Short Fiction* (Athens: Ohio Univ. Press, 1984, pp. 141–52).

Susan Glaspell (1876–1948)

Contributing Editor: Arthur Waterman [p. 1076]

Classroom Issues and Strategies

It's important to show how the details of the play transcend local color and address universal concerns. Students should come to see that the precise setting and time lead to a universal and timeless experience.

Ask students to envision what the play would be like if it were three acts and the background and main characters were fully presented. Point out how the very restrictions of the one-act play enhance the tensions and meaning. The play has been popular since it was first produced and has been seen recently (1987, 1988) on PBS television, which indicates that it appeals to diverse audiences.

Susan Glaspell is an interesting example of the late nineteenth-century woman writer, raised in the local color tradition, who radically altered her life and art after her marriage and moved east. She "came of age" about the same time American writing moved from regionalism to modernism and she helped found the modern movement in American drama. Once her experimental period was over, she returned to fiction and to her earlier themes—much more maturely presented. Whether her retreat back to regionalism was because her husband died or because she felt more secure in the older tradition, no one can say.

Major Themes, Historical Perspectives, and Personal Issues

1. Regional: The play conveys the brutal experience of being a farm wife in Iowa during the latter half of the nineteenth century.
2. Sexual: In this play women are pitted against men—Minnie against her husband, the two women against their husbands and the other men. The men are logical, arrogant, stupid; the women are sympathetic and drawn to empathize with Minnie and forgive her her crime.
3. Mythic: The setting—a lonely, bleak, cold landscape; the main characters are never seen on stage and assume a shadowy, almost archetypal presence; the struggle between them is echoed by the antagonisms between the two women and three men on stage; the result is that a brutal murder is forgiven because of the more terrible tragedy beneath it.

Significant Form, Style, or Artistic Conventions

This play presents most of the qualities of local color writing: exact detail, local speech and customs, a strong sense of place. It avoids some of the excesses of that genre: idealization of character, emphasis on the unique and colorful aspects of the locale, and sentimentality. The demands of the one-act drama, its compression, single set, limited characters, tight plot, single mood—all protect the play from the excesses of its convention and enhance its virtues.

We should also note that the play carefully distinguishes between the affairs of men and the concerns of women. The men intrude on the woman's world, dirtying her towels, scoffing at her knitting and preserves. As we move into the kitchen, the men are left out and the awful details of Minnie's life are revealed to Mrs. Peters and Mrs. Hale, so that when the men return, we see how blind they are and we, the audience, accept their decision not to reveal Minnie's motive.

Original Audience

We know the play was based on an actual trial Susan Glaspell covered as a reporter in Des Moines. In this sense, the play was written for a midwestern audience to dramatize the terrible life of a farm wife, isolated and dependent on her husband for her physical and emotional needs, with the occasional tragic consequences the play depicts. But the play was written after Susan Glaspell had left the Midwest, after she had lived abroad, married, and moved to Provincetown. She had time to ponder the implications of the event and see the tragedy in larger terms, so she was able to transform a journalistic story into a universal drama.

Comparisons, Contrasts, Connections

Zone Gale's "Miss Lulu Bett" (1920) is about a Wisconsin spinster who revolts against midwestern prudishness to seek her own fulfillment. The play has many local color attributes and treats ironically some of the themes in "Trifles."

A better comparison is to be found with Synge's "Riders to the Sea," a one-act tragedy about the lives of fishermen in the Aran Islands. Both plays transcend local color detail to reach mythic concerns, both use a piece of irregular sewing to reveal information, and both present an essential conflict between the men who go out to battle nature, while the women remain to nurture beauty and sustain life.

Questions for Reading and Discussion/ Approaches to Writing

1. If students have been reading someone like Bret Harte, I'd suggest they think about the advantages and disadvantages of local-color writing. Also, I would suggest they examine the one-act play form to see what can and cannot be done with it.
2. I would center on short questions about technique: How does the physical location of the characters help develop the theme? Who are more fully developed, the two women or the three men? Indicate several ways Susan Glaspell conditions the audience to accept the final decision.

Bibliography

See the primary and secondary works listed with the headnote.

Robinson Jeffers (1887–1962)

Contributing Editor: Arthur B. Coffin [p. 1088]

Classroom Issues and Strategies

Many readers/critics feel that Jeffers's most readable poetry is in his lyric poems; others feel that his most powerful verse is in his long narrative poems, which, of course, cannot be anthologized. It is useful—perhaps necessary—therefore to provide students a sense of the larger context in which the lyrics stand and to describe the evolution of Jeffers's personal philosophy, which he called "Inhumanism." Even students who respond readily to Jeffers's reverence for a distant God made manifest in the "beauty of things" (i.e., nature)—and many of them embrace these views instantly—will ask, "Where's this guy coming from?" Consider some of the following suggestions.

One may assign individual students or groups of students narrative poems to read and report on to the class, but, with the exception of "Roan Stallion," this is long and sometimes laborious work. And it is time-consuming in the classroom. The traditional approach of lecturing to provide the necessary context is the most efficient one. (As the bibliography indicates, there is a large body of scholarly work to draw on for this purpose.)

Another possibly more appealing approach from the students' perspective is to introduce Jeffers's *Not Man Apart* (ed. David Brower, Sierra Club, San Francisco, 1965: Ballantine Books, New York, 1969), which, taking its title from a Jeffers line, is a collection of magnificent Ansel Adams photographs of the Big Sur landscape (accompanied by quotes from Jeffers), which has a central role in this poetry.

Hearing these poems is very important, and, whether or not the instructor is a competent reader of these verses, he or she might consider obtaining recordings of William Everson's superb reading of them (available from Gould Media, 44 Parkway West, Mount Vernon, NY 10552-1194; Tape #826—*The Poetry of Robinson Jeffers* by William Everson).

Students respond to Jeffers's concern for the beauty of nature and the divinity he finds there. Often they are receptive to the theme of the destructive nature of human beings, especially to human pollution of the earth. Many students are drawn to what they identify as Jeffers's isolationism, his fiercely held individualism. In addition to questions about Jeffers's religious views and his varied intellectual background, they often ask about the poet himself, biographical data which, in this instance, do not take one far from the texts.

Major Themes, Historical Perspectives, and Personal Issues

With the publication of the long narrative "Tamar" (1924), Jeffers declared his literary independence and attempted to write poetry appropriate to the times as he saw them. In "Self-Criticism in February," which reviews this effort, he wrote, "[this] is not a pastoral time, but [one] founded / On violence, pointed for more massive violence." Like T. S. Eliot and others, Jeffers searched myth and literature for a "usable past," but he employed these materials more radically than his peers, who, he thought, were fading out in effete aestheticism. Generally, Jeffers saw Euripides' vision as more akin to his own than those of Aeschylus and Sophocles; in the Roman poet Lucretius (*On the Nature of Things*, which embodies the materialism of Epicurus) Jeffers found support for his view of nature and divinity; classical mythology and tragedy helped him to structure his personal vision and his poems. American capitalism was morally bankrupt and defacing the landscape; both American politics and international affairs were threatened by "Caesarism"—ruthless leaders and timid followers. The advent of nuclear war seemed to assure the imminent destruction of human beings—but, for Jeffers, not of the world itself—which change, the poet believed, would allow the beauty of the world (the manifest God) to start over again, without the contaminating presence of mankind. His doctrine of Inhumanism—"a shifting of emphasis from man to not-man; the rejection of human solipsism and recognition of the transhuman magnificence"—encourages humans to become "uncentered" from themselves. "This manner of thought and feeling," he wrote, "is neither misanthropic nor pessimistic. . . . it has objective truth and human value. . . ."

Significant Form, Style, or Artistic Conventions

Jeffers's early verses are late-Victorian in manner, reflecting the influences of D. G. Rossetti, A. Swinburne, and G. Moore, but prior to writing "Tamar" he decided to break with modernism, which he saw typified by Mallarmé and his followers. These modernists had forsaken content,

Jeffers believed, in favor of aesthetics, which weakened their verse. His narrative poems are heavily laden with statement and action, and their lines are long and supple after classical models. "Apology for Bad Dreams" and "Self-Criticism in February" tell us nearly all there is to hear about Jeffers's poetic. Despite Jeffers's disclaimer (and the views of critics who agree with him on this point), I see him as a modernist sharing much with other modernists such as Robert Lowell, Eliot, Stevens, and Roethke, who also tried to re-order a fragmented world and to find adequate structures for the task. It may be useful to compare Jeffers's views of religion, order, fictive constructs, and reality with the more sophisticated ones of Wallace Stevens (cf. Stevens's "Sunday Morning," "The Idea of Order at Key West," "The Snow Man," and others).

Original Audience

In several places, Jeffers said that he wrote for all time, not for the moment (even though many of his lyrics of the 1940s are very topical, like carping letters to the editor that criticize world leaders indiscriminately), because he believe poetry should bespeak permanence. His work was very popular during the late 1920s and the 1930s (he appeared on the cover of *Time* magazine), but his audience left him during WWII, when his individualism and their patriotism diverged in a wood. During the 1960s and 1970s, his work was widely translated in Europe, where he gained an enthusiastic readership in the Slavic countries. On this continent, he has been adopted by members of the ecology movement, disaffected members of traditional institutional religions, and academic scholars, who together have revived his reputation. Although Jeffers has been severely slighted in the academic texts of the last decades, he is the poet, I find, that the general student is most apt to have read *before* taking an American literature or poetry course.

Jeffers's disinterest in a particular audience—his writing for all time—simplifies the audience problem in class and permits a wide range of responses.

Comparisons, Contrasts, Connections

Compare Jeffers's themes to Euripides', whose tragedies he used and "adapted" as in Jeffers's Broadway hit "Medea." He follows the Greek closely, but the differences are arresting.

Consider also Lucretius, whose version of Epicurus' materialism attracted Jeffers, who fused it with his pantheistic view of nature.

For another interesting comparison, look at Shelley, whose view of Prometheus and the poet as legislator are reflected in Jeffers. Jeffers's incest theme has been traced to Shelley.

Nietzsche's philosophy appears to have attracted but not to have held Jeffers. Nietzsche's *Thus Spake Zarathustra, Beyond Good and Evil,* and *The Birth of Tragedy* would be the main texts of interest.

Wallace Stevens's interest in the imagination, reality, and fictive constructs provides bases for comparison/contrast.

T. S. Eliot's use of mythic materials and the literary tradition to construct an authentic religious outlook suggests some interesting similarities and dissimilarities.

Eugene O'Neill was similarly preoccupied with Greek tragedy.

Theodore Roethke's mystical view of nature and of the spirit that resides in nature offers fertile possibilities for comparison/contrast.

W. B. Yeats's interest in towers, in social unrest versus change, and in the cycles of nature compare with those of Jeffers.

Ansel Adams's photographs of "Jeffers country" offer opportunities for discerning comparisons/contrasts between visual and literary texts.

Questions for Reading and Discussion/ Approaches to Writing

1. After reading the Jeffers poems included in the text (and any others of his you wish to look at), write two or three pages of response to them. In your brief paper, assume that you are a developer (real estate or commercial, for example), or an environmentalist (perhaps a member of the Sierra Club or other similar group), or a TV evangelist, or some other role of your choice. You should imagine how you think the person you choose to be in your paper would most likely respond to Jeffers's work.

2. You have just been reading Jeffers, and your roommate or brother or sister or parent comes and says, "Reading Jeffers? What does he have to say? Should I read his poems?" Assuming that you and your interrogator are on good terms, write a compact essay summarizing what Jeffers says and include in your response to the last question why you make the recommendation you give. Saying simply "yes" or "no" or "you're too young (or old)" to the last question is to evade its point; develop a reasoned reply. Be specific.

Bibliography

For the instructor in survey courses, the handiest and most comprehensive source is Robert Brophy, *Robinson Jeffers* (Boise: Western Writers Series, 1973), 50 pages.

To keep abreast of Jeffers scholarship, one should consult *Robinson Jeffers Newsletter* (Occidental College, 1600 Campus Road, Los Angeles, CA 90041).

Robert Frost (1874–1963)

Contributing Editor: James Guimond [p. 1099]

Classroom Issues and Strategies

Students often have difficulty appreciating (a) the skill and subtlety with which Frost uses traditional poetic devices such as rhyme and meter; (b) the sparse pleasures he discovers in some of his rural and natural subjects; (c) the bleakness and/or ambiguity of his more "philosophical" poems. Sometimes they also have difficulty understanding that the values he presented in his poems were derived from a type of community or society that was very different from their own: one that was rural, fearful of change, distrustful of technology, proud of craftsmanship, and deeply committed to privacy and self-reliance.

Regarding the formal devices and ambiguity, there is no substitute for traditional "close reading." (Quotes from Frost's essays, "The Constant Symbol" and "The Figure a Poem Makes" can be helpful in this regard.) The sparse pleasures can be seen in poems like "The Pasture" and "The Investment," and the bleakness can be discerned in the endings of "Once by the Pacific" and "Desert Places." The social values can be seen in dramatic poems like "The Fear" and "The Ax-Helve," as well as in "Mending Wall."

When teaching the dramatic poems, it is helpful to discuss their plots and characters with students because Frost sometimes presents these elements in an oblique way.

Students generally respond well to the basic emotional or psychological experiences expressed in Frost's poems. Some of them—for example, ones who have had a philosophy course or two—may raise questions about the implications of poems like "Design."

Major Themes, Historical Perspectives, and Personal Issues

Major themes would include:

1. The limitations and isolation of the individual in either a social or natural environment, plus the related theme of how difficult it is for the self to understand existence.
2. The ambiguity of nature when it is considered as a source of wisdom.
3. Frost's sensitivity to the theme of entrophy, doom, and extinction.

Frost usually deals with personal issues so covertly in his poetry that it is not very fruitful to discuss those topics in detail. If the teacher wishes to do so, however, he/she should consult Thompson's biography. For historical issues, the Cowley and O'Donnell essays in James Cox's *Robert Frost: A Collection of Critical Essays* are helpful.

Significant Form, Style, or Artistic Conventions

Special emphasis should be placed on:

1. His skill in synthesizing traditional formal devices with vernacular speech patterns and language.
2. His ability to develop metaphors.
3. How relatively "unmodern" or traditional he was in relation to some of his contemporaries.

Original Audience

I emphasize that during the 1920s, 1930s, and 1940s Frost had a strong appeal for a conservative readership who did not understand or appreciate modernism very well. Since such readers could be quite influential in academic, editing, and Pulitzer-Prize-judging circles, some of Frost's popularity should be considered in this context.

Comparisons, Contrasts, Connections

Contrasts with Stevens, Williams, Pound, and Eliot are appropriate; and comparisons with Longfellow, Bryant, Robinson, and the British Romantics and Georgians (e.g., Edward Thomas) can be helpful.

Questions for Reading and Discussion/ Approaches to Writing

1. (a) Ask students what it would be like to live on an isolated farm in 1900.
   (b) Find the rhymes in specific poems and discuss why Frost emphasized these words.
   (c) What are the emotional connotations of the images in certain poems?
   (d) Who is the speaker of the poem, and why is he/she speaking?
   (e) How does Frost develop a metaphor in an assigned poem?
2. (a) Comparison-contrast topics work well if they are focused on specific issues like free verse versus traditional meters.
   (b) What is Frost's persona and how does he develop it in a variety of poems?
   (c) How does Frost create conflict or tension in his poems and how does he resolve it?
   (d) How closely does Frost follow his own poetic "rules" as he states them in "The Figure a Poem Makes"?
   (e) Compare the "philosophy of life" which is expressed in a poem like "Directive,'" Design," or "Desert Places" with the ideas in an essay by Ralph Waldo Emerson, such as "Nature."

Bibliography

Many of the essays in James Cox's collection are very good (see the headnote in the text); I have listed those I consider to be particularly useful.

Sherwood Anderson (1876–1941)

Contributing Editor: Martha Curry [p. 1118]

Classroom Issues and Strategies

Teachers should avoid three erroneous approaches to Sherwood Anderson's writings: regarding him primarily as a novelist, as a regional writer, or as author of only one important book, *Winesburg, Ohio.*

Regarding the first error: even in his best novel, *Poor White*, Anderson has difficulty sustaining plot and characterization. Anderson succeeds best in the smaller narrative form of the short story. "Death in the Woods" exemplifies many of the characteristics of the masterpieces of Anderson's story-telling art: direct authorial address to the reader; a circular, not linear, narrative structure; plot subordinated to characterization; simple style and vocabulary; and images drawn from elemental aspects of nature.

Regarding the second error: Although Anderson is one of the many regional writers who chronicle the changes that took place in the Midwest at the turn of the century as a result of industrialization, primary emphasis should be placed on his role as a storyteller.

Regarding the third error: Anthologies should never amputate individual stories from the artistic whole that is *Winesburg, Ohio*. Teachers should urge students to read all of *Winesburg*, pointing out that it is Anderson's best book-length work, but they should also tell students that many of Anderson's best stories are not found in that collection.

Winesburg, Ohio and *Death in the Woods* are not collections of isolated stories but, rather, short story cycles; that is, collections of stories with common themes, imagery, and tone, and often with common setting and characters. An understanding of the short story cycle, from Homer's *Odyssey* to Chaucer's *Canterbury Tales* to Joyce's *Dubliners* will help in understanding Anderson's work.

Students are amazed how contemporary Anderson is. He speaks to their concerns regarding loneliness, fragmentation, and search for beauty and wholeness. They also are intrigued by the artistry that a small work like a short story can achieve.

Major Themes, Historical Perspectives, and Personal Issues

After they study "Death in the Woods," urge students to read the whole of *Winesburg*. Reading the story of Ma Grimes will prepare students for Anderson's central theme of the grotesque. Ma Grimes is one of these grotesques, someone trapped in her own inability to find the "truth" of her life and thus to grow to maturity.

Regarding historical issues: Point out to the students that for ten to twelve years, as he claims both in his *Memoirs* (edited by Paul Rosenfeld [New York: Harcourt Brace, 1942], p. 286) and in his *Writer's Book* (edited by Martha Curry [Metuchen, N.J.: Scarecrow, 1975], p. 28), Anderson tried to write this story to his satisfaction. As we know from a note attached to a holograph housed with the Sherwood Anderson Papers in the Newberry Library in Chicago, Anderson's first attempt to write this story is a short sketch called "Death in the Forest." Chapter

XII of *Tar: A Midwestern Childhood* (Cleveland: Press of Case Western Reserve University, 1969, pp. 129–41), also tells the story of an old woman's death in the woods on a snowy night. A slightly expanded version of this episode, told by a first-person narrator, appeared in *American Mercury* (IX, 7–13), in September of the same year, that is, 1926. Since the 1933 title story in the collection *Death in the Woods* is practically identical with the version of the story that appeared in *American Mercury*, we can assume that Anderson worked on "Death in the Woods" from the mid-1910s, the time he was writing the *Winesburg* stories, until 1926.

When we consider this background concerning the composition of "Death in the Woods," we can see that the story itself exemplifies Anderson's usual method of story telling. Anderson writes and rewrites his stories until he is satisfied with them, just as his narrators try again and again to tell the "real" story hidden beneath surface events. "Death in the Woods," then, is a remarkable example of Anderson's method of composition as well as a remarkably unified short story.

Significant Form, Style, of Artistic Conventions

Attention should always be drawn to the importance of the narrator in Anderson's stories. The narrator in "Death in the Woods" is actually describing the creative method that Anderson uses in writing the story. The central character is not Ma Grimes but the mature narrator who looks back on earlier experiences: the sight of an old, oppressed woman trudging from her farm into town in order to obtain the necessary food for her men and animals; the time he worked for a German farmer who hired a "bound girl"; the moonlit winter night he saw half-wild dogs almost revert to wolves in the presence of the near-death of a human.

In order for the teacher to help students comprehend "the real story I am now trying to tell," the teacher must stress the role of the mature narrator as he struggles to weld his diverse experiences and images into a whole that will bring order out of their diffuseness and beauty out of their ugliness. All of her days Ma Grimes "fed animal life." Only at the end of the story does the reader realize that the most important life Ma Grimes fed was the creative life of the narrator. Thus, the story as a whole demonstrates, as Anderson explains in its final sentence, "why I have been impelled to try to tell the simple story over again." The reader feels, as the story comes to a close, that now, after perhaps ten or twelve years, Anderson has been able to create a beautifully unified work of art.

Original Audience

Since "Death in the Woods" is truly a universal story, even though the setting is a farm and small town at the turn of the century, I do not consider the question of audience or date of composition important.

Comparisons, Contrasts, Connections

Since much of Anderson's fiction relies heavily on his own experiences, the best background materials for teaching "Death in the Woods," to my mind, are primary, not secondary, sources, although excellent critical articles on "Death in the Woods" can easily be found by means of the standard indexes. Nonetheless, the best background information still remains Anderson's own words. Anderson's three autobiographies, *Tar, A Story Teller's Story,* and *Memoirs,* all available in critical texts edited by Ray Lewis White, have excellent indexes that will lead the reader to the appropriate sections.

Questions for Reading and Discussion/ Approaches to Writing

1. Before the students have read the story, point out:
   (a) The various levels of the story: story of Ma Grimes, her relationship to the men and animals in the story, her role as "feeder" of life.
   (b) The function played by the dogs, both literal and symbolic.
   (c) Growth of the narrator from a young boy to a mature artist.
   (d) The difficulty the narrator has in telling the story.
   (e) The many images in the story, both from nature and from art.
2. I have had great success in having students write a short story or character sketch about one of the "grotesques" they meet in everyday life, someone they see on the bus or subway, in the supermarket or on the street, at home or in school. They must approach this character with great respect and love, as Anderson does, and try to imagine and then tell the character's story of isolation, fear, and, ultimately, of beauty.

Bibliography

Read: *Winesburg, Ohio,* a very short book. Several other stories in Maxwell Geismar's *Sherwood Anderson: Short Stories.*

If there is time, read: Chapter XII of *Tar*. "Death in the Forest," edited by William Miller and printed as an appendix to Ray Lewis White's critical edition of *Tar*, pp. 231-36. Selections from White's critical edition of Sherwood Anderson's *Memoirs*.

Chapter I of *Representative Short Story Cycles of the Twentieth Century* by Forest L. Ingram (The Hague: Mouton) for Ingram's theory of the short story cycle.

The Chicago Renaissance in American Letters: A Critical History by Bernard Duffey (Westport, Conn.: Greenwood Press, 1954), Chapter 10, "Three Voices of the Liberation," about Francis Hackett, Harriet Monroe, and Margaret Anderson and the little magazines they founded, and Chapter 11, "The Struggle for Affirmation—Anderson, Sandburg, Lindsay."

Theodore Dreiser (1871–1945)

Contributing Editors: James M. Hutchisson and James L. W. West III
[p. 1127]

Classroom Issues and Strategies

Dreiser's style is unconventional. If students have heard of him, they've heard that he's a clumsy stylist. They also will have difficulty understanding Ida's dilemma in "Typhoon."

The instructor should explain that Dreiser was trained as a journalist whose main duty was to record the who, what, where, when, why and how of a story. Graceful style was a small concern. In fact, some of Dreiser's verbal clumsiness was more or less deliberate. His writing possesses its particular power, its ability to move the emotions, in part because of its bluntness, its lack of grace. Try to imagine "Typhoon" told by a facile stylist, for example, by F. Scott Fitzgerald. It would lose much of its voltage.

It's a good idea to show students how thoroughly trapped and damned Ida Zobel is by an illicit pregnancy. Children of the '80s will likely try to foist their own standards back onto her time and place. Students identify with this story because they feel much peer pressure in matters of sex. Ask them to try to argue sympathetically for Hauptfuhrer. Can it be done? Where did Dreiser's sympathies lie?

Another good theme to discuss is Ida's being "forgiven" by the public, her almost automatic innocence before the court, and her adoption by the wealthy socialite. Dreiser is indicating some things here about the influence of the fourth estate over the administration of justice. We sympathize with Ida, of course, but her exoneration for the killing is suspect. Certainly she still feels great guilt; it is the major motivation for her suicide.

Major Themes, Historical Perspectives, and Personal Issues

Like virtually all of Dreiser's major characters, Ida Zobel in "Typhoon" is a seeker. She searches for beauty and love in a repressive, unenlightened society. She is ignorant and at the mercy of instincts and drives that she does not understand. She is naive enough to be duped by Hauptfuhrer largely because of her obsessively sheltered upbringing. This was ever one of Dreiser's major themes—his hatred of repressiveness and its consequences. The theme fits in well with the general rebelliousness and nonconformity of American writers of his generation and the generation following it.

Significant Form, Style, or Artistic Conventions

Dreiser is best taught as a writer who held philosophically conflicting ideas in suspension simultaneously. His best writing springs from the tensions generated by these opposing ideas. On the one hand he was virtually a textbook naturalist; on the other, a mystic, romantic, and sentimental. He was also a left-leaning social activist, a stance which, strictly speaking, is incompatible with naturalistic beliefs.

Original Audience

The instructor should emphasize that this story was magazine fiction, written to sell. In it, Dreiser was dealing with sensational tabloid material. The story was written in 1926 in order to follow up on the great success of *An American Tragedy*, published in 1925 and also based on a real murder case. The story borrows elements from the *Tragedy*—also from *Sister Carrie* (1900) and *Jennie Gerhardt* (1911), Dreiser's first two novels.

Comparisons, Contrasts, Connections

This story is written in Dreiser's late style, a fragmented, free-association style that attempts to accomplish many of the same things that stream-of-consciousness writers like Joyce and Faulkner were trying to do during the 1920s. Dreiser may have known of *Ulysses;* Faulkner wasn't really on the scene yet. Dreiser *had* been reading Freud and was much interested in the workings of the subconscious mind. One can teach this story as an example of early stream-of-consciousness writing.

Questions for Reading and Discussion/ Approaches to Writing

1. Ask students to reflect on the following before class: guilt and innocence; "peer pressure"; the narrative voice—is it slanted or objective?
2. Have them read a big-city newspaper of the period on microfilm and find similarly sensational material. They might compare the style of reporting ca. 1926 with the style used today and reflect on what this says about changes in American society over the past sixty years.

   Another useful topic is a discussion of free will as it operates (or does not) in "Typhoon." Are these characters in control of their destinies?

   A good short theme can be developed on the last line of the story. How does it resonate back through the entire narrative?

Bibliography

Gerber, Philip. "Theodore Dreiser." Biographical sketch in *Dictionary of Literary Biography*, Vol. 9. Detroit: Gale, 1981.

Griffin, Joseph. *The Small Canvas: An Introduction to Dreiser's Short Stories*, Fairleigh Dickinson, 1985.

Hutchisson, James M. "The Composition and Publication of 'Another American Tragedy': Dreiser's 'Typhoon.'" *Papers of the Bibliographical Society of America* 81: 1 (1987).

Edna St. Vincent Millay (1892–1950)

Contributing Editor: John J. Patton [p. 1154]

Classroom Issues and Strategies

Students have few problems reading Millay's poetry because the poet is forthright in expressing her emotions, ideas, and experiences. Obviously such references as those to Euclid and Endymion require explanation. Occasionally the diction needs some explication because of Millay's fondness for archaic and Latinate words.

Not much more is required than the teacher's ability to clarify some allusions and an occasional word or phrase. Any teacher of modern American literature should also have no problems with the references to city life and to issues of the times, which are generously sprinkled throughout Millay's work. As for accessibility, some benefit will come from placing Millay in the context of the poetry of the 1920s and 1930s as one of those like, for instance, Frost, MacLeish, and Robinson, who carried forward the more traditional verse form and techniques in the face of the experimentalism of Eliot, Pound, Stevens, and W.C. Williams. Millay also wrote on subjects that have a long history in English verse—the natural scene, romantic love, impermanence and death, and even poetry itself and the poet. Some students may therefore possibly view her as "old-fashioned" in contrast to the more experimental poets of her time. What must be emphasized is that Millay and other technically conservative poets flourished alongside the "New Poets," the Modernists, and similar poets and that they produced poetry with less emphasis on intellectualization and more on overt feeling. It is characterized by forthrightness of expression, clarity of diction, and avoidance of ambiguity and of the esoteric and erudite as a source for figurative language.

Millay is one poet in particular whose work benefits from being read aloud in order to do justice to its melodic qualities. In her own recording of some of her poems, Millay emphasizes the song-like nature of much of her verse. Teachers should play this recording for students or, of course, have them read the poems aloud themselves.

Students often raise gender issues. For example, they ask whether it makes any difference that the poet is a woman? Does gender show itself in any apparent way, allowing for those instances where the poet deliberately displays it as in the speaking voice used or the pronoun gender? How is Millay's stance as a "liberated" woman shown in her poetry if at all? Another issue is relevance. In what ways are Millay's poems relevant to today's lives? Are her concerns significant to present-day readers. Is it readily apparent that her poetry dates largely from the 1920s and 1930s?

Major Themes, Historical Perspectives, and Personal Issues

Millay's interest in heterosexual relationships is a major theme in her poetry, whether between husband and wife, as in "An Ancient Gesture," or between disaffected lovers, as in "The Spring and the Fall." Few American poets in this century have written on this subject with the combined artistry and diversity of Millay. "Love Is Not All" and "Oh, Sleep Forever in the Latmian Cave" are from *Fatal Interview*, a fifty-two sonnet sequence that deals with the course of a love affair from beginning to end.

Millay should not, however, be associated exclusively with this kind of poetry. Another major theme is the integrity of the individual, which Millay valued highly for herself as well as for others. "The Return" describes a man who has apparently "sold out" in order to escape into the illusory "comfort" of nature. In "Here Lies, and None to Mourn Him" Millay is describing a humankind that has fatally compromised itself by, perhaps, a reliance on technology (others see it as a comment on war).

A related theme, the integrity of the artist, is touched on in "On Thought in Harness." Millay also had a high degree of social consciousness. She spoke out against the execution in 1926 of the anarchists Sacco and Vanzetti, she wrote about the wars in Spain and China, and she devoted a volume of verse, *Make Bright the Arrows*, to concern about World War II. "Here Lies, and None to Mourn Him" is one of an eighteen-sonnet sequence in this volume.

Significant Form, Style, or Artistic Conventions

Millay's relationship to the poetry of her time should be discussed, as well as her antecedents in verse and her achievements in the sonnet and the lyric. Her immediate contemporaries include notably Cummings, Eliot, Frost, Amy Lowell, Moore, Pound, and Robinson. Millay, like Frost and Robinson, was a conservative in verse form and technique, a "traditionalist." Although highly aware of the work of her contemporaries, she steered clear of all "schools," such as Imagists, Modernists,

Objectivists, etc. Some critics place her in a line of descent from such late-nineteenth-century English poets as Browning and Swinburne.

A widely read person, Millay absorbed influences from sixteenth- and seventeenth-century English poets, hence her devotion to the sonnet form, in which she has no peer in all of American literature. The sonnet "His Stalk the Dark Delphinium" is noteworthy because Millay uses tetrameter verse rather than the more common pentameter. Millay's lyrics display a wide variety of form. Students may gauge her breadth in lyric poetry by contrasting the mixed verse feet and line lengths in "Spring" and its abrupt turns of phrase with the melodic flow of "The Spring and the Fall" and its regularity of form.

Original Audience

Millay continues to appeal to a large audience, as shown by the publication in the fall of 1987 of a new edition of her sonnets. A very large audience of readers in her own time admired her frequent outspokenness, her freshness of attitude, her liberated views as a woman, and the reflection in her poetry of an intensely contemporary sensibility. She is quintessentially modern in her attitude and viewpoint even if her language is often redolent of earlier poets. Although it is true that Millay's poetry has great appeal to women readers, she must not be either presented or viewed as writing solely for women because of the evident limitations it would place on appreciation of her accomplishment.

Comparisons, Contrasts, Connections

To illustrate Millay's mastery of the sonnet, a comparison should be made with Keats as her nearest equivalent. Both display the same ease and control in the form. The sonnets of Sir Philip Sidney, for one, may be used to show Millay's historical connection with the great sonneteering tradition in English. Direct comparison with Shakespeare would be useful only to illustrate her range of achievement—181 sonnets in the new edition.

Millay's lyric poetry can be compared with that of several late-nineteenth-century English lyricists, such as Dowson, D. G. Rossetti, and Housman (Browning and Swinburne have already been mentioned).

Her relationship to older American poets is less clear. She seems to have been little interested in them. Commentators have related her work in ways to that of Emerson and Holmes and perhaps some of Whittier and Longfellow, but not at all to Whitman and Dickinson. As noted above, Millay stands apart from the experiments and innovations in verse in her own time. She should be more meaningfully compared with

Robinson, MacLeish, Frost, and Masters, among others, who, while employing conservative prosodic techniques, expressed a contemporary point of view.

Questions for Reading and Discussion/ Approaches to Writing

1. "Spring": What is suggested about life by images of the empty cup and uncarpeted flight of stairs?

   "The Return": Why is Earth not able to comfort the despairing Man?

   "Here Lies, and None to Mourn Him": What seems to have "cut down" Man (the human race)?

   "Love is Not All": Although love is not "all," would the poet easily give it up?

   "On Thought in Harness": Explain the significance of the title with reference to the poem.

   "Oh, Sleep Forever": Restate the last two lines in your own words.

   "His Stalk the Dark Delphinium": Explain why "all will be easier" when the mind grows its own "iron cortex."

2. The student who selects Millay could read more of her work and then write about a major theme in the work.

   Another possibility is that a student might read further in her sonnets, read sonnets by others, e.g., Sidney, Donne, and Keats, and then write an analytical paper on differences and/or similarities in form, predominant subject matter, diction, etc.

   Another assignment would be to read other American women poets of the time (Crapsey, Teasdale, H.D., Wiley, Amy Lowell) to show any similarities based on their sex.

Bibliography

The following items are recommended because most teachers should have little trouble in gaining access to them and they provide a cross section of opinion and comment:

Cowley, Malcolm. "Postscript: Twenty Years of American Literature." In *After the Genteel Tradition*, edited by Malcolm Cowley, 213–34, passim. New York: W. W. Norton, 1973.

Dash, Joan. "Edna St. Vincent Millay." In *A Life of One's Own*, 116–227. New York: Harper and Row, 1973.

Flanner, Hildergarde. "Two Poets: Jeffers and Millay." In *After the Genteel Tradition*, edited by Malcolm Cowley, 124–33. New York: W. W. Norton, 1937.

Gassman, Janet. "Edna St. Vincent Millay: 'Nobody's Own.' " *Colby Library Quarterly* 9 (1971): 297–310.

Gray, James. *Edna St. Vincent Millay*. Minneapolis: Univ. of Minnesota Press, 1967. Forty-six small pages provide a thoughtful overview.

Hillyer, Robert. "Of Her Essential Voice and Spirit." *New York Times Book Review* (15 April 1954): 5.

Kelmans, Patricia. "Being Born A Woman." *Colby Library Quarterly* 15 (1979): 7–18.

Power, Sister Mary James. "Edna St. Vincent Millay Revels in Her Love of Earth." In *Poets at Prayer*, 19–30. New York: Sheed and Ward, 1938.

Sprague, Rosemary. "Edna St. Vincent Millay." In *Imaginary Gardens: A Study of Five American Poets*, 135–82. Philadelphia: Chilton, 1969.

Untermeyer, Louis. "Edna St. Vincent Millay." In *Modern American Poetry—Modern British Poetry*, edited by Louis Untermeyer, 438–40. New York: Harcourt, Brace, and World, 1962.

Wilson, Edmund. "Epilogue 1952: Edna St. Vincent Millay." In *The Shores of Light*, 744–93. New York: Farrar, Strauss, and Young, 1952.

Alienation and Literary Experimentation

[p. 1163]

Ezra Pound (1885–1972)

Contributing Editor: Betsy Erkkila [p. 1164]

Classroom Issues and Strategies

Pound's announcement of the principles of Imagism in "A Retrospect" provides an excellent introduction to the poetics of literary Modernism. Like Hemingway in prose, Pound turns away from the "emotional slither" and abstract rhetoric of Romantic and Victorian writers toward an emphasis on precision and concision in language and imagery. The poem "In a Station of the Metro" puts Pound's Imagist theory into practice. Pound was struck by the beauty of a crowd of faces he observed in the Metro at La Concorde in Paris; he tried to represent the experience first in a thirty-line poem; then through a Kandinsky-like splash of color; finally, he says, he found the best form for the experience in the model of Japanese *haiku* poetry. The poem interweaves subjective impression with objective expression, presenting in miniature the controlling myth of Pound's work: the discovery of light amid darkness, fertility amid waste, figured in the myth of Persephone in the Underworld.

In teaching "Hugh Selwyn Mauberley" and *The Cantos* you might want to prepare a handout explicating some of the allusions in the poem. You can use Ruthven's *Guide to Personae*, Brooker's *Student's Guide to the Selected Poems of Ezra Pound*, and Kearns's *Guide to Ezra Pound's Selected Cantos*. Begin by asking students to think about the overall import of "Hugh Selwyn Mauberley." On the broadest level, the poem is a compelling critique of the modern age; more specifically, it is about the plight of the artist, and of Pound in particular, in the modern world. Look at the ways the opening section on "E.P." works formally. The poem moves not by linear progression but by the juxtaposition of images as emotional and intellectual complexes; meaning develops not through direct authorial statement but by engaging the reader in a continual process of interpretation.

Major Themes, Historical Perspectives, and Personal Issues

While Pound buries the aesthete figure of his early period in the opening section of "Hugh Selwyn Mauberley," he does not renounce the value of artistic creation as a source of personal and social renewal; he represents and asserts the enduring value of beauty and song in "Envoi," which is modeled on the poem "Go, Lovely Rose" by the seventeenth-century English poet Edmund Waller.

The postwar context of the poem should be emphasized; sections IV and V contain one of the most negative and moving chants against war in modern literature.

Significant Form, Style, or Artistic Conventions

If Pound is the first or only modern writer you are discussing, you might want to begin by discussing the relation between an increasingly complex and allusive form and content among modern writers and the increasing isolation and alienation of the artist in the modern world. Pound went abroad both physically and mentally in his early period, seeking models and masks in past literatures, including Greek (Homer), Latin (Virgil, Ovid, Catullus), Italian (Dante, Arnaut Daniel, Guido Calvalcanti), French Provençal (Bertran de Born), and Chinese (Li Po, Confucius). During the war years, as he began to turn his attention toward the contemporary world, he also turned backward toward the native tradition of Walt Whitman. This turn is evident in the raw and comic exuberance of "Salutation the Second" and in "A Pact," where Pound seeks to come to terms with Walt Whitman.

Comparisons, Contrasts, Connections

Pound's evocation of war might be compared with Eliot's *The Waste Land*, Hemingway's *A Farewell to Arms*, and "The Walls Do Not Fall" in H. D.'s *Trilogy*.

After "Hugh Selwyn Mauberley," Pound turned his main attention to his epic *Cantos*, which he worked on for the remainder of his life. In a letter to W. B. Yeats, he said he intended to write one hundred cantos, modeled on a Bach fugue: "There will be no plot, no chronicle of events, no logic of discourse, but two themes, the Descent into Hades from Homer, a Metamorphosis from Ovid, and mixed with these, medieval or modern historical characters." As Pound's comment suggests, the poem has three analogues: an Odyssean journey, modeled on Homer's *Odyssey*; an ascent through Inferno and Purgatory toward the light of Paradiso, modeled on Dante's *Divine Comedy*; and from Ovid's *Metamorphosis* a series of "magic moments" in which divine energies are revealed in the physical world.

Pound speaks in a personal voice that anticipates the confessional strain in the poems of Allen Ginsberg, Robert Lowell, and Sylvia Plath.

Questions for Reading and Discussion/ Approaches to Writing

Ask students to note how Canto XLV examines the relationship between politics and poetry. Normally, the students respond positively to this poem as a chant against the commercialization of the modern age; in fact, the poem might be compared to Ginsberg's chant against Moloch in section II of *Howl*. Ask the students if there is any problem with the term *usury*, which Pound defined as "A charge for the use of purchasing power, levied without regard to production; often without regard to the possibilities of production." Discuss the ways the charging of interest became—through Christian prohibition—associated with the Jewish people. Is Pound's chant against usury also a chant against the Jews; and insofar as it is, how does this affect our reading and evaluation of the poem?

This discussion should raise some of the same questions about the relationship between politics and poetry, fascism and modernism, that were at the center of the debate about Pound receiving the Bollingen Award for the *Pisan Cantos* in 1949. The same questions, it might be pointed out, are at the center of the reconstruction of American literature. The "Pound Problem" is a telling instance, not only of the ways poetry is political, but of what happens when the poem's politics are "out of tune" with the politics of the dominant culture. One might ask how Pound's anti-Semitism differed in kind and degree from the racism and anti-Semitism that one finds in other major American writers. And why was Pound singled out for persecution at this time?

The "pull down they vanity" section of Canto LXXXI in the *Pisan Cantos* reveals a new attitude of *humilitas* and *humanitas*; Pound speaks in a personal voice that anticipates the confessional strain in the poems of Allen Ginsberg, Robert Lowell, and Sylvia Plath. The *Cantos* are incomplete and inconclusive: they end with two fragments, Cantos CXVII and CXX, which are like the *Cantos* themselves a figure of the fragmentation and incompleteness of the modern world. Pound's final words are at once an apology and an admission of failure: "Let those I love forgive/what I have made." Ask the students if they agree with Pound's final assessment of his epic. Is there, ultimately, any value in his work?

Bibliography

Suggested reading would include: Ruthven's *Guide to Personae*; Brooker's *Student's Guide to the Selected Poems of Ezra Pound*; and Kearns's *Guide to Ezra Pound's Selected Cantos*.

Gertrude Stein (1874–1946)

Contributing Editor: Cynthia Secor [p. 1189]

Classroom Issues and Strategies

Many students will have heard that Stein is "difficult" so they come to her work expecting not to understand. They expect "style" and "experimental strategies," but not content. There exists no cottage industry "explicating" her difficulty, so one does not have easy sources of data such as *Readers' Guide to Gertrude Stein* to which to refer students. In addition, her lesbianism and feminism put off some readers, if they get far enough into the text to see it.

One needs to begin by saying that these texts are the creation of an extremely well-educated woman—an American, a Jew, the child of immigrant parents, a lesbian, and a feminist—whose life experience and literary production bridges the Victorian and modern eras.

Her two enduring concerns are to portray the experience of woman and to explore what it means to present the fact or act of perception—which can be described as how we organize what we see.

How Gertrude Stein organizes what she sees and how she presents "seeing": this is probably enough metaphysics for a beginning.

When students see that the texts are about something, something very serious and important to the author, they relax and "read" the text.

The texts included here allow you to trace the evolution of Stein's style from realistic and naturalistic through abstract and cubist to simple and straightforward. You can also compare and contrast her representation over the years of women, femininity, and culturally determined depictions of women. Bridgman (p. 104) notes this preference in subject matter. Why and how she chose to depict women adds a new dimension to American literary history. My students have enjoyed "opening up" the style only to discover that it really is about "something."

Consider asking your students to write about a subject matter of their own choice in each of the styles represented in the anthology. Ask them to choose something from their own experience that they think will "fit" with that style. Have them comment on what they have learned from the exercise. Does the style determine a range of appropriate experiences? Can you truly use her style with your experience? How does the "fit" fit? When does it not? Did you learn something new about your experience by "seeing" it as Stein would have at the time she used that style? The underlying point here is that her "style" literally changes from text to text. The style is specific to the matter at hand.

Students become engaged with Stein's ideas, values, and experience as a woman. Her response to war interests them. They are interested in her ideas about democracy, race, geniuses, about why ordinary people are worth so much serious attention. They like the children's stories, when we get into what it means to write for children. Detective story buffs get into her ideas about the detecting mind.

My experience has been that once students believe she is serious, they give her serious attention and are fascinated by how she chooses to present the fabric of her life. Hers is a powerful mind and they respond to it. How she turns marginality into centrality is of interest to most of us.

Even so, their question continues to be, "Why is she so hard?"

Major Themes, Historical Perspectives, and Personal Issues

Gertrude Stein is interested in:

> what it is to be an American
> what it is to be a woman
> how people see things
> how people tell stories

She describes her own ordinary experience.

She writes about ordinary, commonplace people in such a manner that the absolute uniqueness of each is captured. This is her contribution to the American tradition of democracy and individualism.

She writes extensively about her life, and her growth into her life, as a major American writer of the twentieth century. She comments on culture, art, politics, and sexuality.

Significant Form, Style, or Artistic Conventions

Begin by showing how her work grows out of the American tradition of realism and naturalism.

Then show how she, in a typically twentieth-century fashion, becomes concerned with how we see what we see. As an American, a first-generation child of European Jewish parents, a woman, a lesbian, a feminist, and an artist, she is fully aware of marginality and centrality and ponders the process by which we organize experience and assign centrality, value, and worth. Remember that she is educated at Harvard University in philosophy and at the Johns Hopkins University in medicine.

She is fully aware that what she is has not historically been treated as fully human, fully civilized. Her literary strategies of a lifetime can be seen to be attempts to portray each life, each point of view, as fully real, absolutely present, and of equal value.

Original Audience

I focus on her willingness to continue writing serious and challenging texts without benefit of a wide contemporary audience. She says she writes for herself and strangers.

Serious writers, common readers, the audiences of her operas, and readers of her autobiographies and essays are variously able to articulate what attracts them and compels their attention. She tries very hard not to be influenced by "audiences."

Comparisons, Contrasts, Connections

Stein is so self-consciously American and so well read that it is fruitful to take her poetry and prose and set it beside such writers as Dickinson, Whitman, James, Wharton, Norris, Dreiser, and see what she does with related subject matter—her forms are radical critiques of the relation between content and form in American naturalism, romanticism, and realism.

Flaubert and Mann are interesting set beside her early prose works. Similarly Hemingway's early short stories are profitably set beside hers. One can see how she evolves a prose style in which the subject matter and the mode of narrative are about equal in weight. It helps to see that she is looking steadily at the "real" world, as she evolves her prose and poetic (and hybrid) conventions.

Cluster T. S. Eliot, Joyce, Pound, and Stein. Often these male contemporaries are on her mind as she does something different. She does not share their interest in the past. She evolves a presentation of female persons independent of patriarchal myth.

Questions for Reading and Discussion/ Approaches to Writing

1. I ask them to recall what was happening politically, socially, and artistically from 1874 to 1946. What events, achievements, personalities, movements, and concepts associated with those years have a bearing on how we perceive women, Americans, immigrants, Jews, lesbians, and geniuses? This lets us look at who "we" are, what we "see," and how it provides for us a context for understanding what Stein is doing with her writing.

2. (a) Consider *Tender Buttons*, "Preciosilla," and *Four Saints in Three Acts*. Characterize Stein's "modernist" strategies. T. S. Eliot and James Joyce add layers of meaning and mythic reference; she seems bent on stripping meaning away and living in a literal present represented as fully as possible. Is this a strategy for writing beyond patriarchy rather than shoring it up or representing fully its complexity?

   (b) Stein's impulse to describe, speculate, and pontificate places her firmly in the tradition of Emerson and others. She writes about herself as a Jew, a lesbian, a Westerner, an American, an expatriate, and a bourgeois Victorian lady of limited but comfortable means. How does she expand our definition of American individualism?

   (c) How does one integrate her comparatively large body of erotic poetry into the American literary tradition? What does it mean that a major American woman writer born in 1874 writes extensively about sex, and that her partner is a woman? How does it enlarge our concept of female sexuality and of female experience?

   (d) It is useful to talk about the tradition of female biography, autobiography, letters, and memoirs, and how this differs from the male tradition. Stein both writes directly about her experience (*Everybody's Autobiography*, *Paris France*) and incorporates it into fiction (*The Making of Americans*, "Ada," and *Ida, A Novel*). How does she extend our understanding of this mode?

   (e) A number of Stein's works, including *Four Saints in Three Acts* and *The Mother of Us All*, have been set to music or produced for the stage. What critical language is appropriate for discussing prose and poetry that experiment with generic conventions and concepts normally applied to scene design, ballet, opera, or piano compositions?

(f) What does it mean that forty years after her death, we still do not have major editions of her letters, her notebooks; scholarly editions of her works; adequate representation in teaching anthologies; study guides that would make her obscurity as clear as we find that of T. S. Eliot, James Joyce, and Ezra Pound?

(g) What did Stein gain and lose by living in a foreign country, where the daily language was other than the language of her childhood, her art, and her domestic life? Hemingway, Wharton, and Baldwin also lived abroad. Why? What other American writers chose to live abroad for long periods of time? Why?

(h) What does it mean that over half of her work was published posthumously and that most of her serious work, when published in her lifetime, was not widely read or understood? What comparison can be made with Emily Dickinson's accomplishment, limitations, and reputation?

Bibliography

Bassoff, Bruce. "Gertrude Stein's 'Composition as Explanation.'" *Twentieth Century Literature: Gertrude Stein Issue* 24, no. 1 (Spring 1978): 76–80.

Benstock, Shari. *Women of the Left Bank: Paris, 1900–1940*. Austin: Univ. of Texas Press, 1986. Chapter Five.

Dubnick, Randa. *The Structure of Obscurity: Gertrude Stein, Language, and Cubism*. Urbana and Chicago: Univ. of Illinois Press, 1984. Chapters Two and Five.

Katz, Leon. "Weininger and *The Making of Americans*." *Twentieth Century Literature: Gertrude Stein Issue* 24, no. 1 (Spring 1978): 8–26.

Kostelanetz, Richard. *The Yale Gertrude Stein*. New Haven and London: Yale Univ. Press, 1980. Introduction.

Secor, Cynthia. "Gertrude Stein: The Complex Force of Her Femininity." In *Women, the Arts, and the 1920s in Paris and New York*, edited by Kenneth W. Wheeler and Virginia Lee Lussier, 27–35. New Brunswick: Transaction Books, 1982.

——. "*Ida*, A Great American Novel." *Twentieth Century Literature: Gertrude Stein Issue* 24, no. 1 (Spring 1978): 96–107.

Sutherland, Donald. *Gertrude Stein: A Biography of Her Work*. New Haven: Yale Univ. Press, 1951. Chapter Four.

William Carlos Williams (1883–1963)

Contributing Editor: Theodora R. Graham [p. 1205]

Classroom Issues and Strategies

Students' assumption that what appears simple is simplistic can be a problem with teaching Williams's poetry. Some students feel the need to sketch in the house, barn, and fields behind the wheelbarrow and white chickens. For others, lack of experience with innovative line breaks and visual effects causes initial confusion. Many do not at first listen for the voice(s). They do not pay attention to speakers and therefore miss the tonal shadings, irony, humor, and other effects, including the sometimes clinical objectivity of poems related to visual art.

I recommend that students read poems aloud from the beginning. I read a poem aloud myself in class as a "possible interpretation" and have students comment on or revise the reading. I also use transparencies of shorter poems, occasionally changing the line breaks in an "edited version" to call attention to Williams's technique of fragmentation (not breaking necessarily with a syntactic unit). In addition, I sometimes use art slides that relate to specific poems (Demuth's "I Saw the Figure 5 in Gold," "Tuberoses"; Picasso's "The Girl and the Hoop"; Sheeler's "Classic Scene").

Students often ask if Williams is usually the speaker in the poem. They wonder how autobiographical his work is and ask whether his work as a doctor really influenced the way he wrote and what he wrote about. Those interested in form ask whether a single sentence, broken up on the page, can be a legitimate poem.

Major Themes, Historical Perspectives, and Personal Issues

Williams champions the American idiom and the "local"—either the urban landscape or one's immediate environment. He pays close attention to ordinary scenes (some purely descriptive; others as compositions as in visual art), the working class and poor. Williams's work often demonstrates the artist's need to destroy or deconstruct what has become outworn and to reassemble or recreate with fresh vision and language. His own "hybrid" background is, in his view, particularly American. He uses his experience as a doctor, married man and father, son and friend, in some of the poems, fiction, and plays. In addition, he demonstrates the need to discover rather than impose order on reality.

Significant Form, Style, or Artistic Conventions

It is important to be familiar with Imagist principles and the serious thrust of Williams's "no ideas but in things," as well as his sometime view of the poem as "a machine made out of words." Students should be aware of inductive process and attempt to relate this to Williams's emphasis on particulars, perhaps comparing it with Frost's statement that a poem does not begin with an idea. But whereas Frost embraced and adapted traditional forms, around 1915 Williams began experimenting in shorter poems with innovative line breaks, speaking voices, and a kind of stripped-down language (as he said of Moore, washing words with acid). Readers of Williams should also be familiar with the Armory Show (1913) and how Cubist fragmentation and photography became sources for new ideas in the arts through Alfred Stieglitz's Gallery "291" and magazine *Camera Work*, through gatherings at the home/ "gallery" of Walter Arensberg in New York City. Since Williams lived a short train ride from the city, he was able to frequent these shows, gatherings, and even studios, like that of Marsden Hartley, with Demuth, a good friend.

That the young Williams was at first influenced primarily by Whitman and Keats and began by writing conventional verse makes his departure from tradition all the more radical.

Original Audience

Point out through a dateline on a transparency the birth dates of Frost, Stevens, Williams, Pound, Moore, and Eliot—and include on the same sheet how old each poet was in 1912 (the date of what is sometimes referred to as the beginning of a poetic renaissance: the start of *Poetry* magazine). Audience was created by editors of little magazines (as new audiences for art were stimulated by opening of small galleries in New York), some—like Williams (see *Contact* I and II)—poets or fiction writers. *Poetry*, *Others*, the *Egoist*, *Criterion* (see *Little Magazines*, ed. F. Hoffman) and other magazines published on both sides of the Atlantic gave poets a place to present their work without considering the strictures of conventional larger-circulation magazines. The *Dial*, edited in the twenties by Marianne Moore, offered a coveted prize, which Williams was awarded.

The audience was not mainstream, not large; but it was generally sophisticated and knowledgeable about new developments in the arts and music. It could also be educated by the writers to be responsive to new work.

Now, of course, the modernists are all anthologized and acknowledged, both in their own rights and as influences for poets of following generations. That does not make them, however, easy to read. And the poems anthologized for secondary-level students often do not present their most controversial, and perhaps interesting, writing.

Comparisons, Contrast, Connections

Students may be asked to discuss how poems begin, or to compare two or more poets' process of revision. They may be asked to compare/ contrast the speakers' dilemmas in Frost's "Design" or other "dark" poems and Williams's "These." They could look as well at the forms each poet has chosen and discuss the possible reasons for what Frost would consider the "playing tennis with the net down" of Williams's verse. One could also discuss Williams's relationship to Pound and the latter's influence on early Williams's, as well as Williams's negative views of Eliot's expatriation and vice versa.

Questions for Reading and Discussion/ Approaches to Writing

1. Students generally have a set of strategies for reading that include giving attention to speaker, setting (time of year, time of day, description, etc.), various devices, audience, etc., that they have adapted to their own use as they become more sophisticated readers. I try not to reduce each writer to a set of questions but do suggest that with Williams they read aloud and look carefully at how Williams develops a speaker, how words—used sparingly—can "tell" more because of juxtaposition or because of their place in a visual composition.

2. Students are particularly interested in interrelations among the arts, in particular with Williams of poetry and visual art. Williams's favorite painter among the Cubists was Juan Gris. Some of his work, because it includes what Williams called "the recognizable object" in a new relation to its context, can be interesting to compare with carefully selected Williams poems (and they can see

Spring and All for Williams's comments on Gris). Too, Williams's work in relation to that of Charles Demuth, Charles Sheeler, and Alfred Stieglitz provides stimulating possibilities. Can a linear art such as poetry come close to resembling a spatial art such as painting or photography?

Bibliography

The secondary bibliography on Williams is very long. An instructor might consult Paul Mariani's edition of the secondary sources, arranged according to periods in Williams's writing, chronologically (published by the American Library Association). And then select more recent articles from this book's lists.

James Breslin's story of *WCW* and Thomas Whitaker's shorter introduction in the Twayne series remain useful.

Specialized studies of Williams and the arts by Bram Dijkstra and Dickran Tashjian provide helpful background.

Williams's *Autobiography* and *I Want to Write a Poem* (ed. Edith Heal) offer insights, not always totally reliable, in the poet's own words.

The *William Carlos Williams Review*, published since 1975, prints articles, reviews, biographical information, unpublished letters, and other manuscripts.

Eugene O'Neill (1888–1953)

Contributing Editor: James A. Robinson [p. 1225]

Classroom Issues and Strategies

Problems with teaching O'Neill include (1) students' lack of acquaintance with drama as a genre, which leads to problems re: point of view, etc.; (2) for *Hairy Ape*, fragmentation of the action and styles—its anti-realism—bewilders some; I often scan the final scenes in discussion in explaining the expressionism of earlier scenes; (3) difficulty with identifying tone: students don't know whether the work is tragedy, comedy, or satire; whether to identify with the hero or laugh at him.

To address these issues (1) emphasize the absence of point of view as an opportunity, not a problem, and use the central conflict to generate theme—in what ways do Yank and Mildred contrast? What do these contrasts represent (socially, sexually, psychologically)? (2) Relate the fragmentation of setting to that found (or made possible) by film as medium; compare other fragmentations to poetry (T. S. Eliot's *The Waste Land*) and fiction (Faulkner) contemporary with the play. (3) Define Yank as both hero and anti-hero (using Esther Jackson's definition in *The Broken World of Tennessee Williams*); identify targets of satire (distorted characters, for example) and ask how they relate to Yank's tragic journey toward awareness and toward death.

Consider approaching this play as an existential text (as Doris Falk does in her book on O'Neill) in which Yank is guilty of "bad faith" in his early identification with something outside of himself—steel—leaving him no place to turn when that identification collapses. Finally, consider a Freudian approach for some scenes like scene 3 with its blatant phallic and vaginal symbolism; you could also see Yank as "id" struggling toward "ego" in some ways, as animal striving to become a human individual.

Major Themes, Historical Perspectives, and Personal Issues

Personal Issues: O'Neill's relationship to women, particularly blaming of mother for his "fall" from innocence; O'Neill's lapsed faith in the Catholic God, leading to a philosophical search similar to Yank's; O'Neill's love of death.

Historical Issues: modern industrial capitalism as destructive of harmony (Paddy vs. Yank) but O'Neill's lack of faith in social solutions (repudiation of Long)

Themes: alienation as major theme, not "belonging"—dramatized in dialogue, setting, sound effects, and character distortions, as well as in action, a quintessential modern theme.

Significant Form, Style, or Artistic Conventions

The primary question is the theatrical mode of expressionism, and why O'Neill chose a style employing distortion and fragmentation for themes of industrialism and alienation.

A related issue is how this expresses the experimental spirit of the '20s and the questioning of American bourgeois culture spearheaded by Mencken and others—particularly the recognition of class divisions apparent in other works, like *Gatsby*.

Original Audience

The Broadway audience of the '20s accepted O'Neill's experimentation, partially because he was promoted by influential critics; but the reviews of *Ape* were mixed. I frankly don't work much with this problem in class, though you could cite reviews from leftist journals about the criticism of capitalism in the play to ignite discussion as to whether this is a central theme.

Comparisons, Contrasts, Connections

As indicated above, the play invites comparison with *The Waste Land* (fragmentation), *The Great Gatsby* (social criticism), as well as with figures like Crane and Dreiser and Jack London (the latter influenced O'Neill, in fact), whose American naturalism emphasized the animal, instinctual behavior of man. Darwinism, the struggle toward evolution (note Yank's emergence from the sea onto land in scene 5) clearly informs the assumptions of the play.

Questions for Reading and Discussion/ Approaches to Writing

For "genre": the key is central conflict (here, Yank vs. Mildred) and how this generates the themes of the play.

For expressionistic aesthetic: point out parallels to/influence of cinema, especially *Cabinet of Dr. Caligari* and *Metropolis*.

Bibliography

Read the *Ape* chapter in Doris Falk, *Eugene O'Neill and the Tragic Tension*; "Eugene O'Neill as Social Critic," *American Quarterly* (Winter 1954; rpt. in Oscar Cargill et al., *O'Neill and His Plays*—which is also useful for O's extra-dramatic utterances, several of which are in *Ape*); the chapter on *Ape* in Timo Tuisanen, *O'Neill's Scenic Images*; the chapter on *Ape* in Travis Bogard, *Contour in Time: The Plays of EO*; and my article, "O'Neill's Distorted Dances," in *Modern Drama* 19 (1976).

Djuna Barnes (1892–1982)

Contributing Editor: Catharine R. Stimpson [p. 1258]

Classroom Issues and Strategies

Problems with teaching Barnes are also opportunities. They include: (1) Her life and complicated childhood, e.g., a suffragist grandmother, a lecherous father; (2) her Bohemian adulthood—she lived and worked in avant-garde circles in New York and Europe and was also bisexual; (3) her comic wit and anguished vision; and (4) the range of her writing. Because she was a professional writer, with no other income for the most part, she took on a gamut of styles (journalism, plays, poems, stories, burlesques). She often parodies older forms, e.g., *Ryder*, the bildungsroman, and picaresque novel. If students don't know the original, they miss her great wit.

Her biography is still emerging, but tell the story of her life. Let students see her courage, adventurousness, and harsher characteristics, e.g., she travelled in hard-drinking circles. Critics/readers are rediscovering and recovering Barnes, seeing afresh how much she did, who she was, what her circles were, how much it mattered that she was a woman writer, how destructive that ghastly childhood was. Make the class part of the process of rediscovering and recovery, part of the adventure. Show students, too, what she was parodying, what part of literary history she was utilizing.

Help students with her dualistic vision, her sense of contradiction and irony. We are born, but born to die. The womb is a tomb. We are corrupt, but we love and desire. We descend in order to ascend.

Major Themes, Historical Perspectives, and Personal Issues

Trace the travails of a young, beautiful, really bright, ironic, bisexual woman making her way in a tough world. Culturally, look at what it means to be modern, to be avant-garde, to go for the new, vital, disorderly, outlawed, carnivalesque. Barnes knew almost everyone, so that she is a way into modern culture, e.g., she interviewed James Joyce. Historically, she is twentieth century. She lived through two world wars, in a world where God had disappeared, though she yearned for faith; in which the corrupt and vile seemed to dominate history.

Significant Form, Style, or Artistic Conventions

Barnes mastered several genres. Use her journalism to show the mass media, especially the mass newspaper. Use her short stories to show a combination of flat realism and the grotesque, the wierd; use *Ladies Almanack*, for one, to show both satire and inside jokes (Barnes was spoofing women's circles in Paris in the 1920s). Use *Nightwood* to show the modern novel, its suspicion of a straight, linear narrative; its interest in consciousness and language and clashing points of view; the darkness of vision, life as a nightwood; its wild humor; its blurring of sexual identifies; its sense of history as a fall. Like a surrealist, Barnes explores the unconscious. Like a symbolist, she incarnates the invisible in a sensible thing.

Original Audience

Barnes was very conscious of writing for specific audiences. She also cared, despite her bohemianism, for the approval of male cultural authorities, especially T. S. Eliot, who endorsed *Nightwood*. Toward the end of her life, Barnes wrote very little, but certain people kept her reputation alive because they loved her, despite her bitter, often destructive, wit, and the difficulty of her work. After her death, feminist critics have helped to reevaluate her. Another biographer, Andrew Field (1983)—who also writes about Vladimir Nabokov—likes quirky, elusive, brilliant, cosmopolitan figures.

Comparisons, Contrasts, Connections

Try teaching her stories with Sherwood Anderson, *Winesberg, Ohio* (1919), for the meticulous observation of despair; *Ladies Almanack* with Gertrude Stein, *The Autobiography of Alice B. Toklas* (1933), for Parisian adventures; *Nightwood* with *Ulysses* for the experimental modern novel; and, for very hard work, the play *Antiphon* with T. S. Eliot's *The Cocktail Party* (1950), for the use of older dramatic forms for metaphysical and psychological exploration.

Questions for Reading and Discussion/ Approaches to Writing

1. I prefer to have students keep journals rather than ask study questions because the journal picks up students' immediate reactions, no matter how hostile they are. If the class is too large, you might ask them to write out their own study questions. If a study question is a necessity, try to get at her sense of family, which is bleak but convinced of the family's necessity; or her sense of differences: how different people can be, perhaps, from "ordinary" life. Though students might not adore this, ask about futility, and, among the deluded, about failure.

2. Barnes was also a good artist. A student might write about her use of pictures, her visual skills, either through her own illustrations or through her vivid, metaphoric, visual language.

Bibliography

Watch for *Silence and Power*, edited by Mary Lynn Broe, forthcoming from Southern Illinois Univ. Press, which uses the lens of feminist criticism.

Douglas Messerli, *Djuna Barnes: A Bibliography* (1975), is an excellent survey of criticism up to the mid-1970s.

Elizabeth Madox Roberts (1881–1941)

Contributing Editor: Sheila Donnelly [p. 1265]

Classroom Issues and Strategies

Problems may arise because Roberts's style is introspective, poetic, and concentrated.

Discuss point of view with emphasis on the use of a central consciousness; provide information about the development and social implications of regionalism; instruct students about the use of symbolism and other figurative devices; prepare them for a complicated story structure. All lead readers toward an appreciation of Elizabeth Madox Roberts.

Until recently students have not been exposed to Roberts's work. Because her short stories are unavailable, my students are familiar with her best novels, *The Time of Man* and *The Great Meadow*. Some students find her complex structure and style of "symbolism working through poetic realism" difficult. Most enjoy the challenge; the characters many times face the perennial problems of youth. More experienced "city kids" have trouble empathizing with the rural mentality—social reality, sense of community—until the basics are explored: love, sex, birth, death—the equalizers.

Major Themes, Historical Perspectives, and Personal Issues

Roberts is concerned with the universal, the "Everyman" theme, as it grows out of her Pigeon River community. She is preoccupied with the intimate connection between the past and the present. Many of her works develop initiation themes through penetrating dramatization of psychological crises. I also think it is important to emphasize her innovative techniques.

Roberts's writing is special to early American literature because of her introspective and poetic style, her sense of southern rural community, her concern for the individual, and her emphasis upon the indomitable human spirit. Her works are primarily concerned with the way individuals apprehend reality.

In contrast to the novels, her stories are highly concentrated: limited in time and space and rendered in swift, artful strokes. But, like her best novels *The Time of Man* and *The Great Meadow*, her stories derive their substance from the characters. Their points of view convey the stories, which oftentimes are variations on the initiation theme. Her best stories in this vein are "On the Mountainside," "The Scarecrow," "The Sacrifice of the Maidens," "Swing Low Sweet Chariot," and "Death at Bearwallow."

Significant Form, Style, or Artistic Conventions

A thorough discussion of regionalism is helpful in introducing Roberts as well as her important place and influence in southern renaissance literature. While a discussion of her admiration for Berkeleian philosophy may be a point of interest and investigation for better students, it is not necessary for the enjoyment of her work.

Original Audience

Roberts can be discussed against the backdrop of the Lost Generation (*The Time of Man* was published in 1926, the same year as Hemingway's

The Sun Also Rises) as well as the movement toward an agrarian revival of the 1920s and 1920s (*I'll Take My Stand: The South and the Agrarian Tradition*). Today, a discussion of her Kentucky women provokes some high-powered and thoughtful commentary on women then and now.

Comparisons, Contrasts, Connections

Comparisons can be made to Ellen Glasgow, Willa Cather, Jesse Stuart, Robert Penn Warren, to name a few. She can also be compared to the many more modern female writers such as Kate Chopin, Zora Neale Hurston, Carson McCullers, Toni Morrison. She can be contrasted to any of the Lost Generation authors. Bases for comparison and contrast lie in personal background, fictional style, theme, region, and current meaningfulness. Mainly, fruitful comparison and contrast is gained from her novels, as her characters are more complex and profoundly developed than those in her short stories. Her works can be contrasted to more short-sighted regional stories, in that they represent "small self-contained centres of life" (Allen Tate), which root in a specific geographical region, adapt to the land, create a pattern of life, and then in turn become aesthetic, taking on universal and archetypal dimensions.

In all her works, Roberts masterfully blends poetry and realism. She, like William Faulkner, is never far from the sweat and agony of human spirit and, like Faulkner too, she believes that humanity will not only endure, but will prevail.

Questions for Reading and Discussion/ Approaches to Writing

1. How do events in your past affect moments, decisions, relationships, etc., in your present, future?
2. What sentiments do you attach to sense stimuli: smells, places, particular events, garments, etc.—the stuff of symbolism?
3. I have had special success with two types of papers:
   (a) Position papers in which students take issue with the characters' responses to particular events. They engage in hypothetical arguments and bring to bear their individual beliefs. These papers tend to generate a more penetrating discussion of all that shapes a character while encouraging students to trust their own analytical skills.

(b) Explication of the text using a quote from the author about her work, which forces students to grapple with an understanding of the author's artistic credo in conjunction with her works. For example, Roberts would say, "Life is from within, and thus the noise outside is a wind blowing in a mirror." This riddling line can be applied to many of her stories and novels, including "Death at Bearwallow."

Comparison/contrast papers with instructor's guidance are also a favorite of mine.

Bibliography

The Southern Review, Autumn 29, no. 4 (1984) has several essays as well as personal reminiscences.

Read Campbell and Foster's study *Elizabeth Madox Roberts: American Novelist* (1956).

See the headnote for a list of secondary sources and additional explication of "Death at Bearwallow" for specific references.

H.D. (Hilda Doolittle) (1886–1961)

Contributing Editor: Susan Stanford Friedman [p. 1278]

Classroom Issues and Strategies

Primary problems in teaching H.D.: Like much modernist poetry (e.g., Pound, Eliot), H.D.'s poetry is "difficult" for students. Mythological and Biblical allusions are common in her poetry. Her Imagist poetry is "impersonal" (like Eliot's)—that is, its relationship to human emotion is often deeply encoded. Her epic poetry is vast and complex in scope; its linguistic, religious, and psychological dimensions are sophisticated and multi-layered. Her perspective as a woman is quite different from the modernist male poets with whom she shares a great deal.

Strategies to teach H.D.: I have found students very responsive to H.D. when I have used the following strategies. Contextualize H.D.'s work in relationship to (1) modernism (students often expect a male poet to be "difficult," but resist having to work hard to read a woman poet); (2) women's poetry and feminist theory—especially feminist concepts of revision of patriarchal myths and traditions; (3) the mythological allusions (get students to relax and see that without footnotes, H.D. provides all the information they need); (4) the musical and syntactic structures of her poetic language. Her Imagist poems can be read as poems about the (female) self resisting stereotypical femininity (they are not "nature" poems). I have had great success in teaching *Trilogy* as a poem about war from a pacifist perspective akin to Virginia Woolf's.

Students are intrigued by the following: (1) Gender. They are fascinated in H.D. as a window into the problems and achievements of women's creativity. They love, for example, to read her famous "sea garden" poems (e.g., "Sea Rose") as encoded statements of female vulnerability and rejection of a suffocating femininity. (2) War and peace. Students are very interested and moved by her response to war. They are intrigued by the goddesses and matriarchal religions. (3) Initially, students are afraid of H.D.—real "poetry anxiety." They think they won't be able to understand it because it has so many allusions. But when they are given a framework for thinking about the poetry, they are very responsive.

Major Themes, Historical Perspectives, and Personal Issues

The headnote summarizes the major themes. To summarize, I think H.D. should be taught with emphasis on the following themes:

1. her attempt to understand the roots of cataclysmic violence and propose a revision of renewal and peace
2. the intersection of the historical and the personal in her stance as a woman
3. her characteristically modernist sense of quest in a shattered and war-torn world
4. her sense of the sacred, manifested in both female and male forms
5. her exploration of language—its magic (as logos), its music, its power as something women can claim to reconstitute gender and a vision of the cosmos

Significant Form, Style, or Artistic Conventions

H.D. should be taught as a modernist and as a woman writer; her Imagist poetry was formally highly innovative, a central influence on modern poetry. Imagism, however, became a craft in the service of larger visions after 1917. In writing epics, H.D. went against the inbuilt masculine conventions of the genre to forge a woman's epic form. The musical quality of H.D.'s poetry should be emphasized—within the *vers libre* tradition, she nonetheless established complex patterns of sound based on assonance, dissonance, internal rhymes, off rhymes, and repetition.

Original Audience

H.D.'s work should always be grounded in its historical period. H.D.'s Imagist verse was written in the exhilarating prewar world of the avant garde and then during the devastating Great War. Her epic poetry was written in the forties and fifties after another great war. Her audience during these years was in effect primarily the avant garde that was "making news" in all the arts. She was not a "popular" poet, but has often been known as a "poet's poet." Since the second wave of feminism, she has been widely read by women and men who are interested in women's writing.

Comparisons, Contrasts, Connections

1. Male modernists: Pound, Eliot, Williams, Stevens, Hughes, Yeats, Lawrence. Like these men, she experimented with poetic language. Like them, she increasingly wrote quest poetry in which the poet figures as a central mythmaking figure creating new meanings in a world whose symbolic systems have been shattered.
2. Female modernist writers: Marianne Moore, Virginia Woolf, Gertrude Stein, Djuna Barnes are modernist women writers with whom H.D.'s reconstructions of gender share a great deal—thematically and linguistically.
3. Fruitful comparisons can also be made with Blake, Dickinson, Dante, Homer.

Questions for Reading and Discussion/ Approaches to Writing

Explication assignments work well with H.D.'s Imagist poems. But the best papers I have received from undergraduates ask the students to examine how H.D. engages in a gender-inflected revisionist mythmaking in her poems. I use Adrienne Rich's concept of "re-vision" ("When We Dead Awaken: Writing as Re-vision" in *On Lies, Secrets and Silence*). The students trace the conventional myth H.D. invokes and then examine thematically and linguistically how she uses and transforms the tradition.

Bibliography

DePlessis, Rachel Blau. *Writing Beyond the Ending: Narrative Strategies of Twentieth-Century Women Writers*. Bloomington: Indiana Univ. Press, 1985. Chapters 5 and 7.

Friedman, Susan Stanford. "Hilda Doolittle (H.D.)." *Dictionary of Literary Biography*. Volume 45. Ed. Peter Quartermain. Detroit: Gale Research, 1986. Broad overview of life and work.

——, and Rachel Blau DuPlessis, eds. *H.D.—Readings*. Madison: Univ. of Wisconsin Press, 1989. A basic anthology aimed at introducing H.D. to teachers and students by reprinting the "essential" H.D. criticism of the past ten years.

Gelpi, Albert. "Re-membering the Mother: A Reading of H.D.'s *Trilogy*." In *H.D.: Woman and Poet*, edited by Michael King, 172–90. Orono, Me. National Poetry Foundation, 1986.

Gubar, Susan. "The Echoing Spell of H.D.'s Trilogy." In *Shakespeare's Sisters: Feminist Essays on Women Poets*, edited by Sandra Gilbert and Susan Gubar. Bloomington: Indiana Univ. Press, 1979.

Morris, Adalaide. "The Concept of Projection: H.D.'s Visionary Powers." *Contemporary Literature* 25 (Winter 1984): 411–37.

Showalter, Elaine. "Feminist Criticism in the Wilderness." In *The New Feminist Criticism*, edited by E. Showalter, 243–70. New York: Pantheon, 1985.

E. E. Cummings (1894–1962)

Contributing Editor: Richard S. Kennedy [p. 1286]

Classroom Issues and Strategies

Sometimes students are not aware that the *visual* presentation of a poem is part of its overall statement. In addition, they are sometimes puzzled by Cummings's unusual linguistic usage: the use of nouns as verbs, other locutions of nouns, etc. (e.g., the world is made of "roses and hello," "of so longs and ashes").

When I call students' attention to ways that words or presentations on the page actually function, this most often brings home an effect that may have been missed (e.g., in the poem "l(a" to point out the way the letter "L" and the word "one" are introduced, as the word "loneliness" and "a leaf falls" are intertwined). Sometimes I simply ask students for their individual responses and find that they really can *feel* the significance of an unusual expression.

I have sometimes begun class by asking, "How does Cummings indicate in his poems that he is a painter as well as a poet?" Another simple approach is to ask, "How does Cummings seem different from any other poet whose work you have read?" I have also asked students at some point in a discussion, "Why are these linguistic presentations that Cummings makes classified as poems?" (This last, of course, is not asked about his sonnets or rhymed stanzaic verses.)

Students vary in their responses, but most of them react deeply to his outlook on life—his valuing of love, nature, human uniqueness. Fewer students appreciate his play with form. Almost all enjoy his humor and satire. Nearly every student joins him in is antiwar stance.

Major Themes, Historical Perspectives, and Personal Issues

Cummings is, in his general outlook on life, an unabashed romantic. He affirms life wholeheartedly in all its multiplicity, but especially in whatever is simple, natural, loving, individual, unique. Above all, he emphasizes feeling and emotion rather than thought or analysis. He rejects those social forces in life that hinder the unique and individual expression of each person's essential being. He is particularly hostile to forces that promote conformity, group behavior, imitation, artificiality. He regards technology and the complexities of civilization as dehumanizing. Above all, he abominates war, which he looks upon as the ultimate negation of human values.

Although Cummings maintains the same general views throughout his life, he is more affirmatively exuberant in his early career and more lightheartedly iconoclastic. In his later career, he is more serene in his response to the basic good things of life and to the beauties of the natural world, but more harshly satiric in his denunciation of what he opposes.

Cummings's play with language, punctuation, capitalization, and his visually directive placement of words on the page are congruent with the new movement in the arts that began in the 1900s in European painting—the movement toward "break up and restructuring" that was part of the revolt against realism in modern art.

Original Audience

Cummings does not address a particular audience, although he assumes that his readers are generally educated in literature and the arts.

Comparisons, Contrasts, Connections

Cummings's work may be associated with the experiments in language and form that are found in the writings of Eliot, Pound, Stein, and Dos Passos. He may be contrasted with writers in the realistic or naturalistic vein, such as Dreiser, Anderson, Robinson, Frost, and Hemingway.

Questions for Reading and Discussion/ Approaches to Writing

1. I have sometimes lectured on his characteristic ideas and attitudes and then asked students to point out which poems illustrate these best. Or I have lectured on his special techniques and expressive devices in order to alert the students to ways of reading and understanding his work.
2. I have sometimes asked students to compare a Cummings sonnet with a conventional one, or to compare a Cummings lyric with one by Frost.

   I have also asked students to point out the likenesses and differences between a specific Cummings work and one by Eliot or Pound.

Bibliography

Richard S. Kennedy's introduction to the typescript edition of *Tulips & Chimneys* by Cummings (Liveright, 1976) summarizes his view of life and his poetic techniques.

Norman Friedman's *E. E. Cummings: The Art of his Poetry* (Johns Hopkins, 1960), Chapters Three and Four, deal clearly with his attitudes and his poetic devices.

T. S. Eliot (1888–1965)

Contributing Editor: Sam S. Baskett [p. 1298]

Classroom Issues and Strategies

For the uninitiated reader, Eliot's poems present a number of difficulties: erudite allusions, lines in a number of foreign languages, lack of narrative structure compounded by startling juxtapositions, a sense of aloofness from the ordinary sensory universe of day-to-day living. For the more sophisticated, Eliot's "modernism," his quest for "reality," may seem dated, even "romantic"; the vision of the waste land, stultifying and bleak; the orthodoxy of "The Dry Salvages" a retreat from the cutting edge of late twentieth-century thought and poetic expression.

To address these problems, explain the most difficult and essential passages, providing some framework and background, without attempting a line-by-line gloss of all the references and their ramifications. The poems, especially *The Waste Land*, should not be treated as puzzles to be solved, but rather, the early poems at least, as typical "modernism" which Eliot "invented" in *The Waste Land* and "Prufrock," a product of symbolism, images, and aggregation. Emphasize that this is all the expression of a personal, intense, even romantic effort by Eliot to get things "right" for himself in his search for order in his life, a validation of his existence, in a word, for "salvation." Emphasize continuing themes, continuing and changing techniques as Eliot attempts to translate, as he said of Shakespeare, his own private agony into something rich, strange, and impersonal.

Students often ask why Eliot is so intentionally, even perversely, difficult? Why the erudite allusions, the foreign languages, the indirectness? What is his attitude toward women? What of the evidence of racial prejudice? What of his aloofness from and condescension to the concerns of ordinary human existence?

Major Themes, Historical Perspectives, and Personal Issues

The symbolism of the waste land, garden, water, city, stairs, etc., as Eliot expresses the themes of time, death-rebirth, levels of love (and attitude toward women), the quest motif on psychological, metaphysical, and aesthetic levels. Dante's four levels—the literal (Eliot's use of geographic place is more basic than has been given sufficient attention), allegorical, moral, and anagogic—are interesting to trace throughout Eliot's developing canon. The relations between geographic place and vision, between the personal, individual talent and the strong sense of tradition, are also significant.

Significant Form, Style, or Artistic Conventions

Eliot's relation to romanticism, his significance in the development (with Pound) of modernism, his role as an expatriate effecting a "reconciliation with America" in "The Dry Salvages" are all important considerations. His techniques of juxtaposition, aggregation of images, symbolism, the use of multiple literary allusions, the influence of Dante are all worth attention, as is his use of "free verse" and many various poetic forms. Note also the musicality of his verse, his use of verbal repetition as well as clusters of images and symbols.

Original Audience

When Eliot's works first appeared, they seemed outrageously impenetrable to many, although he quickly became recognized as the "Pope of Russell Square." This recognition was partly through Pound's efforts, as well as Eliot's magisterial pronouncements in his criticism. Even as he challenged the literary establishment, he was in effect a literary "dictator" during much of his life, despite the shock felt by his followers when he announced in 1927 that he was "catholic, royalist and a classicist." With the religious emphasis of *Ash Wednesday* (1930) and *Four Quartets* (1943), as well as in his plays of the '30s and '40s, it seemed to many that he had become a different writer. A quarter of a century after his death, it is possible to see the continuing figure in the carpet, Eliot as a major figure in modernism, a movement superseded by subsequent developments. His eventual importance has been severely questioned by some critics (e.g., Harold Bloom.)

Comparisons, Contrasts, Connections

Compare Eliot with Pound, Frost, Williams, Stevens. Pound for his influence as "the better craftsman" and for his early recognition of and plumping for Eliot; all of these poets for their combined (but differing) contribution to modernism and the search for reality as a way out of "the heart of darkness." Williams and Stevens (Adamic poets) make interesting contrasts with their different goals and techniques: Williams criticizing Eliot's lack of immediacy, Stevens commenting that Eliot did not make the "visible a little difficult to see."

Questions for Reading and Discussion/ Approaches to Writing

1. What are the similarities and differences in Eliot's protagonists?

    What is the continuing fundamental theme in his work?

    Is "The Dry Salvages" essentially different from his early poems? How so? Are there any continuities?

    Consider the thrust of a particular poem on literal, allegorical, moral, and anagogic levels.

    What is Eliot's attitude toward women?

    What are the techniques by which Eliot's poems achieve intensity?

2. Compare and contrast the protagonists of two poems.

    Trace the quest motif through Eliot's poems.

    How do the late poems ("DS") differ from "Prufrock"? *The Waste Land?*

    Discuss Eliot's attitude toward death as expressed in the poems.

    Discuss Eliot's symbolism, the use of water as a symbol.

Bibliography

Basket, Sam S. "Eliot's London." In *Critical Essays on The Waste Land*, 73–89. London: Longman Literature Guides, 1988. "Fronting the Atlantic: *Cape Cod* and 'The Dry Salvages.' The New England Quarterly LVI, no. 2 (June 1983): 200–19.

Drew, Elizabeth. *T. S. Eliot: The Design of His Poetry*. New York: Charles Scribner's Sons, 1949. Especially pp. 1–30 and relevant passages.

Gordon, Lyndall. *Eliot's Early Years*. Athens: Ohio Univ. Press, 1977. Relevant passages.

———. *Eliot's New Life*. Athens: Ohio Univ. Press, 1988.

Kermode, Frank. "A Babylonish Dialect." In *T. S. Eliot*, edited by Allen Tate, 231–43. New York: Delacorte Press, 1966.

Langbaum, Robert. *The Poetry of Experience*. Chicago: Univ. of Chicago Press, 1985. Relevant passages.

Litz, A. Walton, ed. *Eliot in His Time*. London, 1973. Several useful, illuminating essays.

Martin, Jay, ed. *A Collection of Critical Essays on The Waste Land*. Englewood Cliffs, N.J.: Prentice Hall, Twentieth Century Interpretations, 1968. Several useful, illuminating essays.

Miller, J. Hillis. *Poets of Reality*. Cambridge, Mass.: Belknap Press of Harvard Univ., 1965, 1–12.

Moody, A.D. *T. S. Eliot*. Cambridge: Cambridge Univ. Press, 1979. Relevant passages.

Williamson, George. *A Reader's Guide to T. S. Eliot*. New York: Farrar, Straus & Giroux, 1967.

F. Scott Fitzgerald (1896–1940)

Contributing Editor: John F. Callahan [p. 1333]

Classroom Issues and Strategies

Students often tend to identify Fitzgerald with the nostalgic sensibility of his protagonist, Charlie Wales, and have a corollary tendency to view Fitzgerald as a participant in the excesses of the Jazz Age rather than as a writer who cast a critical eye on his generation's experience.

Fitzgerald's essays serve as important companions to his fiction. I fall back on the trick of photocopying one or more of the following essays: "Echoes of the Jazz Age"; "My Lost City"; "The Crack Up"; "Sleeping and Waking"; or "Pasting It Together." On the relationship between Fitzgerald and Wales, I focus on the overlay of observation and allusion that gives the story a perspective much deeper than Charlie Wales's rather superficial, self-pitying point of view.

Students are very interested in the relationship between Fitzgerald's life and his work and in his sense that the best possibilities of American history are in the past. Their questions include why relationships between men and women seem often bound up with money and social status, and whether or not Fitzgerald maintains a critical detachment from his characters' views of reality.

Major Themes, Historical Perspectives, and Personal Issues

Note the relationship hinted at in the story, between the twenties and thirties, the Boom and the Crash. Also it is important to note that although Wales is once again very well off, despite the Depression, his emotional and psychological stock is precarious. Can personal and historical issues be separated? Again, this is why it is important to use or at least refer to Fitzgerald's essays and letters.

Significant Form, Style, or Artistic Conventions

How, and how successfully, does Fitzgerald's evocative, lyrical prose set up an interplay of identification with and detachment from the protagonist's nostalgic sensibility? To what extent does Fitzgerald's style mirror the story's conflict of sensibility; namely, the contrast between a spare, pared-down modern style showing Hemingway's influence, and a metaphorical, romantic style reliant on a rich, sensuous imagery.

Original Audience

I call attention to Fitzgerald's self-conscious awareness of a double identity as a popular writer of stories for the *Saturday Evening Post* and a serious novelist aspiring to the company of Conrad, Joyce, and James. I consider the relationship, the compatibility between popular and serious fiction in a democratic and vernacular culture.

The issues of freedom and responsibility, the cost of self-indulgent personal behavior seem particularly appropriate to our time.

Comparisons, Contrasts, Connections

The following stories in Volume 2 of the *Heath Anthology* might provide a useful frame of reference: Hemingway's "Hills Like White Elephants"; Porter's "Flowering Judas"; Toomer's "Blood-Burning Moon," "Seventh Street," and "Box Seat." All involve landscape, social milieu, memory, and transitional moments of experience.

Bibliography

The best sources on "Babylon Revisited" are Fitzgerald's essays listed above, a piece called "Ring," written after the death of Ring Lardner, and also Fitzgerald's letters.

Katherine Anne Porter (1890–1980)

Contributing Editor: Jane Krause DeMouy [p. 1349]

Classroom Issues and Strategies

Porter's stories are powerful, but it requires thought and sensitivity to understand the true content of these stories. They should be read for the psychological as well as the representational reality. In addition, her style is highly complex; even the best critics are not very specific in describing exactly what it is Porter does to achieve her impact. She may be difficult for undergraduates to understand, but I think some fruitful discussion can come from focusing on issues of identity. This is an issue that all students know about instinctively; it can lead to interesting discussion to note that Granny Wetherall has had the same problems with identity that many adolescents have; one question becomes whether she has ever shaken them.

Students of Porter would do well to remember the Jamesian principle that art is selection. When Porter, like other artists, chooses certain subjects, she is not only shaping an entity but saying what she considers important, so it is essential to know what she is writing about. Porter does utilize personal experience in her work, but more often than not it is her internal experience that is true, while the factual events have been heightened, dramatized, and symbolized into fiction. In her most complex stories, symbols carry multiple meanings, and the writer's memories are transformed into mythopoeic structures based on the alogical associations common to dreams, rather than precise logical sequences. Since art exists not in facts, but in myth, it is also important to note what she does to change personal knowledge into meaningful, universalized fiction.

Students respond strongly to Porter's theme of rebellion—the wish for independence and personhood.

Major Themes, Historical Perspectives, and Personal Issues

Themes include the conflict between personal freedom and belonging to conventional society; Porter's Miranda/Laura as a female American Adam; the human confusion experienced when one has to confront the passing of the traditions/myths/structures of old southern society into the chaos of a technologically speeded-up, wartorn, and jaded society; biological, cultural, and traditional constraints on women.

Miranda, for instance, has grown up seeing that women are valued for their beauty and ability to bear children; that women who want identity or power can get it only by marrying and bearing children; that land, money, and political voice (real power) belong to men; that women who want these are outcasts.

Miranda's problem is that while she has come to recognize that these practices and beliefs are inherently unjust, they are also part of her cultural imperative. She internalizes the moral "rightness" of these things even as she rejects them. This results in enormous conflict for her. Choosing her culture's values, she is biologically trapped; choosing her self, she must reject everything she has been without knowing what she might be. Being unable—or refusing—to choose results in the emotional paralysis of characters like Laura in "Flowering Judas."

Perhaps most important in approaching a study of Porter are several caveats. Readers must, first of all, be wary of false biographical accounts, and the tendency of reviewers and critics to confuse Porter's fiction with those false accounts. For specific facts, one can consult the only biography, Joan Givner's *Katherine Anne Porter: A Life* (New York, 1983), which carefully tracks a monumental amount of detail to clarify names, dates, and events. It is a diligent compilation of research, but a book that fails to find the personality that charmed lovers, friends, and audiences to the last days of Porter's life. There is no adequate examination of the complex psychology of this important writer, although her stories offer some insight into this.

Significant Form, Style, or Artistic Conventions

"I shall try to tell the truth," she said in "My First Speech," (*Collected Essays*, p. 433), "but the result will be fiction." Porter felt that we really understand very little of what happens to us in the present moment, but by remembering, comparing, and waiting for the consequences, we can begin to understand the meaning of certain events. For her, that process of remembering and comparing takes place as she writes. It is a process clearly recorded in "The Jilting of Granny Wetherall," "The Grave," and "Old Mortality."

Fiction is made, she said, first of legend: those things told to her or read when she was a child. It is also made of memory: her childhood emotional experiences of certain events, as well as present memory: the adult's memory of what happened and explanation to herself of what that meant to the child. This confusion of experiences that took place in and over time is difficult to understand, but humanly true. Each person is a mesh of his or her "child," and what they understand themselves to be in the present, which may be illusory, deluded, or "true" by someone else's objective observation.

It is out of this understanding that Porter creates richly layered characters, events, and conflicts. Characters are who they *were*, who they *are*, who they *think* they were and are, as well as who they are *going to be*—given what happens to them in the story and their capacity to deal with that conflict. It is no wonder that Porter's stories have tremendous impact while being incredibly hard to decipher.

Porter is a master of the twentieth-century short story; it was her metier—so much so that she found it all but impossible to write *Ship of Fools*.

Original Audience

These stories are universal and timeless; however, the diversity of Katherine Anne Porter's experience and stories offers a wealth of teaching approaches. Her stories range from the regional focus of nineteenth-century Texas ("The Grave," "Old Mortality," and others) to the urban sophistication of twentieth-century New York and Mexico ("Theft," "That Tree," "Hacienda") and even to horrible visions of an inverted brave new world, where every man is for himself; moral standards do not exist; and the waste land is realized in loveless sex and human isolation.

Comparisons, Contrasts, Connections

Thematically, the bildungsroman experiences and the loss of innocence recorded in "The Grave" and other stories in "The Old Order" invite comparison with Hemingway's Nick Adams stories, just as do "Pale Horse, Pale Rider" and *A Farewell to Arms*. Like Faulkner, Porter has the historic memory of the southern temper, but it is a more feminine and particular vision, arising from a heightened social awareness that makes her sensitive to social mores, moral values, and the individual strengths that allow a person to survive.

Bibliography

To best understand Porter, one can do no better than to thoroughly read her essays, particularly "Portrait: Old South"; "Noon Wine: The Sources"; the "Introduction to *Flowering Judas*"; and "Three Statements About Writing."

An updated bibliography is expected at this writing, but currently, the standard bibliographies are:

Louise Waldrip and Shirley Ann Bauer, *A Bibliography of the Works of Katherine Anne Porter and A Bibliography of the Criticism of the Works of Katherine Anne Porter* (Metuchen, N.J.: Scarecrow, 1969). For primary sources, Robert F. Kiernan's *Carson McCullers and Katherine Anne Porter: A Reference Guide* (Boston, 1976); and "Katherine Anne Porter" in Duke, Bryer, and Inge, eds. *American Women Writers: Bibliographical Essays* (Greenwood Press, 1983).

Probably the best secondary source, Lodwick Hartley and George Core's *Katherine Anne Porter: A Critical Collection*, is out of print, but available in library collections.

Robert Penn Warren's *Katherine Anne Porter* for the Twentieth Century Views series (Englewood Cliffs, N.J.: Prentice Hall, 1979) also contains some of the seminal critical essays on Porter and essays that represent the critical controversy over *Ship of Fools*.

The newest collection of this kind is Harold Bloom's *Modern Critical Views: Katherine Anne Porter* (New Haven, Conn.: Yale, 1987). Expanded comment on the ideas in this article are in Jane DeMouy's *Katherine Anne Porter's Women: The Eye of Her Fiction* (Austin: Texas Univ. Press, 1983); and those interested in the role of southern women will want to look at Anne Firor Scott's *The Southern Lady: From Pedestal to Politics, 1830–1930*, 1970.

In addition, a fine overview of Porter, including interviews with her contemporaries Robert Penn Warren and Eudora Welty, as well as dramatization of parts of "The Grave" and "The Circus," is available in the one-hour PBS program, "Katherine Anne Porter: The Eye of Memory," American Masterworks Series, produced by Lumiere Productions, New York, 1986.

Marianne Moore (1887–1972)

Contributing Editor: Bernard F. Engel [p. 1370]

Classroom Issues and Strategies

The general student block against poetry often causes difficulties. With Moore, it is useful to observe that she seeks accuracy of statement, that the alleged difficulty of her work does not arise from abstruse symbolism or reference to obscure autobiographical matters, but from precision:

seeking exact presentation, she does not fall back on expected phrasings. The attentive who will slow down and read thoughtfully can understand and enjoy.

Advise students to read through once quickly to get perspective. Then they should read slowly, and aloud. I also advise them that after this first reading they should let the poem sit two or three days, then repeat the process. In class, I read through short poems a few lines at a time, pausing to ask questions; I also ask students to read passages aloud. With undergraduates, I prefer not to spend hours on any one poem. It is better that they read carefully, but without the extended analysis that is appropriate in some graduate classes.

Students need help with the rhetoric and syntax. Professional skimmers all, they need to be shown how to read with care. They rarely raise the abstruse questions of aesthetics or moral philosophy that fascinate the literary critic.

Major Themes, Historical Perspectives, and Personal Issues

Point out:

1. The fact that though there is usually a "moral" point in a Moore poem, the overall aim is aesthetic: the moral is to contribute to the delight, not to dominate it.
2. The way the poems relate to the modernism of Stevens and others.

Significant Form, Style, or Artistic Conventions

In a freshmen class, I focus on the poem itself; with juniors and seniors, I bring out relationships to modernism. The rhetorical form of a poem is usually worth pointing out; metrics should be mentioned, but only in passing.

Original Audience

I mention the fact that until the 1960s Moore's work was considered too difficult for any but the most elevated critics. I also point out that her early admirers were generally male, that only in the last few years have a number of women come to appreciate her. She does not fit the stereotype of woman as emotional (in contrast to supposedly rational man) that many women even yet cling to. Moore, indeed, once remarked that only two or three American women have "even tried" to write poetry—

meaning, one may be sure, Dickinson and herself. (In her last years, she might have added Elizabeth Bishop to her list.)

Early strong objections to her work came from Margaret Anderson of the *Little Review*, who in 1918 asserted that she wrote too intellectually; Anderson reprinted her remarks in 1953. Babette Deutsch in 1935, and again in 1952, voiced similar objections. Some recent feminist critics have also had doubts. Emily Stipes Watts in *The Poetry of American Women from 1632 to 1945* (1977) found Moore practicing a "feminine realism" that "will ultimately be unacceptable"; Watts saw male appreciation of Moore's poetry as condescension. Even Bonnie Costello, one of the best of Moore's readers, has expressed herself as nonplussed at the continuing devotion to Moore's work on the part of some male critics.

Comparisons, Contrasts, Connections

Moore knew and corresponded with Williams, Pound, Eliot, and Stevens. All of them published comments on her, and she in turn wrote of them. There are obvious comparisons and contrasts in the work of these, the chief American modernists.

Questions for Reading and Discussion/ Approaches to Writing

1. I sometimes use study questions. They usually focus on the "mere rhetoric"—what the poem "says": its argument or moral, the way it expresses feeling (with Moore, often the feeling of delight).
2. "Abundance": The poem is remarkable for its detailed observation, presented, of course, in the manner of the nature lover (for example, Thoreau), rather than of the zoologist. Consider why the tone of delight is important, given the intention of the poem's first section.

   "Poetry": In both versions of the poem, Moore's speaker says, "I, too, dislike it. . . ." Why would a lifelong poet say this? What does the speaker like?

   "The Pangolin": The poem starts in a seemingly casual manner—"Another armored animal"—but moves quickly into exact, patient observation of the animal's structure and behavior. Is the speaker coolly rational? Delighted? Or . . . ? What kind of grace is the ultimate subject of this poem?

"Nevertheless": How can a strawberry resemble "a hedgehog or a star-/fish"? How do apple seeds, the rubber plant, and the prickly, pear illustrate the point that "Victory won't come/to me unless I go/to it ..."?

"The Mind Is an Enchanting Thing": What is the difference between "enchanted" and "enchanting"? Explain the paradox in "conscientious inconsistency" (stanza 4).

"To a Chameleon": This text gives the poem in the format printed in the 1967 *Complete Poems*. In the 1981 *Complete Poems*, lines 1 and 2 are combined ("Hid by the august foliage and fruit of the grape-vine"); the last two lines are also combined. What is the effect of this alteration on the shape of the poem? Does it matter?

Bibliography

For students and the hurried instructor, the most convenient assistance may be found by looking up the pages on individual poems in the indexes to the books by Engel (revised edition, Nitchie, Hall, and Phillips). These books deal with all or most of Moore's poetry.

Excellent critical studies by Stapleton, Costello, and others give an overall perspective but usually deal with fewer individual poems.

Louise Bogan (1897–1970)

Contributing Editor: Theodora R. Graham [p. 1380]

Classroom Issues and Strategies

The instructor needs to explain Bogan's often distancing herself from the poem's ideas, creating what Adrienne Rich has called a "mask" or "code." Her use of the more traditional lyric form (though not in most of the poems selected for the anthology) raises questions about her relationship to the experimental verse poets of the prior generation and those of her own were writing. Bogan seems quite accessible—except in poems like "The Sleeping Fury" and "After the Persian," which require calling students' attention to language, imagery, contrasts.

I think that introducing Bogan's more general literary career—and perhaps ideas from her essays, reviews, and Ruth Limmer's edited autobiography will enrich students' understanding of the difficulties women faced as writers and the extraordinary success some achieved as editors (cf. Harriet Monroe, Marianne Moore) and reviewers.

Major Themes, Historical Perspectives, and Personal Issues

A number of Bogan's poems concern love and the woman's need to maintain her identity. She also writes, indirectly, of the poet's demons, the "sleeping fury" that must be addressed in its violence and appeased. Bogan also turns her attention to skillful observation, both of crafted objects (and indirectly to the crafted poem) and of unusual natural things (such as the dragonfly). In "Women" she offers a critique of some women's choice of a restricted, passionless, and dull existence.

Significant Form, Style, or Artistic Conventions

A poem entitled "Rhyme" ends "But once heart's feast/You were to me." A love poem about the rhyme between a man and a woman, the poem could also be read as Bogan's tribute to rhyme itself. In "Women" and "Roman Fountain" she demonstrates a distinct ability and interest in what might have seemed in 1922 and 1935 an old-fashioned technique. (The former consists of 5 stanzas rhyming abcb; the latter, more ingenious, like the fountain it describes, rhymes aabc / aabb / abcabca.) However, other poems selected are dramatically different in formal organization and are unrhymed. Bogan's line breaks, unlike (e.g.) Williams's, generally follow syntactic units. But in "The Sleeping Fury" and "After the Persian" she writes in long lines, form following thought. Both poems contain a kind of elegance, issuing even from the fear and violence of the former.

Bogan's scope is not grand, but her talent in crafting verse and summoning images is noteworthy.

Original Audience

Bogan—like Marianne Moore—was writing for a man's world. Neither made concessions to the popular audience to gain a greater readership. Yet their natural reserve and privacy turned them in a direction away from the more soul-baring tendencies of some of their contemporaries. "The Sleeping Fury" could be about the poet's demon-muse; but it could equally concern her breakdowns, the warring sides of her own personality. That she was poetry editor for the *New Yorker* for many years indicates that she understood a broader public's taste and chose to write a taut, lyric verse.

Comparisons, Contrasts, Connections

It is useful to compare her treatment of natural objects and personal, cloaked subjects with that of Tickings, and with later poets such as Rich and Denise Levertov who do use the personal "I" in more self-revealing ways—but not always.

Questions for Reading and Discussion/
Approaches to Writing

1. I prefer to give students one or two pages of extracts from Bogan's prose writing and Limmer's biographical collection.
2. Those interested in women writers might want to explore the kinds of verse other women of Bogan's generation—particularly those who reached out to a larger audience—chose to write. What were women reading from *Ladies Home Companion* and other popular magazines? How does Bogan's writing compare?

Bibliography

I recommend Bogan's prose and Ruth Limmer's *A Journey Around My Room* extracted as autobiography from Bogan's diaries and other prose.

Ernest Hemingway (1899–1961)

Cobntributing Editor: Margaret Anne O'Connor [p. 1387]

Classroom Issues and Strategies

Most students have already read something by Hemingway, and they come into class with preconceptions. They usually love him or hate him and try to pin labels rather than give his work a new reading. Also they want to concentrate on biography and biographical readings of his works, since most find his well-publicized life even more interesting than his work.

As the headnote to this story suggests, biography is important to understanding Hemingway's approach to writing, but I try to turn students' attention biographically from Hemingway the Adventurer-Philosopher to Hemingway the Writer. Since "Hills Like White Elephants" is much less often anthologized than other Hemingway stories, its newness to students might tempt them to read and reread in order to see how the story fits with other works they've read by him. I approach teaching this taut story as if it were a poem. Word choice and phraseology are keys to its success.

One possible strategy might be to ask two students, a male and a female, to read the dialogue aloud to the class as it were a drama. Then class discussion would move toward tone of voice. Questions of the man's sincerity and the girl's sarcasm would naturally emerge. The less preparation for this exercise the better since a "flat" delivery would remind listeners that Hemingway expects his readers to "interpret."

Students are interested in the philosophy of life they discern from Hemingway's works, the code of behavior his characters follow that gives their lives dignity in the author's eyes. This story seems a self-critique of that code. Careful readers don't believe the girl at the end of the story when she says she's "fine." She's composed herself; she won't make a scene, but she's not "fine." Students want to know how Hemingway has succeeded in making us know that the man is lying to the girl—and perhaps to himself—throughout the story. There's no easy answer to this question, but a close reading of key phrases such as "the only thing that bothers us," "it's perfectly simple," or "I feel fine" will help them see how carefully constructed the story is.

Major Themes, Historical Perspectives, and Personal Issues

"Hills" is a good story to shatter the false impression that Hemingway was insensitive to women. This carefully constructed vignette has a nameless man and woman discussing their relationship against the backdrop of the mountain landscape. As in the very best of Hemingway's novels and stories, the authorial stance is ambiguous; readers must pay close attention to small details to understand the progress of the narrative. Students should be encouraged to focus on the dialogue between the man and girl in order to discern their relationship. The issue of abortion and how each speaker feels about it is central to the story. Yet abortion itself is not the main issue; it is the not-too-subtle pressure "the man" is placing on "the girl" to have the abortion that is the key issue.

Significant Form, Style, or Artistic Conventions

Hemingway's minimalist style in this 1927 story deserves consideration. If Faulkner confuses readers because he offers so many details for readers to sift through in order to understand what's going on, Hemingway confuses by offering so few.

Original Audience

The central issue in this story is the abortion the girl is being pressured to have by her male companion. The author's stance on the issue of abortion is ambiguous, but the story clearly comes out against the male pressuring the female into an abortion that she doesn't seem to want. Pro-choice and pro-life students might want to concentrate class discussion on abortion alone, but the issue of subtle pressure is at the heart of the story.

Comparisons, Contrasts, Connections

Of many possible works of comparison, one of the most fruitful would be Eliot's *The Waste Land*. Compare this rootless couple escaping the commitment of parenthood with Eliot's set of lovers in Book II of his poem. The song of the nightingale "so rudely forced" is "Jug, Jug" which is echoed in the man's choice of a nickname for the girl.

Questions for Reading and Discussion/
Approaches to Writing

1. What's the purpose of the trip the two travelers are taking?
2. Why are the speakers only identified as "a man" and "girl"? How do these designations affect your reading of the story? What nickname does the man use for the girl?
3. How do the descriptions of the landscape relate to the conversation between the two travelers? What about the discussion of drink orders?
4. Note each sentence or paragraph that is not enclosed in quotation marks, and explain how each brief commentary affects your understanding of the characters and the lives they lead.
5. Why does the girl repeat the word "please" seven times? Anger? Hysteria? Fear? Frustration? Why does the man leave her at the table?

6. The railroad station setting is important to the progress—the plot—of the story. How does this physical setting parallel the thematic concerns of the story as well?
7. How does the title relate to the story?

Bibliography

Jeffrey Meyers offers an excellent brief reading of this story in his biography (pp. 196–97).

Wallace Stevens (1879–1955)

Contributing Editor: Linda W. Wagner-Martin [p. 1393]

Classroom Issues and Strategies

The sheer difficulty of apprehending meaning from some of Stevens's poems turns many students away. Yet Stevens is one of the most apt voices for the perfection, and the perfectibility of the poem—the supreme fiction in the writer's, and the reader's, lives. If students can read Stevens's poems well, they will probably be able to read anything in the text.

The elusiveness of meaning is one key difficulty: Stevens's valiant attempts to avoid paraphrase, to lose himself in the brilliant language use, to slide into repetition and assonantal patterns without warning. His work demands complete concentration, and complete sympathy, from his readers. Most students cannot give poetry either of these tributes without some preparation.

Close reading, usually aloud, helps. The well-known Stevens language magic has to be experienced, and since the poems are difficult, asking students to work on them alone, in isolation, is not the best tactic. Beginning with the poems by Stevens might make reading Eliot, Frost, and Williams much easier, so I would make this selection central to the study of modern American poetry.

Major Themes, Historical Perspectives, and Personal Issues

The value of poetry (and all art); the accessibility of great moral, and mortal, themes through language; the impenetrability of most human relationships; the evanescence of formalized belief systems, including religion; the frustration of imperfection; and others. Stevens often builds from historical and/or philosophical knowledge, expecting "fact" to serve as counterpoint for his readers' more imaginative exploits. But this technique is not meant to lead to easy or facile explication. It is a way of contrasting the predictable and the truly valuabe, the imaginary.

Significant Form, Style, or Artistic Conventions

Stevens's intricate stanza and rhyme patterns are a school of poetry in themselves, and each of his poems should be studied as a crafted object. His work fits well with that of T. S. Eliot, as does some of his aesthetic rationale: "Poetry is not personal." "The real is only the base. But it is the base." "In poetry, you must love the words, the ideas and the images and rhythms with all your capacity to love anything at all." "Poetry must be irrational." "The purpose of poetry is to make life complete in itself." "Poetry increase the feeling for reality." "In the absence of a belief in God, the mind turns to its own creations and examines them, not alone from the aesthetic point of view, but for what they reveal, for what they validate and invalidate."

Original Audience

Modernism was so specific a mood and time that students must understand the rage for control of craft, the emphasis on the formalism of the way an art object was formed, and the importance craft held for all parts of the artist's life. Once those conventions are described, and Stevens placed in this period, his own distinctions from the group of modernists will be clearer. ("Not all objects are equal. The vice of imagism was that it did not recognize this." "A change of style is a change of subject." "In the long run the truth does not matter.") Conscious of all the elements of form, Stevens yet overlays his work with a heavily philosophical intention, and the shelves of commentary on his poetry have been occasioned because that commentary is, in many cases, useful.

454 • *The Heath Anthology of American Literature*

Comparisons, Contrasts, Connections

The T. S. Eliot of the *Four Quartets* (likenesses) or the William Carlos Williams of the short poems (differences).

William Faulkner (1897–1962)

Contributing Editor: John Lowe [p. 1406]

Classroom Issues and Strategies

Students are resistance to texts that withhold key information, to narrative that is obscure and/or convoluted, and to characters who don't seem to have "common sense." All of these "sins" appear in Faulkner's work. He also requires a knowledge of southern and American history that many students don't possess.

Begin by emphasizing the pleasures to be gained from unraveling Faulkner's mysteries. Especially focus on his parallels to and differences from the popular myths of southern culture, as found in *Gone With the Wind, North vs. South,* and so on. Approach his works as though they were detective stories (some of them, in fact, are). Do brief presentations of relevant historical materials. Locate the text's place in Faulkner's career, drawing parallels between the character's concerns and the way these issues touched Faulkner as well. When I teach Faulkner's novels, I find it useful to photocopy the genealogy charts of the Compsons, McCaslins, or Sartorises, as the case may be, that are found in Volpe's *A Reader's Guide to William Faulkner.* I also find it useful to focus on Faulkner' acceptance and transcendence of stereotype, always quoting Ralph Ellison's formulation on this aspect of Faulkner's art.

Students very frequently ask if Faulkner really thought of all these things (the hidden references we uncover in symbolism, imagery, and so on) when he penned his stories. They ask if his family owned slaves and how Faulkner felt about it if they did. Some students ask if I think Faulkner was a racist and/or a sexist.

Major Themes, Historical Perspectives, and Personal Issues

Teachers should above all try to focus on:

1. Faulkner's tremendous importance as an interpreter of man's history—and not just southern or American history—at a critical moment when modernism emerged as a questioning, probing tool used to redefine human nature and man's relationship to nature. Issues of sex, class, and above all, race should be explored using a battery of interdisciplinary techniques, including historical, social, anthropological, economic, political, and feminist perspectives. "Barn Burning" has been profitably analyzed by Marxist critics as a class struggle; "A Courtship," superficially a comedy, also yearns for a lost world where red and white men were equals; "Delta Autumn" probes the intersection of material, sexual, racial, and ecological exploitation.

2. All of these issues could and should be profitably connected to the way Faulkner struggled with them in his own life.

   Related themes to bring in from other works the students possibly have read: stories and novels by black writers from the South such as Richard Wright and Zora Neale Hurston; the "new" woman, and Freud's influence on the popular imagination; new perspectives toward democracy after World War I; the shadows cast by both that struggle and the legacy of the Civil War that preceded it; Faulkner's sense of the past, and how it relates to our own concepts of our grandparents and parents; the role of the family in society, and the individual's struggle to belong to and yet break away from both.

   Furthermore, since Faulkner uses mythic/biblical structures in both "Delta Autumn" and "Barn Burning," I ask the students to identify these elements and to demonstrate why they are effective.

Significant Form, Style, or Artistic Conventions

Faulkner needs to be understood in both the context of southern literary traditions and modernism. "A Courtship," for instance, reflects both a modernist's understanding of how Freudian theory can be milked for laughs, and the conventions of frontier/southwestern humor. "Barn Burning," in its employment of Jamesian point of view as confined to Sarty's consciousness, requires detailed analysis of its narrative structures and the consequent effects on the reader. "Delta Autumn" raises point of view as something that changes with age and experience, and questions the idea of a progression in this realm.

Faulkner needs to be related to the other great modernists who so influenced him, especially Joyce and Eliot, and his work should and could be profitably compared and contrasted to the similar but sometimes very different literary experiments of Hemingway, Stein, Fitzgerald, Wright, and so on. "A Courtship" could profitably be related to male bonding stories, especially classic American tales such as *Moby-Dick*, the Deerslayer books, *Huckleberry Finn*. Similarly "Barn Burning" requires an analysis of bildungsroman narratives and psychological fiction.

Original Audience

I try to bring in relevant issues from contemporary life—especially those that have had an impact on my students—in order to emphasize the enduring value of Faulkner's work. The focus on the issues of history, class, gender, and race facilitates this practice.

Comparisons, Contrasts, Connections

"Barn Burning" can easily be contrasted to *Huckleberry Finn*, where a young boy must abandon his father's standards in favor of more humane, just ones, or to a female bildungsroman such as Wharton's *Summer*. The injustice of sharecropping discussed here could be examined alongside other treatments of rural life such as Hamlin Garland's "Under the Lion's Paw" or Richard Wright's "Long Black Song" and "Almos' a Man."

"Delta Autumn" could be contrasted with Cather's "A Wagner Matinee," since both protagonists tragically understand rather late in life that they have sacrificed more than they realized. Its theme of racial intermingling could easily be complemented by Chopin's stories, such as "Désirée's Baby." The idea of a central protagonist deciding on the proper heir for a family keepsake (the hunting horn) may also be found in Alice Walker's "Everyday Use." The theme of the sins of the father descending to future generations is also found in Langston Hughes's play *Mulatto*, and Abraham Cahan's *The Imported Bridegroom*. Ike as an aging figure who compares the generations may be found in Gaines's *The Autobiography of Miss Jane Pittman*, as well as in Cooper's *The Prairie*.

"A Courtship" could profitably be compared with many of Twain's short pieces, with Zora Neale Hurston's treatments of folklore, with male bonding themes in Hemingway's short fiction, with any number of the wonderful sketches of the Old Southwestern humorists, and of course with James Fenimore Cooper's red/white pairs.

Questions for Reading and Discussion/ Approaches to Writing

"Barn Burning"
1. How does one establish individual independence as a teenager? Do you remember any crucial moment in your own life when you realized that you had to make a choice between what your parent(s) and/or family believed and your own values?
2. Is the destruction of another person's property ever something we can justify? Explain.
3. Does it matter that this story is rendered through Sarty's consciousness? What were Faulkner's options, and how would the story be different if he had exercised them?
4. What are the key symbols in the story, and how do they serve the thematic purposes Faulkner had in mind?
5. What is the tone of the story and how is it established?

"A Courtship"
1. How does the setting in a faraway age contribute to the mood of the story?
2. What does a woman usually expect from a suitor during courtship? Why does Herman Basket's sister marry Log-in-the-Creek?
3. If you think this story is funny, how do Faulkner's "writer's tricks" create the humor?
4. How do we know we're dealing with an Indian narrator? Why is this an important aspect of the story and its total effect?

"Delta Autumn"
1. How does the location in a hunting camp function as an appropriate setting for the themes manifest in the story?
2. Why does the story make us reflect on the workings of history, specifically American history?
3. In what ways is Roth Edmonds meant to function as a representative of contemporary man? How is Uncle Ike different from his kinsman?
4. How does Faulkner use withheld information to create a mood of suspense in the story?
5. What are the different uses of the theme of "love" in the story?

I urge the students to choose a story they particularly like; they are then to ask themselves exactly *why* they like it, which will lead them to a topic (the humor employed, a certain character or method of characterization, a fascination with the depiction of the historical period on display, and so on).

Bibliography

"Barn Burning"

Bradford, M. E. "Family and Community in Faulkner's 'Barn Burning.'" *Southern Review* 17 (1981): 332–39.

Franklin, Phyliss. "Sarty Snopes and 'Barn Burning.' " *Mississippi Quarterly* 21 (1968): 189–93.

Fowler, Virginia C. "Faulkner's 'Barn Burning': Sarty's Conflict Reconsidered." *College Language Association Journal* 24 (1981): 513–21.

Hiles, Jane. "Kinship and Heredity in Faulkner's 'Barn Burning.' " *Mississippi Quarterly* 38, no. 3 (1985): 329–37.

Volpe, Edmond L. " 'Barn Burning': A Definition of Evil." In *Faulkner: The Unappeased Imagination: A Collection of Critical Essays,* edited by O. Carey, 75–82. Troy, N.Y.: Whitson, 1980.

"A Courtship"

Bradford, M. E. "Faulkner's 'A Courtship': An Accommodation of Culture." *South Atlantic Quarterly* 80 (1981).

Dabney, Lewis. *The Indians of Yoknapatawpha.* Baton Rogue: LSU Press, 1974. Chapter 4.

"Delta Autumn"

Brooks, Cleanth. "The Story of the McCaslins." In *William Faulkner: The Yoknapatawpha Country.* New Haven: Yale Univ. Press, 1963. Chapter 12.

Grimwood, Michael. " 'Delta Autumn': Stagnation and Sedimentation in Faulkner's Career." *Southern Literary Journal* 16, no. 2 (1984).

Harter, Carol C. "The Winter of Ike McCaslin: Revisions and Irony in Faulkner's 'Delta Autumn.' " *Journal of Modern Literature* 1 (1970): 209–25.

All three stories are treated in Hans Skei's *William Faulkner: The Short Story Career: An Outline of Faulkner's Short Story Writing from 1919 to 1962.* Oslo: Univ. Forl., 1981.

The women in "A Courtship" and "Delta Autumn" are examined in Alexandre Vashchenko's "Woman and the Making of the New World: Faulkner's Short Stories," in *Faulkner and Women,* ed. Doreen Fowler and Ann J. Abadie (Jackson: Univ. of Mississippi Press, 1986), pp. 205–19.

Hart Crane (1899–1932)

Contributing Editor: Margaret Dickie [p. 1433]

Classroom Issues and Strategies

Crane's language is so compressed, multi-layered, and innovative, that often students can make no sense out of it.

The best strategy for dealing with Crane is to encourage students to pay attention to the way words interact, cross-pollinate, and develop in a chain of free associations. Because his language is so metaphorical, students can grasp his meaning more fully if they look for the metaphor embedded in every word. For example, in "Voyages," the sea is figured as a woman, the subject is erotic attraction and dejection, and the movement of the series is in and out of love. The student can best follow this development if she or he makes constant connections between these levels of significance.

Because the poems are so difficult to understand on the level of content, I find that they are good examples of how poems work from word to word. Students can learn how to read poetry from uncovering the various levels of meanings in each word. I send them to the dictionary first to discover all the meanings in every word and then ask them how these meanings work together or pull apart.

Major Themes, Historical Perspectives, and Personal Issues

Crane is the central Modernist love poet. More than any of his contemporaries, he celebrated erotic experience, the world as an eroticized field, and love as the central paradigm. Even when he turned to the myth of America in *The Bridge*, his is concerned with the continent as a woman, with Indian myths of fertility, with the marriage of technology and nature in the new age. His preoccupation with words, with the possibility of poetry in the machine age, forms another major thrust in his poetry, evident in his love poems, his epic, and his later poems about the possibility of expressing love for the world.

Significant Form, Style, or Artistic Conventions

Crane talked about the "logic of metaphor"—by which he imagined his poems developed—as opposed to what he called pure logic. I think that he belongs to the Modernist preoccupation with the associative processes of consciousness. His interest in America as a subject for poetry sets him against T. S. Eliot and connects him to William Carlos Williams.

Original Audience

It is interesting to summarize the early reception of *The Bridge* as a magnificent failure and to set that against more recent readings, which see the long poem as a new form.

Comparisons, Contrasts, Connections

Crane pitted himself against Eliot and *The Waste Land*. He imagined *The Bridge* to be an answer to the negativism and despair of Eliot's work. He intended to celebrate the new age. As he continued to work on his epic, however, he came more and more to share Eliot's despair. He early allied himself with William Carlos Williams, whose *In The American Grain* influenced him as a work about the American land.

Questions for Reading and Discussion/ Approaches to Writing

It is useful to read what Crane said in his letters about what he intended to do in *The Bridge*. I would direct readers especially to letters he wrote to Otto Kahn.

I think that the basic question in reading Crane's poetry is one of development, of detecting how the poem moves from word to word, rather than from point to point. I would ask students to take one word and follow its associations through the poem.

Rolla Lynn Riggs (1899–1954)

Contributing Editor: James W. Parins [p. 1446]

Classroom Issues and Strategies

Riggs's obviously Indian material, "Santo Domingo Corn Dance," for example, might contain references esoteric to some students. His other works will possibly have to be compared to other contemporary poets. For the Indian material, I provide background information as part of the in-class explication/discussion of the poem. The other works will be included in a general discussion of modern poetry using selections from various writers including Eliot and Yeats.

Major Themes, Historical Perspectives, and Personal Issues

A major issue to be emphasized is the assimilation of individual Indians into the large white society. Using biographical materials, we will discuss to what extent Riggs assimilated and what the effects of that process seemed to be on the man and his work.

Significant Form, Style, or Artistic Conventions

The selections included are written in various verse forms. We will discuss the appropriateness of each and try to discover how form affects content and vice versa.

Original Audience

I think original and modern audiences are very similar and do not require much discussion.

Comparisons, Contrasts, Connections

Riggs can be compared with other poets writing at the same time in terms of versification and experimentation.

Questions for Reading and Discussion/ Approaches to Writing

One writing assignment I use is to have the student write an explication of a poem, story, or essay bringing into the discussion such things as narrative and rhetorical technique, versification, genre, style, thematic devices, metaphor, etc. The intended audience is another student in the class who doesn't have a handle on the work.

Bibliography

Dockstader, Frederick J. *Great North American Indians*. New York: Van Nostrand Reinhold, 1977, 243–44.

The Harlem Renaissance

[p. 1456]

Alain Locke (1886–1954)

Contributing Editor: Richard Yarborough [p. 1460]

Classroom Issues and Strategies

One problem I have encountered in teaching Locke's "The New Negro" involves genre—that is, I have found that students tend not to enjoy reading nonfiction prose as much as they do fiction and poetry. In addition, this piece can present students with special difficulties if they do not have a clear enough sense of the historical and cultural context to appreciate the radical social changes on which Locke is commenting.

I try to stress to students the extent to which the developments that Locke is describing resulted from the phenomenon known as the "black migration." They must come to understand how different the Harlem experience was from that of the typical African-American up through World War I. In terms of pedagogical strategy, I encourage them to paraphrase Locke's characterization of these important social changes.

It would be useful if some audio or visual materials were incorporated into the examination of Locke, for it would make the students aware that the Harlem Renaissance was not simply a literary development. (Nor was it limited to Harlem—similar changes were occurring in many major urban areas that had recently received a large influx of blacks.)

On the one hand, students tend to respond sympathetically to Locke's celebration of the move on the part of the younger generation of blacks to reject existing, limited paradigms and racial images. On the other, they sometimes express impatience with Locke's somewhat vague political statements in the essay.

Major Themes, Historical Perspectives, and Personal Issues

Discuss the meaning of the title of the essay. Just what does "New" indicate and, by way of contrast, who is the "Old Negro"?

The importance that Locke places upon Harlem as a "race capital"—the extent to which Harlem drew blacks not just from all parts of the United States but from around the world. What does Locke see as the consequences of such a diverse mix of people of African descent?

Locke's idealism, especially insofar as he views artists and intellectuals as capable of transcending the limitations of parochial thinking and prejudice.

The pan-African implications of the New Negro Movement and the extent to which Locke sees the new race consciousness of American blacks as part of a worldwide phenomenon among oppressed peoples.

The extent to which Locke defines the goals of the "New Negro" as essentially identical to, as he puts it, "the ideals of American institutions and democracy."

The drive toward self-determination as the key to the "spiritual emancipation" that Locke describes.

Significant Form, Style, or Artistic Conventions

I do not generally take the time to discuss Locke's essay in terms of style. I might look at his tone and language—especially as established in the opening paragraph; but I see the essay's primary value as residing in the clarity with which it sets the table for an examination of the creative writing of the Harlem Renaissance.

Original Audience

It is important to recognize Locke's essay as an apologia for an entire generation of black artists and intellectuals. If he is addressing this apologia primarily to white readers, what does he want them to see and how do his arguments and observations relate directly to his goals?

Comparisons, Contrasts, Connections

Locke's essay might be usefully linked with Du Bois's "Of Our Spiritual Striving" (Chapter 1 of *The Souls of Black Folks*) or Hughes's "The Negro Artist and the Racial Mountain" or "When the Negro Was in Vogue." One might also try to locate statements from other early twentieth-century American authors and critics who tended to define the post-World-War-I generation as being somehow radically different from the one that preceded it. The key here is the self-conscious redefinition of self that informs this decade.

Questions for Reading and Discussion/ Approaches to Writing

1. I ask students to make sure that they end up with a clear sense of what Locke means by the phrase "The New Negro."
2. I might ask that the students evaluate a particular Harlem Renaissance writer's work in light of Locke's discussion in "The New Negro."

Bibliography

Baker, Houston A., Jr. *Modernism and the Harlem Renaissance*. Chicago: Univ. of Chicago Press, 1987.

Bontemps, Arna. "The Awakening: A Memoir." In *The Harlem Renaissance Remembered*, edited by Arna Bontemps. New York: Dodd, Mead, 1972.

Huggins, Nathan Irvin. *Harlem Renaissance*. New York: Oxford Univ. Press, 1971.

Kellner, Bruce, ed. *The Harlem Renaissance: A Historical Dictionary for the Era*. New York: Methuen, 1984.

Lewis, David Levering. *When Harlem Was in Vogue*. New York: Knopf, 1981.

Wintz, Cary D. *Black Culture and the Harlem Renaissance*. Houston, Tex.: Rice Univ. Press, 1988.

Jean Toomer (1894–1967)

Contributing Editor: Nellie Y. McKay [p. 1468]

Classroom Issues and Strategies

Toomer's style is difficult, especially in view of earlier African-American literature. To a large extent, Toomer abandoned the predominant naturalistic and realistic representation of the black experience to experiment with newer modernistic techniques. When they first approach these texts, students usually feel that it is well beyond their understanding—that Toomer is engaged in abstractions that are too difficult to comprehend.

Have the students explore all the possibilities for a literal meaning of the metaphors and symbols. "Blood-Burning Moon" is less difficult for them because it has a traditional story line. In "Karintha," for instance, try to get them to see that Toomer is concerned with the sexual and economic oppression of women within their own communities where they should be safe from the former at least.

These selections lend themselves to the visual imagination. Students may find it helpful to think of the "pictures" Toomer's images present as they read and try to understand, also, the written meanings these images present.

Students respond positively to the poetic qualities of the writing, and they enjoy its visual aspects. They have difficulty interpreting the underlying themes and meanings, mainly because the language is seductive and leaves them ambivalent regarding the positive and negative qualities the writer intends to portray. It is best to lead them through one section by reading aloud in class and permitting them to use a number of methods (listening to the words, visualizing the images, etc.) to try to fathom what is going on.

Major Themes, Historical Perspectives, and Personal Issues

1. The significance of black women as representatives of African-American culture. What qualities do women have that are similar to those of the entire group of African-Americans—at least as Toomer saw them?
2. The nature of the richness as well as the pain in African-American culture.
3. The symbolistic aspects of the northern and southern black experience.
4. The role of the black artist—e.g., in "Song of the Son," in which the absent son returns to preserve the almost now-lost culture of his ancestors.

Significant Form, Style, or Artistic Conventions

Toomer is writing at a crucial time in American and African-American literary history. His friends are members of the Lost Generation of writers intent on reforming American literature. His effort is to make a different kind of presentation of African-America through the art of literature. He sees the loss of some of the strongest elements of the culture in the move toward modernization and technology. For example, he captures the beauty and pathos of the experience in "Karintha"; the brutality in "Blood-Burning Moon"; and the imitation of the white culture in "Box Seat."

Original Audience

Cane was written for an intellectual audience who could grasp the nuances the author was interested in promoting. The book sold fewer than 500 copies in its first year, but had enthusiastic reviews from the most avant-garde literary critics. It continues to appeal to intellectuals, especially those who are interested in the ways in which language can be manipulated to express particular life situations.

Comparisons, Contrasts, Connections

Toomer's work can be compared to some of Sherwood Anderson's stories, and to Hart Crane's poetry. The three men knew each other and were friends during the 1920s. They read each other's work and advised each other. Their general thrust was that human beings were alienated from the basic "natural" qualities in themselves, and needed to get back to more of the spiritual values that could be found in closer unity with nature.

Questions for Reading and Discussion/ Approaches to Writing

Cane was a work to celebrate the African-American experience without denying the awful pain and oppression that made the strength of the group so apparent. Paper topics that focus on the history of black America between Reconstruction and the 1920s are useful in showing what a student can learn about Jean Toomer's reasons for the perceptions he revealed in these selections.

Bibliography

The best source on these is the discussion (in chronological order in the book) in the McKay biography of Toomer's literary life and work. The attempt here is to explicate the individual selections in the total book.

Langston Hughes (1902–1967)

Contributing Editor: Charles H. Nichols [p. 1487]

Classroom Issues and Strategies

The primary problems encountered in teaching Langston Hughes grow out of his air of improvisation and familiarity. Vital to an understanding of Hughes's poetry and prose is the idiom, the quality of black colloquial speech and the rhythms of jazz and the blues.

The best strategies for teaching the writer involve the reading aloud of the poetry and prose, the use of recordings and films, the use of the history of the "New Negro" and the Harlem Renaissance.

Major Themes, Historical Perspectives, and Personal Issues

The major themes in Langston Hughes's work grow out of his personal life, his travels, his involvement in radical and protest movements, his interest in Africa and South America as well as the Caribbean.

Significant Form, Style, or Artistic Conventions

In regard to questions of form, style, or artistic convention, the following considerations are relevant to Langston Hughes:

1. His debt to Walt Whitman, Carl Sandburg, and Paul Laurence Dunbar.
2. His enthusiasm for the language and songs of the rural folk and lower-class urban, "street" Negro. As Bontemps once wrote, "No one loved Negroes as Langston Hughes did."
3. His capacity for improvisation and original rhythms. His use of jazz, blues, be-bop, gospel, Harlem slang.

The poetry: Point out the occasion that inspired the poem "The Negro Speaks of Rivers" (cf. *The Big Sea*, pp. 54–56). "The Weary Blues," "Drum," and "Freedom Train" use the idioms of black speech with poetic effect.

Prose: Among Hughes's finest achievements are the Simple stories. Here we have the speech and idiom presented with irony, malapropisms, and humor.

Original Audience

Hughes's audience consisted of his literary friends (Cullen, Van Vechten, Thurman, etc.) as well as the general public.

Comparisons, Contrasts, Connections

Comparisons or contrasts might be made with Sandburg, Whitman, McKay. The bases of such comparisons might be the language and metaphor, the degree of militancy, etc.

Bibliography

Berry, Faith. "Saunders Redding as Literary Critic of Langston Hughes." The Langston Hughes Review V, no. 2 (Fall 1986).

Emanuel, James A. and Theodore L. Gross. *Dark Symphony: Negro Literature in America*. New York, The Free Press, 1968, 191–221, 447–80.

Henderson, Stephen. *Understanding the New Black Poetry: Black Speech and Black Music as Poetic References*. New York: Wm. Morrow & Co., 1973.

Hughes, L. "Ten Ways to Use Poetry in Teaching." CLA Bulletin, 1951.

——. *The First Book of Rhythms* (1954).

Miller, R. Baxter, ed. *Black American Poets Between Worlds, 1940–1960*. Knoxville: Univ. of Tenn. Press, 1986.

——. *The Art and Imagination of Langston Hughes*. Knoxville: Univ. of Kentucky Press, 1988.

O'Daniel, Therman B. *Langston Hughes, Black Genius A Critical Evaluation*. For the College Language Ass'n. New York: Wm. Morrow & Co., 1971, 65 ff. p 171. p. 180.

Countee Cullen (1903–1946)

Contributing Editor: Walter C. Daniel [p. 1510]

Classroom Issues and Strategies

Students who read Cullen need to develop a clear understanding of the temper of the Harlem Renaissance period in U.S. literary development. In addition, they may need help with the classical allusions in "Yet Do I Marvel" and in "Simon the Cyrenian Speaks." Also, students should come to understand the reference to Scottsboro as the poet's criticism of his fellow poet's neglect of what he considers a significant matter (obviously, this requires knowing about the Scottsboro Incident in 1931 and following).

Significant Form, Style, or Artistic Conventions

Countee Cullen is an important figure of the African-American arts movement known as the Harlem Renaissance. Born in Louisville, Kentucky, Cullen was reared in New York City by his paternal grandmother until 1918, when he was adopted by the Reverend Frederick Asbury Cullen. This was a turning point in his life, for he was now introduced into the very center of black activism and achievement. Cullen displayed his talent early; already in high school he was writing poetry, and in his sophomore year at NYU he was awarded second prize in the nationwide Witter Bynner Poetry Contest for "The Ballad of the Brown Girl." Encompassing themes that would remain salient for the remainder of his career, Cullen's first major poem also revealed his unabashed reverence for the works of John Keats. Cullen was firmly convinced that traditional verse forms could not be bettered by more modern paradigms. It was, therefore, the task of any aspiring writer, he felt, to become conversant with and part of a received literary tradition simply because such a tradition has the virtue of longevity and universal sanction.

Cullen's first volume *Color* established him as a writer with an acute spiritual vision. Especially noteworthy in this respect is "Simon the Cyrenian Speaks," a work that eloquently makes use of Matthew 27:32 in order to suggest an analogue between blacks and Simon, the man who was compelled to bear the cross of Christ on his back. Sublimity was not Cullen's only strong point. In "Incident," the reader is brusquely catapulted into the all-too-realistic world of an impressionable eight-year old as he experiences overt racism for the first time on a heretofore memorable ride through the history-filled streets of Baltimore.

In 1927, Cullen edited a significant anthology of black poetry, *Caroling Dusk*, and published two collections of his own, *The Ballad of the Brown Girl* and *Copper Sun*. Representative of Cullen's philosophical development in this period is the multifaceted "Heritage," a poem that summarizes his ambivalent relationship with Christian and pagan cultural constructs.

The 1930s and 1940s saw a change of direction in Cullen's work. His poetry output almost totally ceased as he turned his attention to the novel, theater, translation, teaching, and children's literature. The 1932 novel *One Way to Heaven* was Cullen's response to Carl Van Vechten's 1926 *Nigger Heaven*, a controversial and notorious work exploring the seamy underbelly of Harlem.

Cullen's best work was his poetry; he apparently knew this when he compiled his anthology, with the self-explanatory title *On These I Stand*, shortly before his death.

Original Audience

The Harlem Renaissance period between the two World Wars saw the rise and definition of the "New Negro" in social, political, and literature activities of the nation.

Cullen, along with other formally educated black poets, established a new aesthetic for racial statement.

Comparisons, Contrasts, Connections

Cullen's contemporaries (the best-known ones among the writers) were Gwendolyn Bennett, Langston Hughes, and Claude McKay; contrast the poetic method of social protest by studying poems written by each of these poets.

Cullen has been criticized for taking an elitist attitude toward racial matters and of ignoring social protest. Is this criticism fair to Cullen in light of your reading of some poems written by him and, for instance, Claude McKay?

His first volume of poetry *Color* (1925) revealed an indebtedness to traditional verse forms and an abiding interest in the tenets of Romanticism, characteristics markedly absent from the blues-based folk rhythms of the poetry of Langston Hughes. Cullen looked beyond his own rich heritage for authorial models and chose John Keats, firmly convinced that "To make a poet black, and bid him sing" was a "curious thing" that God had done. So curious, indeed, that the voice of the black poet had to be assimilated to and harmonized with the bearers of an alien literary tradition. In "To John Keats, Poet. At Springtime," Cullen's adulation of the nineteenth-century lyricist is most pronounced: "I know, in spite of all men say/Of Beauty, you have felt her most."

Questions for Reading and Discussion/ Approaches to Writing

1. Identify non-black authors of the 1920s and determine their common themes in contrast with those of black writers.
2. Cullen grew up in a Methodist parsonage as the adopted son of a prominent Harlem pastor. Might the use of paradox about Christian religion and its practices in some of his poetry reflect his home experience? Which works and in which references?
3. Indications of Cullen's fascination with and influence by the English Romantic poets, especially John Keats.
4. Effectiveness of the metaphor of Simon, the Cyrenian to black American life at the time; whether the allusion suggests some theological implications, such as non-redemptive suffering.
5. In the poem "Yet Do I Marvel," Cullen makes an implicit comparison between black poets and the mythical figures of Tantalus and Sisyphus. Explain how this comparison functions within the world of the poem.
6. Lying behind Cullen's title choice for "From the Dark Tower" is the phrase "ivory tower." How does this fact help explain the poem as well as its dedication to Charles S. Johnson?
7. As background to discussion of "Scottsboro, Too, Is Worth Its Song," comment on the historical importance of the Scottsboro Nine case and the trial of Sacco and Vanzetti. Why are these two events paired in Cullen's poem? What was the prevailing poetic current that prevented contemporary concerns from being broached in verse? In answering this last question, compare, for instance, some of the poems written by Wallace Stevens and William Carlos Williams during this period with the poetry of Cullen. Why did Cullen not follow the modernist precepts announced by writers such as T. S. Eliot, Ezra Pound, and Amy Lowell? How does Cullen's allusion to Walt Whitman's lines "I . . . sing myself" and "I sing the body electric" function in the context of this poem?
8. Cullen chooses to set his poem "Incident" in old Baltimore. Why?

9. With reference to "Pagan Prayer," comment on the manner in which African-Americans have used Christian religion as a repository for radical egalitarian hopes. How is Cullen's conception of the religion of the white man different from that of a contemporary Nigerian writer, such as Chinua Achebe in his novels *Things Fall Apart* and *Arrow of God*?

10. How does Cullen accommodate traditions of English poetry to themes of problems of living black in the United States?

11. How active is the poet (Cullen) in taking the position of racial spokesman in the poems? Effective?

Bibliography

Baker, Houston. *Black Literature in America*. New York: McGraw Hill, 1971, 114–58.

Bontemps, Arna. *The Harlem Renaissance Remembered*. New York: Dodd, Mead, 1972.

Daniel, Walter C. "Countee Cullen as Literary Critic" *College Language Association Journal* XIV (March 1972): 281–90.

Davis, Arthur. *From the Dark Tower: African-American Writers 1900–1960*. Howard Univ. Press, 1974.

Wagner, Jean. *Black Poets of the United States*. Urbana-Champaign: Univ. of Illinois Press, 1973. Part II.

Critical discussion of Cullen's poetry was inaugurated by J. Saunders Redding in *To Make a Poet Black*, 1939. More detailed attention was given to his oeuvre in a sympathetic and forthright monograph by Houston A. Baker, Jr., *A Many-colored Coat of Dreams: The Poetry of Countee Cullen*, 1974. Alan R. Shucard in *Countee Cullen*, 1984, provides a complete overview and assessment of Cullen's life and literary endeavors.

Perceptive comments about his novel are contained in Bernard W. Bell's *The African-American Novel and Its Tradition*, 1987.

An invaluable general background of the Harlem Renaissance that also includes comments about Cullen is Nathan Irvin Huggins's *Harlem Renaissance*, 1971. Equally indispensable is Margaret Perry's *A Bio-Bibliography of Countee P. Cullen 1903–1946*, 1971.

Noteworthy articles touching upon particular aspects of Cullen's poetry are:

Davis, Arthur P. "The Alien-and-Exile Theme in Countee Cullen's Racial Poems." *Phylon* 14 (1953): 390–400.

Dorsey, David F. "Countee Cullen's Use of Greek Mythology." *College Language Association Journal* 13 (1970): 68–77.

Webster, Harvey Curtis. "A Difficult Career." *Poetry* 70 (1947): 224–25.

Gwendolyn B. Bennett (1902–1981)

Contributing Editor: Walter C. Daniel [p. 1515]

Classroom Issues and Strategies

Almost always overlooked in discussion about the Harlem Renaissance, Gwendolyn Bennett was, nevertheless, a significant part of the most important artistic movement in African-American history. Chiefly remembered for "The Ebony Flute," a regular column appearing in *Opportunity* that chronicled the creative efforts of the writers, painters, sculptors, actors, and musicians who made Harlem the center of a profound cultural flowering, Bennett was also a poet and short-story writer of considerable skill. "To Usward," for instance, a poem dedicated to Jessie Fauset in honor of the publication of her novel *There Is Confusion*, celebrates the newly discovered sense of empowerment permeating the Harlem community—a community envisioned as a chorus of individual voices at once aware of a rich African cultural heritage and prepared to sing "Before the urgency of youth's behest!" because of its belief that it "claim[s] no part of racial dearth."

More typical of Bennett's lyric voice is the deeply personal "Hatred." Although the motivation for hating is nowhere explicitly revealed, the tragic history of slavery is a barely concealed presence in the poem, welling to the surface as the speaker invokes memory as the agent for understanding her hatred. Unstated, of course, is the hope that memory will also ensure that past savagery is never again repeated. Of her two stories, the most popularly anthologized piece is "Wedding Day," a work that appeared in the sole issue of *Fire!!*, a radical 1926 periodical launched by Langston Hughes, Zora Neale Hurston, and Wallace Thurman with the avowed intent "to burn up a lot of old, dead conventional Negro-white ideas of the past," to validate the folk expression "the blacker the berry, the sweeter the juice."

The tale of Paul Watson, a black American who falsely thought he could flee prejudice in the United States by living as an expatriate in France, "Wedding Day" takes on a dirge-like quality as it recounts the stoical endurance required of black people in coping with contradictory and absurd situations even in a post-World War I Europe many of them helped to liberate.

Although her work was never collected into a single volume, Bennett's poetry and prose was, nonetheless, included in major anthologies of the period such as Countee Cullen's *Caroling Dusk* (1924), Alain Locke's *The New Negro* (1925), and William Stanley Braithwaite's *Yearbook of American Poetry* (1927). Admired for her artistic work on five covers of *Opportunity* and two covers of *Crisis*, praised for her "depth and understanding" of character nuances in her short stories by the playwright Theodore Ward, she was, in the words of James Weldon Johnson, a "dynamic figure" whose keenest talent lay in composing "delicate poignant lyrics."

Questions for Reading and Discussion/ Approaches to Writing

1. Why did the author coin the neologism "usward" as part of the title of the poem "To Usward?"
2. In Chinese culture, what is the significance of ginger jars?
3. In the poem "Advice," Bennett's choice of the word *sophist* is significant. Comment on the etymology and historical circumstances surrounding the first usage of this word.
4. Discuss the importance of Alexander Dumas as a literary figure.
5. The poem "Heritage" centers on a distinct yearning for Africa. Why did the poets of this period stress such a theme?

Arna Bontemps (1902–1973)

Contributing Editor: Charles H. Nichols [p. 1518]

Classroom Issues and Strategies

The primary problems in the teaching of Bontemp's poetry and prose are problems of interpretation. Bontemps is a lucid, sophisticated writer whose use of tone, irony, and symbol achieves subtle and interesting effects. Students need help in interpreting these kinds of figurative language.

In teaching Bontemps it is helpful to read his works aloud and to supply the background information that helps in interpretation. You may want to refer to poems not included in this anthology. "Miracles" is a poem with allusions to the life of Christ. "Let the Church Roll On" uses the familiar setting of the black church. The stark stories from *The Old South* evoke the race relations of the 1930s.

Major Themes, Historical Perspectives, and Personal Issues

The major themes in Bontemps are historical as in *100 Years of Negro Freedom* (1961) and *Black Thunder* (1936). Bontemps has written historical novels on slave revolts and the stunning play *St. Louis Woman*.

Significant Form, Style, or Artistic Conventions

In form and style, Bontemps is deeply influenced by the folk traditions— the spirituals, blues, and jazz. Yet he is also steeped in the finest traditions of English poetry and writes with dignity and a sense of beauty.

Original Audience

Bontemps wrote several works in collaboration with Langston Hughes. He prepared important anthologies and children's books. There have always been audiences for his writing.

Comparisons, Contrasts, Connections

Bontemps might be compared with Jack Conroy or Langston Hughes, writers with whom he collaborated. The basis of each comparison might be their relative concern for historical events or the use of folklore.

Questions f or Reading and Discussion/ Approaches to Writing

1. In the poem "A Black Man Talks of Reaping," the poet presents the bitterness of the black man's experience, yet achieves a universal quality. How does the metaphor of planting and reaping remove the poem from the level of polemics?

Outside reading:

2. (a) "Miracles" is essentially transcendental. Describe the theme of the poem.

(b)   What use does Bontemps make of biblical allusion and religious imagery? How does he use the religious tradition of black people?

Sterling A. Brown (1901–1989)

Contributing Editor: John Edgar Tidwell [p. 1519]

Classroom Issues and Strategies

Two problems come immediately to mind when I consider my past experiences in teaching Brown's poetry. First the relative obscurity of Brown's place in the American literary tradition is the biggest obstacle in teaching Brown because students think his presence in the syllabus requires some big justification.

The second problem, ironically, is much more complicated. Because Brown is a black poet, students are quite willing to interpret his poetry in light of his "blackness," by which they generally mean hard luck, pain, and suffering imposed by "Jim Crow" laws. They are less willing to acknowledge Brown as a poet, one conscientiously crafting and representing experience in poetic form.   Brown's fundamental assertion of a humanistic vision is rooted in the democratic principles of the U.S. Constitution. The way in which this assertion is set forth as compelling poetry sometimes escapes the vision of students, who often want to see him engaged in special pleading. They're often reluctant to see him in a tradition established by Frost, E. A. Robinson, Sandburg, and Masters; at times, a myopia prevents them from seeing how Brown takes aesthetic forms from black folk—the blues, folk tales, work songs— and adapts them for poetic purpose. In short, it is a problem of getting students to understand how Brown is, in fact, an Americanist, whose precepts and examples sought to argue his liberation from, as he considered it, the more narrow designation black writer.

To handle the problem of Brown's relative obscurity, I begin by placing him within a thematic and structural context of black and white writers who sought the "extraordinary in ordinary life." In part, this means illustrating Brown's comment that when Sandburg said yes to his Chicago hog butchers and stacks of wheat, he was moved to celebrate the lives, lore, and language of black folk.

To establish a context of writers using black folk traditions during Brown's era, I begin with Hughes, Hurston, James Weldon Johnson, and

Waring Cuney, among others. I discuss very generally the differing ways they made use of black folk experiences to establish texts and aesthetic contexts. What this permits is a comparative approach; it asks for ways Brown's blues poems, for example, conform and depart from those of Hughes and Cuney.

Of the various presentational techniques I've used, one has been especially useful: listening to Brown reading his own poetry, which is available on several Folkways records. Brown is an exceptional reader, in part because of his background in drama and his reputation for being a raconteur.

Most questions students pose relate to the subtle way in which Brown calls into question the panoply of Jim Crow laws. In Brown's "Old Lem," for example, they ask for clarification about the nonverbal communication suggested by Old Lem's standing with bowed head, averted eyes, and open hands, in contrast to the whites with hands balled in fists and eyes in direct, confrontational stares. The history of these gestures dating from its formalization into law during the early nineteenth century is something they usually don't understand, but come to see when it is explained.

Major Themes, Historical Perspectives, and Personal Issues

How does Brown's work simultaneously refute racial stereotypes *and* affirm the humanity of black life? What is distinctive about Brown's humor? In what ways does it borrow from the vernacular tradition brought to prominence by Twain? How does the theme of the pursuit of democracy figure into Brown's aesthetic vision? How do sociological concerns coalesce with aesthetic pursuits without one overshadowing the other? What innovations in technique and craft can be discerned in Brown's poetry?

Significant Form, Style, or Artistic Conventions

I find the issues of period and school to be particularly interesting. Brown has been vociferous in refuting the term *Harlem* Renaissance. His opposition takes on two points: first, Harlem was *a*, not *the*, center of Negro creative activity during this era. To locate it in Harlem, he continues, is to afford too much credit to Carl Van Vechten and not enough to blacks themselves. Second, he often puns, if this era was the *Renais-sance*, where is the *naissance*? Critics generally include him in the group of writers who came of age during the twenties. Brown questions his inclusion in the group, by preferring to be considered a "lone wolf." And he further questions the neat periodization of the New Negro Movement into the years 1922–1929. A renaissance, he contends, is much longer. One could use Brown's denials, then, as bases for defining problems of period, school, and even aesthetic convention. For example, how does Brown's use of black idiom differ from his immediate predecessors and from writers as early as Paul Laurence Dunbar and his imitators?

Original Audience

Brown himself is his own best spokesman on the question of audience. In terms of an external audience, he confronted "the dilemma of a divided audience." On one hand, a white readership, thoroughly conditioned by racial stereotyping to expect superficial depictions of blacks, sought confirmation of their beliefs in black poetry. Bristling at any hint of a racially demeaning representation of blacks, the audience of black readers sought glorified portraits of blacks, which became stereotypes in another direction. Brown rejected both audiences and instead hypothesized one. The oral or speakerly quality of his poetry depends in part on the audience he creates within his poetry. The dynamics of speaker-listener are central to understanding the performative nature of his work. In Brown's description, poetry should communicate something. (The explanation of "communication" can be inferred from his letter to Langston Hughes, in which he said poets should not follow the elitist path of Pound and Eliot, two poets he considers no longer talking to each other, only themselves.) Communication is accomplished by using forms and structures and the language of black folk.. Such use articulates a vision of the world that celebrates the dignity, humanism, and worth of a people largely misunderstood and misrepresented.

Readers of Brown's poetry today come away with a similar sense of the performative dimensions of his poetry, I think, because much of Brown's poetry holds up today. Even though today's audience may not know the character of racial discrimination in the way Brown experienced it, his poetry has a quality that transcends particular time and place. "She jes' gits hold of us dataway" the speaker in Brown's "Ma Rainey" tells us. Readers of the poem today, like those of an earlier generation, come away with the same feeling.

Questions for Reading and Discussion/ Approaches to Writing

1. The questions I assign are determined by the approach and the poems I use. My approach to the Slim Greer poems, for example, centers on the poem as tall tale. I generally ask students to consult a literary handbook for features of the tall tale and to read the poems in light of their findings. In this same vein, I often assign actual tall tales (such as Roger Welsch's *Shingling the Fog and Other Plains Lies*) or other examples of poetry written in this tradition (such as *Fireside Tales* by Joe Allen), as a way of suggesting Brown's distinctiveness.

2. My paper topics are assigned to extend students' understanding of works we read and discuss in class, by encouraging them to build upon the assigned reading a comparative critical analysis. The issues raised in the first part of this question give students a chance to range beyond class discussion.

Bibliography

For criticism on Brown, the list of works cited at the end of the headnote is extremely useful. One important addition to the list should be:

Jean Wagner, "Chapter 11: Sterling Brown," in his *Black Poets of the United States* (Urbana-Champaign: Univ. of Illinois Press, 1973), 475–503.

Zora Neale Hurston (1891–1960)

Contributing Editor: Robert Hemenway [p. 1535]

Classroom Issues and Strategies

While there are no particular difficulties in teaching Hurston, some students find the dialect hard to understand. To address this problem, I usually read several passages aloud to help students get a "feel" for the voices. Once they've heard Hurston read aloud, they can create her characters' speech in their minds so that it is understandable.

Major Themes, Historical Perspectives, and Personal Issues

Women's issues
Race issues
Interface between oral and written literature

Significant Form, Style, or Artistic Conventions

Short story structure
Representations of an oral culture

Original Audience

Always a complex issue when postulating the audience of a black writer.

Comparisons, Contrasts, Connections

Langston Hughes
Alice Walker

James Weldon Johnson (1871–1938)

Contributing Editor: Arethenia J. Bates Millican [p. 1553]

Classroom Issues and Strategies

Next to James Weldon Johnson's name and date of birth in a biosketch is the familiar catalog of his accomplishments as educator, journalist, lawyer, composer, librettist, poet, novelist, editor, social historian, literary critic, diplomat, fighter for the rights of his people and the rights of all. Yet, he is remembered today, almost exclusively, as the author of "Lift Every Voice and Sing;" and to some degree as the author of the "Creation," the first sermon in *God's Trombones*.

One mythic error is still in vogue for the less ardent student—and that is the indictment leveled against the author who "talks black" but who was never really given to the black ethos. This accusation comes as an error of identification. Some students assume that Johnson himself is the protagonist of the novel, *The Autobiography of an Ex-colored Man*. Actually, the author's friend, "D_____," Douglas Wetmore, is model for the protagonist. Thus, one encounters the problem of coping with an author with name popularity, but who is not known despite his myriad contributions to American and African-American literary culture.

The writer can best be made accessible to students, first, by introducing *Along This Way*, his authentic life story, as well as the history of the Harlem Renaissance and the rise of Marxist ideology. In the index, the entry "Johnson, James Weldon" is a reference guide in chronological order that gives the chance to examine items of choice.

Johnson may stand in clearer relief by using an "exchange" pattern of image-making. For example, discuss W. E. B. Du Bois as a "politician" who engaged in "political" actions at times.

An indirect form of transformation of real life act to art can be traced in an evolutionary process that produced *Trombones*. First, he visited a Jacksonville church during his childhood days where he saw the African shout. Second, he visited "Little Africa." Third, he listened to his father as a gospel preacher. And finally he heard gospel preachers when he was field secretary for the NAACP. The Kansas City sermon spurred these recollections and brought on a feeling that gave him import to black soul, the African communal spirit.

Students usually respond to the following issues:

1. The failure of the "Talented Tenth" to understand the economic imperatives that would involve all Americans.
2. The failure of the Johnson legacy to maintain itself with the onset of Marxism and the rise of proletarian literature.
3. The failure of Fisk and Atlanta universities to play a significant role in building a Johnson file of note.
4. The reason so little is known about J. Rosamond, Johnson's co-editor and collaborator.
5. In a quiet way, Johnson is receiving scholarly interest. Will it be potent enough to take him into the twenty-first century?

Major Themes, Historical Perspectives, and Personal Issues

Exemplary themes of major import in the Johnson canon begin with "Lift Every Voice" and "Bards." They relate to the black presence in America via the peculiar institution, but maintain relevance to the American Dream, "holy hope," and self-realization. Typical themes of historical significance are: freedom and authority; liberty and responsibility; the artist in America; and society and the individual. On the personal level, in terms of the author's race and his innate concerns, the theme of historical reference is stressed in order to give credence to and assess values that originated in Africa. Other themes in the "personal" category are: men's ways with God; the mystical aura of the creative imagination; the power, beauty and "essential rhythm" of indigenous black folk poetry; justice, liberation, and peace.

Significant Form, Style, or Artistic Conventions

Johnson's reputation as a writer rests on his novel and *God's Trombones*. His idea that prose should state facts enables him to write a realistic novel. He treats themes such as namelessness, racial self-hatred, the black mother's ambiguous role, and the white patron/white liberal who appears in the modern novel by blacks.

As a poet, he went through a long evolutionary stage of development. His first poems, *Jingles and Croons*, are written in the "'Dunbar" tradition of accommodation, imitation, and limitation in terms of the two emotions allowed; pathos and humor. The plantation and the minstrel stage are background sources.

When Johnson wrote "Lift Every Voice" in 1900, he had become imbued with the Victorian conventions of English verse. Rudyard Kipling, the poet laureate (the court poet), wrote many occasional poems including "Recessional," which served as a model for the black national anthem in form and structure.

The influence of Walt Whitman, the poet who gave birth to a new American poetry, wrote in free verse. *Song of Myself* set the stage for freedom, individual experiments, and the new theme of egalitarianism that appears in one aspect of Johnson's poem "'Brothers." He used free verse in *Trombones*.

The coming of the New Negro to New York in the post-World War I period, "thoughtwise" and "boywise," combined to form Harlem as the New Jerusalem for blacks. This city became the place for conscious black artists who revered their African past and their southern roots. *Trombones* is grounded in this tradition. It makes use of African rhythms; it employs intonations of southern folk idioms, thus enforcing the power of black speech devoid of the artificial "cant of literary dialect." Therefore, Johnson set the stage for future poets who desired to honor the oral tradition in their conscious literary works.

Original Audience

Black literature written in the nineteenth century and in the first four decades of the twentieth century was written basically for a white reading audience. At that time there were few if any student audiences on any level who studied works by blacks. In black schools great racial personalities were presented to the students during Negro History Week. Now there is Black History Month.

Black literature in class is a phenomenon of the 1960s. Black studies programs became a part of the school curriculum in America. Therefore, the audience in class is a rather new phenomenon.

The class audiences that began as "black" or "white" at first might be one now of new minority constitution; women, handicapped people, elderly citizens, third world students, and/or others. The appeal of the black work to be valid, then, must have appeal to other ethnic groups since the world is now a global village.

For the new class, forums, debates, formal and informal class reports by individual students may enhance interpersonal communication. For the dissemination of facts, the wonders effected by technology are countless. Students may have access to films, recordings, videotapes, and audio tapes for reviewing material introduced earlier in formal class lectures by the professor.

Comparisons, Contrasts, Connections

Fellow novelists of the Harlem Renaissance who honored the theme "passing" (Johnson claimed authorship for *The Ex-colored Man* in 1927) as Walter White's "Flight" (1926), Jessie Fauset's "Plum Bun" (1928), and Nella Larsen's *Passing* (1929) promoted the aesthetic indigenous to African literature: art for life's sake. The "for-life's-sake" element is now dated because these authors were intent on presenting the "better elements" in black life to squelch the ardor of the *Nigger Heaven* (1926) vogue fathered by Carl Van Vechten and adhered to even by Claude McKay in *Home to Harlem* (1928).

Stephen Henderson, author of *Understanding the New Black Poetry* (1973), has indicated that black speech, black song, black music (if one can make such distinctions) are imbued with "experiential energy." On this premise, Johnson, the poet who cultivated his black ethos, is best compared with Langston Hughes (1902–1967).

Questions for Reading and Discussion/ Approaches to Writing

1. Does Johnson's high degree of Euroamerican acculturation deflect from his African-American altruism?
2. Is he rightfully classed as a Victorian in terms of middle-class prudery and respectability?

3. Do you agree with George Kent's view that "his cosmopolitanism always extends his reach and his grasp"? (*In Blackness and the Adventure of Western Culture*, 1972, p. 30).

4. The editors of *The Conscious Voice* (1965) suggest that the poem is the rendering of experience—which also suggests "the intricacy of the poet's involvement in the world." Does Johnson use a suitable aesthetic distance from his subject matter in the poems: "Lift Every Voice" (1900); "Fifty Years" (1853–1913); and "Saint Peter Relates An Incident" (1930)? (Refer to outside sources for latter two poems.)

5. How can one justify the author's use of the compensatory Christian ethic in "Lift Every Voice," "Bards," "Listen Lord"—a prayer—and the sermons in *Trombones* when he himself is an agnostic? (Refer to outside sources for latter two poems.)

6. Three reigning poets influenced Johnson's development as the second outstanding African-American poet: Rudyard Kipling, English: Walt Whitman, American; Paul Laurence Dunbar, African-American. How?

7. Racial violence in the poem "Brothers" (1916) is attended with a plea for brotherhood. What is its advantage over literary dialect?

8. How does the longevity of the oral tradition substantiate its worth in the use of black idiomatic expression in African-American literature?

Suggested paper topics:

Period and Genre: The Color-line Novel

1. Before Johnson (1912)
2. During the Awakening (1915-1920)
3. During the Harlem Renaissance (1920-1930)
4. During the 1960s in Louisiana (Ernest Gaines)

Period:

1. The Influence of the Harlem Renaissance on West African Poets
2. Influence of the African poet, like Leopold Senghor, on African-American Poets during the 1960s

Genre:

1. Poetry by "White" Black Authors
2. Protest Poetry
3. The "Coon Song" on Broadway
4. The Folk Sermon as Literary Genre

Bibliography

Copeland, George E. "James Weldon Johnson—a Bibliography." Master's thesis, School of Library Science at Pratt Institute, Brooklyn, New York, May 1951.

Davis, Thadious. "Southern Standard—Bears in the New Negro Renaissance." In *The History of Southern Literature* 2, 291–313 (1985).

Fleming, Robert. "Contemporary Themes in Johnson's *Autobiography of an Ex-colored Man.*" *Negro American Literature Forum* IV (1970): 120–24.

Johnson, J. W. The first and second book of American Negro Spirituals, 1925, 1925. *God's Trombones*, 1927.

Levy, Eugene. *James Weldon Johnson: Black Leader Black Voices*. 1973. The J. W. Johnson "Prefaces" offer rich critical insight about his work *The Book of American Negro Poetry*, 1922, 1931.

Mcghee, Nancy B. "The Folk Sermon." CLAJ I (1969): 51–61.

Millican, Arethenia Bates. "James Weldon Johnson; In Quest of An Afrocentric Tradition for Black American Literature." Doctoral dissertation, LSU, 1972. Chapters 6, 7, and 10 detail facts on the form and structure of dated poems.

Claude McKay (1889–1948)

Contributing Editor: Elvin Holt [p. 1557]

Classroom Issues and Strategies

I suggest that teachers begin with McKay's love poems. This approach allows students to relate to McKay on a purely human level and prepares them for the discomforting racial themes that dominate some of the other poems.

Students respond to the persistent racism in American society. Some nonblack students want to know why they have to read such poems. Many of them believe the poems are "for black people." Some students object to the eroticism of the love poems.

"Flame-Heart" evokes the Romantic tradition of Wordsworth and Shelley, poets whose work McKay admired greatly. This finely wrought poem, which expresses the poet's deep longing for Jamaica, his beloved homeland, highlights McKay's interest in nonracial themes.

"A Red Flower," one of McKay's most striking love poems, features brilliant conceits similar to those found in the poetry of John Donne and other metaphysical poets. Identify the metaphor in the first and last stanzas of the poem.

In "Flower of Love," McKay presents another example of his passionate, yet controlled, love poetry. Like "A Red Flower," "Flower of Love" turns on an elaborate conceit, recalling the best work of Andrew Marvell. Describe the poem's central metaphor and explain the reference to the South.

"America" is one of McKay's best protest poems. Explain the poem's central theme and describe the prophecy the speaker relates in the final quatrain.

"The Lynching," a moving expression of McKay's outrage against the senseless killings of blacks that marked the early decades of this century, depicts Christ as the victim of the lynching. Is the Christ figure an effective image, considering the context?

McKay's best known poem, "If We Must Die," urges blacks to wage war agains their oppressors. Winston Churchill used McKay's poem to revive the spirit of his countrymen during WWII.

"Harlem Dancer" focuses on a beautiful black woman performing in a nightclub. What is the central theme of the poem? Does the poet articulate a point of view with which black feminists might concur?

"Harlem Shadows" is the title poem from McKay's 1922 collection of poetry. Who or what are the "shadows" mentioned in the poem's title? What does the poem say about the plight of black Americans in general?

Major Themes, Historical Perspectives, and Personal Issues

It is essential that students get a sense of what it was like to be black in America during the early decades of this century. Students must also realize that McKay's Jamaican background made him particularly sensitive to the plight of black Americans.

Significant Form, Style, or Artistic Conventions

It is important to give students a good introduction to the Harlem Renaissance. Students need to know what the writers (blacks) were trying to accomplish. Students should note McKay's dependence upon traditional British forms such as the sonnet.

Original Audience

I help students to understand the social history that shaped McKay's work and determined his first audience. Then I try to help students see why the poems remain fresh and vital to our own time.

Comparisons, Contrasts, Connections

Since McKay was influenced by important British poets such as Wordsworth, Shelley, and Donne, it is useful to compare and contrast his work with that of English Romantic and metaphysical poets. Stylistic similarities are often evident.

Bibliography

James R. Giles's *Claude McKay* is a good book for teachers. The text is well organized, and the index makes it easy to locate specific information.

Anne Spencer (1882–1975)

Contributing Editor: Evelyn H. Roberts [p. 1563]

Classroom Issues and Strategies

Aside from black literature anthologies and general reference sources, limited critical material is available. The poet Anne Spencer can best be made accessible to students in various ways.

1. Relating Spencer's fascination with reading and studying at the Lynchburg Seminary (note, for example, her selection as the commencement speaker).
2. Presenting an overhead transparency of one of her longer poems, "At The Carnival." Most students enjoy this poem and can relate to such an experience—comparing or contrasting with their own carnival and/or county fair experiences.
3. Showing the photographs that appear in J. Lee Greene's *Time's Unfading Garden.*

4. Using selected black literature anthologies placed on library reserve for students who wish to prepare brief oral reports or short papers.

Many of Spencer's poems show dramatic compression and sharpness of image and phrase. She is no pleader of causes, choosing not to comment on the race issue in her published poetry. Yet her biography reveals a wide acquaintance with literary dignitaries, lecturers, and other prominent citizens, black and white, who would appear as public speakers and/or artists in Lynchburg, Virginia.

Students admire Spencer's commitment to maintaining a free, independent spirit, not being hampered or restrained by husband or offspring. They also admire her determination and concentration to create despite the reality that "art is long and time is fleeting." In addition, students applaud both Spencer's (assertiveness as demonstrated by her work for women's suffrage) and her determination to create options that allowed her to pursue her art by diverse routes (as demonstrated by her work as the first black librarian in Lynchburg).

Students are curious about Spencer's statement, published by Countee Cullen (*Caroling Dusk*, p. 47):

"But I have no civilized articulation for the things I hate. I proudly love being a Negro woman; [it's] so involved and interesting. *We* are the PROBLEM—the great national game of TABOO."

Major Themes, Historical Perspectives, and Personal Issues

Like Emerson, Thoreau, Emily Dickinson, Amy Lowell, and Angelina Grimké, Anne Spencer maintained a strong belief in individual freedom and liberty to convey ideas and uphold ideals vital for personal expression. Further, A. Spencer possessed strong individual preferences and exhibited objections to various standards or beliefs that may have compromised her personal ideals. See poems not included in this anthology such as "Wife-Woman," "Neighbors."

Further, Anne Spencer sustained a life-long admiration for poets and the art of poetry. In her poem "Dunbar," she pays tribute to Chatterton, Shelley, and Keats.

Some additional similarities can be cited showing an interrelatedness in the art of the above-mentioned poets. As Emily Dickinson advanced in years, the circle of her world grew ever smaller. Dickinson became a hermit by deliberate and conscious choice. Similarly, Anne Spencer withdrew from the community as the years passed. For Dickinson, her isolation allowed her to become prey to the then-current Emersonian doctrine of "mystical individualism." As a flower of New England transcendentalism, she became a Puritan and free thinker obsessed with the problems of good and evil, of life and death, nature and destiny of the human soul. Toward God, Emily Dickinson exhibited an Emersonian self-possession.

Moreover, Emerson's gnomic style became for Emily Dickinson epigramatic to the point of being cryptic; a quality that Anne Spencer, Amy Lowell, and Angelina Grimké likewise display.

Finally, Anne Spencer in some of her poems—"Requiem," "Substitution," "Wife-Woman"—appears to embrace a pantheistic view that can be compared to Emerson's view in "Hamatreya" of recognizing God in nature.

Significant Form, Style, or Artistic Conventions

Though sometimes coupled with the Harlem Renaissance period, Anne Spencer follows the tradition of neo-Romantic poetry, having composed some poems before the Harlem Renaissance era was clearly identified, or designated. Her poetry communicates a highly personal experience, revealing an arresting image. Her assessment of an experience may be occasionally ironic but discloses her profundity.

Anne Spencer's style reveals her individuality, an affinity for nature imagery, and the conventions of British and American Romantics, as her sensibility to form and color, a rich and varied vocabulary, and a pantheistic philosophy disclose.

An admirer of Robert Browning, one of her favorite poets, who despite his use of the idiom of conversation, achieved remarkable cogent compressed lines, Anne Spencer, likewise, achieved a similar style. Economy of phrase and compression of thought result from numerous revisions of same poem. Compare with Emily Dickinson's extensive and/ or intensive revision strategy.

Original Audience

To help students imagine Spencer's original audience, they are urged to create a yesteryear time capsule list for the poem when first written or published: listing common objects, terms, phrases, scenes, situations existing then but vastly different from the present era. For example:

	BEFORE WWII	SINCE WWII
"At the Carnival" (composed about 1919)	My Limousine-Lady fig-leaf bull-necked man sausage and garlic booth quivering female-thing Gestured assignations heaven-fed Naiad bacilli of the usual Neptune	Gay little girl of the Diving blind crowd quivering female-thing call it dancing Little Diver Carnival-tank

Comparisons, Contrasts, Connections

Both Emily Dickinson and Spencer were philosophical in their observations and perspectives. Dickinson's simple yet passionate style was marked by economy and concentration. She developed sharp intense images, recognized the utility of the ellipsis of thought and verbal ambiguity. Like Anne Spencer, E. Dickinson read extensively and intensively.

Compare E. Dickinson's "Because I Could Not Stop for Death" with A. Spencer's "Substitution" and "Requiem."

Ralph Waldo Emerson created his own philosophy, believing that all forces are united by energetic truth. Though he lectured, and composed many extended prose works, Emerson's poems, like those of Emily Dickinson and Anne Spencer, contain the core of his philosophy. He directed considerable thought to social reform and the growing issue of slavery.

A. Spencer, like Emerson, composed her poems in her garden. She has voiced high ethical, aesthetic, and independent positions on the topics she addresses in her poetry.

Although Anne Spencer did not vividly express her concern for social issues as did Henry David Thoreau and R. W. Emerson, her adult civic and professional life as librarian, and occasionally her poetry, addressed her concern for social and racial progress. H. D. Thoreau conveyed a genuine feeling for the unity of man and nature in *Walden*. His deep-rooted love for one place, Walden, characterized the epitome of his universe. Similarly, Anne Spencer's garden was central to her symbolic, historic, literary, religious imagery and meaning.

Countee Cullen "Foreword" to his work *Caroling Dusk* has asserted that "Anne Spencer [writes] with a cool precision that evokes comparison with Amy Lowell and the influence of a rockbound seacost." (p. xl)

Note: Examine Amy Lowell's "Patterns." Compare techniques and concepts as noted in A. Spencer's poems, e.g., "Substitution," "Lines to a Nasturtium," "For Jim Easter Eve."

Both Angelina Grimké and Spencer studied well their neo-romantic models. Both writers reveal great sensitivity and emotional acuity. Neither is writing for a group or class, or a race, nor do they use the language of complex reasoning and emotional compression. Rather, there is the direct attempt to present and define an emotional experience.

Bibliography

"Anne Spencer." In *Negro Poetry and Drama and The Negro in American Fiction*, edited by Sterling Brown, 65–66. With a new preface by Robert Bone. New York: Atheneum, 1937/1978.

Cullen, Countee, ed. *Caroling Dusk*. New York: Harper, 1927, 47–52.

Green, J. Lee. *Time's Unfading Garden: Anne Spencer's Life and Poetry*. Baton Rouge: Louisiana State Univ. Press, 1977, 204. Since Anne Spencer's poems were published in nearly every major black anthology, it is essential to include Green's work, for the appendix contains the largest collection of her published poems. Spencer never arranged for a collected publication, though she constantly composed poems, and revised many of her earlier pieces through 1974, the year prior to her death. See also Ch. 7, "The Poetry: Aestheticism" and Ch. 8, "The Poetry: Controversy."

Hughes, Langston. "The Negro Artist and the Racial Mountain." *Nation* (23 June 1926): 692–94.

Locke, Alain. "The New Negro; An Interpretation." In *The American Negro: His History and Literature*, edited by Alain Locke, 3–16. New York: Arno Press and The New York Times, 1925/1968.

Primeau, Ronald. "Frank Horne and the Second Echelon Poets of the Harlem Renaissance." In *The Harlem Renaissance Remembered*, edited with a memoir by Arna Bontemps. New York: Dodd, 1972, pp. 247–67.

Stetson, Erlene. "Anne Spencer." *College Language Association* XXI (March 1978): 400–09.

Nella Larsen (1891–1964)

Contributing Editor: Deborah E. McDowell [p. 1566]

Classroom Issues and Strategies

As students become rightly more attuned to representations of gender, race, and class in literary and cultural texts, the subtleties of Nella Larsen's *Quicksand* and *Passing* create interesting problems. Such problems derive from the general tendency of readers to elevate one social category of analysis over all others, often ignoring the interactive working of each on the other: race on gender, gender on class, etc. Readers attentive to class will find the narrow class spectrum of these novels offputting, for they can seem on the surface to be mere apologies for the black middle class, showing little awareness of and bearing on the poverty that the masses of blacks suffered in 1920s Harlem.

While attention to irony, point of view, and rhetorical strategy is essential to reading any text, with Nella Larsen, it is especially so. In *Passing*, for example, understanding that Irene Redfield, from whose perspective much of the novel is told, is an unreliable narrator, is key to understanding the novel. Equally important is the function of Clare and Irene as doubles, a strategy that undermines Irene's authority as the center of racial consciousness, clarifies the points in the narrative's critique of the black middle class, and uncovers the issues of sexuality and class that an exclusive focus on race conceals.

It is useful to read Fannie Hurst's *Imitation of Life* and to show the two film adaptations of the novel.

Students respond to the heightened attention to color and clothing and atmosphere in Nella Larsen's novels and wonder if her concentration on mulatto characters indicates an unmistakeable "privileging" of whiteness.

Major Themes, Historical Perspectives, and Personal Issues

It is important to provide information about 1920s Harlem and the literary and cultural confluences that shaped the Harlem Renaissance. It is critical that the movement be defined not by its "unities," but rather, by its "contraries" and be seen as the site of a class-based contestation over the terms and production of black art. The aesthetic theories, produced by such writers and intellectuals as James Weldon Johnson (Introduction to the *Book of American Negro Poetry*), Alain Locke ("The New Negro"),

Langston Hughes ("The Negro Artist and the Racial Mountain"), W. E. B. Du Bois ("Criteria of Negro Art" and "The Negro in Art: How Shall He Be Portrayed?"), Jessie Fauset (reviews in *The Crisis*), and Zora Neale Hurston ("What White Publishers Won't Print") are all essential readings. None of these attempts to articulate the terms of an emerging "black art" can be divorced from a discussion of the production and consumption of the texts, especially the system of white patronage during the period, which necessarily affected and at times constrained artistic freedom.

Significant Form, Style, or Artistic Conventions

The most obvious tradition in which to situate Larsen's novels must be the novel-of-passing, which problematized questions of race. Deemphasizing "biology," the novel-of-passing provided convenient ways to explore race as a construct of history, culture, and white supremacist ideology. Equally important is the tradition of the novel of manners, as well as the romance.

Original Audience

I note the fact that the audience for Nella Larsen's writings, as for all black writers during the Harlem Renaissance, was primarily white, though a small group of black middle-class intellectuals read them as well.

Comparisons, Contrasts, Connections

Jesssie Fauset's "Plum Bun & Comedy, American Style"
James Weldon Johnson's *The Autobiography of an Ex-colored Man*
Charles Chesnutt's *The House Behind the Cedars*
Edith Wharton's *The House of Mirth*

Questions for Reading and Discussion/ Approaches to Writing

1. The metaphor of passing accrues several layers of meaning. What are they? How do they relate to each other?
2. Whose story is this? Clare's or Irene's?

3. What does this passage mean: "[Irene] was caught between two allegiances, different, yet the same. Herself. Her race. Race: The thing that bound and suffocated her. Whatever steps she took, or if she took none at all, something would be crushed. A person or the race. Clare, herself, or the race. Or, it might be all three."
4. It has been suggested that *Passing* uses race more as a device to sustain suspense than as a compelling social issue. What is the relation of race to subjective experience in the text?
5. What is the significance of narrative endings in Larsen? Why does *Passing* refuse to specify how Clare is killed and who is responsible?

Bibliography

Carby, Hazel. "The Quicksands of Representation." In *Reconstructing Womanhood*. New York: Oxford Univ. Press.

Christian, Barbara. *Black Women Novelists*. Westport, Conn.: Greenwood Press, 1980.

Huggins, Nathan. *Harlem Renaissance*. New York: Oxford Univ. Press.

——. *Voices of the Harlem Renaissance*.

Lewis, David Levering. *When Harlem Was in Vogue*.

McDowell, Deborah E. "The 'Nameless, Shameful Impulse': Sexuality in Nella Larsen's *Quicksand* and *Passing*." In *Studies in Black American Literature*, Volume III, edited by Joe Weixlmann and Houston A. Baker, Jr. Greenwood, Fl.: Penkeville Publishing, 1988.

Tate, Claudia "Nella Larsen's *Passing*: A Problem of Interpretation." *Black American Literature Forum* 14 (Winter 1980).

Wall, Cheryl. "Passing for What? Aspects of Identity in Nella Larsen's Novels." *Black American Literature Forum* 20 (Spring/Summer 1986).

Washington, Mary Helen. "The Mulatta Trap: Nella Larsen's Women of the 1920s." In *Invented Lives*. New York: Anchor/Doubleday, 1987.

Youman, Mary Mabel. "Nella Larsen's *Passing*: A Study in Irony." *College Language Association Journal* 18 (1974).

Blues Lyrics

Conributing Editor: Steven C. Tracy [p. 1581]

Classroom Issues and Strategies

Many students will be totally unfamiliar with the blues tradition and will therefore benefit greatly from the playing of blues recordings in class in conjunction with the selections from blues lyrics printed in the text. In fact, playing these blues selections in class will help introduce the important point that the blues is an oral, not a written, tradition. Asking the students to write down what they hear on the recordings played brings up not only the problems that scholars have deciphering texts but also the issue of how one should render an oral production on the printed page.

Students should be encouraged to respond to the voices of the lyrics. Are they voices of resignation and defeat, of hope and transcendence, of strength and pride, or of some mixture of all of these? What is it that has given the blues their staying power? And what is it that writers like Langston Hughes, Sterling Brown, Al Young, Alice Walker, Shirley Anne Williams, and Allen Ginsberg see in them that makes these writers draw on them for their own writing? Certainly comparing these blues lyrics to various blues poems will help clarify authors' differing attitudes about the blues.

Religious and sexual themes are generally the most controversial. Students question the image of women in the blues and wonder whether the blues singer is weak and self-pitying or strong and self-sufficient. The Furry Lewis lyric is often seen as being bizarre and sick: a good starting point for a discussion of the place of humor in the blues.

Major Themes, Historical Perspectives, and Personal Issues

A number of important subjects are covered in these selections, including love, hate, sex, violence, hope, superstition, religion, and protest, indicating that the blues in fact deal with a range of subjects in a variety of ways. When blues are performed, they often provoke laughter from an audience that identifies with the experience being describe or that appreciates the novel way the experience is described. There are a number of humorous verses here that could be compared for the way they achieve their effects, from Bracey's hyperbole to Carter's prurience to Cox's unexpected assertiveness to the startling images of Wheatstraw and Lewis. Such a discussion would emphasize the idea that the blues, though often discussing sadness and hardships, contain a pretty fair amount of humor. Ellison includes a good discussion of this subject in *Shadow and Act*, as does Garon in *Blues and the Poetic Spirit* (pp. 77–87).

Significant Form, Style, or Artistic Conventions

An advantage to playing the songs for the students is that it allows them to hear how the various stanza structures are fit into the music. For instance, the lyrics of Childers and Wheatstraw are both sung to eight-bar musical stanzas, but the lyric patterns are different. Students can discuss the advantages of one stanza over the other. The selection from "John Henry" is a ten-bar blues ballad, presenting in narrative form the story of the folk-hero whose strength and perseverance in the face of incredible odds is a paradigm for the African-American experience (see Sterling Brown's "Strange Legacies"). The selection from Margaret Carter is from a sixteen-bar vaudeville blues especially, but present in other kinds of blues as well. The rest of the examples included come from twelve-bar blues, but certainly the examples from Jefferson, Bracey, Cox, Robert Johnson, and Holmes are sufficiently different to indicate the possibility of diverse phrasing in the blues, even within what is sometimes considered to be a rather restrictive form.

We can also see in "Got the Blues" the presence of several stock phrases—lines or parts of lines that turn up regularly in blues that are similar to but not the same as the formulaic lines discussed by Parry and Lord. Students might be encouraged to take the first line of stanza two or six and generate an individual rhyme line that completes the thought in some kind of personal manner as a way of helping them understand how tradition has an effect on the individual blues singer.

Comparisons, Contrasts, Connections

The only blues lyric quoted in its entirety here is Blind Lemon Jefferson's "God the Blues," interesting because, rather than developing a single theme, it progresses through associative linkages and contrasts. While some early commentary argued that the blues were often incoherent, more recently texts have been discussed as nonthematic, partially thematic, or thematic, and the presence of such associative linkages and contrasts is important to see and recognize as a textual strategy rather than an example of textual incoherence. Again, students can be encouraged to discern the associations among lines and stanzas the way they might be asked to do for poetry by Pound, Eliot, or Lowell.

Questions for Reading and Discussion/ Approaches to Writing

1. Have students listen to recordings by Langston Hughes, Sterling Brown, Zora Neale Hurston, Ishmael Reed, Michael Harper, Allen Ginsberg, or Jack Kerouac that have musical accompaniment (or are sung performances, in Hurston and Ginsberg) and discuss how the music affects our response to the words.
2. Have students write a blues song and discuss their rationale for choice of stanza form, themes, images, diction, and voice, establishing clearly the relation of their song to the tradition.
3. Have students survey the various methods of transcribing blues lyrics and defend one method as superior to the others.
4. Have students pick a theme developed in a blues-influenced poem by an author like Langston Hughes and search out blues lyrics that deal with a similar theme to see how the literary artist revises the traditional treatment of the theme.

Bibliography

Interviews with blues performers are included in:

Oliver, Paul. *Conversation With the Blues.* New York: Horizon Press, 1965.

Pearson, Barry Lee. *Sounds So Good to Me.* Philadelphia: University of Pennsylvania Press, 1984.

For explanations of unfamiliar words, phrases, and places in blues lyrics see:

Gold, Robert. *Jazz Talk.* New York: Da Capo Press, 1982.

Townley, Eric. *Tell Your Story.* Chigwell, Essex: Storyville, 1976.

Other valuable discussions of blues include:

Ellison, Ralph. *Shadow and Act.* New York: Random House, 1964.

Evans, David. *Big Road Blues.* Berkeley: Univ. of California Press, 1982.

Garon, Paul. *Blues and the Poetic Spirit.* London: Eddison Press, 1975.

Harris, Sheldon. *Blues Who's Who.* New Rochelle, N.Y.: Arlington House, 1975.

Jahn, Jahnheiz. *A History of Neo-African Literature.* New York: Grove Press, 1968.

——. *Muntu: An Outline of the New African Culture.* London: Faber and Faber, 1961.

Jones, Leroi. *Blues People.* New York: Wm. Morrow, 1963.

Oliver, Paul. *The Blues Tradition.* New York: Oak Publications, 1970.

——. *The Meaning of the Blues.* 1960. Reprint. New York: Collier Books, 1972.

——. *Savannah Syncopators: African Retentions in the Blues.* Kibsibm Studio Vista, 1970.

——. *The Story of the Blues.* Philadelphia: Chilton Books, 1973.

Titon, Jeff Todd. *Early Downhome Blues.* Urbana: Univ. of Illinois Press, 1978.

For discussions of the importance of the blues to African-American literature see:

Baker, Houston A., Jr. *Blues, Ideology, and Afro-American Literature.* Chicago: Univ. of Chicago Press, 1984.

Tracy, Steven C. *Langston Hughes and the Blues.*

Williams, Shirley A. "The Blues Roots of Contemporary Afro-American Poetry." In *Chant of Saints*, edited by Michael Harper and Robert Stepto. Chicago: Univ. of Chicago Press, 1979.

Issues and Visions in Modern America

[p. 1587]

John Dos Passos (1896–1970)

Contributing Editor: Robert Rosen [p. 1588]

Classroom Issues and Strategies

The biggest problem will probably be students' lack of historical knowledge. The biographies of *U.S.A.* are slices of history; their broader contexts are alluded to but not spelled out. To appreciate fully the nuances of Dos Passos's language, the significance of his descriptive details, and the force of his sarcasm, a reader needs to know a lot of history.

The teacher probably needs to do some explaining, though he or she should avoid explaining the biographies to death. To appreciate "The Body of An American," students should know something about World War I, which Dos Passos saw and many of his original readers remembered. They should understand such things as the unprecedented carnage of that war (10 million killed and 20 million wounded); the particular brutality of trench warfare; the deeper causes of the war (and of U.S. entrance into the war) that lay behind the noble rhetoric; and the irony of racism at home (alluded to in "The Body of an American") and repression of domestic dissent during and after a war fought, Wilson told Congress, because "the world must be made safe for democracy." "The Bitter Drink" is more difficult than "The Body of an American" because its historical sweep is greater. Perhaps assigning (or even reading aloud) a brief sample of Veblen's writing would help; it would at least give students a sense of his approach and style. (See, for example, the title excerpt "The Captain of Industry" in *The Portable Veblen*, edited by Max Lerner; the last paragraph alone might suffice.)

Major Themes, Historical Perspectives, and Personal Issues

"The Body of an American" is about the waste of war and the public and official cant that surrounds it. These issues should be of interest to students who have friends or relatives facing military service or who are themselves of draft or enlistment age. "The Bitter Drink" is about what it means to be a serious critic of society, to tell the truth and refuse to say "the essential yes." Students soon to begin careers where they may have to compromise their values should find much to discuss.

Significant Form, Style, or Artistic Conventions

Since the excerpts included in the anthology represent only about one percent of the *U.S.A.* trilogy and only one of its four narrative devices (biographies, Newsreels, conventional narratives, and the Camera Eye), teaching these excerpts is very different from teaching *U.S.A.* Should you find time in the course to read *The 42nd Parallel* or *Nineteen Nineteen* or *The Big Money*, you might discuss with students the relationships among the four narrative devices as well as questions about the nature of fiction and the nature of written history raised by Dos Passos's mixing of real historical figures and fictional characters. If students are reading only "The Body of an American" and/or "The Bitter Drink," you might ask them what role they think such "nonfiction" biography might play in a novel. With "The Body of an American," you might also ask about the effect of Dos Passos's running the opening words together, of his juxtapositions of different kinds of language, and of his Whitmanesque listmaking. With "The Bitter Drink," you might discuss how Dos Passos goes about communicating his own attitudes while narrating the life of Veblen.

Original Audience

Though the two excerpts in the text are brief, they should suffice to suggest the radicalism of *U.S.A.* To students surprised by it, you might explain that such views were not so uncommon during the 1930s (though, for Dos Passos, they came even earlier). At the height of the Depression, with no unemployment insurance and meager public relief, over one in four U.S. citizens had no job, and millions more suffered wage cuts and underemployment. People lost all their money in bank failures; families were forced out of their homes and apartments; many went hungry while milk was dumped into rivers and crops were burned to keep up prices. The economic system seemed irrational, and millions marched in protest, fought evictions, joined unions. This was the context of *U.S.A.* for its original readers.

Comparisons, Contrasts, Connections

Almost any other work of fiction from the 1930s might usefully be compared with the excerpts from *U.S.A.* Alongside "The Body of an American" you might read Dalton Trumbo's *Johnny Got His Gun* (1939) or, for contrast, the tight-lipped antiwar fiction in Hemingway's *In Our Time* (1925). For a powerful contemporary comparison, you might look at Vietnam veteran Ron Kovic's *Born on the Fourth of July* (1976).

Questions for Reading and Discussion/ Approaches to Writing

1. With "The Body of an American," you might ask students what kinds of contrasts Dos Passos sets up between the news coverage and political declarations (in smaller print) and the story of John Doe. They'll probably point to such contrasts as the nobility of the rhetoric vs. the ugly actuality of war, the superficiality of the reporting vs. the depth of human suffering, and the impersonality

and abstractness of the public language vs. the personal detail in those lists of possible facts about John Doe and in the many biographical particulars that suggest all that went into making the adult human being whose unidentifiable remains are being buried.

2. With "The Bitter Drink," you might ask what Dos Passos means by Veblen's "constitutional inability to say yes" and why Dos Passos makes this "essential yes" a refrain. Veblen's ideas are as much implied as spelled out, and you might ask students to summarize as much of them as they can infer from the biography. You might also ask them to draw connections between those ideas and Veblen's life. Dos Passos sets this life very firmly in its historical context, and students might discuss the whole sweep of history brought to life in the biography and what patterns and recurring themes they see. Students might also speculate on whether there is too much of the apology in Dos Passos's description of his hero's "woman trouble."

Michael Gold (1893–1967)

Contributing Editor: Barry Gross [p. 1599]

Classroom Issues and Strategies

Because Gold's intentions are didactic, he says what he has to say very directly and his language is very plain. Since he does not deal with any complex or difficult concepts or ideas, his work is immediately accessible to students.

It's useful to provide some statistics for background. For instance, the population density on the Lower East Side, the mortality rate for infants, incidence of tuberculosis and other infectious diseases, etc. It would also be helpful to show pictures, tapes, movies depicting life on the Lower East Side, although there has been a tendency to sentimentalize that life, to make it something to feel nostalgia for, and, hence, it's gotten prettified.

Major Themes, Historical Perspectives, and Personal Issues

The warpings of poverty. The malign effects of unmediated capitalism. The peculiarly American mix and juxtaposition of races, groups, minori-

502 • *The Heath Anthology of American Literature*

ties. The nature of a slum (a slum seems to be a slum regardless of who inhabits it). The threats to the traditional patriarchal structure of family and culture that American ghetto life posed. The role of the mother. The threats to traditional Jewish culture that America posed.

Significant Form, Style, or Artistic Conventions

Note the combination of a journalistic style characterized by short sentences, monosyllabic words, a kind of reportage we think of as Hemingwayesque, and the occasional sketches of sentimentality, exhortation, lament.

Original Audience

To the extent that *Jews Without Money* is written by a member of the Communist Party who called for the overthrow of capitalism, it is very important to locate it in 1930. To the extent that it is a sentimental and intellectual and artistic autobiography, it is not so important to locate it. To the extent that it's a book about being Jewish, some historical placement is necessary. (There will be students, even Jewish students, who will think that "Jews without money" is an oxymoron.)

Comparisons, Contrasts, Connections

The Bread Givers by Anzia Yezierska, *Call It Sleep* by Henry Roth, *Yekl* by Abraham Cahan, *The World of Our Fathers* by Irving Howe, *The Rise of David Levinsky* by Abraham Cahan, *What Makes Sammy Run?* by Budd Schulberg are the most famous of many works that deal with Jewish immigrant life on the Lower East Side. It would also be useful/ interesting to compare and contrast with works by and about other immigrant groups, other minorities, other slum dwellers.

Bibliography

There is much available on the Lower East Side (*World of Our Fathers, The Golden Door,* et al.); the Anti-Defamation League of B'nai B'rith (chapters in all large cities) will usually provide bibliographies, secondary materials, source materials, study guides for educational purposes.

George Samuel Schuyler (1895–1977)

Contributing Editor: Michael W. Peplow [p. 1610]

Classroom Issues and Strategies

Satire, especially the harsher Juvenalian mode, upsets students, who see it as too negative. And when satire deals with an emotional issue such as racial prejudice, it becomes even more controversial. Some students find Schuyler's satire offensive. In addition—though it has universal overtones—"Our Greatest Gift to America" is still a 1920s period piece. Some of the issues and language pose problems for modern students.

I make sure my students have a working definition of satire and, as we read the essay, I discuss the satiric devices Schuyler employs. Once we have finished reading the essay, I ask students to discuss *why* Schuyler chose satire and whether his approach was effective. The more background the students have in Juvenal, Swift, Twain, Ambrose Bierce, and H. L. Mencken (Schuyler's mentor and friend), the better the essay works in class.

I also make sure my students read some "straight" essays that address the racial situation in the 1920s. Articles from the NAACP's *Crisis* are helpful, especially those by its editor, W. E. B. Du Bois (see Daniel Walden, ed., *W. E. B. Du Bois: The Crisis Writings* [Greenwich, Conn.: Fawcett, 1972]). The more exposure students have had to African-American and other minority literatures, the more they will appreciate Schuyler. I give students notes on the Harlem (or New Negro) Renaissance and read passages from Alain Locke's "The New Negro." I tell students about KKK activities and lynchings in the 1920s. I show them copies of *The Pittsburgh Courier*, a leading black newspaper for which Schuyler worked, that featured essays on race pride but included advertisements for skin lighteners and hair straighteners. For the teacher who does not have access to these materials, a valuable resource tool is *The Chronological History of the Negro in America*.

Students sometimes say the essay is too depressing, that Schuyler exaggerates and distorts the way things really were. They feel Schuyler so denigrates blacks that he must have been disgusted with his own people and secretly desired to be white himself. Finally, students say the essay is not relevant because people just aren't prejudiced any longer. Prejudice is not a comfortable thing to admit or discuss in class. It's easier to laugh a bit nervously and go on to the next essay. But questions about present-day prejudices lead to often-dramatic discussions: fraternities or athletes on campus; a racial or religious or national group

(Iranians, for example); AIDS victims and welfare recipients and street people—the list goes on.

Major Themes, Historical Perspectives, and Personal Issues

The historical issues include American racism, the Harlem Renaissance vogue, the tendency of some black publications to preach race pride and at the same time publish skin lightening and hair straightening advertisements, the tendency of some black leaders to profit from American racism, and the all too prevalent belief among whites—and blacks—that "white is right." (You might remind students of an old black saying: "If you're white, you're all right. If you're brown, stick around. If you're black, get back.")

The personal issues include Schuyler's own encounters with racism in the army and during his journalistic tours, his courtship of and eventual marriage to a white woman, and his lifelong belief that America's "colorphobia" was so absurd it merited scathing ridicule.

Significant Form, Style, or Artistic Conventions

1. What literary conventions does Schuyler employ in his satire?
   The purpose of satire is to mock or ridicule human follies or vices. Horatian satire tends to be light, often comic, the assumption being that humans are more foolish than sinful and that they are capable of reformation. Juvenalian satire—Schuyler's mode—is harsh and slashing, the assumption being that humans are so corrupted they are beyond reformation. In an early newspaper column Schuyler wrote that his dominant motive was malice and that his intent was "to slur, lampoon, damn, and occasionally praise anybody or anything in the known universe, not excepting the President of the Immortals." In his long career he rarely praised but did much damning, so much so that he was accused in a *Crisis* editorial in 1965 of being the incurable iconoclast who "dips his pen in his ever-handy [well] of acid."
   In "Our Greatest Gift" Schuyler creates a satiric persona much as his role model Swift did in "A Modest Proposal" and *Gulliver's Travels* (note the reference to "Brobdingnagian"). Schuyler's persona seems to be an intelligent but "plain folks" black man, literate and unafraid to speak the truth. He despises the inner circle of black intellectuals elsewhere for their willingness to capitalize on racial tension and their secret belief that "white is right." He also

despises redneck whites who believe a white skin makes them special. Both groups he sets out to shock; he even uses a number of current racial slurs. By the end of the essay, the persona seems to have become so disgusted with America's "colorphobia" that he sounds like the compleat misanthrope who despairs of ever converting America to rational behavior.

Another technique Schuyler the satirist employs is irony—saying or implying the opposite of what one really believes. Throughout the essay—from the words "greatest gift" in the title, through references to "this enlightened nation" and "our incomparable civilization," to the devastating final paragraph—Schuyler is savagely ironic.

A third technique Schuyler employs is exaggeration. Whether describing black poets, race leaders, or whites, Schuyler's portraits deliberately overstate. His character sketches of three "noble rednecks"—Isadore Shankersoff, Cyrus Leviticus Dumbbell, and Dorothy Dunce—are vintage Schuyler and anticipate his much more extended character sketches in *Black No More*.

2. What literary school does Schuyler belong to?

Schuyler, noted the 1965 *Crisis* editorial, was "a veteran dissenter and incurable iconoclast," one of that "select breed of moral crusaders and apparent social misfits who, as journalists, delighted in breaking the idols of the tribe." He is a direct descendent of Ambrose Bierce, the "caustic columnist" from San Francisco and author of "The Devil's Dictionary" and *The Satanic Reader*, of Brann the Iconoclast, of H. L. Mencken, the founder and editor of *The American Mercury*. He also worked side by side with important 1920s black iconoclasts: Chandler Owen and A. Philip Randolph, Theophilus Lewis and Wallace Thurman, W. E. B. Du Bois and Rudolph Fisher—each of whom was capable of idol-smashing but not on the sustained level that Schuyler was. On an even larger scale, Schuyler, as noted before, was a satirist in the tradition of Juvenal, Swift, and Twain, all of whom he studied and admired.

Original Audience

1. Schuyler's audience was primarily black—the essay appeared in a black publication that was read by the very racial leaders Schuyler lampoons in the first part of his essay. If any whites read it at the time, they would have been those who, in typical Harlem Renaissance fashion, became obsessed with exotic and primitive blacks (see Rudolph Fisher, "The Caucasian Storms Harlem," in Huggins's *Voices from the Harlem Renaissance*; for a good example of

white fascination with blacks, see Carl Van Vechten's melodramatic *Nigger Heaven*).

2. As suggested earlier, today's audience will have difficulty relating to "Our Greatest Gift." White students usually insist that the essay is dated because there are no more lynchings or overt acts of prejudice. Black students are sometimes offended by the racial epithets and the glancing attacks on black leaders. The teacher who wishes to challenge contemporary smugness can have a field day: Is white racism really dead? Do black or other leaders ever capitalize on racial tension? Is there still a "white is right" mentality in America?

Comparisons, Contrasts, Connections

There is no one author to whom Schuyler compares well, though he uses the same satiric devices that Juvenal, Swift, and Twain employ and the same iconoclastic manner that characterized Bierce, Brann, Mencken, Fisher, Lewis, and Thurman.

Questions for Reading and Discussion/ Approaches to Writing

1. (a) Schuyler attacks two groups of people in his essay. Who are they? Is he even-handed in his double attack?

   (b) What is the satire? Distinguish between Juvenalian and Horation satire and decide which mode Schuyler preferred.

   (c) What was the Harlem Renaissance?

2. (a) Have half the class (include the more creative writers) write a satire attacking a controversial issue à la Schuyler. Use a persona, employ irony, and develop two or three exaggerated character sketches. Have the rest of the class write reasoned essays on the same issue. Have the class discuss the best essays from both groups and determine which type of approach—satire or reasoned essay—is more effective, and why.

   (b) Write a response to Schuyler's article assuming the persona of a white racist or a black nationalist in Schuyler's own time.

   (c) First discuss in class and then write an essay on the following: A Modern Response to Schuyler's "Our Greatest Gift to America."

Albert Maltz (1908–1985)

Contributing Editor: Gabriel Miller [p. 1616]

Classroom Issues and Strategies

There are no major problems with teaching Maltz. It is useful, however, for the students to have some historical/social background, particularly concerning the Depression, the rise of radicalism, and its various configurations (why so many writers and intellectuals were attracted to Marxism, Socialism, etc.). Many of Maltz's novels are also grounded in historical events (*The Underground Stream*, *The Cross and the Arrow*, and *A Tale of One January*). You might provide background lectures and readings on the history of the thirties ("Happiest Man on Earth"). For other Maltz pieces, knowledge of radicalism, the radical literary wars, HUAC and the blacklist would be very helpful. Concerning HUAC (House Un-American Activities Committee), many students will be interested in the blacklist, fronts, and the Hollywood Ten (Maltz was part of this group).

Major Themes, Historical Perspectives, and Personal Issues

1. The Depression and displacement and disenfranchisement of the individual.
2. The totalitarian environment and the individual.
3. The ideal of the democratic individual.
4. The individual alone in nature and with the self.

Significant Form, Style, or Artistic Conventions

Discuss the "proletarian novel," the relationship of art and politics, the conventions of realism. Questions of what constitutes a political or radical novel would also be stimulating and useful.

Original Audience

The audience at least in the beginning was the "initiated": radicals who were sympathetic to Maltz's ideas. However, Maltz was always reaching out to a wider audience and would come to reject the restraints of didactic art.

Comparisons, Contrasts, Connections

More well-known writers whose work can be read along with Maltz are Richard Wright, *Native Son* (emphasis on the emerging radical consciousness, questions of class), John Steinbeck, *Grapes of Wrath* (Americans on the road, communal vs. individual) and *In Dubious Battle* (political novel), James Farrell, the Studs Lonigan trilogy (realism, environment, politics); also Jack London and some of Whitman's poems, particularly those emphasizing the ideal of the democratic man.

Questions for Reading and Discussion/ Approaches to Writing

1. I have never taught Maltz but I think questions regarding the effectiveness of presenting character and the characters' relationship to the overriding issues of the story would be productive.
2. Discuss how successfully Maltz integrates didactic aims with "art." Is Maltz's best work at odds with its didactic intent? How does Maltz's work effectively convey the central issues of his time?

Bibliography

Maltz's essays in *The Citizen Writer*; his *New Masses* essay "What Shall We Ask of Writers?" (1946) in which he takes the notion of didactic art to task and for which he was harshly criticized.

Lillian Hellman (1905–1984)

Contributing Editor: Vivian Patraka [p. 1624]

Major Themes, Historical Perspectives, and Personal Issues

What is Hellman's idea of history? Who makes history and how are events in history related? Why does she connect the events of the McCarthy Era to the Vietnam War? What is her conception of the average American's understanding of history? How is this related to the "deep contempt for public intelligence" Hellman ascribes to Nixon? Why does Hellman reserve her strongest sense of betrayal for the intellectuals who did not protest the events of the McCarthy Era? What assumptions about intellectuals did Hellman have to abandon? What qualities does she ascribe to the McCarthyites and their proceedings that should have made them the "hereditary enemies" of intellectuals?

Significant Form, Style, or Artistic Conventions

What kind of credibility does an autobiographical memoir have as compared to a history or a political science book? How convincing is Hellman in establishing her point of view about the McCarthy Era? Is she less convincing because the work identifies itself as someone's opinion? Because she is angry? How does a question like "Since when do you have to agree with people to defend them from injustice?" or a statement like "Truth made you a traitor as it often does in a time of scoundrels" make Hellman's work both persuasive and memorable? Why does Hellman use the word scoundrel and what does she mean by it?

Elsewhere, Hellman has said that in a time of scoundrels, "The pious words come out because you know the pious words are good salesmanship." The idea that the language of morality, of patriotism, and of religion can be manipulated in an entrepreneurial way to capitalize on people's fears applies to more than just the fifties. Are there any examples from contemporary times of this sort of manipulation? Who benefits from it and why? Who is harmed?

Why would Hellman use the phrase "black comedy" to describe activities she considered to be harmful and evil? Why doesn't she call them a tragedy, given that many people's lives were ruined? Elsewhere she says, "One is torn between laughter and tears. It's so truly comic. People were confessing to sins they'd never done; making up lies of meetings they'd been in when they'd been in no such meeting; asking God and the Committee's pardon for nothing but just going into a room and listening to some rather dull talk. . . . And that, to me was the saddest and the most disgusting, as well as most comic. The effect was of a certain section of the country going crazy." What would motivate people to "confess" and "name names" in this manner?

Comparisons, Contrasts, Connections

Hellman has spoken of "the right of each man to his own convictions." Where is the line between having a conviction and being subversive or dangerous and who is allowed to interpret that for us? In what direction is that line currently moving? Playwright Arthur Miller, writing about the McCarthy Era, said "With the tiniest Communist Party in the world, the United States was behaving as though on the verge of a bloody revolution." Who would profit from creating this impression? What kinds of acts can be justified once this impression is created?

Clifford Odets (1906–1963)

Contributing Editor: Michael J. Mendelsohn [p. 1629]

Classroom Issues and Strategies

Instructors need to establish the context—the era of the Great Depression. If Odets occasionally seems dated, he is less so for those who put this play into its 1930s milieu. Consider having student reports or general class discussion on major concerns in the U.S. in the mid-1930s. With some understanding of the Depression decade, it may be less difficult for students to believe that this militant young dramatist was able to present such a play to sympathetic, even enthusiastic audiences.

Major Themes, Historical Perspectives, and Personal Issues

Playwright Odets clearly believed in 1935 that through union solidarity the little man might find a way out of the despair of America's economic and social ills. For many, American society was not fulfilling its true promise; in the big novel of the thirties, *The Grapes of Wrath*, Steinbeck asserted much the same theme. With only a touch of hyperbole, Harold Clurman called *Waiting for Lefty* "the birth of the thirties."

Significant Form, Style, or Artistic Conventions

Techniques of speaking across the proscenium, a scenery-less stage, and planting actors in the audience give instructors plenty to work with. For instructors interested in theatrical links and analogues, Pirandello or Wilder would be appropriate points of departure.

Original Audience

Audience for this work is especially important. It was intended for presentation in union halls before small, typically preconvinced audiences. It is obviously strident, intended to make a militant emotional appeal. Unlike much of our theatre today, it was not intended merely to entertain or inform. Politically, Odets was going through the same sort of youthful flirtation with communism that marked the careers of many of his 1930s contemporaries. Without this sort of context, the play comes off as merely a strident little piece of propaganda.

Comparisons, Contrasts, Connections

Compare with Steinbeck's *The Grapes of Wrath* (1939).

Examine Pirandello or Wilder for some comparison of theatrical techniques of crossing the proscenium and merging actors with audiences.

Questions for Reading and Discussion/ Approaches to Writing

1. What is the unifying plot for all these episodes?
2. Is this play universal, or is it too tied to place (New York) and to time (The Great Depression of the 1930s)?
3. Is the message too blatant? Is the language too strident? Is Odets more a "revolutionary" or "reformer" if you compare, for example, Steinbeck's *The Grapes of Wrath*, a product of the same decade?
4. Which scenes have the greatest impact, and why?
5. Odets has often been praised for his use of vivid, colorful language. Which speeches work well for you? Which are less successful?
6. How successful is the playwright in crossing the proscenium and breaking down the traditional separation between audience and action? Why does he use this technique?

Bibliography

Brenman-Gibson, Margaret. *Clifford Odets*. Boston: Atheneum, 1981, 299–306.

Clurman, Harold. *The Fervent Years*. New York: Hill and Wang, 1957, 138–42.

Mendelsohn, Michael. *Clifford Odets*. New York: Everett/Edwards, 1969, 21–6.

Murray, Edward. *Clifford Odets*. New York: Frederick Ungar, 1968. Ch. 1.

Weales, Gerald. *Clifford Odets*. Indianapolis: Pegasus, 1971. Ch. 3.

Meridel LeSueur (b. 1900)

Contributing Editor: Elaine Hedges [p. 1648]

Classroom Issues and Strategies

To read "Women on the Breadlines," students need to know about the Depression of the 1930s; presumably this piece of writing will be read in that context. Especially important is that our popular notion of the Depression includes images mainly of *men* standing in breadlines or selling apples! But women, who also suffered unemployment or were abandoned by husbands seeking work elsewhere, were also affected. LeSueur was one of the few writers to attend to the situation of women in the Depression. On the whole the piece is very readable and should not present difficulties.

Women students respond very positively to "Annunciation"—to its style and its discussion of the feelings of a woman during pregnancy. I haven't taught it to male students. It would be interesting to ask them if they can identify with any of the experiences or feelings in the story, and whether they think these are important experiences and feelings. (Stories about pregnancy and childbirth are rare in our literature. Women readers are expected to identify with male stories/myths: hunting whales, going to war. Can male readers learn to identify with female experiences?)

Major Themes, Historical Perspectives, and Personal Issues

The major historical issue in "Women on the Breadlines" is the Depression. Instructor might want to ask why women have tended to be ignored in accounts of it.

The theme of the relation of human beings to nature, of human life cycle to the natural life cycle, is important in the conception and development of the story "Annunciation."

Historically, the story was written during the Depression of the 1930s, and the hope and qualified optimism in the story are set against that background of poverty and uncertainty. Does this work to make the life/nature theme more powerful?

Significant Form, Style, or Artistic Conventions

"Women on the Breadlines" is a piece of journalism. Is it also "literature"? The style is one of deliberately short, simple sentences. This suggests "objective" reporting or emphasis on fact, but is it a deliberate literary style? Is it appropriate to the way of life and the feelings of the women being described? Note also that LeSueur employs imagery in this (deceptively) simple style: e.g., a scrub woman with hands "like watersoaked branches." Can students find other effective uses of figurative language?

Is this kind of personal journalism, which was cultivated in the thirties, similar to any today?

Also examine the structure of the piece. Does it develop like a short story? What are the differences between journalistic feature stories and literary short stories?

What is the effect of the first-person point of view?

In "Annunciation" the language and imagery through which the woman in the story increasingly associates herself with nature, culminating in the vision of the pear tree, are significant.

Is she a believable first-person narrator? What does she think it important to reveal about herself?

Original Audience

Students may have to read "Annunciation" carefully, or be told something about the Depression, in order to appreciate the poverty-stricken background and the loneliness of the woman. A contemporary audience would have picked up on these immediately.

Comparisons, Contrasts, Connections

Compare to Steinbeck's *Grapes of Wrath*. How does LeSueur present her male and female characters as contrasted to Steinbeck's presentation of men and women?

Bibliography

Hedges, Elaine, ed. *Ripening: Selected Work, 1927–1980 of Meridel LeSueur*. New York: Feminist Press, 1982. See the Introduction.

Thomas S. Whitecloud (Chippewa) (1914–1972)

Contributing Editor: Daniel F. Littlefield, Jr. [p. 1662]

Classroom Issues and Strategies

Present "Blue Winds Dancing" as you would any well-written essay.

The social implication of being Indian in an Anglo-dominated society gets lost for students in the larger issue of simply feeling "at odds" as a result of "gaps"—social, political, generational, etc.

Major Themes, Historical Perspectives, and Personal Issues

1. Self-identify, self-realization
2. Individual caught between two cultures
3. Culture loss and acculturation

Significant Form, Style, or Artistic Conventions

Stress the essay structure (this one is neatly divided; how do the three parts interlock, structurally, thematically?)

Stress the use of rich visual imagery. Which *seem* to be drawn from Indian heritage, which not? Is there any difference in the effects of each?

Original Audience

It fits into the context of the whole scene of social disruption in the Great Depression, heightened in this case by the sense of being kicked loose, out of touch with two cultures.

For contemporary readers, it speaks to the large theme of searching out roots, self-realization.

Comparisons, Contrasts, Connections

For earlier generations of Indian writers who deal with the theme of being caught between cultures, see Copway and Apes, Eastman and Bonnin. For later writers, see Welch and Erdrich.

Further Explorations of an "American" Self

[p. 1668]

Robert Penn Warren (1905–1989)

Contributing Editor: Robert H. Brinkmeyer, Jr. [p. 1669]

Classroom Issues and Strategies

I don't think teachers will encounter any serious problems. Warren is a very accessible poet, with a strong sense of narrative and a nonintimidating diction, both of which students generally enjoy.

Warren's great concern with the historical vision and the meanings found in memory and the past are distinctly southern. For students with no background in southern literature, these interests may seem forced, even bizarre in their intensity. A general overview of some of the major themes of twentieth-century southern literature would help put Warren into perspective.

The poetry speaks for itself, but I do think, as I have said, that discussing Warren's "southernness" is an effective way to begin a discussion of him. One might go from there into a discussion of which poems clearly evoke a southern perspective and which don't—and then, why and why not, which are more effective, etc.

Students generally respond well to Warren's poetry, particularly to that in which the persona struggles with problems of identify and meaning. The poetry selected here is quite varied, so questions arise about continuities/discontinuities in terms of subject matter and poetic vision between the poems, and about the different stanza forms and the lines employed by the poet. Warren's depiction of the natural world—the hawk, for instance—is quite striking, and students like to discuss this aspect of his work.

Major Themes, Historical Perspectives, and Personal Issues

1. The self in the world, particularly one's relationship with nature.
2. The meaning and significance of history.

3. The limits of the creative imagination and human knowledge.
4. The quest for meaning in continuities and in the assimilation of the self with the world outside it.

Significant Form, Style, or Artistic Conventions

Topics for questions might include: the significance of narrative and the dramatic in Warren's verse; the effectiveness of a diction that frequently tends toward the colloquial; the contrast between Warren's narrative verse ("Amazing Grace in the Back Country") and his poetry of statement ("Fear and Trembling"); the role of the persona; the form of Warren's verse, including stanza and line.

Original Audience

In "Infant Boy at Midcentury" one might discuss what was happening (and had just happened) in the world at midcentury, particularly in light of and in contrast to Warren's traditional upbringing and sympathies.

Comparisons, Contrasts, Connections

Three southern poets with similar interests come to mind: John Crowe Ransom, whose verse is more formal and controlled than Warren's; Allen Tate, who explores in his poetry the tensions arising from problems of history, time, and identity; and James Dickey, whose verse is strongly narrative. In addition, look at any of the confessional poets, but particularly Robert Lowell; a comparison with them is fruitful in trying to establish whether Warren's poetry should be read as confessional.

Bibliography

Section One, "Warren the Poet," in James Justus, *The Achievement of Robert Penn Warren*.

Chapter Two, "His Mature Manner," in Calvin Bedient, *In the Heart's Last Kingdom: Robert Penn Warren's Major Poetry*.

"Introduction: The Critical Reckoning," in Victor Strandberg, *The Poetic Vision of Robert Penn Warren*.

"Sunset Hawk: Warren's Poetry and Tradition," by Harold Bloom in Walter B. Edgar, ed., *A Southern Renascence Man: Views of Robert Penn Warren*.

John Crowe Ransom (1888–1974)

Contributing Editor: Martha E. Cook [p. 1681]

Classroom Issues and Strategies

Students often find the allusive language and the level of diction difficult; sometimes they also seem bored by the subject matter. Also, more experienced students tend to stereotype Ransom as a neo-Confederate and/or to be confused by the lack of "southern" subjects.

Focusing on Ransom's use of language, his wit and irony, seems to be the best route to exploring his themes on a level that students will respond to. Moving from the particular to the universal works even for the poems that seem to be fairly abstract; certainly the theme of "The Equilibrists" is one that students can react to once they have discovered or uncovered it. Using the kind of close analysis practiced by the New Critics is invaluable in studying Ransom's poetry.

Reading Ransom's poetry aloud is a very good strategy, since reading aloud reveals a lot of the liveliness that students sometimes miss on the printed page and also illuminates the ironic tone.

Students seem to be interested in the themes of transience and mutability and in the dichotomy of the body and the soul. They also sometimes get involved with Ransom's work by following up allusions to myths and legends.

Major Themes, Historical Perspectives, and Personal Issues

Themes: tradition, ritual, myth; mutability; the transience of life and love; death; the dichotomy of body and soul.

Historical issues: Ransom's relationship to the Fugitive group and the little magazine, *The Fugitive;* Ransom as a New Critic; the relationship of a classical education to modernism in poetry; the 1920s and reaction to the Great War.

Personal issues: Ransom's life as a teacher and editor; his experience as a Rhodes Scholar and as a soldier in the war; his strong classical education.

Significant Form, Style, or Artistic Conventions

Ransom is so closely related to the metaphysical poets whom he knew so thoroughly that exploring this aspect of his style and form is particularly useful, as is any consideration of his juxtaposition of different levels of diction and his use of surprising words or word forms. He can be seen in the context of the Southern Renaissance of the 1920s or specifically as part of the Fugitive movement, primarily in his concern with tradition and traditional values, though not in his use of southern subjects. As one of the New Critics, his critical theories are important both for their own value and as they provide an avenue into the poetry.

Original Audience

A different approach to Ransom that I have found invaluable is to place him in the context of the outpouring of literature in the 1920s and to relate his experiences in the war to those of Hemingway, Faulkner, Dos Passos, etc., one reason I particularly wanted to include "Crocodile." The Fugitives are often seen as a group unrelated to other writers in the 1920s, but especially Ransom's European experiences can be compared to those of his contemporaries.

Comparisons, Contrasts, Connections

Ransom can be productively compared to other Fugitive poets, especially to Allen Tate in his wit and irony; to metaphysical poets, both early and modern; to the tradition of the elegy; and to other writers who explore the same subject matter, for example, "Philomela" to *The Waste Land*.

Questions for Reading and Discussion/ Approaches to Writing

1. I tell them to be sure to look up the definitions of any unfamiliar words, and I also mention particular works we have already read that might be relevant, such as other poems on death, war, love, etc. Usually Eliot would precede Ransom or immediately follow, so I might warn students to watch for parallels and contrasts.
2. Specifically, students usually do best with Ransom when they focus on his use of language. In general, I find it useful to have students draft their own ideas, using support from the particular work, before they go to outside sources for a historical context or other critics' views.

Bibliography

Morton, Claire Clements. "Ransom's 'The Equilibrists.' " *Explicator* 41 (Summer 1983): 37–8.

Pratt, William. "In Pursuit of the Fugitives." In *The Fugitive Poets*. New York: Dutton, 1965, 13–46.

Rubin, Louis D., Jr. "John Crowe Ransom: The Wary Fugitive." In *The Wary Fugitives: Four Poets and the South*. Baton Rouge: Louisiana State Univ. Press, 1978, 1–63.

Tate, Allen. "Gentleman in a Dustcoat." *Sewanee Review* 76 (Summer 1968): 375–81.

Young, Thomas Daniel. "The Fugitives: Ransom, Davidson, Tate." In *The History of Southern Literature*, edited by Louis D. Rubin, Jr., and others. Baton Rouge: Louisiana State Univ. Press, 1985, 319–32.

Anzia Yezierska (1882?–1970)

Contributing Editor: Sally Ann Drucker [p. 1688]

Classroom Issues and Strategies

Because Yezierska often uses a first-person narrator who speaks with a great deal of emotional intensity, readers sometimes assume that her stories are strictly autobiographical. In addition, her use of Yiddish-English dialect can obscure the fact that she crafted these stories deliberately and carefully. Readers unfamiliar with Yezierska may focus on how these stories relate to episodes in her life, rather than on her vivid characters, rich imagery, and adept use of dialect.

It can be helpful to discuss one of Yezierska's purposes in writing—to immerse the reader in the ghetto experience. (She also wished to explore her own feelings, and to earn a living in the process.) In addition, although most readers come from backgrounds totally different from that of her characters, her stories can be discussed in terms of contemporary problems encountered by new immigrants, ghetto youth, working-class employees, and women.

Photos of Lower East Side tenement scenes or films such as *Hester Street* (based on *Yekl*) are useful to set up a visual context for Yezierska's writing.

Yezierska's most-taught novel is *Bread Givers*. In that book, the patriarchal father represents traditional Jewish ways. Because of the negative aspects of the father-daughter relationship, students who are not familiar with Jewish culture come away with a skewed view of it. Even in Yezierska's other works, what the heroine is giving up in order to become Americanized—family and culture—may not be readily apparent, given the heroine's economic and status gains from the process. These issues can be clarified in class discussion.

Major Themes, Historical Perspectives, and Personal Issues

The processes of acculturation and assimilation, and the positive and negative effects of these processes, are ongoing themes in Yezierska's writing. Her work is particularly interesting for its presentation of immigrant women's pursuit of the American Dream.

Significant Form, Style, or Artistic Conventions

Yezierska's work has been called sentimental and melodramatic. It is important to understand that in the Yiddish language tradition that she came out of, emotionality was expected, particularly for women. Her work fuses aspects of realism (attention to detail) and romanticism (characters' idealism), ultimately making it difficult to categorize.

Original Audience

Yezierska's stories were first published in magazines that had a general readership. She wrote primarily for mainstream Anglo-American audiences of the '20s, although her work was certainly seen by Jewish-Americans and other ethnic readers as well. Contemporary audiences, particularly female readers, respond especially to the immigrant waif characters as women who forged cultural and economic identities by their own strength, energy, and perseverance.

Comparisons, Contrasts, Connections

Other works on immigrant Jewish life:

Yekl, by Abraham Cahan
Jews Without Money, by Michael Gold
Call It Sleep, by Henry Roth
The Promised Land, by Mary Antin

Questions for Reading and Discussion/ Approaches to Writing

1. It can be useful to ask about conflicts described in her writing: in this story, old vs. new, expectations vs. reality, in other stories, Jewish tradition vs. American opportunity, parent vs. child.
2. General: Oral histories—students interview members of their families, focusing on questions of cultural transitions, such as rural vs. urban, one decade vs. another, immigrant conflicts, etc. Papers—on working-class women in early twentieth-century literature, on the Americanization process in literature.
3. Specific: Papers comparing this story with some of Yezierska's others in *Hungry Hearts* or *Children of Loneliness*.

Bibliography

Baum, Charlotte, et al. *The Jewish Woman in America*. New York: Dial Press, 1976. Chapters 3, 4, 5, 91–162.

Drucker, Sally Ann. "Yiddish, Yidgin & Yezierska." *Modern Jewish Studies Annual VI* (1987): 99–113.

Henriksen, Louise Levitas. "Afterword About Anzia Yezierska." In *The Open Cage: An Anzia Yezierska Collection*. New York: Persea Books, 1979, 253–62.

Kessler-Harris, Alice. "Introduction." In *The Open Cage: An Anzia Yezierska Collection*. New York: Persea Books, 1979, v–xiii.

Pratt, Norma Fain. "Culture and Radical Politics: Yiddish Women Writers, 1890-1940." *American Jewish History* 70, no. 1 (Sept. 1980): 68–90.

Yezierska, Anzia. "Mostly About Myself." In *Children of Loneliness*. New York: Funk & Wagnalls, 1923, 9–31.

John Steinbeck (1902–1968)

Contributing Editor: Cliff Lewis [p. 1697]

Classroom Issues and Strategies

Students read Steinbeck as a social critic or merely as a story teller. The task is to define Steinbeck as a writer in the mode of the twenties. One must define such terms as illusion, mythic, archetype, depth psychology, and symbol in establishing his artistic process. Secondly, one must show a student the ongoing conflict in Steinbeck's work between expectation and change, consciousness and altered circumstances.

Students love reading Steinbeck: I cite passages from his letters to indicate his artistic interests in the above ideas. I point out particular details in the works to support my interpretations. In "Flight," I have them look for description of an Indian; I explore similar conflicts and ways of perceiving in our daily lives. For a discussion of "Flight," I ask them to define the stereotypical Indian brave, stereotypical Mexican children, the role of school and education in cultural assimilation.

I offer the view of Steinbeck as a modern artist who sees the artist's role as analogous to a psychiatrist's: to know thyself. If each work is seen as dealing with a different human drive—sexual repression, religious quest, rejection, self-hate, security and certainty of tradition, the need to belong, etc.—Steinbeck's work takes on a pattern. By all means, link such drives to similar ones readily found in students' lives.

Major Themes, Historical Perspectives, and Personal Issues

Themes to emphasize: Indian cultural conflicts; western migration; individualism and social cooperation; evolutionary changes that occurred in religious beliefs; man's evolutionary development and the primeval feelings and attitudes he may have kept and the ways they are manifested; later feelings about his failings as family man, artist, and man of conscience.

Significant Form, Style, or Artistic Conventions

Steinbeck tried to find an organic means of expression for each book that he wrote. He considered his work to be experimental. He intentionally used a documentary style for *Grapes*, the fabular for *The Pearl*, the picaresque for *Tortilla Flat*, and so on. Generally he belongs to the

myth-symbol school of the twenties. Dreams, the unconscious, reoccur-
ring myths, symbolic characters—these qualities are characteristic of
what Jung called the "visionary" style. Realism, Steinbeck once noted, is
the surface form for his interest in psychology and philosophy. To this
Grapes is no exception. I'd add that his work about Indians follows the
outlines of tragedy. Finally point out that Steinbeck's work included film
scripts, plays, and political speeches and war propaganda.

Original Audience

Although Steinbeck's work is rooted in pre-World War II California, he
attempted to write of human impulses that defied any historical
moment. The use of biological allusions, pagan imagery, religious titles,
and his treatment of human drives are meant to be universal. The conflicts of his works are indeed those of our age: economic security,
changes in values, a sense of alienation—see his *Travels*—social changes
beyond our grasp As his subject is change and efforts to deal with it, his
art is timeless.

Comparisons, Contrasts, Connections

For his treatment of the mob psyche and the group, one can find similarities in N. West. Hemingway's cultural changes in Spain, the existential world of his characters, and the industrialization of Faulkner's South
parallel Steinbeck's social dynamics. In all, pastoral worlds disappear.
Both Hawthorne and Faulkner share Steinbeck's recognition of the
power of myth; Hemingway, like Steinbeck, recognizes unfulfilled religious needs. In Hemingway's style Steinbeck found a model for his own.
Yet the classics are also influential: Milton on *In Dubious Battle*, the
Arthurian legends on Indians and his nonconformists, *Winesburg* on the
early short stories, "Everyman" on *The Wayward Bus* among others. And
everywhere are the Bible and *The Golden Bough*.

Questions for Reading and Discussion/ Approaches to Writing

1. To teach "Flight," I would direct students: To define the stereotype of an Indian and to locate supporting details. To locate cultural artifacts Pepe abandons in his regression backward to a primeval state. To ask what are the duties of Pepe's peers and the consequences. To explain the significance of the landscape starting with Pepe's home. To define manhood as Pepe understood it and explain whether his concept changed. To discuss what is pursuing Pepe—an abstraction?

2. Any of the above questions will do. And what is the role of the mother? Or ask questions about illusion, the definition of myth and symbol, the use of biological or animal imagery and its purpose.

Bibliography

See pertinent sections of Jackson Benson's biography. A collection of essays I'm editing on the above issues will soon be published by Edwin Mellen Press. R. Astro's book has good material on Steinbeck and philosophy and science.

Two *Steinbeck Study Guides* edited by T. Hayashi have good general information on Steinbeck's writings. P. Lisca's updated *Wide World of John Steinbeck* remains a valuable study.

Saunders Redding (1906–1988)

Contributing Editor: Eleanor Q. Tignor [p. 1711]

Classroom Issues and Strategies

I have not as yet taught Redding, but I have taught other black American authors who are from the same period, who treat similar themes, or who use a similar form. I do not anticipate any problems in teaching him.

He can be made accessible, as well as universal, on a personal, biological, racial, and historic basis. (*No Day of Triumph*, Chapter One, is clearly a family narrative.)

Major Themes, Historical Perspectives, and Personal Issues

1. The black American's double consciousness—being black and being American; its effect on self-development and on relations with others, black and white.
2. The role of the family (family philosophy and patterns, goals and values) in shaping offspring—the nurturing but also sometimes the hindrances.
3. Slavery and its effects on blacks—on personal development and behavior, on family life in the next generation and generations to come.
4. Slavery and its effects on whites, especially the master/slave "relationship."
5. The tragic mulatto—caught between being black and (not) being white.
6. Intra-racial skin color consciousness and conflict.
7. The educated Negro and the "Negro burden": extraordinary responsibility "to uphold the race"; related theme—being better than whites in order to succeed.
8. The hold of religion on blacks, especially poorer blacks.
9. The black American folk past and its vestiges, especially its effects on blacks of little education.
10. The author as family member and individualist, as man of reason and humanist.

Significant Form, Style, or Artistic Conventions

1. The effects of a text that merges personal and social history.
2. Objectivity versus subjectivity in this highly personal text.
3. Passionate tone and satirical humor.
4. Precise language.
5. Influence of the thinking of W. E. B. Du Bois (see especially *The Souls of Black Folk*); anti-Booker T. Washington philosophy (see Du Bois's *The Souls of Black Folk* and Washington's *Up from Slavery*).
6. Writing as catharsis (see the rest of *No Day of Triumph* and especially *On Being Black in America*).
7. Skill in blending exposition, dialogue, and anecdote in the creation of a highly readable text.
8. Incorporation of black folk materials (songs, tales, prayers).

Original Audience

In 1942, most black Americans and other Americans who knew and were sensitive to the conditions of slavery and the post-slavery years would have had no difficulty with Redding's thesis and tone. The history may need to be sketched in for present-day students; skin color consciousness and the history of the slave and the free black must be understood to get the impact of each of the grandmothers on Redding, the boy.

Comparisons, Contrasts, Connections

1. Du Bois's *Souls of Black Folk* (1903) should be a major comparison. See Du Bois's chapter on Booker T. Washington (III: "Of Mr. Booker T. Washington and Others," in *Souls of Black Folk*) and Washington's *Up from Slavery*.
2. For the theme of being black in America, also highly personal as well as social responses, see for comparison: Richard Wright's "The Ethics of Living Jim Crow" (in Richard Wright's *Uncle Tom's Children*); James Baldwin's "The Discovery of What It Means to Be an American" and "Nobody Knows My Name: A Letter from the South" (both essays in Baldwin's *Nobody Knows My Name*); Maya Angelou's *I Know Why the Caged Bird Sings*.
3. For facts and commentary on slavery, see Redding's *They Came in Chains*, as well as any slave narratives taught in the course.
4. For an understanding of the stereotyping of the mulatto and other black stereotypes in American literature, see Sterling A. Brown's "Negro Character as Seen by White Authors," *Journal of Negro Education*, 2 (1933), reprinted in *Dark Symphony*, ed. James A. Emanuel and Theodore Gross (New York: The Free Press, 1968).
5. For autobiographical comparison/contrast with other black boys who became famous men, see Richard Wright's *Black Boy* and Langston Hughes's *The Big Sea* (Part I, Chapters 2–16).

Questions for Reading and Discussion/ Approaches to Writing

1. State your impressions of the Redding daily household. Support your impressions, explaining how you arrived at them.
2. State and explain the tone of Redding's opening to the chapter, prior to his introduction of Grandma Redding.
3. Contrast Grandma Redding and Grandma Conway, as they appeared to Saunders Redding, the boy.

4. Does Redding, the man, in retrospect, admire either grandmother, neither, or one more than the other? Explain.
5. Through their different manners of death and Redding's description of each death, what is implied about each of the grandmothers?
6. Who in the chapter is "troubled in mind?" Give your analysis.
7. Using Redding's style of writing as a model, write an analysis of your own "roots."

Pietro Di Donato (b. 1911)

Contributing Editor: Helen Barolini [p. 1719]

Classroom Issues and Strategies

The lack of perception of Italian-American authors as literary and the general lack of knowledge concerning the body of Italian-American writing is an obstacle to be overcome. In particular with Di Donato's classic work, *Christ in Concrete*, there is the question of linguistic uniqueness—a result of transposing Italian thought forms into English. This lends richness and texture to the work, but must be explained.

The Italian-American author and his/her work can be examined in terms of the general theme of the outsider and can be related to authors of other groups, bridging the narrow ethnic theme to the more general one. Students are interested in issues of workers' exploitation, what impels immigrants toward the American dream, and what the country was like fifty years ago as compared to today.

The language can be dealt with by showing how language forms thought patterns, and so viewpoints. However, beneath the uniqueness lies the same human feelings and their expression.

There is a film version of *Christ in Concrete* that could be useful to promote classroom discussion.

Major Themes, Historical Perspectives, and Personal Issues

Di Donato's *Christ in Concrete* is an achievement in giving literary form to the oral culture of the immigrant peasant transformed into urban worker. His is a prime example of the proletarian novel of the 1930s.

Significant Form, Style, or Artistic Conventions

Di Donato created an American language that accommodated the oral culture of his protagonists, a language that reflects the texture of the peasant-worker discourse. It is important to note that dignity and intelligence are not the social prerogatives of the more articulate social group.

Original Audience

Di Donato's work was written in the 1930s period of the Depression, social protest, and growing interest in socialist solutions for the ills of the world and its workers. It was hailed, at its appearance, as "the epithet of the 20th Century." In some ways it continues to be extraordinarily actual, as witness the collapse of the building in Bridgeport during the summer of 1987 that duplicated the tragedy of *Christ in Concrete* with the loss of workers' lives.

Comparisons, Contrasts, Connections

Di Donato can be related to Clifford Odets, another writer of social protest, who had some influence on him. Also, compare with the lyric proletarianism of Steinbeck's *Grapes of Wrath* and with John Fante's evocation of his mason father in *The Brotherhood of the Grape*.

It could be useful, also, to link Di Donato with the passionate outcry of James Baldwin in *Go Tell It on the Mountain* or with the working-class women of Tillie Olsen's *Yonnondio*.

Questions for Reading and Discussion/ Approaches to Writing

1. I think it is useful to have some perspective on the social conditions of the times in this country as reflected in *Christ in Concrete*.
2. Study the techniques of characterization. What makes a character live, or, on the other hand, fade? What makes a successful character?

   How do Di Donato's Italian-American working-class characters relate to all people everywhere?

Bibliography

Esposito, Michael P. "The Evolution of Di Donato's Perceptions of Italian Americans." In *The Italian Americans Through the Generations*. Proceedings of the 15th annual conference of the American Italian Historical Association. Staten Island: AIHA, 1986.

———. "The Travail of Pietro Di Donato." MELUS 7, no. 2 (Summer 1980): 47–60.

Sinicropi, Giovanni. "Christ in Concrete." *Italian Americana* 3 (1977): 175–83.

Viscusi, Robert. "The Semiology of Semen: Questioning the Father." In *The Italian Americans Through the Generations*. Proceedings of the 15th annual conference of the American Italian Historical Association. Staten Island: AIHA, 1986.

———. "De Vulgari Eloquentia: An Approach to the Language of Italian American Fiction." In *Yale Italian Studies*, 1, no. 3 (Winter 1981): 21–38. An interesting commentary on language usage.

Mourning Dove (Okanogan) (1888–1936)

Contributing Editor: Kristin Herzog [p. 1728]

Classroom Issues and Strategies

Students tend to see these stories as folklore, not realizing their complexity and philosophical background. They cannot measure the difficulty of translating a corporate tradition into the narrative voice of an individual writer. They will wonder for what audience the stories were written.

Consider approaching Mourning Dove from the world of American Indian spirituality, especially since the sweat-house tradition is still alive in some tribes.

In order to teach the excerpts from *Coyote Stories*, a basic understanding of the trickster figure in the legends of various tribes is necessary. Though the trickster's shape can be Raven, Blue Jay, Raccoon, Crow, or Spider, and though his function differs in detail, he is most frequently Coyote, the creature of playful disguises and clever self-seeking, the breaker of taboos, teller of lies, and creator of possibilities. He is the restlessly moving, ever-changing, indomitable spirit of survival. Coyote is always at the mercy of his passions and appetites; he holds no moral or social values, yet through his actions all values come into being. Trickster tales give humorous vent to those impulses that the tribes had to repress in order to maintain social order.

Major Themes, Historical Perspectives, and Personal Issues

Mourning Dove had to surmount almost incredible obstacles to become an author, and she personifies the ambivalent position of many ethnic women writers. Besides the lack of education and the ordeal of daily life in migrant labor camps, she had to contend with suspicious members of her tribe who did not see any purpose in giving away their sacred stories or who expected payment for telling them since some ethnologists had established that custom.

She also had to deal with the two men who made her publications possible: Lucullus McWhorter and Heister Dean Guie, the former an eminent scholar and faithful friend, the latter a journalist who wanted to establish a reputation as illustrator and editor. Both badgered her continually with questions of verification for certain customs' names or spellings. Both considered themselves authorities on the selection of stories "proper" for a white audience and on the addition of notes. Guie decided to eliminate at least ten tales from the final manuscript because they dealt with subjects like incest, transvestism, and infanticide. Donald Hines has retrieved these stories from Mourning Dove's manuscripts and has restored all the tales as closely as possible to her original version.

Significant Form, Style, or Artistic Conventions

Most difficult to grasp for the white reader is probably the concept of power. Usually an individual's power derived from or was related to an animal to which he or she felt kinship. Power for the Okanogans is not identical with what we call the mind or the soul, but instead is more like the Christian concept of a guardian angel—a force that protects and leads. When a young girl or boy received power, they also received a "power song" that was their very own. Thus power is immediately related to words.

Original Audience

When the oral tradition entered the literary mainstream, it first had to take on the conventions and proprieties of white literature. Only decades later was the mainstream audience able to understand orality "in the raw." In Mourning Dove's time, the often bizarre or obscene behavior of Coyote could easily be understood as reflection on Okanogan morals. Besides, *Coyote Stories* was written first of all for children.

Comparisons, Contrasts, Connections

Compare with Zitkala-Sa in terms of "translating'" tribal traditions into white western narrative form.

On the surface, of course, the story of "'The Spirit Chief Names the Animal People" is simply entertaining and educational. But, like any creation myth, it expresses a complex "philosophy." The animal people's need for "names" points to the coming of humans with a new kind of speech. But there were "tribes" already inhabiting the earth together with the animal people, and they were threatened by "people-devouring monsters." In a type of "Fortunate Fall" parable, it is the Coyote, the bragging, bungling fool, who by divine mercy is given the task of conquering these monsters. His special power may at times falter, but if he dies, his life can be restored by his twin brother, Fox, or by "others of the people."

The reader trained in the Judeo-Christian tradition may want to compare this story with biblical images and concepts. The Spirit Chief is "an all-powerful Man Above"—as McWhorter's note phrases it—but he has a wife who could be compared to the Sophia of the Hebrews: she participates in the creation and is the human, commonsensical aspect of the divinity who knows what the people need.

Questions for Reading and Discussion/
Approaches to Writing

1. Compare the creation myths of various world religions or of various American Indian tribes. What do they have in common?
2. In what sense did Mourning Dove herself become a "trickster"? How do these stories compare with fairy tales and fables?

Bibliography

Allen, Paula Gunn. *The Sacred Hoop: Recovering the Feminine in American Indian Traditions.* Boston: Beacon Press, 1986, 81–4, 151.

Astrov, Margot. *American Indian Prose and Poetry.* Quoted in Mary V. Dearborn, *Pocahontas's Daughters: Gender and Ethnicity in American Culture.* New York: Oxford Univ. Press, 1986, 28.

Fisher, Dexter. Introduction. In *Cogewea, the Half-Blood: A Depiction of the great Montana Cattle Range*, by Hum-ishu-ma, v–xxix. Lincoln: Univ. of Nebraska Press, 1981.

——. "The Transformation of Tradition," 87.

Hines, Donald M. ed. *Tales of the Okanogans, Collected by Mourning Dove.* Fairfield, Wash.: Ye Galleon Press, 1976, 14.

Radin, Paul. *The Trickster: A Study in American Indian Mythology.* New York: Philosophical Library, 1956; rpt. New York: Greenwood Press, 1969.

Schöler, Bo. Introduction. In *Coyote Was Here: Essays on Contemporary Native American Literary and Political Mobilization.* Aarhus, Denmark: Dept. of English, Univ. of Aarhus, 1984, 9.

Yanan, Eileen. *Coyote and the Colville.* Omak, Wash.: St. Mary's Mission, 1971, 29.

John Joseph Mathews (Osage) (1894–1979)

Contributing Editor: Andrew O. Wiget [p. 1735]

Classroom Issues and Strategies

The principal issue in *Sundown* is the notion of progress. Students frequently identify progress with material improvements in life-style or increasingly complex technology. This selection questions whether those are the true marks of civilization. To see this, however, students must realize that this selection comprises two parts, each of which portrays a different moment, widely separated in time in the life of the principle character, Chal Windzer. Chal (short for "Challenge," so named because his father wanted him to be a challenge to the new generation) is a teenager in the first section, still closely identified with some element of his traditional Osage lifestyle. Note, however, that he is moving rapidly toward accepting the values of Anglos, as is suggested by his distance from the group of Indians he encounters during the storm.

The second section of the story occurs over a decade later. Chal has gone off to the University of Oklahoma where he has been exposed to prejudice, bigotry, and romance. Falling in love with a white girl, he comes to despise his Indian appearance and later tries to pass himself off as a Spanish (not Mexican) gentleman. During World War I, he serves in the Army Air Force as an aviator and develops a passion for flying, which fulfills his need for a career. He loves the excitement, the danger, the thrill of flying. After serving in the Army Air Force, he returns home where he falls back into an indolent life-style, marked by long periods of drunkenness. He is just coming out of one of these periods, referred to in the last section of this selection, when he attends the hearings at which Roan Horse speaks.

In addition to providing background plot information, I also certainly call attention to certain literary devices. For example the oil derricks symbolize both the march and retreat of "progress." I'd also remind students a little bit of the history of this period of time. Osages were exempted from the provisions of the Dawes General Allotment Act, along with the Five Civilized Tribes, because they held their land under patented title, not by treaty. The surface of their reservation land had been allotted and much of it alienated through sale, but the mineral rights were retained by the Osage tribe in common and leases were given out. In the 1920s, royalties from these leases brought the tribe up to 20 million dollars per year, divided equally, amounting to around 25 thousand dollars per capita. A county court in Oklahoma had declared the Osages incompetent to manage their estates and had appointed guardians who charged a fee to manage these estates. Between exorbitant fees and the malfeasance of these guardians, much money and land was lost to the Osages.

In 1925, Congress transferred supervision of these mineral rights from the county court alone to the county court working in conjunction with the Osage agency. The federal investigators referred to in the last section are not only members of Congress but agents of the Federal Bureau of Investigation. The so-called "Osage Oil Murders" are a historical event of great notoriety and served to establish the credibility of the FBI as a law enforcement agency. As Mathews indicates, a conspiracy evolved to murder people who owned rights to oil land so that their inheritors would receive those rights. By murdering the inheritors, the conspirators planned to channel those rights into the hands of one person, an Anglo man who had married an Osage woman. She was the last person on the hit list, which today still leaves a trail of twenty-four unsolved murders and bombings.

The Osage oil boom needs to be understood in the context of the free-for-all capitalist economy of the 1890s and the first two decades of this century, during which the excesses of the Robber Barons were finally curbed by the creation of federal regulatory agencies. From the point of view of Indians in Oklahoma, however, the real question that needs to be asked is this: What happens to a community of people who go from a subsistence economy, based on communal land, barter, and credit, to an excess of cash, in the neighborhood of 25 thousand dollars per person per year (at the value of the 1920s dollar), all within the space of one generation ? How does such a change affect people's values, beliefs, and behaviors?

Students seem concerned about the ambivalence of the ending, especially about whether or not Chal is really capable of being a challenge to his generation, as his father had hoped. After reading about Chal's life of indolence, it is difficult for students to believe that he will make such a bold move, requiring such a commitment of effort, especially if that move is motivated only by observing the very brief appearance of Roan Horse. On the other hand, Chal has shown the desire to be a warrior, and he has great ambitions. Does the ending mark a real turning point in his life?

Major Themes, Historical Perspectives, and Personal Issues

I would highlight the structure of the boom town society that appears in the beginning of the selection. I would indicate the characters' attitudes toward the upcoming storm (bad for business, dangerous) and contrast that with the attitudes of some of the older Indians, such as Black Elk. In between we have younger Indians, such as Sun-On-His-Wings and Chal.

The various attitudes that each of these people takes toward the onset of the storm and toward the damage that the storm does provide a keen insight into the different sets of values that are coming together under the pressure of "progress" and assimilation in this reservation community.

Significant Form, Style, or Artistic Conventions

I would point to the oil derricks as a symbol of "progress"; I would also look at the change in Chal's character between the first section and the second section. It's especially important that students try to understand

Chal's apparent indifference and his drunkenness as a response to an excess of easy money in the absence of compelling community values. The recognition of this, on Chal's part, is what moves him to respond so affirmatively to Roan Horse's brief speech.

Original Audience

This book was published in the 1930s, where it met a receptive audience of people in the middle of the Depression, who understood the tremendous personal cost and human devastation that was brought about by the unchecked exploitation of natural resources and poor people. In this context, especially, American Indians were highlighted as an oppressed minority within the United States. In 1928 the Meriam Report, commissioned by the U.S. government, found that Indians had a mortality rate twice as high as the white population, an infant mortality rate three times as high as the white population, and that in spite of all this, the government had been spending only fifty cents per year on the health care of each Indian. Statistics like this shocked the nation, and Indians became the object of renewed federal attention. Under the Roosevelt administration, the U.S. government took a number of important steps to redress these failures of its trust relationship, though many of them, such as the Indian Reorganization Act (1934), which allowed tribes to form their own governments with written constitutions, were controversial. Nevertheless, Mathews's work needs to be seen as speaking to the notion that the major difficulties on Indian reservations come from what today we would call a "culture of poverty." And that these can be remedied by government treatment.

Comparisons, Contrasts, Connections

Insofar as Mathews gives us a good picture of the transition on Indian reservations, he can be compared usefully to Oskison and Bonnin. Lynn Riggs's play *The Cherokee Night* also gives a good picture of the deculturation that has been visited upon American Indians as a result of the abuses in the trust relationship that they had with the U.S. government.

Questions for Reading and Discussion/ Approaches to Writing

1. How do the oil derricks mark the changes in the life of the Osages and also in the personal history of Chal? Why is Chal impressed by Roan Horse's speech?

2. In the first section of the story a young Indian comments about Black Elk: "His body is here but his mind is back in a place where we lived many years ago." How does this observation reflect the forces that are creating the conflict in this story?

3. At the very end of the story, Chal says that he is going to go off to Harvard Law School and become an orator. What do you think is the likelihood of Chal fulfilling this stated goal? How would you support your judgment?

Bibliography

Wiget, Andrew. "Modern Fiction." In *Native American Literature*. Boston: Twayne, 1985.

Wilson, Terry. "Osage Oxonian: The Heritage of John Joseph Mathews." *Chronicles of Oklahoma* 59 (1981): 264–93.

Younghill Kang (1903–1972)

Contributing Editor: Elaine H. Kim [p. 1747]

Classroom Issues and Strategies

Students will generally be unfamiliar with Korean history and society, both past and present. They will also have trouble with Kang's archaisms. To address these problems, provide extensive socio-historical background and place the work within United States literary context, especially the Asian-American literature context.

Teach Kang in tandem with Korean-American women writers (e.g., Ronyoung Kim, *Clay Walls*, 1987) depicting the same period. Also, consider comparing Kang to the following:

1. Contemporary Korean-American writers (e.g., T.Y. Park, *Guilt Payment*, 1983).
2. Chinese, Filipino, and Japanese portrayers of community life (e.g., Louis Chu, Bulosan, Milton Murayama).
3. "Refugee" writing (e.g., Wendy Law-Jone, *The Coffin Tree*, 1983).

Major Themes, Historical Perspectives, and Personal Issues

Consider the following possibilities:

1. Immigrant (as opposed to sojourner) view.
2. Class perspectives when facing race discrimination.
3. Portrait of early Korean-American community life, through three major characters and a narrator.

Original Audience

East Goes West was written by a nonwhite immigrant for an Anglo audience at a time of intense anti-Asia activity in the United States.

Comparisons, Contrasts, Connections

Compare with Carlos Buloscun, *America Is in the Heart*; Lin Yutang's work, "selling" China to western readers. Examine the class perspective of immigrants vs. elite sojourners.

Bibliography

Give them one of my overview essays on Asian American lit., e.g., from
American Studies International Fall 84
Cultural Critique Spring 87
Columbia Literary History of the U.S. (1988)

Carved on the Walls: Poetry by Early Chinese Immigrants (1919–1940)

Contributing Editors: Him Mark Lai, Genny Lim, Judy Yung [p. 1755]

Classroom Issues and Strategies

Because of the exclusion of racial minorities such as Chinese Americans from our American education and their continuous stereotyping in the popular media, most people do not have the historical or literary background to understand and appreciate Chinese poetry as written by the early immigrants at the Angel Island Immigration Station.

The headnote includes background information on the history of Chinese Americans and their detention experience at Angel Island as well as explanations of the literary style and content of the Chinese poems. We have also included footnotes to explain the literary and historical allusions used in the poems. It is important that students be aware of this background material in their reading of the poems as well as their significance as part of the earliest record of Chinese-American literature and history written from the perspective of Chinese immigrants in America.

As you teach these selections, consider a stimulation exercise where students can experience how Chinese immigrants must have felt as unwelcomed aliens arriving at Angel Island. As students read these poems, they are made aware of the impact of discriminatory laws. They also learn to appreciate a different poetic style of writing. On the other hand, most students are puzzled by the historical context of the poems and by the larger moral issues of racism.

Major Themes, Historical Perspectives, and Personal Issues

The poems express strong feelings of anger, frustration, uncertainty, hope, despair, self-pity, homesickness, and loneliness written by Chinese immigrants who were singled out for exclusion by American immigration laws on the basis of race. As such, they are important fragments of American history and literature long missing from the public record as well as strong evidence that dispels the stereotype of Chinese Americans as passive, complacent, and illiterate.

Significant Form, Style, or Artistic Conventions

Most of the poems were written in the 1910s and 1920s, when the classical style of Chinese poetry was still popular and when feelings of Chinese nationalism ran strong. Of the 135 poems that have been recovered, about half are written with four lines per poem and seven characters per line. The remainder consist of verses with six or eight lines and five or seven characters per line. The literary quality of the poems varies greatly, which is understandable considering that most immigrants at this time did not have formal schooling beyond the primary grades. Many poems violate rules of rhyme and tone required in Chinese poetry and incorrect characters and usages often appear. However, these flaws do not appear in the translation, in which we chose to sacrifice form for content.

Original Audience

The Angel Island poems were written as a means to vent and record the response of Chinese immigrants to the humiliating treatment they suffered at the Angel Island Immigration Station. They were intended for other Chinese immigrants who would follow in the footsteps of the poets. But as read now, they are an important literary record of the experience and feelings of one group of immigrants who, because of their race and a weak motherland, were unwelcomed and singled out for discriminatory treatment.

Comparisons, Contrasts, Connections

The only other work published so far that would serve as a useful tool of comparison in terms of form and content is Marion Hom's *Songs of Gold Mountain: Cantonese Rhymes from San Francisco Chinatown* (Berkeley: University of California Press, 1987)—a collection of Chinese folk rhymes first published in 1911 and 1915. It would also be useful for students to read about the European immigrant experience at Ellis Island in order for them to see the different treatments of immigrants to America due to race.

Questions for Reading and Discussion/ Approaches to Writing

1. (a) What are the themes of the Angel Island poems and how do they reflect the historical circumstances for Chinese immigrants coming to the United States between 1910 and 1940?
   (b) How would you describe the nameless poets based on your reading of the Angel Island poems?
2. (a) Compare and contrast the Angel Island poems with those written by another American poet in the early twentieth century.
   (b) Show how the image of Chinese immigrants as reflected in the Angel Island poems confirms or contradicts prevailing stereotypes of Chinese-Americans in the popular media.

Bibliography

Lai, Him Mark, Genny Lim, and Judy Yung. *Island: Poetry and History of Chinese Immigrants on Angel Island, 1910–1940.* San Francisco: HOC-DOI Project, Chinese Culture Foundation, 1980.

Lowe, Felicia. "Carved in Silence." A film about the Chinese immigration experience at Angel Island, 1988, available from Felicia Lowe, 398 11th Street, San Francisco, CA 94103; video available from National Asian American Telecommunications Association, 346 9th Street, 2nd Floor, San Francisco, CA 94103.

Mark, Diane Mei Lin and Ginger Chih. *A Place Called Chinese America*. Dubuque: Kendall/Hunt Publishing Company, 1982.

Contemporary Period

1945 to the Present

Prose

Richard Wright (1908–1960)

Contributing Editor: John M. Reilly [p. 1786]

Classroom Issues and Strategies

Among sympathetic readers, there is an assumption that Wright is documentary, that his works can be read as elementary sociology. If these readers are familiar with literary movements, they also assume he can be classed as a naturalistic author displaying the experience of victims. Readers of a negative disposition are inclined to class Wright as an exponent of hate, an unreasonable writer who is not sensitive to the complexities of moral experience.

For all of these readers, a useful approach is to focus on the narrative point of view, the third person narration (or what is technically labeled free, indirect discourse or narrated monologue) that places us within the consciousness of the protagonist. This introduces a complexity of mind, an experience of identification (but not identity) that can illustrate how we and the protagonist are "inside" of statistics or documentary, how we experience life as though we had choice and cannot be victims.

I would recommend for study of "The Man Who Was Almost a Man" some consideration of how Wright revised his work to make it less and less "realistic," more and more symbolic. This approach allows for treatment of the issue of universality. Student discussion often centers around guilt and freedom. The most commonly asked questions have to do with a tendency to allegorize the underground journey. While exploring what Wright might intend by some of his choices of settings that the character enters, it is possible to suggest that they are categorical and take him into dominant institutions while exposing the workings of the social values.

Major Themes, Historical Perspectives, and Personal Issues

The focus on point of view is also helpful for drawing attention to the interest Wright has in social psychology, which dramatizes in narrative the consciousness of a character as the crossroads of social forces (race, class) and personal impulses and self-creation. Wright is dedicated to study of the production of personality and the arousal of a self-directive being. This, after all, is the substance of African-American history: how oppressed people create a world, a culture, and remake personalities the dominant group seeks to eradicate.

Significant Form, Style, or Artistic Conventions

The challenge is to describe "protest" literature as a repudiation of the dominant discourse on race without allowing readers to believe that rejection of the dominant literary styles is to become nonliterary. Wright should be seen as a major voice of African-American modernism (see the emphasis on the black self, the effort in his work to found a subjectivity). That's his literary period. His school may well be called protest. But the selection in the anthology requires attention to the language of symbolism—the charged objects and language of racial discourse.

Original Audience

The audience in the 1940s and 1950s may have been less receptive to the symbolic element, less attuned to the existentialist outlook of a black writer. The greatest distinction of audiences, however, lies in the historical experiences of white and black readers. The protagonist is, like Bigger Thomas, a Stagger Lee, a "baadd man"; and in his story he "signifies" on white culture by use of the elements of black culture. Obviously, different people will see these differently. (See Claudia Mitchel-Kernan, "Signifying," *Mother Wit from the Laughing Barrel*, ed. Alan Dundes, Prentice-Hall, 1973, pp. 310–28.)

Comparisons, Contrasts, Connections

Compare with Ralph Ellison, *Invisible Man*, for the use of perception imagery as well as the subterranean symbolism; Albert Camus, *The Stranger*, for the experience of a protagonist who finds the assumptions of normality collapsing.

Questions for Reading and Discussion/ Approaches to Writing

1. (a) What is the meaning of Dave's final remark?
   (b) Compare this work to a crime story. Who is Wright's criminal?
2. (a) Discuss the creativity of the protagonist.
   (b) Suggest why Wright chose not to indicate the name or "vital statistics" of his protagonist.

Bibliography

Bakish, Davis, "Underground in an Ambiguous Dreamworld." *Studies in Black Literature* 2 (Autumn 1971): 18–23.

Davis, Charles T., and Michel Fabre. *Richard Wright: A Primary Bibliography*. Boston: G. K. Hall, 1982. Information on revisions and evolving form of story.

Everette, Mildred. "The Death of Richard Wright's American Dream: 'The Man Who Lived Underground.' " *CLA Journal 17* (1974): 318–26.

Fabre, Michel. "From Tabloid to Myth: 'The Man Who Lived Underground.' " *The World of Richard Wright*. Jackson: Univ. of Miss. Press, 1985, 93–107.

Gelfant, Blanche. "Residence Underground: Recent Fictions of the Subterranean City." *Sewanee Review* 83 (2975): 406–38.

Goed, William. "On Lower Frequencies: The Buried Men in Wright and Ellison." *Modern Fiction Studies* 15 (1970): 483–501.

Hyman, Stanley Edgar. "Richard Wright Reappraised." *The Atlantic* 225 (March 1970): 127–32. Addresses critically the protest vs. symbolism in Wright's work with "The Man . . ." as an example of his finest writing.

Reilly, John. "Self-Portraits by Richard Wright." *Colorado Quarterly* 20 (Summer 1971): 31–45. On revisions and the author's personal investment in "The Man . . .".

Eudora Welty (b. 1909)

Contributing Editor: Jennifer L. Randisi [p. 1796]

Classroom Issues and Strategies

Like many lyric novelists, Welty is easy to read. She therefore seems (to many students) very simple. They like her, generally, and don't want to ruin their enjoyment by having to analyze her.

I like to begin by looking at what makes Welty seem simple (her lovely sentences, her homey metaphors, her "impulse to praise"). The difficulty here is not a lack of accessibility, but rather that Welty seems too accessible, too superficial. The challenge is to get students to read Welty seriously, critically, analytically.

Welty has said that except what's personal there's so little to tell. I'd start where she did: with the hearts of the characters she's writing about—the universal emotions they share with us. Why do we feel a certain way about the story? The situation? The character? What is evoked? How is Welty able to evoke a certain response from us? What values does Welty hold? (This is something she shares with writers like Faulkner, Flannery O'Connor, Katherine Anne Porter, Walker Percy, and Alice Walker. There are values here; these people believe in certain things and the community shares both a value system and a sense of what words like "love" and "compassion" mean.)

As with most of the southern writers, Welty's humor, her use of the grotesque, and her dialogue are often initial difficulties for students, who tend to take her too seriously and thus miss the fun she's having. Welty's books often work the way folk or fairy tales do; students aren't used to this.

Major Themes, Historical Perspectives, and Personal Issues

Major themes include the problem of balancing love and separateness (the community and one's sense of self), the role and influence of family and the land ("place"), and the possibilities of art (storytelling) to inform life. Welty is also very concerned with resonances of classical mythology, legend, and folk tale, and with the intersection of history and romance.

Significant Form, Style, or Artistic Conventions

Welty clearly owes something to fellow Mississippian William Faulkner, and to the oral tradition of the South. She has a terrific ear, reproducing cadences of dialect and giving much insight into her characters by allowing her readers to hear them talk. Welty's work also owes something to the grotesque as developed in the American South.

Original Audience

Since Welty hasn't been grouped with writers critical of the South (her issues are neither political nor social in a broad sense), her work hasn't been read much differently over the years. She's been criticized for not attacking the South; that has never been her interest or her aim.

Comparisons, Contrasts, Connections

Any of the southerners writing in the twentieth century could be compared to Welty in terms of voice, violence, attitude toward the land, feelings about community, and ways of telling a story. Faulkner, Flannery O'Connor, Katherine Anne Porter, Walker Percy—even Alice Walker—would be good to start with.

Questions for Reading and Discussion/ Approaches to Writing

1. I like to start with what students see. I think study questions (except for general questions relating to the elements of the story—point of view, character, theme) direct their reading toward what they think I want them to see rather than allowing them to see what they see.
2. I am fond of the short paper (2–3 pages) and of the directed journal. The former allows students to focus on a very specific problem or concern; the latter allows students to carry issues from one author to the next, or from one book to the next. I like assigning a formal paper from one of the journal entries.

Bibliography

Welty's essay "Place in Fiction" is very good. Welty's book of photographs, *One Time, One Place*, is a nice companion piece, as is her collection of essays, *The Eye of the Story*. Peggy Prenshaw's *Conversations with Eudora Welty* has some helpful information and I think her collection of essays (*Eudora Welty: Critical Essays*) and John F. Desmond's (*A Still Moment: Essays on the Art of Eudora Welty*) are both worthwhile reading.

My chapter on *Losing Battles* (in *A Tissue of Lies*) is quite good on that particular book.

Tillie Lerner Olsen (b. 1912)

Contributing Editor: Deborah S. Rosenfelt [p. 1812]

Classroom Issues and Strategies

Olsen's work is relatively easy to teach since it addresses themes of concern to contemporary students and since its experiments with language remain within the bounds of realism. *Tell Me a Riddle* is among the most difficult of Olsen's works and some students have trouble for two reasons: they are unfamiliar with the social and political history embedded in the novella and they are confused by the allusive, stream of consciousness techniques Olsen employs for the revelation of that history's centrality in the consciousness of the protagonist.

Since the knee-jerk negative reaction to "communists" is often a problem, I make sure I discuss thoroughly the historical soil out of which *Tell Me a Riddle* grows. Sometimes I show the film *Seeing Reds*. I always read students a useful passage from *A Long View from the Left: Memoirs of an American Revolutionary* (Delta, 1972, p. 8) by Al Richmond.

Showing the film version of *Tell Me a Riddle* can be a good strategy for provoking discussion. The film itself is one of the rare representations of older people's lives and one of the few in which an older woman figures as the protagonist. Reading passages from Olsen's *Silences*, especially the autobiographical ones, also proves helpful and interesting to students.

Students respond most immediately and deeply to Eva's rage and anger about the sacrifices her life has involved. They also get into painful discussions about aging and dying, and about the limited options for the elderly in American society. The questions they ask include the following: Why won't the grandmother (Eva) hold her grandchild? Please help us figure out the configuration of family relationships in the story (here it helps if students have also read the other stories in the *Tell Me a Riddle* volume). Why doesn't Eva want to see the rabbi in the hospital? Where do they go when they go to the city on the beach (the answer to that one is Venice, California, an area near Los Angeles that houses an old Jewish community lovingly documented in the book and film, *Number Our Days*). Why won't David let her go home again?

Major Themes, Historical Perspectives, and Personal Issues

Tell Me a Riddle is very rich thematically, historically, and personally. Its central themes include the confrontation with aging, illness, and death; the deprivations and struggles of poverty; the conflicts, full of love and rage, in marital relations; the family, especially motherhood, as a site of both love and nurturance and of repression; the burying of women's sense of self and the silencing of their capacities for expression over years of tending to the needs and listening to the rhythms of others; the quest for meaning in one's personal life; and the affirmation of hope for and engagement on behalf of a freer, more peaceful, more just and humane world.

The themes of *Tell Me a Riddle* are in many ways the themes of Olsen's life. Olsen's parents took part in the 1905 revolution and became Socialist Party activists in the United States. Olsen herself became a Communist in the years when communism as a philosophy and as a movement seemed to offer the best hope for an egalitarian society. Eva is modeled partly on Olsen's mother, who died of cancer, as does Eva.

I see Olsen as belonging to a tradition of women writers in this country associated with the American left, who unite a class consciousness and a feminist consciousness in their lives and creative work.

Significant Form, Style, or Artistic Conventions

In *Tell Me a Riddle* Olsen is deliberately experimental, fracturing chronological sequence, using stream of consciousness techniques to represent the processes of human consciousness, insisting on the evocative power of each individual word. Though remaining within the bounds of realism, she draws fully on the techniques of modernist fiction to render a humanistic and socially impassioned vision rare in modernist and post-modernist writing.

Original Audience

The question of audience is, I think, less relevant to contemporary writers than to those of earlier centuries. I do speak about Olsen's political background and about her special importance for contemporary women writers and readers. It is also important that the stories of the *Tell Me a Riddle* volume were written during the McCarthy era. All of them, especially *Tell Me a Riddle*, subtly bear witness to the disappointment and despair of progressives during that era, when the radical dreams and visions of the thirties and forties were deliberately eradicated. Olsen's family was one of many to endure harassment by the FBI. *Riddle*'s topical allusions to Nazi concentration camps and the dropping of the atomic bomb at Hiroshima, and David's yearning for a time of belief and belonging contribute to the subtext of anguish and betrayal so characteristic of the literature of the period.

Comparisons, Contrasts, Connections

I find it useful to compare *Tell Me a Riddle* to other works by women authors that record the tensions of "dual life," especially those which, like *Riddle*, deploy an imagery of speech and silencing not only to delineate the protagonist's quest for personal expression but also to develop her relationship to processes of social change. Among the many works that contain some configuration of these themes and images are Agnes Smedley's novel *Daughter of Earth*, Harriet Arnow's *The Dollmaker*, Maxine Hong Kingston's *The Woman Warrior: Memoirs of a Girlhood among Ghosts*, much of the poetry of Audre Lorde and Adrienne Rich, Alice Walker's *The Color Purple*, and Joy Kogawa's *Obasan*.

As stories of "secular humanist" Jewish family life, the work might be compared with Grace Paley's fiction or Meridel LeSueur's *The Girl*.

As part of the tradition of working-class writers, she could be compared with Rebecca Harding Davis's *Life in the Iron-Mills*, Agnes Smedley's *Daughter of Earth*, Mike Gold's *Jews Without Money*, Henry Roth's *Call It Sleep*, and Fielding Burke's *Call Home the Heart*.

As a story exploring the consciousness of one who is dying, students might want to compare *Riddle* to Tolstoi's *The Death of Ivan Ilych*.

Questions for Reading and Discussion/
Approaches to Writing

1. What is the immediate cause of the conflict in this story? Does the author take sides in this conflict? Does this conflict have a resolution? What underlying causes does it suggest?
2. Try to explain or account for the story's title. What about the subtitle?
3. Who is the "hero" of this story? Why?

4. This is a story about a woman dying of cancer. Did you find it "depressing" or "inspiring"? Why?
5. Why is Eva so angry about the appearance of the rabbi in the hospital? What does she mean by "Race, human; religion, none"?
6. What do we learn about Eva's girlhood? Why do we learn it so late in the story?
7. Discuss Jeanne's role in the story.
8. Is David the same man at the end of the story as he was at the beginning? Explain your answer.

Bibliography

Olsen's personal/critical essays, those in *Silences* and that in *Mother to Daughter, Daughter to Mother*, are very important sources of insight and information. Especially recommended: pp. 5–46 in *Silences*, "Silences in Literature" (1962), and "One Out of Twelve: Writers Who Are Women in Our Century" (1971).

Other recommended reading:

Coiner, Constance. "Literature of Resistance: The Intersection of Feminism and the Political Left in Tillie Olsen and Meridel LeSueur." In *Politics of Literature: Toward the 1990's* edited by Lennard Davis and Bella Mirabella. New York: Columbia Univ. Press, forthcoming.

Orr, Elaine Neil. *Tillie Olsen and a Feminist Spiritual Vision.* Jackson: Univ. Press of Mississippi, 1987. Especially Chs. II and IV.

Rosenfelt, Deborah. "From the Thirties: Tillie Olsen and the Radical Tradition." *Feminist Studies* 7:3 (Fall 1981): 371–406.

Carlos Bulosan (1913–1956)

Contributing Editors: Amy Ling and Oscar Campomanes [p. 1840)

Classroom Issues and Strategies

Some readers may be repulsed by what they consider an overly negative portrayal of American society. Their reactions range from incredulity to discomfort to rejection of what they consider to be exaggeration. Other readers are quick to dismiss Bulosan on aesthetic criteria, believing *American Is in the Heart* to be autobiographical and sociological, rather than "literary." The issue of genre is another problem area: his fiction seems autobiographical, his poetry prosy, his short stories read like essays and his essays like short stories.

Providing students with biographical background on Bulosan, showing that he was primarily a writer rather than a farm laborer/factory worker, and giving them historical information on Philippine immigration will set this text into its proper context. This text is primarily a novel and at the same time, as Carey McWilliams has pointed out, "it reflects the collective life experience of thousands of Filipino immigrants who were attracted to this country by its legendary promises of a better life."

If a slide show on Philippine immigration is obtainable, it would provide useful information. The film *Manongs* from Visual Communications in California is an excellent introduction.

As students read Bulosan, they ask, "Who is this man? What group does he belong to? What are his concerns? Is the plight of the immigrant today different than it was in the 1930s and 1940s?"

Major Themes, Historical Perspectives, and Personal Issues

Bulosan's major theme is exile and return—the effect of departure from home and the necessity to return to the Philippines in order to make sense of the exile's experience in the United States because of the colonial status of the Philippines.

His second purpose is to record his own, his family's, and his friends' experiences and lives, their loneliness and alienation.

Significant Form, Style, or Artistic Conventions

Bulosan wrote with an eye to violating literary conventions, as mentioned above. As a political activist and labor organizer, he also believed that creative literary activity and social purpose cannot be separated. Some of his later stories are magic realist in style. "Silence" is certainly meant to be read as symbolic rather than literal.

Original Audience

Bulosan, at the beginning of his career, wrote for a mainstream American audience, and was placed in the position of cultural mediator, a bridge between the Philippines, which America wanted to know better during WWII, and the U.S. Late in life, he consciously cultivated a Filipino audience, sending stories back to the Philippines, most of which were rejected. In the 1970s, he was "rediscovered" by Asian-Americans delighted to have found a spokesperson as prolific and multifaceted as he.

Comparisons, Contrasts, Connections

In his unadorned, deceptively simple prose style, he resembles Hemingway; in his social concerns, Steinbeck's *Grapes of Wrath*. Bulosan may be compared with Maxine Hong Kingston in that both were critically acclaimed by a wide audience but denounced by certain portions of their own community who accused them of having "sold out." With Kingston he also shares a reliance on peasant forms of storytelling as well as the seeming incoherence of their works and the question of genre.

Questions for Reading and Discussion/ Approaches to Writing

1. The students may be directed to think about whether there are distinguishing characteristics to Filipino immigrant experience setting it apart from Chinese, Japanese, Korean, or any European group.
2. Ask students to keep a journal of their random reactions to the text. On a sheet of paper, have them record quotes, phrases, or words from the text that were particularly significant to them; on the right-hand side of the sheet, they are to record their reactions. Later they write a one-page statement of their responses, setting up a dialogue between themselves and their instructor. The instructor then makes a response and dittoes up the dialogue that the entire class can enter into the dialogue. Finally the class writes papers on the entire classroom-wide dialogue.

Bibliography

Amerasia Journal 6:1 (1979). Special issue devoted to the writings of Carlos Bulosan.

"Carlos Bulosan" 500-word biographical entry in the *Encyclopedia of the American Left*, by Oscar Campomanes (Brown University).

Evangelista, Suzanne Potter. *Carlos Bulosan and His Poetry*, A *Biography and an Anthology*. Seattle: Univ. of Washington Press, 1985.

Campomanes, Oscar, and Todd Gernes. "Two Letters from America: Carlos Bulosan and the Act of Writing." MELUS (Spring 1990): forthcoming.

San Juan E., "Tunnelling Out of the Belly of the Beast." In *Crisis in the Philippines*. South Hadley, Mass.: Bergin & Garvey, 1986.

Ralph Ellison (b. 1914)

Contributing Editor: Linda Wagner-Martin [p. 1843]

Classroom Issues and Strategies

The very familiarity of Ellison's name—and that of *Invisible Man*—makes teaching just a segment of it difficult. Students will have stereotypical ideas of what the book says, what Ellison intends, and many of them will have had courses in African-American literature that have been heavily political and will have studied the way James Baldwin reacted to Ellison, the way Wright felt about him, etc. In other words, some of these students will have to be taught to simply read what Ellison creates, as text, as carefully crafted post-modernist writing, filled with irony, humor, complaint, and above all, care. The influence of black language and music rhythms is key.

As we read, we need to forget that this is a major text by a black author and study it, at first, as we would any piece of writing. A second approach considers the work's racial and language characteristics; it is sometimes effective if we just read parts of it without the consideration of its ethnic qualities.

Major Themes, Historical Perspectives, and Personal Issues

Major themes are alienation, in the great American tradition from the nineteenth century; separateness of black from black, as well as black from white; disenfranchisement from cultural norms and attitudes; sheer loneliness, and its role as catalyst in helping the Invisible Man create his language, his lament; the role of names and lack of names; cultural signals about belonging, possession, place. Most significant themes in American art and literature eventually appear in this novel.

Bibliography

Refer to the headnote in the text for complete information.

Saul Bellow (b. 1915)

Contributing Editor: Allan Chavkin [p. 1855]

Classroom Issues and Strategies

In the past some students complained that Bellow was too pessimistic and too difficult to understand. Those objections were prompted by *Herzog*, but "Looking for Mr. Green" does not possess the difficult style or dark subject matter of *Herzog*. Perhaps the only real problem will be convincing students that the story is not as simple as it seems.

I think the best strategy is to focus on specific parts of the story by asking a series of specific questions. This particular story can be approached on two different levels, for it is both a realistic depiction of a relief worker's dedicated attempt to search for an unemployed, crippled black man in the slums of Depression Chicago in order to deliver a welfare check and a symbolic quest to discover the relationship between reality and appearances.

My approach to the story is generally conventional—asking questions and prompting class discussion on key issues. Another possible approach would be to play all or part of an excellent unabridged audio-recording of the story by Books on Tape, P. O. Box 7900, Newport Beach, CA 92658–7900, and discuss the interpretation that the Books-on-Tape reader gives to the story.

Students often respond actively to the following issues raised by "Looking for Mr. Green":

1. Money as a formative influence on the creation of identity.
2. The problem of the noncompetitive in a highly competitive society.
3. The clash between idealism and cynical "realism," between the noble idealist and the cynic.
4. The quest of a stubborn idealist in an irrational world.
5. Racism and stereotyping.

Major Themes, Historical Perspectives, and Personal Issues

Historical Issues and Themes: How does society help the downtrodden (in this story an unemployed, crippled black man) in bad economic times (e.g., the Depression)? The story also examines the problems of race, class, and gender. Other issues that the class might focus upon are: the plight of the noncompetitive in a capitalistic, highly competitive society; how money influences character; the alienation of the urban black man.

Personal Issues and Themes: How does an idealistic humanist (i.e., the typical Bellow hero) reconcile noble ideas with the harsh facts of the human condition? Is man essentially a victim of his situation or is he the master of his fate? What is Bellow suggesting about the problem of human suffering and evil? The relationship of the individual to his society? The relationship of appearance to reality? The clash between the human need to order and make sense of life according to moral principles and life's amoral disorder, discontinuity, irrationality, and mystery?

Significant Form, Style, or Artistic Conventions

The story can be discussed as a bildungsroman; as a parable; as a symbolic quest; as a realistic depiction of the Depression and of the alienation of the urban black man.

Original Audience

The story was published in 1951, and the 1950s audiences are not radically different from the audiences of the 1990s. In short, I don't discuss this question in class.

Comparisons, Contrasts, Connections

The story might be compared with some works by such black writers as Baldwin, Wright, and Ellison, or any other writers who have written about the Depression (e.g., Steinbeck). The story could be compared to some stories by such naturalistic writers as Dreiser and London who are also concerned with the free will vs. determinism theme. An interesting comparison would be with Fitzgerald, who wrote on the formative influence of money on the self. The idea that illusion is necessary for the survival of self in a harsh, predatory world is a central theme of modern American drama (O'Neill, Tennessee Williams, and Miller), and this story might be compared to the most important modern American plays. Bellow's depiction of women might be compared to that of other writers.

Questions for Reading and Discussion/
Approaches to Writing

1. (a) What is the purpose in the story of Grebe's supervisor Raynor? What is Bellow's attitude toward Raynor's cynical "wisdom"? Is concern for the individual anachronistic? For philosophical studies?

   (b) What is the purpose of the encounter with the Italian grocer who presents a hellish vision of the city with its chaotic masses of suffering humanity?

   (c) The old man Field offers this view of money—"Nothing is black where it shines and the only place you see black is where it ain't shining." Discuss. What do you think of the scheme for creating black millionaires? Why does Bellow include this scheme in the story?

   (d) What is the purpose of the Staika incident in the story? Raynor sees her as embodying "the destructive force" that will "submerge everybody in time," including "nations and governments." In contrast, Grebe sees her as "the life force." Who is closer to the truth?

   (e) The word "sun" and sun imagery are repeated throughout the story. Discuss.

2. (a) Discuss the theme of appearance vs. reality.

   (b) Bellow ends the story with Grebe's encounter with the drunken, naked black woman, who may be another embodiment of the spirit of Staika. Why does Bellow conclude the story this way? Has Grebe failed or succeeded? Is he deceiving himself?

   (c) David Demarest comments: "Grebe's stubborn idealism is nothing less than the basic human need to construct the world according to intelligent, moral principles." Discuss.

   (d) Believing that "Looking for Mr. Green" needs to be seen "as one of the great short stories of our time," Eusebio Rodrigues argues that the Old Testament flavors it. This story is "a modern dramatization of Ecclesiastes." Discuss.

Bibliography

Chavkin, Allan. "The Problem of Suffering in the Fiction of Saul Bellow." *Comparative Literature Studies* 21 (Summer 1984): 161–74.

Demarest, David. "The Theme of Discontinuity in Saul Bellow's Fiction: 'Looking for Mr. Green' and 'A Father-to-be.' " *Studies in Short Fiction* 6 (Winter 1969): 175–86.

Fuchs, Daniel. *Saul Bellow: Vision and Revision.* Durham, N.C.: Duke Univ. Press, 1984, 287–89.

Opdahl, Keith Michael. *The Novels of Saul Bellow.* Univ. Park: The Pennsylvania State Univ. Press, 1967, 100–103.

Rodrigues, Eusebio L. "Koheleth in Chicago: The Quest for the Real in 'Looking for Mr. Green.' " *Studies in Short Fiction* 11 (1974): 387–93.

Hisaye Yamamoto (b. 1921)

Contributing Editor: King Kok Cheung-Mare [p. 1871]

Classroom Issues and Strategies

Students are generally unfamiliar with Japanese-American history and cultural sensibilities. It is useful to spend some time introducing Japanese-American history and culture, especially the practice of "picture bride" (which sheds light on the marriage of Mr. and Mrs. Hayashi) and the style of communication among Issei and Nisei.

It would be helpful to analyze "Seventeen Syllables" in terms of a double plot: the overt one concerning Rosie and the covert one concerning Mrs. Hayashi. Students often relate to the interaction between mother and daughter and are appalled by Mr. Hayashi's callousness.

Major Themes, Historical Perspectives, and Personal Issues

1. The relatively restrained interaction between Issei (first generation) and Nisei (second generation) as a result of both cultural prescription and lanaguage barrier;
2. The historical practice of "picture bride," according to which the bride and the groom had only seen each other's photos before marriage;
3. The theme of aborted creativity; and
4. The sexual and racial barriers faced by the author herself, who came of age in an internment camp during World War II.

Significant Form, Style, or Artistic Conventions

Stress the narrative strategies of the author, especially her use of naïve narrator. While Yamamoto may have been influenced by the modernist experimentation with limited point of view, she also capitalizes on the scant verbal interchange between her Japanese-American characters to build suspense and tension.

Original Audience

The work has always been intended for a multicultural audience, but the reader's appreciation will undoubtedly be enhanced by knowledge of Japanese-American history and culture.

Comparisons, Contrasts, Connections

1. James Joyce (*Dubliners*) for the use of naïve narrator;
2. Grace Paley for the interaction between husbands and wives, between immigrant parents and their children; and
3. Wakako Yamauchi and Amy Tan for the relationship between mothers and daughters.

Questions for Reading and Discussion/ Approaches to Writing

1. (a) How do cultural differences complicate intergenerational communication in "Seventeen Syllables?"
   (b) Are there any connections between the episodes about Rosie and those about her mother?
   (c) What effects does the author achieve by using a limited point of view?
2. (a) How does Yamamoto connect the two plots concerning Rosie and her mother in "Seventeen Syllables"?
   (b) Analyze the theme of deception in "Seventeen Syllables."
   (c) Compare the use of the daughter's point of view in Hisaye Yamamoto's "Seventeen Syllables" and Grace Paley's "The Loudest Voice."
   (d) Compare the communication between parents and child in "Seventeen Syllables" and in Grace Paley's "The Loudest Voice."

Bibliography

Cheung, King-Kok. "Introduction." *Seventeen Syllables and Other Stories* by Hisaye Yamamoto. New York: Kitchen Table, 1988, xi–xxv.

Crow, Charles L. "The *Issei* Father in the Fiction of Hisaye Yamamoto." *Opening Up Literary Criticism: Essays on American Prose and Poetry.* Edited by Leo Truchlar. Salzburg, Aus.: Verlag Wolfgang Neugebauer, 1986, 34–40.

——. "A MELUS Interview: Hisaye Yamamoto." *MELUS* 14.1 (1987): 73–84.

Kim, Elaine H. *Asian American Literature: An Introduction to the Writings and Their Social Context.* Philadelphia: Temple Univ. Press, 1982. Chapter 5.

McDonald, Dorothy Ritsuko, and Katharine Newman. "Relocation and Dislocation: The Writings of Hisaye Yamamoto and Wakako Yamauchi." *MELUS* 6.3 (1980): 21–38.

Yogi, Stan. "Legacies Revealed: Uncovering Buried Plots in the Stories of Hisaye Yamamoto." *Studies in American Fiction* 17.2 (1989): 169–81.

Grace Paley (b. 1922)

Contributing Editor: Rose Yalow Kamel [p. 1882]

Classroom Issues and Strategies

Problems with teaching "The Loudest Voice" include students' unawareness of Jewish-American history and culture; an unfamiliarity with idioms and cadences of New York speech; a literalness that makes it difficult to appreciate Paley's irony and humor.

To address these problems, consider sharing photographs of and exchanging stories about students' immigrant grandparents. Encourage discussions of similarities between Jews and other immigrant populations.

Show films about the Jewish immigrant experience—*Ellis Island, Hester Street,* and segments of *Raisins and Almonds* all explore how first generation immigrants adapted to mainstream culture in New York

City. Implicit is the conflict between first and second generation immigrants explored in "The Loudest Voice."

For projects, consider the following:

1. Oral testimony projects: Students who elect to do oral testimony projects in which the narrators are older immigrants become more sensitive to first-person point of view, the function of memory, repetition, tonal variation, narrative ellipses. All of these devices Paley uses in her narratives.

2. Guest speakers: Foreign students—Hispanic, Asian, African—who reflect the latest wave of immigration can be invited to share their experiences adapting to the language and belief system of mainstream America. Whether oral or written, this kind of communication makes Paley more accessible to them and also to other students.

3. Essays: Students may write essays on the story focusing on the American teacher's point of view in describing the Jewish children in his/her class who need to be assimilated into American culture.

My students are preprofessional ethnics (Italian, Polish, Irish, Korean). Nostalgic, they respond strongly to family holidays, customs, food, and are interested in differences between old and new world tradition. On the other hand, they tend to be politically conservative and xenophobic, arguing that since their grandparents came to this country and realized the American dream, why can't the blacks do likewise? On the Yiddish/English conflict in "The Loudest Voice," they rail against bilingual education, failing to understand Paley's point that adaptable children can assimilate both languages.

Major Themes, Historical Perspectives, and Personal Issues

Focus on the influence of the American Dream on children of immigrants; the drive for upward mobility in order to realize it; the problem of deciding what aspect of ethnic heritage to retain, what to give up in order to assimilate in the promised land.

More subtly depicted is the theme of gender stereotyping. Paley depicts the socialization in public school of a young girl who successfully avoids conformity and passivity because her father and teacher encourage her to be assertive.

Significant Form, Style, or Artistic Conventions

Paley uses stylistic collage—fragments and ellipses, a merging of past and present tense—that conveys a sense of wholeness in which setting, character, point of view coalesce and render with absolute fidelity a small urban world. Tonal irony as well as a near-perfect ear for dialogue make Paley a writer's writer.

Structurally, Paley's stories resemble women's diary writing—fragmented, fact-focused, immersed in the transitory, seemingly disconnected aspects of daily life that define women's lives.

Original Audience

The reading audience for "The Loudest Voice" in the 1960s was probably similar to the urban, college-educated, cosmopolitan audience for Paley's stories today. She speaks as well to an audience of younger readers familiar with Hispanic and Asian tensions about holding on to traditional beliefs while seeking to enter mainstream culture by assimilating and becoming upwardly mobile.

Comparisons, Contrasts, Connections

Anzia Yezierska's "The Fat of the Land" from *Hungry Hearts and Other Stories by Anzia Yezierska* (New York: Persea, 1985) addresses the problem of young bilingual Jewish women trying to assimilate in the promised land. A comparison can be made between Yezierska's sentimentality and Paley's irony. Also comparable is Tillie Olsen's "I Stand Here Ironing," revealing similar parent-child tensions rooted in class struggle and ethnicity. In this first-person narrative, however, told from the mother's point of view, Emily the daughter becomes a social misfit, unable to conform to the stereotype of pretty blonde girl child. Unlike Shirley Abramowitz in "The Loudest Voice," Emily is shy, underachieving, unable to believe in herself unless she can play to the crowd as a stage comedian.

Questions for Reading and Discussion/ Approaches to Writing

1. (a) Write an essay focusing on the importance of place in your life. To what extent does place influence identity?

   (b) Write a first-person narrative focusing on your memory of exploring an experience or discovering an idea markedly different from those of your parents.

2. Compare the neighborhood settings in two other Grace Paley stories, "An Interest in Life" and "The Long-Distance Runner." Discuss the way settings in these stories make the first-person narrator feel integrated or marginal in her community.

Bibliography

A Bintel Brief: A Bundle of Letters to the Jewish Daily Forward, ed. Isaac Metzer (New York: Ballantine, 1971) is a compendium of letters written by Jewish immigrants describing their conflicts adapting to America. This small paperback provides a cultural background for the time, setting, and background of this story.

Blanche Gelfant, "Grace Paley: Fragments for a Portrait in Collage" (*New England Review*, 3: 285) is a lucid analysis of Paley's narrative style.

"To Aggravate the Conscience: Grace Paley's Loud Voice" in Rose Kamel, *Aggravating the Conscience: Jewish American Literary Foremothers in the Promised Land* (New York: Peter Lang, 1989, 115–49) is an analysis of Paley's short fiction in context with her life and beliefs.

Norman Mailer (b. 1923)

Contributing Editor: Barry H. Leeds [p. 1888]

Classroom Issues and Strategies

To begin with, any approach to teaching Norman Mailer's work must take into consideration his flamboyant and controversial public image, which often obscures critical responses to the works. Amazingly, many college students will not recognize Mailer's name at first; but those who do will very probably be armored in negative preconceptions, often based on incomplete or erroneous information.

The selections from *The Armies of the Night* presented in the anthology provide an opportunity to deal effectively with this issue: Mailer is ultimately shown, not as an unconscionable egotist presenting himself as his own hero, but as a rather self-deprecating narrator/protagonist. For example, crossing the line of MP's in his act of civil disobedience, he describes himself as a somewhat ridiculous figure:

"It was his dark pinstripe suit, his vest . . . the barrel chest, the early paunch—he must have looked like a banker himself, a banker, gone ape!" (pp. 150–151, Signet edition).

Again, before being arrested, Mailer feels, almost unwillingly, that "a deep modesty was on its way to him . . . as well as fear, yes now he saw it, fear of the consequences of this weekend in Washington . . ." (Signet, p. 93).

This emerging new sense of self leads to a crucial realization: "No, the only revolutionary truth was a gun in the hills, and that would not be his, he would be too old by then, and too incompetent, yes, too incompetent said the new modesty, and too showboat, too lacking in essential judgment . . ." (Signet, p. 94).

Yet despite the constant interplay here (as in his life and work as a whole) between the performer and the thoughtful commentator, what looms far larger is Mailer's evocative capacity to strike to the heart of an issue of national significance in his prose. Consider the forceful and moving conclusion to *The Armies of the Night*, entitled "The Metaphor Delivered" (Signet, p. 320).

The unusual point of view used here, which was to become a hallmark of Mailer's nonfiction of the 1970s provides interesting possibilities for a discussion of point of view and genre.

Major Themes, Historical Perspectives, and Personal Issues

The historical themes are obvious from the nature of *The Armies of the Night* and its relationship to the Vietnam War. Mailer's preoccupation with existential choice, personal courage, and integrity are evident in the passages selected.

Significant Form, Style, or Artistic Conventions

As I have explained in my headnote, Mailer's development from a derivative and naturalistic vision in *The Naked and the Dead* (1948) to a unique and highly existential one in later works such as *An American Dream* (1965) is evident in *Armies of the Night*. The concept of the "nonfiction novel" and the unusual third-person participant/narrator point of view are important in any discussion of *Armies* and Mailer's subsequent work.

Original Audience

It is interesting and important to discuss the significance (or perceived insignificance) of those events recounted in *Armies of the Night* to today's students. Further, my footnotes will to some degree ameliorate unfamiliarity with particular people or events.

Comparisons, Contrasts, Connections

Parallels can be drawn to Hemingway's *Green Hills of Africa* (1935), Tom Wolfe's *The Electric Kool-Aid Acid Test* (1968) and even *The Education of Henry Adams* (1907). Further, Mailer's early work, notably *The Naked and the Dead* (1948) was influenced profoundly by Farrell, Dos Passos, and Steinbeck.

Questions for Reading and Discussion/
Approaches to Writing

1. Do you find Mailer's use of himself as a third-person participant effective or confusing? This book, which won both a Pulitzer Prize and the National Book Award, has often been cited, along with Tom Wolfe's *The Electric Kool-Aid Acid Test* (1968) as an example of the "new journalism." But a similar point of view was used by Henry Adams in *The Education of Henry Adams* as early as 1907, and the concept of a "nonfiction novel" dates back at least as far as Ernest Hemingway's *Green Hills of Africa* (1935). Does this relatively unusual form attract or repel you?
2. Mailer writes (Signet, p. 63): "The American corporation éxecutive . . . was perfectly capable of burning unseen women and children in the Vietnamese jungles, yet felt a large displeasure and fairly final disapproval at the generous use of obscenity in literature and public." Do you agree with Mailer that depersonalized governmental violence is more obscene than the use of four-letter words?
3. Consider Mailer's final statements in "The Metaphor Delivered." Do you feel that Mailer, despite his antiwar civil disobedience, is a patriot? Do the U.S. Marshals who think him a traitor love their country more? Were you emotionally moved by this conclusion?
4. These events took place more than twenty years ago. Do they seem to have any bearing on your life, and on the America you live in today, or do they seem like ancient history? Are the participants (e.g., Robert Lowell, Dwight MacDonald) familiar or alien to you?

5. Can you envision any future national situation in which similar demonstrations might occur? Are there any that you might find justifiable?

Bibliography

Chapter 8, "The Armies of the Night," in *The Structured Vision of Norman Mailer* by Barry H. Legs (NYU Press, 1969) seems to help render the book more accessible to my students. Also:

Lennon, J. Michael, ed. *Critical Essays on Norman Mailer*. Boston: G. K. Hall, 1986.

Manso, Peter. *Mailer: His Life and Times*. New York: Simon and Schuster, 1985.

John Okada (1923–1971)

Contributing Editor: King Kok Cheung-Mare [p. 1900]

Classroom Issues and Strategies

Students need historical background concerning World War II and the internment of Japanese-Americans. Explain how people often internalize the attitudes of the dominant society even though the attitudes may seem unreasonable today.

Major Themes, Historical Perspectives, and Personal Issues

Historical context is crucial to the understanding of *No-No Boy*, since the novel explores unflinchingly the issues of Japanese-American identity. Is it half Japanese and half American, or is it neither? After the bombing of Pearl Harbor, Japanese-Americans in various coastal states—Washington, Oregon, California—were interned on account of their ethnicity alone. Camp authorities then administered a loyalty questionnaire that contained two disconcerting questions: "Are you willing to serve in the armed forces of the United States in combat duty wherever ordered?" and "Will you swear unqualified allegiance to the United States of America and faithfully defend the United States from any or all attacks of foreign or domestic forces, and forswear any form of allegiance or obedience to the Japanese Emperor, to any other foreign government, power, or organization?"

These questions divided the Japanese-American community and aggravated generational conflict. In some cases the parents still felt attached to their country of origin, while their American-born children—*nisei*—strived for an American identity. In other cases, the parents wanted to be loyal to America, but their children were too bitter against the American government to answer yes and yes.

Significant Form, Style, or Artistic Conventions

Okada commands a style that is at once effusive and spontaneous, quiet and deep. He has a keen eye for subtle details and psychological nuances that enables him to capture the reserved yet affectionate inter-action of Kenji's family.

Yet Okada seldom lingers on one key. He can change his note rapidly from subdued pathos to withering irony, as when he moves from depicting the silent grief in Kenji's household to exposing racism at the Club Oriental where Kenji feels totally comfortable because his being Japanese there does not call attention to itself. At that very moment, there is a commotion at the entrance: the Chinese owner reports that he has to prevent two "niggers" from entering the club with a Japanese. The one place where Kenji does not feel the sting of racial prejudice turns out to be just as racist as others.

Comparisons, Contrasts, Connections

Compare *No-No Boy* with Joy Kogawa's *Obasan* and Jeanne Wakatsuki Houston and James Houston's *Farewell to Manzanar*. All three books describe the adverse impact of the internment on Japanese-American families.

Questions for Reading and Discussion/ Approaches to Writing

1. (a) Why does Ichiro feel alienated?
   (b) Why is Ichiro rejected by the people in his own ethnic community? Who are the exceptions?
   (c) How would you characterize the interaction in Kenii's family?

2. (a) Compare the dilemmas of Ichiro and Kenji.
   (b) Who is responsible for Ichiro's suffering? Ichiro himself? His family? The Japanese-American community? America at large?

Bibliography

Book-length literary works that dwell on the Japanese internment include:

Farewell to Manzanar by Jeanne Wakatsuki Houston and James O. Houston (Boston: Houghton Mifflin, 1973)

Journey to Washington by Daniel Inouye and Lawrence Elliot (Englewood Cliffs, N.J.: Prentice-Hall, 1967)

All I Asking for Is My Body by Milton Murayama (San Francisco: Supra, 1975)

Upon Their Shoulders by Shelley Ota (New York: Exposition, 1951)

Nisei Daughter by Monica Sone (Boston: Little, Brown, 1953)

For a detailed study of the relation between historical circumstances and literature see:

Elaine Kim's *Asian American Literature: An Introduction to the Writings and their Social Context* (Philadelphia: Temple Univ. Press, 1982)

Brief surveys of Chinese American and Japanese-American literature: *Three American Literatures* edited by Houston A. Baker, Jr. (New York: MLA, 1982)

See also Dorothy Ritsuko McDonald, "After Imprisonment: Ichiro's Search for Redemption in *No-No Boy*," MELUS 6.3 (1979): 19–26.

James Baldwin (1924–1987)

Contributing Editors: Trudier Harris and John Reilly [p. 1912]

Classroom Issues and Strategies

Problems surround Baldwin's voicing the subjectivity of characters, the great sympathy he awards to the outlook of the marginalized. Students normally meet the underclass as victims perhaps objectified by statistics and case studies. For that matter, students who are not African-American have difficulty with the black orientation arising from Baldwin's middle-class characters: the artists and other, more conventionally successful people.

The strategies flow from the principle that people do not experience their lives as victims, even if popular social autobiographical essay *Notes of a Native Son*—the portion where he recounts contracting the "dread, chronic disease" of anger and fury when denied service in a diner—might be useful in raising the issue of why Baldwin says every African-American has a Bigger Thomas in his head. The anger may become creative, as might the pain. A companion discussion explores the importance of blues aesthetic to Baldwin: the artful treatment of common experience by a singular singer whose call evokes a responsive confirmation from those who listen to it. In addition, an exploration of the aesthetic of popular black music would also enhance the students' understanding.

Within a literary context, the strategies should establish that fictional narrative is the only way we know the interior experience of other people. The imagination creating the narrative presents an elusive subjectivity. If a writer is self-defined as African-American, that writer will aim to inscribe the collective subjectivity under the aspect of a particular character. Of course, the point is valid for women writers and other groups also, as long as the writers have chosen deliberately to identify themselves as part of the collective body.

Major Themes, Historical Perspectives, and Personal Issues

Themes of personal importance include the significance of community identification, the communion achieved in "Sonny's Blues" for example; the conflicted feelings following success when that requires departure from the home community; the power of love to bridge difference. The chief historical issue centers on the experience or urbanization following migration from an agricultural society. The philosophical issue concerns Baldwin's use of religious imagery and outlook, his interest in redemption and the freeing of spirit. Interestingly, this philosophical/religious issue is often conveyed in the secular terms of blues, but transcendence remains the point.

Significant Form, Style, or Artistic Conventions

Baldwin's frequent use of the first-person narration and the personal essay naturally associates his writing with autobiography. His fiction should be discussed in relation to the traditions of African-American autobiography which, since the fugitive slave narratives, has presented a theme of liberation from external bondage and a freeing of subjectivity to express itself in writing. As for period, his writing should be looked at as a successor to polemical protest; thus, it is temporally founded in the 1950s and 1960s.

Original Audience

In class I ask students to search out signs that the narrative was written for one audience or the other: What knowledge is expected of the reader? What past experiences are shared by assumption? Incidentally, this makes an interesting way to overcome the resistance to the material. Without being much aware that they are experiencing African-American culture, most Americans like the style and sound of blues and jazz, share some of the ways of dress associated with those arts and their audiences, and know the speech patterns.

Comparisons, Contrasts, Connections

One can make a comparison with *Benito Cereno* and *Native Son*. The basis is the degree of identification with African-Americans accomplished in each. How closely does the writer approach the consciousness of the black slave and street kids? Measure and discuss the gap between the shock felt by Delano and the communion of the brothers in Baldwin's story.

Questions for Reading and Discussion/ Approaches to Writing

Keeping in mind that James Baldwin's first experiences with "the word" occurred in evangelical churches, see if that influences his use of the "literary word."

What does Baldwin's short story tell you about the so-called ghetto that you could not learn as well from an article in a sociology journal?

College students are responsive to questions of the ethics of success. They may raise it with this story of "Sonny's Blues" by wondering why the narrator should feel guilty and even by speculating about what will happen to the characters next.

Bibliography

" 'Sonny's Blues': James Baldwin's Image of Black Community." *Negro American Literature Forum* 4, no. 2 (1970): 56–60. Rpt. in *James Baldwin: A Collection of Critical Essays*, edited by Keneth Kinnamon, 139–46. Englewood Cliffs, N.J.: Prentice-Hall, 1974. Also rpt. in *James Baldwin: A Critical Evaluation*, edited by Theman B. O'Daniel, 163–69. Washington, D.C.: Howard Univ. Press, 1977.

Flannery O'Connor (1925–1964)

Contributing Editor: Beverly Lyon Clark* [p. 1935]

Classroom Issues and Strategies

My students have trouble dealing with the horror that O'Connor evokes—often they want to dismiss the story out of hand, while I want to use it to raise questions. Another problem pertains to religious belief: either students lack any such belief, which might make a kind of sense of O'Connor's violence, or else they possess it, and latch onto O'Connor's religious explications at the expense of any other approach.

I like to start with students' gut responses—to start with where they already are and to make sure I address the affective as well as the cognitive. In particular, I break the class into groups of five and ask students to try to build consensus in answering study questions.

In general, the elusiveness of O'Connor's best stories makes them eminently teachable—pushing students to sustain ambiguity, to withhold final judgments. It also pushes me to teach better—to empower students more effectively, since I don't have all the answers at my fingertips. My responses to O'Connor are always tentative, exploratory. I start, as do most of my students, with a gut response that is negative. For O'Connor defies the humanistic responses I value—she distances the characters and thwarts compassion. Above all, O'Connor's work raises tantalizing questions. Is she, as John Hawkes suggests, "happily on the side of the devil"? Or, on the contrary, does the diabolical Misfit function, paradoxically, as an agent of grace? We know what O'Connor wants us to believe. But should we?

---

*With thanks to LynAnn Mastaj and her classmates for comments on these questions.

Major Themes, Historical Perspectives, and Personal Issues

One important context that I need to provide for my students is background on O'Connor's Christianity. The most useful source here is O'Connor's own essays and lectures, which often explain how to read her works as she would have them read. Certainly O'Connor's pronouncements have guided much of the criticism of her work. I'll summarize some of her main points:

She states that the subject of her work is "the action of grace in territory held largely by the devil" (*Mystery and Manners* 118). She tries to portray in each story "an action that is totally unexpected, yet totally believable" (118), often an act of violence, violence being "the extreme situation that best reveals what we are essentially" (113). Through violence she wants to evoke Christian mystery, though she doesn't exclude other approaches to her fiction: she states that she could not have written "A Good Man Is Hard to Find" in any other way but "there are perhaps other ways than my own in which this story could be read" (109).

In general O'Connor explains that she is not so much a realist of the social fabric as a "realist of distances" (44), portraying both concrete everyday manners and something more, something beyond the ordinary: "It is the business of fiction to embody mystery through manners . . . (124). She admits too that her fiction might be called grotesque, though she cautions that "anything that comes out of the South is going to be called grotesque by the northern reader, unless it is grotesque, in which case it is going to be called realistic" (40). And she connects her religious concerns with being southern, for, she says, "while the South is hardly Christ-centered, it is most certainly Christ-haunted" (44).

I also find it important to address the question of racism in the story. Is the story racist? I ask. Is the grandmother racist, in her comments on cute little pickaninnies and her use of "nigger"? Does the narrator endorse the grandmother's attitude? And what do we make of her naming a cat Pitty Sing—a pseudo-Japanese name that sounds less like Japanese than like a babytalk version of "pretty thing"? Is O'Connor simply presenting characteristically racist attitudes of not particularly admirable characters? I find Alice Walker's comments helpful here, on O'Connor's respectful reluctance to enter the minds of black characters and pretend to know what they're thinking.

Comparisons, Contrasts, Connections

O'Connor is usually compared to writers who are southern or gothic or Catholic or some combination thereof: e.g., William Faulkner,

Nathanael West, Graham Greene. Louise Westling (in *Sacred Groves and Ravaged Gardens: The Fiction of Eudora Welty, Carson McCullers, and Flannery O'Connor* [Univ. of Georgia Press, 1985]) has made fruitful comparisons with Eudora Welty and Carson McCullers, though most critics seem to find it difficult to discover points of comparison with other women writers.

Questions for Reading and Discussion/ Approaches to Writing

The following questions can be given to students in advance or used to guide discussion during class:

1. What qualities of the grandmother do you like? What qualities do you dislike? How did you feel when The Misfit killed her? Why?
2. How would you characterize the other members of the family? What is the function of images like the following: the mother's "face was as broad and innocent as a cabbage and was tied around with a green head-kerchief that had two points on the top like a rabbit's ears" and the grandmother's "big black valise looked like the head of a hippopotamus"?
3. How does O'Connor foreshadow death and the encounter with The Misfit?
4. What does the grandmother mean by a "good man"? Whom does she consider good people? What are other possible meanings of "good"? Why does she tell The Misfit that he's a good man? Is there any sense in which he is?
5. What is the significance of the discussion of Jesus? Was he a good man?
6. What is the significance of the grandmother's saying, "Why you're one of my babies. You're one of my own children"?
7. What is the significance of The Misfit's saying, "She would of been a good woman if it had been somebody there to shoot her every minute of her life"?

There are, of course, no absolute answers to these questions; the story resists easy solutions, violates the reader's expectations.

Bibliography

Other O'Connor stories well worth reading and teaching include "The Displaced Person," "The Artificial Nigger," "Good Country People," "Everything That Rises Must Converge," "Revelation," and "Parker's

Back" (all in *The Complete Stories* [Farrar, 1971]). O'Connor's essays have been collected in *Mystery and Manners* (Farrar, 1969).

As for secondary sources, the fullest biography so far, at least until O'Connor's long-time friend Sally Fitzgerald completes hers, is Lorine M. Getz's *Flannery O'Connor: Her Life, Library and Book Reviews* (Mellen, 1980).

For discussion of O'Connor's social, religious, and intellectual milieux see Robert Coles's *Flannery O'Connor's South* (Louisiana State Univ. Press, 1980).

A fine companion piece is Barbara McKenzie's photographic essay, *Flannery O'Connor's Georgia* (Univ. of Georgia Press, 1980).

Three collections of essays provide a good range of criticism on O'Connor:

1. *The Added Dimension: The Art and Mind of Flannery O'Connor*, ed. Melvin J. Friedman and Lewis A. Lawson (1966; rpt. Fordham Univ. Press, 1977).
2. *Critical Essays on Flannery O'Connor*, ed. Melvin J. Friedman and Beverly Lyon Clark (Hall, 1985).
3. *Flannery O'Connor*, ed. Harold Bloom (Chelsea House, 1986).

The Friedman and Clark collection, for instance, includes the Walker and Hawkes essays alluded to above: John Hawkes, "Flannery O'Connor's Devil," *Sewanee Review* 70 (1962): 395–407; Alice Walker, "Beyond the Peacock: The Reconstruction of Flannery O'Connor," *In Search of Our Mothers' Gardens* (Harcourt, 1983).

Further expositions of diverse approaches—religious, formalist, feminist, psychoanalytic, poststructuralist—appear in some thirty book-length studies and hundreds of articles.

Rolando Hinojosa-Smith (b. 1929)

Contributing Editor: Juan Bruce-Novoa [p. 1948]

Classroom Issues and Strategies

Most students know nothing about the author or the context of this selection. Useful information can be found in Hinojosa's interview included in *Chicano Authors, Inquiry by Interview* (Juan Bruce-Novoa).

I find it useful to ask students to write an accurate version of something they have experienced as a group: a short reading, a brief video, or even a planned interruption in class by an outsider. They then must consider the differences in the accounts of the same event. Sometimes I ask them to write an accurate description of an object I place in their midst; then we compare versions.

They respond to the element of different versions and observe how justice, represented in the newspaper reports, is not necessarily served. They ask if the person is guilty, raising the question of what is guilt.

Major Themes, Historical Perspectives, and Personal Issues

The major themes are the search for an accurate version of any event in the midst of the proliferation of information; the conflict between oral and written texts; the historical disregard for the Chicano community in South Texas and elsewhere; and the placement of the author in the role of cultural detective.

Significant Form, Style, or Artistic Conventions

The basic form is that of a criminal investigation, related to the detective story. Yet it breaks with the genre in that it does not resolve the case by discovery of the culprit; instead, the frame of the story maintains its position, and—if anything—gets worse.

Fragmentation does not bother students much now. The small units emphasize the post-modern experience of life as short sound bites.

The style is marked by shifts in voices, an attempt to capture the community in its speech patterns.

Original Audience

I establish the period of Chicano renewal (1965–1975) and the need expressed then in literature to search for communal history. It was aimed at an audience then that would sympathize with the victim, considering itself an abused and ignored group in a society controlled by the forces represented in the newspaper clippings that frame the story. This has changed. Now audiences are much less sympathetic to marginal peoples, and even Chicanos are not as willing to accept the old version of oppression of minority groups.

Comparisons, Contrasts, Connections

Faulkner's creation of a fictional county in several works coincides well with Hinojosa's project. The use of multiple voices to give different perspectives is quite similar.

Questions for Reading and Discussion/ Approaches to Writing

1. I ask students to consider what is history. What is news reporting? What is a fact? I often ask them to look up the etymology of fact and consider its relation to manufacture.
2. Assign the reporting of an imaginary event; give them the basic facts and characters and even an official summary statement. Then have them reconstruct the fragments as seen from one perspective. Compare the papers.

Bibliography

Refer to the headnote in the text for complete information.

Martin Luther King, Jr. (1929–1968)

Contributing Editor: Keith D. Miller [p. 1957]

Major Themes, Historical Perspectives, and Personal Issues

Context for "I Have a Dream"

Unfortunately, many students remain blissfully unaware of the horrific racial inequities that King decried in "I Have a Dream." In 1963, southern states featured not only separate black and white schools, churches, and neighborhoods, but also separate black and white restrooms, drinking fountains, hotels, motels, restaurants, cafes, golf courses, libraries, elevators, and cemeteries. Blacks were also systematically denied the right to vote. In addition, southern whites could commit crimes against blacks—including murder—with little or no fear of punishment. The system of racial division was enshrined in southern custom and law. Racism also conditioned life in the North. Although segregationist practices directly violated the Fourteenth and Fifteenth Amendments of the

Constitution, the federal government exerted little or no effort to enforce these amendments. Leading politicians— including John Kennedy, Robert Kennedy, and Lyndon Johnson— advocated racial equality only when pressured by King, James Farmer, John Lewis, and other activists who fostered nonviolent social disruption in the pursuit of equal rights. Fortunately black students are often knowledgeable of the civil rights era and can help to enlighten the rest of the class.

Content for "I Have a Dream"

"I Have a Dream" has been misconstrued and sentimentalized by some who focus only on the dream. The first half of the speech does not portray an American dream but rather catalogs an American nightmare. In the manner of Old Testament prophets, Frederick Douglass's "What to the Slave Is the Fourth of July?" oration, and John Lewis, King excoriated a nation that espoused equality while forcing blacks onto "a lonely island of poverty in the midst of a vast ocean of material prosperity."

Context for "I've Been to the Mountaintop"

By the time of King's final speech, the heyday of the civil rights movement was over. Large riots in major cities and the divisive issue of the Vietnam War had shattered the liberal consensus for civil rights and created an atmosphere of crisis.

Content for "I've Been to the Mountaintop"

King clearly wanted to energize his listeners on behalf of the strike. He analyzed the Parable of the Good Samaritan, identifying the Memphis strikers with the roadside victim and urging his listeners to act the part of the Good Samaritan. He also arranged the strike in a historical sequence that featured the Exodus, the cultural glory of Greece and Rome, the Reformation, the Emancipation Proclamation, the Great Depression, and—late in his address—the lunch counter sit-ins for civil rights and his major crusades in Albany, Birmingham, and Selma. By placing the struggle in Memphis in the company of epochal events and his own greatest achievements (neglecting to mention his more recent, unsuccessful campaign in Chicago), King elevated the strike from a minor, local event to a significant act in the entire American drama.

Significant Form, Style, or Artistic Conventions

Black Folk Pulpit: "I Have a Dream"

Important in reaching King's enormous and diverse audience were the resources of black folk-preaching. These resources included call-and-response interaction with listeners; calm-to-storm delivery that begins in a slow, professorial manner before swinging gradually and rhythmically to a dramatic climax; schemes of parallelism, especially anaphora (e.g., "I have a dream that . . ."); and clusters of light and dark metaphors. Black students can frequently inform their classmates about these time-honored characteristics of the black folk pulpit that give life to King's address.

Black Folk Pulpit: "I've Been to the Mountaintop"

Elements of the folk pulpit that animate "Mountaintop" include call-and-response interaction; calm-to-storm delivery; the apocalyptic tone of much evangelistic, revivalist preaching ("The nation is sick. Trouble is in the land."); and the updating of a prominent analogy of black Christians equating blacks with Old Testament Hebrews and slaveowners with the Egyptian Pharaoh. King resuscitated the analogy by labeling his opposition as Pharaoh and by urging solidarity among Pharaoh's oppressed and segregated slaves. Concluding "Mountaintop," King boldly likened himself to Moses and foretold his own death prior to blacks'/Hebrews' entry into the Promised Land.

Familiar Symbolism: "I've Been to the Mountaintop"

As with "I Have a Dream," King defined his appeal by explaining nonviolence and by applying standard patriotic and religious symbols to his effort. His protest became an exercise of the First Amendment; an attempt to rebuild a New Memphis akin to a New Jerusalem; a later chapter in the book of Exodus; and in his last sentence, a merging of his vision with that of "The Battle Hymn of the Republic."

Original Audience

King spoke "I Have a Dream" to an immediate crowd of 250,000 followers who had rallied from around the nation in a March on Washington held in front of the Lincoln Memorial. His audience also consisted of millions across the nation and the world via radio and television.

Important in reaching King's enormous and diverse audience were the resources of black folk-preaching. These resources included call-and-response interaction with listeners.

King's audience in "Mountaintop" consisted of 2,000 ardent and predominantly black followers gathered to support the cause of striking garbage workers in Memphis, Tennessee.

Comparisons, Contrasts, Connections

Old Testament prophets, Frederick Douglass's "The Fourth of July" oration, and John Lewis.

In "I Have a Dream" are the voices of Lincoln, Jefferson, Shakespeare, Amos, Isaiah, Jesus, Handel's *Messiah*, "America the Beautiful," a slave spiritual, and the black folk pulpit.

Bibliography

For a valuable analysis of King's 1963 address, see Alexandra Alvarez, "Martin Luther King's 'I Have a Dream': The Speech Event as Metaphor," *Journal of Black Studies* 18 (1988): 337–57.

I also encourage teachers to compare and contrast "I Have a Dream" with Frederick Douglass's "The Fourth of July" (*Rhetoric of Black Revolution*, ed. Arthur Smith, Boston: Allyn and Bacon, 1970, pp. 125–53.)

Useful for such a discussion is Robert Heath, "Black Rhetoric: An Example of the Poverty of Values," *Southern Speech Communication Journal* 39 (1973): 145–60.

For background on King, see James Cone, "Martin Luther King, Jr.: Black Theology—Black Church," *Theology Today* 40 (1984): 409–20.

Playing records or audio-video tapes of King's speeches substantially facilitates discussion of the oral dynamics of the black pulpit that nurtured King and shaped his address. The PBS series "Eyes on the Prize" is especially useful. "I Have a Dream" is available from Nashboro Records and, under the title *Great March on Washington*, from Motown Records. Tapes of these and many other addresses by King are available from the Southern Christian Leadership Conference in Atlanta.

Paule Marshall (b. 1929)

Contributing Editor: Dorothy L. Denniston [p. 1969]

Classroom Issues and Strategies

Our strategy for approaching Marshall's fiction is to explain the "Middle Passage" to illustrate the placement of blacks all over the world (African diaspora). It might also be helpful to discuss the notion of traditional African cyclical time, which involves recurrence and duration, as opposed to Western linear time, which suggests change and progress.

The cyclic approach applies thematically (Da-duh's symbolic immortality) and structurally (the story comes full circle). Also important is the traditional African view of the world as being composed of dualities/opposites that work together to constitute a harmonious moral order. (For a more complete explanation, see Marshall's "From the Poets in the Kitchen" in *Reena and Other Short Stories*.)

Consider also discussing the African oral tradition as a recorder of history and preserver of folk tradition. Since it is centered on the same ideas as written literatures (the ideas, beliefs, hopes, and fears of a people), its purpose is to create and maintain a national identity, to guide social action, to encourage social interaction, and simply to entertain. The oral arts are equally concerned with preserving the past to honor traditional values and to reveal their relevance to the modern world. Marshall's craftsmanship is executed in such a dynamic fashion as to elicit responses usually reserved for oral performance or theater.

Students readily respond to similarities/differences between black cultures represented throughout the diaspora. Once they recognize African cultural components as positive, they reevaluate old attitudes and beliefs and begin to appreciate differences in cultural perspectives as they celebrate the human spirit.

Major Themes, Historical Perspectives, and Personal Issues

A major theme is the search for identity (personal and cultural). Marshall insists upon the necessity for a "journey back" through history in order to come to terms with one's past as an explanation of the present and as a guiding post for the future. For the author, in particular, the story becomes a means to begin unraveling her multicultural background (American, African-American, Afro-Caribbean). To be considered foremost is the theme embodied in the epigram: the quality of life itself is threatened by giving priority to materialistic values over those that nourish the human spirit.

Significant Form, Style, or Artistic Conventions

Questions of form and style include Marshall's manipulation of time and her juxtaposition of images to create opposites (landscape, physical description, culture). This suggests an artistic convention that is, at base, African as it imitates or revives in another form the African oral narrative tradition. In fact, Marshall merges Western literary tradition with that of the African to create a new, distinctive expression.

Original Audience

All audiences find Marshall accessible. It might be interesting to contrast her idyllic view of Barbados in "To Da-duh" with her later view in the story "Barbados." The audience may wish to share contemporary views of third world countries and attitudes toward Western powers.

Comparisons, Contrasts, Connections

Both Toni Morrison and Paule Marshall deal with ancestral figures (connections to the past) to underscore cyclical patterns or deviations from them. Morrison's *Song of Solomon* (1977), *Tar Baby* (1981), or *Beloved* (1988) might be effectively compared to Marshall's *Praisesong for the Widow* (1983), *Brown Girl, Brownstones* (1959), or *The Chosen Place, the Timeless People* (1969).

Questions for Reading and Discussion/ Approaches to Writing

Discuss the use of African and Caribbean imagery and explain why it is essential to Marshall's aesthetic.

Bibliography

Barthold, Bonnie. *Black Time: Fiction in Africa, the Caribbean and the United States.* New Haven: Yale Univ. Press, 1981.

Brown, Lloyd. "The Rhythms of Poetry in Paule Marshall's Fiction." *Novel: A Forum on Fiction* 7, no. 2 (Winter 1974).

Christian, Barbara. *Black Women Novelists: The Development of a Tradition, 1982–1976.* Westport, Connecticut: Greenwood Press, 1980.

Marshall, Paule. "Shaping the World of My Art." *New Letters* (Autumn 1973).

Review especially the following:

——. "From the Poets in the Kitchen." In *Reena and Other Short Stories,* 3–12. Old Westbury, New York: The Feminist Press, 1983.

Mbiti, John S. *African Religions and Philosophies.* New York: Doubleday and Co., 1970.

Donald Barthelme (1931–1989)

Contributing Editor: Linda Wagner-Martin [p. 1979]

Classroom Issues and Strategies

The brevity and irony of Barthelme's work are sometimes surprising to students. Again, the high modernist quality—every word crafted for its purpose, but caught in a web of style and form that makes the whole seem artlessly natural—must be explained. Students may have read less contemporary fiction than modern and what contemporary fiction they have read may well be limited to the genres of romance, science fiction, and mystery. As with any period of art, the determining craft and language practices need explication.

In the case of such a short selection, ask students to write about the work at the beginning of the class—and again at the end, once discussion has finished—something simple like "What were your reactions to this work?" Then ask them to compare their two answers (without a grade, of course) with the hope of showing them that reading must be an active process, that they must form opinions. And in this author's case, getting his readers to respond is his first priority.

Major Themes, Historical Perspectives, and Personal Issues

People's inability to learn to live in their culture. The omnipresent romantic attitudes that society continues to inscribe, whatever the subject being considered. At base, the belief that people will endure, will eventually figure it out. Barthelme's fiction is, finally, positive—even optimistic—but first readings may not give that impression.

Significant Form, Style, or Artistic Conventions

Discuss the way humor is achieved, the interplay between irony and humor, the effects of terse and unsentimental language—students must be given ways of understanding why this story has the effect it does.

Contemporary fiction—whether minimalist or highly contrived parodic or allusive and truly post-modern—needs much more attention in the classroom. Connections must be made between writing students already understand, such as Hemingway's, and more recent work, so that they see the continuum of artistry that grows from one generation to the next.

Original Audience

Anticonservative in many ways, Barthelme's fiction taunts the current society and its attitudes at every turn. The teacher will have to be subtle in not claiming that "we all" think the way Barthelme does, or the legions of all-American conservatives will be on his/her doorstep; but the fiction itself can do a great deal.

Comparisons, Contrasts, Connections

Barthelme is given as a kind of example of this school, which includes Ray Carver, Jayne Anne Phillips, etc. Interesting approaches can be created by contrasting this fiction with much of that by writers of minority cultural groups—James Welch, Alice Walker—to see how such fiction differs.

Bibliography

Refer to the headnote in the text for complete information.

E. L. Doctorow (b. 1931)

Contributing Editor: Linda Wagner-Martin [p. 1982]

Classroom Issues and Strategies

Doctorow is an accessible writer, with few techniques that are troublesome to this media-trained student body. His juxtaposition of times and story lines, his sly parodies and jokes, his precise description all make reading his work interesting yet not terribly difficult. Doctorow's writing is usually not a closed system, though knowing about other texts and a great deal of American literature can enrich the primary reading experience.

Students deserve to be told in advance the kinds of skilled effects they should be alert to. Doctorow is a consummate craftsman who prides himself on milking every sentence for numerous effects. Students should know that reading him once, while pleasant, may not be enough.

In the case of this novel, there is much historical information that should be conveyed—including the fact that the Rosenberg case is still not settled decisively. Contradictory opinions still exist.

Major Themes, Historical Perspectives, and Personal Issues

Conflicts between conservative and liberal; historical patterns of conservative power at odds with humane behavior; issues of Doctorow's using sentiment (i.e., genuine feeling) in focusing on the children of the alleged traitors to evoke sympathy for their plight, as well as to create a framework for his narrative.

Significant Form, Style, or Artistic Conventions

Doctorow is the contemporary novelist who draws heavily from previous literature for both form and theme: for example, his recent *Billy Bathgate* (1989) bears much resemblance to Melville's *Billy Budd*, though it appears to be the Dutch Schultz story, just as his *Ragtime* was another amalgam of figures and episodes from the U.S. historical past. In this earlier fiction, the historical events are used less as a scaffolding for a more immediate story than as the structure of the narrative. We are urged to follow what seems to be an accurate retelling of the Rosenberg's story—but it is not, in some respects. It conflates the purpose of historically based fiction for its own ends. Doctorow has long been interested in John Dos Passos and his use of the historical within his fiction. Doctorow's complex uses of the past are a study in themselves.

Original Audience

Doctorow as a political writer would be one focus of the course, along with a great many other writers included in the contemporary section of the book. That *The Book of Daniel* appeared in 1971, in an era still suffused with the liberalism of the 1960s, is important. Audiences were more receptive to his evocation of sympathy in those years than they might be now. The references to the biblical text and to the figures of the children as they face inimical culture, strangely unsympathetic to their plight, add to the layers of irony that the author manages to achieve.

Comparisons, Contrasts, Connections

The writers of the 1930s and some contemporary writers (primarily black, Chicano, or female) share political aims, some more clearly stated than Doctorow's. While Carolyn Forché in her poems wants to create an atmosphere of action, Doctorow uses the political as a way into the humane. He does not ask the reader to make amends for the Rosenberg's punishment, or to find their children; he asks their pity for people caught in such a plight.

Bibliography

Refer to the headnote in the text for complete information.

Toni Morrison (b. 1931)

Contributing Editor: Linda Wagner-Martin [p. 1993]

Classroom Issues and Strategies

Expect some resistance to subject matter (menstruation, cross parents, the eventual rape of Pecola by her father, and the loveless home of the Breedlove family), which is complicated by the fact that Morrison is such a prominent black writer. *The Bluest Eye* could, of course, be a story of white characters. Students must be introduced to the fact that Morrison creates several plots, so that the poignant story of Pecola Breedlove is not seen as emblematic of all black daughters. The narrator and her sister are also black children, and their family not only survives, but teaches them how to survive—and prosper.

Expect to encounter the same resistance to much literature by women writers: that it is depressing (and therefore, somehow, unreal). "Real" literature is morally uplifting, no doubt.

Using what students already know about Morrison (probably *Beloved*, perhaps *Song of Solomon*), the instructor can discuss the importance of knowing the oeuvre of the writer's output and show how this excerpt from Morrison's first novel (1970) in some ways foreshadowed her later fiction. To create strong characters in *Beloved*, who kill their infant daughter rather than see her become a slave, is just a further development for the author who makes human interaction funny, believable, and touching in *The Bluest Eye* excerpt. Powerfully realistic diction and brilliantly sketched description make this excerpt work like a poem, and students should be led through some of its lines as if it were poetry.

Major Themes, Historical Perspectives, and Personal Issues

The abuses of poverty; the inhumanity of one needy person toward another; the public reaction to incest and resulting pregnancy; racial prejudice and class prejudice (wealthy blacks, or lighter skinned blacks, and their attitudes toward the Breedloves); social attitudes toward such "women's problems" such as prostitution, concepts of female beauty, the role of the mother.

Significant Form, Style, or Artistic Conventions

Morrison's techniques in this fiction are closer to modernist practices than to post-modernist. She begins with a set of excerpts from an elite school reader, blurring the words and letters as a black child—whose life is so remote from this paradigm of Dick and Jane, parents, white house, pets—admits being unable to understand either language or concepts. This distancing, of which the reader is reminded throughout the novel when lines from this section appear as chapter titles and epigraphs, creates the mood of puzzlement that dominates the text. The characters are puzzled by everything that happens; even Claudia as narrator cannot understand what she is describing, and her nostalgic recollections are dotted with apologies and explanations after the facts. Life is no fairy tale, and Morrison wrenches all the meaning possible from her anti-fairy tale. Growing up, as in Annis Pratt's study, means growing.

Original Audience

Placing the book at the beginning of the current feminist movement may help—issues such as women's bodily functions and incest were hardly the topic of a lot of fiction twenty years ago—but its blend of racial and gender depictions probably makes it key. The controversy over what African-American critics were studying (largely literature by black men) and what feminist critics were studying (largely literature by white women) needs to be described. There was no approach, no classroom, in which black women writers, despite their important tradition in literature, would regularly be taught. For Morrison to write such a novel in this context bespoke her own steady direction, one that subsequent novels have continued to explore.

Comparisons, Contrasts, Connections

Compare with Zora Neale Hurston, Alice Walker, Margaret Walker, and other black women writers who explore similar (if veiled) themes. But also look at the range of women authors included here, and the high modernists—Faulkner, Dos Passos—whose craft influenced Morrison in ways that might be less obvious.

Bibliography

Refer to the headnote in the text for complete information.

John Updike (b. 1932)

Contributing Editor: George Searles [p. 2007]

Classroom Issues and Strategies

One valid objection to Updike is that he is too narrowly an interpreter of the WASP/yuppie environment, a realm of somewhat limited interest; another is that his work proceeds from a too exclusively male perspective. The former concern will, of course, be more/less problematic depending on the nature of the college (more problematic at an urban community college, less so at a "prestige" school). The latter charge, however, provides the basis for fruitful discussion in any academic environment.

First, it's important to point out what Henry James once said, to the effect that we must grant an author's donnée and evaluate only in terms of what is made of it. But in Updike's case, it's also necessary to stress that his real concerns transcend his surface preoccupations. Although he's often described as a chronicler of social ills, really he's after larger game—the sheer intractability of the human predicament. Students must be shown that in Updike the particular is simply an avenue to the universal.

In addition to Updike's stories, students should be referred to the magazine articles listed in the bibliography and to the 1979 short story collection *Too Far To Go*, which reprints all the previous "Maples" stories, along with several then-new ones including "Separating." Also useful is the videotaped television special based on that collection. Another instructive exercise is to compare this story with some of Updike's early poems, particularly "Home Movies"—a little gem in its own right.

Indeed, there's a direct echo of this poem near the story's conclusion: "We cannot climb back . . ./ To that calm light. The brief film ends" is rendered in "Separating" as "You cannot climb back . . . you can only fall."

Most students seem better able to respond to Dickie and his siblings than to Richard or Joan. Younger students sometimes belabor rather secondary or irrelevant concerns: e.g., Why isn't the rock band identified? Why does John eat the cigarette?

Major Themes, Historical Perspectives, and Personal Issues

During the course of his long and prolific career, Updike has produced a series of interlocking short stories about Richard and Joan Maple, an upwardly mobile but unhappy couple whose ill-fated union closely parallels Updike's own first marriage to his college sweetheart, Mary Pennington. As critic Suzanne Henning Uphaus has neatly summarized it:

"The stories, written over a span of twenty-three years, follow the outward events. . . . Dick Maple, like Updike, married in the early fifties when he was twenty-one; both couples had four children, separated after twenty-one years, and finally received one of the first no-fault divorces granted in the state of Massachusetts."

This is probably the place from which to launch a classroom treatment of a story like "Separating."

Consider the protagonist's bleak assertion in Updike's *Roger's Version*: "There are so few things which, contemplated, do not like flimsy trapdoors open under the weight of our attention into the bottomless pit below" (74). Surely this has much to do with Dickie's baleful question "Why?" at the end of "Separating," and his father's perception of the boy's query as "a window thrown open on emptiness."

Significant Form, Style, or Artistic Conventions

Updike is acknowledged as a master stylist. "Separating" provides ample evidence of his skill in this area. Note, for example, the story's subtle but relentless accumulation of negative imagery. Again and again, key details reinforce Maple's inner sense of inadequacy, failure, and dread. Simultaneously, however, these images are juxtaposed with details of an ironically playful nature, thereby establishing a balance of sorts between angst and whimsy, a tone of amused negation that's perfectly suited to Updike's view of the human condition.

Original Audience

As this is a contemporary story, the "when/now" issue is not relevant. As for audience, I think that Updike sees himself writing for people more or less like himself: WASP, affluent, etc. But again, it's important when teaching Updike's work to show that the problems his characters confront are in a broad sense everyone's problems: responsibility, guilt, mortality, etc.

Comparisons, Contrasts, Connections

Updike is an exceptionally autobiographical writer. Perhaps that's the place to begin with a story like "Separating." Although this approach violates several critical tenets, it will get things rolling, and will lead ideally to discussion of the relationship between fiction and autobiography . . . how writers transmute personal experience into art. Comparisons can be drawn in this regard between Updike and Philip Roth and John Irving. Useful, too, is a consideration of the several *New Yorker* stories by Updike's son David: "Separating" from another angle.

Questions for Reading and Discussion/ Approaches to Writing

In a lower-level course (e.g., Freshman Comp, Intro to Lit) Updike's work—and especially a story like "Separating"—can generate good "personal experience" papers, as so many students today have first- or second-hand knowledge of separation and divorce.

Obviously, the story also lends itself exceptionally well to treatments of the whole "responsibility to self vs. responsibility to other" idea.

In an upper-level course, more strictly "literary" topics emerge.

Bibliography

Atlas, James. "John Updike Breaks Out of Suburbia." *The New York Times Magazine* (10 December 1978): 60–64, 68–76.

Howard, Jane. "Can a Nice Novelist Finish First?" *Life* (4 November 1966): 74–82.

Kakutani, Michiko. "Turning Sex and Guilt into an American Epic." *Saturday Review* (October 1981): 14–22.

———. "Updike's Struggle to Portray Women." *The New York Times* (5 May 1988).

"View From the Catacombs." *Time* (26 April 1968): 66–75.

Ernest J. Gaines (b. 1933)

Contributing Editor: John F. Callahan [p. 2016]

Classroom Issues and Strategies

The simplicity and tautness of Gaines's "The Sky Is Gray" sometimes lulls students to sleep and leads them, at first, not to look for some of the abiding, archetypal patterns in this story. Partly, this is due to the young boy's voice. Given the changes in race relations between the time in which the story was set, then written, and now, students need to read very carefully to pick up the nuances of this 1940s social milieu.

Instructor and students should read large chunks of the story outloud. Secondly, background on this milieu is very helpful; for this reason I urge that Gaines's essay "Miss Jane and I" (*Callaloo* 1, no. 3 [May 1974]) be offered as a companion to the story.

Students often ask about the actuality of segregation—they wonder whether Gaines's details are accurate. In addition, they ask whether the story's voice is consistently that of the young boy James.

Major Themes, Historical Perspectives, and Personal Issues

The story is about a young boy having to grow up earlier than he might have wished or than the adults in his family might have wished because his father is serving in World War II. The boy's mother must be father as well as mother to James. He learns about courage and dignity, about pain, and about the love and will that make pain bearable. The story also shows breaks in the color line enforced by Jim Crow laws and customs.

Significant Form, Style, or Artistic Conventions

How authentic are young James's voice and point of view? How (and why) does Gaines rely on the oral tradition of storytelling in his fiction?

Original Audience

Gaines has said over and over again that he writes especially for young people, with particular reference to the young whites and, preeminently, the young blacks of the South. That is worth exploring along with three different layers of time: (1) the story's time of the 1940s; (2) the writer's time of the mid-1960s; and (3) the reader's changing moment.

Comparisons, Contrasts, Connections

Other relevant stories in Vol. 2 of the anthology include: Faulkner's "Barn Burning"; Steinbeck's "Flight"; Wright's "The Man Who Was Almost a Man"; Ellison's *Invisible Man*, Chapter 1; and McPherson's "A Solo Song: For Doc."

Questions for Reading and Discussion/ Approaches to Writing

1. When does James become a man?
2. How does James come into his own voice?

Bibliography

See the special issue of *Callaloo* 1, no. 3 (May 1978) devoted to Gaines and his work.

Callahan, John F. "The Landscape of Voice in Ernest J. Gaines's *Bloodline*." *Callaloo* 7, no. 1 (Winter 1984): 86–112, especially pp. 86–90, 96–99.

N. Scott Momaday (Kiowa) (b. 1934)

Contributing Editor: Kenneth M. Roemer [p. 2038]

Classroom Issues and Strategies

In several areas, teachers of *Rainy Mountain* are in agreement. For example, whether an instructor uses excerpts or the entire book (the University of New Mexico paperback is the best classroom edition), acquainting students with a few of Momaday's other works can help them to establish important thematic, generic, and cultural contexts for reading *Rainy Mountain*. Especially relevant are the two sermons delivered by the Kiowa Priest of the Sun in Momaday's novel *House Made of Dawn* (1968) and Momaday's essay "The Man Made of Words" (available in Geary Hobson's anthology *The Remembered Earth* [1979]), which outlines the major phases of composition of *Rainy Mountain* and sets forth Momaday's theory of language.

Beyond recommending an acquaintance with *House Made of Dawn* and "Man Made of Words," there is little agreement among teachers of *Rainy Mountain* about how much "background" information students "need to know" in order to "understand" Momaday's book. This apparent confusion can become the focus for classroom discussions of an important question: How can works frequently omitted from literary canons and characterized by unfamiliar subject matter and unusual forms of expression be made accessible and meaningful to "typical" college students? One approach to this question is to ask students to complete their first readings and initial discussions of the excerpts from *Rainy Mountain* before they have received any background information; students should even be discouraged from reading the headnote. The initial discussion can center on questions about what type of writing the excerpts represent (e.g., should they be in a poetry section?) and about what types of information (if any) they think they need to understand the excerpts.

Major Themes, Historical Perspectives, and Personal Issues

The forms and themes of *Rainy Mountain* suggest numerous other classroom strategies many of which are described in detail in Part Two of *Approaches to Teaching Rainy Mountain* and in my *College English* essay on teaching survey courses (37 [1976]: 619–24).

The importance of landscape in Momaday's book also suggests a way to bridge discussions of nineteenth-century classic American literature and *Rainy Mountain*. As J. Frank Papovich has argued in "Landscape, Tradition and Identity" in *Perspectives on Contemporary Literature* (12 [1986]: 13–19), students should be made aware that there are alternatives to the concept of the American landscape articulated in the myth of the isolated male hero escaping from domesticity and society to confront the challenges of the wilderness. By contrast, Momaday's nature is a place teeming with intricate networks of animal, human, and cosmic life connected by mutual survival relationships, storytelling traditions that embrace social gatherings at his grandmother's house as well as the growth of a babe into the Sun's wife, and an imagination that can transform an Oklahoma cricket into a being worthy of kinship with the moon.

Significant Form, Style, or Artistic Conventions

Autobiography, epic, sonnet, prose-poem, history, folk tale, vision, creation hymn, lyrical prose, a collection of quintessential novels—these are a few of the labels critics, scholars, and N. Scott Momaday have used to describe *The Way to Rainy Mountain*.

Comparisons, Contrasts, Connections

I recommend comparisons between Momaday's written excerpts and parallel Kiowa oral narratives or pictorial histories (e.g., comparing the buffalo story in XVI to the narrative in Boyd, Vol. 2 [70–73] or comparing the descriptions in XVII of how women were treated to Mooney's accounts drawn from Kiowa calendar histories [280, 281, 294]).

Within the context of American literature courses, various comparative studies can be made between *Rainy Mountain* and other more familiar works. Instructors interested in narrative structure can compare Momaday's discontinuous and multivoiced text to poetic works by Masters, Eliot, and Pound and to prose works by Anderson and Faulkner.

Momaday's treatment of identity formation can be compared to other authors' attempts to define how personae who—because of their ethnic heritage, gender, or class status—had to integrate creatively the apparently unrelated elements of their mainstream and nonmainstream backgrounds and experiences.

Questions for Reading and Discussion/ Approaches to Writing

One participatory approach to the identity issue is to require students to select a significant landscape in their own backgrounds and to use this selection as the basis for composing three-voice sections modeled on the structure of *Rainy Mountain*.

Bibliography

Roemer, Kenneth M. *Approaches to Teaching Momaday's The Way to Rainy Mountain*. New York: MLA, 1989.

Nicholasa Mohr (b. 1935)

Contributing Editor: Frances R. Aparicio [p. 2048]

Classroom Issues and Strategies

Mohr's writings are quite accessible for the college-age student population. There is no bilingualism, her English is quite simple and direct, and her stories in general do not create difficulties in reading or comprehension.

Major Themes, Historical Perspectives, and Personal Issues

1. The universal theme of "growing up" (bildungsroman), and in her case in particular, growing up female in El Barrio.
2. The theme of the family; views of the Hispanic family and the expectations it holds of its members, in contrast to its American counterpart.
3. Sexual roles in Latino culture; traditional versus free vocations (for men).
4. Mother/daughter relationships; tensions, generational differences.
5. Women's issues such as career versus family, the economic survival of welfare mothers, dependency and independence issues.

Significant Form, Style, or Artistic Conventions

The autobiographical form is quite predominant in Mohr's writings, as is James Clifford's concept of "ethnobiography," in which the self is seen in conjunction with his/her ethnic community. And Mohr employs traditional storytelling, simple, direct, accessible, chronological use of time, logical structure.

Original Audience

It is important to read many of Mohr's works as literature for young adolescents. This explains and justifies the simplicity and directness of her style.

Comparisons, Contrasts, Connections

Fruitful comparisons could be made if we look at other Latina women who also write on "growing up female and Hispanic in the United States": Sandra Cisneros's *The House on Mango Street* (Houston: Arte Público Press, 1983); *Cuentos by Latinas*, eds. Alma Gómez, Cherríe Moraga, and Mariana Romo-Carmona (New York: Kitchen Table Women of Color Press, 1983); and Helena Maria Viramontes's *The Moths and Other Stories* (Houston: Arte Público Press, 1985). Viramontes's stories promise fruitful comparisons with Mohr's *Rituals of Survivals*.

In addition, Mohr has been contrasted to Piri Thomas's *Down These Mean Streets*, another autobiographical book in which El Barrio is presented in terms of drugs, gangs, and violence. I would propose a comparison to Eduard Rivera's *Family Installments* as yet another example of ethnobiography.

Finally, interesting contrasts and parallelisms may be drawn from looking at North American women writers such as Ann Beattie and the Canadian Margaret Atwood; while class and race perspectives might differ, female and feminist issues could be explored as common themes.

Questions for Reading and Discussion/ Approaches to Writing

1. Study questions: Specific questions on text, characters, plot, endings, issues raised. More major themes could also be explored such as: How do we define epic characters, history, and great literature? Where would Mohr's characters fit within the traditional paradigms?
2. Writing assignment: Students may write their own autobiography; experiment with first- and third-person narratives; contrast female students' writings with male students'.

   Paper topics: (a) Discuss role of women within family and society in Mohr's stories; (b) discuss Mohr as a feminine or feminist writer; (c) analyze the Hispanic cultural background to her stories *vis-à-vis* the universal themes.

Bibliography

Not much has been written on Nicholasa Mohr's work per se. The following are good introductory articles, and the Rivero article is particularly good for the study of bildungsroman in Latina women's writings:

Acosta-Belén, Edna. "The Literature of the Puerto Rican National Minority in the United States." *The Bilingual Review* 5:1–2 (Jan.–Aug. 1978): 107–16.

Cruz, Arnaldo. "Teaching Puerto Rican Authors: Modernization and Identity in Nuyorican Literature. *ADE Journal* (December 1988).

Mohr, Nicholasa. "On Being Authentic." *The Americas Review* 14:3–4 (Fall-Winter 1986): 106–109.

——."Puerto Rican Writers in the United States, Puerto Rican Writers in Puerto Rico: A Separation Beyond Language." *The Americas Review* 15:2 (Summer 1987): 87–92.

Rivero, Eliana, "*The House on Mango Street*: Tales of Growing Up Female and Hispanic." Tucson: Southwest Institute for Research on Women, The Univ. of Arizona, Working Paper 22, 1986.

Tomás Rivera (1935–1984)

Contributing Editor: Ramón Saldívar [p. 2056]

Classroom Issues and Strategies

The primary problem centers on the question of narrative form. Rivera's novel is written in nonsequential chronology, with a multiplicity of characters, without an easily identifiable continuous narrator, and without a strictly causal narrative logic. While each of the selections is coherent within itself, students will need to be prepared for the apparent lack of continuity from one section the work to the next.

I begin with a careful discussion of the first selection, "The Lost Year," to show that there is, at least in sketchy form, the beginnings of a narrative identity present. As in other modernist and post-modernist writings, in Faulkner's *As I Lay Dying*, and *Go Down, Moses*, for example, or in Juan Rulfo's *Pedro Paramo*, the narrative is not expository, attempting to give us historical depiction. It offers instead complex subjective impressions and psychological portraiture. Students should be asked to read the first selection looking for ways in which the narrative does cohere. Ask: Who speaks? Where is the speaker? What does the speaker learn about him/herself here even if only minimally? As students proceed to the following selections, it is appropriate to ask what this unconventional narrative form has to do with the themes of the work.

Rivera's work is openly critical of and in opposition to mainstream American culture. What does it accomplish by being oppositional? What does it share with other "marginal" literatures, such as African-American, feminist, gay and lesbian, or third world writings? Instead of attempting to locate Rivera within American or modernist writings, it might be useful to think of Rivera's place within the group of other non-canonic, antitraditional, enraged writings.

Students are sometimes misled by the apparent simplicity of the first selection: they might need to be carefully alerted to the question of identity being posed there. Also, the historical context of racial violence and political struggle may need to be constructed for students: they may want to see these stories as exclusively about the plight of *individuals* when in reality Rivera is using individual characters as *types* for a whole community.

Major Themes, Historical Perspectives, and Personal Issues

General Themes: The coming to maturity of a young child, as he begins to get a glimmer of the profound mystery of the adult world. The child, apparently a boy, raises in the second selection the traditional *lehresjahre* themes, having to do with the disillusionment of childhood dreams.

Specific Themes: This coming to maturity and the posing of universal existential questions (Who am I? Where do I belong?) takes place within the specific historical and social context of working-class life and political struggle of the Mexican-American migrant farmworker of the late 1940s and 1950s in Texas.

Universal themes are thus localized to a very high degree. What does this localizing of universal themes accomplish in the novel? Also, the question of personal identity is in each of the three selections increasingly tied to the identity of the community (*la raza*). The stories thus also thematize the relationship between private history and public history.

Significant Form, Style, or Artistic Conventions

Questions of style are intimately involved with questions of substance in these selections. Rivera claims to have been influenced by his reading in Joyce, Proust, Faulkner, and the great Latin American novelists. Rivera also acknowledged that he had been profoundly influenced by the work of the great Mexican-American anthropologist and folklorist Américo Paredes, whose ethnographic work realistically pictured turn-of-the-century life in the Southwest. Why does this work about the "local" theme of life in the American Southwest offer itself in the form of high modernism? Would not a more straightforward socialist realism have been more appropriate for the themes it presents?

Original Audience

The work was originally written in Spanish, using the colloquial, every-day cadences of working-class Spanish-speaking people. Bilingual instructors should review the original text and try to point out to students that the English translations are but approximations of a decidedly *oral* rhythm. Written at the height of the Chicano political movement and in the midst of an often bitter labor struggle, at times Rivera's work bristles with anger and outrage. The turmoil of the late 1960s and early 1970s plays a large role in the tone of the work.

Comparisons, Contrasts, Connections

Rivera claimed to have been influenced by many modern authors, Faulkner chief among them. A useful discussion of the relationships between form and theme might arise by comparing Rivera's work with Faulkner's *As I Lay Dying*, or *Absalom, Absalom!* What does narrative experimentation have to do with social realism? Why does an author choose nontraditional narrative techniques? What does one gain by setting aside causally motivated character action?

Questions for Reading and Discussion/ Approaches to Writing

1. Many of the questions posed by this study guide might be fruitfully addressed to students before they read Rivera's work. Especially useful are those questions that ask students to think about the relationship between form/content and that take into account the historical/political circumstances of the period during which these stories were written.

2. Students might consider in the piece entitled "And the Earth Did Not Devour Him": Why does the earth not devour him? What does the narrator learn and why does this knowledge seem so momentous? Concerning the last selection, "When We Arrive," students might discuss the journey motif: Where are these migrant workers going? What will they find at the end of the road?

Bibliography

Ramón Saldívar, "A Dialectic of Difference: Toward a Theory of the Chicano Novel," in *Contemporary Chicano Fiction*, ed. Vernon E. Lattin (Binghamton, N.Y.: The Bilingual Press, 1986), pp. 13–31, includes a discussion of the selections. *International Studies in Honor of Tomás Rivera*, ed. Julian Olivares (Houston: Arte Público Press, 1985) is an excellent collection of essays on *And the Earth Did Not Devour Him*.

Thomas Pynchon (b. 1937?)

Contributing Editor: Richard Pearce [p. 2065]

Classroom Issues and Strategies

Problems in teaching Pynchon are contradictory. On the one hand, students feel that the story is superficial and limited to the stereotype of the sixties they know from television. On the other hand, even by the end of this short section, they begin to feel overloaded—too much coincidence, too much happening.

To address these problems, emphasize the comedy. Deal with the problem of coincidence and overloading head on. List all the events and coincidences; discuss them. Work with elements of popular culture: radio, television, rock music, advertising, technology. Relate all the plots to the vague sense that someone or some organization may be plotting. Ask what we know about Pierce Inverarity. Relate to the post-World War II development of the suburbs, automobiles and superhighways, plastics, electronics, and the military-industrial complex. Focus on two goals: (1) understanding the decentered novel—too much going on for us to grasp, to understand what's important, to distinguish the good guys from the bad guys (and later radicals from reactionaries); and (2) recognizing that everything is connected. End with questions about this paradox: Is it positive—the ultimate democratic novel, where there are no hierarchies, where people from all classes and many subcultures will become interconnected, and where a woman can take on the role of hero (and Oedipus)? Is it negative—a writer running out of control, the ultimate paranoic nightmare, a random world where there is no connection and no meaning?

Major Themes, Historical Perspectives, and Personal Issues

Focus on the modern problems of (1) ordinary people being controlled by big business, the media, government, and (2) having access to so much information that we can't grasp connection or meaning.

Significant Form, Style, or Artistic Conventions

See the discussion of post-modernism in the head. Have students identify as many styles and allusions as possible—from pop (the Shadow, Baby Igor) to Papa (Oedipus). See how they relate, or don't relate.

Original Audience

By understanding the complex context of the sixties, we can understand the novel's pertinence today.

Bibliography

See the chapters on *Lot 49* in Joseph Slade's *Thomas Pynchon* (New York: Warner, 1974); Tony Tanner's *Thomas Pynchon* (London and New York: Methuen, 1982); and Alan Wilde's *Middle Grounds: Studies in Contemporary American Fiction* (Philadelphia: Univ. of Pennsylvania Press, 1987).

See also my brief introduction to *Critical Essays on Thomas Pynchon* (Boston: G. K. Hall, 1981), which was reprinted in *American Writers: A Collection of Literary Biographies* III, Part 2, ed. A. Walton Litz (New York: Scribner's, 1981).

Among the most important critical works is the chapter on Pynchon in Tony Tanner's *City of Words: American Fiction 1950–1970* (New York: Harper and Row, 1971), reprinted in *Twentieth Century Views of Thomas Pynchon*, ed. Edward Mendelson (Englewood Cliffs, N.J.: Prentice-Hall, 1978).

One of the most intelligent discussions of *The Crying of Lot 49* is the chapter in Thomas H. Schaub's *Pynchon: The Voice of Ambiguity* (Urbana:

University of Illinois Press, 1981), reprinted in *Critical Essays on Thomas Pynchon*, ed. Richard Pearce (Boston: G. K. Hall, 1981).

Setting *Lot 49* in the context of this anthology is Wendy Steiner's essay in *Reconstructing American Literary History*, ed. Sacvan Bercovitch (Cambridge, Massachusetts: Harvard Univ. Press, 1986).

Joyce Carol Oates (b. 1938)

Contributing Editor: Eileen T. Bender [p. 2072]

Classroom Issues and Strategies

In a time of instant fare—both literal and intellectual—Joyce Carol Oates is most demanding. Several of her more recent novels (she has published eighteen as of 1988) are, like the nineteenth-century work she parodies, voluminous. Oates has produced an amazing variety of excellent work in all genres: novels, short fiction, drama, critical essays, poetry, reviews of contemporary writing and ideas. She reads, edits, and teaches, currently holding a chair professorship at Princeton University. She defeats those readers who want artists to fit certain categories. Extremely well-read, and at home in the classroom, Oates is often deliberately elusive.

While she calls her writing "experimental," Oates's individual works are highly accessible—at least at first glance. Often, as in "Where Are You Going, Where Have You Been?" they begin in familiar territory. The central characters and the scenes are vivid and recognizable. Details (in this case, the drive-in teen culture, the sibling rivalry, the snatches of popular songs) enhance the sense of *déjà vu*. Yet by the end, dark and violent forces surface to baffle conventional expectations, of both character and plot. Once again, the so-called "Dark Lady of American Letters" creates a disturbance, challenging the reader to think of both fiction and reality with new and deeper understanding.

Because of the variety of her work, Oates can be viewed as a "woman of letters." Students will be interested in a writer who is constantly engaged in public discussion (in print most frequently) of the arts: they should watch for her letters to the editor, interviews, essays, and reviews in the *New York Times*, and the popular press.

Oates's work itself can be approached at different levels of sophistication. It is always interesting to explore the many allusive patterns in her fiction. Several of her short stories are meant as explicit imitation of famous forebears (e.g., "The Dead," "Metamorphosis," "The Lady With the Pet Dog"), and those can be read in tandem to see the complexity of Oates's relationship to literary tradition.

In "Where Are You Going, Where Have You Been?" Oates makes an ordinary tale extraordinary by juxtaposing two powerful legends: the modern rock hero (the story is dedicated to activist-song writer Bob Dylan), and the ancient demon lover. Drawing together these threads, Oates is able to tell a chilling tale of a young adolescent, tantalized by glamorous surfaces, unable to resist more satanic designs. In this case, the "accessible" story needs to be peeled back, in order for Oates's intentions and the full sense of the work to be understood.

In responding to this story, students are disturbed by the violence that erupts from ordinary reality, and question its function or purpose—especially if they view literature as a kind of moral lesson or as an escape into a world elsewhere (the romantic paradigm). They will ask questions about the author herself, surprised that so academic and soft-spoken a person is capable of describing such violence in her stories. These responses provide an ideal occasion to discuss the creative process, and the difference between author and character, biography and literature, reality imagined and imaginative reality.

Major Themes, Historical Perspectives, and Personal Issues

At the center of much of Oates's work is concern about the singular power of the self, and the high cost of the struggle for autonomy. In this, she is like those contemporary "third force" psychologists she has studied and admired (chiefly Maslow and Laing) who posit a different human ideal: communion rather than mastery. Readers might focus on the patterns of selfhood and the possibilities for relationship in her work.

Oates also calls herself a "feminist" although she does not like the restrictive title of "woman writer"; rather, she prefers being described as a woman who writes. In her exploration of character and relationships, the nature of love and sexual power are frequently at issue. Again, this would be a fruitful topic for further reading and discussion, using Oates's own essays on androgyny, feminism, and the special circumstances of the "woman who writes" as starting point.

Oates is not only an avid student of literature and reader of history, psychology, and philosophy; she is a keen interpreter of the contemporary scene, concerned in her work with issues relevant to most modern readers. Besides feminist questions, her work has dealt with politics, migrant workers, medical and legal ethics, urban riots, and, most recently, boxing. Such work is immediately accessible to students. It also allows Oates to expose her own sense of the wonder and mystery of human character and personality.

Significant Form, Style, or Artistic Conventions

Interestingly, among her "imitations" and allusive fictions, Oates has tested almost every major literary school or set of conventions: naturalism, existentialism, social realism, detective stories, epic chronicle, romance. Presenting excerpts from Oates's novels would not only show her versatility, but would convey the way literature has an important and imposing influence on the modern writer.

While the story in this anthology unfolds chronologically, and appears conventional, the more surrealistic subtext imposes itself and frustrates the fairy-tale or "happy ending" quest. The subversion of one convention by another here is not only interesting in its own right, but enforces Oates's thematic design.

Original Audience

"Where Are You Going, Where Have You Been?" is of course a contemporary story; yet it also rests on a diminishing sense of recent history. It was written for an audience who had a vivid sense of the tumultuous American '60s, with its antiwar activism, folk and rock music, and emergent "youth culture." If indeed the hippies of that time are the yuppies of today, it would be important for students to reacquaint themselves with the work Bob Dylan (the story's dedicatee) and others represented, as well as the perilous uncertainty of those times, which would have heightened the risks of adolescent passage.

Comparisons, Contrasts, Connections

While Oates has been variously compared and contrasted with Welty, Faulkner, Steinbeck, and even Dreiser, one of the more interesting writers with whom she might be compared is Flannery O'Connor. (Oates even wrote a moving poem about her, following O'Connor's death.) "Where Are You Going, Where Have You Been?" can best be compared with O'Connor's "A Good Man Is Hard to Find," in which gratuitous and even mindless violence bursts through and destroys the pious confidence of O'Connor's ordinary country people. Both Oates and O'Connor emphasize the reality and presence of evil. But in O'Connor's case, the imminence of evil transforms visible reality into mere illusion. For

Oates, naivete (not innocence) is dangerous in a perennially fallen but vividly real world.

Questions for Reading and Discussion/ Approaches to Writing

Questions useful *before* reading the selection would concern the two "legends" that are important to the story: Dylan and Demon.

1. Why is this story dedicated to Bob Dylan?
2. Who is Arnold Friend? Do you think he is appropriately named? What is the significance of his car? His clothing? His language?
3. When and why does Connie begin to question his identity? What impact does her confusion have on her own personality? How are "personality" and "identity" displayed and defined in this story?

Additionally, students may need more background on Dylan and the '60s to understand Oates's view of the demonic aspect of those times in America.

In dealing with this story, students might be asked to put themselves in the place of Connie's sister or one of Connie's "real" friends, describing Friend or their perception of what has happened. The title should be discussed. Students can be asked to find the Dylan lyric that gives the story its title, play it for the class, and lead a discussion of the culture and politics of the '60s; photographs of that time could be especially useful in picturing the look and style Friend tries to emulate. Students might write about the danger of "codes": their power to distort perception.

Another approach could be aesthetic: specifically, viewing the story not as realistic but surrealistic. Here, paintings of modern masters such as Magritte or Dali could illustrate the hauntingly familiar contours of the surrealistic imagination—another possible written assignment. Oates herself refers to an earlier surrealist, Bosch, in the title of an early novel, *A Garden of Earthly Delights*. That painting might generate a lively discussion of Oates's vision of evil.

Bibliography

Bender, Eileen T. *Joyce Carol Oates, Artist In Residence*. Bloomington: Indiana Univ. Press, 1987.

Clemons, Walter. "Joyce Carol Oates: Love and Violence." *Newsweek*, 11 (Dec. 1972): 72–77.

Creighton, Joanne. *Joyce Carol Oates*. Boston: G. K. Hall, 1979.

Friedman, Ellen. *Joyce Carol Oates*. New York: Ungar, 1970.

Kazin, Alfred. *Bright Book of Life*. New York: Atlantic/Little, Brown, 1973.

Norman, Torburg. *Isolation and Contact: A Study of Character Relationships in Joyce Carol Oates's Short Stories*. Goteburg, Sweden: Gothenburg Studies in English 57, 1984.

Wagner, Linda. *Critical Essays on Joyce Carol Oates*. Boston: G. K. Hall, 1979.

Michael Herr (b. 1940)

Contributing Editor: Raymund Paredes [p. 2086]

Classroom Issues and Strategies

The major problem in teaching Herr is that, given the poor historical knowledge of most U.S. college students, they often know little about the Vietnam War, its causes and sources of conflict. Furthermore, some students will not know the military terms used in the selection.

It's probably necessary and certainly a good idea to provide some sort of historical context for the consideration of Herr's work. This can be done by assigning supplementary reading or lecturing on the history of the Vietnam War. As a Vietnam War veteran myself, I relate my own personal experiences of the war to students to compare with Herr's. If you, or any older students, have direct experience with the Vietnam era, this is a useful approach. There are many good films about Vietnam (both feature and documentary) that could complement Herr's book.

Students respond very strongly to the graphic depiction of the inhumanity and insanity of the war. They want to know more about the causes of the Vietnam War and the political climate of the United States at the time.

Major Themes, Historical Perspectives, and Personal Issues

The major themes in the excerpted passage are the dehumanizing and brutalizing influences of war, particularly the way war renders soldiers incapable of functioning in "normal" social circumstances; the relationship between the writer's style and presentation of the war and the drug culture of the 1960s and 1970s; and the author's view that the war was fundamentally immaterial, even more so than other wars. Key here is Herr's use of the Spanish phrase "la vida loca" (the crazy life). On a personal level, Herr emphasizes his troubling, even macabre, attraction to the war, its combination of bloodshed, madness, camaraderie, and heroism.

Significant Form, Style, or Artistic Conventions

Dispatches is an extraordinary work stylistically, a brilliant execution of the speaking styles of young American soldiers: fast paced, full of slang, very much shaped by popular culture (films, television, rock and roll music) and the drug culture. Herr is also adept at capturing the officialese of the U.S. military establishment. Many of the formal and stylistic qualities of *Dispatches* connect Herr to postmodernism.

Original Audience

Dispatches is a very contemporary book in terms of its values, its point of view, a book about young people written by a young person.

Comparisons, Contrasts, Connections

Herr's work can be compared to that of other writers about the Vietnam War and with the so-called "new journalists" such as Tom Wolfe. The second connection is especially interesting. Students might note how Herr uses literary/fictional techniques—figurative language, characterization, narrative development—in what is ostensibly, as indicated by the title, a work of journalism. Students might look at other treatments of the Vietnam War—both fictional and journalistic—to compare points of view about the war, its impact on the humanity of the soldiers, etc.

Questions for Reading and Discussion/ Approaches to Writing

1. What is the author's attitude toward the war? What are the effects of the war on human behavior? From your knowledge, is Herr's position on the war widely shared?

2. How would you describe Herr's style? In what ways is Herr's style compatible (or not) with its subject? From what sources does Herr draw his images, his metaphors? How does this compare with the practices of other writers? In what sense is the notion of "la vida loca" symbolic of both the literary situation and the temper of the times?

Bibliography

Other books on Vietnam are very useful. I recommend: Stanley Karnow's *Vietnam*, Neil Sheehan's *A Bright Shining Lie*, Wallace Terry's *Bloods*, and Philip Caputo's *A Rumor of War*.

Maxine Hong Kingston (b. 1940)

Contributing Editor: Amy Ling [p. 2094]

Classroom Issues and Strategies

The primary problem for any initial reading of Kingston's *Woman Warrior* is the question of genre or form. Is this text nonfiction? (It won the National Book Critics Circle Award for the best book of nonfiction published in 1976.) Since the word "memoirs" is in the title, is it autobiography? Or is it a piece of imaginative fiction, which seems most apparent in the "White Tigers" chapter included in this anthology. *The Woman Warrior*, of course, is all of the above, sequentially and simultaneously, a collage of genres.

As Kingston does not maintain a unity of genre, neither does she maintain a unity of diction. "White Tigers" begins with a colloquial tone, a Chinese-American woman speaking informally about her Chinese-American female upbringing. It then goes into a conditional tense and a storytelling mode—"The call *would* come from a bird that flew over our roof"—into a narration filled with magical details, described at times in a matter-of-fact manner, at other times in an elevated, poetic style. Then, without warning, the language and the subject matter lapse abruptly from the fanciful to the everyday in the sudden line, "My American life has been such a disappointment." In diction and language also, *The Woman Warrior* is an amalgamation.

In terms of content, "White Tigers" has been called, by one critic from the People's Republic of China, "a version of the Kung Fu movie interspliced with a Western." (See David Leiwei Li's article, "The Naming of a Chinese American "I" Cross-Cultural Sign/nification in *The Woman Warrior*," in *Criticism* 30:4, Winter 1988, p. 506.) According to Li, "Kingston's artistic match-making of the Kung Fu and the Western in the representation of the Chinese myth is an exploitation of the general audience who will be, one may argue, more responsive to formulaic genres." (506)

Major Themes, Historical Perspectives, and Personal Issues

Since her mother's talking-story was one of the major forces of her childhood and since she herself is now talking-story in writing this book, stories, factual and fictional, are an inherent part of Kingston's autobiography. Finding one's voice in order to talk-story, a metaphor for knowing oneself in order to attain the fullness of one's power, becomes one of the book's major themes.

As the second chapter of a five-chapter book, "White Tigers" is best understood in the context and thematic structure of the entire work. The book's first chapter, "No Name Woman," tells the story of the paternal aunt who bears a child out of wedlock and is harried by the villagers and by her family into drowning herself; the family now punishes this taboo-breaker by never speaking of her, by denying her her name. "No Name Woman" presents the cautionary tale of woman as victim; "White Tigers," however, provides the model to emulate, woman as victor. This pattern, woman as victim opposed to woman as victor, is repeated throughout the text in succeeding chapters.

Significant Form, Style, or Artistic Conventions

One of the distinctive accomplishments of *The Woman Warrior* is that it crosses boundaries between genres, dictions, styles, between fact and fiction, as it crosses the boundaries between cultures, Chinese and American. In the collage of style and form, in the amalgam of language and content, in the combination of Chinese myth, family history, and American individualism and rebelliousness, Kingston defines herself as a Chinese-American woman. Thus, the book would appear to be primarily autobiographical in thrust, though not wholly factual in content.

Original Audience

The Woman Warrior is decidedly a product of the sixties, of the civil rights and women's liberation movements.

Comparisons, Contrasts, Connections

Like other women and ethnic writers such as Leslie Marmon Silko, Toni Morrison, and Adrienne Rich who appropriated and revisioned myths for their own uses, so Kingston appropriated the tale of the legendary Fa Mulan for her own purposes. The original ballad of the Chinese woman warrior is recorded in a fifth-century ballad of 62 lines; Kingston elaborates on this ballad, adding the fanciful details of the long and arduous training period with the two immortals in the mountains and her nurturing by animals and other natural forces. Kingston's most significant addition, however, is the woman warrior's marriage and childbearing while still in armor disguised as a man. In the original ballad, Mulan performs these roles sequentially; in Kingston's version, simultaneously. With this change, Kingston crosses gender barriers, making her woman warrior into a superwoman who is not bound by gender differences and separate spheres but who can perform successfully in warfare, a traditionally masculine role, and at the same time bear children, an exclusively feminine role.

Questions for Reading and Discussion/ Approaches to Writing

1. In the first chapter of *The Woman Warrior*, Kingston questions other Chinese-Americans as to what is Chinese tradition and what is the movies. What elements in "White Tigers" are typical of a Kung Fu movie? Which portions of this selection are decidedly not?
2. Kingston allies "wives and slaves" and opposes them to heroines and swordswomen. In the Chinese tradition as Kingston portrays it why was the position of wife such an undesirable one?
3. Using evidence outside the text, has Kingston succeeded in any way as a literary "woman warrior"? Has she herself inverted the woman as victim into woman as victor? How?

Bibliography

Blinde, Patricia Lin. "The Icicle in the Desert: Perspective and Form in the Works of Two Chinese American Women Writers." *MELUS* 6.3 (1979): 51–71.

Cheung, King-Kok. " 'Don't Tell': Imposed Silences in *The Color Purple* and *The Woman Warrior*." *PMLA* 103 (1988): 162–74.

Chua, Chen Lok. "Two Versions of the American Dream: The Golden Mountain in Lin Yutang and Maxine Hong Kingston." *MELUS* 8.4 (1981): 61–70.

Juhasz, Suzanne. "Towards a Theory of Form in Feminist Autobiography: Kate Millet's *Fear of Flying* and *Sitar*; Maxine Hong Kingston's *The Woman Warrior*." *International Journal of Women's Studies* 2.1 (January-February 1979): 62–75.

Kingston, Maxine Hong. "Cultural Misreadings by American Reviewers." In *Asian and Western Writers in Dialogue: New Cultural Identities*, edited by Guy Amirthanayagam, 55–65. London: Macmillan, 1982.

Li, David Leiwei. "The Naming of a Chinese American "I": Cross-Cultural Sign/nifications in *The Woman Warrior*." *Criticism* 30:4 (Winter 1988): 506.

Ling, Amy. "Thematic Threads in Maxine Hong Kingston's *The Woman Warrior*." *Tamkang Review* 14 (1983–4): 5–15.

Rabine, Leslie W. "No Paradise Lost: Social Gender and Symbolic Gender in the Writings of Maxine Hong Kingston." *Signs* 12.3 (1987): 471–92.

Bobbie Ann Mason (b. 1940)

Contributing Editor: Linda Wagner-Martin [p. 2115]

Classroom Issues and Strategies

There are few problems, except for those of tone and mood identification. Mason's seemingly artless style and unsophisticated characters throw readers off guard: this fiction is easy, and perhaps less meaningful than something more challenging. But the same kind of explicative tactics that are appropriate with Cather or Fitzgerald will work with Mason and should be applied.

The South is just now producing quantities of good fiction, and Mason should be seen as a part of that renaissance. Whether the impetus is the breaking of cultural mores, the racial conflicts that remain centered in that region, or the legacy of oral storytelling, the outcome is the same—a body of excellent, and varied, fiction, much of it written by women. Mason's story is particularly suitable for discussing each of these elements—and for seeing how she achieves her deft control of the fictional line.

Major Themes, Historical Perspectives, and Personal Issues

Countless "domestic" fictions have given readers marriage as the expected happy ending. "Shiloh" shows the happiness that results from marriage dissolved and posits a number of problems in women's (and men's) expectations of the blessed union. Setting the troubled marriage on the Civil War battlefield adds to the irony and poignancy, and it also points to the southernness of the situation (women in the South are traditionally conservative, mindless, and domestic).

Significant Form, Style, or Artistic Conventions

In some ways a minimalist story (like those of Ray Carver), Mason's work achieves a quantity of effects through a sketch-like suggestion. Placing her fiction in the context of other contemporary writing is very important, and contrasting it with the selection by Louise Erdrich might be a useful technique for showing how formal Mason's craft is.

Original Audience

Because this is so contemporary, the question of historical difference is not important.

Bibliography

Refer to the headnote in the text for complete information.

James Welch (Blackfeet-Gros Ventre) (b. 1940)

Contributing Editor: Linda Wagner-Martin [p. 2126]

Classroom Issues and Strategies

Students are completely unfamiliar with this author and with the plight of Native Americans in the United States during the 1980s and 1990s. Welch's fiction is immediately accessible. Students find it powerful. They shirk from its relentlessly depressing impact, but Welch has written *Winter in the Blood, The Death of Jim Loney,* and much of his poetry to create that impact. His writing is protest literature, so skillfully achieved that it seems apolitical.

Sometimes hostile to the completely new, students today seem to be willing to rely on canon choices. Once Welch is placed for them, they respond with empathy to his fiction.

The general setting of the culture, the hardships generations of Native Americans have learned to live with, the socioeconomic issues make deciphering characters' attitudes easier. The strengths of the Indian culture need to be described as well, because students in many parts of the country are unfamiliar with customs, imagery, and attitudes that are necessary in reading this excerpt.

Welch's precision and control must be discussed. Students must see how they are in his power throughout this excerpt. Further, they must want to read not only this novel, but the others as well.

Major Themes, Historical Perspectives, and Personal Issues

It is also good to emphasize the choice of art as profession. For Welch, giving voice to frustration has created memorable fiction and poetry. His most recent novel, *Fools Crow,* does much more than depict the alienation of the contemporary Native American man—but to do so, he draws on nineteenth-century history as the basis of his plot.

Significant Form, Style, or Artistic Conventions

Questions of realism and how realistic writing is achieved: characterization, language, situation, emphasis on dialogue rather than interior monologue.

Questions of appropriateness: What is believable about the fiction, and how has Welch created that intensity that is so believable? Why is a plot like this more germane to the lives Welch describes than an adventurous, action-filled narrative would have been?

Original Audience

The issue of political literature (which will occur often in selections from the contemporary section) will need attention. How can Welch create a sympathetic hero without portraying the poverty and disillusion of a culture? How can he achieve this accuracy without maligning Native Americans? These issues are the same faced by Toni Morrison in *The Bluest Eye*: How many readers will assume that Pecola's father rapes her because he is a black man? Yet Morrison gives the reader several kinds of black families, most of them admirable, showing that race is not the issue here. In Welch's spare text, there are no foil families, so his risk is somewhat greater.

Comparisons, Contrasts, Connections

Hemingway and Richard Wright are obvious choices for comparison but the differences are important as well. Wright relied in many cases on dialect, with language spelled as words might have been pronounced, and Hemingway used carefully stylized language in his quantities of dialogue, so that identifying characters by place or education was sometimes difficult. Welch creates a dialect that is carefully mannered, as if the insecure speaker had modeled his language, like his life, on the middle-class TV image of a person and a family.

Bibliography

Refer to the headnote in the text for complete information.

James Alan McPherson (b. 1943)

Contributing Editor: John F. Callahan [p. 2139]

Classroom Issues and Strategies

Students are unfamiliar with the railroads and the extent to which black men were a fraternity in the service jobs on the trains. There is some need to explain the argot of railroading, to familiarize students with the vocabulary and syncopated accents of the black vernacular.

Involve students with the rich variations of the oral tradition. Get them telling stories, in particular stories of how they met and came to know people of very different backgrounds because of summer jobs. It helps to read chunks of the story out loud.

Students are often interested in Youngblood's attitude toward the storyteller and the storyteller's attitude toward Doc Craft.

Major Themes, Historical Perspectives, and Personal Issues

The complexity and richness as well as the hardships of the lives lived by black traveling men; the initiative and kinship developed by the black workers; the qualities of the trickster; also the ways racism surcharges the attempts by blacks and whites to master situations and each other. Once again, the fact that the story is told by an old-timer about to quit (in 1964 or so) to Youngblood—the college student in a temporary job— about working on the road for the last twenty years or more sets up important contrasts between the past and the present, particularly the impact of technology on older ways of work and life.

Significant Form, Style, or Artistic Conventions

The relationship of oral storytelling as an initiation ritual to McPherson's craft of fiction writing, particularly his resolve to initiate readers of all races into a facet of their culture passing quickly out of sight.

Comparisons, Contrasts, Connections

See Baldwin's "Sonny's Blues"; Ellison's *Invisible Man*, Chapter 1; Walker's "Nineteen Fifty-Five"; and Silko's "Lullaby."

Questions for Reading and Discussion/ Approaches to Writing

What is the significance of the name Doc Craft?

Bibliography

Ellison, Ralph and James McPherson. "Indivisible Man." *Atlantic*. (December 1970): 45–60.

McPherson, James. "On Becoming an American Writer." *Atlantic* 242, no. 6 (December 1978): 53–7.

Alice Walker (b. 1944)

Contributing Editor: Marilyn Richardson [p. 2156]

Major Themes, Historical Perspectives, and Personal Issues

1. The bemused black women for whom a creative, witty, and compassionate union with the universe is as natural as breathing.
2. The volcanic forces that go into the creative life and work of a heroine like the narrator. See her account of her encounter with Bessie Smith.
3. The theft of black music by white musicians who do not understand what they are performing.

Significant Form, Style, or Artistic Conventions

The narrative voice in this story is deceptively informal and uneducated. Gracie Mae Still is in fact extremely subtle and sophisticated. The reader must put aside assumptions about her speech and learn from her on her own terms.

Bibliography

"Alice Walker Reads 'nineteen fifty-five' " and an "Interview with Alice Walker" in which she discusses the story are tapes available from The American Audio Prose Library, P.O. Box 842, Columbia, MO 65205.

Leslie Marmon Silko (Laguna) (b. 1948)

Contributing Editor: Norma C. Wilson [p. 2167]

Classroom Issues and Strategies

When I first began to read Silko's poetry and fiction, I attempted to use the critical methods I had used in my prior study of European and American literature. I sought primary sources of the traditional stories that appeared in her work. But I soon found that very little of the traditional literature of the Lagunas had been recorded in writing. I realized that I needed to know more of the background—cultural and historical—of Silko's writing.

In the spring of 1977, I arranged to meet with Silko at the University of New Mexico. She explained to me that her writing had evolved from an outlook she had developed as a result of hearing the old stories and songs all her life. She also led me to a number of helpful written sources, including Bertha P. Dutton and Miriam A. Marmon's *The Laguna Calendar* (Albuquerque: Univ. of New Mexico Press, 1936) and the transcript of an interview with Mrs. Walter K. Marmon in the Special Collections Department of the Zimmerman Library, U.N.M. Another source I've found helpful is Leslie A. White, "The Acoma Indians" (*Forty-seventh Annual Report of the Bureau of American Ethnology*, Washington, D.C.: U.S. Government Printing Office, 1932).

One can use the videotape, *Running on the Edge of the Rainbow*, produced by Larry Evers at the University of Arizona, Tucson. I often begin looking at Silko's writing by using a transparency of her poem "Prayer to the Pacific." Students frequently come to think in new ways about their relationships to nature and about the exploitation of Native American people and the natural earth. They ask such questions as, "Did the government really do that to the Navajos?"

Major Themes, Historical Perspectives, and Personal Issues

In teaching "Lullaby," the idea of harmony is essential—the Navajo woman is balanced because she is aware of her relation to the natural world, that she is a part of it and that is the most important relationship. This allows her to nurture as the earth nurtures. One should emphasize forced changes in the Navajo way of life that have resulted from the encroachment of industry and the government on Navajo land. Today the struggle centering on Big Mountain would be a good focus. Of course, alcoholism and the splitting up of Indian families would be other important issues to focus on.

Significant Form, Style, or Artistic Conventions

It is important to note that Silko's fiction is a blending of traditional with modern elements. And just as "Lullaby" ends with a song, many of Silko's other works are also a blend of prose and poetry.

Original Audience

"Lullaby" seems to be a story from out of the 1950s. We talk about the U.S. government's relocation policy during that decade. Relocation was an attempt to remove Indians from reservations and relocate them in urban environments. We also discuss the long history of the U.S. government removing Indian children from their families and culture. Recently this kind of removal has been somewhat reversed by the Indian Child Welfare Act, which gives tribes authority over the placement of the children enrolled in these tribes.

Comparisons, Contrasts, Connections

One might compare and contrast Silko's work with that of Simon J. Ortiz. One might also consider comparing and contrasting it with the work of James Wright, Gary Snyder, and Louise Erdrich.

Questions for Reading and Discussion/ Approaches to Writing

One might ask the students to look up specific places mentioned in the story on a map—Cebolleta Creek, Long Mesa, Canoncito, etc.

1. Discuss the importance of the oral tradition in Silko's writing.
2. Discuss the structure of Silko's fiction. Is it linear or cyclic?
3. What is the image of woman in Silko's fiction? Compare or contrast this with the images of women in the broader context of American society and culture.
4. What criticisms of American society are implicit in Silko's fiction?
5. What Navajo cultural values are evident in the story "Lullaby"?

Bibliography

Silko, L. M. "An Old-Time Indian Attack Conducted in Two Parts." In *The Remembered Earth*, edited by Geary Hobson. Albuquerque: Univ. of New Mexico Press, 1979.

Fisher, Dexter. "Stories and Their Tellers—A Conversation with Leslie Marmon Silko." In *The Third Woman: Minority Women Writers of the United States*. Boston: Houghton Mifflin, 1980.

Aurora Levins Morales (b. 1954)

Contributing Editor: Frances R. Aparicio [p. 2175]

Classroom Issues and Strategies

Since Levins Morales's major book is authored in collaboration with her mother, Rosario Morales, it would be appropriate to present her work in this context. Instructors could familiarize themselves with *Getting Home Alive* and make a selection of texts in which the dialogue—as well as the differences—between mother and daughter is exemplified.

Major Themes, Historical Perspectives, and Personal Issues

Major themes in Aurora Levins Morales's work: identity as a female minority in the U.S.; feminism; multiple identity (Puerto Rican, Jewish, North American), also inherited versus self-defined identities; concept of *immigrant*; Jewish culture and traditions; mother/daughter relationships; importance of language, reading, words, and writing; remembering and memory as a vehicle to surpass sense of fragmentation and exile/displacement; images of spaces and cities; "internationalist" politics.

Significant Form, Style, or Artistic Conventions

Heterogeneous forms and texts constitute Levins Morales's writings. *Getting Home Alive* is a collage of poems, short stories, lyrical prose pieces, essays, and dialogues. Note the importance of eclectic style: she is lyrical, subdued at times, sensorial, and quite visual in her imagery. She does not belong to any major literary movement; her writings cannot be easily categorized into one style or another, though they definitely respond to the preoccupations of other U.S. women of color.

Comparisons, Contrasts, Connections

Fruitful comparisons can be drawn to the works of other women of color, such as Cherríe Moraga, *Loving in the War Years* in *Cuentos: Stories by Latinas*, eds. Gómez, Moraga, Romo-Carmona (New York: Kitchen Table Press, 1983). Levins Morales has been particularly influenced by Alice Walker. In addition, I believe comparisons and contrasts with mainstream U.S. feminist writers would also prove valuable.

Questions for Reading and Discussion/ Approaches to Writing

1. Study questions would deal with textual analysis and with clarifying references to Spanish words, places in Puerto Rico or El Barrio, and other allusions that might not be clear to students.
2. (a) Have students do their own version of "Child of the Americas" in order to look into their own inheritance and cross-cultural identities.

   (b) Paper topics might include the importance of multiple identity and "internationalist" politics; comparison and contrast of mother's and daughter's experiences, points of view, language, and style; meaning of language, reading, and writing for Levins Morales; an analysis of images of space, borders, urban centers, mobility, exile, displacement; contrast to Nuyorican writers from El Barrio: how would Levins Morales diverge from this movement, and why should she still be considered as representative of Puerto Rican writers in the United States?

Bibliography

Benmayor, Rina. "Crossing Borders: The Politics of Multiple Identity," *Centro de Estudios Puertorriqueños Bulletin* 2:3 (Spring, 1988): 71–77.

Rojas, Lourdes. "Latinas at the Crossroads: An Affirmation of Life in Rosario Morales and Aurora Levins Morales's *Getting Home Alive*." In *Breaking Boundaries: Latina Writing and Critical Reading*, edited by A. Horno-Delgado, E. Ortega, N. Scott, and N. Saporta-Sternbach. Amherst: Univ. of Mass. Press, 1989, 166–77.

Louise Erdrich (Chippewa) (b. 1954)

Contributing Editor: Andrew O. Wiget [p. 2180]

Classroom Issues and Strategies

One problem in teaching *Love Medicine* is the intensity of religious experience, which many students in today's secular society may have difficulty relating to. Another is the surrealistic imagery that Marie Lazarre uses in describing her relationship with Sister Leopolda. And yet a third is understanding the historical and cultural context of reservation life at this period of time in the 1930s.

In terms of the historical and cultural context, I would point out to students that Indian reservations in the 1930s were notorious for their poverty, their high mortality rate, their chronic unemployment, and the destruction of the fabric of Native American social and cultural forms. One of the principal policies of the United States government was to transform Native Americans into carbon copies of Anglo-Americans, and one of the principal ways that they hoped to accomplish this, ever since the Grant administration in the 1870s, was through religion.

During the 1870s, the Native American communities were allocated among the various major Christian sects, and missionary activity was understood to be an agent of social and cultural transformation. The objective was to get rid of the Indian while saving the man. Culture was imagined as a number of practices and behaviors and customs, which—if they could be changed—would eliminate all the historic obstacles to the Indians' participation in Anglo-American culture. Of course, if they were eliminated, so would the Indian nest be eliminated. Religion then is hardly a simple spiritual force, but an agent of the interests of the Euro-American majority. Such an understanding, I think, should help students appreciate the intensity with which Marie and Sister Leopolda enter their confrontation.

A fine introduction to this story would be to spend a good deal of time focusing on the first paragraph, trying to understand the tone of the narrator and also the structure of her vision of herself, which she repeats later in the story. I would use the imagery and the tone as a way of developing the narrator's sense of herself, and I would try to account for her intense antagonism to the "black robe women on the hill."

Most students are puzzled by the intensity of the antagonism, and they have real questions as to whether or not Marie or Leopolda or both are crazy. Students tend to think that they're crazy because of the surrealistic imagery and because of the intensity of the emotion, which strikes

most of them as excessive. Students need to realize that religion, especially when it is the lens through which other issues are magnified, can
become the focus of such intense feelings, and that when one's feelings
are so intense, they frequently compel the creation of surrealistic
imagery as the only means to adequately shape what one sees.

Major Themes, Historical Perspectives, and Personal Issues

I think that there are two major themes that could be addressed in this
story. The first is to understand religion, as described in the previous
question, as a field upon which two different sets of interests contest
their right to define the terms by which people will understand themselves and others. For all the black comedy in this story, the battle that
Leopolda fights with the Dark One over the soul of Marie Lazarre is
understood by both Leopolda and Marie as a very real battle. Leopolda
represents a set of values, and so does the Dark One. Marie is understood as struggling to choose between the values of the Dark One and
the values of Sister Leopolda, and these values are cultural as well as
spiritual, for it is precisely the Indian character of Marie—her pride, her
resistance to change, her imagination—that Leopolda identifies with the
Dark One.

A second theme is to view the formation of identity in bicultural
environments as an enriching, rather than an impoverishing, experience. Too often in bicultural situations, Indian protagonists are represented as being helpless, suspended in their inability to make a decision
between two sets of values offered to them. The John Joseph Mathews
novel *Sundown* is an example. In this story, however, Marie Lazarre
chooses, and she chooses to identify herself as an Indian over and against
the black robe sisters precisely by turning their own naivete against
them. The "veils of faith" that she refers to early in this story not only
prevent the sisters from seeing the truth, but they also obscure their
faith from shining forth, like the Reverend Mr. Hooper's veil in
Hawthorne's story "The Minister's Black Veil."

Significant Form, Style, or Artistic Conventions

This story succeeds principally as a study of characterization. I would
ask students to pay special attention to matters of tone and point of view.
Since this story is told in the first person, I would ask them, on the basis
of what they have read, to form an opinion of Marie Lazarre and, secondly, to develop some sense of her judgment of Sister Leopolda. I

would ask them to look especially at the imagery and the language that Marie uses to describe her encounters with Leopolda and to describe herself, as the basis for their opinions.

Original Audience

The audience for whom this story is written is contemporary, but differs from the students we meet in university settings by perhaps being older and therefore more familiar with a traditional religiosity. Students who are not Catholic may need to know something about Catholicism, especially the role of nuns, and the historic role of missionaries in relationship to Indian communities. Other explicitly Catholic references, such as to the stigmata, are explained by their context in the story.

Comparisons, Contrasts, Connections

This story can be usefully contrasted with some of Flannery O'Connor's stories, which focus on the discovery of real faith, especially from a Catholic perspective. The emphasis on surrealistic imagery provides interesting connections with poems like those of Adrienne Rich; since this is a retrospective narrative, one might usefully compare this probing of a formative event from narrator's past with Rich's poem "Diving into the Wreck." Insofar as this offers us a sensitive and imaginative teenage minority narrator, the story invites comparisons with the work of Toni Morrison and Alice Walker. In Native American terms, useful comparisons would be to Gertrude Bonnin's "Why I Am a Pagan," as well as John Oskison's "The Problem of Old Harjo."

Questions for Reading and Discussion/ Approaches to Writing

1. I've never used questions ahead of time for this particular story, though if I did, I think they would be addressed to issues of characterization and tone.
2. An interesting assignment, because this story is told from Marie's point of view, is to retell the encounter between Marie and Sister Leopolda from Sister Leopolda's perspective. This would require students to formulate characterizations of Leopolda and of Marie, which would be useful touchstones for evaluating their comprehension of the issues on which the conflict in this story rests.

Bibliography

Erdrich, Louise. "Whatever Is Really Yours: An Interview with Louise Erdrich." *Survival This Way: An Interview with American Indian Poets.* Tucson: Univ. of Arizona, 1987, 73–86.

Wiget, Andrew. "Singing the Indian Blues: Louise Erdrich and the Love that Hurts So Good." *Puerto del Sol* 21:2 (1986): 166–75

Drama

Tennessee Williams (1911–1983)

Contributing Editor: Thomas P. Adler [p. 2190]

Classroom Issues and Strategies

Students may tend to respond to the heroines, especially in Williams's earlier plays up through the end of the 1940s, differently from what he intended because their value system is not the same. His sensitive, poetic misfits who escape from reality into a world of illusion/art are likely to seem too remote, too soft. The very things that Williams values about them—their grace, their gentility—nowadays may appear dispensable adjuncts of life in an age when competition and aggressiveness are valorized among both sexes. So students need to be sensitized to Williams's romantic ideals and to what he sees as the civilizing, humanizing virtues.

It helps to place Williams in context as a southern dramatist, and also as one who propounds the feminizing of American culture as a counter to a society built on masculine ideals of strength and power. Students also need to understand that Williams is a "poetic" realist, not simply in his use of a lyrical rhetoric but in his handling of imagery, both verbal and visual. If they attend carefully to his command of visual stage symbolism, they can oftentimes discover the necessary clues about Williams's attitude toward his characters.

Any discussion of "Portrait of a Madonna" will necessarily focus upon Williams's characterization of his sexually frustrated and neurotic heroine, whose upbringing in a succession of southern rectories, under the nay-saying and guilt-inducing "shadow" of the church and of the cross, has left her totally unprepared for life and prey to crazed delusions. Miss Collins becomes almost the archetypal unmarried daughter, restricted by the responsibility of caring for an aged mother, sensing the social pressure to be sexual and yet denied any morally sanctioned expression of these feelings, finally forced into madness as a result of unrealistic expectations. The image of the Madonna and Child becomes central to an understanding of the play: the Virgin and Mother whom Lucretia costumed for the Sunday School Christmas pageant; the children she visits twice a year on religious holidays with her scrapbooks of Campbell soup kids; Richard's many children; the fabricated "child" to be born of a woman virginal in body and heart, defiled only in her dreams.

Brief though it is, Williams's play is amenable to many critical approaches other than the psychological and feminist. A formalist approach might examine the way in which Williams structures his play—as he later will *Streetcar*—around a series of dichotomies: past/present; memory/fact; gentility/brutality; shadow/light; sanity/insanity; freedom/repression; virginal/defiled; harmless illusion/harmful delusion. A literary-historical approach could place the work within the tradition of southern gothicism, while a sociocultural framework could explore the way in which the myth of southern chivalry curtails Lucretia's independence, as well as the way in which utilitarian technology threatens the artistic sensibility (elevator cage as machine played off against the music on the gramophone). A generic approach might consider the possibilities for seeing the play as a tragedy, while a biographical approach might trace the relationship between Lucretia and Williams's own schizophrenic sister Rose.

Major Themes, Historical Perspectives, and Personal Issues

Central thematic issues include the question of illusion and reality, the relationship between madness and art, and the role of the artist in society, as well as the necessity to respond compassionately and nonjudgmentally to the needs of God's sensitive yet weak creatures who are battered and misunderstood. Historically, Williams's relation to the myth of the cavalier South should be explored. Finally, Williams's close identification with his heroines needs to be seen in light of his relationship with his schizophrenic sister Rose, as he admits in his *Memoirs*, the most intensely emotional attachment in his personal life.

Significant Form, Style, or Artistic Conventions

Although "Portrait" itself is essentially a realistic, albeit somewhat poetic, play, Williams himself should be approached as an innovator of a new "plastic" theater, a practitioner, along with Arthur Miller, of what some have termed "a theatre of gauze." To handle this aspect of Williams's aesthetic, the instructor might either read or reproduce as a handout the dramatist's Production Notes to *Glass Menagerie*, along with Tom's opening narration in that play, which really differentiates Williams's practice—"truth in the pleasant disguise of illusion"—from the strict realism—"illusion that has the appearance of truth"—of others.

Original Audience

The choice of the one-act play form itself tells something about Williams's intended audience. Rather than aim at a commercial production, "Portrait" seems more appropriate for an amateur (academic or civic) theater presentation, where the interest will be largely on character and dialogue rather than production values. Thus, it appears intended for a limited audience of intense theatergoers. From the perspective of the dramatist, it serves partly as a "study" for larger work(s), in much the same way that a painter might do a series of studies before attempting a full canvas. And so, in a sense, the artist too is his own audience.

Comparisons, Contrasts, Connections

Lucretia Collins bears comparison with other Williams heroines in "The Lady of Larkspur Lotion," *The Glass Menagerie, A Streetcar Named Desire,* and *Summer and Smoke.* Students might also contrast the way Miss Collins escapes from the sociocultural milieu that constricts her freedom with the heroines' responses in Susan Glaspell's short play "Trifles" and William Faulkner's short story "A Rose for Emily."

Questions for Reading and Discussion/ Approaches to Writing

1. (a) Consider the dramatic function(s) of the minor characters, the Porter and the Elevator Boy, in the play.
   (b) Could "Portrait of a Madonna" have been expanded to a full-length work? To accomplish that, what else might Williams have dramatized? Would anything have been lost in the transformation?

2. (a) The director of the original production of "Portrait" had Lucretia exit clutching a doll. What, if anything, would justify such an interpolation in Williams's text, and what might be the impact on the audience?

   (b) Discuss the theater metaphor in "Portrait": the minor characters as onstage audience; the bedroom, scene of illusions, as stage; Mr. Abrams as stage manager/director at end, etc.

   (c) In what way does Williams's characterization of Lucretia Collins lead the audience to conclude that he considered her story "tragic"?

Bibliography

Critical Studies:

Londré, Felicia Hardison. *Tennessee Williams*. New York: Frederick Ungar, 1979, pp. 46–7.

Taylor, Jo Beth. "*A Streetcar Named Desire*: Evolution of Blanche and Stanley." *Publications of the Mississippi Philological Association* (1986): 63–4.

Wolf, Morris Philip. "Casanova's Portmanteau: *Camino Real* and Recurring Communication Patterns of Tennessee Williams." In *Tennessee Williams: A Tribute*, edited by Jac Tharpe, 258–59. Jackson: Univ. Press of Mississippi, 1977.

Production Reviews:

Atkinson, Brooks. *The New York Times* (26 April 1959): Sec. 2, p. 1.

Oliver, W. E. Rpt. in *Dictionary of Literary Biography Documentary Series: Volume Four/Tennessee Williams*, edited by Margaret A Van Antwerp and Sally Johns, 77–8. Detroit: Gale Research Company, 1984.

The New York Theatre Critics Reviews 20, no. 11 (20 April 1959): 320–23.

Lorraine Vivian Hansberry (1930–1965)

Contributing Editor: Jeanne-Marie A. Miller [p. 2201]

Classroom Issues and Strategies

The primary problem that might be encountered is the student's lack of familiarity with black American drama. The images of blacks on the early American stage reflected their place in American life. Dramatic expression, exclusively by white authors, made of them contented, faithful slaves or servants, tragic figures of mixed blood, and comic characters. The comic figures were dominant.

Despite prejudice and racism, black playwrights were known in the American theater as early as 1823 when a play entitled *King Shotaway*, written by Mr. Brown (whose first name is uncertain) was produced by the African Grove Theater and Company. Also in the nineteenth century, William Wells Brown, a former slave, published *The Escape; or, A Leap for Freedom* (1858), and William E. Easton's play *Dessalines* was produced in Chicago (1893). From the beginning, the concern of most black playwrights has been the realistic depiction of the black experience.

During the twentieth century, growing out of the increased interest of American writers in folk material, came a renewed interest among white playwrights in blacks as source material for drama. Consider, for instance, Eugene O'Neill's *The Emperor Jones* (1920). The 1920s, the period of the Harlem Renaissance, also introduced the first serious (that is, nonmusical) dramas by black playwrights on Broadway—for example, Willis Richardson's *A Chip Woman's Fortune* (1923) and Garland Anderson's *Appearances* (1925).

One of the most popular plays on Broadway during the 1930s was *The Green Pastures* (1930), a black folk fable written by Marc Connelly, a white playwright. As the Depression worsened, plays that protested against the social and economic conditions that sorely afflicted people were produced. Paul Peters and George Sklar's *Stevedore* (1934), for example, centers on a black militant hero who defends his rights as a man and a worker on the New Orleans docks.

Though blacks were gaining some experience on Broadway, in community theaters, and in drama groups in black institutions of higher learning, it was the Federal Theater Project, which grew out of the Depression and provided work for unemployed theater people, that gave a major boost to blacks in theater. The post-World War II years found some white playwrights concentrating on the tense situation that existed when black soldiers, who had been in Europe fighting for democracy, returned to a segregated America. For instance, *Strange Fruit* (1945), a drama adapted from a novel by its author Lillian Smith and her sister Esther, makes a bitter commentary on racial segregation, intolerance, and injustice in this country.

Two dramas by black playwrights reached Broadway in the 1940s: white playwright Paul Green and Richard Wright's *Native Son* (1941) and Theodore Ward's *Our Lan'* (1947). The play *Native Son* is a dramatization of Wright's powerful novel about Bigger Thomas and the corrosive effects of American society on him. *Our Lan'* concerns a group of newly freed slaves who search for economic independence and security during the latter days of the Civil War and the early Reconstruction Period.

Ironically, as the heightened period of the civil rights movement of the 1950s produced a plethora of plays by black writers affected by the mood of the country, white playwrights who employed black themes and characters returned to the traditional images of blacks. Consider, for instance, Berenice Sadie Brown, a black cook, in Carson McCullers's *A Member of the Wedding* (1950) and the black slave from Barbados who confesses to being a witch in Arthur Miller's *The Crucible* (1953) (the setting is the Salem witchcraft trials in 1692).

During the 1950s Off Broadway teemed with plays by black writers: William Branch's *Medal for Willie* (1951) and *In Splendid Error* (1955); Alice Childress's *Trouble in Mind* (1955) and Loften Mitchell's *Land Beyond the River* (1957), for example. At the end of the decade, twenty-eight-year-old Lorraine Hansberry made her debut on Broadway with *A Raisin in the Sun* (1959). She was the first black woman to have a play produced on Broadway and the first black playwright and youngest playwright to win the New York Drama Critics Circle Award. The production was significant in other ways. Not only were the playwright and the cast, except for one, black, but so were the director and some of the investors. Blacks came out in large numbers to see this award-winning work that truthfully depicts a black working-class family who triumphs over the debilitating conditions of the ghetto. With *Raisin* American drama and blacks reached a new milestone. The play has been translated into over thirty languages and produced in many countries. In 1961 it became a film and in 1973 a Tony Award-winning musical.

Major Themes, Historical Perspectives, and Personal Issues

Some of the major themes of her works are as follows: the slave system and its effect on Americans; the deprivation and injustice suffered by blacks because of racism; moral choices; deferred dreams of black Americans; self-determination of African countries; ability to control one's own destiny; negative effects of voguish movements; and relationships between men and women. The major historical and personal issues that should be emphasized are slavery and the Civil War; contrasting portraits of slavery; the civil rights movement of the 1950s and 1960s, whose antecedents were in the black protest and revolt of slaves, such as Hannibal in *The Drinking Gourd*; and feminism.

Significant Form, Style, or Artistic Conventions

Hansberry followed the trend of realism. In her dramas she wished to illustrate character. As an artist she believed that all people had stature and that there were no dramatically uninteresting people. She searched for the extraordinary, the uniqueness in the ordinary. She embraced the social nature of art, and she dissected personality as it interacted with society. Her dramatic style included the use of colloquial speech, a sense of the rhythm of language, the use of symbolism, and departures from realistic speech into the lyrical.

Original Audience

Hansberry wrote for the general theater audience. The particular audience for whom *The Drinking Gourd* was written was the general television audience of 1960. The drama was commissioned by NBC for producer-director Dore Schary to initiate a series of ninety-minute television dramas commemorating the centennial of the Civil War. This drama was a pre-*Roots* work, which was to have exposed audiences to a portrait of slavery by a black writer. Since *Roots* was presented on television during the 1970s, audiences seem to be better educated about a black writer's point of view about the issue of slavery.

Comparisons, Contrasts, Connections

At the center of *The Member of the Wedding* (1950), a drama by Carson McCullers, a white writer, is a black cook who holds together the white family for whom she works. Unlike McCullers's play, in which the black cook's family is hardly ever seen, Hansberry's *A Raisin in the Sun* dramatizes the story of a black domestic and *her* family. It is a story told from inside the race. *The Drinking Gourd* treats the family relationships of a slave-owning family and their slaves.

Other dramas about slavery with which *The Drinking Gourd* may be compared and contrasted are the following by white authors: George L.

Aiken's *Uncle Tom's Cabin* (1852), a dramatization of Harriet Beecher Stowe's novel; Dion Boucicault's *The Octoroon* (1859); James D. McCabe, Jr., *The Guerrillas* (1863); and James A. Herne's *The Reverend Griffith Davenport* (1899). The earliest extant play by a black writer is also about slavery: William Wells Brown's *The Escape* (1858).

Questions for Reading and Discussion/ Approaches to Writing

Some study questions that students might find useful are as follows:

1. (a)   What is Hansberry's background?
   (b)   What is her philosophy of art?
   (c)   How does she move from the particular to the universal in her plays?
   (d)   How does she use language in her plays?

Paper topics that have proved useful are as follows:

2. (a)   The role of women in Hansberry's plays
   (b)   Family relationships
   (c)   Language in Hansberry's plays
   (d)   Love between man and woman
   (e)   Relationships between women and men

Bibliography

The introductions to *Les Blancs: The Collected Last Plays of Lorraine Hansberry*, written by Julius Lester for the 1972 edition and by Margaret B. Wilkerson for the 1983 edition, as well as the critical backgrounds by Robert Nemiroff in each of these editions.

The collection of essays and the bibliography that appear in the special issue of *Freedomways* (vol. 19, no. 4, 1979) entitled "Lorraine Hansberry: Art of Thunder, Vision of Light."

The first two chapters on Hansberry's life in Anne Cheney's book *Lorraine Hansberry*, Boston: Twayne Publishers, 1984.

A film entitled *Lorraine Hansberry: The black Experience in the Creation of Drama*, Princeton, N.J.: Films for the Humanities, 1976.

Edward Albee (b. 1928)

Contributing Editor: Carol A. Burns [p. 2263]

Classroom Issues and Strategies

The Zoo Story is accessible to most students even in introductory courses, and few students have difficulty in recognizing Albee's central point about the paucity of human relationships. However, teachers need to lead students to recognize how well crafted and "of a piece" the play is as well as how powerful (and equivocal) the play's final statement is.

I usually begin by encouraging students to see that while Jerry and Peter are obviously very different (not just in their life-styles but in their desire to reach and to be reached by other people), Jerry was only a short time ago as withdrawn from others as Peter (e.g., his relationships with women, his "please" and "when" letters). And, more importantly, the milieux in which Peter and Jerry live are similarly sterile. Peter's family life seems vapid. Jerry's rooming-house is a "zoo" in which all the residents are carefully separated from one another. The landlady is the one person who seeks contact with someone else and she is as psychically spent as her appearance suggests. She does not wish to establish an emotional relationship with Jerry; he is merely "the *object* of her sweaty lust" (my italics) which can easily be satisfied by a delusion. Initially, Jerry, in simply wanting to be left alone (like Peter, like most people, Albee would say), responded to the very different overtures from both the landlady and her dog by appeasement—conjure a fantasy for the lady, throw some meat to her dog—designed to gain him "solitary free passage." Jerry's "fall from physical grace" suggests his fall from spiritual grace as well, manifested in his blithe indifference to others.

A good question here for students is what Jerry learned from his encounter with the dog. Ironically, the dog was different from most people in that it tried to reach him. Indeed, Jerry finally regards the dog's attempt to bite him as an act of love for just this reason. And Jerry's feeding the dog was truly a hostile act because he was trying to prevent contact. Therefore, although Jerry gains his initial objective, "solitary free passage," he eventually understands that he has lost—"and what is gained is loss." Jerry learns that in his fallen world, the only contact that seems possible is with an animal, that it is hurtful (of course, any contact is potentially hurtful), and that it ultimately fails. Ironically, again, the dog recalls Jerry to his human nature and Jerry realizes that human relationships are now bestial (or worse). That Jerry is able to wrestle such an illumination from his innocuous tussle with his landlady's dog is testimony to his intelligence and sensitivity.

However, Peter is less willing to undergo the conversion process and he resists recognition of the truth implicit in Jerry's dog story. Having learned that in our present inhumane state, simple kindness alone no longer works, Jerry continues to use his mixture of kindness and cruelty to reach Peter because "the two, combined, together, at the same time, are the teaching emotion." Students are usually quick to see the metatheatrical nature of the play, the extent to which the director-actor Jerry leads the unknowing Peter through a preplanned scenario. The kindness and cruelty characteristic of Jerry's conversation with Peter early in the play now becomes physical as he first tickles and then shoves Peter off the bench that is an image of Peter's isolation. Cruelty than clearly takes the upper hand as Jerry physically and verbally assaults Peter. In fact, he whips Peter's feelings up to a frenzy so that he can engineer his own death at Peter's hands.

However bleak the play's final statement is, Jerry does succeed at what he so obviously set out to do, i.e., make contact with another person and convey his message to him. Peter's final understanding and the extent to which Jerry has reached him is communicated not with words alone but also with his "pitiful howl" of "OH MY GOD!" It is the howl of an animal. Peter is finally aware of people's basic animal nature, "what other people *need*." Interestingly, the zoo image carries both negative and positive connotations—people live in a zoo separated from one another by cages of their own making, but they can destroy their bars by recognizing their own basic animal nature. To become an animal is to become more fully human; as Peter says to Jerry, "You're an animal, too." This and Jerry's several repetitions of Peter's words, particularly the latter's final words, "Oh . . . my . . . God," suggest not only the men's unity but the respect Jerry now accords Peter.

Bibliography

Bennett, Robert B. "Tragic Vision in *The Zoo Story*." *Modern Drama* 20: 55–66.

Bigsby, C. W. E. *Albee*. Edinburgh: Oliver, 1969.

———, ed. *Edward Albee: A Collection of Critical Essays*. Englewood Cliffs: Prentice-Hall, 1975. See articles by Brian Way and Rose Zimbardo.

Coh, Ruby. *Edward Albee*. Minneapolis: Univ. of Minnesota Press, 1969.

Gabbard, Lucina P. "At the Zoo: From O'Neill to Albee." *Modern Drama* 19: 365–74. Compares *Zoo* to O'Neill's *The Hairy Ape*; provides some historical perspective on *Zoo*.

Nilan, Mary M. "Albee's *The Zoo Story*: Alienated Man and the Nature of Love." *Modern Drama* 16:55–59. Sees Jerry as incapable of genuine contact with other people.

Wallace, Robert S. *"The Zoo Story*: Albee's Attack on Fiction." *Modern Drama* 16:49–54. Sees *Zoo* as criticism of people's affinity for fiction instead of experience; deals with some metatheatrical aspects of *Zoo*.

Poetry

Theodore Roethke (1908–1963)

Contributing Editor: Janis Stout [p. 2280]

Major Themes, Historical Perspectives, and Personal Issues

Personal Background: Roethke had extremely ambivalent feelings about his father, who was managing partner in a large greenhouse operation in Saginaw, Michigan.

Significant Form, Style, or Artistic Conventions

"Frau Bauman, Frau Schmidt, and Frau Schwartze"

The three "ancient ladies" preside over processes of growth (both vegetable and the poet's own) almost as personifications of natural forces, or even the three Fates. Their presence, like Mother Nature's, is somewhat ambiguous; there is a note of threat in their tickling of the child and in their night presence. The three women's vigor and authority should be noted, as well as their avoidance of limitation by sex-role stereotypes: clearly female (they wear skirts, they have a special association with the child), they also climb ladders and stand astride the steam-pipes providing heat in the greenhouse.

"Root Cellar"

"Root Cellar" and "Big Wind" represent the celebrated "greenhouse poems," a group characterized by close attention to details evident only to one who knows this particular world very well—as Roethke did. They are distinguished from, say, Wordworth's nature poems in that they celebrate equally the natural processes themselves and the human effort and control involved. They share Wordsworth's ability to appreciate the humble or homely elements of nature. Here, in particular, we see Roethke's wonder at the sheer life process even when manifested in forms that would ordinarily seem ugly or repellent.

"Big Wind"

We might say "Big Wind" celebrates the tenacity of human effort in the face of hostile natural forces, an effort that wrests out of chaos the beauty of the roses. However, that idea should not be pressed so far as to exclude the creative force of natural vitality. Nature and human effort join together in producing roses. The greenhouse itself, shown as a ship running before the storm, seems almost a living thing.

"The Lost Son"

"The Lost Son" illustrates three major elements in Roethke's work: surrealistic style; reflection of his own psychological disorders; and mysticism, his vision of spiritual wholeness as a merging of the individual consciousness with natural processes and life-forms.

1. "The Flight" is a poem of anxiety about death and loss of identity.
2. "The Return" associates wellness with the greenhouse world of childhood. The return spoken of is the return of light and heat—or full heat, since the greenhouses would scarcely have been left unheated on winter nights. The plants are both an object of the poet's close observation and a representation of his life.

"Meditations of an Old Woman"

Probably the most far-reaching question that can be asked of students, but also the most difficult, is, What difference does it make that the speaker is an old woman? Old, we can understand; we think of wisdom, experience, release from the distractions of youth. Buy why not an old man? One tempting answer is that our society has typically seen passivity and the passive virtues (patience, for instance) as feminine.

"Elegy"

Not often anthologized, this funerary tribute approaches a fusion of comedy with high seriousness. Aunt Tilly is a wonderfully strong, assertive, independent-minded woman who both fulfills traditional roles (housewife, cook, nurse, tender of the dead) and transcends them. The comedy emerges in the last stanza when Aunt Tilly comes "bearing down" on the butcher who, knowing he has met his match, quails before her indomitability and her clarity of vision.

Bibliography

Seager, Allen. *The Glass House* (1968).

Stout, James P. "Theodore Roethke and the Journey of the Solitary Self." *Interpretations* 16 (1985): 86–93.

Sullivan, Rosemary. *Theodore Roethke: The Garden-Master* (1975).

Elizabeth Bishop (1911–1979)

Contributing Editor: Carole Doreski [p. 2293]

Classroom Issues and Strategies

Bishop's poems are highly accessible and do not present problems for most mature readers. I have found that more students come to hear the poetry of Bishop when they commit some of her work to memory. I often challenge students to find the poetry first and then discuss the theme. This encourages them to begin to find relationships among form, language, and topic.

Significant Form, Style, or Artistic Conventions

Bishop's voice communicates rather directly to beginning readers of poetry. What is difficult to convey is the depth of expression and learning evidenced in these poems. Her work shows not merely experience but wisdom, the ability to reflect upon one's life, and that makes some poems difficult for younger readers.

For younger women readers, Bishop often seems old-fashioned, fussy, or detached. This perplexed the poet in that she felt that she had lived her life as an independent woman. This "generation gap" often provides an interesting class opportunity to talk about historical, cultural, and class assumptions in literature—and how those issues affect us as readers.

Students are often quite taken by Bishop's regard for animals. With the spirit of a Darwinian naturalist, the poet is willing to accord the natural world intrinsic rights and purposes. The dream-fusion world of the Man-Moth provides many students with an opportunity to discover this avenue into Bishop's world.

Original Audience

Bishop presents a curious "generational" case in that the circumstances of her childhood (raised by her maternal grandparents and an aunt) skew some of her references in favor of an earlier time. The kitchen setting in "Sestina" (not in this anthology), for example, seems more old-fashioned than Robert Lowell's interior scenes in "91 Revere Street." Otherwise her poems may be seen as timely—or timeless.

Comparisons, Contrasts, Connections

In the British lyric tradition, Bishop, by admission and allusion, draws heavily from Herbert, Hopkins, Wordsworth, Tennyson, Keats, and Blake.

Most pertinent American contrasts are with her mentor Marianne Moore (large correspondence at the Rosenbach Museum, Philadelphia), her friends Robert Lowell (correspondence at Houghton Library, Harvard University; Vassar College Library, Poughkeepsie) and May Swenson (correspondence at Washington University Library, St. Louis).

Questions for Reading and Discussion/ Approaches to Writing

1. "The Man-Moth"
   (a) This is but one of Bishop's many dream poems. In what ways does Bishop demonstrate her interest in and reliance upon surrealism?
   (b) How does Bishop attempt to humanize her exile through a multitude of sensory impressions? Are they effective?
   (c) The final stanza addresses the reader. How does Bishop intensify her creature's humanity through his ultimate vulnerability? Are we made to feel like the man-moth?

2. "Filling Station"
   (a) As Bishop describes setting and inhabitants of this "family filling station," she deliberately builds upon the initial observation, "Oh, but it is dirty!" Why dwell upon and develop this commentary? Does it suggest a missing family member? Is this station without a feminine presence?
   (b) The scale of the poem seems deliberately diminutive. Does this intensify the feminine quality of the poem? Is this intentional?
   (c) The closing stanza returns a sense of order or at least purpose to this scene. The symmetry of the cans lulls the "high-strung automobiles" into calmness. With the final line, "Somebody loves us all," does Bishop suggest a religious or maternal caretaker for this family?
3. Describe the voice and tone in a single poem. The casual humor of Bishop's world is often missed by casual readers (obsessed with travel and loss as themes).
4. Bishop owes much to her surrealist heritage. Sleep and dream states animate the worlds of the "Man-Moth" and "Crusoe in England." Such an essay would allow students to discover a new topical frame for discussion of experience, language, and poetic form.
5. A useful technical assignment would be to discuss Bishop's reliance upon simile rather than metaphor as her chief poetic device to link her world with the reader's. It says something critical about Bishop's belief in the limits of shared knowledge, experience.

Bibliography

Primary Works

North & South, 1946 (Houghton Mifflin Poetry Award); *Poems: North & South—A Cold Spring* (Pulitzer Prize, 1956); *Questions of Travel*, 1965; *The Complete Poems*, 1969 (National Book Award); *Geography III*, 1976; *The Complete Poems, 1927–1979*, 1983; *The Collected Prose*, 1984.

Secondary Works

Candace MacMahon, *Elizabeth Bishop: A Bibliography, 1927–1979*, 1980; Lloyd Schwartz and Sybil Estess, *Elizabeth Bishop and Her Art*, 1983; Harold Bloom, *Modern Critical Views: Elizabeth Bishop*, 1985; Robert Dale Parker, *The Unbeliever: The Poetry of Elizabeth Bishop*, 1988; Thomas J. Travisano, *Elizabeth Bishop: Her Artistic Development*, 1988.

Robert Hayden (1913–1980)

Contributing Editor: Robert M. Greenberg [p. 2301]

Classroom Issues and Strategies

It's important to get students to fully appreciate Hayden's effects of sound, image, and atmosphere. For better appreciation of the poems' aural qualities, have students read such selections as "Summertime and the Living . . . " and "Mourning Poem for the Queen of Sunday" out loud.

Discuss a condensed narrative poem such as "Tour 5" as a short story. This should permit a discussion of the evolving point of view of the travelers and the evolving psychological quality of the imagery.

Point out also Hayden's control of voice. "Summertime," for example, is spoken in the idiom of the black church, as if by a chorus of mourners; and if one reads the final lines to mean that the congregation *did* suspect her of misbehaving, then the poem becomes a masterpiece of wryness and irony.

Students are interested in questions like the following:

1. Is it possible to be both an ethnic and a universal (or liberal humanist) writer? What constitutes universality? What constitutes successful treatment of ethnic material?
2. Can a writer from a minority group write for a general educated audience without giving up in resonance what he gains in breadth of audience and reference?

Major Themes, Historical Perspectives, and Personal Issues

Major themes are tension between the imagination and the tragic nature of life; the past in the present; the nurturing power of early life and ethnically colored memories.

Significant Form, Style, or Artistic Conventions

Precede discussion of form and style with a discussion of the function of a particular type of poem. For example, Hayden wrote spirit-of-place poems such as "Tour 5," which depend heavily on imagery; folk character poems such as "Mourning Poem for the Queen of Sunday," which depend on economy of characterization and humor; and early neighborhood poems such as "Summertime and the Living . . .," which depend on realism mixed with nostalgia, fancy, or psychological symbolism.

Original Audience

It is important to realize Hayden always wrote for a general literate audience, not exclusively or even primarily for a black audience. The issue of audience for him relates to the issue of the role of a poet.

Comparisons, Contrasts, Connections

Yeats as an ethnic-universal poet compares to Hayden.

Questions for Reading and Discussion/ Approaches to Writing

1. "Tour 5"
   (a) Discuss the human situation the poem describes. Consider its treatment of both the external and internal aspects of the experience for the travelers.
   (b) Discuss the allusive quality of the adjectives used in the first stanza to convey a festive mood and in the last three lines to convey the violence of the Civil War and the cruelty of slavery.
   (c) Discuss what makes this a poem of the first order. Conciseness, controlled intensity, human drama, eloquence, and powerful symbols are some of the qualities you might touch on.
2. "Summertime and the Living . . ."
   (a) Discuss Hayden's use of a third-person restrospective point of view to write about childhood. (It gives him the ability to be both inside and outside the child's perspective.)
   (b) Discuss the sound of words and their connection with sense. Hayden is highly conscious of the aural dimension of language.
   (c) What is the function of the title, which is taken from a song in George and Ira Gershwin's opera *Porgie and Bess*?
3. "Mourning Poem for the Queen of Sunday"
   (a) Discuss the viewpoint of the speakers about the murdered diva. Discuss the final two lines. Are they at all ironic? Are the speakers totally surprised?
   (b) Discuss the importance of tone throughout the poem.

(c)   Discuss the poem's atmosphere and how elements other than tone contribute to the black church feeling.

Bibliography

Greenberg, Robert M. "Robert Hayden." In *American Writers: A Collection of Literary Biographies*, Supplement II, Part I, edited by A. Walton Litz, 361–83. New York: Charles Scribner's Sons, 1981. Has biographical, critical, and bibliographical material.

Hayden, Robert. *Collected Prose: Robert Hayden*, edited by Frederick Glaysher. Ann Arbor, Mich.: Univ. of Michigan Press, 1984. Has excellent interview material with Hayden about particular poems.

John Berryman (1914–1972)

Contributing Editor: Joseph Mancini [p. 2306]

Classroom Issues and Strategies

Students are likely to experience difficulty "decoding" Berryman's language and thus, like many early critics, dismiss it as the incoherent babbling of a habitually drunk poet. Much of his early poetry is, indeed, constructed of ill-conceived contortions of language that purportedly create fresh expressions of feeling but instead bury it; yet the language of *Homage* and the *Dream Songs* is not repressive but rather expressive of multidimensional realities. Another problem sometimes arises when students actually begin to understand how Berryman uses language: they can become "inebriated" with the wit for its own sake rather than seeing it as being shaped by the feelings it in turn shapes.

In an interview with Jan Howard, Berryman provided the primary key for solving both problems: students and other readers must learn to read him not "with their eyes . . . [but rather] with their ears." "The harmony lies also in the hear [sic] of the persuaded," claims Henry, Berryman's persona, in a posthumously published song. In another such song, Henry states, "The Song was made in darkness to be set alit/ obstacles placed by the singer in the way of it) / but a hearer like a new friend." Thus, the best strategy to help make Berryman's language accessible to students is to stress the necessity of their "collaborating" with the Trickster/Poet/Friend by reading the poems aloud again and again, inside and outside class, until they can hear the puns and multiple meanings of syntactical segments. Also close reading, especially in class, of a few poems work better as a collaborative technique than trying to cover vast reaches of Berryman's work.

To help students hear acutely the often conflicting tones or voices in the *Songs*, I will coach several students in learning to read together, at one, the same lines, each person reading with a different affect. Or with the more explicit dialogue songs, I will have two students each play one of the personae in response to the other. Another strategy for the more ambitious students is to have them imitate a Berryman song and read it in class.

Students often ask about Berryman's life and loves, with particular attention to his suicide and the suicide of his father. They will also inquire about his relationships with other contemporary poets, especially Lowell, and earlier poets like Frost and Eliot. Occasionally, students will be so stunned by the expressive quality of Berryman's language that they will question how conscious he was of crafting his work to reveal so many dimensions. Still another issue that arises is the link between drinking and inspiration: Berryman often thought that he could not write adequately without simultaneously boozing.

Significant Form, Style, or Artistic Conventions

In "From the Middle and Senior Generations," one of Berryman's essays in the posthumously published *The Freedom of the Poet*, Berryman lists a series of motives for writing poetry, the most important being a "freeing," the enabling of the poet "gradually, again and again, to become almost issues of living and dying, particularly by suicide; problems of relationships with lovers, parents, children, other poets, and God in various manifestations, Western and Eastern; and the means whereby poetry could be fashioned as an explorative and healing tool." In *The Dream Songs*, these themes and questions of form give rise to many enigmas that critics have wrestled with; among the most important are the following:

1. An enduring issue among scholars of *The Dream Songs* is the nature of Berryman's relation to his persona, Henry, and to Henry's counterpart, Sir Bones.
2. An issue that has stirred much debate among Berryman scholars centers on whether *The Dream Songs* is a unified work.
3. Though the title of Berryman's major work seems explicitly to invite the critic to investigate the significance of dreams and dream theory in relation to the *Songs*, few critics have accepted the invitation.

Original Audience

I treat this issue by noting Berryman's longstanding enquiry into the nature of "personal" versus "impersonal" poetry. Berryman's audience for his apprentice poetry was largely influenced by the Eliotic dictum against "personal poetry." Berryman's allegiance to Eliot's proscription was quite evident in his 1939 review of *The Personal Heresy: A Controversy by C. S. Lewis and E. M. W. Tillyard.* Yet his later intense attention to the more personal works of Yeats, Pound, Whitman, and Lowell, especially noted in his essays on these men collected in *The Freedom of the Poet*, helped lead him to address another audience, one that saw that "poetry comes out of personality." In *Homage* and *The Dream Songs*, Berryman can be seen as trying to create an utterance at once communal and personal, objective and subjective, for an audience more eclectic in its aesthetic taste.

Comparisons, Contrasts, Connections

Comparing Lowell's *Life Studies*, Whitman's *Song of Myself*, and Pound's *Hugh Selwyn Mauberly* (each poem or book in whole or in part) with Berryman's 77 *Dream Songs* would reveal the stable and changing characteristics of a long tradition of personal poetry by poets Berryman respected and critiqued in print.

Students might also wish to compare "personal" poems by men with those composed by women, such as Anne Sexton and Sylvia Plath (who is featured in the *Songs*).

Berryman also learned a great deal about aesthetic "reserve" from Stephen Crane's prose and poetry (see his *Stephen Crane*, 1950).

During his graduate years, Berryman also became a Shakespearean scholar and learned thereby much about the dramatic elements in poetry. See also *The Freedom of the Poet* for critiques of other writers Berryman emulated in part.

Questions for Reading and Discussion/ Approaches to Writing

1. (a) What does the concept of "confessional" or "personal" poetry mean to you?
   (b) In your view, can there by any justification for a poet's writing in a language that is not immediately comprehended?
   (c) What for you is the relationship between neurosis and the capacity of a poet to "plumb the depths"?

(d) Is there any way in which poetry can be considered a tool for spiritual healing?

2. (a) In engaging with a poet like Berryman who requires "close listening," the student will be most productive if he/she chooses a song that touches his/her heart and mind and spends hours doing a line-by-line reading.

(b) Students may also do profitable work linking Berryman's themes and forms to psychological schemas, including those of Jung, Freud, Fritz Perls, and Reich, with particular attention to the issues associated with dreams and language.

(c) In addition, *The Freedom of the Poet* is a useful tool for students to use in tracing some of Berryman's views about the nature and purpose of poetry. Comparisons with other confessional poets might also prove fruitful.

Bibliography

Arpin, Gary. *John Berryman: A Reference Guide*. Boston: G. K. Hall, 1976.

Conarroe, Joel. *John Berryman: An Introduction to the Poetry*. New York: Columbia Univ. Press, 1977.

Haffenden, John. *The Life of John Berryman*. Boston: Routledge & Kegan Paul, 1982.

Mancini, Joseph, Jr. *The Berryman Gestalt: Therapeutic Strategies in the Poetry of John Berryman*. New York: Garland Publishing, 1987.

Simpson, Eileen. *Poets in Their Youths: A Memoir*. New York: Random House, 1982.

Gwendolyn Brooks (b. 1917)

Contributing Editor: D. H. Melhem [p. 2311]

Classroom Issues and Strategies

Brooks's work is generally accessible. Occasionally, however, and more likely in some earlier works, like *Annie Allen* and individual poems like "Riders to the Blood-red Wrath," intense linguistic and semantic compression present minor difficulties.

My book *Gwendolyn Brooks: Poetry and the Heroic Voice* can be used as a guide to her published works. As holds true for most poetry, Brooks's should be read aloud. In the process, its power (boosted by alliteration), the musicality, and the narrative are vivified and made easily accessible.

Although I have not had the opportunity to teach Brooks extensively, students seem taken with identity poems like "The Life of Lincoln West" and the didactic "Ballad of Pearl May Lee," which was Hughes's favorite. The narrative aspect seems to be especially appealing. As these are not in this anthology, you may wish to recommend them as exra reading.

Major Themes, Historical Perspectives, and Personal Issues

Themes include black pride, black identity and solidarity, the black humanism and caritas, a maternal vision. Historically, racial discrimination; the civil rights movement of the fifties; black rebellion of the sixties; a concern with complacency in the seventies; black leadership.

Significant Form, Style, or Artistic Conventions

Brooks was influenced at first by the Harlem Renaissance. Her early work featured the sonnet and the ballad, and she experimented with adaptations of conventional meter. Later development of the black arts movement in the sixties, along with conceptions of a black aesthetic, turned her toward free verse and an abandonment of the sonnet as inappropriate to the times. She retained, however, her interest in the ballad—its musicality and accessibility—and in what she called "verse journalism."

Comparisons, Contrasts, Connections

In the earlier works: Langston Hughes, Paul Laurence Dunbar, Merrill Moore, Edna St. Vincent Millay, Claude McKay, Ann Spencer.

In the later works: Amiri Baraka, Haki R. Madhubuti, and again, Hughes.

Bibliography

Gwendolyn Brooks: Poetry and the Heroic Voice, by D. H. Melhem (Univ. Press of Kentucky, 1987) chronologically discusses each major work in a separate chapter; biographical introduction; biocritical, prosodic, and historical approach; discusses correspondence with first publisher.

See also *A Life Distilled* (essays), ed. M. K. Mootry and G. Smith (Univ. of Illinois Press, 1987).

Gwendolyn Brooks, by Harry Shaw (Boston: Twayne, 1980), presents a thematic approach.

Robert Lowell (1917–1977)

Contributing Editor: Linda Wagner-Martin [p. 2323]

Classroom Issues and Strategies

Lowell's poetry is more difficult than readers expect, deceptively difficult. Since many students come to him expecting an accessible poet (after all, he's one of those "confessionals"), they sometimes resent having to mine his poems for the background and the allusive sources they contain. Attention to an explicative preparation usually helps. "New Critical" methods are very appropriate.

Major Themes, Historical Perspectives, and Personal Issues

The combination of the historical with the personal is one of Lowell's most pervasive themes. His illustrious and prominent family (the Lowells) created a burden for both his psyche and his art. The reader must know history to read Lowell. The human mind in search, moving with intuitive understanding (as opposed to a reliance on fact), sometimes succeeding, sometimes not, is Lowell's continuing theme.

Significant Form, Style, or Artistic Conventions

A range of forms must be studied—Lowell is the most formal of poets, even toward the end, with the so-called "notebooks." Studying his intense revision (hardly a word left unchanged from the original version to the final) and examining his effort to skew natural language into his highly concentrated form are both good approaches.

Original Audience

Consider the whole business of the confessional, as Lowell moved from the historical into his unique blend of the personal and the historical.

Address the issue of location. Boston, the New England area, held not only Lowell's history but the country's.

Comparisons, Contrasts, Connections

Compare Lowell's poetry to that of Berryman, Jarrell, Schwartz, Sexton, and Plath.

Bibliography

Refer to the headnote in the text for complete information.

Lawrence Ferlinghetti (b. 1919)

Contributing Editor: Helen Barolini [p. 2332]

Classroom Issues and Strategies

Ferlinghetti's work is immediately accessible and appealing, and these qualities should be emphasized. He uses everyday language to articulate his themes. A problem could be his critique of social problems in America; conservative students may find him too sharply satiric about their image of this country. You might note that although Ferlinghetti articulates the "outsider" view of society, he also espouses hope for the future; for instance, poems like "Popular Manifest" (not in this anthology) give a sense of vision and expectation.

Tape recordings of Ferlinghetti reading can be effective.

Major Themes, Historical Perspectives, and Personal Issues

Ferlinghetti is a political activist and his poetical career spans and reflects thirty years of U.S. political history.

His personal voice brings poetry back to the people. He has done this not only as a poet, but as a publisher, editor, translator, and discoverer of new talent.

Significant Form, Style, or Artistic Conventions

Ferlinghetti has been prominently identified with the Beat Movement of the 1950s. It is important to consider the Beat Movement as an ongoing part of American bohemianism, and to contrast it, for example, with the expatriate movement of post-World War I.

The hip vocabulary can well be examined, and the beat experience of alienation can be connected with other marginals in the society.

Original Audience

The work of Ferlinghetti can be placed in the specific social context of the beat movement in the fifties—beats were the anarchists in a time of general post-war conformism.

Comparisons, Contrasts, Connections

Ferlinghetti can certainly be compared with his fellow beats, like Allen Ginsberg and Gregory Corso, and contrasted with other poets of the time—for instance, the more mannered Wallace Stevens. There is also much to compare, stylistically, with E. E. Cummings.

Questions for Reading and Discussion/ Approaches to Writing

1. With this particular poet, the most effective approach is to plunge right into the work. He elicits the questions.
2. Discuss the San Francisco Renaissance, which centered around Ferlinghetti's City Lights Bookstore.
3. What is the counterculture in America?

Bibliography

General

Charters, Samuel. *Some Poems/Poets: Studies in American Underground Poetry since 1945.* Oyez, 1971.

The Postmoderns: The New American Poetry Revised. N.Y.: Grove, 1982.

Particular

Cherkovski, Neeli. *Ferlinghetti: A Biography*. N.Y.: Doubleday, 1979.

Hopkins, Crale D. "The Poetry of Lawrence Ferlinghetti: A Reconsideration." *Italian Americana* 1, no. 1 (Autumn 1974): 59–76.

Kherdian, David. *Six Poets of the San Francisco Renaissance*. Fresno, Cal.: Giligia Press, 1967.

Vestere, Richard. "Ferlinghetti: Rebirth of a Beat Poet." *Identity Magazine*. (March 1977): 42–4.

Richard Wilbur (b. 1921)

Contributing Editor: Bernard Engel [p. 2339]

Classroom Issues and Strategies

Students sometimes have difficulty with syntax that is out of the ordinary and with expression that uses original imagery and metaphors.

I approach teaching Wilbur by kidding students a bit about becoming tied up when they see verse in print, pointing out that they spend hours a day listening to it in pop songs that employ traditional rhyme and metrics, and plentiful, though stale, images, metaphor, and symbols.

Then I come at the poem with a businesslike approach: deal with it as one would a prose statement. After coming to a version or versions of what it "says," I elaborate on other possibilities, and explain—or ask students to explain—images, metaphors, unusual diction. Though I touch on metrics, I do not emphasize them in undergraduate classes.

I use reading questions to start students' thinking and to indicate the direction I'd suggest they take. Questions of traditional vs. open form led to heated discussion ten years ago. There is less fervor today, but the matter can still spark discussion. Students' questions are usually about the meaning of an expression. When aesthetic-philosophical questions arise, they come from me. Some statement in their text headnote usually can prompt reflection and discussion.

Major Themes, Historical Perspectives, and Personal Issues

1. The contrast between Wilbur's relatively tight control and the open form advocated by Williams, Olson, and others.
2. Wilbur's relation to the poetic modernists and to such of his contemporaries as Jarrell.

Original Audience

I discuss possible reasons for the fact that Wilbur, though well known and much honored, has not been recognized as one of the leading figures, and also the probability, as I see it, that his work will outlast the more fashionable. He is an academic poet in the good sense of that term—learned, employing civilized wit, highly skilled in technique.

Comparisons, Contrasts, Connections

The bases are the apparent differences between the various poets' works. Since undergraduates will usually be reading poems by several writers in a term, comparisons and contrasts come readily.

David Hill's book has several passages discussing critics who compare Wilbur's work with that of Robert Lowell, Howard Nemerov, and others. Useful comparison could also be with Richard Eberhart—a poet who is equally convinced that the flesh is poetry's environment, but is nevertheless much more willing to move into mysticism and exclamation. Peter Viereck contrasts Wilbur, an "Apollonia," with Theodore Roethke, a "Dionysian," in *The Last Decade in Poetry* (Nashville: George Peabody College for Teachers, 1954).

Compare Wilbur's vigorous defense of traditional patterns, metrics, and rhyme with Charles Olson's essay "Projective Verse" or similar arguments for open form.

Questions for Reading and Discussion/ Approaches to Writing

" 'A World Without Objects Is a Sensible Emptiness' "

1. This poem expresses Wilbur's repeated conviction that "mirages" are not enough, that "all shinings" must be worked out in the world of sensory reality. Compare Emerson's insistence in "The American Scholar" on knowing "the meal in the firkin, the milk in the pan."

2. The title's quotation is from Meditation 65 in Thomas Traherne's *Second Century*. Asserting that one lacking someone or something to love would be better off having "no being," Traherne says: "Life without objects is a sensible emptiness, and that is a greater misery than death or nothing." David Hill discusses the poem on his pages 62–5.

"Pangloss's Song: A Comic-Opera Lyric"

1. Students should note how Wilbur uses humor to avoid the distasteful in this lyric (and observe that the word "syphilis" does not appear).
2. Without attempting to impose too much philosophical freight on this *jeu d'esprit*, one might observe that the poem satisfies Wilbur's insistence that the idealist must be aware of realities.

"In the Field"

1. In mythology, Andromeda (Stanza 3) was rescued from a sea monster by Perseus; Wilbur has observed that Euripides' lost play *Andromeda* may have told of her transformation into a constellation.
2. Discuss the assertion of the last two stanzas that "the one/ Unbounded thing we know" is "the heart's wish for life."

"The Mind-Reader"

1. Students should be able to explain the seemingly unimportant analogy in the first stanza because the speaker comes back to it again and again.
2. In what ways does the poem suggest that the speaker is indeed wise, rather than merely weary or cynical?

I generally prefer that undergraduates avoid the library: they should write on ideas that come to them in their own reading of Wilbur and other poets in the course. They may follow up on statements or hints in their textbooks and in class presentations. I'd rather they read the poems themselves several times, instead of haunting the library for abstruse articles they won't understand. A little library work is necessary, of course, for junior and senior English majors.

Bibliography

The best help for the harried instructor and the undergraduate student will come from:

Comparing headnotes and footnotes in anthologies—most prominent ones contain poems by Wilbur.

Checking discussions entered in the index to David Hill, *Richard Wilbur* (Twayne, 1968)—now somewhat out of date, but still useful.

Consulting the early but still useful essay by Wilbur himself, "The Bottles Become New, Too:" (*Quarterly Review of Literature* VII [1953]: 186–92; reprinted in Wilbur's *Responses: Prose Pieces: 1973–1976* [1976]: 215–23).

Consulting Bruce Michelson's thoughtful "Richard Wilbur," pp. 335–68 in Ronald Baughman, ed., *Contemporary Authors: Bibliographical Series—American Poets* (Detroit: Gale Research, 1986), volume 2.

James Dickey (b. 1923)

Contributing Editor: Jennifer Randisi [p. 2349]

Classroom Issues and Strategies

The accusation that Dickey is only interested in a male audience can be a problem. His settings are like those of Hemingway: nature, the wilderness, war. Women initially feel quite put off.

There is enough inner life—enough concern with intuition, "being," locating oneself in the moment—so that students realize Dickey is not concerned with mastering the world, but rather the opposite, a kind of skeptical merging with it. For all the violence, this is a "feminine" outlook. Students are surprised by Dickey's language, his perception.

There are many ways into Dickey's work, depending upon where in a course and in what kind of a course you are using him. For instance, begin with his background as a southerner, his involvement in war, his feelings about his dead brother, Eugene, as one approach. For another approach, begin with his place in American poetry (Who came before him? Whom did he "father"?).

Students are often confused by the violence. They want to know why it's there—what function it serves. They like the poems but have difficulty analyzing the tone. Often women students find Dickey too much of a "male" writer—too concerned with hunting and war.

652 • *The Heath Anthology of American Literature*

Major Themes, Historical Perspectives, and Personal Issues

Themes include the tension between maintaining control and relinquishing it (whether the landscape is war, the hunt, or the self), the transforming power of art (and the artist's vision), and the ways in which individuals can find a new, more immediate, relationship with the external world. Dickey's work explores borders of all kinds: conscious and unconscious, inner and outer, living and dead.

Significant Form, Style, or Artistic Conventions

Dickey has been characterized as a modern romanticist. He is direct and accessible in his early poems, although his tone and thought are often quite complex. His poems written in the 1970s experiment with a longer, nearly prosaic line of verse. In both his poems and novels, Dickey is interested in pushing the limits of the form.

Original Audience

Dickey often writes about the war. While his experience comes from World War II and Korea, the idea of war—the impersonal relation between men—continues to be a relevant issue. This notion is often counterbalanced by the hunt—an arena offering an opportunity for a pure, intensely personal relationship, between hunter and hunted.

Comparisons, Contrasts, Connections

Dickey's skepticism has been compared to that of Yeats and the transfiguring joy he often expresses in his poems has been compared to that of Theodore Roethke. His preoccupation with the morality of action and guilt for war link him with other southerners, both poets and anarchists. His concern with the natural world (its joys and terrors) can be compared to that of Robert Frost.

Questions for Reading and Discussion/ Approaches to Writing

1. I like assigning short (2–3 pp.) very focused papers asking students to respond to a specific idea or issue suggested in the poem.
2. Useful papers could also trace thematic aspects through several poems.

3. Or ask students to look at Dickey's comments about his writing. There are many interviews, written and taped.

Bibliography

Conversations with James Dickey is useful, as are the essays in *The Imagination as Glory: The Poetry of James Dickey*.

Mari Evans

Contributing Editors: Joyce Joyce and John Reilly [p. 2358]

Classroom Issues and Strategies

In her Afro-centric writing, Evans challenges readers to accept that she directs her words to African-Americans. Tone and references in the poetry make these uninvited readers feel excluded. In response, they may be dismissive.

This must be directly confronted with some discussion of the "special orientation" of other writers. Does Robert Frost write for the descendants of Irish and Italian immigrants in the New England cities? If not directly, then does he obliquely say something to the urban citizens, to us? In addition, the apppearance of vernacular speech in writing sanctioned as poetry creates a stir of interest in the question of whether or not there is an inherently acceptable language for literature.

Major Themes, Historical Perspectives, and Personal Issues

Mari Evans puts a high value upon culture, which makes the language of a poem and the alleged commercialism of other poets cause for battle. In her belief that control of language can make a difference and that a poem is an act of resistance and social construction, this dissident poet calls for an exploration of the theory of culture. The valorization of culture must be associated with the black liberation movement, black political power, and the ideas of revolution advanced in those causes during the 1960s and 1970s.

Significant Form, Style, or Artistic Conventions

The free verse form, reflecting a belief in the native orality of poetry and the political need to "perform" poetry in the community, helps to define the meaning of Evans's remark that poems are wholes. This poetry can be related to other performative lyrics such as the blues and popular song.

Original Audience

This is a fundamental issue for Evans. She has rejected the double consciousness identified by W. E. B. Du Bois in *Souls of Black Folk* (1913) by addressing her work to a black audience. This can be studied in class, at the risk of denaturing the poetry, by talking about it as a technique of a school of poetry and by a brief discussion of the new black aesthetic developed by Larry Neal, Amiri Baraka, Hoyt Fuller, et al.

Comparisons, Contrasts, Connections

Evans may be compared with Allen Ginsberg in order to show the similarity of avant-garde positions regarding popular American culture. This places Evans in a literary, historical context that illustrates a shared purpose among authors seeking to create a new voice. She may be compared to Gwendolyn Brooks with an eye to the creation of a character. For example, looking at "We Real Cool" and "I Am a Black Woman" could lead to a useful discussion of the uses of voice to characterize.

Questions for Reading and Discussion/ Approaches to Writing

1. Prepare annotations for the historical references in the second stanza of "I Am a Black Woman."
2. Look back at the poetry of Emily Dickinson and note the similarities and differences between Dickinson's "I Dwell in Possibility" and Evans's "conceptuality."

Bibliography

Evans's own critical writing is most illuminating. Her book *Black Women Writers* is an excellent source of statements.

Denise Levertov (b. 1923)

Contributing Editor: Joan F. Hallisey [p. 2363]

Classroom Issues and Strategies

With an adequate introduction to her life and works, Denise Levertov is not a difficult author. Levertov can best be made accessible to students when they are familiar with the poet's own prose reflections on poetry, the role of the poet, and "notes" on organic form. You might prepare an introduction to her work by making reference to her quite precise discussion of these themes in *The Poet in the World* (New Dimensions, 1973) or *Light Up the Cave* (New Dimensions, 1982).

Consider using tapes of Levertov reading her own poetry. The most recent cassette, "The Acolyte" (Watershed), contains a fine sampling from her earlier poetry through *Oblique Prayers*. Encourage students to listen both to her poetry readings and interviews and to incorporate either in their class or seminar discussions and presentations or as material for their research papers. When students are doing a class presentation, strongly urge them to be certain that their classmates have copies of the poems they will be discussing.

Students respond very favorably to Levertov's conviction that the poet writes more than "[she] knows." They also respond positively to the fact that an American woman "engaged" poet has spoken out strongly on women's rights, peace and justice issues, race, and other questions on human rights.

Students may ask you if Levertov is discouraged in the face of so much darkness and disaster evident in the late twentieth century. This presents a good opportunity to have the students examine "Writing in the Dark" (if you can obtain this poem) and "The May Mornings."

Major Themes, Historical Perspectives, and Personal Issues

Levertov's work is concerned with several dimensions of the human experience: love, motherhood, nature, war, the nuclear arms race, mysticism, poetry, and the role of the poet. If you are teaching a women's literature course or an upper-level course focusing on a few writers, several of these themes might be examined. In a survey course, you might concentrate on three themes that include both historical and personal issues: poetry, the role of the poet, and her interest in humanitarian politics.

Significant Form, Style, or Artistic Conventions

Levertov in "Some Notes on Organic Form" tells the reader that during the writing of a poem the various elements of the poet's being are in communion with one another and heightened. She believes that ear and eye, intellect and passion, interrelate more subtly than at other times, and she regards the poet's "checking for accuracy," for precision of language that must take place throughout the writing not as a "matter of one element supervising the others but of intuitive interaction between all the elements involved"(*The Poet in the World*, p. 9).

Like Wordsworth and Emerson, Levertov sees content and form as being in a state of dynamic interaction. She sees rhyme, echo, reiteration as serving not only to knit the elements of an experience "but also as being the means, the sole means, by which the density of texture and the returning or circling of perception can be transmuted into language, apperceived" (Ibid., p. 9).

You might point out that as an artist who is "obstinately precise" about her craft, Levertov pays close attention to etymologies as she searches for the right words, the right image, the right arrangement of the lines on the page. It will be helpful for students to be able to recognize other poetic techniques that Levertov uses in her poetry: enjambment, color, contrast, and even the pun to sustain conflict and ambiguity. Levertov will sometimes make use of the juxtaposition of key words and line breaks.

Levertov does not consider herself a member of any particular school.

Original Audience

Levertov has said, on several occasions, that she never has readers in mind when she is writing a poem. She believes that a poem has to be not merely addressed to a person or a problem *out there*; but must come from *in here*, the inner being of the poet, and it must also address something *in here*.

It is important to share Levertov's ideas with the students when you discuss audience. One might stress the universality of some themes: familial and cultural heritage, poetry, and the role of the poet/prophet in a "time of terror." There is a "timeless" kind of relevance for these themes, and they need not be confined to any one age.

Comparisons, Contrasts, Connections

There is enough evidence to suggest that a fruitful comparison might be made between several of Muriel Rukeyser's finest poems ("Akiba," "Kathe Kollwitz" [*Speed of Darkness* 1968], "Searching/Not Searching" [*Breaking Open*, 1973]) and some of Levertov's poems on comparable themes.

Questions for Reading and Discussion/
Approaches to Writing

1. (a) What kinds of feelings do you have about the Holocaust? About nuclear war?
   (b) What do you think the role of the poet should be today? Do you think she/he should speak out about political or social issues? Why? Why not?
2. (a) Several of Levertov's poems can be used for a writing sample and subsequent discussion at the beginning of the course. Brief poems that students respond strongly to are: "The Broken Sandal," (Levertov's *Relearning the Alphabet*, p. 4), "Variation on a Theme from Rilke," (Levertov's *Breathing the Water*, p. 3), and "Knowing the Way" (Levertov's *Footprints*, p. 57).
   (b) One might give a short assignment to compare the themes, tone, and imagery of Levertov's "The Broken Sandal" with Adrienne Rich's "Prospective Immigrants—Please Note."
   (c) Discuss the imagery and tone in Levertov's "The May Mornings" and Lucille Clifton's "Breaklight."
   (d) Examine several of Levertov's poems on poetry and the role of the poet in light of Ralph Waldo Emerson's call for the "true" poet in several of his essays, most notably in "The Poet," "Poetry and the Imagination," and "The American Scholar."

Bibliography

Denise Levertov's *The Poet in the World* (1973) and *Light Up the Cave* (1982), both from New Dimensions, are essential primary source materials for a deeper understanding of the poems included in the text.

"The Sense of Pilgrimage" essay in *The Poet in the World* and "Beatrice Levertoff" in *Light Up the Cave* offer valuable background material for teaching "Illustrious Ancestors."

See also the introduction to her poetry by Miss Levertov in *The Bloodaxe Book of Contemporary Women Poets*, edited by Jeni Couzyn, Bloodaxe Books, 1985, pp. 73–79.

Robert Creeley (b. 1926)

Contributing Editor: Thomas R. Whitaker [p. 2369]

Classroom Issues and Strategies

"Hart Crane"

Dedicated to a friend of Crane who became a friend of Creeley, this is the opening poem in *For Love*. Is it a negative portrait or a sympathetic study of difficulties central to Creeley's own career? Certainly it contains many leitmotifs of Creeley's poetry: stuttering, isolations, incompletion, self-conscious ineptness, the difficulty of utterance, the need for friends, the confrontations of a broken world.

"I Know a Man"

The colloquial anecdote as parable? How does the stammering lineation complicate the swift utterance? Why should the shift in speakers occur with such ambiguous punctuation—a comma splice? According to Creeley, "drive" is said not by the friend but by the speaker.

"For Love"

The closing poem in *For Love*, this is informed by the qualities attributed to Crane in the volume's opening poem. "For Love" is one of many poems to Bobbie—wife, companion, muse, and mother of children—that wrestle with the nature of love, the difficulty of utterance, and a mass of conflicting feelings: doubt, faith, despair, surprise, self-criticism, gratitude, relief. The poem is a remarkable enactment of a complex and moment-by-moment honesty.

"Words"

This poem drives yet further inward to the ambiguous point where an inarticulate self engages an imperfectly grasped language. Not the wife or muse but "words" seem now the objects of direct address, the poem's "you." Nevertheless, the poem's detailed phrases and its movement through anxious blockage toward an ambiguously blessed release strongly suggest a love poem.

"America"

Though seldom an explicitly political poet, Creeley here brings his sardonic tone and his belief in utterance as our most intimate identity to bear on the question, What has happened to the America that Whitman celebrated? "The United States themselves are essentially the greatest poem," Whitman had said in his Preface to the 1855 *Leaves of Grass*. And he had often spoken of the "words" belonging to that poem, as in "One's-Self I Sing" and in the reflections on "the People" in *Democratic Vistas*.

"America" modulates those concerns into Creeley's own more quizzical language. We may read it as a dark response, a century later, to Whitman's "Long, Too Long America" in *Drum-Taps*. For Creeley's more extended response to Whitman, see his *Whitman: Selected Poems*.

Significant Form, Style, or Artistic Conventions

In "Projective Verse" Charles Olson quotes Creeley's remark that "Form is never more than an extension of content." Creeley liked, as an implicit definition of form, a Blakean aphorism that he learned from Slater Brown: "Fire delights in its form." His central statement of open poetics, involving "a content which cannot be anticipated," is "I'm Given to Write Poems" (*A Quick Graph*, pp. 61–72).

It is useful to know that, when reading his poetry aloud, Creeley always indicates line-ends by means of very brief pauses. The resultant stammer—quite unlike the effect of Williams's reading—is integral to Creeley's style, which involves a pervasive sense of wryly humorous or painful groping for the next line.

Comparisons, Contrasts, Connections

William Carlos Williams told Robert Creeley, "You have the subtlest feeling for the measure I have encountered anywhere except in the verses of Ezra Pound." For Creeley's relation to Williams, see his essays in *A Quick Graph* and Paul Mariani, "Robert Creeley," in *A Usable Past* (Amherst: Univ. of Mass. Press, 1984). For his relation to Pound, see "A Note on Ezra Pound" (*A Quick Graph*), and for his sustained and mutually valuable relation to Charles Olson, see again *A Quick Graph*.

Perhaps the class would like to compare "Hart Crane" with Robert Lowell's "Words for Hart Crane" in *Life Studies*. Two views of Crane, two modes of portraiture, and two historically important styles of mid-century American verse; these plus "The Broken Tower" itself would make a fascinating unit of study.

Bibliography

Mariani, Paul. "Robert Greeley." In *A Usable Past: Essays on Modern and Contemporary Poetry*. Amherst: Univ. of Mass. Press, 1984, pp. 184–202.

Olson, Charles. *Selected Writings*.

Williams, William Carlos. *A Quick Graph*. Pp. 61–72; 99–120; 151–84.

Allen Ginsberg (b. 1926)

Contributing Editor: Linda Wagner-Martin [p. 2376]

Classroom Issues and Strategies

Teaching Ginsberg requires addressing rampant stereotypes about the beats and the kind of art they created; i.e., the drug culture, homosexuality, Eastern belief systems, and, most important, the effects of such practices on the poem.

By showing the students what a standard formalist 1950s poem was, I have usually been able to keep them focused on the work itself. Ginsberg's long-lined, chart-like poems are so responsive to his speech rhythms that once they hear tapes, they begin to see his rationale for form. Connections with Whitman's work are also useful.

Major Themes, Historical Perspectives, and Personal Issues

Ginsberg's dissatisfaction with America during the 1950s prompted his jeremiads, laments, "Howls." When his macabre humor could surface, as it does in "A Supermarket in California," he shows the balance that clear vision can create. His idealism about his country marks much of his work, which is in many ways much less "personal" than it at first seems.

Significant Form, Style, or Artistic Conventions

Consider the tradition of American poetry as voice dependent (Whitman and William Carlos Williams) rather than a text for reading. The highly allusive, ornate, "learned" poems of an Eliot or Stevens have much less influence on Ginsberg's work, although he certainly knows a great deal about poetry. His poems are what he chooses to write, and he makes this choice from a plethora of models.

Original Audience

Ginsberg's work can usefully be approached as protest as well as lament. Connections with racial minorities can help define his own Jewish rhythms.

Comparisons, Contrasts, Connections

Walt Whitman	Robert Creeley
William Carlos Williams	Langston Hughes
Theodore Roethke	Lawrence Ferlinghetti
Gary Snyder	Etheridge Knight
Denise Levertov	Pedro Pietri

Bibliography

Refer to the headnote in the text for complete information.

John Ashbery (b. 1927)

Contributing Editor: David Bergman [p. 2387]

Classroom Issues and Strategies

Students are sometimes put off by their inability to paraphrase the poems line by line. This problem is minimized by the selection in the text, which has centered around Ashbery's more linear narrative, but the selection does not completely obviate the problem, nor would one wish to avoid it since it is fundamental to Ashbery's style and method. Students are also disturbed by his often paradoxical adages and free-flowing imagery. Finally, students generally don't have the literary, historical, or cultural background to grasp Ashbery's frequently allusive manner.

Students should be encouraged to explore the connections between seemingly unrelated passages. These connections are probably best found if the student is encouraged to move freely through the poem at first, finding whatever connection he or she can spot. Richard Howard convincingly argues that each Ashbery poem contains an emblem for its entire meaning. If allowed time, students usually find such emblems. Second, drawing connections between Ashbery's method and such graphic methods as collage and assemblage often helps. Students, of course, should be reminded to read the notes.

I have found it useful to present Ashbery in relation to the visual arts, in particular the shifting perspective of comic strips, the surprising juxtapositions of collage and assemblage, the vitality of abstract impressionism, and the metaphysical imagery of de Chirico.

Major Themes, Historical Perspectives, and Personal Issues

The selection highlights three major themes or questions running through Ashbery's work: (1) the problem of subjective identity—Whose consciousness informs the poem? (2) the relationship between language and subjectivity—Whose language do I speak or does the language have a mind of its own? (3) the connection between subjectivity, language, and place—What does it mean to be an American poet?

Significant Form, Style, or Artistic Conventions

Ashbery has long been interested in French art, especially dada and surrealism. Such interests have merged with an equally strong concern for poetic form and structure, as evinced by the sestina of "Farm Implements" and the 4 x 4 structure (four stanzas each of four lines) of "Paradoxes and Oxymorons," a structure he uses through *Shadow Train*, the volume from which the poem was taken. Ashbery's combination of surrealism and formalism typifies a certain strain of postmodernism.

Original Audience

Obviously Ashbery is writing for a highly sophisticated contemporary audience. The decade he spent in France provided him with an international perspective.

Comparisons, Contrasts, Connections

Frank O'Hara, Kenneth Koch, and James Schuyler are or were close friends of Ashbery; together they formed the nucleus of what is sometimes dubbed the New York School of Poetry. The dream-like imagery bears some resemblance to Berryman and Ginsberg. Whitman provides a particularly vital touchstone to an American tradition.

Questions for Reading and Discussion/
Approaches to Writing

How do comic strips (and other forms of popular art) inform both the content and the style of Ashbery's poems? Who is speaking in an Ashbery poem? What is American about John Ashbery?

Bibliography

Altieri, Charles. "John Ashbery." In *Self and Sensibility in Contemporary American Poetry*. New York: Cambridge Univ. Press.

Berger, Charles. "Vision in the Form of a Task." Lehman, 163–208.

Bergman, David. "Introduction: John Ashbery." In *Reported Sightings: Art Chronicles 1957–87*. New York: Knopf, 1989, xi–xxiii.

——. "Choosing Our Fathers: Gender and Identity in Whitman, Ashbery and Richard Howard." *American Literary History* 1 (1989): 383–403.

Lehman, David, ed. *Beyond Amazement: New Essays on John Ashbery*. Ithaca: Cornell Univ. Press, 1980.

Anne Sexton (1928–1974)

Contributing Editor: Diana Hume George [p. 2395]

Classroom Issues and Strategies

Anne Sexton's poetry teaches superbly. It is accessible, challenging, richly textured, and culturally resonant. Her work is equally appropriate for use in American literature, women's studies, and poetry courses. The selections in this text represent many of the diverse subjects and directions of her work.

Three problems tend to recur in teaching Sexton; all are interrelated. First, the "confessional school" context is troublesome because that subgenre in American poetry is both misnamed and easily misunderstood; Sexton has been the subject of inordinately negative commentary as the first prominent woman poet writing in this mode. Second, contemporary readers, despite the feminist movement, often have difficulty dealing with Sexton's explicitly bodily and female subject matter and imagery. Finally, readers often find her poetry depressing, especially the poems that deal with suicide, death, and mental illness.

If the course emphasizes historical context, a sympathetic and knowledgeable explanation of resistance to the confessional mode is helpful. (Ironically, if historical context is not important to presentation of the material, I suggest not mentioning it at all.) Academic and public reactions to the women's movement, even though Sexton did not deliberately style herself as a feminist poet, will help to make students understand the depth and extent of her cultural and poetic transgressions. The third problem is most troubling for teaching Sexton; teachers might emphasize the necessity for literature to confront and deal with controversial and uncomfortable themes such as suicide, mortality, madness. A discussion of the dangers of equating creativity and emotional illness might be helpful, even necessary, for some students. It's also important to demonstrate that Sexton wrote many poems of celebration, as well as of mourning.

Students often want to know how and why Sexton killed herself. They want to disapprove, yet they are often fascinated. I recommend one of two approaches. Either avoid the whole thing by not mentioning her suicide and by directing students toward the poems and away from Sexton's life; or engage the issue directly, in which case you need to allow some time to make thoughtful responses and guide a useful discussion that will illuminate more than one life and death.

Major Themes, Historical Perspectives, and Personal Issues

A balanced presentation of Sexton would include mention of her major themes, most of which are touched upon in the selection of poems here: religious quest, transformation and dismantling of myth, the meanings of gender, inheritance and legacy, the search for fathers, mother-daughter relationships, sexual anxiety, madness and suicide, issues of female identity.

Significant Form, Style, or Artistic Conventions

The problem of placement in the confessional school can be turned into an advantage by emphasizing Sexton's groundbreaking innovations in style and subject matter. Sexton's early poetry was preoccupied with form and technique; she could write in tightly constrained metrical forms, as demonstrated in *To Bedlam and Part Way Back* and *All My Pretty Ones*. She wrote in free verse during the middle and late phases of her poetic career. Most important is her gift for unique imagery, often centering on the body or the household.

Original Audience

Many of Sexton's readers have been women, and she has perhaps a special appeal for female readers because of her domestic imagery. She also found a wide readership among people who have experienced emotional illness or depression. But Sexton's appeal is wider than a specialist audience. She is exceptionally accessible, writes in deliberately colloquial style, and her diversity and range are such that she appeals to students from different backgrounds.

Comparisons, Contrasts, Connections

Among other confessionals, she can be discussed in context with Robert Lowell, Sylvia Plath, John Berryman, W. D. Snodgrass. Among women poets, she shares concerns of subject and style with Adrienne Rich, Denise Levertov, Sylvia Plath, Alicia Ostriker, and, in a different way, Maxine Kumin. It's also appropriate to mention her similarities to Emily Dickinson, another female New England poet who wrote in unconventional ways about personal subjects, religion, and mortality. Because she was a religious poet whose work is part of the questing tradition, she might be usefully compared with John Donne and George Herbert. Since many of her poems are spoken from the perspective of a child speaker, the standard literary tradition for comparative purposes can include Blake and Wordsworth, Vaughan and Traherne. Extraliterary texts that illuminate her work include selections of psychoanalytic theory, especially Freudian.

Questions for Reading and Discussion/ Approaches to Writing

1. I try to avoid giving students a predisposition to Sexton, and instead discuss difficulties and questions as they arise in discussion.
2. (a) Examine the range of Sexton's subject matter and poetic style.
   (b) Pick a theme in a Sexton poem and trace it in other poems she wrote.
   (c) In what sense is Sexton a religious poet? A heretic?

    (d)   Examine several surprising, unconventional images from several Sexton poems. What makes them surprising? Successful?

    (e)   If Sexton is confessional, what is it that she is confessing?

    (f)   Compare one of Sexton's "Transformations" with the original version in the Brothers Grimm.

    (g)   Select another poet with whom Sexton can be compared, such as a confessional poet, a feminist poet, a religious poet, and discuss similarities and differences in their perspectives.

    (h)   What are some of the possible uses for poetry that speaks from the perspective of madness or of suicide?

Bibliography

Excellent articles on Sexton are most readily available in recent and forthcoming anthologies of criticism. Instructors can select articles that bear most directly on their concerns.

Sexton: Selected Criticism, edited by Diana Hume George (Univ. of Illinois Press, 1988) includes many previously published articles from diverse sources in addition to new criticism, as does *Anne Sexton: Telling the Tale*, edited by Steven E. Colburn (Univ. of Michigan Press, 1988).

Original Essays on Anne Sexton, edited by Frances Bixler (Univ. of Central Arkansas Press, 1988) contains many new and previously unpublished selections.

The G. K. Hall anthology of criticism on Sexton, edited by Linda Wagner-Martin, is in preparation.

J. D. McClatchy's *Anne Sexton: The Poet and Her Critics* (Indiana Univ. Press, 1978) is the original critical collection.

Diane Wood Middlebrook is writing a biography, which will be published by Houghton Mifflin.

Critics who specialize in Sexton or who have written major essays on her, whose works will be found in most or all of the above anthologies, include Alicia Suskin Ostriker, Diane Wood Middlebrook, Diana Hume George, Estella Lauter, Suzanne Juhasz, and Linda Wagner-Martin.

Adrienne Rich (b. 1929)

Contributing Editor: Wendy Martin [p. 2409]

Classroom Issues and Strategies

Rich's poetry is extremely accessible and readable. There are few allusions that cannot be understood. However, from time to time, there will be references to events or literary works that will not be immediately recognized by students. This material or these references are glossed in the text so the student can understand the historical or literary context.

Other problems occur when there is fundamental hostility to the poet over feminism. The instructor will have to explain that feminism simply means a belief in the social, political, and economic equality of women and men. Explain, also, that Rich is not a man-hater or in any way unwilling to consider men as human beings. Rather, her priority is to establish the fundamental concerns of her women readers.

Major Themes, Historical Perspectives, and Personal Issues

It is important to read these poems out loud, to understand that Rich is simultaneously a political, polemical, and lyric poet. It is important also to establish for the poems of the '60s, the Vietnam War protests as background as well as the feminist movement of the '60s and '70s.

It is also important to emphasize that in many respects the '60s and '70s were reaction to the confinement of the '50s and the feminine mystique of that period. In addition, stress that the political background of the poems by Adrienne Rich connects the personal and the political.

Significant Form, Style, or Artistic Conventions

Rich employs free verse, dialogue, and the interweaving of several voices. She evolves from a more tightly constructed traditional rhymed poetry to a more open, loose, and flexible poetic line. The instructor must stress again that poetic subjects are chosen often for their political value and importance. It is important once again to stress that politics and art are intertwined, that they cannot be separated. Aesthetic matters affect the conditions of everyday life.

Original Audience

Adrienne Rich has written her poetry for all time. While it grows out of the political conflicts and tensions of the feminist movement and the antiwar protests, it speaks of universal issues of relationships between men and women and between women and women that will endure for generations to come.

Comparisons, Contrasts, Connections

The feminist activists poets like Audre Lorde, June Jordan, Carolyn Forché would be very useful to read along with Rich. Also it might be useful to teach poets like Allen Ginsberg and Gary Snyder who were, after all, poets of the beat movement of the late '50s and early '60s. They were poets with a vision, as is Rich.

Questions for Reading and Discussion/ Approaches to Writing

1. It might be useful to discuss the evolution of the more free and more flexible line that begins with Whitman and the greater flexibility of subject matter that also begins with Whitman and Dickinson and to carry this discussion on through William Carlos Williams and Allen Ginsberg to discuss the evolution of the free verse that Rich uses.
2. Any writing topic that would discuss either the evolution of flexible poetics or aesthetics—that is, a concern with people's actual lived experiences, for the way they actually talk and think.

   In addition, in the case of Rich, any paper that would link her to other women writers of the twentieth century (and the nineteenth, for that matter) would be useful. Rich is often quoted as an important cultural critic who provides the context for feminist thought in general in the twentieth century. It might also be useful to assign parts of her prose, essays either in collected essays or in *Of Woman Born*.

Bibliography

I would highly recommend my own book: *An American Triptych: The Lives and Work of Anne Bradstreet, Emily Dickinson, and Adrienne Rich*. I am recommending this book because it provides both a historical and an aesthetic context for the poetry of Rich. It links her to earlier traditions that have shaped her work and demonstrates effectively how American

Puritanism and American feminism are intertwined. It gives a lot of biographical material as well as historical background and literary analysis.

Gary Snyder (b. 1930)

Contributing Editor: Thomas R. Whitaker [p. 2418]

Questions for Reading and Discussion/ Approaches to Writing

"Riprap"

As Snyder tells us in his first volume, riprap is "a cobble of stone laid on steep, slick rock to make a trail for horses in the mountains." In *Myths & Texts* (p. 43), he calls poetry "a riprap on the slick rock of metaphysics." This poem may suggest the "objectivism" of William Carlos Williams— "No ideas but in things"—and yet it finally evokes an infinite, everchanging system of worlds and thoughts. Such idealism, of course, also enters Williams's *Paterson*. Central to the poetics of both Williams and Snyder are strategies that enable particulars to evoke a pattern and so provide a link with the universal. What strategies can the class find here? Some poems for comparison: "Mid-August at Sourdough Mountain Lookout" and "Piute Creek" in *Riprap*, and "For Nothing" in *Turtle Island*—all concerned to relate "thing" and "mind" or "form" and "emptiness."

"Vapor Trails"

How does this poem relate aesthetic patterns, natural patterns, and the patterns of human violence? Is the poem finally a lament over such violence? Or a discovery of its beauty? Or a resignation to its naturalness? Or all or none of these? Can the class trace the shifting tone of the meditation from beginning to end?

This poem, too, has affinities with Williams's work. See, for example, such studies of symmetry and craft as "On Gay Wallpaper" and "Fine Work with Pitch and Copper." Does the ironic use of "design" at the end of "Vapor Trails" obliquely recall the concerns of Robert Frost's "Design"?

"Wave"

This poem, like others in *Regarding Wave*, links various manifestations of energy—inorganic, organic, sexual, linguistic, mental—through images and etymologies that evoke a cosmic wave, motion, or dance. Snyder's riprap, a human construction that enables a mental ascent, seems now to have yielded more fully to the perception of patterns inherent in natural process, patterns in which we dancingly participate.

Wave: wife. As that analogy develops, does the poem suggest that nature is our muse and that the energy of all sentience and all cosmic process is fundamentally sexual?

Would the class enjoy some visual analogies to "the dancing grain of things/of my mind"? If so, you might look at the photographs and calligraphy in Lao Tsu, *Tao Te Ching*, translated by Gia-Fu Feng and Jane English (New York: Random House, 1972).

"It Was When"

This reverie over moments when Snyder's son Kai might have been conceived is both a love poem to his wife Masa and a celebration of the "grace" manifest in their coming together. Its imagery, cadences, and reverence for vital processes strongly recall the poetry of D. H. Lawrence. The class might like to make comparisons with Lawrence's "Gloire de Dijon" and perhaps other poems in *Look! We Have Come Through!*

"It Was When" is a densely woven pattern of alliteration and assonance. How do those sound effects cooperate with the poem's cadences and its meanings?

You may want to consult other poems in *Regarding Wave* that continue Snyder's meditation on his marriage and Kai's birth: "The Bed in the Sky," "Kai, Today," and "Not Leaving the House."

"The Egg"

This is another poem in a rather Lawrentian mode. Among its issues: What does the "egg" hold in potential? Can the body it generates—the body of one's own son—be a kind of articulate utterance, a manifestation of organic syntax? And can that utterance express the whole process of cosmic evolution?

The epigraph comes from Robert Duncan's "The Structure of Rime I," *The Opening of the Field* (New York: New Directions, 1960, p. 12). In the sequence begun by that poem, Duncan explores language, the psyche, the organism, and the cosmos in ways that Snyder here recapitulates from his own point of view. In "The Egg" and "snake" is, among other things, the *kundalini* of Tantric yoga, a movement of energy from the body's sexual "root" to the "third eye," an organ of transcendental vision in the forehead. How does the poem ask our attention to mediate between the concrete particulars of Kai's lively body and such evolutionary and cosmic implications?

Comparisons, Contrasts, Connections

Snyder often plays variations on the imagist mode in which Ezra Pound and William Carlos Williams did much of their earlier work. D. H. Lawrence's love poems and animal poems are also important antecedents, as are Kenneth Rexroth's meditations amid Western landscapes and his translations from Japanese poetry.

Central to the poetics of both Williams and Snyder are strategies that enable particulars to evoke a pattern and so provide a link with the universal.

Bibliography

Rothenberg, Jerome. *Technicians of the Sacred*, 2nd ed. Berkeley: Univ. of California Press, 1985.

——. *Shaking the Pumpkin*. New York: Doubleday, 1972.

Etheridge Knight (b. 1931)

Contributing Editor: Patricia Liggins-Hill [p. 2424]

Classroom Issues and Strategies

Students often lack the knowledge of the new black aesthetic, the black oral tradition, and contemporary black poetry, in general. I lecture on major twentieth-century black poets and literary movements. In addition, I provide supplementary research articles, primarily from *BALF* (*Black American Literature Forum*) and *CLA* (*College Language Association*).

Since Knight has read his poems on various college campuses throughout the country, I use tapes of his poetry readings. I also read his poetry aloud and invite students to do likewise, since his punctuation guides the reader easily through the oral poems.

Students, black and white, identify with the intense pain, loneliness, frustration, and deep sense of isolation Knight expresses in his prison poetry. They often compare their own sense of isolation, frustration, and depression as college students with his institutional experience.

Students often ask the following questions:

1. Why haven't they been previously exposed to this significant poet and to the new black aesthetic?
2. How did Knight learn to write poetry so well in prison with only an eighth-grade education?
3. What is the poet doing now? Is he still on drugs?
4. What is the difference between written and transcribed oral poetry?

Major Themes, Historical Perspectives, and Personal Issues

Knight's major themes are (1) liberation and (2) the black heritage. Since slavery has been a crucial reality in black history, much of Knight's poetry focuses on a modern kind of enslavement, imprisonment; his work searches for and discovers ways in which a person can be free while incarcerated. His poems are both personal and communal. As he searches for his own identity and meaning in life, he explores the past black American life experience from both its southern and its African heritage.

Knight's poetry should be taught within the historical context of the civil rights and black revolutionary movements of the 1960s and 1970s. The social backdrop of his and other new black poets' cries against racism were the assassinations of Malcolm X, Martin Luther King, Jr., John and Robert Kennedy, also the burning of ghettos, the bombings of black schools in the South, the violent confrontations between white police and black people, and the strong sense of awareness of poverty in black communities.

What the teacher should emphasize is that—while Knight shares with Baraka, Madhubuti, Major, and the other new black poets the bond of black cultural identity (the bond of the oppressed, the bond formed by black art, etc.)—he, unlike them, has emerged after serving an eight-year prison term for robbery from a second consciousness of community. This community of criminal is what Franz Fanon calls "the lumpenproletariat," "the wretched of the earth." Ironically, Knight's major contribution to the new aesthetic is derived from this second sense of consciousness which favorably reinforces his strong collective mentality and identification as a black artist. He brings his prison consciousness, in which the individual is institutionally destroyed and the self becomes merely one number among many, to the verbal structure of his transcribed oral verse.

Significant Form, Style, or Artistic Conventions

Consider the following questions:

1. What is the new black aesthetic and what are Knight's major contributions to the arts movement?
2. What are the black oral devices in Knight's poetry and what are his major contributions to the black oral tradition?
3. What are the universal elements in Knight's poetry?
4. In the "Idea of Ancestry" and "The Violent Space," how does Knight fuse various elements of "time and space" not only to denote his own imprisonment but also to connote the present social conditions of black people in general?
5. How does Knight develop his black communal art forms in his later poems "Blues for a Mississippi Black Boy" and "Ilu, the Talking Drum"?
6. What are the major influences on Knight's poetry? (Discuss the influences of Walt Whitman, Langston Hughes, and Sterling Brown.)
7. How does Knight's earlier poetry differ from his later poems? (Discuss in terms of the poet's voice, tone, and techniques, e.g., oral devices, imagery.)

Original Audience

Knight addresses black people in particular, and a mixed audience in general. He uses a variety of communal art forms and techniques such as blues idioms, jazz and African pulse structures, as well as clusters of communal images that link the poet and his experience directly to his reader/audience. For the latter, the teacher should use examples of images from "The Idea of Ancestry" and "The Bones of My Father" (if this poem is available).

Comparisons, Contrasts, Connections

Langston Hughes, Sterling Brown, and Walt Whitman are the major influences on Knight's poetry. Knight's "Idea of Ancestry" flows in a Whitmanesque style and his "Blues for a Mississippi Black Boy" stems from the transcribed oral, blues poetic tradition of Hughes and Brown.

He has indicated these influences in "An Interview with Etheridge Knight" by Patricia L. Hill (*San Francisco Review of Books* 3, no. 9 [1978]: 10).

Questions for Reading and Discussion/ Approaches to Writing

1. (a) How does Knight's poetry differ in content, form, and style from that of the earlier oral poets Hughes and Brown? How is his poetry similar to theirs?

   (b) How does Knight's poetry differ in content, form, and style from that of Baraka, Madhubuti, and the other major new black aesthetic poets? How is his poetry similar to theirs?

2. (a) The Western "Art for Art's Sake" Aesthetic Principle vs. the New Black Aesthetic.

   (b) The Importance of Knight's Prison "Lumpenproletariat" Consciousness to the New Black Aesthetic.

   (c) The Major Poetic Influences on Knight's Poetry.

   (d) The Written and Oral Poetry Elements in Knight's Poetry.

   (e) Whitman's vs. Knight's Vision of America.

   (f) Knight's Open and Closed Forms of Poetry.

Bibliography

Nketia, J. H. Kwalena. *The Music of Africa.* New York: W. W. Norton, 1974.

Sylvia Plath (1932–1963)

Contributing Editor: Linda Wagner-Martin [p. 2430]

Classroom Issues and Strategies

Students usually begin with the fact that Plath committed suicide and then read her death as some kind of "warning" to talented, ambitious women writers. (The recent biography by Stevenson only supports this view, unfortunately.) What must be done is to get to the text, in each case, and read for nuance of meaning—humor, anger, poignance, intellectual tour de force. Running parallel with this sense of Plath as some inhuman persona is a fearful acknowledgment that women who have ambition are not quite normal. Plath receives a very gender-based reading. A good corrective is to talk about people who have tendencies toward depression, a situation that encompasses many men as well as women.

Focus on the text and ready information about the possible biographical influence on that text. Often, however, the influences are largely literary—Medea is as close a persona for some of the late poems as Plath herself—Eliot, Stevens, Merwin, Yeats, etc. Criticism is just now starting to mine these rich areas. Some attention to the late 1950s and early 1960s is also helpful: seeing the poetry and *The Bell Jar* as the same kind of breakthrough into the expression of women's anger as Betty Friedan's or Simone de Beauvoir's seems to be useful.

Hearing Plath read from her own late work is always effective: she has an unusual, almost strident voice, and the humor and gutsiness of the 1962 poems comes across well. Caedmon has one recording that has many of the late poems backed with Plath's interview with Peter Orr for the BBC, taped on October 30, 1962 (many of the poems she reads were written just that week, or shortly before). The PBS *Voices and Visions* Plath segment is also fairly accurate and effective.

As mentioned above, the fact of Plath's suicide seems primary in many students' minds. Partly because many of them have read, or know of, *The Bell Jar*, it is hard to erase the image of the tormented woman, ill at ease in her world. But once that issue is cleared, and her writing is seen as a means of keeping her alive, perhaps the study of that writing becomes more important to students: it seems to have a less than esoteric "meaning."

Major Themes, Historical Perspectives, and Personal Issues

Themes include women's place in American culture (even though Plath lived the last three years in England, thinking wrongly that she had more freedom in England to be a writer); what women can attempt; how coerced they were by social norms (i.e., to date, marry, have children, be a helpmeet, support charities); the weight society places on women—to be the only support of children, to earn livings (Plath's life, echoing her mother's very difficult one, with little money and two children for whom she wanted the best of opportunities); the need for superhuman talent, endurance, and resourcefulness in every woman's life.

Significant Form, Style, or Artistic Conventions

Versatility of form (tercet, villanelle, many shapes of organic form, syllabics), use of rhyme (and its variations, near rhyme, slant rhyme, assonance), word choice (mixed vocabularies)—Plath must be studied as an expert, compelling poet, whose influence on the contemporary poetry scene—poems written by men as well as women—has been inestimable. Without prejudicing readers, the teacher must consider what "confessional" poetry is: the use of seemingly "real" experience, experience that often is a supreme fiction rather than personal biography; a means of making art less remote from life by using what might be life experience as its text. Unfortunately, as long as only women poets or poets with abnormal psychiatric histories are considered "confessional," the term is going to be ineffective for a meaningful study of contemporary poetry.

Original Audience

Although most of Plath's best poems were written in the early 1960s, the important point to be made is that today's readers find her work immensely immediate. Her expression of distrust of society, her anger at the positions talented women were asked to take in that society, were healthful (and rare) during the early 1960s, so she became a kind of voice of the times in the same way Hemingway expressed the mood of the 1920s. But while much of Hemingway's work seems dated to today's students (at least his ethical and moral stances toward life), Plath's writing has gained currency.

Comparisons, Contrasts, Connections

The most striking comparison can be made between the early work of Anne Sexton and Plath (Plath learned a lot from Sexton), and to a lesser extent, the poems of Theodore Roethke. W. D. Snodgrass's long poem "Heart's Needle" was an important catalyst for both Sexton and Plath, as was some of Robert Lowell's work, and, to some, John Berryman's (but he was more influenced by Sexton and Plath than the other way around). If earlier Plath poems are used, Wallace Stevens and T. S. Eliot are key. And, in moderation, Ted Hughes's early work can be useful—especially the animal and archaic tones and images.

Bibliography

Susan Van Dyne's essays on the manuscripts are invaluable (see *Centennial Review*, Summer 1988).

See also the *Massachusetts Review* essay, collected in Wagner's *Sylvia Plath: Critical Essays* (Boston: G. K. Hall, 1984).

Wagner's Routledge collection, *Sylvia Plath: The Critical Heritage* (1988) includes a number of helpful reviews.

Linda Bundtzen's *Plath's Incarnations* (Univ. of Mich., 1983) and Steven Axelrod's 1990 study from Johns Hopkins, along with the Wagner-Martin biography of Plath, are useful.

Sonia Sanchez (b. 1934)

Contributing Editors: Joyce Joyce and John Reilly [p. 2440]

Classroom Issues and Strategies

There is a widespread feeling that protest and politics are either inappropriate to literature or, if acceptable at certain times, the time for it has now passed.

The whole course will be founded upon an acceptance of the fact that there are no *a priori* definitions for literature. Poetry is what the poet writes or the audience claims as poetry. The real issues are whether or not the poet sets out a plausible poetics (one neither too solipsistic nor so undiscriminating as to dissolve meaning) and whether or not the practice of the poet has the local excitement and disciplined language to make it asthetically satisfying. Upon these premises, the study of Sonia Sanchez can proceed with attention to her idea of revolutionary poetry associated with nation building, as it was discussed in the 1960s and 1970s.

Operating on the assumption that there is some common tradition underlying work of poets who declare ethnicity (African-American) as their common identity, useful discussion is possible about ways Sanchez differs from Michael Harper and Jay Wright. What differences in aesthetic and practice account for the relative complexity of Harper and Wright when contrasted with Sanchez? But, then, what allows us to consider them all black poets? Surely not merely the selection of subject matter?

Major Themes, Historical Perspectives, and Personal Issues

The historical and political are boldly set out in Sanchez's poetry. The personal may be overlooked by the hasty reader, but the poetry develops a persona with a highly subjective voice conveying the impression of a real human being feeling her way to positions, struggling to make her expressive declarative writing conform to her intuitions and interior self. This tension once observed makes all the themes arranged around the black aesthetic and black politics also accessible.

Significant Form, Style, or Artistic Conventions

The "eye" devices (lowercase letters, speed writing, fluid lines) along with the free form of verse and vernacular word choice are avant-garde devices seen in the work of many other poets. The point here is to see them associated with an aesthetic that privileges the oral and musical. For Sanchez it would be valuable to point to the frequency with which African-American poets allude to jazz performers, even making their lines sound like a musical instrument, just as, historically, musical instruments imitated the sounds of voice in early jazz and blues. This would make the vigor of the poem on the Righteous Brothers understandable, for music is a talisman of African-American culture. It would also set up a useful contrast between poetry written for print and poetry written to simulate the ephemerality of performed music or song.

Original Audience

For Sanchez these questions have great importance, for she has undergone important changes that have brought the spiritual and personal more forward in her verse. Dating her poems in connection with political events is very important. One might, for example, talk about an avowedly nationalist poetry written for struggle to assert values believed to be a source of community solidarity. There are many parallels to suggest, including the writing of Irish authors in English, Jewish-American writers adapting the sounds of Yiddish to an exploration of traditional values in English, etc. Following the nationalist period of her work we see a shift of focus. One must ask students if the elements centered in the newer poems were not already present before. The appropriate answer (yes) will permit assertion of the developing nature of a writer's corpus, something worth presenting in all courses.

Comparisons, Contrasts, Connections

"Just Don't Never Give Up on Love" could be contrasted with confessional verse such as Plath's "Daddy" to distinguish the ways feeling can be distanced. Similarly the feminist voices of Adrienne Rich and Marge Piercy can introduce subtle distinctions when contrasted with the same Sanchez narrative/poem. What, we might ask, is the basis of distinction: formal or attitudinal?

Questions for Reading and Discussion/ Approaches to Writing

1. Recalling the use made of the mask by Paul Laurence Dunbar, consider what differences have occurred to change the meaning of that image in the 88 years until Sanchez published "Masks."
2. A society may be culturally diverse; yet, that does not mean that cultures are similarly powerful or influential. Discuss the way that Sonia Sanchez and other revolutionary black poets ssee the relationship between their culture and that of the dominant white society.

Bibliography

Palmer, Roderick. "The Poetry of Three Revolutionists: Don L. Lee, Sonia Sanchez, and Nikki Giovanni." *CLA Journal*, xv (Sept. 1971): 25–36. Rpt. in *Modern Black Poets*, edited by Donald Gibson. Englewood Cliffs, N.J.: Prentice-Hall, 1973, 135–46.

Amiri Baraka (LeRoy Jones) (b. 1934)

Contributing Editor: Marcellette Williams [p. 2448]

Classroom Issues and Strategies

The typical problems in teaching Baraka's poetry have to do with what has been called his "unevenness"—perhaps more accurately attributable to the tension inherent in balancing Baraka's role as poet and his role as activist—and the strident tone of some of his poems—also related to his political activism.

Both problems are probably best addressed directly by inviting the students to describe or characterize their impressions of the impetus for the poems as they read them (stressing "their reading" is critical and complements what current reading theory regards as the essential role of the reader in any reading paradigm), then asking them to substantiate textually those impressions. Such a strategy finesses the temptation to engage in a definitive debate of the politics of the time as the genesis and raison d'etre of Baraka's poetry. Further, such a strategy allows students to explore the aesthetics as well as the politics of his poetry and understand better the inter/inner-(con)textuality of the two.

Because the "sound" of Baraka's poetry is essential to texturing or fleshing out its meaning, readings aloud should contribute to discussions as well as to the introduction to his work.

Students respond almost always to the intimacy of Baraka's poems; sometimes they are offended by that intimacy, and this posture often leads to discussions of poetic necessity. Students also raise the question of the paradox of Baraka's clear aesthetic debts and his vehemence in trying to tear down that very Western ideal.

Major Themes, Historical Perspectives, and Personal Issues

It is important to emphasize the themes of death and despair in the early poems, moral and social corruption with its concomitant decrying of Western values and ethics, the struggle against self-hatred, a growing ethnic awareness, and the beneficent view of and creative energy occasioned by "black magic."

The issues to focus on historically involve the racial tenor of the decades represented by his poetic output as well as the poetic aesthetics of imagism, projectivism, and Dadaism—all of which influenced Baraka to some extent.

From the perspective of personal issues, his bohemian acquaintances of the fifties (Olson and Ginsberg, for example), his marriage to Hettie Cohen, his visit to Cuba, his name change, the death of Malcolm X, and his Obie for *The Dutchman* are all important considerations.

Significant Form, Style, or Artistic Conventions

It is appropriate to refer to the question of "school," here again in the context of the poet's use of sound and images as the articulation of form and meaning. I would further encourage the students to pay careful attention to Baraka's use of repetition—at the lexical, syntactic, semantic, and phonological levels. What is its effect? Does it inform? If so, how? Are there aspects of the poems one might regard as transformations? If so, what might they be? What effect might they have? How might they function in the poem?

Baraka's consideration of the significance of "roots" appears to evolve in his poetry. How might you characterize it?

Original Audience

A consideration of progenitors and progeny provides a convenient point of departure for a discussion of audience for Baraka's work. Students interested in imagism and projectivism, for example, will certainly value Baraka's efforts as an effective use of those aesthetic doctrines toward the shaping of poetry of revolution appropriate for the time.

Baraka's influence is apparent in the poetry of Sonia Sanchez and Ntozake Shange. What aspects of this influence, if any, might contribute to considerations of audience with regard to time and poetry?

Comparisons, Contrasts, Connections

In considering Baraka's conscious use of language for poetic effect, comparisons with William Carlos Williams (for the use of the vernacular and the idiom) and with Ezra Pound (for its communicative focus) are appropriate. Sometimes in discussions of Baraka's early poems, the criticism compares them in tone and theme—moral decay and social disillusionment—with Eliot's *Waste Land*.

Questions for Reading and Discussion/ Approaches to Writing

1. Frank Smith discusses the "behind the eyeball" information a reader brings to text. Louise Rosenblatt discusses the expectations and experiences a reader brings to "transact" or negotiate meaning with text. Given these considerations of the reader, prediscussion questions might be designed to elicit from the reader whatever information or preconceptions he/she has about the author and/or his work. If the students are totally unfamiliar with Baraka, then questions eliciting experiential responses to the broad issues of theme or technique would be appropriate—"What, if anything, do the terms social fragmentation and/or moral decay mean to you?" "What would you imagine as a poetic attack on society? Or a poetic ethnic response to a dead or dying society?"

2. Writing assignments and topics for the students are derived from the assumption that as readers their participation is essential to meaning. Topics are not generally prescribed but, rather, derived from the questions about and interest in the author and his (Baraka's) work. These assignments sometimes take the form of poetic responses, critical essays, or "dialogues" with Baraka.

Bibliography

Brown, Lloyd W. "Baraka as Poet," Chapter 5, in Lloyd W. Brown's *Amiri Baraka*, Boston: Twayne Publishers, 1980, 104–35.

Harris, William J. "The Transformed Poem." In *The Poetry and Poetics of Amiri Baraka: The Jazz Aesthetic*. Columbia: Univ. of Missouri Press, 1985, 91–121.

Lacey, Henry. "Die Schwartze Bohemien: 'The Terrible Disorder of a Young Man'" and "Imamu," both found in Henry Lacey's *To Raise, Destroy, and Create*. Troy, New York: The Whitstone Publishing Company, 1981, 1–42, 93–162.

Soller, Werner. "Who Substitutes for the Dead Lecturer?: Poetry of the Early 1960s." In Werner Soller's *Amiri Baraka/LeRoi Jones: The Quest for a Populist Modernism*, New York: Columbia Univ. Press, 1978, 83–95.

Audre Lorde (b. 1934)

Contributing Editor: Claudia Tate [p. 2455]

Classroom Issues and Strategies

The primary problem in working with this writer is the difficulty in securing the entire corpus of her published work. Most libraries have only those works published after 1982. Many of those published prior to this date are out of print.

To address this issue, I have made special orders for texts that are still in print and asked the library to place them on reserve. In other cases, I have selected specific works from these early texts and photocopied them for class use.

Students need to be taught to empathize with the racial, sexual, and class characteristics of the persona inscribed in Lorde's work. Such empathy will enable them to understand the basis of Lorde's value formation.

Students immediately respond to Lorde's courage to confront a problem, no matter what its difficulty, and to her deliberate inscription of the anguish that problem has caused her. Both the confrontation and the acknowledged pain serve as her vehicle for resolving the problem.

Major Themes, Historical Perspectives, and Personal Issues

Lorde's work focuses on lyricizing large historical and social issues in the voice of a black woman. This vantage point provides stringent social commentary on white male, middle-class, heterosexual privilege inherent in the dominant culture, on the one hand, and on the disadvantage accorded to those who diverge from this so-called standard. In addition, students should be aware that there have historically been racial and class biases between white and black feminists concerning issues that centralize racial equality, like enfranchisement, work, and sexuality.

Significant Form, Style, or Artistic Conventions

Students studying Lorde's poetry should familiarize themselves with the aesthetic and rhetorical demands of the lyrical mode. In addition, they should be prepared for the high degree of intimacy inscribed in Lorde's work.

Comparisons, Contrasts, Connections

Comparisons can be drawn with Adrienne Rich, June Jordan, and Ntozake Shange in order to stress the intimacy of the woman-centered problematic that informs and structures Lorde's work.

Bibliography

Selections from *Some of Us Are Brave*, eds. Barbara Smith et al, *Sturdy Black Bridges*, eds. Gloria Hull et al, and *Color, Sex, and Poetry*, Gloria Hull.

Jay Wright (b. 1935)

Contributing Editor: Phillip M. Richards [p. 2461]

Classroom Issues and Strategies

The greatest difficulty of Wright's poems is their obscurity. In reading his later poems, in particular, students have trouble discovering dramatic situation, persona, and tone. Some familiarity with Wright's own statements about his poetic undertaking is desirable.

Often the central dramatic action of the poem is the contemplation of past events or the attempt to recover a community's experience. One might ask students, what is the purpose of these historical quests? Jay Wright's poems often dramatize a persona's attempt to discover his continuity with past ancestors and events. The poetry attempts to recapture historical experience as a means of establishing the poetic persona's personal identity.

Major Themes, Historical Perspectives, and Personal Issues

The crucial themes in Wright are the poet's quest to establish himself as a member and artist-spokesman for his tribe (African-Americans, Africans, and Hispanics). The poet seeks to establish this sense of kinship by dramatizing the historical and psychological continuities that link him with his ancestors. Wright's books, then, are quests for identity by means of historical understanding.

Significant Form, Style, or Artistic Conventions

Wright's poetry is closely allied to the Black Mountain school as it is examined by the work of Charles Olson.

Original Audience

The bulk of Wright's published poetry was written during the 1960s and 1970s during a period of interest in the African roots of the African-American experience. Some of the work of *The Homecoming Singer* (Wright's first book) shows the influence of the beat movement. Significantly, he alludes to early poems by Amiri Baraka, which were influenced by the same beat ethos.

Comparisons, Contrasts, Connections

Wright's attempts to link himself with an African past reflect a central theme in twentieth-century black poetry. Wright's efforts in this connection recall poems on Africa by Langston Hughes and Countee Cullen. One might compare the primitivism of Hughes's and Cullen's early poetry with Wright's attempts to give cultural specificity to African ritual. Wright's historical themes also link him to the historical poetry of Robert Hayden as well as to that of Michael Harper.

T. S. Eliot is a hidden influence in much of Wright's work. The early poems in *The Homecoming Singer* feature a youthful, male, self-mocking persona much like that of "Portrait of a Lady" or "The Love Song of J. Alfred Prufrock." Wright's ritualistic poems that meditate upon history and its meaning owe something to *Four Quartets*.

Bibliography

The best introductions to Wright appear in *Callaloo* 6 (Fall 1983), which includes good essays by Stepto and Barrax, and a highly theoretical essay by Kutzinski.

Jay Wright's own statement on his poetic craft, "Desire's Design, Vision's Resonance" in *Callaloo* 10 (Winter 1987): 13–28, is also extremely useful.

Vera Kutzinski's chapter on Wright in her book, *Against the American Grain: Myth and History in William Carlos Williams, Jay Wright, and Nicolas Guillen*, is the most comprehensive critical statement on Wright's poetry.

Marge Piercy (b. 1936)

Contributing Editor: Estella Lauter [p. 2468]

Classroom Issues and Strategies

I have taught Piercy's poems in a Women in Literature course offered for credit in general education and in a course on American Women Poets. Most students find her very direct and accessible, but some are unnerved by her openness in expressing her feelings and describing her experience while others are daunted by her high expectations of herself and other human beings. Students generally profit from small group discussions where they can share related experiences and discuss the pressures Piercy's poems exert on them.

If I had enough time to use one of her novels in relationship to the poems, it would be wonderful to contrast their highly researched, intricate plots with the structures of the poems. Her own voice in the poems is direct; it's fascinating to see how she suspends it in the novels for various narrative purposes.

Major Themes, Historical Perspectives, and Personal Issues

Piercy's poems raise important issues related to feminism, ecology, imperialism, civil rights, religious heritage, love, and effective relationships. Often one issue leads to another. Like Thoreau, she works at living ethically and peacefully in an environment ravaged by greed, anxiety, and fear.

Significant Form, Style, or Artistic Conventions

In own brief introduction to *Circles on the Water* (1985), Piercy writes that she intends "to be of use" for readers rather than for other poets, to "give utterance to energy, experience, insight, words flowing from many lives." Although the voice is always hers, the experiences sometimes belong to others. Line length and rhythm follow from the material. She writes political and/or didactic poetry as necessary, out of a belief that poets belong to a social context and speak for constituencies; but the primary purpose of poetry from her point of view is to align the psyche, to heal the alienation of thought and feeling, and to "weld mind back into body seamlessly." Whitman is one of her models. Although she does not name Levertov as an influence, she must have profited from Levertov's articulation in the sixties of an organic theory of poetry.

Original Audience

I talk about Piercy's ability to speak for women, to open up subjects that haven't been understood. I've heard her read three times to audiences with varying degrees of sophistication, and I've spoken with her at length about her political concerns. So I share these experiences with the students. (Others could speak from her forthright essays in *Parti-colored Blocks* or from her essay in *Contemporary Authors*.) I always tell the story of her first reading of the poems about her mother that appear in *My Mother's Body*. It was at a National Women's Studies Conference, and she told the audience that she had brought the poems not knowing whether or not she would be able to share them. Their warm response allowed her to do so. She talked about the pain of writing poems that address issues too difficult for others to hear. This always turns out to be an encouraging story for students who write without an audience.

Comparisons, Contrasts, Connections

Piercy shares many concerns with Denise Levertov, Adrienne Rich, and Audre Lorde. All four are political poets who share a deep concern for women and who value the capacity to care, but they have very different styles, voices, attitudes, feelings, blind spots, and so on. Levertov refuses to identify herself as a feminist, for example, as the others do. Rich never speaks about her relationship with her mother and rarely deals with her biological sister, whereas Lorde is relatively open about both, Piercy has a long sequence on her mother, and Levertov has a sequence on her sister. Levertov, Rich, and Piercy handle their Jewish heritage differently; Piercy's celebration of her feminist and Jewish sources is more like Lorde's response to her African heritage. And so on. This kind of comparison helps students to understand and respect differences among women.

Questions for Reading and Discussion/ Approaches to Writing

1. I prefer to give students several poems on the same general subject and ask them to work out the differences and similarities in point of view in discussion. This seems to give more room for them to experience the poems.
2. In Piercy's case, several topics keyed to her poem cycles work exceptionally well: the value of marriage ("The Chuppah"); mother-daughter relationships ("What Remains"); the lunar calendar ("The Lunar Cycle"); the tarot cards ("Laying Down the Tower"); the power of religion ("The Ram's Horn").

Bibliography

The most useful materials to date are Piercy's own essays in *Parti-colored Blocks* and *Contemporary Authors,* but a few articles have appeared and a bibliography of her writings has been compiled by Elaine Tuttle Hansen and William J. Scheick in Catherine Rainwater and W. J. Scheick, eds.,

Contemporary American Women Writes: Narratives Strategies (Lexington: Univ. Press of Kentucky, 1985).

See also:

Contoski, Victor. "Marge Piercy: A Vision of the Peaceable Kingdom." *Modern Poetry Studies* 8 (1977): 205–16.

Wynne, Edith J. "Imagery of Association in the Poetry of Marge Piercy." *Publications of the Missouri Philological Association* 10 (1985): 57–63.

Ishmael Reed (b. 1938)

Contributing Editor: Michael Boccia [p. 2475]

Classroom Issues and Strategies

Ishmael Reed frequently offends readers, who feel that they and the institutions they hold sacred (the church, American history, schools, etc.) are attacked and ridiculed by him. His humorous exaggerations and sharp barbs are misunderstood partly because satire and irony are so often misunderstood. In addition, most students are ignorant of the many contributions to American culture made by blacks and other minorities. Black and minority contributions in every field are highlighted in Reed's work. Reed often lists his historical, mythical, or literary sources in the text itself and has his own version of history, politics, literature, and culture.

Pointing out that Reed is a jokester and a humorous writer often makes his work more palatable to students. Once they begin to laugh at Reed's humor, they can take a more objective look at his condemnations of society. Of course, students refuse to accept his version of history, politics, and religion. Most commonly, students want to know if Reed's version of the "truth" is really true. They challenge his veracity whenever he challenges their beliefs. This permits me to send them off to check on Reed's statements, which proves rewarding and enlightening for them.

Of course, Reed does not want readers to accept to single viewpoint; he wishes our view of reality to be multi-faceted. In Reed's Neo-HooDoo Church many "truths" are accepted. In fact, one source that is extremely helpful in understanding Reed's viewpoint is the "Neo-HooDoo Manifesto" (*Los Angeles Free Press* [18–24 Sept. 1969]: 42.

Major Themes, Historical Perspectives, and Personal Issues

Reed covers the gamut of issues, writing about politics, social issues, racism, history, and just about everything else. Most of his satire is aimed at the status quo, and thus he often offends readers. It is important to remind students that he is writing satire, but that there is truth to his comic attacks on the establishment. Closely related to his allusions to black artists and history are his themes. He views the counterculture as the vital force in life and hopefully predicts that the joyous side of life will triumph over the repressive side.

His radical beliefs appear as themes in his work. Knowledge of the cultures (popular, American, African, etc.) Reed draws upon is very helpful. Knowing about black history and literature is very valuable and can best be seen through Reed's eyes by reading his own commentary. *Shrovetide in Old New Orleans* is especially helpful in this area.

Reed's vision of history cries out for the recognition of minority contribution to Western civilization. Estaban (the black slave who fed the Pilgrims), Sacajawea (the Native American woman who helped Lewis and Clark) and many other minority contributors are referred to in Reed's work, and because students are often ignorant of these contributions, some small survey of black history is very useful.

Significant Form, Style, or Artistic Conventions

Reed's originality is rooted in his experimental forms, so introducing the traditional art forms that Reed distorts often helps readers understand his experiments. A survey of the forms of novels, journalism, television and radio programs, movies, newsreels, popular dances, and music will help students understand the fractured forms Reed offers.

The symbols Reed selects also reflect the eclectic nature of his art, in that the symbols and their meanings include but transcend traditional significance. Reed will blend symbols from ancient Egypt with rock and roll, or offer the flip side of history by revealing what went on behind the veil of history as popularly reported. In all cases one will find much stimulation in the juxtaposition of Reed's symbols and contexts.

Original Audience

The students are often angry at the satire of their culture. The provocation that they feel is precisely the point of Reed's slashing wit. He wants to provoke them into thinking about their culture in new ways. Pointing this out to students often alleviates their anger.

Comparisons, Contrasts, Connections

Introducing students to Swift's "A Modest Proposal" is an effective way to clarify how Reed's satire functions. Few readers think that eating babies is a serious proposal by Swift, and once satire is perceived as an exaggeration meant to stir controversy and thought, students are willing to listen to Reed's propositions.

Placing Reed in literary context is difficult because he writes in numerous genres and borrows from many nonliterary art forms. No doubt his innovations place him with writers like Joyce and Blake, and his satire places him among the most controversial writers of any literary period.

Certainly his use of allusion and motif is reminiscent of T. S. Eliot or James Joyce, but Reed likes to cite black writers as his models. Reed feels that the minorities have been slighted and a review of some of the black writers he cites as inspiration is often helpful to students.

Questions for Reading and Discussion/ Approaches to Writing

Students respond well to hunting down the literary, historical, and topical references in the poetry. I often ask them to select a single motif, such as Egyptian myth, and track it through a poem after researching the area.

Bibliography

I strongly recommend reading Reed on Reed: *Shrovetide in Old New Orleans*, especially "The Old Music," "Self Interview," "Remembering Josephine Baker," and "Harlem Renaissance."

For a detailed discussion of his literary and critical stances see John O'Brien, "Ishmael Reed Interview," *The New Fiction, Interviews with Innovative American Writers*, David Bellamy, ed. (Urbana: University of Illinois Press, 1974): 130–41.

For a view of the Dionysian/Appollonian struggle as portrayed by Reed, see Sam Keen, "Manifesto for a Dionysian Theology," *Transcendence*, Herbert W. Richardson, ed. (Boston: Beacon Press, 1969): 31–52.

For a general overview, see Henry Gates, "Ishmael Reed," *The Dictionary of Literary Biography* 33.

Half of *The Review of Contemporary Fiction* 4.2 (1984) is devoted to Reed.

Michael S. Harper (b. 1938)

Contributing Editor: Herman Beavers [p. 2483]

Classroom Issues and Strategies

Harper's poems often prove difficult because he is so deft at merging personal and national history within the space of one metaphor. One must be aware, then, of Harper's propensity toward veiled references to historical events. One can think here of a series of poems like "History as Apple Tree." The result, in a series like this, is that the reader cannot follow the large number of historical references Harper makes—in this case, to the history of Rhode Island and its founder, Roger Williams. The poems can be seen as obscure or enigmatic, when, in fact, they are designed to highlight a mode of African-American performance. In the same manner that one finds jazz musicians "quoting" another song within the space of a solo, Harper's use of history is often designed to suggest the simultaneity of events, the fact that one cannot escape the presence of the past.

Harper's interviews are often helpful, particularly those interviews where he discusses his poetic technique. Harper is a storyteller, a performer. He is adept at the conveyance of nuance in the poems. A valuable strategy is teaching Harper's poems in conjunction with a brief introduction to modern jazz. Team teaching with a jazz historian or an ethnomusicologist while focusing on Harper's strategies of composition is a way to ground the student in Harper's use of jazz as a structuring technique in his poems. Moreover, it allows for dialogue between literary and musical worlds. Since Harper's poems are often about both music and the context out of which the music springs, such a dialogue is important for students to see. As far as history is concerned, pointing the student toward, for example, a history of the Civil War or a biography of John Brown will often illuminate Harper's propensity to "name drop" in his poems. What becomes clear is that Harper is not being dense, but rather he sees his poetic project as one of "putting the reader to work."

You might introduce Harper by showing the film *Birth of a Nation* in order to flesh out Harper's revisionary stance toward myth. Using the film as a kind of counter-milieu, one can point out that Harper's poetry is designed to create a renewed, more vital American mythos. Also, a class where the students can hear John Coltrane's *A Love Supreme* album will prove invaluable to understanding Harper's jazz poems.

Students often protest the inaccessibility of the poems: e.g., "I don't understand this poem at all!" There are often questions regarding Harper's use of the word "modality." Also they do not understand Harper's use of repetition, which is designed to evoke the chant, or the poem as song.

Major Themes, Historical Perspectives, and Personal Issues

Harper is very concerned in his poems with the "American tradition of forgetfulness." In his poetry, one finds him creating situations where the contradictions between oral and written versions of history are brought into focus. Because Harper thinks of poetry as a discourse of song, the poems utilize improvisation to convey their themes. The intent of this is to highlight the complexity of American identity.

Harper's personal issues are, further, not necessarily distinguishable from the historical in this poems. If one were to point to a set of events that spur Harper's poetic voice, it would be the deaths of two of his children shortly after birth. Harper's poems on the subject express not only the personal grief of his wife and himself, but also the loss of cultural possibility the children represent. As a black man in a country so hostile to those who are black, Harper's grief is conflated into rage at the waste of human potential, a result of American forms of amnesia.

In short, the historical and the personal often function in layered fashion. Thus, Harper may use his personal grief as the springboard for illuminating a history of atrocities; the source of grief is different, but the grief is no less real.

Significant Form, Style, or Artistic Conventions

While Harper does not write in "forms" (at least of the classical sort), his work is informed by jazz composition and also several examples of African-American modernism. Clearly, Sterling Brown, Ralph Ellison, and Robert Hayden have each had an impact on Harper's poetry, not only formally, but also in terms of the questions Harper takes up in his poems. I would also cite W. H. Auden and W. B. Yeats as influences.

Formally and stylistically, Harper's poetry derives from jazz improvisation. For example, in one of his poems on the jazz saxophonist John Coltrane, Harper works out a poem that doubles as a prayer-chant in Coltrane's memory. What this suggests is that Harper does not favor symmetricality for the mere sake of symmetricality; thus, he eschews forms like the sonnet or the villanelle. One does find Harper, however, using prosody to usher the reader into a rhythmic mode that captures the nature of poetry as song as opposed to written discourse.

Original Audience

Harper's poems have indeed been widely read. However, his work has undergone a shift in audience. When he came on the scene in the late sixties, the black arts movement produced a large amount of poetry, largely because of poetry's supposed immediacy of impact. For that reason, I believe Harper's work was read by a number of people who expected militancy, anger, and a very narrow subject matter. However, one can see that his work has a different stylistic quality than that of many of his contemporaries who claimed to be writing for a narrower audience. Harper's poetry is more oriented toward inclusiveness, thus his poems utilize American history as a poetic site rather than just relying on a reified notion of racial identity that is crystallized into myth. Thus, after the sixties, Harper's audience became more clearly located in the poetry establishment. Though he still writes about musicians and artists, his readership is more specialized, more focused on poetry than twenty years ago.

Comparisons, Contrasts, Connections

Compare Harper with Brown, Ellison, Auden, and Yeats, as well as James Wright, Philip Levine, and Seamus Heaney. Hayden, Wright, and Yeats can, in their respective fashions, be considered remembrancers. That is, their work (to paraphrase Yeats) suggest that "memories are old identities." Hence, they often explore the vagaries of the past. A fruitful comparison might, for example, be made between Harper's and Hayden's poems on Vietnam. Brown and Harper are both interested in acts of heroism in African-American culture and lore. Ellison and Harper share an inclusive vision of America that eschews racial separatism in favor of a more dualistic sense of American identity.

Questions for Reading and Discussion/ Approaches to Writing

The letter-essay is extremely effective. Here the student writes a letter to Harper, a figure who appears in one of his poems, the instructor in the class, a classmate, etc., and engages the poems through their own personal response to the poems. The exercise allows students to feel more comfortable posing questions as part of their inquiry and also provides an opportunity to reflect on the poem's impact on their lives both experientially and exegetically.

Bibliography

See the interview with Harper in John O'Brien's *Interviews with Black Writers*. Also see his interview in *Ploughshares*, Fall 1981.

Read Robert B. Stepto's essay on Harper's work in the anthology *Chant of Saints* (Urbana: Univ. of Illinois Press, 1979) and his essay on Harper's poems in *The Hollins Critic* (1976).

Michael G. Cooke has a chapter on Harper in his book *Afro-American Literature in the Twentieth Century* (New Haven: Yale Univ. Press, 1985).

Bernice Zamora (b. 1938)

Contributing Editor: Juanita Luna Lawhn [p. 2491]

Classroom Issues and Strategies

One of the major problems that I have encountered teaching this author is the problem of dealing with a second language. In several of her poems, Zamora utilizes both Spanish and English within the same text.

Another problem that I have encountered is the religious symbolism that Zamora alludes to in her work. For example, if a student reading the poem "Penitents" is not familiar with the religious beliefs practiced by the Penitents, then the message that Zamora is attempting to present is not received as clearly and effectively as it is when the student has been familiarized with the religious background of the Penitents.

Another problem that I have encountered teaching Zamora is the problem caused by the use of intertextuality. While all her pieces stand on their own, unless the student is made aware of the author's intertextual references, the poems are limited to the images that are created within the work. Knowledge of the works that are intertextually woven in her poetry permits the reader to transcend space and time limitations.

To make Zamora more accessible, translate Spanish phrases, refer students to outside reading that explains the religious beliefs of the Penitents, and encourage students to read poets—such as Robinson Jeffers, Gullivec, Shakespeare, and Hesse—whose works serve as the intertextual basis for some of Zamora's poetry.

I recommend that Zamora's work be viewed from a feminist perspective, giving special attention to the serpent motif that is present throughout her work and relating the serpent motif to the symbolism associated with goddesses.

I would also recommend that her work be studied from a third world perspective. From this perspective, the student can take into consideration race, class, and gender.

Major Themes, Historical Perspectives, and Personal Issues

The major themes that the writer develops are freedom, justice, love, hate, violence, death, assimilation, and isolation. Some of the issues that the writer develops are the entrapment of women in a man's world, socially and politically; the violence that permeates communities that are deprived economically and educationally; the violence that women as well as men suffer because of the double standards in social values and mores.

Significant Form, Style, or Artistic Conventions

I recommend Bruce-Novoa's article, "Bernice Zamora y Lorna Dee Cervantes: Una estetica feministra."

Original Audience

When I speak of Zamora's work, I give a brief background of the Chicano literary movement. I indicate that Zamora's work was published and distributed by a Chicano publishing company and its audience was an ethnic audience, especially one that was well versed in American literature. I also indicate that she was one of the first major Chicana poets who published her work in book form. While her work is not limited to a feminist audience, it does lend itself to be read by one who is a feminist in the U.S. as well as by third world women. Because of the present trends to include minority writers in American literature anthologies, her audience has been expanded to reach a cross section of U.S. society.

Comparisons, Contrasts, Connections

Since Bernice Zamora is presented as one of the representatives of the Chicana poet, it would be wise to recommend readings by other Chicana poets. The following is a representative list of works by Chicana poets:

Cervantes, Lorna Dee. *Emplumada*. Pittsburgh: Univ. of Pittsburgh Press, 1981.

Cisneros, Sandra. *My Wicked Wicked Ways*. Bloomington, Indiana: Third Woman Press, 1987.

Corpi, Lucha. *Palabras de Mediodia/Noon Words*. Trans. Catherine Rodriguez-Nieto. Berkeley: El Fuego de Aztlan Publications, 1980.

Moraga, Cherrie. *Loving in the War Years: Lo que nunca paso por los labios*. Boston: Southend Press Collective, 1983.

Villanueva, Alma. *Bloodroot*. Austin, Texas: Place of Herons Press, 1977.

I recommend that her work be compared and contrasted with the work of Adrienne Rich, Marge Piercy, and Judith Ortiz Cofer.

Questions for Reading and Discussion/ Approaches to Writing

1. (a) Define *Aztlan*.
   (b) Define *Nahault*.
   (c) Define *community*.
   (d) Define *ritual*.
   (e) What is the universal symbolism of the serpent?
2. (a) Discuss several feminist issues that Zamora confronts with her poetry (the entrapment of women in a man's world, the issue of double standards in society, the exclusion of women from sacred rituals in a community, the exclusion of women in arts, and the function of women in society as objects to be utilized by men to serve their own needs).
   (b) Trace the serpent leitmotif in Zamora's work.
   (c) According to Zamora's poetry, what is the artist's role in society?
   (d) Trace the androgynous images in Zamora's poetry.

Bibliography

Eger, Ernestina N. *A Bibliography of Criticism of Contemporary Chicano Literature*. Berkeley: Univ. of California Chicano Studies Library Publication, 1982.

Lawhn, Juanita. "Victorian Attitudes Affecting the Mexican Woman Writing in *La Prensa* during the Early 1900s and the Chicana of the 1980s." In *Missions in Conflict*, edited by Renate Von Bardeleben, Dietrich Briesemeister, and Juan Bruce-Novoa. Tübingen, W. Germany, Gunter Narr Verlag, 1986.

Penitentes of New Mexico, edited by Carlos E. Cortez. New York: Arno Press, 1974.

Simon Ortiz (Acoma Pueblo) (b. 1941)

Contributing Editor: Andrew O. Wiget [p. 2495]

Classroom Issues and Strategies

The principal problem with Ortiz's poetry from a student perspective is that it is so intensely political and that it takes a political view of past events. Students can be reactionary and feel that what is past is past, and that there has been too much of a tendency to cast aspersions upon America's reputation in recent years. This jingoism is often accompanied by a belief that poetry should not be political, but rather should concern itself with eternal truths. These are not problems that are associated with Ortiz's poetry exclusively, of course, but are part of the naive vision of poetry that teachers of literature struggle to overcome.

I think it's very important to begin this poem with a reflection upon the historical experiences of Native Americans. Begin with the historical epigraph describing the Sand Creek Massacre of Black Kettle's band which gives this poem sequence its name. That particular massacre is very well documented and students should spend some time trying to understand the forces that came together to create that massacre: Colonial Chivington's own political ambitions; his ability to mobilize the fears and anxieties of the frontier Colorado communities; his success at taking advantage of the militarization of the frontier during the Civil War; the remoteness of Chivington's forces from federal supervision; and the nonresistance of the Indians.

A second important issue to be discussed is how we all use key events in the past to give us a sense of what our history is, emphasizing that the historical memory of people is selective and formed for very contemporary reasons.

I think that there are certain key lines in the poetry that are worth looking at in some detail. In addition, I ask students to look at the relationships between the epigraphs and the poems, how each speaks to the other. Finally, I ask students how these poems as a group, framed as they are by the boldfaced short poems about America, and prefaced by the historical statement concerning the Sand Creek Massacre, all work together to create a unified statement.

The poems move between some very concrete historical references (on the one hand) such as those to Cotton Mather, Kit Carson, and Saigon, and (on the other hand) to some highly surrealistic imagery and abstract language. Students frequently have difficulty bringing the two together, and it's helpful to explore some of Ortiz's more provocative statements as a way of creating the matrix of values from which the poetry emerges.

Major Themes, Historical Perspectives, and Personal Issues

The major theme of Ortiz's poem sequence is that Euro-Americans were as much victims of their own ambitions and blindness as were Native Americans, and that the recognition by Euro-Americans that they have victimized themselves is the first step toward the beginning of a healing of America that will be based on a common appreciation of our shared responsibility for her future.

Significant Form, Style, or Artistic Conventions

Certainly the principal formal question will be the juxtaposition of the epigraphs, with their blunt ideological focus, and the poems, with their convoluted syntax and high rhetoric. It would be important to remind students, I think, that Ortiz's cycle of poems about the American historical experience is only one example in a long history of poetry about the American historical experience that stretches back through Hart Crane's *The Bridge* and Whitman's *Leaves of Grass* to early national poems such as Trumbull's *The Columbiad*.

Original Audience

I don't think the original audience for this poetry is significantly different from the student audience, except perhaps in their political orientation (the students may be more conservative). These poems were written at the end of the seventies and represent in some sense a considered reflection upon the traumatization of the American psyche by the domestic turmoil of the 1960s, the loss of confidence evoked by Watergate, and crisis of conscience provoked by the Vietnam War. Most of the students who will be reading these poems for the first time remember none of those events.

Comparisons, Contrasts, Connections

Certainly I think Whitman, whom Ortiz does admire greatly, can be invoked. Ortiz tries to cultivate a prophetic voice and a historical vision similar to Whitman's. I think he may also be effectively contrasted with many writers for whom a historical criticism of America's past terminates in an attitude of despair. Ortiz has transformed anger into hope through compassion.

Questions for Reading and Discussion/ Approaches to Writing

I would look at the first poem and ask students what is meant by the juxtaposition of the lines "No waste lands,/No forgiveness," Or to look at the third poem, which may be an even more provocative example, and ask them why Ortiz believes he should have stolen the sweater from the Salvation Army store, and why, in the end, he didn't.

Bibliography

Ortiz, Simon. "The Story Never Ends: An Interview with Simon Ortiz." In Joseph Bruchoc, *Survival This Way: Interviews with American Indian Poets.* Tucson: Univ. of Arizona, 1987, 211–30.

———. "Sending a Voice: The Emergence of Contemporary Native American Poetry." *College English* 46 (1984): 598–609.

Wiget, Andrew. "Contemporary Poetry." *Native American Literature.* Boston: Twayne, 1985.

———. *Simon Ortiz.* Boise State Univ. Western Writers Series, Number 74. Boise: Boise State Univ., 1986.

Janice Mirikitani (b. 1942)

Contributing Editor: Shirley Lim [p. 2501]

Classroom Issues and Strategies

Students need to learn about the internment of Japanese-American citizens during World War II. You might consider reading historical extracts of laws passed against Japanese-Americans during internment or passages from books describing camp life. If possible, show students paintings and photographs of internment experience. Students tend to resist issues of racism in mainstream white American culture; counter this tendency by discussing the long history of persecution of Asians on the West Coast.

Deal with the strong aural/oral quality of Mirikitani's writing—the strong protest voice.

Student often raise questions about the poet's anger: How personally does the reader take this? How successfully has the poet expressed her anger and transformed it into memorable poetry? What kinds of historical materials does the poet mine? Why are these materials useful and significant?

Major Themes, Historical Perspectives, and Personal Issues

Themes are the historical documentation of legislation against Asians in the U.S.; internment during World War II; Mirikitani's own experience in Lake Tule during World War II; economic and psychological sufferings of Japanese-Americans during that period; position of Asian-American women historically and politically.

Significant Form, Style, or Artistic Conventions

Consider the issue of protest and oral poetry; traditions of such poetry in black literature in the 1960s and 1970s; influence of "black is beautiful" movement on Mirikitani.

Original Audience

Consider the didactic and socio-political nature of the writing: a divided audience; her own people and an audience to be persuaded and accused of past prejudices. Much of her poetry was written in the 1970s at the peak of social protests against white hegemony.

Comparisons, Contrasts, Connections

Compare her poems with Sonia Sanchez and Don L. Lee, for example, on socio-political and minority concerns.

Questions for Reading and Discussion/ Approaches to Writing

1. Personal accounts or observations of racism at work in their own society.
2. How they themselves perceive Asian-Americans; their stereotypes of Asian-American women.

Bibliography

Refer to Mini Okubo's books on camp life, the movie of the Houstons' book on Manzanar, and newspaper accounts of the recent debate and settlement of repayments to Japanese-Americans for injustice done to them by the U.S. Governmentt during their internment period.

Pedro Pietri (b. 1944)

Contributing Editor: Frances R. Aparicio [p. 2509]

Classroom Issues and Strategies

As with other Nuyorican poets, the language switching and references to either Spanish or Puerto Rican culture need to be explained. Preparing a handout with a glossary and giving a small introduction to life in El Barrio (perhaps with photos, pictures, or videos) might also be helpful.

Pedro Pietri has produced two records, "Loose Joints" and "One is a Crowd" (Folkway Records). If available, they would be good for classroom use.

Some students might have a difficult time understanding the anger and the bitterness of Pietri's voice against "the system," an issue for disagreement and discussion.

Major Themes, Historical Perspectives, and Personal Issues

Pietri's poetry is political poetry in its most direct sense: a poetry of denunciation, directed to create a cultural consciousness among the members of the Puerto Rican community. Other themes are the demythification of authority figures and social institutions (government, schools, church, "the system"); alienation in contemporary urban life; a surrealistic search for the truth in the irrational and the absurd.

Significant Form, Style, or Artistic Conventions

"Puerto Rican Obituary" can be read as a parody of an epic poem (the dream and the search and the epic deeds of a nation inverted), and within an antiaesthetic attitude. Again, as in Laviera, this is oral poetry to be recited and *screamed*. In *Traffic Violations*, Pietri's poetry falls within the surrealistic mode, fragmented images, search for the absurd in everyday life, irrational, surprising metaphors and imagery, humor, and sarcasm.

Original Audience

Though quite contemporary, Pietri's poetry has to be understood in terms of its original objective of addressing the masses as oral poetry. This is important in order to achieve a true understanding of his use of popular language, anger, and antiaesthetic style.

Comparisons, Contrasts, Connections

I believe that fruitful comparisons may be drawn if one looks into Allen Ginsberg and other poets of the beat generation and of the '60s (as poetry of social denouncement, protest, and harsh, antiacademic language). Also compare with contemporary African-American poets who deal with urban themes, alienation, and social injustice.

Questions for Reading and Discussion/ Approaches to Writing

1. For "Puerto Rican Obituary," questions dealing with theme: What is it denouncing? How are the "puertorriqueños" portrayed? Analyze image of *death*. Would you define it as an "epic" poem? What is the use of Spanish in the poem? Consider the poem as an example of urban literature; define the Utopian space that Pietri proposes.

2. Paper topics might deal with Puerto Rican migration; use of Spanish and English (for aesthetic effort); functions of humor and irony; analyze the poems as "outlaw" literature.

Bibliography

Two general articles on Puerto Rican writers discuss Pietri's work:

Cruz, Arnaldo. "Teaching Puerto Rican Authors: Modernization and Identity in Nuyorican Literature." *ADE Journal* published by the Modern Language Association (December 1988).

Acosta-Belén, Edna. "The Literature of the Puerto Rican National Minority in the United States. *The Bilingual Review* 5:1–2 (Jan.-Aug. 1978): 107–16.

Roberta Hill Whiteman (Oneida) (b. 1947)

Contributing Editor: Andrew O. Wiget [p. 2519]

Major Themes, Historical Perspectives, and Personal Issues

The most important consideration in Whiteman's poetry is her unification of both the personal and historical sense of loss. In poems like "In the Longhouse, Oneida Museum," "Dream of Rebirth," and "Scraps Worthy of Wind" she has internalized the loss and alienation that have come from the Oneida experience of removal. This historic consciousness is echoed by her own personal loss in the death of parents and the loss of loved ones. It is a sense of loss that creates tremendous longing, a longing edged with anger, that's reflected in poems like "Underground Water" and "Scraps Worthy of Wind."

Significant Form, Style, or Artistic Conventions

As the headnote to this section indicates, Whiteman owes a lot to Richard Hugo, and so her poetry falls squarely within the mainstream of contemporary American poetry. Thus, it should not present any unusual difficulties in terms of form or imagery or rhetorical strategy for the reader. Whiteman is very much a classic poet, if contemporary poetry can be said to have produced "classical" poets, and pays a good deal of attention to form. Call the reader's attention to her use of line breaks and the tremendous balance of stresses in her lines. Also she moves very keenly between abstract language of great rhetorical power and very concrete immediate images that haunt the mind. A reference probably lost on students in "Lines for Marking Time," for instance, is the comparison of the inside of an operating radio of the old-fashioned tube design to "a shimmering city." I would also ask students to formulate their sense of the tone of these poems.

Comparisons, Contrasts, Connections

Whiteman compares favorably to a number of contemporary poets for whom the loss of contact with their ethnic, occupational, or cultural past has been one of the defining factors in the formation of their identity. She would work very well with others from different traditions such as Cofer, Song, and Mirikitani, as well as other poets for whom the burden of memory has been a dominant theme. Her "Underground Water" is usefully compared to Adrienne Rich's "Diving into the Wreck." Historically, one could read Roberta Hill Whiteman's poetry as a response to the deculturation of American Indians reflected in other writings in the anthology by Native Americans, including John Joseph Mathews, John Milton Oskison, and Gertrude Bonnin.

Questions for Reading and Discussion/ Approaches to Writing

1. What about these poems reveals them to have been written by an Indian author? How would you describe the writer's attitude toward the past? What seems to be this writer's overriding concern?
2. Find a line or image from these poems that you think best represents the interest or personal vision of this author, and use it to explore her poetry.

Bibliography

"Massaging the Earth: An Interview with Roberta Hill Whiteman." In *Survival This Way: Interviews with Native American Poets*, edited by Joseph Bruchac, 329–35. Tuscon: Univ. of Arizona, 1987.

Wiget, Andrew. "Review of *Star Quilt*." *American Indian Culture and Research Journal* 8 (1985): 92–6.

Wendy Rose (Hopi) (b. 1948)

Contributing Editor: C. B. Clark [p. 2525]

Classroom Issues and Strategies

The main problem with teaching Rose is the students' lack of knowledge of American Indians. Reading out loud is a problem, again because students do not have background knowledge about Indian culture and history to enable them to pick up on comments about imperialism, removals, atrocities, resentments, etc.

For the most part, students respond only to the tragedies. They miss the joy, the beauty, the lyricism of the poetry because they are not sophisticated enough to appreciate it.

Major Themes, Historical Perspectives, and Personal Issues

Themes are colonialism, imperialism, dependency, nostalgia for the old ways, reverence for grandparents, resentment for conditions of the present, plight of reservation and urban Indians, sense of hopelessness, the power of the trickster, feminism as synonymous with heritage, deadly compromise, symbolism of all that has been lost (such as land), tension between the desire to retrieve the past and the inevitability of change, arrogance of white people, problems of half-breeds (or mixed-bloods).

Significant Form, Style, or Artistic Conventions

Rose uses free verse. She is aware of classical European form but chooses not to use it. In addition, she is less an oral poet using chants and more of a lyric poet. She is not in any school, except American Indian.

Original Audience

I ask this question: Is there an audience outside American Indians? A second audience, of course, would be the students in class. A third audience would be the general reader.

Questions for Reading and Discussion/ Approaches to Writing

1. What are major themes of Hopi religion? Who are the Hopi? Where do they live? Why do they live atop mesas? Where do the Hopi claim to come from? How did they get to where they are today? What contemporary problems do they face? What is the Hopi relationship to the outside world? Who are some Hopi leaders today? How do the Hopi view the world?
2. Hand out a reading list on the Hopi, containing ethnographic, historical, and contemporary works. Hand out a theme list, containing topics like manifest destiny or acculturation. Hand out a subject list, with subjects like alcoholism, jails, and kachinas. Then, ask students to write an essay using Rose's works in reference to any of these topics.

Bibliography

No single biographical or critical work exists on Rose. Information must be gleaned from critical pieces, collections, and book reviews. Additionally, information can come from autobiographical statements preceding selections printed in anthologies of American Indian works.

Rose is included in Joseph Bruchac's *Survival This Way*, Swann and Krupat's *I Tell You Now*, and Andrew Wiget's *Native American Literature*.

Víctor Hernández Cruz (b. 1949)

Contributing Editor: Frances R. Aparicio [p. 2533]

Classroom Issues and Strategies

Perhaps the most basic difficulty for students is the highly abstract and introspective nature of Cruz's poetry. It may seem hermetic at times, and partly this is due to the use of imagery, words, and references that originate in Hispanic culture or mythology. Also, his poetry demands a reader who is familiar with both English and Spanish since he frequently plays with both languages.

I would advise students to read carefully and aid them by preparing a glossary or handout that would clarify the difficult references. (The problem is that not all English teachers have access to the meaning of local references to Puerto Rican towns, Indian gods, mythological figures.)

I would emphasize the important of the concrete poetry movement in relation to Cruz's work. The importance of the collage text, the use of space, the page, the graphics, and the significance of *play* as integral elements in the reading of a poem, could be clearly explained by a visual presentation of concrete poems from Brazil, Europe, and the United States.

Major Themes, Historical Perspectives, and Personal Issues

Urban life; meaning of language as an identity construct; importance of the cultural and historical past and how it flows into the present; importance of music and drugs as a basis for the poet's images; Hispanic culture and identity: how is it reaffirmed through literary creation?

Significant Form, Style, or Artistic Conventions

Focus on the importance of collage or hybrid texts; influence of concrete poetry; linguistic mixtures and lucid bilingualism; concept of metaliterary texts; contemporary American poetry: free verse, fragmentation, minimalism, surrealism.

Comparisons, Contrasts, Connections

Compare and contrast with Allen Ginsberg and other poets of the beat generation (use of imagery based on drugs, music of the '60s, influence of surrealism and irreverent language); an additional comparison to E. E. Cummings, as well as to the concrete poets, would be helpful in terms of use of space, punctuation, and the page as signifiers. Contrast with poets like Pedro Pietri and Tato Laviera, in which the elements of popular culture are central to the understanding of their works (Cruz is much more introspective and abstract, and does not fit totally into the paradigm of Nuyorican aesthetics).

Questions for Reading and Discussion/ Approaches to Writing

Study questions will focus mostly on the assigned text and would require students to identify major theme, use of language and imagery, and aesthetic effect of each poem.

Paper topics would focus on major themes. For example:

1. Discuss how "Speech changing within space," the epigraph to *By Lingual Wholes*, encapsulates Víctor Hernández Cruz's poetics.
2. Would you agree that English is transformed or affected by Spanish in Cruz's works? If so, how is this achieved?
3. Discuss the presence of Hispanic culture within contemporary, urban life in the United States, as it is reflected in Cruz's literature.
4. Analyze Cruz's texts as an example of urban literature: how do his point of view, attitudes, imagery, and rhythms create a sense of life in American cities?
5. Write on Cruz's use of music and drugs as basis for his poetic imagery.

Bibliography

Acosta-Belén, Edna. "The Literature of the Puerto Rican National Minority in the United States." *Bilingual Review*, Vol. 5, no. 1 and 2. Jan.-Aug. 1978, 107–16.

Cruz, Arnaldo, "Teaching Puerto Rican Authors: Modernization and Identity in Nuyorican Literature." *ADE Bulletin*. MLA, Dec. 1988, 45–51.

Cruz, Víctor Hernández, "Mountains in the North: Hispanic Writing in the USA." *The Americas Review*, 14: 3–4 Fall/Winter 1986, 110–14.

Carolyn Forché (b. 1950)

Contributing Editor: Constance Coiner [p. 2538]

Classroom Issues and Strategies

Students will need some introduction to the situation in El Salvador at the time when Forché went there as a journalist/poet/human rights investigator, 1978–80 (two of the three poems included in this anthology are among her "El Salvador" poems). Students will naturally be curious about the U.S. role in El Salvador, both when Forché was there and since.

In "A Lesson in Commitment" (*Triquarterly* [Winter 1986]: 30–8) Forché recounts the events that led to her going to El Salvador—an interesting, even amusing story that students will welcome. Consider also "The Military Web of Corruption," *The Nation* (October 23, 1982, 391–39), by Forché and Leonel Gomez. Then address the controversy concerning "political poetry" in the U.S. An essential article is "El Salvador: An Aide Memoire" (*The American Poetry Review* [July/August 1981]: 3–7). This article both prefaces and theoretically frames the "El Salvador" poems.

An audiocassette is available of Forché reading poems from *The Country Between Us* from Watershed Tapes, P. O. Box 50145, Washington, D.C. 20004.

"The Colonel"

This poem has incredible impact. It silenced 320 students when I read it in a UCLA literature class and provoked lively fifty-minute discussions in several freshman composition classes. Forché felt a similar response to it at her readings.

Forché invented the term "documentary poem" for "The Colonel," and even though none of the other poems in *The Country Between Us* is a prose-poem, "The Colonel" nevertheless represents the collection in the following ways: In the twentieth century the lyric has become by far the preponderant poetic poem, but Forché is a storyteller, her poetry predominantly narrative. Because she wants her readers to experience what she witnessed in El Salvador from 1978–80, she consciously resists lyricizing experience. She employs lyric and manipulates form, but *in calculated relation to bourgeois forms.*

In the journalistic way that it sets the scene, "The Colonel" takes little poetic license, and the reader trusts that it has not caricatured the truth; even visually, with its justified right-hand margin, the piece resembles a newspaper report more than a poem. If we were overwhelmed by a sense of craft, of manipulation, we would be suspicious; as a savvy political strategist, however, Forché lowers Americans' defenses. She tells the truth, but knows that certain forms make better conduits for it than others.

"Because One Is Always Forgotten"

This is the last of the poems in the first section ("In Salvador," 1978–80) of *The Country Between Us* and makes an excellent pedagogical companion piece to "The Colonel." As in her documentary poem, Forché writes—it bears repeating—in calculated relation to bourgeois forms, calling attention to the limits of inherited poetic forms and at the same time insisting that poetry can be used for political as well as aesthetic purposes. The obverse of "The Colonel," which appears artless, this elegy in couplets is the most highly structured piece in the book.

The poem begins with blank verse, the reigning meter in English poetry since Shakespeare. But the meter breaks (Forché adds and drops beats) as if to suggest the traditional forms necessarily strain or snap under the weight of political imprisonment, torture, murder.

"As Children Together"

This selection gives us a sense of Forché's Detroit working-class roots. In *Gathering the Tribes* and *The Country Between Us*, a thread runs from Slovakia and Anna, the immigrant grandmother, through Detroit— where her grandmother continued as a role model, her father worked as a tool and die maker, and her mother bore seven children before attending college—to El Salvador. "As Children Together" reveals that Forché "always believed . . . that there might be a way to get out" of her girlhood poverty. Although she escaped the relief checks and the battered men, in her poetry and in her identification with oppressed people, the poet has never left Detroit, has not abandoned her class.

"As Children Together" also links Vietnam to El Salvador. Young men from Forché's working-class neighborhood were drafted or seduced into enlisting in the army that went to Vietnam when their more privileged counterparts found alternatives to military service. They returned, if they returned at all, listless, bitter, and ill-prepared for civilian jobs. Forché's girlhood friend Victoria, to whom the poem is addressed, lives in a trailer near their hometown with a husband mentally broken by the Vietnam War. It was during Vietnam that Forché came of age, and it schooled her for Central America.

Major Themes, Historical Perspectives, and Personal Issues

1. U.S. imperialism.
2. The difference between poetry that calls attention chiefly to form and poetry like Forché's that's formally interesting as well as socially and politically engaged.
3. *The Country Between Us* (from which "The Colonel" and "Because One Is Always Forgotten" are taken) resonates with a sense of *international kinship*.
4. Merging of personal and political.

Significant Form, Style, or Artistic Conventions

In the twentieth century, the lyric has become the preponderant poetic form, but Forché is a storyteller, her poetry predominantly narrative. Because she wants her readers to experience what she witnessed in El Salvador from 1978–80, she consciously resists lyricizing experiences. Forché has said that "the twentieth-century human condition demands a poetry of witness."

Original Audience

The particular audience for Forché's poetry is the American people. Monsignor Romero, the Archbishop of San Salvador who was assassinated while praying at mass by a right-wing death squad, urged Forché to return to the U.S. and "tell the American people what is happening." Poets do not often so purposefully address such a wide audience. The class should discuss in what ways Forché's poems effectively address the wide popular audience she seeks. She wants to speak to more people than the "already converted."

Comparisons, Contrasts, Connections

Denise Levertov, Muriel Rukeyser, Adrienne Rich, Pablo Neruda—these are anti-imperialist, politically engaged writers whose lives and literary texts promote a global as well as private kinship.

The private anguish of Sylvia Plath's later poems (e.g., "Daddy," "Lady Lazarus") provides a provocative contrast to the very public issues of human rights violations addressed in "The Colonel" and "Because One Is Always Forgotten."

Bibliography

Forché, Carolyn. "El Salvador: An Aide Memoire." *American Poetry Review* (July/August 1981): 3–7.

———. "A Lesson in Commitment." *Tri-Quarterly* (Winter 1986): 30–8.

Greer, Michael. "Politicizing the Modern: Carolyn Forché in El Salvador and America." *The Centennial Review* (Spring 1986): 160–80.

Useful interviews include Kim Addonizio and John High's in *Five Fingers Review* 3 (1985): 116–31, and Constance Coiner's in *The Jacaranda Review* (Winter 1988).

Joy Harjo (Creek) (b. 1951)

Contributing Editor: C. B. Clark [p. 2543]

Classroom Issues and Strategies

Students have problems reading Harjo because they have next to no knowledge about American Indian culture and history. It's important to make certain that students read the biographical notes and footnotes provided in the text. Consider also using audiotapes of Harjo reading and discussing her own work.

Students usually only respond to tragedies. They are not sophisticated enough to grasp the joy and beauty of the lyricism of the poetry. They are, however, interested in contemporary Indians.

Major Themes, Historical Perspectives, and Personal Issues

Imperialism, colonialism, dependency, nostalgia for the old ways, reverence for grandparents and elders, resentment of conditions of the present, plight of reservation and urban Indians, natural world, sense of hopelessness, power of the trickster, idea that the feminine is synonymous with heritage, deadly compromise, symbol of all that has been lost (such as the land), tension between the desire to retrieve the past and the inevitability of change, the arrogance of white people, problems of half-breeds (or mixed-bloods).

Significant Form, Style, or Artistic Conventions

Harjo uses free verse. She is aware of classic European form, but chooses not to use it. She does try oral chant, as in "She Had Some Horses." She is not in any school, except American Indian.

Original Audience

Ask the question: Is there any audience outside American Indians? The second audience is the student, and the third is the general reader.

Questions for Reading and Discussion/ Approaches to Writing

1. Who are the Creeks? What is their origin? What impact did removal have on the Five Civilized Tribes? Where are the Creeks today? How are they organized? What was the role of the Christian missionary? What is traditional Creek religion? What is a Stomp Ground? Does Harjo travel much and is that reflected in her poetry?

2. Hand out a reading list, containing ethnographic, historical, and contemporary works on the Creeks. Hand out a theme list, containing such items as removal, acculturation, identity. Hand out a subject list containing topics such as removal, alcoholism, and jails. Ask the students to write an essay on each of the lists. Require some library research for the essays, which will provide background for the poetry.

Bibliography

There are no separate works on Harjo. Bits on her can be found in critical pieces on her work, in collections, in autobiographical pieces, and through interviews.

Published works that deal in part with her include Joseph Bruchac's *Survival This Way* and Andrew O. Wiget's *Native American Literature*, part of the Twayne series.

Garrett Hongo (b. 1951)

Contributing Editor: Amy Ling [p. 2550]

Classroom Issues and Strategies

Explain that Hongo's themes and craft are evident even in the small selection we have in this text. The title poem of his first book, *Yellow Light*, emphasizes the centrality of the Asian perspective by ascribing a positive, fertile quality to the color commonly designating Asian skin and formerly meaning "cowardly." By focusing his sights on the common person in the midst of her or his daily rounds, as in "Yellow Light," "Off from Swing Shift," and "And Your Soul Shall Dance," by describing their surroundings in precise detail, by suggesting their dreams, Hongo depicts his people's dignity.

Major Themes, Historical Perspectives, and Personal Issues

The work of any Asian-American writer is best understood in the context of the black civil rights and the women's liberation movements of the 1960s and 1970s. These movements by African-Americans and women led Asian Americans to join in the push for change. Asian-Americans as a group had endured racial discrimination in the U.S. for over a century, from the harassment of Chinese in the California gold mines to the internment of thousands of Japanese-Americans during World War II. Furthermore, the last three wars the United States had engaged in had been fought in Asia, a fact that further consolidated a sense of community among the hitherto disparate Asian groups in this country

Significant Form, Style, or Artistic Conventions

In Hongo's volume *Yellow Light,* we no longer find a dependence on language and rhythm borrowed from African-American culture nor strident screams of bitterness and anger. Hongo is at home in his skin, positive about his background and the people around him, confident in his own voice, concerned as much with his craft as with his message.

Hongo's poems paint portraits of the people around him, and he invests his people with dignity and bathes them in love. Pride in an Asian-American heritage shines through in the catalogue of foods in "Who Among You Knows the Essence of Garlic?" Hongo's eye has the precision of seventeenth-century Flemish still-life painters, but his art is dynamic and evokes the sounds, smells, and tastes of the foods he describes.

He has combined the consciousness of the late twentieth-century ethnic nationalist with the early twentieth-century imagist's concern for the most precise, the most resonant image, and added to this combination his own largeness of spirit.

Comparisons, Contrasts, Connections

The examples of Inada and Chin excited Garrett Hongo, who was encouraged by their work to do his own.

Frank Chin displayed his artistic and verbal talent, making his claim for a place in American history and expressing his deep ambivalence about Chinese-Americans in his plays. "Chickencoop Chinaman" was a dazzling display of verbal pyrotechnics but underlying the surface razzle-dazzle is a passionate throbbing of anger and pain for the emasculation and evisceration of Chinese men in the United States.

Lawson Fusao Inada was another visible and vocal model for younger Asian-American writers. His book of poetry *Before the War* provided a range of models and styles from lyrical musings, to sublimated anger from a Japanese-American perspective, to colloquial outbursts inspired by black jazz and rhythms.

Hongo acknowledges other models and mentors as well: Bert Meyers, Donald Hall, C. K. Williams, Charles Wright, and Philip Levine.

Bibliography

Hongo, Garrett, Alan Chong Lau, and Lawson Fusao Inada. *The Buddha Bandits Down Highway* 99. Mountainview, Cal.: Buddhahead Press, 1978.

——. *River of Heaven.* New York: Alfred A. Knopf, 1988.

Kodama-Nishimoto, Michi, and Warren Nishimoto. "Interview with Writer Garrett Hongo: Oral History and Literature." *Oral History Recorder* (Summer 1986): 2–4.

Tato Laviera (b. 1951)

Contributing Editor: Frances R. Aparicio [p. 2562]

Classroom Issues and Strategies

Laviera's poetry is difficult to read because of the linguistic puns and his mixture of English and Spanish, which presupposes not only a bilingual reader, but one who is also familiar with references to Puerto Rican folklore, colloquialisms, history, music, and in general to the popular culture of both Puerto Rico and of the Puerto Ricans in New York.

Give handouts or glossaries that explain local references and Spanish words; also it might be helpful to try to translate Spanish phrases and words, in order to show the unique value of bilingualism within Laviera's poetry, and the fact that most of it is untranslatable.

It would be wonderful to recite Laviera's poems aloud and to introduce them to the students as such, as oral poetry. One might also relate his poetry to the tradition of rapping in New York City. Again, students need to clarify references to Puerto Rico and El Barrio with which they might be unfamiliar. They respond to issues of bilingual education, social criticism, and language (Spanish in the United States).

Major Themes, Historical Perspectives, and Personal Issues

Major themes are tension between Puerto Rican and Nuyorican societies and identity; language and bilingualism as ethnic identity markers; life in El Barrio; music and popular culture; denouncement of social institutions such as schools, Puerto Rican and U.S. governments, the Catholic church, etc.; major context of the history of Puerto Rican immigration to the U.S. and Operation Bootstrap in the 1940s and 1950s; presence of African-Caribbean and African-American cultures.

Significant Form, Style, or Artistic Conventions

Laviera's poetry best exemplifies the new genre of bilingual poetry in the United States. Discuss historical context of bilingual literature in other countries, aesthetic innovation within contemporary literature, political stance, use of oral speech and traditions versus written, academic and intellectual poetry; relate to Mexican-American poets, and to African-American poets of the 1960s.

Original Audience

This is poetry meant to be sung and recited. Originally addressed to the Puerto Rican community in New York and presented in the Nuyorican Café, it is poetry for the masses.

Comparisons, Contrasts, Connections

There is a good basis for comparison with Alurista, the Mexican-American poet who was the first to publish bilingual poetry in this country. (See *Floricanto en Aztlán*.)

Questions for Reading and Discussion/ Approaches to Writing

Study questions for Laviera would try to help students contextualize his poetry both historically and aesthetically. For example:

1. How would you describe El Barrio in New York? How does Laviera present it in his poems?
2. After reading Laviera's poems, how would you define poetry? What kind of language is appropriate for poetry? Would Laviera's work fit into your definition?

A good and challenging writing assignment is to ask students to write their own bilingual poem (using any other language they may know). Discuss problems and effects.

Paper topics would include textual analysis of one poem, a discussion of the functions of language and bilingualism, and its problems; language and ethnic identity; the functions of humor and irony.

Bibliography

Juan Flores, John Attinasi and Pedro Pedraza, Jr., "La Carreta Made a U-Turn: Puerto Rican Language and Culture in the United States," 110:2 *Daedalus* (Spring, 1981): 193–217; Wolfgang Binder, "Celebrating Life: The AmeRícan Poet Tato Laviera," Introduction to *AmeRícan* by Tato Laviera, 1985, 5–10; Juan Flores, "Keys to Tato Laviera," Introduction to *Enclave* by Tato Laviera, 1985, 5–7; Frances Aparicio, "La vida es un spanglish disparatero: Bilingualism in Nuyorican Poetry," *European Perspectives on Hispanic Literature of the United States*, ed. Genvieve Fabre, 1988, 147–60.

Judith Ortiz Cofer (b. 1952)

Contributing Editor: Juan Bruce-Novoa [p. 2568]

Classroom Issues and Strategies

Ortiz Cofer is quite clear and accessible, although students have questions about who she is and why she uses Spanish.

I present the students something from my own cultural background, with allusions to Mexican history and culture. Then I ask them to jot down what has been said. We compare the results, finding that those who do not share the background will choose different elements out of the material than those who come from a background similar to my own. We discuss the function of ethnic identification through shared allusions about the drawing of the ethnic circle around some readers, while excluding others, even when the latter can understand the words.

Students respond to the theme of the abandoned female, which often results in discussions of the single-parent family.

Major Themes, Historical Perspectives, and Personal Issues

The theme of male absence and women who wait is perhaps the major one touched on here. Also, there is the historical theme of Puerto Ricans and other minorities in the military as a way of life that both gives them mobility yet divides their families.

The colonization of Puerto Rico by the U.S. and the division of its population into island and mainland groups is reflected in the division of the family.

Significant Form, Style, or Artistic Conventions

This is confessional poetry, but with a twist. The author walks a fine line between writing for her own group and writing for the general audience. Thus she introduces Spanish and some culture items from the island, but recontextualizes them into English and U.S. culture. The style becomes an intercultural hybrid.

Original Audience

There is the Puerto Rican audience that will bring to the poems a specific knowledge of cultural elements that they share with the poet. This audience will place the poem in a wider catalog of cultural references. The non-Puerto Rican audience must draw only from the information given, and will perhaps apply the situations to universal myth or archetypes.

Comparisons, Contrasts, Connections

You can compare her well to many other women writers, especially in the sense of women alone in a male world.

Questions for Reading and Discussion/ Approaches to Writing

1. I ask them to consider what is the function of ethnic writing. How does it work for insiders as compared to outsiders? They should try to determine at what point ethnic writing becomes incomprehensible to outsiders, and what it means to open it to readers beyond the ethnic circle.
2. Write on the theme of the distant patriarch in U.S. contemporary life.
3. Write on the pros and cons of foreign language in literature.

Bibliography

Refer to the headnote in the text for complete information.

Gary Soto (b. 1952)

Contributing Editor: Raymund Paredes [p. 2572]

Classroom Issues and Strategies

As a Chicano working-class poet, Soto sometimes uses figurative language that might be unfamiliar to and difficult for some readers. Occasionally, he uses a Spanish word or phrase. As a poet with a strong sense of kinship with people who are poor, neglected and oppressed, Soto tries to create poetry out of ordinary working-class experience and images. All this is very different from typically bourgeois American poetry.

It is useful to connect Soto's work to contemporary events in Mexican-American experience. Reading a bit about Cesar Chavez and the California farm worker struggle places some of Soto's sympathies in context. General reading in Chicano (or Mexican-American) history would also be useful. It is also useful to consider Soto among other contemporary poets whose sensibilities were shaped by the post-1960s struggles to improve the circumstances of minority groups and the poor.

Urge students to try to see the world from the point of view of one of Soto's working-class Chicanos, perhaps a farm worker. From this perspective, one sees things very differently than from the point of view generally presented in American writing. For the tired, underpaid farm worker, nature is neither kind nor beautiful, as, for example, Thoreau would have us believe. Soto writes about the choking dust in the fields, the danger to the workers' very existence that the sun represents. Imagine a life without many creature comforts, imagine feelings of hunger, imagine the pain of knowing that for the affluent and comfortable, your life counts for very little.

Students are generally moved by Soto's vivid and honest presentation of personal experiences, his sympathy for the poor, and the accessibility of his work. They generally wish to know more about Mexican-American and Mexican cultures, more about the plight of farm workers and the urban poor.

Major Themes, Historical Perspectives, and Personal Issues

Despite Soto's distinctiveness, he is very much a contemporary American poet. Like many of his peers, he writes largely in an autobiographical or confessional mode. As an intensively introspective poet, he seeks to maintain his connection to his Mexican heritage as it exists on both sides of the border. His work often focuses on the loss of a father at an early age, on the difficulties of adolescence (especially romantic feelings), and the urgency of family intimacy. On a broader level, Soto speaks passionately on behalf of tolerance and mutual respect while he denounces middle- and upper-class complacency and indifference to the poor.

Significant Form, Style, or Artistic Conventions

Again, Soto is very much a contemporary American poet, writing autobiographically in free verse and using images that are drawn from ordinary experience and popular culture. His sympathies for the poor are very typical of contemporary writers from ethnic or underprivileged backgrounds. It is also important to note that some of Soto's poetry has been influenced by the "magical realism" of modern Latin American writing, especially García-Márquez.

Original Audience

Although Soto is a Chicano poet in that his Mexican-American heritage is a key aspect of his literary sensibility, he nevertheless aims for a wider audience. He clearly wants a broad American audience to feel sympathies for his poetic characters and their circumstances. The product of a contemporary sensibility, Soto's poetry is topical and vital.

Comparisons, Contrasts, Connections

Again, as an autobiographical poet, Soto can be compared with such figures as Robert Lowell, John Berryman, and Sylvia Plath. His working-class sensibility is reminiscent of James Wright, Philip Levine (who was Soto's teacher at California State University, Fresno). His celebration of certain Chicano values and denunciation of bigotry is comparable to that of other Chicano poets such as Lorna Dee Cervantes.

Questions for Reading and Discussion/ Approaches to Writing

1. Students might be asked to look for clues in his work as to ethnic background, economic status, and geographical setting.

   Furthermore, they might be asked to consider certain formal qualities of his work: Where do Soto's images and symbols come from? Does Soto attempt to make his work accessible to ordinary readers?

2. Soto's work is fruitfully compared to other autobiographical poets (Lowell, Berryman, Plath) and to working-class poets such as Wright and Levine.

   Soto's book *The Tale of Sunlight* (particularly its final section) might be studied for its elements of "magical realism."

   Soto, of course, can be studied in connection to other Chicano poets such as Lorna Dee Cervantes and Umar Salinas.

Bibliography

Probably the most useful general source of information on Soto (complete with various references) is the article on Soto in *The Dictionary of Literary Biography*, volume 82, "Chicano Writers" (1989).

Lorna Dee Cervantes (b. 1954)

Contributing Editor: Juan Bruce-Novoa [p. 2579]

Classroom Issues and Strategies

Students often dislike the strident tone of "Poem for the Young White Man." Even Chicanos now get turned off by it. The feminism has the same effect on the men. Why is she so hostile toward males, they ask? Some now say that she is passé, radicalism being a thing of the sixties. I prepare the students with information on feminist issues, especially on the single-parent families, wife abuse, and child abuse. I also prepare them by talking about racial and ethnic strife as a form of warfare, seen as genocide by minority groups.

I use Bernice Zamora's poetry as an introduction. Her alienation from the male rituals in "Penitents" produces the all-female family in "Beneath . . . ." The sense of living in one's own land, but under other's rules (Zamora's "On Living in Aztlán"), explains the bitterness of "Poem for the Young White Man." And both of the poets eventually find a solution in their relation to nature through animal imagery.

Major Themes, Historical Perspectives, and Personal Issues

The historical theme of the disappearance of the nuclear family in the United States is primary here. There is also the effect of urban renewal on ethnic and poor communities whose neighborhoods were often the targets for projects that dislodged people from an area. In "Crow" there is the theme of finding a link in nature to counter urban alienation.

On the personal level, Cervantes's family history is reflected autobiographically in "Beneath . . . ."

Significant Form, Style, or Artistic Conventions

Cervantes uses the form of the narrative poem, with a few key metaphors. Her confessional mode is reminiscent of Robert Lowell's. Her style is conversational, direct, unpretentious.

Original Audience

Although her audience was and is generally "third worldist" and Chicano, these poems show a range of different target audiences. "Beneath . . ." is a feminist poem, appealing greatly to women. When it was first published there was little discussion of the issue of female heads of households in Chicano circles because few wanted to admit to the problem in the Chicano community. Now the discussion is much more common.

"Poem for . . ." had great appeal in the closing days of the radical movement, but has since faded to a smaller audience of Chicanos who have heard the radical poetry to the point of exhaustion. However, mainstream liberals like "Poem for . . ." because it speaks as they assume all minorities should speak, harshly, bitterly, and violently. They love it, even when it is not as well written as Lorna's other poems, and when it represents a contradiction in her philosophy.

Comparisons, Contrasts, Connections

I compare her to Margaret Atwood in their sense of women being submerged and needing to surface by finding their own traditions. They both have a capacity for stringent statement when pushed by violent circumstances. Both have strong links to nature, in which their ancestors cultivated, not only food, but their culture.

Carlos Castaneda's theory of the enemy is significant for Cervantes.

Questions for Reading and Discussion/ Approaches to Writing

1. Students are asked to consider the significance of mainstream construction projects on local communities; from here they are asked to ponder the cycle of change and its victims.
2. Write on the links between "Beneath . . ." and "Poem for . . . ."
3. Write on Cervantes's view of the world as a threat to existence and what she offers as a response.

Bibliography

The best article is my "Bernice Zamora and Lorna Dee Cervantes," *Revista Iberoamericana* 51, 132–33 (July-Dec. 1985): 565–73. See also Cordelia Candelaria's *Chicano Poetry*.

Cathy Song (b. 1955)

Contributing Editor: Shirley Lim [p. 2585]

Classroom Issues and Strategies

The main problem with teaching Song is students' lack of knowledge of Hawaiian immigrant history and of Asian-Japanese cultural markers and materials. Offer entry points by discussing ethnic immigrant history and cultural embedding of images and themes.

Use posters of Utumara woodcuts and Georgia O'Keeffe paintings to make imagistic style come alive for students; also discuss narratives of picture brides.

Students are interested in issues of family/kinship networks. They question how Song's networks are different from their own, looking for specific cultural markers.

Major Themes, Historical Perspectives, and Personal Issues

Asian immigrant into Hawaii, plantation culture; picture-bride customs; Asian emphasis on filial pieties, family ties; the poet's painterly interests in themes and style—these are among Song's themes.

Significant Form, Style, or Artistic Conventions

Consider: imagistic conventions forming part of modernist, Williams's school of thought; the influence of aesthetics drawn from visual arts, also part of Williams's convention; Song's style of compression, density, natural rhythms of everyday speech.

Original Audience

Her poetry is in every way contemporary; her audience is intimately drawn into the observations.

Comparisons, Contrasts, Connections

Good comparisons would be with William Carlos Williams and early Adrienne Rich.

Questions for Reading and Discussion/ Approaches to Writing

1. Have students write down some of their own family history.
2. Discuss mother-daughter relationships.
3. What are the most fundamental elements of modern American poetry?

Bibliography

I recommend my own review in *MELUS* (Fall 1983).

Index of Authors